AGESILAOS

AGESILAOS

and the Crisis of Sparta

Paul Cartledge

The Johns Hopkins University Press
Baltimore

For Judith Portrait again
(and not because I said I would)

First published in 1987 by
The Johns Hopkins University Press
701 West 40th Street
Baltimore, Maryland 21211

Library of Congress Cataloging-in-Publication-Data

Cartledge, Paul
Agesilaos and the crisis of Sparta.

Bibliography: p.
Includes index.
1. Agesilaos, II, King of Sparta.   2. Sparta
(Ancient city)—History.   3. Greece—History—
Spartan and Theban Supremacies, 404–362 B.C.
4. Greece—Kings and rulers—Biography.   I. Title.
DF232.A33C37   1987   938'.906'0924 [B]   86-27450
ISBN 0-8018-3505-4

Printed and bound in Great Britain

Contents

Part Four: Conclusions

Appendices

Illustrations

Preface

Of the making of books on ancient Sparta there is, it seems, no end. 'Statistically', as I commented in reviewing Hooker 1980,[1] 'a book on ancient Sparta can be expected roughly every two years'. Yet another such book requires justification, therefore, especially to those who (unlike me) have waded through the entire torrent of modern bibliography let loose by Manso 1800-1805 and generously sampled in the extraordinary endnotes to Tigerstedt 1965-74, or even through the more easily negotiable selections of Vagiakakos/Taïphakos 1975, Clauss 1983 and Ducat 1983.

Two kinds of justification are in principle available: new matter, new manner. Since it would not be unfair to say that the 23 incomplete lines of a fragmentary and not certainly datable Spartan treaty on stone (Peek 1974; but see Cartledge 1976a, 1978b, Kelly 1978b, Gschnitzer 1978) constitute the most substantial recent addition to the documentary evidence, and since there is little immediate prospect of startling archaeological and literary discoveries bearing directly and obviously upon the history of Classical Sparta, only the latter kind can in practice be legitimately used.

In one of my earliest articles, published a decade ago now (Cartledge 1975), I set out briefly and rather dogmatically my guiding principles of historiography and sketched how they might some day be applied to the best attested period of Spartan history, the 'age of Xenophon' between about 430 and 360 (BC – as are all dates in this book except where specifically designated otherwise). I see no good reason to alter those principles; indeed, the publication of a fundamental study of the ancient Greek class struggle (Ste. Croix 1981, corr. repr. 1983) has rather served to confirm my belief in their utility for explaining the literally vital features of ancient Sparta and other Greek societies – as I have indicated in a review of Ste. Croix in the *English Historical Review*. However, the angle of vision contemplated in that early article has been changed in the present study so as to give a different, quasi-biographical slant to what might be called 'the age of Agesilaos' (Agesila*os* not Agesila*us* for the reasons given by Freeman 1893, xvi-xvii, though I go further than he in the same direction without, I hope, being guilty of what the playwright-turned-historical novelist John Arden has stigmatized as an 'unpalatable academicism'; cf. Cartledge 1979, xv). An attempted justification of this approach and a statement of my aims are given in Chapter 1. Here a few preliminary words to clarify the book's scope and organization may be found helpful.

[1]All works cited thus by author's name and year of publication are listed in the Bibliography (pp. 461-87), together with others that I have used but not had occasion to cite specifically in the main body of the book. I have not made use of anything published after 1983.

In my previous book (1979), which was based ultimately on a 1975 Oxford doctoral thesis on Spartan archaeology and history in the pre-Classical era, I was principally concerned to elucidate the ways in which Sparta's internal and external history was conditioned in its broad outlines by the natural and human resources at the Spartans' disposal within the frontiers of their uniquely large and unusually rich *polis* (state and territory) in the southern Peloponnese of mainland Greece (see Fig. 1 on p.2). This was a regional study, an exercise in geographical history, setting out what I took and still take to be the proper regional framework within which all Spartan history should be viewed. I deliberately avoided detailed discussion of Spartan political, military, social and other institutions, except in so far as these were integrally related to this basic geographical framework, in order to try to bring out as sharply as possible the indispensable advantages of this approach. In the present book the balance of emphasis and discussion is reversed: 'Biography', as the young Edmund Clerihew Bentley sagely observed, 'Is different from Geography. Geography is about Maps, While Biography deals with Chaps'. But the method and conclusions of *Sparta and Lakonia*, which may be regarded as both a prefatory and a companion volume, are here largely presupposed.

Meanwhile, after completing the doctoral thesis, I have produced a series of articles on some or all aspects of several key Spartan institutions or practices (see Bibliography, pp. 465-6). These are informed by the same comparative perspective that I have sought to apply in this book and are all in some way and to some degree relevant to its concerns. The specialist reader who requires more narrowly technical discussion or fuller bibliographical reference on such topics as hoplite warfare, literacy, pederasty, the status of married women, or diplomacy will have to refer back to them. But the book has been written for a wider readership than specialist ancient Greek historians; and it is with the needs of non-specialists and general readers in mind that I have dispensed with distracting footnotes or endnotes, kept appendices to a necessary minimum, and aimed to say everything of substantial importance in a continuous text broken only by essential references to the ancient texts or to the modern, secondary literature.

The text is divided into four main sections: introductory, thematic, narrative and synoptic. The *thematic* chapters, which form the bulk of the book, have to some extent been written so that they can be read out of sequence by readers who are, for example, particularly interested in the mechanics of political decision-taking at Sparta, in Helotage, or in warfare. But the order of the chapters is initially determined by the progression of major episodes in the development of Agesilaos' career. It is to be hoped that the repetitions inevitably entailed by this mode of exposition will not be found irksomely excessive. The *narrative* section cannot of course be wholly comprehended in isolation from the thematic. But perhaps it may at least serve undergraduate and non-specialist readers in some sort as a highly condensed history of Greece from the Spartan standpoint in the last decade of the fifth century and the first four decades of the fourth. Such readers may prefer to read this section after the introductory section to provide themselves with a chronological framework for approaching the thematic chapters. It is also particularly for them that the Chronological

Table and Glossary of Abbreviations used for source-references have been included.

'The labour of writing a biography,' Bernard Crick has reflected (1982,39), 'like the education of a child, involves a prolonged and strange mixture of love and critical distance, of commitment and restraint.' Studying Agesilaos has not, I confess, stirred in me any feelings that could remotely be described as love, or even affection. But critical distance, commitment and restraint will, I venture to hope, be discovered to be present in the appropriate quantities.

It remains for me to thank all those individuals or bodies who have contributed materially towards the eventual publication of this study. Among my academic colleagues I would single out, invidiously, C.D. Hamilton, S.J. Hodkinson, D.H. Kelly, G.E.M. de Ste. Croix and J.B. Salmon; but J.A. Crook, P.D.A. Garnsey and my other ancient historian colleagues in Cambridge, besides showing exceptional kindness to a metic (admittedly a privileged one), have kept me on my mettle as well. So too the students to whom I have lectured or whom I have supervised over the past six years in Cambridge are owed a collective debt of gratitude for making me rethink my position on more problems than it is comfortable to recall. The facilities of the Classics Faculty Library, now rehoused in pleasant, purpose-built surroundings, and the unlimited helpfulness of the Assistant Librarian Miss June Ethridge and the former Faculty Clerk Mrs Iris Hunter were indispensable aids to study.

The Leverhulme Research Awards Committee through a most generous grant made it possible for me to inspect personally all the major Boiotian battlefields in the 'dancing-ground of Ares' as well as to refresh and extend my knowledge of Lakonian topography.

Cambridge   P.C.
Spring 1985

Abbreviations and Sources

Greek

(Claudius) Aelian(us): *V*(aria) *H*(istoria) = Poikilê Historia in 15 Books; second half of C2 AD

Ain(eias) Takt(ikos): *c.*355

Aisch(ines): *c.*390-315

Andok(ides): *c.*440-after 392/1

Anth(ologia) Pal(atina): collection in 15 Books made in C10 AD of Greek poetry from Archaic times onwards

Arist(otle): 384-322
   E(thica) *N*(icomachea)
   Lak(edaimoniôn) *Pol*(iteia): produced within Aristotle's School, not necessarily by A. himself; fragments only survive (ed. V. Rose)
   Phys(ics)
   Pol(itics)
   Rhet(oric)

(L. Flavius) Arr(ianus Xenophon): *Anab*(asis) in 7 Books; ? *c.* AD 125

Ath(ênaiôn) *Pol*(iteia): ascribed to Aristotle (but see Rhodes 1981a); 330s/320s

Athen(aios, *Deipnosophistai* = Banqueting Sophists); *c.* AD 200

Dem(osthenes): 384-322

Dio Chrys(ostom): *c.* AD 40-115; eighty speeches survive, including two by a pupil

Diog(enes) Laert(ius): Lives and Opinions of the Philosophers in 10 Books; ? early/late C3 AD

Dion(ysios) Hal(ikarnassios): *Lys*(ias) = lit. crit. of Athenian orator Lysias (*c.*459-380); last third of C1 BC

D-K: *Die Fragmente der Vorsokratiker*, 5th to 7th edns, by H. Diels, ed. with additions by W. Kranz

DS/Diod.: Diodorus Siculus, Bibliotheca in 40 Books; *floruit c.*60-30

FGrHist.: *Die Fragmente der griechischen Historiker*, ed. F. Jacoby, 1923-58

Hdt.: Herodotus; *c.*480s-after 429

Hell(enika) Ox(yrhynchia): ? second quarter of C4; cited after V. Bartoletti, Teubner edn 1959

Hesiod: *W*(orks and) *D*(ays); *c.*700

Inscriptions
  IDélos: Inscriptions de Délos, Paris, 1926-
  IG: Inscriptiones Graecae, Berlin, 1893-
  M/L: A Selection of Greek Historical Inscriptions to the End of the Fifth Century
    B.C., edited by R. Meiggs and D.M. Lewis, Oxford, 1969 and repr.
  SEG: Supplementum Epigraphicum Graecum
  Tod: see Tod 1948
  W/V: see Wickersham/Verbrugghe 1973

Isok(rates): 436-338
  Arch(idamos): speech placed in mouth of Archidamos (later III) of Sparta
  Ep(istulae): most of the nine letters attributed to Isok. are believed authentic

Lucian: *De hist*(oria) *conscr*(ibenda); 160s

Lys(ias): *c*.459-380

Paus(anias): Description of Greece in 10 Books (III: Lakonia; IV: Messenia); written *c*.
  AD 160-180

Plat(o): *c*.428-347
  Alk(ibiades)
  Hipp(ias) *Ma*(jor)
  Protag(oras)
  Rep(ublic)

Plut(arch): *c*. AD 46-after 120
  i. *Lives* (cited according to the Budé edn numeration)
    Ages(ilaos II of Sparta), followed by *Comp*(aratio) *Ages*(ilai et) *Pomp*(eii)
    Alex(ander the Great)
    Alk(ibiades)
    Art(axerxes II Mnêmôn of Persia)
    Fab(ius Maximus Cunctator)
    Kim(ôn)
    Kleom(enes III of Sparta)
    Lyk(ourgos), followed by *Comp*(aratio) *Lyc*(urgi et) *Num*(ae)
    Lys(andros)
    Nik(ias)
    Pelop(idas)
    Sol(on)
  ii. *Mor*(alia) (cited according to the Loeb edn)

(Julius) Poll(ux): Onomastikon in 10 Books, dedicated to emperor Commodus

Polyain(os): Strategemata in 8 Books, dedicated to emperors Marcus Aurelius and Lucius
  Verus

Polyb(ios): *c*.200-after 120

Ps(eudo)-Her(odes): Peri Politeias; rhetorical exercise perhaps by Herodes Atticus (to
  whom it was attributed in antiquity); H.A.'s dates are AD 101-*c*.177

Speusippos: *Ep*(istula ad) *Phil*(ippum); 343/2

Stob(aios) = Ioannis from Macedonian Stoboi: *Flor*(ilegium); ? early C5 AD

SV: H. Bengtson (ed.), Die Verträge der griechisch-römischen Welt vol. II, Munich
  1962, rev. edn 1975

Theop(ompos): *FGrHist.* 115; *c.*378-after 323

Thuc(ydides): *c.*455-after 400

Xen(ophon): *c.*430-after 355
  Ages(ilaos II)
  Anab(asis)
  Hipp(archikos)
  Cyr(opaedia)
  LP/Lak(edaimoniôn) *Pol*(iteia)
  Mem(orabilia)
  Smp: Symposium

Latin

Cic(ero): 106-43
  De Div(inatione)
  Ep(istulae)
  Phil(ippics)

(Sextus Julius) Frontinus: *Strat*(egemata); second half of C1 AD

Justin: M. Iustinus Iunianus, *Epitome* of Pompeius Trogus' *Historiae Philippicae*; ? C2 AD

(Cornelius) Nep(os): *c.*99-24
  Ages(ilaus)
  Chabr(ias)
  Lys(ander)
  Pelop(idas)
  Tim(otheus)

Tac(itus): *Ann*(ales); first quarter of C2 AD

PART ONE

Introduction

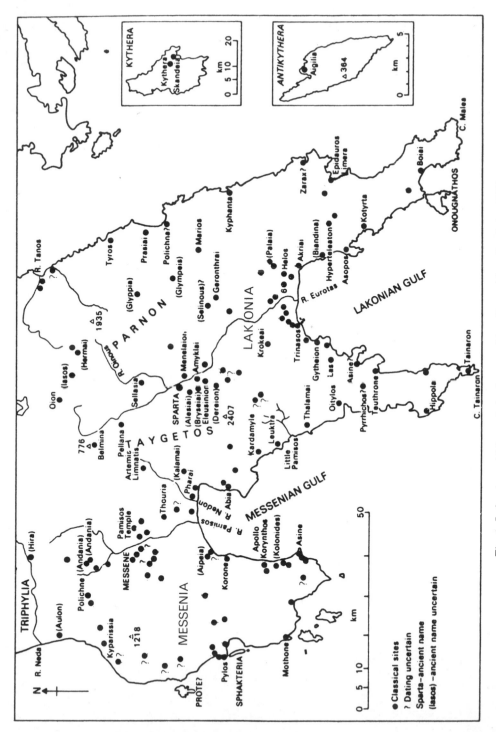

Fig. 1. Lakonia and Messenia in the age of Agesilaos. After Cartledge 1979

1

A Life in the Day of Agesilaos

Men make their own history, but they do not make it just as they please; they do not make it under circumstances chosen by themselves, but under circumstances directly encountered, given and transmitted from the past. The tradition of all the dead generations weighs like a nightmare on the brain of the living. (Karl Marx, *The Eighteenth Brumaire of Louis Bonaparte*)

Le problème que nous pose constamment Agésilas est celui de déterminer sa part de réponsabilité propre. (Bommelaer 1981, 188)

The history of ancient Sparta is replete with paradoxes. Not the least of them is that her greatest military victory destroyed the model military state. In 404, at the conclusion of the Athenian War (see Chapter 4), Sparta stood at the apex of the Aegean Greek world. Yet within half a century she had been reduced to the status of a mere Peloponnesian squabbler. This *pentêkontaëtia* is arguably the most absorbing, as it is certainly the best documented, period in all Spartan history. For once, too, the overworked expression 'crisis' (cf. Le Roy Ladurie 1981, ch. 9; Finley 1982, 208) is entirely apt, since it was then that Sparta's future subordinate rôle in Greek and world history was decided.

As one of the two Spartan kings, reigning from about 400 to 360, Agesilaos II presided over both Sparta's greatest imperial expansion and her eclipse as a major power. In an extraordinary coda to a remarkable career he died in his mid-eighties while returning from service as a mercenary general in Egypt which he had undertaken in a desperate bid to refill Sparta's coffers (Chapter 15). How was the mighty fallen! Just two decades earlier, in the 380s, Agesilaos had been nearly as much King of Greece as Philip II of Macedon was to be after 338. But it is not only Agesilaos' personal *peripeteia* or his equally startling previous ascendancy that excite the historian's curiosity. Of the many noteworthy features of his long, eventful and revealing reign it will be enough to draw attention here to three.

In the first place, when he succeeded his half-brother Agis II on the Eurypontid throne (Chapter 7), most Greeks outside Sparta must have asked about him what Cyrus the Great of Persia was reported to have asked about the Spartans in general a century and a half earlier (Hdt. 1.153.1): who on earth is he? However, as I shall hope to show (esp. Chapter 3), although Agesilaos was not expected to succeed Agis, he was far from unprepared or unfitted to rule. A member of the Eurypontid royal house but yet not in direct line of succession, and born lame in one leg to boot, Agesilaos was exceptionally well placed to view both ordinary Spartan society and high Spartan politics from the inside as well as the outside. For the first half of his long life, indeed until after he had exceeded the average life-expectancy at birth of a Greek male in his day, he experienced the lifestyle of an ordinary Spartan, so far as that was possible for a prince of the blood royal. He passed through the uniquely rigorous system of public education prescribed for all Spartans except the heirs-apparent, and in the process he participated, with far-reaching consequences, as junior partner in a pederastic relationship of the accepted Spartan type. It was not before he had completed over half of his obligatory forty years of active military service that he was elevated as if out of the blue to what passed in Sparta for the purple.

Secondly, from the institutional point of view the reign of Agesilaos is most interesting and important for the light it sheds on the nature of Spartan political organization. Grote was of the opinion, which he expressed with characteristic pungency, that 'the Spartan Kings were not kings at all, in any modern sense of the term; not only they were not absolute, but they were not even constitutional kings' (1888, vol. VII, 404-5). All ancient political theorists, however much they might disagree among themselves as to the correct positive characterization of the Spartan polity (Chapter 8), would have agreed with Grote that it was not a kingdom (*basileia*). Yet under Agesilaos, as to some extent under the Agiad Kleomenes I (*c.*520-490) before him though in very different ways and vastly changed circumstances, the full potential of the kingship for the active exercise of preponderant political power was realized. If the fourth century in Greece as a whole was in a sense the age of monarchist opinion (Chapter 22), this was due not just to extra-constitutional absolute monarchs like Dionysios I of Syracuse or to the constitutional monarchs of Macedon but also in some measure to Agesilaos.

Thirdly, the reign of Agesilaos spanned a crucial period not merely of Spartan but of all Greek and indeed all 'western' history. Unwittingly by her aggressively expansionist imperialism Agesilaos' Sparta helped to dig the grave of the politically independent Greek *polis*,[1] a creative experiment that was to be largely interred by the successive efforts of the Macedonians and the Romans. This aspect of Agesilaos' reign raises most sharply the two most ticklish and significant problems of causation. How far, in what ways and for what reasons was Agesilaos himself personally responsible for Sparta's imperialist policies? And what was the nature of the connection between Spartan imperialism and the crisis of Sparta? Hence the title of this book, which was chosen to underline the importance of these problems without implying a prejudgment of the answers and was chosen on the assumption that the historian's primary and ultimate function is the explanation of the most widely significant historical events and processes (see Chapter 21).

These three features of Agesilaos' reign far from exhaust the reasons for

---

[1]'City-state' is the conventional translation, but it is potentially seriously misleading. For not all *poleis* had a properly urban centre, as Sparta did not, and an essential feature of the *polis* was the large extent to which it identified town and country.

studying his career. By ancient standards the life of Agesilaos at least after his unheralded accession is unusually fully documented (Chapters 5,22). Xenophon, one of our main surviving narrative sources for all Greek history between about 410 and 360, was also a personal friend and political client of Agesilaos (Chapter 9) besides being his first 'biographer'. Indeed, his encomium known simply as the *Agesilaos* is one of the earliest examples of the biographical genre in western literature. Most of the other major historians and publicists of the fourth century could not, even had they wished to, avoid commenting on what may properly be called the Agesilaos phenomenon (see esp. Theop. 115F321). The later extant sources, who drew directly or indirectly on these, include two more biographers of Agesilaos, most notably Plutarch. Finally, Agesilaos himself has been handed down to us as preternaturally loquacious for a Spartan, in the sense that in the Plutarchan collections of 'Apophthegms' more supposedly *ipsissima verba* are attributed to him than to any other king, commander or private person, Greek or non-Greek, not excluding those of the ubiquitous, omniprovident but mainly if not entirely fictitious Spartan lawgiver Lykourgos.

However, this apparent abundance of ancient testimony should not be allowed to mislead. Not only are all these sources less than wholly objective or 'scientifically' critical, but they fail individually and collectively to provide enough of the kind of material needed to write what would count today as a true biography of Agesilaos. This is so even if biography be defined minimally as 'an account of the life of a man from birth to death' (Momigliano 1971, 11). *A fortiori* the rather romantic conception of biography as 'poetry with a conscience' advanced by Robert Gittings (1978) cannot begin to be entertained in the present context. For the supposed *ipsissima verba* just mentioned (to which add perhaps Page 1981, no. CLXIV) are of course strictly figments of other people's imaginations; the one-word inscription consisting of the name 'Agesilaos' that someone cut on an architectural member at Ephesos need have nothing to do with our Agesilaos (despite Börker 1980); and probably the closest we can get physically to Agesilaos the man is to inspect the substantial circular structure that has been plausibly identified with the 'circular building' (4.5.6) in which he was sitting in 390 reviewing the booty he had taken from the Perachora promontory of the Corinthia when news was conveyed to him of the savaging of a Spartan regiment (Chapter 12). In fact, of ancient political figures only Cicero and perhaps the Roman Emperor Julian (but see Athanassiadi-Fowden 1981, v) qualify for properly biographical treatment in the post-Lytton Strachey sense of an account of their inner as well as their public lives.

This conception of biography, however, has recently been challenged by Bernard Crick (1982, 29-39), who has advanced the contrary conception of 'external' biography as opposed to a (spuriously) empathetic character sketch. This 'external' conception he also distinguishes from and places above the 'Life and Times' approach, on the grounds that 'such a formula, unless a man has a great effect on events,is mainly padding'. This may well be so in many cases. But since there is no possibility of an 'internal' biography of Agesilaos, or indeed of any kind of biography except a narrowly 'political' one; and since it can and will be argued that Agesilaos did have 'a great effect on events', there would seem to be no objections to the 'Life and Times' approach in his case. Indeed, it has much to recommend it.

Negatively speaking, by concentrating attention as much on 'the crisis of Sparta' as on 'King Agesilaos' it should obviate the danger of distorting the general history of a period to suit the needs of a character-study. For, as Sir Ronald Syme has said (1939, 7), 'undue insistence upon the character and exploits of a single person invests history with dramatic unity at the expense of truth'; or, more epigrammatically (Syme 1974, 481), 'Biography offers an attractive approach to history, or a substitute'. Positively, the relative richness of biographical information that is available and the fact that Agesilaos not merely participated in but actively shaped Spartan society, culture and politics over several decades make it possible to use his career as a kind of prism to refract the light reflected by the economic, social, political, diplomatic, military and other facets of the Spartan crisis. In other words, an examination of the career of Agesilaos under these heads can be regarded as at the least a convenient expository device for writing a total history of Sparta in an epoch when she was at the centre of Greek affairs east of the Straits of Otranto.

Besides these particular reasons for wishing to study Agesilaos and Sparta, the time has come for a work of synthesis that takes advantage of the recent spate of monographs on aspects of Greek history in the hitherto relatively neglected first half of the fourth century (cf. Hamilton 1982d, 297-8, 317-18). Periodization, though, is the bane of all historians unless the 'periods' isolated are treated with reserve for what they are, mere conventions and conveniences. The student of Marc Bloch who wrote in an essay that in French history the eighteenth century (AD) began in 1714 and ended in 1789 (Bloch 1954, 182) was unconsciously doing us all a service. For it is a sheer coincidence that the great war between Sparta and Athens ended so close to the end of what we happen to call the fifth century and that the reign of Agesilaos began at more or less exactly the same time as the fourth. A new 'century', in other words, does not necessarily mean a new era or epoch of history, especially as those Greeks who were actually making the relevant history had no universally acknowledged system of time-reckoning let alone our BC/AD (or BCE/CE) division. It is therefore dangerous in the extreme to speak glibly of 'the crisis of the fourth century' as if the year 399 marked a radical discontinuity or even a significant break with all that had gone before – and in particular with 'the glory that was Greece' (meaning usually 'Periklean' Athens). On the other hand, it is no less clear that the Aegean Greek world had been importantly and permanently altered by the Athenian War and that if one were to select a date for the beginning of 'the fourth century' in a qualitative sense 404 would serve as well as any. Whether or not it is helpful to speak of a general crisis occurring in this qualitatively defined fourth century remains to be seen (esp. Chapter 15).

A final reason for studying Agesilaos in some detail today is that he has enjoyed and indeed still enjoys a flourishing *Nachleben*. His moral character above all has fascinated European writers and thinkers within the so-called 'Spartan tradition' brilliantly evoked by Elizabeth Rawson down into our own century. In a sense she is of course right that Agesilaos 'has never recovered from the eighteenth-century reaction against the princely warrior' in favour of 'the ideal ... of a more modest and socially responsible figure' (Rawson 1969, 226, 223). Yet it is also true that, as E. Zierke observed in his useful résumé of modern scholarship (1936, 22), 'one could almost establish a wave-like movement in the development of views on Agesilaos'. J.C.F. Manso (1800-1805) began the modern scholarly study of Sparta and so provides the first scholarly example of the reaction noted by Rawson. But his debunking view was countered by Plass and his in turn by Körtum. However, no full-dress study of Agesilaos appeared nor was any consistent attempt made to apply Niebuhrian *Quellenforschung* (cf. Christ 1972) to the sources for his career until the monograph of G.F. Hertzberg (1856). This landmark in Agesilaos studies is assessed separately in Appendix I. But Hertzberg, too, misguidedly tried to strike a balance in the debate over Agesilaos' moral character by arguing that it had been good until the Peace of Antalkidas of 386 (Chapter 11) but degenerated thereafter. This compromise was hardly calculated to appeal to A. Buttmann (1872), whose 'portrait of the life of a Spartan king and patriot' published two years after the Battle of Sedan achieved the near-impossible feat of outdoing Xenophon's encomium. The wheel, to change Zierke's metaphor, had come full circle.

Scholarly debate over Agesilaos is still lively, though happily it is no longer couched – at least not explicitly – in Tacitean moralizing or pseudo-psychological terms. But Buttmann's panegyric was the last monograph of any length devoted to his career. Zierke's Frankfurt dissertation, good as far as it goes, occupies only seventy-eight pages and is concerned with selected topics of Agesilaos' reign in its public aspects. Yet this is both the earliest and the longest of the 'main discussions' cited in a powerful but apologetic and ultimately unconvincing assessment by G.L. Cawkwell (1976a; cf. now 1983). More can, I believe, be done with the available material, especially in the light of two recent studies of Lysander (Rahe 1977, Bommelaer 1981). For Lysander served Agesilaos as a model both to follow and to avoid following (Chapter 6). I cannot and of course do not claim to have solved definitively the causal problems outlined earlier in this introductory chapter. Causation is a difficult web to unpick even when all the threads are distinctly visible and in good condition. But by incorporating the results of more than a century and a half of scholarship, by taking into account all the available evidence and by approaching it within the conceptual framework summed up in the quotation from Marx printed above, I hope to have been able to produce a new synthesis, a fresh starting-point for further research on a subject of permanent significance and perennial fascination.

2

Sparta at the Birth of Agesilaos

There never was a nation whose greatness was more empty than theirs: the splendor they lived in was inferior to that of a theatre, and the only thing they all could be proud of, was, that they enjoyed nothing. (Bernard Mandeville, *The Fable of the Bees*)

The birthdate of Agesilaos, like most details of his personal life, is not securely established. But for the reasons rehearsed in the next chapter a date of 445 or perhaps a little later should not be unduly wide of the mark. Which means that Agesilaos was born at a conjuncture in Spartan history scarcely less significant than the one in Macedonian history at which Alexander the Great is alleged to have drawn his first breath almost a century later (Plut. *Alex.* 3.8). For in the winter of 446/5, following the Greek equivalent of the Potsdam Conference, the Spartans and Athenians agreed to carve up the Aegean Greek world between them into two great power blocs.

The full text of the protocol now known as the Thirty Years' Peace (really Truce, since the Greek term was *spondai*) does not survive. But a copy inscribed on a bronze stele (pillar) erected under the watchful eyes of Zeus and Hera in the great Panhellenic sanctuary of Olympia was reportedly still visible and legible six centuries or so later (Paus. 5.23.4). Only seven clauses of the Peace are known for certain, and even of these the precise wording cannot be determined for lack of a surviving copy: (1) it was to last for thirty years; (2) Athens was to cede some territories acquired over the past fifteen years during the so-called 'First Peloponnesian War', notably the two ports of neighbouring Megara on the Corinthian and Saronic Gulfs; (3) a non-aggression formula provided that neither side should make an armed attack on the other if arbitration by a third party were requested; (4) each side was to have and to hold what it possessed when the other terms had been observed; (5) lists of the allies on either side were to be appended in writing to the treaty-document, and such listed allies might not then change sides; (6) states not so listed might ally themselves to either side in the future; and (finally, so far as the evidence goes) (7) Argos was explicitly mentioned as being free to conclude a private *entente* with Athens outside the framework of the Peace, should the two parties be so desirous.

The key clause is (4). Thereby the Spartans in effect recognized the Athenian

Empire (*archê*), a concept to which we shall return in Chapters 6 and 14; while for their part the Athenians acknowledged Sparta's control of what we call the Peloponnesian League. This multi-state alliance is the first major element in the birthright of Agesilaos that needs to be discussed. In fact, to paraphrase Voltaire's acid remark about the Holy Roman Empire, the Peloponnesian League was neither (exclusively or entirely) Peloponnesian nor (strictly) a league (see further Chapter 13). But like other misleading modern inexactitudes, such as 'colony' for *apoikia*, 'Peloponnesian League' is too deeply entrenched in current jargon to be conveniently uprooted; and there is in any case no obvious alternative formula to pick out this specially privileged group of Sparta's subordinate allies. What matters more, of course, is the significance of the League for Sparta. Briefly, it was both the shield whereby she protected her vulnerable domestic power-base, a 'security cocoon that Sparta had patiently woven around herself' (Legon 1981, 275), and also the diplomatic and military instrument through which she claimed and expressed the status of one of the two major powers of Aegean Greece in 445 while simultaneously suppressing the counter-claim of Argos to hegemony in the Peloponnese. Let us outline the latter function first.

The origins of the Peloponnesian League (soundly discussed by Wickert 1961; less satisfactorily by Moretti 1962, 5-95, esp. 76-81) are mostly lost in the mists of Herodotean logography. For although they fall squarely within the period *c.*550-479 chosen for special enquiry (*historiê*) by the Father of History, Herodotus was not the historian to be slowed down by diplomatic and constitutional niceties, and there is no documentary evidence certainly datable before 479 to put flesh on his narrative skeleton. The single pre-Hellenistic Spartan treaty of alliance that has been preserved on stone, that with the otherwise unknown Aitolian Erxadieis, cannot be unquestionably dated and does not unequivocally fall within the admittedly rather loose framework of the Peloponnesian League constitution (Peek 1974 and Gschnitzer 1978 agree on a date of *c.*500-475, but see Cartledge 1976a, 1978b; Kelly 1978b). It is indeed possible to query whether the League ever had anything that might usefully be called a 'constitution', in this or any period down to its effective dissolution in the mid-360s. But my own view is that its rudimentary constitutional structure did at least make it a *Bündnissystem*, a system of alliance, though not a *Staatenbund* or league (cf. Ste. Croix 1972, 104,117; Gschnitzer 1978, 33; against those cited in Ste. Croix 1972, 104n.45, to whom add Kelly 1975, 52-69). If the title be conceded, and if we may legitimately draw on Xenophon, who is by far our most prolific source, as well as fifth-century evidence, then the constitution of the Peloponnesian League in 445 may be summarized on the following lines.

The name of the League was 'The Lakedaimonians (Spartans) and their allies (*summachoi*)'. League members, it seems virtually certain, were allied individually by written treaty to Sparta alone and did not necessarily have any formal ties among themselves. Officially all allies were autonomous, and a clause to that effect may have been routinely inserted in the individual treaties (it does not appear in the Erxadieis treaty, but this is incomplete). That is, they had in theory the right to make their own *nomoi* (positive laws) and so, according to Greek notions of *nomoi*, might choose their form of political constitution and administer legal justice as they wished (Ste. Croix 1972, 98-9). In practice, however, the Spartans were careful to ensure that as a matter of convenience as well as ideology the allied states generally continued to be governed more or less as they were when first received into alliance, by well-disposed oligarchies (Thuc. 1.19,144.2 are clear statements of this Spartan principle; cf. 5.31.6). This well illustrates a general rule of Greek interstate relations and vocabulary, that 'the independence of the "autonomous" states stands always in the shadow of a stronger power' (Ostwald 1982, 1; following Bickerman 1958, 327-32, 334-7,343).

The claim of such oligarchies to govern rested in the first instance on their wealth and sometimes too on their supposed aristocratic birth, but ultimately on Spartan support and the threat or promise of Spartan military intervention. Relations with these friendly oligarchies were cemented by personal ties of ritual guest-friendship (*xenia*) involving especially the two Spartan royal houses; and, as with the client-kings of the Roman Empire, the sons of allied oligarchs might be sent to Sparta for a taste of the peculiarly Spartan brand of education discussed in the next chapter and so become known as *trophimoi xenoi* (5.3.9).[1] It was a short step – and one that notably Agesilaos was not afraid to take – from favouring such regimes to intervening militarily in an ally's internal affairs to impose or prop up a client or puppet oligarchy against the wishes of the majority of its citizens (cf. Ste. Croix 1954/5, 20n.5). Such intervention could be represented as fulfilling the absolute moral obligation of the aristocratic code to help one's friends (and harm one's enemies). Less politely put, it was an infringement of an ally's *autonomia* (see further Chapters 11 and 13 on this concept) and a technique of *Realpolitik*.

The allies, as mentioned above, were not necessarily bound formally to each other, and when the League as such was at peace wars between individual member-states were permitted or at least did occur (e.g. Plut. *Kim.* 17.1; Thuc. 4.134.1; contrast 5.4.36-7). But if an ally was attacked by a non-League member, Sparta was bound by the terms of the treaties to give aid 'with all strength in accordance with her ability' (*panti sthenei katto dunaton*) and *vice versa* if Sparta was so attacked – something which did not in fact happen on a large scale until 370/69 when the attackers crucially included revolted ex-members of the League (Chapters 12-14). In the case of aggressive action by the League as a whole, however, the relationship between Sparta and the allies was not one of equality and reciprocity (Ste. Croix 1972, 298-9). For the allies were required to swear to have the same friends and enemies as the Spartans (hence they became *summachoi*, since a *summachia* in its original, full sense was an offensive as well as a defensive alliance), whereas the Spartans did not necessarily or even usually take the reciprocal oath. Moreover, probably from the outset allies had to swear to 'follow the Spartans whithersoever they might lead' (e.g. 2.2.20, 4.6.2, 5.3.26, 6.3.8). This clause was a suitable reflection of Sparta's military preponderance, it is true, but formally it also robbed the allies of their *eleutheria* or freedom to determine their own foreign policy and so converted them into subjects and Sparta into their *hêgemôn* or leader. It was perhaps this *Hegemonieklausel* which

---

[1]Where no other indication is given such references are to Xenophon's *Hellenika*.

encouraged Herodotus to describe most of the Peloponnese from as early as the mid-sixth century as 'already subjugated (*katestrammenê*)' by Sparta (Hdt. 1.68.6, with Ste. Croix 1972, 108-10).

This glib generalization, however, disguises a process that was by no means automatic. The earliest known alliance, which may have served as a model for the rest, was concluded between Sparta and Tegea around 550 (*SV* 112). It would at least be symbolically apt if this were indeed the first alliance. For Tegea was the nearest *polis* to Sparta, it was one of the two major states of Arkadia (the other being Mantineia), and Arkadia was the single most vital geographical area of the Peloponnese outside their own home territory with which the Spartans had to deal. By allying with the Tegean oligarchy Sparta sought to prise her neighbour away from the embrace of Argos, Sparta's chief rival for the hegemony of the Peloponnese (e.g. Thuc. 5.40.3); to use Tegean influence and manpower in S.W. Arkadia to contain the ever potentially rebellious Messenian Helots; and to ensure that the obvious overland approach to her home territory was in safe and friendly hands. To make doubly sure of Argive acquiescence, a heavy defeat was inflicted on Argos by Sparta in about 545 and the disputed frontier region of Thyreatis (also known as Kynouria) was annexed to the Spartan *polis*. Within twenty years Sparta was almost certainly allied to Corinth, who controlled the vital Isthmos land-route and had a significant navy (cf. Cartledge 1982, 258 and n.83),[2] and perhaps soon after to Megara on the far, eastern side of the Isthmos (cf. Legon 1981, 143-5). For even though Corinth and Megara like many neighbouring Greek states were far from always enjoying the best of relations with each other, they also both saw the virtue of an alliance with Sparta that might provide aid against other hostile neighbours such as Argos and Athens besides shoring up their existing oligarchic regimes. Not only was the Isthmos now secure but Argos was hemmed in on the north as well as the south. By 491, it appears (Ste. Croix 1972, 333-5; but see now Figueira 1981), the aristocratic oligarchy of the island state of Aigina was also a Peloponnesian League ally, and Argos had again been soundly trounced, probably in 494. But the Persian invasions of 490 and 480-479 precipitated a generation of Peloponnesian instability for Sparta, fomented latterly by a revived Argos and abetted by an expansionist Athens (Cartledge 1979, ch.11). Stability was only restored – but not entirely satisfactorily and in the event temporarily – by the Peace of 446/5.

So far as the Peloponnesian League's constitution is concerned, a major development had occurred in or around 504. To be more accurate, a Spartan alliance was then transmogrified into something more deserving of the title 'Peloponnesian League'. Henceforth an inner circle of League allies was distinguished from the broader Spartan alliance which also comprised *ad hoc* alliances concluded later by Sparta outside the League framework (Ste. Croix 1972, 102-5; cf. Cargill 1981 for a similar distinction in the fourth century between allies of Athens who were members of the Second Athenian League and allies who were not). For Peloponnesian League members the

---

[2]J.B. Salmon, *Wealthy Corinth* (Oxford, 1984) unfortunately appeared after this book was finished: see my review in *CR* n.s. 35 (1985), 115-17.

hegemony-clause was now so modified that Sparta's decision to commit them to an aggressive war against an external enemy was no longer sufficient for League action. The decision of the Spartan Assembly had first to be ratified by a majority vote of allied representatives or mandated delegates (which they were is not known, but more likely the former) meeting in a Congress summoned by Sparta and usually held in Sparta over which a Spartan chairman presided.

Each ally regardless of size had one vote (among themselves Greek oligarchs could be as fiercely egalitarian as Greek democrats), and majority decisions were binding on the minority unless a dissenting ally could claim a prior religious obligation as a legitimate exemption (below). Should Sparta's decision for war be duly ratified, as in 432, then Sparta as *hêgemôn* levied the League army, herself contributing the commander-in-chief (normally a king) and designating Spartan officers (*xenagoi*) to levy the stipulated amount of allied troops; and it was Sparta who determined when and where the combined force was to muster. In these circumstances Sparta's influence naturally weighed heavily, but the outcome of a Congress was by no means necessarily a pure formality: the first Congress on record (Hdt. 5.91-3) in fact rejected the Spartan proposal in *c.*504 for war on Athens to reinstate Hippias as tyrant, and this was not the last time that Corinth, exploiting her strategic indispensability, was successfully to lead the allied opposition to Sparta's will. On the other hand, the League's decision-taking machinery ensured that the *hêgemôn* could not be committed against her will to spearheading a foreign policy of which she disapproved (cf. Ste. Croix 1972, 110-12). That permanent advantage to Sparta greatly overbalanced individual setbacks like that of *c.*504.

The conclusion of Peace by the League, as for instance in 446/5, was similarly subject to a majority vote of an allied Congress, and again the obligation to abide by the majority decision was binding. But in 421 the Corinthians, in a small minority on this occasion, claimed exemption from the League decision to ratify the Peace of Nikias by appealing to what they represented as a universally applicable exemption-clause. An 'impediment of gods or heroes', they alleged (Thuc. 5.30.3), made it impossible for them to swear to observe the Peace because that would mean breaking existing treaties with their allies in northern Greece (even though they were outside the Peloponnesian League). Since treaties, like much other public business in Classical Greece, were ultimately religious in content – in the sense that they were constituted by the oaths sworn in the name of gods or heroes (hence the erection of copies in sanctuaries such as Olympia) – this claim to exemption on the ground of a prior religious obligation was presumably valid (cf. Ste. Croix 1972, 118-20). It has been doubted whether an organization which tolerated so widely-cast an 'escape-clause' could have been effective as a power-unit, but this is to underestimate the Spartans' notorious religiosity (Hodkinson 1983, 273-6) and to overlook the fact that outright secession from the alliance was not permitted. Even if in Corinth's case the alleged impediment was merely a trumped-up excuse for prevarication and disobedience, it was at any rate nicely calculated to undermine Sparta's legitimacy as *hêgemôn*.

So long as Sparta observed the letter of her individual treaties with her allies and duly sought and received their collective approval of those foreign policies which involved League action, no ally had a strictly legal justification for refusing to 'follow whithersoever Sparta might lead' or to abide by peace-terms ratified by a League Congress – apart perhaps from the 'gods or heroes' exemption. If, nevertheless, an ally failed to fulfill its obligations, whether negatively by for example refusing to contribute its stipulated contingent to a League expedition or positively by, say, allying with a declared enemy of Sparta and the League, that constituted revolt and Sparta was fully justified in coercing the ally without the need to call a League Congress. Cases of genuine dispute, however, might arise when Sparta was either, as in 421, preternaturally weak or, as in 404 and 386, exceptionally strong. Then Sparta might either make unusual concessions to particularly formidable dissident allies (as to the Boiotians in 420 and the Mantineians some time after 418: see Chapters 14 and 13) or act strictly *ultra vires* in coercing and punishing allies who had in various ways exploited her earlier weakness (as the Eleians in the late 400s, and the Mantineians and Phleiasians in the 380s: Chapter 13). In the grey area between less than one hundred per cent obedience and outright revolt it was relative power rather than narrow legality that determined Sparta's behaviour towards a recalcitrant ally. But that behaviour, as I shall hope to demonstrate, was always conditioned by the maxim *salus patriae, suprema lex*. Sparta's conception of her own best interests, or rather the conception entertained by the group that at any time happened to be dominant within the Spartan political hierarchy, always guided her actions rather than any altruistic or even impersonal considerations of justice or morality. (Not that Sparta was peculiar in this respect, then or now.)

Which brings us naturally to the final aspect of the Peloponnesian League to be considered here. Each individual treaty between Sparta and her Peloponnesian League allies possibly contained, as the separate treaty of defensive alliance with Athens in 421 certainly did (Thuc. 5.23.2), a clause binding the ally to lend Sparta assistance in the event of a revolt by the 'slave class' (*douleia*, used here as the collective noun for *douloi*), that is by the Helots. It was perhaps in fulfilment of this obligation that Mantineia (5.2.3) and Aigina (Thuc. 2.27.2, 4.56.2) had given aid during the great revolt of the 460s (Cartledge 1979, 219-20). At any rate, it would not be at all surprising if some such provision had been inserted in the treaties at an appropriate moment after that revolt had been eventually crushed. But whether they all contained such an explicit provision or this obligation was tacitly subsumed under the 'friends and enemies' clause, it was without question the Helots who provided the link between the Peloponnesian League as the instrument of Spartan power abroad and the League as shield of Sparta's highly vulnerable domestic power-base. For the Helots were both the ultimate foundation of Spartan might, a sort of earthy caryatid like George Orwell's grimy Wigan coalminers, and Sparta's Achilles heel. 'Most Spartan institutions', as Thucydides (4.80.3) famously put it, 'have always been designed with a view to security against the Helots'.[3] The history of Sparta, it is not too much to say, is fundamentally the history of the class struggle between the Spartans and the Helots (cf. Cartledge 1979, ch.10; and see further Chapter 10).

[3] Or, according to a different interpretation of the Greek word-order: 'So far as the Helots are concerned, most Spartan institutions have always been designed with a view to security.'

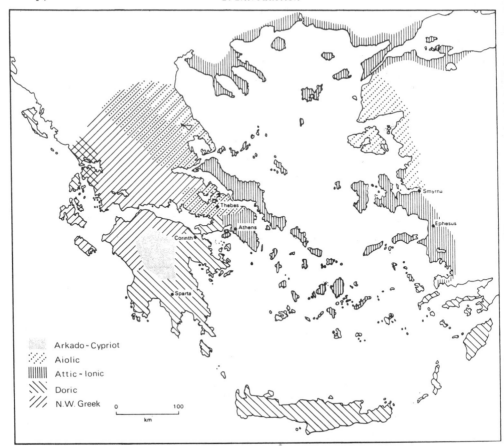

Fig. 2. The distribution of Greek dialects in the age of Agesilaos. After R.J.A. Talbert (ed.), *Atlas of Classical History* (London & Sydney 1985)

By the mid-tenth century Sparta on the Eurotas River had been settled by Greeks speaking the Doric sub-dialect of West Greek – or proto-Doric, to be absolutely precise (Fig. 2). The origins and early history of the settlement are enveloped in the fogs of what is often hopefully called 'tradition'. For the Spartans' somewhat humorously alleged interest in *archaiologia* (Plat. *Hipp. Ma.* 285d), that is in tales of the past including stories about the foundations of cities, was not, and for the most part could not have been even if it had been felt desirable, translated into reliable history either by Spartans or by concerned outsiders. From a welter of conflicting modern hypotheses one fact stands out starkly. The origins of the Spartan state in its historical form are inextricably tied up with the forced labour pumped out of the class of state-serfs known as Helots (*Heilôtai*).

In the mid-fifth century, Thucydides (1.101.2) reveals, most Helots were the descendants of the ancient Messenians who had been enslaved long ago (in fact in the wars of the eighth and seventh centuries: Cartledge 1979, ch.8), and as a result all Helots were known generically as 'Messenians'. Historically, though, the first Helots had been created not in Messenia but in Lakonia, the nuclear territory of the Spartans in southern Peloponnese to east of the 2407m Taygetos massif (Fig. 1). In the eighth century the Spartans had transferred their imperialist attentions from the valley of the Eurotas to that of the Pamisos, but the subjugation of the Messenians (an amalgam of more or less recently settled peoples) had cost them far more time, manpower and resources than they could have wished. It was to meet this challenge that the Spartans transformed themselves into the first hoplite republic in Greece through a unique package of reforms the bulk of which seems to have been passed in the first half of the seventh century.

Again the details are obscure, but the essence of the reforms was fourfold. *Economically*, Spartan citizenship was tied to possession of an allotment (*klaros*) from the produce of which a Spartiate (full Spartan citizen) was required to pay monthly a fixed minimum contribution to a common mess (*sussition, suskanion* and other terms: Chapter 3). *Militarily*, all Spartiates became hoplites, that is heavy-armed infantrymen, and the organization of the army was somehow (obscurely to us: Appendix II) linked to that of the messes: 'All the citizens were "equal" and equally aristocrats, in that all belonged to a military organisation based on common feasts' (Murray 1981, 1308). *Politically*, the Assembly of hoplite Peers (*Homoioi*, as they perhaps now began to call themselves) won the right to a say at least in matters of peace and war. And *socially*, in order to produce the desired uniformity, solidarity and unquestioning obedience and discipline, a comprehensive system of public education known as the *agôgê* (literally 'raising', a term appropriate to cattle) was rigidly enforced by the central authorities of the state (Chapter 3); though this was only one element in a concerted assault on family or any other ties that might pull in a direction counter to the perceived needs of the *polis* as a whole.

By the end of the seventh century the Messenian Wars of aggrandisement were at long last over. But though subjugated the Helots, especially but not only the Messenians, remained a constant lurking threat to internal order, and each year the Spartans ritually declared war on their enemy within (Arist. fr. 538). It was the Helot threat, too, which decisively influenced the switch away from outright imperialist aggression to the diplomatic initiative of the sixth century that culminated in the formation of the Peloponnesian League. It is revealing that in the document marking the end of a long period of hostility the Tegeans were specifically ordered by the Spartans not to give refugee Messenians citizen rights in Tegea (Arist. fr. 592, with Jacoby 1944). But the Helots were not the only factor within the border of the Spartan state that influenced this diplomatic shift.

In tandem with the creation of the Helots the Spartans had developed a third force within the population of Lakonia and Messenia. The Perioikoi, as their name denotes, 'lived round about' the Spartans and Helots. In the Classical fifth and fourth centuries there were perhaps as many as eighty Perioikic settlements farming the less fertile land along the hilly margins of the Eurotas and Pamisos valleys or occupying coastal sites from Thyrea in N.E. Lakonia round to

Kyparissia in N.W. Messenia. Their origins are obscure and probably diverse (Cartledge 1979, ch. 7), but their status as it had evolved by the fifth century was apparently uniform and is easier for us to grasp (Cartledge 1979, ch.10). The Perioikoi were personally free, unlike the Helots, and in their own individual communities, which could with some degree of plausibility be called *poleis*, they enjoyed a form of local autonomy. But vis-à-vis Sparta they had no public political rights whatsoever, even though in military contexts they might share the designation 'Lakedaimonians' with the Spartans; and probably for most of them their private rights of landholding and marriage and civil contract were conditional upon the good will of the suzerain. It is noteworthy that the Spartan kings owned tracts of land in many of the Perioikic *poleis* (Xen. *LP* 15.3), and the Perioikoi may have been required to make some financial contribution to the central Spartan exchequer. What is certain is that militarily they were wholly at the Spartans' beck, acting as an early warning system and first line of defence against rebellious Helots within Lakonia and Messenia and at latest by the early fifth century obliged to contribute to the regular Lakedaimonian army on expeditions beyond the frontiers. Indeed, as Spartiate manpower declined sharply (Chapters 4 and 10), so Perioikic military service became progressively more vital until by 425 they were actually brigaded in the same units with Spartiate hoplites (Chapters 4, 12, App. II).

Some slight positive evidence exists (esp. 5.3.9) for the kind of social differentiation within the Perioikic communities that we might in any case have suspected, and it is reasonable to suppose that Sparta treated her Perioikic subjects analogously to her Peloponnesian League subject allies inasmuch as she will have taken care to ensure that they were controlled by the wealthy and ideologically pliant few. In short, Sparta's relations with the Perioikic *poleis* could well have provided the original idea and model for the Peloponnesian League (cf. Cartledge 1980b, 107-8).

From the seventh century onwards, then, Sparta had turned herself into a uniquely large, rich and well-integrated state, specifically a new-model military state based ultimately on the exploitation of the Helots. As Thucydides (1.18.1) acutely observed, the achievement of domestic stability at an early date (though he put it too early) was a major source of Sparta's great strength and had enabled her to intervene in the affairs of other states. By creating in addition the Peloponnesian League Sparta had both consolidated her domestic power-base and extended her influence and power abroad. It was as *hêgemôn* of the League that Sparta as of right led the thirty or so loyalist Greek states to victory over the invading Persian horde in 480-479. Sparta deserved her place at the head of the roll of honour inscribed on the Serpent Column victory-monument erected in the Panhellenic sanctuary of Delphi (M/L 27 = Fornara 1983, no.59).

As has already been remarked, however, the generation following this victory brought severe problems for Sparta, especially in the Peloponnese. Divisions over policy between leading Spartans and differences with key Peloponnesian League allies had been exploited both by Argos and by Athens who, thanks to her new navy, was rapidly becoming the other Greek super-power. These difficulties were compounded by a destructive earthquake that hit Sparta in about 465 and was followed at once by a massive revolt of the Helots. The latter were always apt to take advantage of their masters' misfortunes and on this occasion received support from two Perioikic communities in Messenia. Finally, Sparta found herself involved willy-nilly in the so-called First Peloponnesian War of *c*.460-445 against Athens and her allies. With Athens fought Megara, who was perhaps the first Peloponnesian League member to have revolted from Sparta by allying with an enemy state (Cartledge 1979, 226). This alliance with Megara, as we saw from the terms of the Thirty Years' Peace, had given Athens direct access to the Corinthian Gulf. It had also enabled her to muzzle Corinth yet more tightly by settling a colony of Helot rebels fresh from the great revolt at the mouth of the Gulf in Naupaktos. Hence Sparta's involvement in the War through what Thucydides would have called *anankê* or necessity, and her first major military involvement in central Greece beyond the Isthmos since the late sixth century to try to break Athens' stranglehold on the land-route through the Megarid.

By 446 Sparta seemed at last to have extricated herself from imminent disaster. She had won an important set-piece hoplite battle at Tanagra in Boiotia in 458 or 457 and had survived a Helot revolt, a seaborne raid on her own territory and the loss of Aigina to Athens. Indeed, as the Agiad king Pleistoanax led a Peloponnesian League army into Attika following the return of errant Megara to the fold, Athens, preoccupied with the revolt of her neighbouring Euboian allies, was apparently at his mercy. Yet soon after crossing the Athenian frontier Pleistoanax withdrew and Athens was able to restore her position in Euboia before proceeding to the conference table to negotiate the Thirty Years' Peace. The Peace was concluded, and Pleistoanax may have hoped to take the credit for an agreement that on paper should obviate some of the difficulties experienced by Sparta since the Persian Wars. Instead, Pleistoanax was put on trial, found guilty of bribery and compelled to go into exile in company with a close political associate. This unfortunately ill-documented affair opens a (rather dirty and cracked) window onto the determination of policy at Sparta and the fierce struggles for power within the Spartan political hierarchy.

While on campaign beyond the frontiers of Lakedaimon (the official name of the Spartan state) the king deputed to command the army was virtually an absolute monarch – virtually, because even here two of the five annually selected chief executive officials called Ephors or 'Overseers' accompanied him to perform the function indicated by their title (see further Chapter 8). Once back in Sparta, though, the king could in effect be called to account by being put on trial before his peers. In such cases the thirty-man Gerousia ('Senate' would be a precise equivalent), which included the two kings *ex officio*, sat as a supreme court together with the Ephors. Through their exclusive power of jurisdiction in these and other capital cases (Ste. Croix 1972, 349-50) the Gerontes (literally 'old men', who had to be at least 60 and so beyond military age) wielded a strong retrospective influence over the conduct of foreign and domestic policy. Prospectively too, it seems that they fulfilled a probouleutic (pre-deliberative) function in relation to the warrior Assembly, whose prerogative it was to decide on matters of peace and war (Chapter 8). What, then, lay behind the prosecution and conviction of Pleistoanax in 446/5?

Sparta, as noted in Chapter 1, could not properly be described as a *basileia* or kingdom. Yet for reasons to be fully explored later (esp. Chapters 7,8,9 and 12), a king might achieve a position of dominance in Sparta above and beyond his formally limited powers, provided that he was scrupulous to observe the Spartan proprieties and skilful in manipulating the extensive funds of patronage at his disposal. Pleistoanax, however, had the galling humiliation of twice seeing his eirenic or at least physically non-aggressive policy towards Athens undermined by his political opponents at home. Not only was he exiled in 445 but within five years Sparta was prepared to violate the Peace (Cartledge 1982, 261-2). His second peace initiative, which culminated in the Peace of 421 (conventionally named after the Athenian Nikias but it could as well be called the Peace of Pleistoanax), had an even shorter active life.

The opposition to this Peace was led by two of the Ephors of 421/0 (Thuc. 5.36.1), and it is a reasonable surmise that at least a majority of the Ephors had voted for his condemnation in 446/5 too. But it would be wrong to see the determination of policy in Sparta simply in terms of a struggle between the kings and the Ephors. Rather, when there were two or more policy options, as there always were in our period, the Spartan political hierarchy tended to crystallize into two or more factions in which individuals Ephors might or might not be prominent. (It is remarkable how few Ephors achieved the kind of prominence that ensured the preservation of their names, let alone their deeds.) At the head of these factions, whether merely as figureheads or as their guiding forces, stood the two kings. For traditionally (Hdt. 6.52.8) the kings agreed to disagree with each other, for all that when in Sparta they lived perforce in quite intimate proximity as fellow-members of the royal mess and might develop feelings bordering on affection regardless of their political differences (esp. 5.3.20). Exceptionally, as in the case of a Brasidas or a Lysander, a man born outside the royal families might achieve political prominence for a spell. But it is a fair measure of the vulnerability of these extra-regal power groupings that Lysander wished to alter the Spartan constitution so as to make himself eligible for selection as king (Chapter 6), while both he and Brasidas achieved far greater power and glory outside than in Sparta. As for the Ephors who led the opposition to the Peace of 421, it is doubtful whether they would have achieved much without the tacit support of Pleistoanax' rival King Agis. His father Archidamos II had doubtless voted against Pleistoanax in 446/5, just as he himself was to vote against Pausanias in 403.

Some Spartiates, in other words, were more equal than others, as is only to be expected in a hierarchically ordered and gerontocratic military society. But what one would not expect to find in such a society as Sparta advertised herself to be is the survival of prerogatives associated not just with wealth but also – in the case of the kingship and, I believe, the Gerousia – with birth. In the kernel of Spartan egalitarianism festered the cancre of hereditary privilege. To outsiders like Herodotus and Thucydides Sparta may have seemed at least by normal Greek standards remarkably stable politically. But it was a stability shot through with aggressive competitiveness and constant, sometimes unbearable tensions at all levels. It was partly for this reason that the Thirty Years' Peace was destined to run for less than half its intended span. But before we consider the outbreak and significance of the Athenian War (Chapter 4) we must first look more closely into the circumstances of the birth and upbringing of Agesilaos.

3

Agesilaoupaideia: Educating Agesilaos

[Deformed persons] will, if they be of spirit, seek to free themselves from scorn; which must be either by virtue or malice: and therefore let it not be marvelled if sometimes they prove excellent persons; as was Agesilaus. (Francis Bacon, *Essay* XLIV 'Of Deformity')

All I say is, kings is kings, and you got to make allowances. Take them all round, they're a mighty ornery lot. It's the way they're raised. (Mark Twain, *Huckleberry Finn*)

Agesilaos was unusually short by Spartan standards (cf. Xen. *LP* 1.10,2.6), and he suffered the further potentially grave disability of being lame in one leg from birth. His height, or rather lack of it, gave rise to the apocryphal anecdote that his father had been fined by the Ephors for marrying a short woman who would produce not kings but kinglets (Plut. *Ages.* 2.6, from Theophrastos; *Mor.* 1d; Athen. 13.566d; cf. Ste. Croix 1972, 352); this would presumably have been after an accusation of 'bad marriage' (*dikê kakogamiou*: Poll. 3.48). His lameness was brought up against him in the succession-dispute that followed the death of Agis II and nearly scuppered his chances of becoming king (Chapter 7). This episode, which incidentally proves that he was congenitally lame,[1] demonstrates that 'lameness' of birth, illegitimacy in other words, was regarded – at least at the time – as a greater political disability than lameness of body (Vernant 1982, 22; for ancient attitudes to deformity in general cf. Den Boer 1979, ch.7).

   Yet despite or perhaps, as Bacon would have it, because of these physical disadvantages Agesilaos showed himself second to no Spartan in physical endeavour and achievement, even if his stature and gait did provoke the typically Greek tendency to mock a man's natural impairments. By the close of his long and for the most part frenetically active life his body was seared with scars from war-wounds (Plut. *Ages.* 36.3), and he died, not at Sparta on his humble pallet in his quaintly antiquated but probably not genuinely antique dwelling (Xen. *Ages.* 8.7), but on the coast of N. Africa en route home from yet another campaign (Chapters 15-16).

   There was no age-limit for commanders in ancient Greece (Finley 1981b,

---

[1]Otherwise the crafty Lysander would undoubtedly have deflected his opponents' quasi-religious attack by pointing out that his man had been lamed in battle or a riding accident or whatever.

156-7), whereas it was a matter for comment when U.S. President Reagan ordered the retirement of eighty-one year-old Admiral Hyman Rickover at the end of 1981. Indeed, it was said (Plut. *Pelop.* 2.7) that a general should die in old age if not of old age. Agesilaos was a veritable *makrobios*. Plutarch (*Ages.* 36.3,40.3) says that he was over eighty when he set sail for Africa and eighty-four when he died. This does not conflict with Xenophon's vaguer statement that he was about eighty at the start of this campaign (*Ages.* 2.28). The precise date of his death cannot be fixed with absolute certainty. But a good case has been made from the standpoint of Egyptian history for the winter of 360/59 (Kienitz 1953, 156-7, followed by Cawkwell 1976a, 63n.8; *contra* Kelly 1975, 31-5 who prefers 359/8). If Plutarch's exact figure of eighty-four be accepted – and he was either using what looks like a good chronographic source or drawing on the fruits of his own researches in the Spartan archives (*anagraphai: Ages.* 19.6) – then Agesilaos will have been born in 445 or more probably 444. To this conclusion Xenophon's assertion (*Ages.* 1.6) that he was 'still young' (*eti neos*) when he acceded in or just before 400 (Chapter 7) has seemed an obstacle. But rather than take the drastic step of emending to 'no longer young' (*ouketi*) I suggest that here as elsewhere Xenophon may silently have been employing a Spartan technical term. For it has been cogently argued (Wade-Gery 1958, 73, 82) that in a military context 'the youth' (*hê neotês*: Hdt. 9.12.2) comprised the Spartiate year-classes from twenty to forty-four inclusive and so meant something akin to the Roman *iuniores*. Agesilaos, at forty-three or forty-four, would just have qualified as a *neos* at his accession, and there would be particular point to Xenophon's saying that he was 'still' young.

By 445 or 444 his father Archidamos II had already reigned for at least a quarter of a century (cf. Hereward 1956) and was approaching the officially defined threshold of 'old age' in Sparta, if indeed he was not already over sixty. Agesilaos was a product of his second marriage (Plut. *Ages.* 1.1; see Fig. 3). The first had been contracted, no doubt for pecuniary and status reasons, with his own step-aunt and terminated by her death. His second marriage was to a woman who was young enough to remarry and bear a child (Teleutias) after the

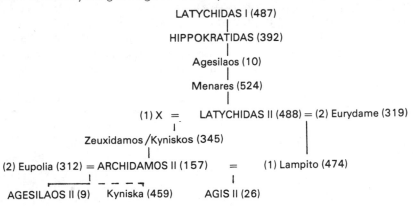

Fig.3. The ancestry of Agesilaos (numbers in brackets after Poralla 1913; broken line = filiation uncertain)

death of Archidamos (in at latest winter 427/6) and who was perhaps still alive in 391 (an inference from 4.4.19). Since Spartan girls seem typically to have been married at around the age of twenty (Cartledge 1981b, 94-5), Archidamos should have taken his second wife somewhere in the earlier 440s – that is, not long before the birth of Agesilaos as we might have anticipated.

We happen to know the names both of Agesilaos' mother, Eupôlia, and of his maternal grandfather, Melesippidas, probably thanks to the personal archival research of Plutarch mentioned above. Their horsey, ergo aristocratic nomenclature suggests that once again Archidamos had married prudently on grounds of social and economic status, even if the stature of his second wife was not all that it might have been (see further Chapter 9). Two facts, though, about the infant Agesilaos are rather surprising at first sight. The first (as already remarked by Michell 1952, 110n.3) is that he was allowed to survive. The second is his name.

As to his surviving, the decision to rear him was presumably not taken solely by Archidamos, since in Sparta that prerogative was ordinarily transferred in part from the natural father to the community as represented by the appropriate tribal elders (Plut. *Lyk.* 16.1-2; cf. Xen. *LP* 6.1-2). So if royal babies were treated in the usual Spartan way, as may perhaps be inferred from the survival of Damaratos (later King Damaratos) and Agesilaos' rival Latychidas whom their fathers had considered illegitimate, one might have expected that the lameness of Agesilaos would have counted decisively against him and that he would have joined other rejects at the foot of the aptly named Apothetai chasm. It is possible that his lameness was not markedly obvious at first, though this is perhaps unlikely in view of the fact that Spartan infants were not swaddled. So other explanations may be canvassed. His later life would suggest that in all other respects he was a well-formed and healthy specimen and so perfectly capable of coping with the rigours of the ritualistic or hygienic wine-baths that constituted the first of a whole series of public examinations to which Spartan males were subjected. It may have been felt that as he was not in direct line for the Eurypontid throne his lameness would not make him a potential liability as commander-in-chief or conversely that Agis might die prematurely and so leave Archidamos and the Eurypontids without a direct successor. But there is also a more intriguing, more sociological explanation available: that Agesilaos was reared chiefly because Sparta was already experiencing severe manpower shortage and so required all male infants who were not utterly incapacitated to be raised.

As for his name, there are two royals called Agesilaos attested before our Agesilaos. The earlier belonged to the other house, that of the Agiadai. His regnal dates are wholly conjectural, but *c.*815-785 may be an acceptable guess (Forrest 1980, 21). The other homonymous royal predecessor was a direct ancestor, in fact a paternal great-great-great-grandfather. He appears in the Eurypontid list rehearsed by Herodotus (8.131.2), who explicitly remarks that he did not reign. The nature and functions of this Herodotean list have been discussed in my earlier book (Cartledge 1979, App. 3). I argued there that it was a king-list which mainly served to legitimate the title of the Eurypontids to rule as direct descendants both of the pre-Dorian hero-god Herakles and of the eponymous Euryp(h)on. However, in its uppermost reaches this list contains two suspiciously *ben trovato* names, Prytanis and Eunomos. Their retrospective insertion tends to confirm the information conveyed elsewhere by Herodotus (6.51) that the house of Eurysthenes, that is the Agiads, was 'the more honoured of the two inasmuch as it is the senior branch'. In the fourth century further surgery was deemed necessary, and Soös was grafted onto the Eurypontid tree to make the tally of reigning sovereigns from the two houses precisely equal (Figure 7).

The origins of the Spartan dyarchy will forever be uncertain, but it seems a reasonable inference that the Agiads owed their superior honour to the fact that at one time they had been the sole ruling house. The first joint kings are likely to have been the first to whom joint action is attributed, namely the Agiad Archelaos and the Eurypontid Charilaos (or Charillos), whose reigns can be dated in the second quarter of the eighth century (Cartledge 1980b, 98). Archelaos was not the first Agiad to bear a name compounded of *laos* (people). In this he had been preceded by Leobotas (or Labotas) and Agesilaos I. But Charilaos was the first such Eurypontid, and there may be significance in the emulous choice of a name with a root stretching back at least to Late Bronze Age times. At Mycenaean Pylos, it seems, the Lawagetas (leader of the *laos*) was a dignitary second in importance only to the Wanax or High King.

But in the early seventh century an innovation in royal nomenclature is clearly detectable, the use of a name compounded with *damos*. This word too had antecedents in the Mycenaean world, where it seems to have meant a local village community (Ventris/Chadwick 1973, Index s.v.). In the historical period, however, *damos* had acquired another, politically significant meaning, and it was probably no accident that the first Spartan king to bear a *damos*-name was the Eurypontid Archidamos I whose reign is plausibly located around 660-45. For it was precisely in the first half of the seventh century that the Spartan *damos*, in the sense of the non-aristocratic mass of ordinary Spartan citizen warriors, won formal political recognition (Chapter 2). It would not have been surprising if the supposedly junior royal house had moved rather more smartly with the times and sought to ingratiate itself with the Spartan commons. Archidamos I's two immediate successors bore *laos*-names, but beginning with Damaratos (born *c*.550) eight of the remaining fourteen Eurypontid kings sport *damos* nomenclature. Our Agesilaos, then, is a throwback to a bygone era in his name as in so much else (a substantive point missed in Sergent 1976, 3-29, a wilfully selective and perverse when not demonstrably erroneous discussion of Spartan royal nomenclature).

The singularity of Agesilaos' early life by no means ends here. Once past his seventh birthday he was taken from his father's house and enrolled in a 'pack' or 'herd' (*boua, agela*) with his coevals thereby embarking upon the gruelling endurance test and obstacle course that served boys up to the age of eighteen as an education in Sparta. Nothing unusual in that, it may be thought: every boy was compelled to go through the 'upbringing' or 'raising' (*agôgê*) in what Simonides therefore called 'mantaming' Sparta (*damasimbrotos: ap.* Plut. *Ages.* 1.3; cf. Vermeule 1979, 101, 235n.22). What made it remarkable in the case of Agesilaos was that he subsequently became king. For the heirs-apparent were exempted from this otherwise universal obligation (Plut. *Ages.* 1.4, with Cartledge 1978a, 28-9), so that Spartan kings typically had not shared the education of their compatriots. In this respect as in others Agesilaos was the prototype for Xenophon's fictional Cyrus the Great who in the *Cyropaedia* experienced precisely the same *paideia* as the Persian Honoured Equals (*Homotimoi*, reminiscent of the Spartan Homoioi; but see Carlier 1978, 141-3).

Plutarch is our sole witness to this exemption, and an unreliable Hellenistic writer (Teles fr. 3 Hense) may formally contradict it. But there are powerful extrinsic reasons for accepting Plutarch's testimony even if it is not possible to say what his ultimate source of information was. First, the Spartans could have wanted to avoid the risk of a poor performance in the *agôgê* by their future kings and warlords. Second, they could have esteemed other qualities than those of brute toughness and unquestioning obedience drilled in by the educational regime as essential for their leaders. But over and above these is a third reason, the exceptional status of the Spartan kings both in life and in death which may properly be called charismatic (Chapters 7, 16). It would have been entirely consonant with this peculiar regal status if the heirs-apparent had not been treated as other Spartan boys were. For the latter, successful passage through the *agôgê* was a requirement of full Spartan citizenship and so membership in the elite cadre of the Homoioi or 'Peers' (3.3.5; Xen. *LP* 10.7, 13.1,7; *Anab.* 4.6.14; Arist. *Pol.* 1306b10; with Shimron 1979). Exemption from the *agôgê* would therefore mark out the kings from boyhood as standing on a superior plane even to that of the Homoioi. It would have institutionalised their charismatic status.

Conversely, the fact that a king had gone through the *agôgê* and passed all its formidable tests with flying colours could only have enhanced the quasi-divinity with which the Spartan kingship was hedged. Such was the position of Agesilaos, as it had been before him of the Agiad Leonidas (rightly noted by Hertzberg 1856,2), the quintessential Spartan hero-king. How important success in the *agôgê* might be is also illustrated, I believe, by the succession-dispute between the Agiad half-brothers Kleomenes (1) and Dorieus. Kleomenes was the heir-apparent and *ex hypothesi* exempted from the *agôgê*; so when Dorieus challenged his right to the throne on grounds of his own superior manly virtue (*andragathia*) as displayed among his age-mates (Hdt. 5.42.1), this is most naturally interpreted as a reference to his performance in the *agôgê*. In short, the *Agesilaoupaideia* or education of Agesilaos helps explain both why he became king and, I shall argue, the quality and significance of his reign.

It also exemplifies a peculiar and peculiarly important structural feature of Spartan society, the full implications of which may be better appreciated through comparative analysis. Long ago striking similarities were noticed between the *agôgê* and cycles of male initiation in so-called 'primitive' tribal societies, similarities both in form and in detail. But these earlier interpreters did not always sufficiently realize that 'What anthropology illuminates about Sparta ... are certain aspects of her lost early history rather than the Sparta from which the fossilized evidence comes' (Finley 1975, 116-17). Comparative ethnography should be used as a kind of geological tool to lay bare the strata of cultural deposit below those exposed for us by the surviving literary sources (cf. Cartledge 1981a, 24). For Sparta and the tribal societies of the anthropologists are in evolutionary perspective not strictly analogous entities. Even the Archaic Spartans of the eighth century were not a *Naturvolk* or 'primitive' people. Still less was Classical Sparta in technical anthropological parlance a 'small-scale community' or 'pre-state society'. Thus while anthropology might be used to disclose the hypothetical or hidden origins of certain historical Spartan customs or cultural complexes, by itself it could not explain why these customs had 'survived' or took the form they did in, say, the third quarter of the fifth century when Agesilaos was undergoing the *agôgê*. In short, anthropology alone could not account for the function of the *agôgê* in relation to the structure of Spartan society in Agesilaos' youth.

The developed *agôgê* as recorded in the pages of Xenophon, Plutarch and other even more inferior writers was a mainly secular educational cycle with important religious elements. If we speak of it as a process of 'initiation', this has to be understood primarily in a metaphorical or secular sense. In cross-cultural perspective puberty is the change of life most often chosen as the moment to symbolise the threshold over which the initiand must pass from immaturity to adulthood and full membership of the adult community. In Sparta the developed *agôgê* betrays a trace of puberty-rite initiation inasmuch as the instruction and supervision of the boys were intensified after they had reached the age of twelve. But this intensification was not an end in itself. It was subordinated to the overall aim of the *agôgê*. Hypothetically, this process of subordination could have occurred as the state organization of Sparta rose above the primitive structure of the age-set system in the eighth-seventh century. The age-sets were maintained – in technical language the *agôgê* is a graded age-set system – but only the year-classes from the thirteenth onwards kept or were now given the archaic-sounding names preserved for us in late glosses on manuscripts of Herodotus and Strabo (Tazelaar 1967, whose schema is rightly accepted by Hodkinson 1983,245-51, in his excellent brief characterisation of the *agôgê*). The emphasis was placed on the years from twelve to social as opposed to sexual maturity. For the overriding aim of this educational cycle was military, the production of exemplary adult male warriors.

'From the very beginning of boyhood they are trained and disciplined for land warfare', noted one of Xenophon's fervently pro-Spartan speakers (7.1.8; cf. Xen. *Mem.* 3.5.15-16; other references *ap.* Whibley 1896, 119). This was a necessity not a luxury or quaint conservatism for a society the very existence of which was constantly menaced by the Helots (Chapter 10). In other societies such as our own warfare can be a way of expressing socially undesirable behaviour in a socially acceptable form (Harrison 1973, 4). But for the Spartans their behaviour in war was a natural extension of the mores drummed into them through the rigours of the *agôgê*. The cycle should therefore be seen as educational not just in the narrow sense that it imparted technical skills but also in the sense that it was the chief means of socializing the Spartan youth, of attuning them to the ideals of the adult members of the community and in particular those of the old men beyond military age. If socialization was complete – and even in 'totalitarian' Sparta it was not always so – the Spartan youth internalized the values of their elders (and *ipso facto*, according to Spartan ideas, betters) and made them their own. Above all else, they were expected to digest the message that a noble death in battle was infinitely preferable to an ignoble life (e.g. Xen. *LP* 9.1, with Loraux 1977). 'With your shield or on it', an apophthegm attributed by Aristotle (*ap.* Stob. *Flor.* 7.31) to Gorgo daughter of Kleomenes I and wife of Leonidas, summed this attitude up, besides nicely suggesting how women, precisely the non-military half of the Spartan population, were integrated within the dominant masculine warrior code. The positive glorification of such a death was reinforced negatively by the prospect of richly varied sanctions of dishonour (*aidôs, aischunê*: Thuc. 1.84.3).

More pragmatically the future Spartan hoplite learned through the *agôgê* the asceticism of campaign (cf. Gernet 1983, 171-2) in regard to food, clothing and bedding that enabled him to make the transition from life in Sparta with the minimum of adjustment. He also learned the cardinal battlefield virtues of discipline, including self-discipline (*sôphrosunê*: Isok. 12.116), vigilance (*phulakê*: Thuc. 2.11.9), obedience to authority (*peitharchia*) and unflinching toughness in the face of the enemy (*andreia*, literally 'manliness'). Not only did enrolment in a *boua* or *agela*, itself part of a 'squadron' (*ila*), accustom him to military organization, but mock battles were staged and fought with remarkable no-holds-barred savagery (Paus. 3.14.8-10). Indeed, a propensity to physical violence was fostered at all levels and in all spheres inside and outside the bounds of formal competitions in what became known as the 'boys' contest' (*paidikos agôn*). The line was drawn at actual homicide, and the penalty for manslaughter was exile (Xen. *Anab.* 4.8.25; cf. Plut. *Mor.* 233f (34)), since apart from the ritual pollution incurred this was wasteful of indispensable manpower. But anything short of homicide was tolerated, indeed officially sanctioned. Corporal punishment for failure was inflicted with relentless brutality by the young adults known as 'Whip-bearers' (Xen. *LP* 2.2) and by any other adults who happened to be on hand, the Spartans (as often) holding an extreme version of a general Greek theory – in this case that pain was an integral element in the learning process.

Overall supervision of the young was officially one of the many duties of the Ephors, but it was the special responsibility of the Paidonomos (literally 'boy-herd') who was somehow selected from among the youngest adults. This top-level supervision was a function of the fact that Sparta was the only state in all Greece to prescribe a comprehensive system of public education for all boys and it well illustrates the Spartan genius for minute organization. But it may also help to explain the Spartans' notorious inability to conduct themselves with tact and moderation in positions of authority outside Sparta once they were freed from the prying glances and strong right arms of their peers and seniors (cf. Chapter 6). Equally, the negative emphasis on punishment for any deviation from a predetermined and externally imposed line of behaviour accounts for their characteristically one-dimensional and inflexible interpretation of Sparta's best interests in foreign relations.

The overridingly physical character of Spartan education is clear enough. Literacy and music were not entirely neglected (Cartledge 1978a); but deep literacy was confined to the elite few, and music was apparently wholly restricted to public manifestations of competitive choral singing and to various kinds of dancing (valued because it was conducive to the sense of rhythm that could be important in hoplite warfare) rather than used for private cultivation and amusement. It was predominantly this physical emphasis of the *agôgê* that Aristotle (*Pol.* 1338b11-19; cf. 1271b2-6, 1333b11-21) had in mind when he sharply criticised the Spartans for mistaking one part of virtue, courage, for virtue itself and for being so singlemindedly fixated on instilling courage into the young as to 'render them like wild animals'. Training in virtue, he concluded, 'should not follow the Spartan model' (*Pol.* 1334a40-b3). Aristotle of course was writing or speaking in the 330s with the benefit of hindsight. By then the argument from success deployed in favour of the *agôgê* by Xenophon had collapsed, and Aristotle judged that the Spartans, now that they no longer ruled over others, were not a happy people. As usual the philosopher was on to something important, and the causal connection between Sparta's military ideal and way of life at home and her conduct of foreign policy will be explored in later chapters. Here, though, I am more interested in the other ways in which the *agôgê* helped to mould and reinforce the structure of Spartan society and especially in the effects of Agesilaos' passage through it on his future conduct as king.

Like many tribal initiatory cycles the *agôgê* served as an instrument for reinforcing the dominance of the adult male initiates over the non-initiated children and, less obviously but no less forcefully, over the female half of the citizen population. Spartan girls were, it seems, educated in some sense other than merely trained by their mothers and grandmothers for the domestic tasks that were the exclusive lot of other Greek girls; but they do not seem to have had anything comparable to the boys' *agôgê* and what training they did receive was chiefly designed to make them good mothers of male warriors. The *agôgê* provided socially therapeutic channels for aggression, even if manslaughter might occasionally occur. It reinforced masculine solidarity in a society where the atmosphere of masculine exclusiveness was peculiarly intense even by the standard of the 'men's club' that a Greek *polis* typically was. It symbolised through an elaborate series of rituals – the Gymnopaidiai, Karneia and Hyakinthia religious festivals are of special relevance here – the passage from family to community, from *oikos* to *polis*, a passage of peculiar resonance in Sparta where the community (*koinon*) was all in all and the ideal of 'doing one's own thing' allegedly lauded in democratic Athens was anathema. Finally, and not least, it was in the *agôgê* that the process of elite-formation began.

To take the last point first, Africanists studying age-set systems among pastoral tribes have commented on the 'politics' of age-setting (e.g. Almagor 1978; Baxter/Almagor 1978). They have remarked that the position achieved by an individual within his set may influence for the future such crucial political variables as access to social privilege, to marginal economic resources, and to ritual benefits. The same was true of Sparta, *mutatis mutandis*. Sparta was indeed the most rigidly hierarchical of all Greek societies and social mobility here was in general extremely limited. But the *agôgê* provides a partial exception to this rule. For success in the *agôgê* might bring a youth born of humble parentage or in reduced economic circumstances to the attention of the Spartan elite, those whom Herodotus (7.134.2) calls 'well-born and exceptionally wealthy'. The contacts thus established – and in Sparta they could be of a peculiarly intimate nature – might have the same effect on one's life-chances as being sent to a 'good' school and going on to Oxford or Cambridge can have in a country like Britain today. Such was the experience of Lysander, whose relationship with Agesilaos had more influence on the course of the latter's career than any other single factor.

Lysander (to use the familiar Latin form of the Greek Lysandros) was through his father Aristokritos an aristocrat by birth, being no less a 'descendant of Herakles' than the Agiads and Eurypontids. But Phylarchos, a third-century historian of sorts who knew Sparta at first hand (*FGrHist.* 81F43, followed by Ael. *VH* 12.43), reports that Lysander was also a *mothax*. Since as an adult Lysander was one of the Homoioi and indeed a member of the Spartan elite, *mothax* status was possibly a temporary and clearly not an irremediable stigma, and the *mothakes* (probably identical with the *mothônes*) cannot have been one of the plethora of inferior categories spawned by the Spartan social system that were apparently known collectively as 'Inferiors' (*hupomeiones*, a term attested only at 3.3.6). What little evidence there is suggests that they were marked out from the other Homoioi by their origins and circumstances of recruitment (cf. Lotze 1962). To borrow the phrase of Arnold Toynbee (1969,343-6), they were 'Homoioi by adoption'. That is to say, being disqualified by family circumstances from embarking upon the *agôgê* unaided, they were 'adopted' figuratively by some other qualified Spartan and put through under his auspices together with his own son or sons. This would have been another way of achieving the end specified by Xenophon (*LP* 1.7-9) for the Spartans' unique marital practices (a husband might either introduce an outsider to beget children for him out of his wife or himself procreate through another man's wife), namely 'to obtain brothers for their sons who share in their patriline (*genos*) and power (*dunamis*) but have no claim to inherit'.

What family circumstances might have disqualified Lysander? One theory (embraced uncritically by Rahe 1977) has it that all *mothakes* were sons of Helot mothers. But if so, why did Aristokritos bother to redeem Lysander from the ranks of the bastards (*nothoi*, attested explicitly at 5.3.9) when he already had a legitimate son or had a chance of fathering one (viz. Libys)? An alternative and surely preferable explanation is that Lysander was a *mothax* because his father had been too poor to put him through the *agôgê* himself (cf. Lotze 1962, esp. 433-4). Plutarch (*Lys.* 1.3) expressly states that Lysander was brought up in poverty, and we know that poverty in the form of inability to pay mess-dues excluded a man from the Homoioi and so presumably consigned him at least temporarily to the Inferiors (Arist. *Pol.* 1271a26-36; cf. Xen. *LP* 10.7). I am of course aware that 'the *peripeteia* of the self-made man, especially if (paradoxically) he is of high birth, has always been the stock-in-trade of romantic biography' (Badian 1976, 38); but it still strikes me as significant that Libys was nowhere described as a *mothax*. When he started on the *agôgê*, Aristokritos was no longer or, more plausibly, not yet impoverished.

Whatever the true explanation, the fact that Lysander – like Gylippos and Kallikratidas allegedly (Ael. *VH* 12.43) – triumphed over his *mothax* origins not only to achieve full Spartan citizenship but eventually to scale the political heights indicates the degree of social mobility that was possible through the *agôgê* and almost certainly also illustrates the social transformation Sparta was undergoing in the latter part of the fifth century through pressure of *oliganthrôpia* (shortage of citizen manpower). It remains to explain how Lysander may have clawed his way to the top in the Spartan beast-house.

Before his appointment as Admiral of the Fleet (*nauarchos*) in charge of Sparta's Aegean war-effort in 408 or 407, there is just one solid clue to the slight puzzle of his sudden emergence. At some stage in his career he had become the lover (*erastês*) or in Spartan parlance the *eispnêlas* (inspirer) of Agesilaos. The mechanics of homosexual courtship in Sparta are very imperfectly known, and the nature and functions of male homosexuality or rather pederasty only slightly better. But I hope I have been able to establish, partly through using ethnographic parallels, that in the fourth century and almost certainly by the second half of the fifth pederasty at Sparta had a public and official character; that it was normal for a Spartan boy to enter into a pederastic relationship after his twelfth birthday with a young adult but unmarried Spartan; and that this relationship was considered to be an integral part of the boy's education and so intimately connected to the ideals and institutions of the *agôgê* (Cartledge 1981a). My further suggestion that the pederastic relationship could also have a political dimension in the narrow sense of that word was more adventurous and tentative but I believe no less sound. This has obvious relevance to the relationship of Lysander and Agesilaos and perhaps also to Lysander's earlier career (see too Chapter 9).

Agesilaos became Lysander's beloved (*erômenos, paidika*, in Spartan the 'hearer', *aïtas*) somewhere between 433 and 428, an intriguing eddy in the maelstrom of international affairs in those years. That Lysander was in a position to woo and win the most eligible boy of his age-group argues powerful character and powerful contacts, which is what we would expect from the evidence of his career after 408. A good case has been made that Lysander owed his emergence into political prominence to the patronage of Agis II (Rahe 1977). If we combine this with his earlier personal relationship with Agesilaos, a common factor becomes apparent in the shape of Archidamos II, father to both Agis and Agesilaos. In other words, if my explanation of Lysander's *mothax* status is correct, the man who took the promising son of the impoverished aristocrat Aristokritos under his wing and put him through the *agôgê* was very likely a member of Archidamos' circle. The hypothesis of a connection between Aristokritos and Archidamos is not inconsistent with the fact that Aristokritos was able to maintain his hereditary *xenia* with a Libyan princeling (DS 14.13.5-6 – hence the name of his son Libys), since such external relationships probably required royal approval. A possible *quid pro quo* may be detected in the horses raced so successfully at Olympia by Archidamos' daughter and Agesilaos' (full?) sister Kyniska (cf. Chapter 9): Cyrenaica was a notable supplier of fine steeds. Alternatively, the postulated connection between Archidamos and Lysander could have been established later, for example on the hypothesis that Lysander's *andragathia* in the *agôgê* had won him election to the elite royal bodyguard of the 300 Hippeis (Chapter 12). The outbreak of the Athenian War in 431 would have given the roughly twenty-five year-old Lysander a splendid opportunity to win his spurs under the eyes of Archidamos.

Those are possible reconstructions of Lysander's experience of the *agôgê*. I shall return to his career and its effects on Agesilaos later (Chapter 6). First it remains to round off our discussion of Agesilaos' adolescence. When almost half a century later Agesilaos was giving his reasons for not voting for the execution of Sphodrias in 378, he is reported to have said that it was 'difficult to put to death a man who as a *pais*, as a *paidiskos* and as a *hêbôn* had consistently behaved in a wholly exemplary fashion' (5.4.32). These three words, untranslatable exactly into English, are the Spartan technical terms for three age-grades. During the period of the *agôgê* from the age of seven to eighteen the Spartan male was a *pais*, literally a child or boy. Between the ages of eighteen and twenty he became a *paidiskos*, 'child-ish' or 'child-like', halfway between boyhood and manhood. At twenty he came of age, attaining full adult citizen status, so that in a military context the ten youngest year-classes for example were called 'the ten from *hêbê*' (*ta deka aph' hêbês*). What concerns us immediately is what a *paidiskos* might spend his time doing.

At Athens the eighteen- and nineteen-year-olds were known as *ephêboi* ('on the threshold of *hêbê*'), and at some time in the third quarter of the fourth century an organized system of military training was introduced for them, a form of national service known as the *ephêbeia* (?Arist. *Ath. Pol.* 42, with Rhodes 1981a, 493-510; Vidal-Naquet 1981, 151-74). This regularization and formalization of what had previously been arranged *ad hoc* and not a universally obligatory public duty was part of a general tendency of the period towards increased professionalism in warfare (Chapter 15). Earlier, as Aristotle (*Pol.* 1338b24ff.) noted, such professionalism had been the preserve of the Spartans; indeed, he added sniffily, it was merely the fact that they alone drilled their young rather than the quality of the training that explained their former military supremacy. From this we might fairly infer that, once the *agôgê* proper had been completed, the Spartans somehow maintained the pressure of discipline and labour imposed in its final stage by prescribing rigorous exercises for those aged eighteen or nineteen.

That indeed is just what Xenophon (*LP* 3, deleting with Cobet *eis to meirakiousthai* from 3.1; cf. Tazelaar 1967, 147-8) says was done for Spartan *paidiskoi* in contrast to boys of their age in other Greek states. But what he conspicuously does not mention (except perhaps at *LP* 2.7, where he is ostensibly dealing with the *paides*) is the form of training undergone by those *paidiskoi* who served as *kruptoi* in the Krypteia or Secret Service. Whether Agesilaos himself participated in the Krypteia is not known for certain, though the mention of a Hegesileos (Attic-Ionic for Agesilaos) in a sadly truncated papyrus that has been convincingly interpreted as describing the Krypteia (P. Lond. 187, with Girard 1898 and (new readings) 1900, 872n.9) makes it a plausible hypothesis. But this remarkably revealing institution in any event necessarily occupies an important place in the discussion of Spartan education.

Two versions of the Krypteia, a hard and a soft, are contained in the ancient literary sources. The 'soft' version is presented by the generally pro-Spartan Plato (*Laws* 633bc, cf. 760e, 761b, 763b). In a consideration of Spartan practices instituted for the purpose of war Plato's Athenian interlocutor (a surrogate for Plato himself) cites gymnastic exercises and common meals. To these the

Spartan interlocutor Megillos (perhaps to be identified with Poralla 1913, no. 513) adds hunting and, as a broad category, the endurance of pain – 'a very conspicuous feature of Spartan life', as he rightly says. Under the latter general heading Megillos cites boxing matches and whippings,[2] which would both affect the *paides*; then the Krypteia, during which the participants go without shoes and bedding even in winter; and finally the Gymnopaidiai, the annual festival of the 'Naked Boys' in which the men display extraordinary endurance of the summer heat. This sequence apparently confirms that the Krypteia was the speciality of those between the status of boys and men, but Megillos' picture of the Krypteia as a kind of glorified endurance test in which the only sufferers of pain were the Spartan youths is monstrously one-sided.

Or at least it is if we are to believe the radically different 'hard' version that Plutarch found in the work on the Spartan *politeia* compiled under the direction of Plato's most distinguished pupil, Aristotle, a thinker who consistently and cogently took a far less favourable view of Sparta than his master (Cloché 1942). According to the Aristotelian *Lak. Pol.* (fr. 538, *ap.* Plut. *Lyk.* 28), the Ephors annually on taking office (in late autumn) made a solemn declaration of war upon the Helots in the name of the Spartan state. The express aim of this declaration was to exonerate in advance from the taint of blood-pollution any Spartan who should happen to kill a Helot; and it was under cover of this precautionary exemption that the members of the Krypteia fulfilled their primary function of doing away with unwanted Helots, according to the Aristotelian version. This they did by going out into the country, presumably in Messenia as well as or rather than in Lakonia (hence the need for the special mountain-leggings called *kalbateinai* mentioned in the London papyrus), lying hidden by day and coming out at night to perform their dirty business.

The kindly Plutarch could not believe that Lykourgos could have sanctioned let alone invented such a dreadful institution and salved his conscience by ascribing its introduction to the aftermath of the particularly savage Messenian revolt of the 460s during which for example a detachment of 300 Spartans was annihilated (Hdt. 9.64.2, cf. 35.2). Modern historians of course need neither be as squeamish as Plutarch nor indeed adopt a moralizing attitude of any kind, however outlandish they may find this hitherto unparalleled example of a ruling class ritually declaring war in a literal sense upon its entire workforce (see further Chapter 10). They need merely turn to a splendid pioneering article (Jeanmaire 1913) in which a French historian amply demonstrated through a host of especially African ethnographic parallels the striking similarities between the Krypteia and the final phase of male initiation rites in tribal societies.

Jeanmaire's hypothesis about the ultimate origins of the Krypteia has been brilliantly confirmed by another French historian (Vidal-Naquet 1981, 151-74, excellently translated into English in Gordon 1981), who has pointed out that the *kruptoi* were a sort of anti-hoplites. Whereas the adult citizen hoplites fought heavily-armed and en masse in the heat of a summer's day, the members of the Krypteia hunted their prey alone and at night even during the winter, armed

---

[2]Perhaps a covert reference to the curious rite of Xen. *LP* 2.9, discussed by Den Boer 1954, 261-74; but it may have a wider application.

only with a dagger and wearing the barest minimum of protective clothing. Such a reversal of the norms of adult society is utterly typical of the final phase of the adolescent initiation rites studied by anthropologists across a very broad spectrum of natural and social environments and levels of technical development (see works cited in Cartledge 1981a). The best explanation of the Krypteia, in other words, is that it represents a re-institutionalization or re-adaptation of an existing initiation rite in order for it to serve not merely a social but also a police function. If Sparta may under certain circumstances properly be described as a police state, the Krypteia offered the appropriate kind of paramilitary training for those who were destined to be the superintendents and chief constables of this society. It would therefore have been entirely appropriate for Agesilaos to have participated in the Krypteia, and the stress in the sources on his model performance in the *agôgê* is consistent with the suggestion that he did in fact do so. It is not absolutely certain whether all Spartan ephebes took part or only a select number of them, but if selection was involved Agesilaos is unlikely to have been overlooked.

After his twentieth birthday and the completion of the necessary rites of transition and incorporation, a Spartan youth became a *hêbôn*, an adult in the social sense. But in order to reach political maturity, that is acquire full citizen status as a Spartiate, yet another hurdle had to be jumped. He had to be elected to a common mess (*suskanion* or 'common tent' appears to have been the technical term, at least on campaign, but *andreion, philition, pheidition* and the generic *sussition* are variously attested). Concerning recruitment to the messes we know only one thing for certain: that it was effected by unanimous vote of all existing members, one 'blackball' (in fact a squashed pellet of bread) being sufficient to eliminate a candidate (Plut. *Lyk.* 12.9-11). We do not know what determined a candidate's choice of mess nor on what grounds he might be rejected. As for the composition of a mess we know only that it contained men of all ages (Xen. *LP* 5.5), but there may also have been some mixing of rich and poor in the same mess (*LP* 7.4, cf. 5.3). However, it is reasonable to infer from the selection procedure and from the character of Spartan society as a whole that some messes were more desirable, more socially exclusive, than others and that within a mess – small as it was (fifteen members, according to Plutarch) – there would develop a hierarchy of some kind whether based on wealth, seniority, attainment or a combination of these (cf. Hodkinson 1983, 253-4). So too we may confidently assert that the very principle of messing in this way contributed materially to fostering the oligarchic character of the Spartan *politeia* as a whole (see further Chapter 8).

Spartan heirs-apparent did not go through the *agôgê*. Logically, therefore, they could not put themselves forward for election to a mess in the ordinary way. Instead they must have been recruited automatically on attaining their majority to the royal mess, in which both kings and their respective entourages (selected at least in part by themselves) dined together at public expense (Hdt. 6.57; Xen. *LP* 15.4-5, *Ages.* 5.1, *Hell.* 5.3.20). No doubt they were not strangers to their new messmates, since it was the Spartan custom to allow boys to sit in on the communal meal (Xen. *LP* 3.4; Plut. *Lyk.* 12.4-5, *Mor.* 236f). Agesilaos, however, having gone through the *agôgê* and (probably) Krypteia, was perhaps technically eligible for a non-royal mess. But it would be easiest to imagine that in about 425 or 424 he began to dine in the same mess as his half-brother Agis II. Here too, I suspect, Lysander was to be found, if not as a regular member then at least on occasion enjoying the extra ration provided as a privilege to enable the kings to entertain a favoured guest (Xen. *LP* 15.4, *Ages.* 5.1).

What then, in conclusion, were the main benefits or disadvantages that may have accrued to Agesilaos and Sparta from his being a king who unusually had experienced to some considerable extent the ordinary upbringing of a typical Spartan boy and youth? Plutarch (*Ages.* 1.4-5) remarked sententiously that 'it was his peculiarity to achieve the position of ruler only after he had first learned to obey. Which is why he was to show himself of all kings by far the most in harmony with his subjects. For he united with his naturally commanding and regal disposition the common touch and the kindly affability he had learned from the *agôgê*'. The rapport with ordinary Spartans that Plutarch singles out here and in his account of Agesilaos' accession (*Ages.* 3.5) is undoubtedly an important part of the truth. But that was by no means all the *agôgê* meant to Agesilaos and so to Sparta. It is a well-known psychological fact that those who best survive brutal ordeals in education or other forms of social learning and initiation tend to be the greatest sticklers for maintaining the brutality unchanged. Tacitus (*Ann.* 1.20) summed it up in four words when speaking of a notoriously ferocious disciplinarian on the Pannonian front in AD 14 who had risen from the ranks: *eo inmitior quia toleraverat* ('he was harsher precisely because he had himself endured (the discipline)'). In this as in other areas of Sparta's social regimen Agesilaos was to prove dramatically and, I believe, fatally conservative. He lacked the independent and broader vision that his times required and that the different upbringing of the heirs-apparent made possible though by no means always actual.

Agesilaos was, in short, the incarnation of the typical Spartan to a significant extent, a classic product of the Spartan system of education. The very particular flavour of that education is, as often, best appreciated through a comparison. Describing the origins of formal education in early modern France, Michel Foucault (1977) noted three factors conducing to the success of disciplinary power: hierarchical observation, normalizing judgment, and the examination. For the first of these, he argued, the new educationists had 'an almost ideal model' ready to hand, namely the military camp. Since Sparta was appropriately likened in antiquity to a permanently sited armed camp, Foucault's description of the temporary camp as an educational model has a peculiarly literal relevance to Sparta and Spartan education and is far more revealing than the once popular analogy of the British public school: 'the short-lived, artificial city, built and reshaped almost at will; the seat of a power that must be all the stronger, but also all the more discreet, all the more effective and on the alert in that it is exercised over armed men. In the perfect camp, all power would be exercised solely through exact observation; each gaze would form a part of the overall functioning of power' (1977, 171). It was in such a milieu and from such a base that the Spartans decided to fight the Athenian War.

4

The Athenian War

Until then Greece had walked with her feet well planted on the ground, but that war shook her from her foundations like an earthquake. (Paus. 3.7.11)

For what can war but endless war breed? (Milton 'On the Lord General Fairfax')

In the winter of 373/2 the temple of Pythian Apollo in the Panhellenic shrine of Delphi, the navel of the earth, was destroyed by earthquake and/or fire. Some three years later a subscription-list was opened, and contributions for the rebuilding of the temple from both individuals and states were brought from all corners of the Greek world (Tod 140 = W/V 43; cf. Tod 133.8-10 and generally Roux 1979). Sparta put a premium on maintaining a special relationship with Apollo of Delphi (cf. Zeilhofer 1959) and to that end the kings had the enormous privilege of appointing the four officials called Pythioi as permanent ambassadors (*theopropoi*) to his sanctuary (Hdt. 6.57.2,4; Xen. *LP* 15.4; Cic. *De Div.* 1.43.95). Let us suppose for the sake of argument that it was as Pythioi that the epigraphically attested Antileon and Echeteles (Poralla 1913, nos 100,339) were deputed to bring Sparta's contributions to the rebuilding fund in the 360s or 350s. What would they have seen?

As they entered the precinct and set foot upon the Sacred Way they would have found towering above them immediately to their left the so-called 'Navarchs' Monument' (Fig. 4.1). This grandiose memorial had been erected to commemorate the Spartans' or more precisely Lysander's triumph over the Athenian fleet at Aigospotamoi in 405 (see further Chapter 6 on the monument). That 'battle' had finally rung down the curtain on the prolonged tragedy of the Athenian War – or Peloponnesian War as it is more usually called thanks to the Athenian Thucydides. The Spartan victory had eventually been won with and could not have been won without massive financial aid from Persia. Yet just beyond the Navarchs' Monument there stood in jarring juxtaposition the Athenians' memorial of the famous victory they had snatched from the Persians at Marathon in 490, that Greece might still be free.

After Aigospotamoi and the end of the War in spring 404 Sparta stood at the apex of the Greek world east of the straits of Otranto. A generation later, her pride had been humbled – as the memorial opposite the Navarchs' Monument will have sharply reminded our notional Pythioi. For this had been recently

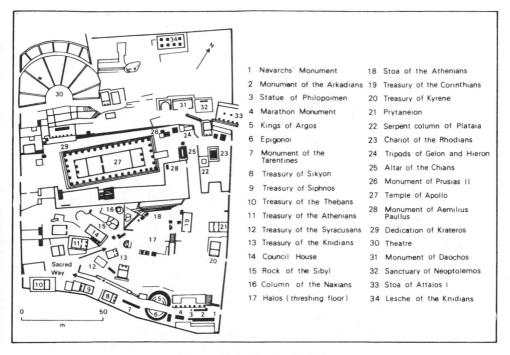

1 Navarchs' Monument
2 Monument of the Arkadians
3 Statue of Philopoimen
4 Marathon Monument
5 Kings of Argos
6 Epigonoi
7 Monument of the Tarentines
8 Treasury of Sikyon
9 Treasury of Siphnos
10 Treasury of the Thebans
11 Treasury of the Athenians
12 Treasury of the Syracusans
13 Treasury of the Knidians
14 Council House
15 Rock of the Sibyl
16 Column of the Naxians
17 Halos (threshing floor)
18 Stoa of the Athenians
19 Treasury of the Corinthians
20 Treasury of Kyrene
21 Prytaneion
22 Serpent column of Plataia
23 Chariot of the Rhodians
24 Tripods of Gelon and Hieron
25 Altar of the Chians
26 Monument of Prusias II
27 Temple of Apollo
28 Monument of Aemilius Paullus
29 Dedication of Krateros
30 Theatre
31 Monument of Daochos
32 Sanctuary of Neoptolemos
33 Stoa of Attalos I
34 Lesche of the Knidians

Fig. 4.1. Delphi. After Talbert

erected by the politically united Arkadians, the neighbours and for long the allies of Sparta, to commemorate the defeats inflicted on Sparta in 370/69. Beyond the Arkadian monument stood a niche containing ten bronze statues of mythical ancestors erected about the same time by the men of Argos, Sparta's traditional enemy and rival in the Peloponnese; this was said to commemorate the share taken by Argos in resurrecting the *polis* of Messene in 369 following the liberation of the Messenian Helots from Spartan ownership and control after some three centuries. Another hundred metres or so beyond the Argive niche, to left of and just off the Sacred Way, there stood yet another memorial of the downfall of Spartan power: the so-called 'Treasury' put up by the Thebans in proud advertisement of their stunning victory over the Spartans at Leuktra in 371.

The shrine of Delphi, in other words, was a gigantic war-memorial (cf. Pritchett 1974, I, 98-100), serving to illustrate all too clearly the paradoxical combination of Panhellenic solidarity and inter-Hellenic internecine warfare that characterized Greek history in our period as in others. But our Pythioi might also be forgiven for reflecting somewhat sombrely on the instability of fortune (or Fortune) and empire, as Herodotus (1.5.4, 207.2) and Thucydides' Perikles (2.64.3) had already been moved to do when the Athenian War was in prospect or its infancy. War was indeed a harsh teacher (Thuc. 3.82.2).

At least one of the memorials mentioned, however, the Lysander monument as it may fairly be called, speaks more to us and to its original public than this rather banal truism. For it was designed not merely to advertise the merits and providential status of Lysander to the world at large but also and more especially to advance his cause in the domestic power-struggle that had raged in Sparta during the Athenian War and showed no signs of abating once it was over. The natural response of King Agis II, formerly the patron and latterly the rival of Lysander, was to erect his own counter-monument at Delphi. Echoing perhaps the terms of the treaty imposed on Athens (2.2.20) and thereby arrogating to himself the credit for the victory which he felt had gone unduly to Lysander, Agis had himself described in his dedicatory inscription as 'king of both the land and the sea' (Plut. *Mor.* 467f, cf. *Lys.* 21.1; Arist. *Pol.* 1306b31-3; Athen. 543b).

Struggle among the Spartan political hierarchy was by no means a novelty. But the Athenian War by its length, its difficulty, and above all its ultimately successful outcome had hugely raised the stakes in the game of Spartan place-seeking and policymaking. Or, to change the metaphor, it had heightened the multiple tensions which lay behind the determination of policy and the distribution of political influence: tensions between the Spartans and the Helots, between the Spartans and the Perioikoi, between the Spartans and their allies inside and outside the Peloponnesian League, between the League and the outside world, between full Spartan citizens and Spartans of variously inferior status, and amongst the Spartiates themselves (cf. Will 1972, 444).

The Spartans had been far from unwilling to declare war on Athens in 432 (below); but the overconfident expectation that it would soon be won may well have weighed heavily with many of them, especially the completely untried younger men who formed the majority of the Assembly (cf. Thuc. 2.8.1; and Bloedow 1981, 140-2). As it turned out, the Athenian War was almost a thirty years' war, a generation long. Inevitably therefore it changed many things about Sparta and the wider Greek and Aegean world, many of them irreversibly. More parochially, it took Agesilaos from adolescence to mature adulthood and the threshold (though he could not have known this) of regal power. The aim of this chapter is to give an idea of how far the Sparta that Agesilaos came to lead differed from the Sparta of his boyhood. This will bring sharply into relief the need of postwar Sparta for flexible and innovative statesmanship that Agesilaos was so signally to fail to satisfy.

Towards the end of a penetrating essay on Classical Spartan society M.I. Finley (1981a, 40) conveniently listed the principal innovations flowing from Sparta's extended participation in genuinely military and not merely militaristic activity.[1] These innovations include severe pressure on manpower leading to a dangerously liberal incorporation of non-Spartiates into the regular Spartan army and unprecedented opportunities for ambitious individuals involving wide travel abroad in breach of the traditional xenophobia and the temptations of enrichment through the possession of coined money. 'The system,' Finley comments, 'could not and did not long survive'. To see whether that judgment is fair and accurate is part of the point of this book, but no one will dispute that

---

[1] I cannot accept, though, the literal implication of his remark that Sparta was drawn into the Athenian War 'against her will', not even with the qualifying 'almost'.

the Athenian War did not merely precede but actually precipitated the Spartan crisis. I shall examine preliminarily five areas of significant change and one of significant continuity.

(i) Manpower shortage and changes in Spartan army-organization

Aristotle, looking back from the privileged vantage-point of the 330s, laconically ascribed the demise of Sparta as a great power to *oliganthrôpia*, the shortage of citizen military manpower. It is notorious that the ancient Greeks were unbureaucratic and had no penchant for keeping detailed population statistics on a regular and continuous basis. But since warfare was endemic, they all had to have a fair idea of their available military effective, at least of their front-line hoplite troops. This was especially true of the oligarchies of the Peloponnesian League in which the hoplite muster-list (*katalogos*) could also serve as a citizen-register. Occasionally these *katalogoi* found their way into the surviving narrative histories or into the systematic analysis of the Greek *polis* by Aristotle for whom the size of the citizen body was a politically crucial variable.

Thus we are able to gain a rough but, I think, reasonably reliable notion of the scale of *oliganthrôpia* suffered by Sparta between the early fifth century and the second quarter of the fourth century from Herodotus (7.234.2) and Aristotle's *Politics* (1270a29-32). The former puts into the mouth of the exiled Spartan ex-King Damaratos in 480 the statement that Sparta had a potential fighting force of 8000. Whether this figure includes men beyond military age, that is over sixty, is unclear, and of course Damaratos may have exaggerated to suit his argument. But despite modern objections to this total (e.g. Beloch 1906, 53,73 – 6000 max.; Cozzoli 1979, 59-73 – unconvincing attempt to show that 5000 was the total effective; *contra* Kromayer 1903, 194), a round 8000 is not inconsistent with the round 5000 said to have marched out to do battle at Plataia the following year (Hdt. 9.10.1,11.3,28.2,29.1), especially as these are stated to have been 'the youth' (*hê neotês*: see Chapter 3).

Aristotle for his part in the context of a stinging critique of the Spartan property-regime contrasted the potential with the actual Spartan citizen fighting strength:

> although the land was sufficient to support 1,500 cavalry and 30,000 heavy infantry, the number fell to below 1,000. The sheer facts have shown that these arrangements were bad: one single blow was too much for Sparta, and she succumbed owing to the shortage of men (trans. T.J. Saunders)

By 'the land' Aristotle can only mean the territory owned by the Spartans (as opposed to the Perioikoi) within the *polis* before the loss of Messenian land in 370/69; 'these arrangements' are the Spartan system of land-tenure; and the 'single blow' is clearly the Battle of Leuktra in 371. If Aristotle is rightly taken to be saying that Sparta's citizen effective had already fallen below 1000 before Leuktra, he was guilty of some exaggeration. But not much. Modern estimates, based ultimately on Xenophon's figures for Spartiates at Leuktra (6.1.1, 4.15,17), would not push it above 1500 (e.g. Ste. Croix 1972, 332 – 1200; Cozzoli 1979, 11 – 1400). In the battle itself they lost 400 men. So how Cary (1926,

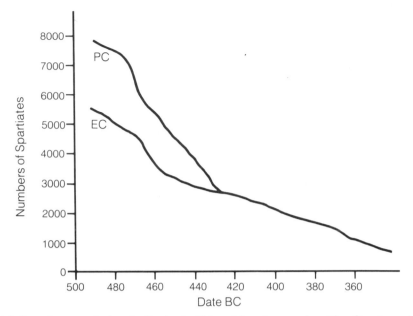

Fig. 4.2. Spartiate population decline in the fifth and fourth centuries. After Cavaignac 1912

186-7) could think that the disastrous decline in Spartan citizen numbers belongs to the second half of the fourth century is a bit of a mystery. By 371, in fact, Spartan citizen military manpower had plummeted to about one fifth of what it had been a century earlier (Fig. 4.2). The causes of this decline will be discussed later (Chapter 10). What concerns me now are the effects the decline had on the Spartan effort in the Athenian War and the measures Sparta took to counteract those effects.

In this respect the eighth and ninth years of the Athenian War, 425/4 and 424/3, were clearly pivotal. In a speech attributed to him by Thucydides (1.80.3) in 432 Archidamos II the senior Spartan king and general had used the fact that Athens was the most populous state in Greece as an argument for delaying a declaration of war. By 426 Sparta was no nearer winning the war than in 431 but at least the Great Plague of Athens had seriously undermined the demographic argument: by the count of Thucydides (3.87) no less than 4,400 Athenian hoplites and 300 cavalrymen had fallen victim to it, together with untold numbers of ordinary Athenians too poor to equip themselves with heavy armour or a horse. Yet within two years it was Sparta not Athens which had sued for peace on manpower grounds, and that not as the result of an actual loss but in order to forestall the potential loss of just 120 or so Spartan citizens who had surrendered to the Athenians on the island of Sphakteria off the Messenian coast and were being held hostage at Athens (Thuc. 4.38.5).

Two generations or so later (on the date see Chapter 5) Xenophon began his essay on the Spartan polity thus (*LP* 1.1):

I was reflecting one day on the fact that, although Sparta has one of the smallest populations, it has become the most powerful and famous of all Greek states, and I wondered how this could have come about. However, when I examined the way of life of the Spartiates, I ceased to be surprised (trans. J.M. Moore)

But in 425 Sparta had been willing to abandon a war begun amid a great fanfare of altruistic liberation propaganda for the selfish purpose of recovering a mere handful of their men. Her 'way of life' obviously was not a complete explanation of her power and fame if it was unable to triumph over such a small diminution (some three per cent) of the citizen body. In the immediate term the capture of these men, together of course with the permanent occupation by Athens of Messenian Pylos, resulted in panic measures of repression against the Helots. In the longer run it forced Sparta to the bargaining table in 422/1 at a serious disadvantage to Athens. Ultimately it contributed to the social upheaval of which we get a brief but highly illuminating glimpse shortly after the accession of Agesilaos (Chapter 10).

The panic measures taken against the Helots for fear of a repetition of the revolt of the 460s were threefold. Some 2000 of the most energetic among them were liquidated after a selection. For the first time, at least in the Athenian War, a regular force of cavalry and archers was raised to act as mobile defence units in the event of Helot uprisings. And 700 Helots armed as hoplites were despatched on a mission far away from Spartan territory expressly to reduce Helot numbers at home. Comment on the first two of these measures is reserved for later (Chapters 10, 12). The third, however, was not just unprecedented but occasioned what is in the present context the most significant episode in the first phase of the Athenian War.

Helots had of course been called upon to fight before, and Sparta was not the only Greek state to employ its servile population in war. But this was the first, and almost the last, time that Sparta equipped unemancipated Helots as hoplites, that is heavy-armed front-line infantrymen. The experiment was conducted with typical Spartan caution. These Helot hoplites were not to serve as members of the regular Spartan phalanx. Instead, along with 1000 Peloponnesian mercenaries (also the first of their kind to be recruited by Sparta in the war: cf. Chapter 15), they were to operate as a small commando unit under the exceptionally able and enterprising (and therefore in the eyes of the Spartan authorities suspect) Brasidas. Moreover, they were to serve in a theatre almost as far from home base as it was possible to reach by land, on the northern, Thracian shore of the Aegean.

I shall return to the military and political significance of Brasidas' Thracian campaign shortly. As for these Helots, they performed so satisfactorily that the Spartans took a further step along the road to incorporating men of Helot origin in the regular phalanx. At some time between 424 and 421 they created the status of Neodamôdeis. Literally 'new *damos*-men', in fact they were Helots liberated expressly for military purposes and not incorporated in the social and political structure of the Spartan *damos*. In 421 Neodamôdeis were being used for garrison duty only (on the sensitive frontier with Elis), so far as we know. But in 418 at the (First) Battle of Mantineia they were to be found fighting in the phalanx alongside the Brasideioi ('Brasidas' men'). The very name of the latter, even if it was unofficial, indicates their special and separate status: they were the survivors from Brasidas' original 700 Helots who in 421 had been collectively manumitted by act of the Spartan Assembly (Thuc. 5.34.1, 67.1,71.3,72.3). Only once more, in 413 (Thuc. 7.58.3), do we hear of unemancipated Helots being used as hoplites, again in a small band despatched far, far away from Sparta (to Sicily) and again ranked with Neodamôdeis. Thereafter it is Neodamôdeis alone and in ever increasing numbers who appear in the sources until the status was apparently discontinued after 369 (for a possible last use in 360/59 see Chapter 15).

In other words, in order to compensate for the serious and irreversible decline of Spartiate manpower (and incidentally to divide the Helots against themselves), the Spartans between 424 and 369 resorted to the desperate expedient of tapping the (alarmingly) abundant manpower reserves of their servile population. No matter how docile the Helots selected for promotion in this way may have proved, and however useful this device may have been thought to be as a means of forestalling united Helot opposition or insurrection, it nevertheless represented a serious breach in the principle of the citizen militia, the very principle upon which the post-reformation Spartan state had been founded and the source of Sparta's proud military tradition.

This was not, however, the first such breach of that principle. It was the last rather than the first resort, as could have been predicted. The earlier, decisive breach involved the Perioikoi. As noted earlier (Chapter 2) they were obligated like Sparta's Peloponnesian League allies to follow the Spartans whithersoever they might lead by land and sea. Indeed, they did not even have the right of collective veto on a Spartan decision available in theory to those allies nor, almost certainly, the right to claim a prior religious obligation as a legitimate exemption from the duty to follow. Bronze figurines depicting hoplites in full rig had been dedicated in Perioikic sanctuaries in both Lakonia and Messenia before the end of the sixth century, but our first evidence for the use of Perioikic hoplites in the regular Spartan army concerns the Persian Wars of 480-479. At Plataia, it seems clear, they were brigaded separately from the Spartiates, just as the Brasideioi and Neodamadeis were at Mantineia in 418. This was only to be expected given the strict correspondence between the Spartan way of life, in which the Perioikoi did not share, and Spartan military organization. In fact it is something of a mystery how the Perioikoi at Plataia had been recruited and trained, though it is pretty certain that they were mainly landowners who had the necessary wealth and leisure to equip themselves as hoplites and take time away from their fields.

The number of Perioikoi called up in 479 is said to have precisely equalled that of the Spartiates: 5000. Since there were some eighty Perioikic communities all told, this probably did not represent so high a proportion of their potential hoplite manpower as the Spartan contribution, which appears to have constituted some two thirds. However, between the Persian Wars and the beginning of the Athenian War Spartan full citizen numbers dropped dramatically (not gradually, as Cawkwell 1983 would have it), by something between a third and a half; and in 425, as we have seen above, this *oliganthrôpia* had manifested itself in a most telling manner so far as Sparta's attitude to the war-effort was concerned and led to desperate measures of control against the Helots. But Thucydides' precise information on the Pylos débâcle does not only reveal how few Spartiates it took to make Sparta sue for peace. It also shows, when read in the most straightforward way, that some time after 479 and before 425 Sparta had effected a remarkable army reform (for the organization before the reform see Appendix II).

This is the tally Thucydides gives, in a suitably spare, military-minded style:

> There died on the island [Sphakteria] and there were taken alive the following numbers: in all 420 hoplites crossed over to the island; of these, 292 were brought back alive [to Athens], the rest were killed. The number of those captured alive who were actually Spartiates was *c.*120.

Who, then, were the 170 or so non-Spartiates captured alive? In the account of the fighting preceding their surrender Thucydides consistently refers to the guard as a whole (420 men) as 'Lakedaimonians'. Theoretically, this term could be used of Spartans of less than full citizen status, men who in this case would have been degraded for economic rather than military reasons. But that explanation of the 170 seems to be excluded by the way Thucydides (4.8.1) describes the troops used for the Pylos campaign: first 'the Spartiates and those of the Perioikoi who lived nearest', then 'the other Lakedaimonians'. The non-Spartiates captured on Sphakteria were, in other words, Perioikoi.[2]

The procedure whereby the Spartans selected the relays of garrisons for the defence of Sphakteria is described by Thucydides (4.8.9) as follows: 'they kept sending the hoplites across to the island, drafting them by lot from all the *lochoi*. The last of the relays, the one that was actually caught, numbered 420 hoplites together with their Helots.' Much unfortunately is obscure about Spartan army organization, and Thucydides has complicated matters enormously by referring to six *lochoi* at the Battle of Mantineia when he should (I believe: cf. Cartledge 1979, 253-7) have referred to six *morai*. Whatever the explanation of Thucydides' error, it is clear to me that the *mora*, which was certainly in being by 403 (2.4.31), had already been introduced by 418. I am only slightly less confident that it was in existence by 425. For the neatest explanation of the composition of the relay of 420 is that advanced by Arnold Toynbee (1969, 373-4,376-7,382-3,391). He postulated that this was the sum of twelve *enômotiai*, one *enômotia* of thirty-five men having been selected by lot from each of the twelve *lochoi* (there being two *lochoi* to a *mora*).

The *enômotia*, literally a sworn brotherhood, was the lowest and smallest unit of the Spartan army. Each *enômotia* had probably always consisted notionally of one Spartiate from each of the forty active-service year-classes from twenty to fifty-nine inclusive. The number of actual members of an *enômotia* on campaign

---

[2]Similarly at 5.57.1 Thucydides makes no explicit mention of Perioikoi among the 'Lakedaimonians' who marched out in full force (*pandêmei*) in high summer 418; but their presence may be inferred from the fact that, when the 'Lakedaimonians' had marched out earlier *pandêmei* (5.54.1), the *poleis* – that is the Perioikic *poleis* (implicitly distinguished from Sparta's allies at 5.54.2) – did not know where they were going. See further Ste. Croix 1972, 345-6.

would depend on the number of year-classes the Ephors decided to call out. But if Toynbee's hypothesis about the composition of the 420 men on Sphakteria in 425 is right, it follows that Perioikoi now formed part of the regular establishment and were brigaded with Spartiates in the same regiments; it is perhaps unlikely, though, to judge from passages like 3.5.7 or 5.1.33, that they were mingled at the level of the *enômotia*. This was not like incorporating Gurkhas in a British regiment, which is more or less what Alexander the Great did not shrink from doing when he incorporated oriental cavalrymen into his new Macedono-Iranian Hipparchies. But it did certainly mark a major concession to the reality of Spartiate *oliganthrôpia* and a major infringement of the principle of the one-to-one correspondence between the Spartan citizen body and the regular Spartan hoplite establishment – an infringement that would have been felt the more strongly in a military society such as Sparta. For the Perioikoi could not be admitted to the common messes, although conceivably in exceptional cases (the sons of the *kaloikagathoi* Perioikoi mentioned at 5.3.9 perhaps) they might have experienced the *agôgê*. And even if they were formed into their own separate *enômotiai*, this still represented a significant weakening of the emotive and practical meanings of that unit, which admirably harnessed the potential of what American military analysts like to call 'small group dynamics' (Keegan 1978, 51, cf. 71). I have wondered whether Xenophon's comment (*LP* 11.7) that only soldiers brought up under the 'laws of Lykourgos' are capable of fighting on even after the phalanx has been disrupted might not be a veiled reference to these incorporated Perioikic hoplites.

When this drastic innovation was effected we can only guess. But the losses caused by the earthquake of *c*.464 followed by the knife-edge victory at Tanagra in 458 or 457 – 'a damned nice thing – the nearest run thing you ever saw in your life', as someone might have commented – will surely have set the naturally conservative Spartan military hierarchy to thinking furiously about a change; and the Peace of 446/5 could have provided the occasion to introduce one. Indeed, it is possible that the Spartans were influenced in some degree by the newly established (or re-established) Boiotian Confederacy, for at least after 447 the Boiotian federal army was recruited by *merê* ('wards': Chapter 14) and that term is cognate with *morai* or 'divisions'.

However that may be, the reform clearly proved successful enough. So far as the Spartans were concerned, this was a form of organization based neither on Dorian tribe nor on locality, as earlier forms of organization had been (Appendix II). Instead, 'men were just drafted in as the army needed them' (Wade-Gery 1958, 73). This served administrative convenience at a time of shrinking citizen manpower, but it would also have had the effect of strengthening the army structure as a whole against its parts. As to the Perioikoi, the success is not entirely surprising; for the incorporated Perioikoi were no doubt heavily acculturated to Spartan ways and perhaps even more Spartan than the Spartans, as people in their sort of situation often are (e.g. Eualkes of Geronthrai: Cartledge 1979, 257, 313; cf. generally Holladay 1977, 124). None the less, training will have been something of a problem, especially in the matter of drill, even if most of the front-line fighters (*promachoi*) and file-leaders (*prôtostatai*) were Spartiates (Delbrück 1975, 55) and the phalanx in and of itself 'carries along with it even the moderately trained man and the moderately brave man' (Delbrück 1975, 151). So too maintenance of an *esprit de corps* will have been complicated by the reform, despite such external devices as the *lambda* for 'Lakedaimonians' emblazoned on all shields (4.4.10; cf. Tod 130.4-5). These were two of the factors that were eventually to give the Thebans a decisive edge, but in 432 the Spartan Assembly voted for the Athenian War in the confident expectation that victory would be theirs within three years at the very outside. That was only their first mistake.

(ii) Changes in strategy and tactics

At different times and speeds between roughly 700 and 600 all the major states of mainland Greece south of Thessaly introduced what has become known as 'the hoplite reform' (Snodgrass 1965, variously corroborated or modified by Cartledge 1977; Salmon 1977; Holladay 1982, esp. 94-7). Thereafter, until the fifth century in the case of Athens and the third century for most other states, the massed phalanx of heavy-armed infantrymen known from their large, two-handled shields as hoplites constituted their principal fighting force. Precisely why the reform was made or accepted is not entirely clear, not least because we lack the good contemporary written evidence that might settle the issues. But that the motives were importantly moral and social as well as narrowly technological and military still seems to me to be as true of hoplite fighting as it was of the development of cavalry supremacy in the Middle Ages (Howard 1976, 14).

On its chosen ground, the relatively few flat or flattish plains where the bulk of a state's food-supply was ideally grown, the hoplite phalanx proved efficient enough in set-piece battles for well over two centuries. But during the Athenian War its limitations began to be decisively exposed, and under a century later Philip of Macedon's victory at Chaironeia demonstrated the superiority even in good hoplite country of combined cavalry and infantry manoeuvres involving the use of a significantly re-equipped phalanx trained to a level of professional proficiency beyond anything then known in Greece. Sparta, typically, was slow to adapt to the new Macedonian phalanx; it was not introduced there until the third quarter of the third century by a king, Kleomenes III, whose reign was revolutionary in the political and economic spheres too. Sparta may also have been relatively slow to introduce the hoplite reform in the first place, perhaps close to the middle of the seventh century. But when she did make her move, she moved emphatically and in such a way that her new model army became the envy or terror of her many foes and widely recognised as the *doyen* of developed hoplite warfare. The Battles of Thermopylai and Plataia set the seal on this reputation, and it was to this hoplite tradition that Agesilaos was heir, though he proved unable to maintain it.

The various complementary reasons for Sparta's acknowledged hoplite superiority can be (and were by Aristotle, as we saw in Chapter 3) boiled down to one: in a world of amateur militias Sparta's citizen hoplites were the only soldiers who could be aptly described as professionals. They were in Xenophon's view (*Mem.* 3.9.2) the hoplites par excellence or in Plutarch's graphic phrases 'craftsmen and technicians of the art of war' (*technitai kai sophistai tôn polemikôn*: *Pelop.* 23.4) and 'artisans of war and devotees of Ares' (*polemou cheirotechnai kai therapontes Areôs*: *Comp. Lyc. et Num.* 2.6). This professional status was achieved negatively by transferring to the subjugated Helots the sole responsibility for producing the edible necessities of life in the fertile plains of Lakonia and Messenia and by debarring all Spartan citizens from manual crafts except that of the soldier (Plut. *Ages.* 26.4-5; but see Cartledge 1976b). Positively, the unique feature of Sparta's version of the hoplite reform was that it made all Spartan citizens members of the hoplite phalanx in contrast to the one third or so of the citizenry in most other Greek states who could afford the expense of hoplite equipment (cf. Ste. Croix 1972, 35n.65) and the time needed to train and fight away from their fields. It is unclear how precisely the Spartan hoplite came by his arms and armour, but I am still inclined to believe that it was not by any 'market' mechanism. Rather, the provision of hoplite equipment could have been somehow centrally administered, perhaps even by requisitioning the relevant goods and materials from the Perioikoi. If so, the primary qualification for Spartan citizenship would have been identical with that for service in the regular hoplite establishment, namely the continuing ability to contribute a fixed minimum of natural produce to the common mess to which one had been elected after successful passage through the *agôgê*.

Uniformity of martial accoutrements, which in Sparta uniquely was extended to clothing (the *phoinikis* or short red cloak was 'the very symbol of Spartan militarism': Connolly 1981, 45) and coiffure (hair was grown long from the age of thirty specifically for its military function), was one of the two main ways of enabling the self-styled Homoioi or 'Peers' – who were in fact enmeshed in a complex web of inequalities – to experience a sort of 'warrior communism' (Weber 1978, 1153), a genuine and tangible degree of mutual parity. The other way was through what Thucydides' Perikles decried as 'laborious training' (*epiponos askêsis*: 2.39.1), meaning that in his eyes the Spartans were mere automatons rather than the 'natural' warriors produced under the Athenian system – or lack of one. To the Spartans themselves this critique would have seemed a great compliment. For although their military training proper in hoplite drill and weapon-training probably did not begin in earnest until they became fully fledged citizen warriors at twenty, they had been under civic discipline for ultimately military ends for some fourteen years already (Chapter 3).

Once past the age of politico-military majority the overriding emphasis in training for a Spartan was on drill. In an era of close-quarter warfare when technology was likely to give only temporary and marginal advantages, it was their drill which gave the Spartans the edge over their opponents. In the case of hoplite-style warfare at any rate, Keegan seems to me incorrect to state that the functions of drill for long-service armies are 'choreographic, ritualistic, perhaps even aesthetic, certainly much more than tactical' (1978, 33). For battle between hoplite armies was traditionally a graceless and unimaginative affair in which weight of numbers counted for as much as if not more than skill in the manipulation of spear and sword. But to make numbers tell, cohesion and timing were of the essence: hence the Spartans' proper emphasis on music (Plut. *Lyk.* 21.3-4, *Mor.* 238b) and dancing (cf. Wheeler 1982, esp. 227,230-3) as being indispensable aids to the development of a sense of rhythm and the ability to march in step (e.g. Thuc. 5.10.5, with Pritchett 1974, I, 107 on 'rhythm-conscious' Brasidas). Most of our specific evidence for the various drill-dependent manoeuvres – deployment from column into line, marshalling the ranks to varying depths, opening ranks, countermarching to reverse front or flanks, inclination or extension of wings against the enemy's flanks – applies to the reorganized army of the fourth century, but it would seem to apply *a fortiori* to the period before the Athenian War. All these could be accomplished with machine-like precision in the set-pieces that hoplite battles typically were.

Set-piece battles, however, were thin on the ground in the Athenian War. The Spartans' initial grand strategy of invading Attika annually by land just before the cereal harvest failed to provoke the Athenians into committing themselves to an encounter they would assuredly have lost and it failed no less signally to compel them to come to terms to avoid starvation. Their grand strategy, to be blunt, was null and void *ab initio* (Brunt 1965; cf. Moxon 1978). This lesson was soon grasped by Brasidas, whose experiences – as commander of a mobile detachment in 431, Ephor in 431/0 and naval commander and adviser in 429, 427, and 425 – had given him an unusually broad view of this heterogeneous war (generally Thuc. 4.81.1). His strategic genius is clearly to be seen behind the foundation of the military colony of Herakleia Trachinia in 426 (Chapter 14); but it was only after the Pylos disaster, and even then with considerable reluctance due apparently to envy, that the Spartan authorities were prepared to allow him to launch a new strategic initiative and open a new front in Thrace. The composition of his wholly non-Spartiate force has been commented on above; it foreshadowed the kind of force Sparta was to use in her Asiatic campaigns of the 390s (Chapter 12).

Thrace was also the breeding-ground of a kind of soldier later to make a considerable impact upon Greek warfare – but again one with the potentialities of which the Spartans were very slow to come to terms. The peltast, who took his name from his usually wicker shield, was more lightly armed and mobile than the hoplite. He could be used in formation but not to deliver the knock-out blow in a set-piece encounter. His special utility was in more broken fighting on uneven, hilly terrain, the sort of terrain that constitutes most of Greece (cf. Grundy 1948, I, 243). From the non-Greek Thracians the peltast's values were first learned by the Greeks of Chalkidike, and as early in the Athenian War as the Battle of Spartolos in 429 (Thuc. 2.79) he showed what damage he in association with cavalry could inflict on hoplites on ground that was not of their choosing. In 422 Brasidas at Amphipolis became the first Spartan to command large numbers of them (Thuc. 5.6). But it was not until the fourth century, under the leadership of the Athenian Iphikrates above all, that peltasts were able to teach Spartan hoplites a tactical lesson they would never forget (Chapter 12).

However, the Pylos disaster of 425 had already shown how vulnerable they could be to light-armed tactics (Best 1969, 20-4; Wilson 1979), despite their attempts to increase mobility by abandoning the metal helmet and breastplate (Anderson 1970, 21-3, 29-37). For although the Spartans had used some kind of light-armed troops in the time of Tyrtaios (*gumnêtes*: fr. 11.35-8; *gumnomachoi*: P.Oxy. 3316.14), they had (like most other Greek states) failed to develop this arm. The chief reason for the Spartans' failure appears to be ideological, a combination of snobbery and military nostalgia. Just as the cannon and hand-gun 'degraded war, putting as they did the noble man-at-arms at the mercy of the vile and base born' (Howard 1976, 14), so arrows – contemptuously dismissed as 'spindles' (women's implements) by one of the Spartiates captured on Sphakteria (Thuc. 4.40.2) – were unable to distinguish the noble and brave from the cowardly. For battle to be 'gentlemanly' it had to take place between social equals (cf. Keegan 1978, 98, 103n, 322). None the less, as we have seen, in the year following the Pylos disaster the Spartans did belatedly raise a force of archers.

A similar ideological point was made apophthegmatically by Agesilaos' son Archidamos in a context of about 370, when he saw a missile shot by the newly-developed Sicilian catapults (Plut. *Mor.* 191e, 219a (8)): 'By Herakles! the valour (*aretâ*) of a man is no more!' These catapults were designed to disrupt the defence of a fortified position and had first been extensively developed under the patronage of Dionysios I of Syracuse (405-367), who is said to have been the first general to possess a full siege apparatus (cf. Tarn 1930, 102-3). But the potential of artillery for sieges was not to be realized completely until the reigns of Philip and Alexander of Macedon (cf. Arist. *Pol.* 1330a34-31a18; and generally Garlan 1974). In this department too Sparta was notoriously backward. Their siege of little Plataia, which occupied two whole years and was prosecuted essentially by the traditional method of circumvallation (after a rather half-hearted flirtation with rams, combustible weapons and a siege-mound) has rightly been called 'a museum of the besieger's art' (Grundy 1948, I, 288-9).

The Battle of Mantineia in 418 was the last set-piece hoplite battle of the Athenian War fought in mainland Greece. Although it resulted eventually in a resounding Spartan victory, a combination of overconfident or incompetent generalship, insubordination and perhaps some loss of morale had nearly brought disaster; and in retrospect this battle may be seen as the beginning of the end of Sparta's unquestioned hoplite dominance. It is not insignificant that, unlike Plutarch as cited above, Xenophon (*LP* 13.5) applied the expression 'craftsmen in warfare' to the Spartans' scrupulous observance of the religious proprieties thought likely to secure the favour of heaven in advance of battle rather than to their military evolutions on the battlefield. Besides, victory at Mantineia very far from ended the Athenian War, and it was paradoxically at sea rather than on the land that it was decided in Sparta's favour – a striking illustration of the dictum placed by Thucydides (1.122.1) in the mouth of his Corinthian speakers at Sparta in 432 that 'war least of all proceeds on fixed conditions but rather in and of itself for the most part devises ways of responding to the immediate circumstances.'

To their credit the Spartans did in the final phase of the Athenian War adapt perforce to circumstances in two crucial ways. In place of annual invasions of Attika they adopted the relatively new strategy of *epiteichismos* (cf. Westlake 1983a), spectacularly deployed against them at Pylos since 425, by occupying the Athenian fort of Dekeleia from 413 to the end of the war. This proved a far more effective economic weapon. Nevertheless, as other Thucydidean speakers no less presciently put it in 428 (Thuc. 3.13.5), 'it is not in Attika, as one may think, that the war will be decided but in the area from which Attika draws its sustenance and support'. The Mytilenaian ambassadors were referring to Athens' Aegean Empire and more particularly to the Bosporos and Hellespont bottlenecks through which the literally vital wheat-supply of Athens was transported annually from the northern shores of the Black Sea. But to win the War in this theatre demanded supremacy at sea, and there were powerful reasons why the Spartans should have been slow, diffident, reluctant to commit themselves wholeheartedly to this element from early on in the Athenian War.

To begin with, the Spartans had no naval tradition. The location of Sparta some fifty kilometres inland, the fact that its chief port of Gytheion was a Perioikic town, the acquisition of military and political supremacy without the need for a regular fleet, the huge expense of maintaining a fleet as opposed to the relative cheapness of conventional hoplite warfare, the rudimentary character of Spartan public finance and lack of a convertible currency, the self-sufficient and overwhelmingly agrarian economic base of Lakonia and Messenia, the inevitability of relying mainly on Perioikoi and Helots to fit out, crew and command the ships – all these factors conspired to make the Spartans the landlubbing power par excellence (e.g. Thuc. 4.12.3). Not that the Spartans were totally without naval experience before the Athenian War (cf. Pareti 1961 (1908/9), 1-19); but that experience was hardly encouraging – a further reason for Sparta's reluctance to 'go naval' from the start.

In 524, during what Herodotus slightly inaccurately called 'the first expedition to Asia of the Lakedaimonian Dorians', the Spartans had failed to overthrow the Samian tyrant Polykrates and had suffered a defeat at sea (Hdt. 3.54-6; cf. Cartledge 1982). No doubt the bulk of the 'large' fleet was provided by their Corinthian allies, but this was not an auspicious start to a programme of maritime expansion, if such a programme there was. It is noticeable that no king was entrusted with naval command either in 524 or in *c.*512 when one Anchimol(i)os led a Spartan invasion of Attika by sea. Perhaps there was some sort of taboo against it (a suggestion of Lewis 1977,45). If so, it was broken down by the Persian Wars of 480-479 as a consequence of the Spartans' overall command of the loyalist Greeks both by land and by sea. Despite the honours showered upon him at Sparta the non-royal admiral of 480, Eurybiadas, had not covered himself with glory at sea, and in 479 the naval command was assumed by King Latychidas (Leotychides) II.

The decisive Battle of Mykale, however, was won more on the Asiatic mainland than on the water, and following the battle Latychidas had been unwilling to prosecute the war against the Persians any further in the Aegean. Indeed, so far from burning to complete the liberation of those Aegean Greeks still under Persian control, 'the Peloponnesians' (which must include Latychidas) had proposed to remove the Ionian Greeks of Asia from their homes and resettle them on the Greek mainland in the coastal towns of those Greeks who had taken the Persian side during Xerxes' invasion (Hdt. 9.106.2-3). We shall return to the wider significance of this proposal (Chapter 11). Here it is sufficient to note that this quietist and isolationist policy had been reversed by the time of the 478 campaigning season, when Regent Pausanias, fresh from his land victory at Plataia, devoted his energies to beating back the Persians by sea. But the decision of the Spartan home authorities (abetted no doubt by Latychidas) to recall him that same year and to relinquish the leadership of the Greeks against Persia to Athens and her new naval alliance meant the end of any serious Spartan military involvement in the Aegean until 412.

In naval terms the Athenian War had begun disastrously for the Spartans. Deprived by diplomacy of the fleet of Kerkyra (Corcyra) before the War broke out, the Spartans relied primarily on Corinth in this sphere. But not only did large Athenian fleets make virtually unimpeded raids all round the Peloponnese and begin to establish the ring of bases that was completed in 424. In 429 the Athenian admiral Phormion delivered a stinging lesson in seacraft to the Corinthians in their own home waters, the Corinthian Gulf (Thuc. 2.79-92). The timidity and total ineffectiveness of the Spartan admiral Alkidas when he ventured into the eastern Aegean in 427 (Thuc. 3.16.3ff) were not therefore inexplicable; and when in 425 the Spartans suffered the crowning misfortune of losing practically the entire Peloponnesian fleet to the Athenians (Thuc. 4.16.3 – they were not returned), it was clear that the only way they could hope to defeat the Athenian fleet was on the land, that is by capturing Athenian bases. But Spartan counsels were not directed and executed by an Alexander the Great; and Brasidas, who made a stab at putting such a strategy into effect, was himself stabbed in the back by the home authorities for reasons to which we shall shortly return (Chapter 6). In short, 'ce que les Péloponnésiens accompliront sur mer avant 412 relèvera de l'anecdote' (Will 1972, 319).

By 412, however, the balance of naval power had shifted dramatically, thanks to the calamitous failure by the Athenians to capture Syracuse, let alone all Sicily. In the course of the Sicilian Expedition of 415-413 they lost most of their fleet and the best-trained Aegean Greek sailors then available. They were thereby more than half disarmed. If Sparta could secure the necessary cash to construct ships and pay crews, there was a chance at last of outright victory in a war they had begun a score of years before. But – and it was an enormous 'but' – obtaining that cash and re-gearing the system of higher military command to an unfamiliar mode of protracted warfare in unfamiliar surroundings with largely non-Spartan troops might involve not just a temporary re-orientation of diplomacy and military operations but a threat to the very fabric of traditional Spartan society – war being, as Von Clausewitz famously put it, the continuation of policy with the admixture of other means. Within a comparatively short space of time precisely that threat did indeed materialize, so it is worth outlining briefly the main non-military implications forced upon Sparta by the final, naval phase of the Athenian War. The modalities and consequences of these changes will be explored in detail in succeeding chapters. But to conclude this section it may be pointed out that by the time of the Battle of Arginousai in 406 the ships on the Spartan side were reportedly better sailers than the Athenians' (1.6.31) and that in Lysander Sparta produced an admiral superior to any the Greek world had known since Themistokles or perhaps Phormion.

(iii) Finance

The Athenian War if any demonstrates the truth of Cicero's often echoed dictum that unlimited money is the sinews of war (*nervi belli: Phil.* 5.2.5). The prudent Archidamos had reportedly warned his over-eager and inexperienced audience of this in 432 (Thuc. 1.83.2; cf. Plut. *Mor.* 190a and – wrongly attributed to Archidamos III – 219a(7)). The embassies sent in the early years of the War to the Great King of Persia were presumably designed to elicit cash (Thuc. 2.7,67; 4.50), but they failed and Sparta technically remained in a state of war with Persia until 412. Then the decision was taken to prosecute the war at sea with all due vigour, so that the need for a steady and large income became overwhelming. Since the Spartans themselves were unable or unwilling to pay even an extraordinary war-levy (Thuc. 1.80.4; cf. Arist. *Pol.* 1271b10-17, with Andreades 1915, 1933; Lotz 1935, 336-7) and reluctant from religious scruple to 'borrow' from the sacred treasures at Olympia and Delphi (cf. Thuc. 1.121.3,143.1); since the Peloponnesian League levied no tribute and maintained no central war-fund (Thuc. 1.19, 141.3-5, 142.1); since extraordinary contributions by Lakonizing states and individuals (such as those listed on the uncertainly dated M/L 67) could not provide enough funds regularly enough; and since the King of Macedon, who potentially had access to huge reserves of gold and silver (cf. Ps.-Her. *Peri Pol.*24), was unreliable, there was no other available source of the required amounts of cash on a constant basis than the Great King and his two western Asiatic satraps, Tissaphernes (based on Sardis) and Pharnabazus (based on Daskyleion).

The timing was opportune. Athens had recently broken her non-aggression pact with Persia (Thuc. 8.5,19,28,54; with A. Andrewes in Gomme 1981 *ad locc.*), and the King was temporarily free to turn his mind away from Judaean, Egyptian and Median troubles to the Aegean. His price for aid, however, was politically high. He not only wanted his satraps to make good the arrears of tribute stopped by Athenian naval power for the past half century. He also wanted his claim to the sovereignty of all Asia recognized and with it his right to (as the Asiatic Greeks saw it) infringe the autonomy of the Greek cities in Asia. But this was a price that the Spartans to begin with fell over themselves in their eagerness to pay, despite the high-sounding liberation propaganda which they had used to mask their real motives for starting the Athenian War and which Brasidas had employed to great effect in Thrace between 424 and 422. In cold fact the Spartan war-cry of 'freedom' was but 'a catchword without real meaning, but with an appeal, ready and compulsive, for those who do not think' (Glover 1917, 364; see further Chapter 11).

(iv) Spartans abroad

According to Thucydides (4.81.2), 'in the later war after the Sicilian events the upright conduct and intelligence of Brasidas were the chief factors in arousing enthusiasm for the Spartans among the allies of Athens, of whom some had experience of Brasidas' behaviour at first hand, others judged of it by repute'. Since Brasidas had died in 422, this is a pretty damning comment on the conduct and intelligence of his successors from 413 on, and Thucydides' later remark (4.81.3) that 'the reputation (Brasidas) acquired for excellence in all departments left behind the firm expectation that the other Spartans would be like him' can only be taken as ironic, as it was no doubt meant to be (see further Chapter 6). For the various Spartan officials who were despatched to the Aegean theatre – navarchs (*nauarchoi* or Admirals of the Fleet), harmosts (*harmostai, harmostêres*), other commanders – proved themselves the very reverse of tactful, generous, astute and fairminded towards Athens' subjects and former subjects. They neither walked softly nor did they merely carry a big stick. According to Thucydides (1.77.6, quoted in full in Chapter 6), Athenian speakers at Sparta in 432 had looked back to the conduct of the war against Persia in 480-78 and observed that the Spartans, should they ever take over the Athenian Empire, would quickly forfeit the good will they enjoyed on account of the fear Athens inspired. This 'prediction' was of course fulfilled when the power of individual Spartans abroad in the period after the Athenian War was at a pitch never before (and never again) attained (Xen. *Anab.* 6.6.12; Isok. 4.111; 6.52).

Ostensibly the Athenian speakers had in mind above all the erratic and possibly treasonous behaviour of Regent Pausanias in 478. But that their words had a more general application even the Spartan authorities were not able or willing to deny. Archidamos, for example, reportedly (Thuc. 1.85.1) used the threat posed to the Spartan way of life as an argument against the war in prospect; and the Spartans' notorious 'expulsions of foreigners' (*xenêlasiai*: see further Chapter 13) are just the most vivid illustration of the manner in which Sparta 'regulated and controlled all of the relations between her citizens and outsiders in an attempt to insure that public concerns take precedence over private' (Rahe 1977, 49n.62). This goes a long way towards explaining why since at least the Persian Wars kings in command abroad had regularly been accompanied by two Ephors and after 418 by boards of ten, fifteen or thirty 'advisers' (*sumbouloi*), and why from the earliest years of the Athenian War Spartan naval commanders had been similarly advised (or supervised). But not all Spartan commanders were thus restricted. For a time at least Brasidas in Thrace, King Agis at Dekeleia and Lysander in the Aegean were able to turn their military and diplomatic successes to personal account and build up power-bases more or less independent of control from home. However, their independence and success tended to exaggerate the envy and distrust of one's peers that the Spartan *agôgê* by its tense combination of emulation and egalitarianism helped to inculcate from an early of age especially among the social and political elite (Chapter 3). The sharpness of political rivalry at Sparta was greatly honed as a result.

(v) Spartan domestic conflicts

In connection with the particularly vicious and bloody *stasis* (civil strife) that broke out on Kerkyra in 427 Thucydides (3.82.2) commented that thereafter the entire Greek world was similarly convulsed. There were no oligarchs and democrats in Sparta in the same sense as there were in Kerkyra. But there were rich and poor Spartans, and it is a very remarkable fact that during the Athenian

War Sparta was not exempt from this universal *stasis*. It is remarkable because traditionally Sparta was held to have been free from *stasis* for centuries (Thuc. 1.18.2; Lys. 33.7) and this supposed feature of Spartan society was one of its chief attractions for non-Spartan sympathizers. Such ideologues were not to be confused by reality (Chapter 22).

Sparta notoriously 'did not wash her linen in public' (Gomme 1956, 358), which made things easier for the Lakonizing ideologues and makes them harder for us. But the *arcana* of Spartan politics can, I believe, be penetrated by using the evidence available, especially that of Xenophon. Detailed discussion is best reserved for later (esp. Chapters 6, 8-10), but it may be useful to establish some preliminary guidelines here. First, a question of terminology. 'Factions' is the wrong word to describe the rival groupings within the Spartan political elite if it is taken to mean something like the political parties of modern representative democracies with their fixed membership and programmes. It is harmless enough, though, if used to refer to the more or less temporary groupings of influential men around some recognized leader, usually a king but occasionally an annual office-holder such as an Ephor (e.g. Xenares: Thuc. 5.46.4) or a navarch (Lysander). Personality, ideology, policy – all these were inextricably intermingled in the process of factional rivalry that on occasion split the elite quite literally down the middle (Paus. 3.5.2: the trial of Pausanias in 403). The extraordinary circumstances of the Athenian War, and especially the opportunities for personal enrichment to which the bribe-prone Spartans easily succumbed, provoked unprecedented internal political upheavals, of which the degradation of the Pylos returnees for fear that they would start a revolution in 421 (Thuc. 5.34.2) and the execution of Thorax for the possession of coined money in 404 (Chapter 6) are just two striking examples. The lead given by the 'haves' was smartly followed by the 'have-nots' under Kinadon in 399 – or would have been but for Sparta's well-laid contingency plans to meet such a threat of revolt by the many dispossessed.

(vi) Sparta and the allies

Of the existing tensions affecting Sparta that were exacerbated by the Athenian War it remains only to consider those between Sparta and her allies, especially those of the Peloponnesian League (cf. Chapter 2). Notionally at least it was on behalf of her allies that Sparta declared war on Athens in 432, in the following circumstances. There had from the start been an important section of Spartan opinion opposed to the Peace of 446/5, or at least to the chief Spartan peacemaker Pleistoanax. In the light of relations between Sparta and Athens since the Persian Wars it is not unreasonable to suppose that this section took a 'hawkish' view of the growth of the Athenian Empire, believing that it should be cut off at the roots. Already by 441/0, it may be argued (Cartledge 1982, 261-3), the 'hawks' were in the ascendant over the 'doves' who argued for peaceful co-existence with the Athenians and mutual respect for the two great powers' respective spheres of influence. For in that year the Spartan Assembly probably decided to assist the Samians in their attempted revolt from Athens in flagrant breach of the Thirty Years' Peace. Nothing in fact came of that decision since as in *c.*504 the Corinthians persuaded a majority of the Peloponnesian League allies against such an intervention – though it is of course another matter whether they did so on the highminded principle of upholding 'Greek law and custom' as Thucydides (1.41.1) makes them claim in the Athenian Assembly in 433.

Within a decade of 441/0, however, the Corinthians had changed their minds. In 432 at a meeting of the Spartan Assembly they urged their *hêgemôn* (leader – of the Peloponnesian League) to declare war on Athens on the grounds that the Athenians had broken the Peace in two incidents involving cities originally founded by Corinth, Kerkyra in north-west Greece and Poteidaia in Chalkidike. Other allies of Sparta, notably Megara and Aigina, also alleged Athenian breaches of the Peace, to which (if Thucydides may be believed) an Athenian delegation which happened to be in Sparta on some other, unspecified business was given a right of reply. Thereafter, all foreigners were requested to withdraw, and in closed session the Spartan Assembly voted overwhelmingly that the Athenians had broken the Peace. This was tantamount to an outright declaration of war, although diplomatic formalities continued during the winter of 432/1 and hostilities were precipitated by an incident (an attack on Plataia by Thebes) which involved neither Sparta nor Athens directly.

The proceedings of this crucial Assembly meeting will be re-examined later (Chapter 8) for the light they shed on the process of public decision-making at Sparta. Here I am more especially concerned with the underlying issues and – what is equally relevant – the way Thucydides chose to represent and explain them. For in order to dramatize the significance of this meeting and to exhibit the factors governing the process of deliberation through which interstate relations were conducted, Thucydides wrote up four of the speeches delivered in this momentous debate. All four of course raise the usual problem of fidelity to their originals, a problem that is hardly resolved by Thucydides' own account (1.22) of why and how he wrote the speeches included in his History. But this problem is particularly acute in connection with the two Spartan speeches, respectively by King Archidamos and the Ephor Sthenelaïdas. Not only were they delivered in closed session (like the exchanges in the so-called Melian Dialogue: Thuc. 5.84-113), but their arguments and their effect have to be reconciled with Thucydides' personally expressed view on the origins or cause of the Athenian War. To paraphrase the latter, the Spartans according to Thucydides had no realistic alternative to making war on Athens since Athenian power had grown to such an extent that it was now encroaching upon the alliance on which the Spartans' security depended. It was therefore out of a prudential fear for their own position, and not out of respect for the legal, moral and emotional arguments brought forward by their allies, that the Spartans unavoidably declared the Thirty Years' Peace a dead letter and so began a major war (cf. Ste. Croix 1972).

The speeches of Archidamos (1.80-85) and Sthenelaïdas (1.86), followed by the brief account of the overwhelming vote for war (1.87), at once support and range beyond Thucydides' analysis of the causes of the war (1.23.5-6, 88,118.2). In this vital test-case at least it seems to me that speeches, narrative and authorial judgment form a unified, mutually reinforcing set. The very fact that

Archidamos' long, reasoned and reasonable speech is trumped (not answered) by Sthenelaïdas' quintessentially laconic, seven-sentence exhortation indicates beautifully just how overwhelming was the feeling in favour of war at Sparta among his predominantly young, that is under forty, and largely un-battlescarred audience. Sthenelaïdas merely asserts the to him patent guilt of Athens and refers to only half of what Thucydides in a strikingly odd phrase calls 'the truest explanation' (*alêthestatê prophasis*) of why the war broke out, that is the growth of Athenian power. He does not of course describe his reaction to this as one of fear for Spartan security. Instead, he couches his brusque appeal to the conservative and war-hungry Spartans in the timeless moral-legal terms of conventional Greek ethics in a way calculated to give a semblance of legitimate justification to their bellicosity: the Spartans, he says, must help their friends and harm their enemies. 'Vote then for war, Spartans, and be worthy of Sparta! Do not let the Athenians grow more powerful! Let us not utterly betray the allies but rather let us go forward to battle against the wrongdoers fortified by the help of the gods!'

The reader of Thucydides, looking back on the Athenian War in its entirety, can only be astonished by this improvident warmongering and nod even more vigorously with approval at the sagacity of the elder statesman Archidamos who foresaw how difficult the war would be to win. And such of course was the intention of Thucydides, whatever may have been the relationship between the words he put in the king's mouth and the speech the king actually delivered to the Spartan Assembly in 432 (cf. Wassermann 1952/3; 1963/4, 290). But Thucydides surely had another, ironical purpose too. For the one thing Sparta did pretty consistently during the War, from as early as 425, was betray her allies of the Peloponnesian League in the sense that she fought for her own and not their interests.

In 425, as we have seen above, the Spartans were ready to make peace for the sake of recovering a small number of Spartiate prisoners. Spartan talk of peace, friendship and alliance with Athens (Thuc. 4.19.1) was all very fine, but the Athenian Empire was still intact, the Peloponnesians were experiencing severe economic hardship and in the circumstances the peace terms would have been even more humiliating for Sparta and unacceptable to some of her principal allies than those granted four years later by a considerably weakened Athens. As it was, in 421 four Peloponnesian League allies including the two most powerful refused to swear to the Peace of Nikias on the grounds that it did not sufficiently accommodate their interests. They were Corinth, the Boiotian Confederacy, Megara and Elis. Each had a territorial claim which the terms agreed by Sparta did not acknowledge. But over and above these they were all highly suspicious of the clause which gave Sparta and Athens *carte blanche* to alter any of the other clauses by mutual consent without reference to their respective allies (Thuc. 5.18.11). When shortly afterwards Corinth formed a secret pact with Argos and then together with Elis and Corinth's allies in Thrace openly joined an anti-Spartan Peloponnesian entente headed by Argos the first adherents of which were Mantineia and her allies – well, Sparta must have felt that civilization as she had known it was approaching its end.

Sparta did of course extricate herself from this imbroglio and went on eventually to win the Athenian War. But the mutual resentment and sense of betrayal felt by Sparta and some of her principal allies welled up once again immediately after its successful outcome, and within a decade of its end Sparta was actually at war with a coalition led by Corinth, Boiotia, Argos and Athens (Chapter 14). That war, like the Athenian War, was won by Sparta only with the aid of the Great King of Persia, the principal beneficiary of some four decades of inter-specific bloodletting by the major Greek states. If there was a lesson for the by now middle-aged Agesilaos to learn from all this, it has to be said that he failed to learn it. For him, unlike Dr Johnson's scoundrel, patriotism very narrowly conceived was always his first refuge.

One incident during the Athenian War most nearly captures and summarizes what was to be the consistent position of Agesilaos on interstate relations – the Plataian affair of 429-7. Little Plataia, ironically enough on the advice of a Spartan king, had sought and received an alliance with Athens in the late sixth century rather than be swallowed up in a Boiotian federation dominated by her powerful neighbour Thebes. The Thebans accordingly bided their time until in the uneasy interval between the Spartan declaration of war in 432 and the first Peloponnesian invasion of Attika in 431 they sought to infiltrate and take over Plataia by force of arms. The attempt failed, but communications between the Spartans and Boiotia were strategically vital and Plataia unfortunately stood in their way. Hence the long siege of Plataia begun by Archidamos in 429 and completed two years later. On the surrender of the Plataians the Spartans sent out an investigative and judicial commission of five. One of these, Aristomelidas, was probably the future father-in-law of Agesilaos and so doubtless a client of Archidamos (cf. Chapter 9). A long and eloquent plea for mercy was addressed to the commissioners by two Plataians, one of whom was a *proxenos* or official representative of Spartan interests at Plataia and had the richly symbolic name and patronymic Lakon ('the Spartan') son of Aeimnestos (a name shared by the Spartiate who killed the Persian commander-in-chief at the Battle of Plataia: Hdt. 9.64.2). The judges, however, were unmoved and merely asked each of the more than 200 Plataian captives individually their original question: have you done the Spartans and their allies any service in the war (Thuc. 3.52.5, 68.1)? All replied in the negative and were promptly put to the sword, 'a horrifying example of war psychosis' (Bengtson 1969, 171-2).

A year later the Spartans razed the city of Plataia to the ground but made a show of reverencing the sacred character of the site, the factor on which the Plataians had to a large extent rested their appeal for clemency in 427. Thucydides, though, was not deceived, and no more should we be. 'The Spartans took this line with Plataia largely or wholly on account of the Thebans, whom they regarded as useful to them at this stage of the war' (3.68.4). Agesilaos no doubt enjoyed hearing the tale from his father-in-law, since it chimed with what a Byzantine opponent on trial for his life at Sparta aptly called 'the one absolute criterion of honour and justice' for the Spartans, namely their conception of their country's interest (Plut. *Alk*. 31.8; cf. Thuc. 5.105.4). But it was not to Aristomelidas that Agesilaos owed his basic precepts of statecraft. In that regard his principal mentor was Lysander, as we shall see (Chapter 6) after we have ended the preliminaries by surveying the sources of evidence for Agesilaos and the crisis of Sparta.

5

Agesilaos, Xenophon and the Sources of Evidence

Every one likes flattery; and when you come to royalty you should lay it on with a trowel. (Benjamin Disraeli, letter to Matthew Arnold)

If (Xenophon) had lived in modern days, he would have been a high-class journalist and pamphleteer; he would have made his fortune as a war-correspondent; and would have written the life of some mediocre hero of the stamp of Agesilaus. (Bury 1909, 151-2)

Lysander had more influence on the conduct of Agesilaos as king than any other individual (Chapter 6). But it was a 'self-appointed Spartan' (Jacoby 1955, 614), not a Spartan by birth, who most closely identified with Agesilaos' aspirations and outlook during his reign and who took it upon himself to sing the praises of his dead patron, mentor and friend to a by no means unanimously favourable (despite Isok. *Ep.* 9.1) world. That eulogist – or rather apologist (cf. Dümmler 1901, I, 271) – was the Athenian-born Xenophon, who felt 'a genuine elective affinity' (Taeger 1957, 120) for the Spartan king. His *Agesilaos* began thus as it meant to continue:

I am aware that it is no easy matter to compose an encomium that will do justice to the virtue and reputation of Agesilaos. Nevertheless, the attempt has to be made. For it would not be well if a perfectly good man (*teleôs anêr agathos*) should receive no laudations, however inadequate, precisely because of his perfection.

Few if any now doubt that Xenophon was the author of the *Agesilaos* (the opposite view prevailed in Hertzberg's day) or that it was written or at least published by him immediately after the death of Agesilaos in or about the winter of 360/59. Would that the authenticity and compositional chronology of all the works ascribed to Xenophon were so clearcut. For the historian of Sparta in the age of Agesilaos the doubts are particularly irksome, concerning as they do the chronography of the *Hellenika* and both the chronography and the authenticity of the pamphlet entitled *Lakedaimoniôn Politeia*. Neither title may in fact be Xenophon's own, and both are more or less misleading, as we shall see. The *Hellenika* purports to be a narrative history of Greece from 411 to 362, a period which subsumes all but the tail-end of Agesilaos' reign, and the *Lak. Pol.* is a short essay devoted to a selection of Spartan customs and institutions as they were in theory and/or practice during this same era. It would therefore be pleasant if we could be sure who wrote and published them and when. Without that basic information it becomes virtually impossible to answer the perhaps more significant question, why these three compositions were given to the public.

Again, the case of the *Agesilaos* seems the most straightforward. If we take the proem quoted above at face value, Xenophon believed that Agesilaos was a 'perfectly good man' and so felt that he should do his humble and inadequate best to pay his hero's goodness its due meed of honour. But there was of course much more to it: a personal desire to reciprocate a patron's benefactions and to help a friend as friends were honour-bound to do (cf. Chapter 9); a quasi-philosophical desire to promote the ideal of aristocratic or rather kingly leadership (cf. Chapter 22); a propagandistic desire to defend the career of Agesilaos against his detractors inside and outside Sparta (cf. Dümmler 1901, I, 271, 274); and not least perhaps a literary desire to make his mark in the relatively new biographical genre of writing (cf. Stuart 1928, esp. ch.3; Momigliano 1971, 50-1; Russell/Wilson 1981, xv; Plezia 1982). All four motives, and maybe others besides, must be kept firmly in mind when evaluating the *Agesilaos* as evidence for the history of Agesilaos and Sparta rather than Xenophon's credo and personal relationship to its subject (see generally Breitenbach 1967, 1701-7; and more tendentiously Higgins 1977, 76-82).

The status of the *Lak. Pol.* is rather more ambiguous (Ollier 1934; Bordes 1982, 165-203; out on a limb in rejecting its authenticity is Chrimes 1948). In language and style the work is undeniably Xenophontic (Richards 1907, 40-7,67-72), unlike the polemical pamphlet entitled *Athenaiôn Politeia* which became incorporated certainly erroneously among the manuscripts of genuinely Xenophontic works. But in the process of manuscript transmission one chapter, the fourteenth, somehow was inserted out of its proper place – or so it has seemed to almost all modern readers. This has allowed scholars the luxury of interminable and irreconcilable argument over whether it should be replaced at the beginning or the end of the work, over the date of the chapter's composition, and indeed whether it was ever published by Xenophon himself. This putatively misplaced chapter is written in a spirit that is unquestionably hostile to the Spartans of the writer's own day who are said to obey 'neither the god nor the laws of Lykourgos' (14.7). Yet the other fourteen chapters, at least on a straightforward or – as some would have it (e.g. Strauss 1939; Higgins 1977, 65-75; Carlier 1978, 136n.12,160n.64) – superficial reading, mostly laud Spartan institutions and customs to the skies for inculcating exemplary moral and physical virtues and for engendering thereby unparalleled material power and prosperity for the state.

Thus, whether the fourteenth chapter belongs at the beginning or (as most believe) the end, the pamphleteer seems here to be contrasting the Spartans' glorious and admirable past with their sordid present, or the ideal with the real Sparta. The chronographical question therefore is whether the deterioration in Sparta's mores and power, which the author attributes to impiety and abandonment of the laws of Lykourgos, occasioned the pamphlet as a whole or just the misplaced chapter. If the former, then the *Lak. Pol.* was presumably not written before at the earliest 378 (the date of the foundation of the Second Athenian League – Chapter 14 – to which there may be an oblique reference at *LP* 14.6); and putatively it could have been composed as some kind of explanation or apology for Sparta's fourth-century failure (rather as the spuriously Xenophontic *Ath. Pol.* was written in part to explain Athens' fifth-century success), if indeed it was not also Xenophon's *apologia pro vita sua*. On the other hand, supposing the misplaced chapter to be an afterthought, one might argue that the bulk of the *Lak. Pol.* was written at some time before the decisive battle of Leuktra in an almost wholly laudatory spirit and perhaps even (as suggested by Wilamowitz 1884, 272) at the instigation of Agesilaos whose influence is all-pervasive (cf. Ollier 1934, xxxv-vi,45,71,72,74).

Chronological certainty is impossible of attainment. We lack even such 'objective' stylometric arguments as have been deployed in the debate over the relative and absolute chronology of the *Hellenika* and its alleged constituent 'parts' (below). My own mind is therefore open. But on balance I incline to the unitarian view that would place the composition of the entire *Lak. Pol.* after Leuktra and indeed after the death of Agesilaos. For the *Agesilaos* shows that as late as 359 Xenophon could still see fit to compose a work in which the praise of an individual Spartan – admittedly an outstanding and so rather exceptional individual (cf. Rawson 1969, 48) – could not but rub off to some degree on his state. And in that work (*Ages.* 2.23) Xenophon went out of his way specifically to exonerate Agesilaos from responsibility for the reverses Sparta suffered from the early 370s onwards, especially the disaster of Leuktra, as if to imply that at least Agesilaos had not ceased to obey the god and the laws of Lykourgos. The direct and damning criticism levelled at the Spartans collectively at *LP* 14 would of course have been out of place in a eulogy, but it strikes me as just the sort of thing Xenophon would have been moved to write in the thoroughly disillusioned spirit manifested in the conclusion to the *Hellenika* (certainly written no earlier than 362) and would have felt able to publish after Agesilaos was safely dead and buried.

In writing that last sentence I have invoked Xenophon's biography to account for his literary activity and so run the risk of at best perpetrating the intentional fallacy or at worst arguing in a circle from the date of a work to Xenophon's intellectual and spiritual development and back again. I do not see how these risks can be avoided when independent biographical information is so scarce (cf. Rahn 1981 on one major incident, and generally Anderson 1974b, more speculatively Delebecque 1957) and the chronology of the works so insecure. The risks can at least be minimized, however, by making assumptions explicit and confessing openly to speculation. All assumptions and speculations involving biographical information depend ultimately on just two available sources: Xenophon's own writings and a longish passage in Diogenes Laertius' *Lives of the Philosophers* (2.49-58, with Wilamowitz 1881, 330-5) which besides those writings was able to use a lawcourt speech concerning a grandson of Xenophon. A cautious 'brief life' might be reconstructed on the following lines.

Xenophon was born into an upper-class Athenian family early in the Athenian War. A 'natural conservative' (Glover 1917, 174), he duly received the conventional, decidedly athletic education deemed appropriate to youths of his

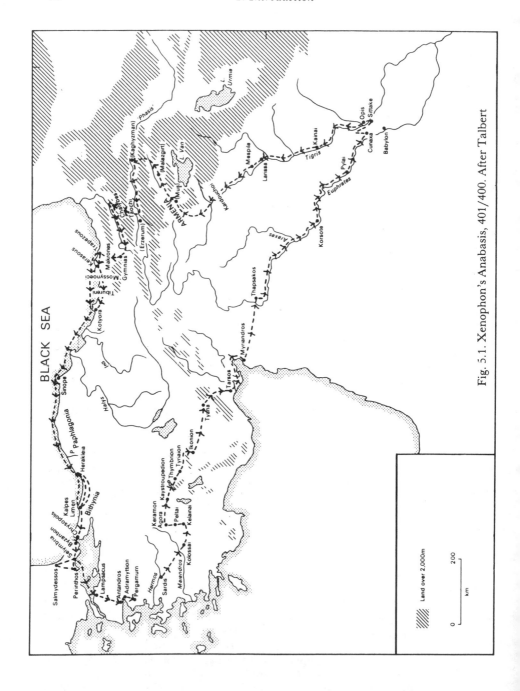

Fig. 5.1. Xenophon's Anabasis, 401/400. After Talbert

station, until in his teens he fell in with and under the spell of Sokrates. From him Xenophon received a kind of higher education, though it is open to question whether this affected his intellectual development and moral outlook as deeply as Xenophon clearly wanted others to believe. After participating as a cavalryman in the traumatic last years of the Athenian War and probably also in the even more traumatic domestic upheaval that followed it (thereby compromising himself politically; cf. Rhodes 1981a, 458), he decided in 402 to become a soldier of fortune like many thousands of others in these troubled times (cf. Chapter 15). Together with a Theban family friend he left Athens for Asia to enlist as a junior officer in the large Greek mercenary force being assembled by the Persian pretender Cyrus with the covert connivance of the suzerain of Greece, Sparta (Chapter 11). The foolhardy death of Cyrus at Cunaxa in Mesopotamia in 401 robbed the expedition of its point, and the Greek mercenaries were compelled to make their painful way back from the heart of Asia to Greek civilization harried by Persian troops, native tribesmen, inclement weather and unfamiliar terrain.

Xenophon's account of this famous 'march up country' survives as the *Anabasis*, but it is generally agreed that this was not the first participant account to be published and that the *Anabasis* was composed many years after the epic events (Breitenbach 1967, 1639-44). It is none the less a uniquely revealing document for the history of Greek society in the aftermath of the Athenian War, for relations between Greece and Persia, for the economic and political condition of the western reaches of the Persian Empire and of the outer barbarian fringes of the Aegean Greek world (Fig. 5.1), and for the new professional attitude to the writing of technical military literature that characterises the fourth century. After a demoralizingly hostile reception by the Spartan commander at the Bosporos and some service with a Hellenized king of Thrace, the surviving remnant of the so-called Ten Thousand mercenaries – including Xenophon, who was by now their overall commander – was absorbed in 399 into the Spartan army despatched to liberate the Greeks of Ionia from Persian control (3.1.11-28 of the *Hellenika* has been thought to betray autopsy). After three years of desultory fighting punctuated by truces the Spartans decided to increase their commitment and for the first time in their history send out a king to campaign on the continent of Asia. It was thus in 396 that Agesilaos and Xenophon first met.

Presumably during the first year of Agesilaos' campaign Xenophon retained his command of the Kyreioi ('Cyrus' men'). But in 395 that post was reallocated by Agesilaos to a Spartan (3.4.20), so Xenophon either took a subordinate command or, more likely, went on to the staff of Agesilaos. The *Lak. Pol.* (13.7) usefully details the members of a commanding king's staff on campaign: 'all full Spartan citizens (Homoioi) who are fellow-members of the royal mess, together with seers, doctors, flute-players, commanding officers and any volunteers who happen to be present.' It is not difficult to place Xenophon in the latter category. At any rate Xenophon remained with Agesilaos until the king was urgently recalled in 395/4 to cope with the major threat to Spartan suzerainty posed by a grand coalition of important Greek states including Xenophon's native Athens. Weep though he might (cf. 4.2.4), Xenophon stoically returned with Agesilaos (and some camels: 3.4.24) to Greece – or, as he put it in the *Anabasis* (5.3.6), to

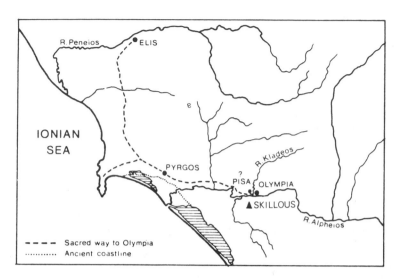

Fig. 5.2. Skillous and the north-west Peloponnese. After J. Swaddling, *The Ancient Olympic Games* (London 1980)

Boiotia. There Agesilaos fought and won the Battle of Koroneia (Chapter 12); and even if Xenophon did not join in the actual fighting (it seems he disapproved of the tactics adopted by Agesilaos: 4.3.19; *Ages.* 2.12), we could have been virtually sure that he was an eyewitness without the explicit testimony of Plutarch (*Ages.* 18.2) to that effect. For the battle provoked from his pen the 'most poetic moment of description in the whole of the *Agesilaus*' (Henry 1967, 152, on *Ages.* 2.14). No doubt, too, he was among those first off the mark to crown Agesilaos with wreaths for his victory.

Politically speaking, it was immaterial whether Xenophon had taken up arms against his fellow-countrymen (*Ages.* 2.6) at Koroneia or not. His mere presence with the army of Agesilaos was treasonable enough, and it was perhaps now that he was formally exiled from Athens on a charge of Laconism (*Anab.* 7.7.57) if indeed he had not been exiled earlier – perhaps around 399, when Sokrates was executed – on a charge of Medism (cf. *Anab.* 3.1.5).[1] Either way a return to Athens in 394 was barred, and Xenophon availed himself of this possibly not unwelcome circumstance to settle in the Peloponnese. At first he lived in Sparta, later on an estate at Skillous in Triphylia a short distance south of Olympia (*Anab.* 5.3; Diog. Laert. 2.52; Paus. 5.6.5; see Fig. 5.2. The actual site is claimed to have been identified.) This estate was granted to him by the Spartans, presumably at the instigation of Agesilaos who may now fairly be described as Xenophon's patron (cf. Chapter 9). It was also reportedly at the suggestion of Agesilaos (Plut. *Ages.* 20.2) that Xenophon's two sons were put through the Spartan *agôgê* thereby qualifying for membership of the class of *trophimoi xenoi*

[1]The chronology of Xenophon's career with special reference to 401-392 is discussed by Rahn 1981, who plumps for the later date but uses arguments of very variable weight.

('Spartan-raised foreigners'); some of these volunteered for service in the
Spartan army at Olynthos in 381 (5.3.9; cf. Chapter 13). This gives a particular
poignancy to Xenophon's description of the *agôgê* in the *Lak. Pol.* (2-4).

What exactly Xenophon was doing when and where between 394 and his
death (in the later 350s?) is almost entirely conjectural. The unusually full
treatment by him of certain episodes and campaigns in the Corinthian War (4.5;
4.6) has suggested to some that he was writing as an eyewitness; and he could
have heard the Olympic Oration of Gorgias in 392 and the homonymous
Oration also delivered at Olympia by another Sicilian, Lysias (33), probably in
384. His exile was conceivably revoked formally in 386 under the terms of or in
consequence of the Peace of Antalkidas (Chapter 11), but it seems Xenophon
preferred the squire's life on his Skillous estate to a return to Athens. In 371,
however, Sparta's defeat at Leuktra gave the men of Elis their chance to reclaim
Triphylia, of which Sparta had deprived them in 400 (Chapter 13), and
Xenophon was obliged to abandon his paradisal haven. He may actually have
been making one of his no doubt frequent visits to Sparta when news of the
Leuktra defeat was brought there during the annual Gymnopaidiai festival
(6.4.16), since this was an occasion when friendly foreigners were welcomed
(Xen. *Mem.* 1.2.61; cf. Plut. *Kim.* 10.6). But rather than remain permanently in
Sparta it seems he chose to remove himself to Corinth. How long he stayed here
is unclear. Some particularly vivid descriptions (e.g. 7.1.18-19) suggest autopsy
in the 360s, and he may have died in Corinth as an ancient tradition had it. On
the other hand, the 360s witnessed a rapprochement between Sparta and Athens
in face of the mutual threat from Thebes (Chapter 14), and the fact that
Xenophon's sons were fighting for Athens on the same side as Sparta in 362
must mean that by then if not long before Xenophon himself was entitled to
return to his native city. The publication of four works with a specifically
Athenian content – the *Hipparchicus, Oeconomicus, Memorabilia* and especially the
Poroi, the last quite closely datable around 355 – could signify that Xenophon
did indeed return to Athens at the finish. But whether he had remained since his
teens ever 'the simple and restrained Socratic' (Higgins 1977, 66; cf. Tigerstedt
1965, 176) and had returned to Athens 'sage now, as well as heroic' (Higgins
1977, 143) seems to me an entirely different question.

It is also a very relevant question as we turn to consider what is in several
ways Xenophon's most puzzling production, the *Hellenika* or 'Greek History'.
The title, as noted earlier, may not be Xenophon's. It is certainly inapt. For the
work's geographical scope rarely extends beyond the Peloponnese, and its choice
and treatment of material are esoteric, sometimes almost capricious. *A History of
My Times*, the title under which it is translated in the Penguin Classics series, is
altogether more suitable. For that admirably captures the personal, memoirist
flavour of the work.[2] Why, then, did he write it? Was it because he 'quite closely
resembles a familiar British figure – the retired general, staunch Tory and
Anglican, firm defender of the Establishment in Church and State, and at the
same time a reflective man with ambitions to write edifying literature' (Irwin

[2]The title of the late Lord Butler's memoirs would be almost equally appropriate: *The Art of Memory:
Friends in Perspective*.

1974, 410)? Or, having tried his hand at all the other prose genres, and being indeed a pioneer in more than one, did he wish to enter the lists as a serious writer of *historia* in the tradition of Herodotus and Thucydides? Or did he perhaps aim to conflate the two, that is to manipulate history to teach philosophy by examples, employing a deceptively simple but in fact subtly allusive literary manner for the purpose? All three views have their modern advocates; my own coincides most nearly with the first. But let us begin by considering the second possibility.

In one crucial respect Xenophon was unfortunate in choosing to start his *Hellenika* more or less (in fact rather less than more) where Thucydides had unavoidably ended his history of the Athenian War. Judgment of Xenophon's value as a historian has tended to be passed in the form of a comparison between him and his great predecessor. Eduard Meyer may have summed up the general nineteenth-century opinion when he characterized Xenophon as 'a really well informed and truthful reporter'; but Barthold Niebuhr, the Danish pioneer of source-criticism in ancient history (Christ 1972, ch. 3), and George Grote, an English disciple of Niebuhr, had earlier registered a very different, utterly hostile view (cf. Cartledge 1979, 261). The future lay with Niebuhr and Grote. In 1908 there was published a longish, fragmentary papyrus of another fourth-century continuator of Thucydides (P. Oxy. 842), whose approach and performance so far as they could be properly assessed far more closely approximated to those of Thucydides than did those of Xenophon. To those with eyes to see, the defects of the *Hellenika* when viewed as if it had been written in a post-Thucydidean spirit now became glaringly apparent.

In the first place, it is partial in both senses, both displaying bias or prejudice and committing sins of omission. As to the former, Xenophon is quite clearly hostile towards Thebes (esp. 7.5.12) and to a lesser extent Athens, whereas on the whole and in general he is favourable towards Sparta. This does not mean that individual Spartans, not excluding Agesilaos, are not criticized directly or by imputation (e.g. 4.5.5ff, 5.3.16, 5.4.1,13; cf. Cloché 1944; Delebecque 1957, 67). But to Xenophon Sparta was of existing states the nearest to his ideal of a disciplined society in which the anonymous masses were led by and submissive to their betters, and most Spartans were ideally at least essentially good men raised in a climate conducive to what Xenophon counted as virtue.

As for Xenophon's omissions, they are quite frankly scandalous – *if* he is to be regarded as a deutero-Thucydides. 'The silences of Xenophon have ceased merely to amaze; they have become a scandal' (Cawkwell 1973, 57; cf. Parke 1927, 159). To explain them away on the grounds of an artistic desire to avoid derailing his narrative (Higgins 1977, 174-5n.136) is hardly cogent. To take only the most striking examples, he omits to describe both the formation of the grand alliance that fought the Corinthian War against Sparta and the foundation of the Second Athenian League in 378, which was ostensibly designed to counter Sparta's breaches of the Peace of Antalkidas. He does not explain the rise of Thebes (through control and consolidation of the Boiotian Confederacy, establishment of the elite force known as the Sacred Band – mentioned only obliquely at 7.1.19 – and other military reforms, and skilful diplomacy) or narrate the careers of her great leaders of the 370s and 360s. In fact, Epameinondas, the individual most responsible for defeating the Spartans at Leuktra, is not introduced by name until a context of 366 (7.1.41; cf. Griffith 1950, 246; generally Westlake 1975), Pelopidas, instigator of the liberation of Thebes from a Spartan garrison in 379/8 and principal commander of the Sacred Band, not until a context of 367 (7.1.34) – and that one which was in Xenophon's eyes thoroughly disreputable. Xenophon omits to mention specifically in their proper place, though he does later imply their occurrence, the liberation of the Messenian Helots and refoundation of Messene in 369 or the creation of an Arkadian federation and the foundation of Megalopolis as federal capital between 370 and 368. Finally, he fails altogether to notice what Cawkwell (1979, 341n.) has called 'arguably the most important diplomatic affair of his age, viz. the Arcadians' appeal to Athens in late 370 B.C., which Athens rejected, and their recourse to Thebes which led to the Theban expedition to the Peloponnese in winter 370-69 B.C.' Clearly Xenophon was an exception to Plutarch's generalization that the Greeks never appreciated the solemnity, sanctity and mystery of silence.

Hostility to Thebes (as opposed to individual Thebans) could at a pinch be invoked as a catch-all explanation for these startling omissions. But that cannot possibly account for other apparently odd features of the work: inaccuracy of detail, capricious unevenness in the selection and treatment of episodes, unscrupulous inconsistency of method in exposing his story. It begins to look very much as though Xenophon cannot have been even trying to be a second Thucydides, whereas the author of the papyrus history justly dubbed the *Hellenika Oxyrhynchia* clearly was (see further below). Hence a new and potentially more fruitful approach has been pursued quite vigorously in recent times. Instead of regarding and condemning Xenophon as a Thucydides manqué it is suggested that he should be evaluated on his own merits as a writer of a very different kind, not in fact as a historian at all in the modern, Thucydidean sense of a (notionally) disinterested and critical explicator of the human past. But this more tolerant attitude can lead to very different conclusions. On the one hand, there are those who, regretting that Xenophon did not try to emulate Thucydides, characterize the *Hellenika* as memoir-literature and variously ascribe its historiographical defects to solipsism, platitudinous moralizing, absence of research, and lapses of memory. On the other hand, others welcome the *Hellenika* as a positive because fundamentally anti-imperialist contribution to the ideology or even philosophy of international relations, a subtly allusive tract for sorry times in which 'there was even more uncertainty and confusion in Greece after the battle [of Mantineia] than there had been previously' (7.5.27).

Both these responses seem to me partly right, partly wrong. High intelligence, piercing insight and scrupulous concentration can be combined with an extreme lucidity of expression such as Xenophon's (witness Voltaire and Flaubert, for instance), and a simple style of writing should not automatically be identified with a simplified view of life. Xenophon, moreover, can at times be subtle, allusive, ironical. However, I find it hard to equate *his* subtlety with high intelligence, *his* allusiveness with piercing insight, *his* irony with scrupulous concentration. Besides, the omissions listed above are flagrant, hardly subtle, and the caprices of inclusion and treatment are too easily and convincingly explained on the memoirs hypothesis for any other to be needed. All that can and should, I think, be salvaged from the case for Xenophon the thinker is a handful of banal moral platitudes which sort only too well with the kind of plain man's guide to Sokratic thinking that he provides in the *Memorabilia*. As Mary Renault's fictional Alexias puts it in her novel *The Last of the Wine*: 'Man or boy, I have never found in Xenophon anything mean or base. He was always a practical man, honourable, religious, with a set of fixed ethics, not wrong but circumscribed. Point out to such a man a clear and simple good, and he will follow it over the roughest country you like to show him.'

On the other hand, if the *Hellenika* is essentially memoirs, it is so only in a special sense. For Xenophon is consistently and doubtless self-consciously reticent about his own part in the events he recalls (cf. Anderson 1974b, 146). Thus it is in the *Anabasis*, not the *Hellenika*, that he tells of his return from Asia to Greece in 394, his exile, and his settling at Skillous; and it is only a modern inference from the nature of the reportage that Xenophon was, say, on the spot in Sparta when news of Leuktra arrived. If Xenophon ought not to be judged as if he had tried and failed to emulate Thucydides, neither should any estimate of the *Hellenika* overlook the mask of impersonality that he deliberately assumed in composing the work. However, when that has been said and all due allowances have been made, the *Hellenika* does all the same seem most usefully characterized as the memoirs of an old man. Leaving aside temperament and political opinions, the chief differences between Thucydides and Xenophon are twofold.

The first lies in their respective attitudes to the gathering and sifting of information. As Thucydides (1.22) tells his readers explicitly, he made it a principle not to write down the first story that came his way nor even to be guided by his own general impressions; and thanks to his exile, which as he puts it gave him 'rather exceptional facilities for looking into things', he 'saw what was being done on both sides, particularly the Peloponnesian' (5.26.5). Xenophon, by contrast, rarely felt the need to search for information beyond the circle of his immediate experience and acquaintance, that is principally among Agesilaos' laconophile and oligarchic clientele consisting of the 'best men', 'those people who had the best interests of the Peloponnese at heart' (7.4.35; 5.1; cf. 5.2.7).

This radically different attitude to data-collection reflected the second major difference between them, that of overall purpose. Whereas Thucydides was concerned to explain interstate behaviour in such a way that politicians in the future might find his work useful as a textbook of statecraft, Xenophon was primarily a moralist, interested in pointing the ethical lessons of individual or collective behaviour however ineffectual that might be in terms of *Realpolitik* (esp. 5.1.4; 7.2.1). A touchstone of their different mental outlooks is their perception of the role of the supernatural in history. Thucydides scoffs unblushingly at those who believe that the gods intervene directly and decisively in human affairs through oracles, portents and other suchlike superhuman manifestations. Xenophon, however, after noting ironically that in 379 Spartan supremacy had apparently been at last well and truly established, could then write: 'Many examples could be given both from Greek and from foreign history to show that the gods are not indifferent to irreligion or to evildoing' (5.4.1; cf. Sordi 1951, 336-7). The example he chooses to give here is Sparta's defeat at Leuktra some eight years later, which he 'explains' as the result of divine retribution for Sparta's illegal and sacrilegious seizure of the Theban akropolis in 382. But as Cawkwell (1979, 45) has well remarked, 'The hand of God is an explanation that dulls the quest for truth', and the same can be said of Xenophon's persistent moralizing.

On balance therefore I incline to view the *Hellenika* as a characteristic and predictable product of the kind of man sketched in brief by the philosopher T.H. Irwin (quoted above). If I were to choose a sentence to serve as a motto for his oeuvre as a whole, it would be one taken from the *Kynegetikos* (13.5 – though that work is not certainly by Xenophon): 'My object is to give utterance to correct conceptions that meet the needs of readers well schooled for virtue.' This view of the *Hellenika* at any rate seems to me to embody 'the most rigidly minimalist theory of its purpose' which is all that the work's 'inconsequentiality' will allow (Tuplin 1981, 8).

I have left to the end of this brief discussion of the *Hellenika* the question of its date or dates of composition. Was it all written after the Battle of Mantineia (362) and indeed well after it, as some passages (e.g. 6.4.37) undoubtedly were? Or was it written in two or more stages, the resultant 'parts' being subjected to more than one redaction? The extreme 'unitarian' view would place the composition of the whole in the 350s, the extreme 'analyst' position would postulate up to four chronologically separable 'parts'. But the consensus appears reasonably enough to adopt an interpretation somewhere between these two poles and to draw a single line at 2.3.9: 'All this [money] Lysander handed over to the Spartan authorities at the end of the summer' (of 404). This is not where Thucydides would have terminated his history, had he lived to complete it. He believed (5.26.1) that the Athenian War ended with the Spartan occupation of the Long Walls and the Peiraieus, a point already reached in the *Hellenika* at 2.2.23. But then the fact that Xenophon broadly continued Thucydides' unfinished history in the chronological sense should not be pressed harder than any other point of comparison between them. Besides, the chief arguments for ending 'Part I' of the *Hellenika* at 2.3.9 are stylometric. Xenophon's use of particles, it has been claimed, and his choice of synonyms in the putative Parts I and II of the *Hellenika* and in the passages of the *Hellenika* (Books 3 and 4) and of the *Agesilaos* that correspond to each other, often to a large extent verbally, indicate the following order of composition: *Hell.* Part I, *Agesilaos*, *Hell.* Part II (2.3.11-7.5.27, 2.3.10 being interpolated; for a review of the earlier discussions see Henry 1967, 108-33).

The stylometric argument for a break in composition has been contested, and 'Part II' (or at least Books 3 and 4) of the *Hellenika* has even been placed before 'Part I'. I am no stylometer, but I am at least satisfied by the ten or so more or less securely datable passages in Books 3-7 that these five books were cast in their published form in the 350s, after the death of Agesilaos and the publication of the *Agesilaos*. This explains why the *Hellenika* may in my view fairly be called not just memoirs but the memoirs of an old man, for Xenophon was by then seventy or thereabouts. No doubt Xenophon would have echoed the words of an indisputable Athenian sage of an earlier epoch: 'I grow old ever learning many things' (Solon fr. 18); but it would not be otiose to point out to him that one thing he failed signally to learn was a proper concern for posterity. If all I had to go on was that which is contained in the *Hellenika*, or even that together with the *Agesilaos* and *Lak. Pol.*, I could not in all conscience be sitting here today writing this book.

Fortunately for us if not for the reputation of Xenophon he was not the only ancient author to take up the quill where Thucydides perforce had laid it down. We know the names of three others who did so, and we have additionally three papyrus fragments of a historian who did likewise but who is not certainly let alone necessarily to be identified with any of the three whose names we happen to know. Of these three or four historians, two – the (probably) Athenian Kratippos and the Boiotian Daimachos of Plataia – are just names to us, unless of course Kratippos is in fact the author of the papyrus history (as argued recently by Accame 1978a; *contra* Lehmann 1976). But that unknown and in the present state of the evidence strictly unknowable historian (Bloch 1940,303-41, is still valid despite the new Florence and Cairo fragments; cf. Bonamente 1973, 13-19) and Theopompos of Chios are both figures of considerable historiographical stature, whose very different merits make the loss of most of their respective *Hellenika* all the more lamentable.

First, then, the papyrus author, who is known to science alternatively as P (for papyrus author) and the Oxyrhynchos Historian (from the context in Egypt which produced the papyri; cf. generally on Roman Oxyrhynchos, Turner 1952). I shall call him[3] P, since this seems an appropriately colourless label. It is of course impossible to deliver a final judgment on a historian on the basis of about 1200 surviving lines, but the little we have (to Bartoletti 1959 add now the Cairo fragment published by Koenen 1976 and accepted as his by e.g. Lehmann 1977) suffices to show that P was far closer in approach and execution to Thucydides than was Xenophon. Where it is possible to compare P and Xenophon directly, for example over the autumn 395 campaign of Agesilaos in Asia Minor (see Chapter 12), the differences between them leap to the eye. While Xenophon was clearly concerned primarily with the personality of Agesilaos and so concentrated on episodes that lent themselves to more picturesque or dramatic treatment, P as a good military historian sturdily ignored the incidentals retailed by Xenophon and allowed the reader to see clearly the truth Xenophon strove to obfuscate, namely that Agesilaos achieved no notable victories. P's flat, 'antirhetorical' style (Bonamente 1973) was an admirable vehicle for this approach.

In two respects, indeed, P seems to be superior even to his exemplar Thucydides. In chapter 16 (Bartoletti's numeration) he gives an explicit and reasonably detailed account of the Boiotian Confederacy as it was constituted in 395 at the outbreak of the Corinthian War. Thucydides in his usual manner had simply taken that organization for granted, though he provided isolated details

[3]'Him', despite the delightfully eccentric view of Ehrhardt 1970, 225, that P is the daughter of Thucydides.

which permit comparison and contrast with P's picture of the constitution after Thucydides' period. Secondly, at several points P shows himself interested in the rivalry of factions within the protagonist states and so brings out the connection in some detail between domestic politics and the determination of foreign policy that Thucydides again as a rule tended to overlook. On the other hand, whereas Thucydides could in no sense be accused of being pro-Spartan or indeed of taking one state's side against another, P does seem to share Xenophon's general preference for Sparta and hostility to radical democrats; at least, he gives credence to informants who supported a pro-Spartan, that is broadly oligarchic, line in domestic politics. Unlike Xenophon, however, he was not unduly impressed by Agesilaos and does not allow his political bias to unbalance his picture of an opponent of Agesilaos such as Konon.

These points of comparison and contrast with Thucydides and Xenophon are enough to demonstrate that P, unlike Xenophon, was a historian in the proper sense and indeed a historian of the first rank: 'sober and well-informed, positively greedy for facts' (A. Andrewes in Gomme 1981, 208). It is therefore pleasant to know that P's history, in contrast to Xenophon's, was appreciated from early on in antiquity and had a fairly flourishing *Nachleben*. Three separate papyri from Roman Egypt attest to P's continued popularity half a millennium later, and that despite the flatness of his prose style. Historiographically, though, far more significant is the fact that he was used in preference to Xenophon by the first Greek 'universal' historian Ephoros of Kyme in Aiolis (Barber 1935, esp. ch.3). Ephoros, like Theopompos, was traditionally (cf. Tigerstedt 1965, 490-1 n.867) a pupil of the Athenian rhetorician Isokrates, who founded Athens' first institute of advanced learning in the 390s. This was not exactly a school of post-Thucydidean historiography. On the contrary, Isokrates and his pupils did much to ensure that Thucydides should lack for a significant immediate posterity. 'The new science of the past succumbed not least to the fascination of rhetoric' (Tigerstedt 1965, 206). By these practitioners history was employed as a servant rather than obeyed as a master (cf. Baynes 1955, 144-67; Welles 1966); and their concern with the way in which 'facts' were presented to the reader rather than with substantiating their truth tended to blunt any instinct for critical investigation.

However, in contrast to his fellow-pupil, Ephoros chose not to continue Thucydides but rather to compose a history of Greece in thirty books from the so-called Dorian Invasion in the eleventh century down to his own day, the third quarter of the fourth. Most of this massive work is lost, apart from a handful of isolated quotations or supposed quotations that are rather optimistically called 'fragments' (collected in Jacoby, *FGrHist*. 70). It has, though, been partly preserved for us at second hand by the Sicilian Greek universal historian Diodoros, who in the later first century wrote 'a sort of manual of what everyone needs to know about history' (Hornblower 1981, 23). Diodoros' usual practice in compiling his *Bibliothêkê* ('Library of History') appears to have been to follow one main source at a time; and for Books 11 to 15, it is generally agreed (following Volquardsen 1868), that source was Ephoros, the historian whom Diodoros most admired. Books 14 and 15 almost exactly cover the reign of Agesilaos (though they contain a good deal of material, especially on Sicily, not directly relevant to his career).

Unfortunately Diodoros was a largely uncritical and often inefficient compiler, guilty of topographical and other factual errors, of self-contradiction, confusion and omission. His peculiar quality has been admirably conveyed by O. Murray in a review of Hornblower 1981: 'His amazing versatility in all styles of history from chronicle to utopian romance is combined with such incredible incompetence in execution and such a complete lack of the most elementary historical abilities that one is forced to recognise the characteristics of the chameleon, changing colour with each new source, but basically a rather stupid and sleepy lizard.' It is therefore fortunate that there are enough testimonia and quotations of Ephoros by other sources to enable us to form a rough estimate of his overall value.

Like Isokrates and Theopompos, and in his different way Xenophon, Ephoros was prone to moralize. In politics he seems to have been clearly pro-Athenian and therefore (though less unambiguously) anti-Spartan, but his political judgments were anyway superficial (cf. Barber 1935, 58). In style his history was frosted with the glitter of Isokratean rhetoric. On the other hand, he was not entirely devoid of characteristics that we should approve. He claimed (F110) that personal investigation and practical experience were the first qualities of a historian; he distinguished between history-writing and show-piece rhetorical compositions (F111); and he read widely if on the whole uncritically in the available written sources. His chief value for our purposes, as can now be seen more clearly by comparing Diodoros with P, is that he represents a tradition independent of and in some cases markedly superior to that of Xenophon. Earlier in discussing the supposed layers of composition of Xenophon's *Hellenika* I borrowed from Homeric scholarship the terminology of 'analyst' and 'unitarian'. When comparing the Xenophontic and Ephoran traditions it is useful to borrow from the terminology of scholarship on the sources for Alexander the Great. Thus if Xenophon represents the 'official' tradition on Sparta and Agesilaos, Ephoros represents the 'vulgate', the ultimate begetter of which appears to have been P.

This parallel, however, is only useful up to a point. For P, who wrote no later than 346, seems not to have carried his history beyond the Peace of Antalkidas in 386; and what written sources if any lie behind Ephoros' account of 386-360 is unclear: perhaps no more and no less than lie behind Xenophon's sweeping reference (7.2.1) to 'all the historians'. But at least we may now assert with some confidence that parts of Book 13 and Book 14 of Diodoros descend ultimately from P via Ephoros. If the corresponding books of Xenophon's *Hellenika* were written anything up to forty years after the events they describe, then we may with even greater confidence take a step that would have made Eduard Meyer blench, that is actually prefer Diodoros to Xenophon in a case of radical and irreconcilable conflict over the alleged facts. The *locus classicus* of such a factual conflict, perhaps, concerns Agesilaos' Asiatic campaign of summer 395, in particular the battle fought in the environs of Sardis (discussed at some length in Chapter 12).

Theopompos did not even get as far as P, his *Hellenika* coming to an end with a bump in 394. This was not because he thought that year marked a turning-point in Greek history so much as because he became diverted into his *Philippika*, literally 'Matters relating to Philip'. The rise of Philip II of Macedon, whom Theopompos appropriately dubbed the most extraordinary man Europe had yet produced, goaded the Chiot historian into composing the first general Greek history to be written around the exploits of a single individual. None the less, like P, he too found occasion to digress backwards in time outside the strict chronological parameters of his subject, and the *Philippika* appears to have dealt with practically the whole eastern Mediterranean in the fourth century down to the 330s, not to mention extended forays into fifth-century history.

Both P and Theopompos continued Thucydides. There the parallel between them ends. The true parallel to Theopompos is Macaulay (except that the Greek historian, being a pessimist, was a Macaulay in reverse): both at any rate believed that history should be written as a form of improving polemic. The *bête noire* of Theopompos was democracy, which he equated with moral depravity and decadence. The ancient tradition (*FGrHist.* 115T2) that his father was expelled from Chios for favouring pro-oligarchic Sparta is therefore wholly credible (cf. Chapter 14). That expulsion occurred in the 370s, probably, and Theopompos remained an exile until the reign of Philip's son Alexander. Like Xenophon, Theopompos approved the Spartan way of life (F102), but he too could be critical of individual Spartans (F192) – though he praised both Agesilaos (F22,100,107,321) and Lysander (F20,333) – and even, unlike Xenophon, of certain Spartan institutions (F122). His pro-Spartan outlook should not be exaggerated. The extent and force of his moralizing, however, it is scarcely possible to overestimate; one ancient critic (T20; cf. Lucian, *De hist. conscr.* 39) thought his severity of judgment surpassed even that of the assizes in Hades. But what makes the moralising particularly repugnant to modern taste is that it was tricked out with all the devices of Isokratean rhetoric. A final defect worth mentioning is Theopompos' fatal weakness for a good, that is a tall, story. Unverified gossip was by his hands elevated to the status of historical fact; or, as a distinguished modern historian of Philip has brilliantly put it, he 'combined the industry and devotion of the first-rate historian with the flair of the second-rate journalist for misrepresentation by hyperbole' (G.T. Griffith in Hammond/Griffith 1979, 285; cf. generally von Fritz 1941b; Connor 1968, 1-18, 117-29). One example is F321 (*ap.* Plut. *Ages.* 10.10), where he says that Agesilaos was acknowledged to be the greatest and most glorious of his contemporaries. Even Xenophon (6.4.28) preferred Jason of Pherai, while a modern historian might award that palm to Dionysios of Syracuse.

There is far less of Theopompos available to us than there is, thanks to Diodoros, of Ephoros. But Theopompos was widely read in antiquity, and not only by the grammarians and lexicographers who ransacked him for oddities of syntax and vocabulary. He would merit the space allotted to him here if for no other reason than that he was used extensively by a writer who was neither a historian nor a contemporary but who was very widely read indeed in the literature of the fourth century and very likely had a first-hand knowledge of all four authors so far discussed in this chapter. This polymathic writer is Plutarch, 'the sage of Chaironeia' (Mahaffy 1906,339) in Boiotia, who among a vast output composed a series of Parallel Lives of the great Greeks and Romans in the late first and early second centuries AD. Fifty of these brief Lives survive, and they include two that are of the most obvious relevance to the subject of this book: the *Agesilaos* (paralleled with Pompey) and the *Lysander* (paralleled with Sulla; for bibliography see Tigerstedt 1974, 521-2n.942). In the *Lysander* (30.2), which was written before the *Agesilaos* (cf. Jones, C.P., 1966), Plutarch perspicaciously observed that Theopompos 'deserves more credence when he praises than when he blames'.

It was for remarks like that that in the Renaissance the Lives were regarded as 'a mirror ... of human nature' (Russell 1966, 139); but historians of Agesilaos and Sparta must, regrettably no doubt, confine themselves to narrower, technical questions concerning their reliability as historical sources: above all, how many and what type of authorities did he consult for the relevant Lives; what literary and philosophical considerations might have led him to adapt, manipulate or distort the material he found in his sources; and how far did the political assumptions and institutions of his own day, the early Roman Empire, affect his picture of the distant past? These questions cannot be answered in detail here, and indeed the answers are a matter of controversy even among Plutarch specialists (e.g. Stadter 1965; Russell 1973, esp. ch.6; Wardman 1974; Pelling 1976, 1980). But it is, I think, certain that Plutarch had direct access to the fourth-century writers discussed above, although – like Macaulay – he would have called on the resources of a stupendous memory rather than riffle through a sheaf of file-cards when referring to or quoting verbally from them (as in the Theopompos citation). In addition to no less than 150 historians of various hues and calibres Plutarch consulted philosophers, antiquarians, commentators on comic plays and so on from all the centuries between the fifth BC and his own. In the *Agesilaos*, for instance, he cites by name the following historians: Thucydides (5c), Xenophon, Theopompos, Kallisthenes, Theophrastos, Douris, Hieronymos of Rhodes and Dioskorides (all 4c); it is a certain inference too that, like his Roman predecessor in the field of short biography, Cornelius Nepos, he relied heavily on Ephoros (cf. Sachse 1888); and the number of citations is not in any case necessarily a guide to Plutarch's direct reading of an author. On top of all this he also apparently conducted a piece of personal, first-hand research in the process of compiling the *Agesilaos*. Irritated by the fact that Xenophon (*Ages.* 8.7) had failed to give the name of a daughter of Agesilaos, and noting the complaint of Dikaiarchos (fr. 65 Wehrli) that nothing was known of either Agesilaos' daughter or Epameinondas' mother, Plutarch 'discovered in the Spartan *anagraphai* that Agesilaos' wife was named Kleora and his daughters Eupolia and Proauga' (*Ages.* 19.9-10). No more unfortunately is known of these written archives (cf. Tigerstedt 1974, 520-1n.926), but this passage is a salutary reminder that Plutarch was a man of indefatigable curiosity with first-hand experience of Sparta and by no means simply a hack compiler wholly dependent on other people's written productions. That, however, was just what Nepos was, and his mini-biographies merely offered 'a sort of crash course to help the ordinary reader in a literary world where ignorance of things Greek was no longer tolerable' (Wiseman 1979, 157; cf. Jenkinson 1973).

What matters to the historian, though, is the selection Plutarch made from the various sources he consulted and the emphases he gave to what he selected. Both unfortunately were determined by his ultimately moralizing purpose (e.g.

Nik. 1.3) rather than by a concern for getting the facts right or explaining the role of the individual subject in the wider historical process. Even though in Plutarch's case the gulf between biography and history was not as great as in that of, say, Nepos, we have to take the full measure of Plutarch's own repeated affirmations (*Alex.* 1.2; cf. *Galba* 2.5, *Fab.* 16.6) that he was writing *bioi* not *historiai*. Hence his emphasis on the subject's education, where his unalterable *phusis* (nature) was first revealed and acquired characteristics (*êthê*) first developed.[4] Hence his pin-pointing of debuts, climaxes and reversals of fortune for literary effect. Hence, finally, his preoccupation with great personalities, whom he represented as larger than life exemplars of virtue and vice. In short, Plutarch's interpretation through selective presentation of his subjects is a very unsure guide indeed to the historical realities, especially as it is coupled with chronographic laxity and a weakness of insight into the political conditions of the (to him) unimaginably different Greek past. Still, thanks to his industry, he can preserve for us vital pieces of information not to be found in, say, Xenophon that are ultimately derived from, say, Ephoros and so from P; thanks to his greater objectivity (or at least Boiotian patriotism), he may, unlike Xenophon, openly and directly criticize Agesilaos for his excessive indulgence towards his subservient friends, his lust for power, his ambition and self-interest, his ungrateful treatment of Lysander, his degrading service as a mercenary on behalf of a man he then betrayed, and his occupation of Thebes in peacetime in contravention of human and divine justice; and thanks to his concern with character (cf. Dodds 1933, 105), he may record anecdotes (cf. Chapter 1), gestures and other apparent trivia that do in fact cast an unfamiliar and revealing light on the more prominent personalities.[5] For these not inconsiderable mercies we should be duly thankful.

The other main source of written evidence for Agesilaos and Sparta is epigraphy. The collection and study of inscriptions have been at the core of ancient history since the nineteenth century when historians of more recent periods such as Leopold von Ranke began to emphasize the unique qualities of documentary records as historical sources (see generally F. Millar in Crawford 1983, 80-136). Regrettably, though, the ancient Greeks before the Hellenistic period were the least bureaucratic of people. Even Classical Athens, the most prolific producer of inscribed documents, did not establish a permanent, centralized 'public record office' until the end of the fifth century. In Sparta, where of set purpose the laws were not written down even on perishable material, one would not expect the documentary habit to have put down deep roots (cf. Cartledge 1978a); and it is noticeable that it was foreigners – Hellanikos of Lesbos, Charon of Lampsakos – who are credited with the *editiones principes* of respectively the list of victors at the annual Karneia festival and a list of officials (kings or Ephors).

---

[4]The Greeks had nothing that we would call a psychological theory, and they regarded the man as father of the child rather than *vice versa*; cf. Dihle 1956, 76-82.

[5]John Dryden was particularly caught by the way Plutarch could portray the hero as an ordinary domestic human being: 'You may behold ... Agesilaus riding on a hobby-horse among his children. The pageantry of life is taken away; you ... find the demi-god a man' (Preface to his 1683 translation).

The reason why Classical Athens is the most abundant source of public, official state inscriptions is not simply or even primarily because the city of Athens has been more intensively explored in modern times than any other ancient Greek city. It is because from 507 to 322, with a couple of brief intermissions, Athens was a democracy, and an integral part of the ideology of democracy was the professed belief in the public availability of relevant documentation, especially of those documents that recorded laws and other public decrees. Sparta, whose constitution was *sui generis* but, I shall argue (Chapter 8), is best characterised as a peculiar form of oligarchy, lacked a comparable ideological motivation, though texts of treaties were published on stone in the town of Sparta itself (e.g. Peek 1974, found on the Akropolis) and at Amyklai a short way south from at least the later fifth century (Thuc. 5.18.10 – the Peace of Nikias).

Spartan citizens, that is to say, were probably functionally literate in the minimal sense that they could read and write simple messages, but only high-ranking Spartan officials would need to be able to employ literate skills on a regular basis. This situation is reflected in the comparative dearth of private inscriptions from Sparta, and that is not a small loss. For all inscriptions, whether public or private, can of course become historical evidence under certain circumstances – a fact that is obscured by the criminally misleading title of M.N. Tod's otherwise admirably useful collections of *Greek Historical Inscriptions*. However, texts of treaties, decrees and other state documents are naturally more obviously relevant to international and domestic policymaking than private inscriptions such as dedications of offerings to the gods. The small number of Spartan inscriptions in Tod's second volume is therefore significant. This is a part, though far from the whole, of the reason why Sparta never produced a historian in anything like the modern sense (cf. Chapter 22).

Inscriptions need not be written only on stone, bronze or clay and deposited in public sacred or secular precincts. Coins, too, carry superscriptions as well as images which can provide historical information (see generally M.H. Crawford in Crawford 1983, 185-233). Again, Sparta stood aside from the mainstream of Greek practice in this respect; and the state forbore to strike coins until the early third century when King Areus identified himself with the state in the un-Spartan manner of a Hellenistic god-king. For domestic purposes iron spits had continued to serve as a money of account and a standard of value, though not necessarily as a means of payment and exchange, long after coinage had been invented towards the end of the seventh century. But the influx of coined silver and gold into Sparta following the triumph of Lysander at the end of the Athenian War occasioned a crisis. As we shall see (Chapter 6), this was resolved formally by the decisions that, although the state might continue to use money minted elsewhere for official purposes such as the payment of mercenaries, it would not strike a Spartan currency and that the possession of coined money by individual Spartans was to be or (formally) remain illegal. Spartans, however, had notoriously sticky fingers, and the ban on private possession was ever more openly flouted. Yet the number of foreign coins actually recovered from Lakonia in modern times is minute. In fact, our best evidence for their arrival apart from the literary sources is an official Spartan document probably of the early fourth century that records contributions to a Spartan war-fund (M/L 67 = Fornara 132).

Lastly, there is the mute evidence of archaeology which can only be made to speak clearly and unambiguously with the aid of the written sources but in any case 'seldom speaks the language of historical events' (A.M. Snodgrass in Crawford 1983, 137-84, at 166). I have stated elsewhere (Cartledge 1979, esp. ch. 1 and App. 1) my views on the kind of information archaeology can legitimately be made to convey to the historian, more socio-economic than political or diplomatic, and have set out at some length in that same work the available archaeological evidence from and pertaining directly to Sparta and Lakonia. There will be further occasions to use archaeological material in the present book, but it had better be stated firmly at the outset that comparatively little can be brought to bear directly for explanatory purposes on the Spartan crisis. In this respect archaeology is no more and no less helpful than the few immediately relevant inscriptions and coins.

The burden of explanation, therefore, has to full squarely on the shoulders, rather bowed and sagging though they may be, of the literary sources. I conclude this chapter by laying down some guidelines for establishing from these sources what Thucydides (1.22.2) called 'the deeds of the transactions', the facts, that is, as opposed to their interpretation (though I am aware that this is not an absolute disjunction).

Rahe (1977), when dealing with the career of Lysander between 407 and 403, preferred as a rule the testimony of what I have labelled the 'vulgate' descended from P to that of the 'official' tradition sponsored by Xenophon, with four exceptions: viz., where the vulgate account clashed with common sense; where Ephoros abandoned P's annalistic framework and so confused the chronology (the confusion being compounded by Diodoros who compiled annalistically); where the biases of Ephoros added extraneous material to the vulgate tradition; and where Xenophon's exceptional familiarity with Spartan institutions seemed to deserve trust. To me, however, it does not seem possible on principle to prefer the vulgate to the official tradition; rather, each case of a conflict should be evaluated on its individual merits. For even though Xenophon can apparently commit extraordinary sins of omission and commission, there is no overriding reason to suppose that P was any more factually infallible than his model Thucydides, however much more seriously he took the job of getting the facts right than Xenophon did. Besides, P probably did not carry his history beyond the Peace of Antalkidas in 386, so there is even less reason to suspend disbelief of Diodoros' fifteenth Book than of Books 13 and 14. Otherwise Rahe's criteria strike me as eminently sane and cogent, though I would emphasize more than he the peculiar contribution of Xenophon. It may be an exaggeration to assert that 'without this chapter [*sc. Hell.* 3.3, the account of the conspiracy of Kinadon] the obscurity surrounding ancient Sparta would be ten times more opaque' (Cawkwell 1979, 161n). But it is none the less due to Xenophon above all that the present attempt to penetrate 'the secrecy of the state' (Thuc. 5.68.2) was initially conceived and that it can be represented as in principle not an entirely hopeless enterprise.

PART TWO

Themes

6

Agesilaos, Lysander and Spartan Imperialism

For when the authority of princes is made but an accessary to a cause, and that there be other bands that tie faster than the band of sovereignty, kings begin to be put almost out of possession. (Francis Bacon, Essay XV 'Of Seditions and Troubles')

There was a saying in Sparta that 'Greece could not have endured two Lysanders'. This is an understatement of the case ... Greece and Sparta would have found a single Lysander beyond their endurance. (Cary 1927, 32)

It is no accident, I suppose, that the Greeks had no word for imperialism; no word, that is, corresponding to our word, developed out of 'empire', and echoing 'empire' easily, if eerily, through many an empty mind. (Griffith 1978, 143)

Had Agesilaos not become king in succession to one of his half-brothers, Agis II, his remembrance would probably be as bright, or rather as dim, as that of his other half-brother, Teleutias. Even so, the record of Agesilaos' exploits before his accession remains a total blank, despite some more or less informed modern guesses. And although we may agree that he had profited from the *agôgê* (Chapter 3) and enjoyed high standing in Sparta by the time Agis died, the decisive factor in his elevation to the Eurypontid throne ahead of Agis' belatedly recognized son Latychidas was assuredly the intervention on his behalf by Lysander.

The precise circumstances of Agesilaos' accession and the potential and actual significance of the kingship at Sparta are the subjects of the three following chapters. Here the known career of Lysander, with special reference to the years 407 to 403, will be scrutinized from three points of view. First, an attempt will be made to assess the influence of Lysander's career in general and his relationship with Agesilaos in particular upon the character of the latter's reign. Second, Lysander warrants examination in his own right, since he was both a product and a major contributory cause of the strains placed on the traditional structure of Spartan society by the Athenian War. Third, the character of Spartan imperialism as a whole and especially the brand of it inspired by Lysander and practised between 404 and 394 will be assessed.

Considering the impact of Lysander on Greek and indeed Eurasian history, his deeds are not very fully commemorated in the surviving literature, and in respect of chronology the sources fail us almost disastrously. Two recent studies (Rahe 1977; Bommelaer 1981, esp. 61-2, 135-6, 171, 197), both scrupulously exact in their scholarship, place major episodes in different years, not only within the period 410-406 where this problem systematically affects all Greek history (cf. Lotze 1964, 72-86; Robertson 1980), but also in the two years following the Battle of Aigospotamoi. Yet it is impossible to make complete sense of Spartan politics in these years unless the physical movements of Lysander can be precisely dated – as they cannot: 'We are uncertain about his mere physical movements in almost every month in the crucial period between Aigospotamoi and Pausanias' settlement at Athens' (Andrewes 1971, 206). On the other hand, to the literary evidence we can add the uniquely immediate and authentic testimony of archaeology and some informative contemporary inscriptions.

In general terms the literary sources for Lysander cover the same range as those for Agesilaos. There is therefore no need to repeat the general remarks of the previous chapter. But whereas Agesilaos on the whole received a favourable press, Lysander – partly for that very reason – was saddled with a poor one (Prentice 1934; Bommelaer 1981, 25-45, 234-41). Brief comment on Xenophon and Plutarch will sufficiently illustrate the hazards of a search for Lysander. In the *Agesilaos* Xenophon is reticent to the point of complete and utter silence about Lysander, for the obvious and tendentious reason that he did not wish to dilute his hero's eulogy by making him owe any part of his alleged success to Lysander (not, *pace* Bommelaer 1981, 27n.11, because Xenophon changed his mind about Lysander). Silence had the further not incidental advantage of obliterating the ugly personal feud that erupted between the two men during the first year of the Asiatic campaign (Chapters 9 and 11), when Agesilaos displayed the very reverse of *philetairia* (comradely affection and loyalty) in demoting and humiliating Lysander and doing so in a manner uncomfortably reminiscent of the ruthless guile that was one of Lysander's own salient characteristics. This contretemps could not of course be expunged from the *Hellenika* (3.4.7-10). But it is not dwelt on there either, and Xenophon is astonishingly reticent about the possible constitutional implications of their disagreement. Thus the general impression conveyed by Xenophon is an attitude of respectful but cool appreciation of Lysander (cf. Westlake 1969, 216-24).

Plutarch's *Lysander* is one of his better Lives from the historiographical point of view. Bommelaer, indeed, has classified it among his 'main' sources, on the ground that Plutarch made a determined effort to get his facts right especially when they implied a moral judgment of Lysander. In this regard, however, as indeed in its structure, outlook and range of interests, the *Lysander* is a microcosm of Plutarchan biography (analysed as such by Russell 1966, at 151-4). What gives it some added interest is that Plutarch, after his usual wide reading in Xenophon, Theopompos, Ephoros, Theophrastos and others, and a consistent use of his familiar comparative technique, presents a slightly more favourable portrait of Lysander than that of the consensus of non-Xenophontic sources. Or rather a more favourable picture of Lysander's character and characteristics (*êthê*), since it was the supposed corruption of Spartan mores by Lysander's introduction of a mass of coined money that for Plutarch – as for Xenophon and other writers ancient and modern (see Chapter 21) – set Sparta on the road to ruin, whereas Lysander himself remained remarkably impervious to its seductions and died a (relatively) poor man.

For all the diligence of his research, though, Plutarch could discover no more than his immediate or mediate sources could about Lysander's background and career before he was appointed navarch (*nauarchos*) or Admiral of the Fleet in the Aegean theatre of the Athenian War in 408 or 407. (He came out, according to the chronology I follow, in spring 407, but his year of office may technically have begun late in 408: Bommelaer 1981, 70-9, 83-95.) His alleged *mothax* origins and his intimate connection with Agesilaos in his twenties are both compatible with the inference that he stepped out on the road to a distinguished public career under the aegis of Archidamos II (Chapter 3). What little we know of his relations with Archidamos' elder son and successor Agis before Agis very temporarily sided with Pausanias against him in the summer of 403 (Chapters 8 and 14) may indicate that Agis had inherited Lysander as a client from his father (cf. Ste. Croix 1972, 145,147; Rahe 1977, 9). Lysander's appointment as navarch presumably therefore had the support of Agis, if indeed it was not actually made on Agis' personal recommendation.

Unfortunately, though, we do not know how navarchs were selected, and Bommelaer's laboriously argued suggestion that Lysander had something to do with a change in the date at which they took up their office is to explain *ignotum per ignotius*. Equally if not more plausibly, the position had only become a regular office (*archê*) after the disastrous defeat in 410 at Kyzikos in the Propontis, where the Spartans in effect lost an entire fleet (on the suggested regularization see Sealey 1976; on the sources for the battle Andrewes 1982). In accordance with the widespread Greek republican principle that was also applied to the other major executive office, the Ephorate (Westlake 1976; see further Chapter 8), tenure of the annual navarchy could not be legally repeated (2.1.7; DS 13.100.8; Plut. *Lys.* 7.3). But that law could be circumvented and was, twice, in the case of Lysander by giving him a notionally subordinate naval command.[1]

Whatever the reasons, or qualifications, for his appointment, Lysander proved magnificently equal to his new task. But even Lysander could not have achieved his military, political or diplomatic objectives without cash, and it was therefore providential that his arrival in the Aegean coincided with the arrival in Western Asia Minor of the sixteen-year-old Persian prince Cyrus (the Younger). Relations between Sparta and Persia will be the subject of Chapter 11. Suffice it to say here that in order to secure funds for the Aegean war Sparta in 412/11 had made a Faustian compact with Darius II, Great King of Persia, through his western supremo Tissaphernes. In exchange for money to pay crews and secure the necessary supplies for building and maintaining a warfleet big enough to challenge Athens' hitherto unquestioned naval supremacy, the Spartans had conceded the sovereignty of Asia, including the Greek *poleis* therein (or so the Persians understood), to Persia. The cash, however, had not been readily forthcoming at first, partly because the Great King had other things besides the Athenian War on his mind, in part because Tissaphernes and the other Aegean

[1] To our knowledge only Pollis *may* have held two navarchies, separated by nearly twenty years: Poralla 1913, no. 621; but I am inclined to suppose this to be a case of homonymy, like that of for example Leon (ibid. no. 482, with A. Andrewes in Gomme 1981, 69).

satrap Pharnabazus competed with each other for prestige and influence rather
than co-operated for the greater good of Persia or Sparta, and partly because
Tissaphernes' set policy was to support Sparta only sufficiently to enable her to
keep on terms with Athens so that the two Greek powers might exhaust each
other. Pharnabazus was appreciably more open-fisted and even risked his neck
in the Spartan cause – as he later and with some chagrin is said to have
reminded Agesilaos (4.1.32; see further Chapter 11); but his efforts had little to
show for themselves in the way of solid military successes. The arrival of Cyrus,
son of Darius by Parysatis, transformed the situation. It also marked a change
of direction in the counsels of the Persian court, though if we are to believe the
apparently well informed Ktesias this was induced by the machinations of
Parysatis rather than any long-term strategic considerations (cf. Rahe 1977,
1-7). Anyhow, Cyrus and Lysander struck up a remarkable and for Sparta (and
Lysander) remarkably fruitful relationship. Pay for crews was increased both in
amount and in regularity, and at Notion near Ephesos in late 407 or early 406
the Spartans won their first major naval victory of the War (Andrewes 1982).

   The generosity of Cyrus was not of course disinterested. Victory for Sparta in
the Athenian War, so long as Sparta respected the terms of the treaty of 411
(which I do not believe to have been substantially modified by a putative 'Treaty
of Boiotios' – see Chapter 11), would mean the achievement by 'cheque-book
diplomacy' of an objective that had been on the Persians' agenda since the
Persian Wars of 480-79. Asia would once more be the King's in fact as well as
name, tribute would again flow to Susa as of right from the Greeks as well as the
non-Greeks of Asia. But Cyrus, and Parysatis, had an ulterior personal motive
too. Although Cyrus was the first son to be born to Darius after his accession in
425/4 (for the date see Lewis 1977, 70ff.), he was not the eldest legitimate son. If
there was to be a fight for the Persian throne after Darius' death, as there had
been on earlier such occasions, then who better than the Spartans to lend the
necessary military aid? Even if Sparta herself was short on citizen manpower,
she might contribute men from among her subordinate classes, or at least permit
and even further the recruitment of hoplite mercenaries; again, this would not
have been the first time such Greek troops had been involved in a Persian
dynastic struggle (cf. Rahe 1980a; and Chapter 15).

   What Lysander thought, or knew, of his youthful paymaster's long-term aims
for securing the throne of Persia is not recorded. But it is more likely than not
that he would have favoured them. For during the course of his navarchy it
quickly became apparent that he too had towering political and not merely
military, personal as well as patriotic, ambitions; and in little more than a
decade the power of Persia was to become a decisive factor in Greek domestic
politics (Chapters 11 and 14). It is not therefore inconceivable that the acutely
farsighted Lysander had already had ideas of turning the navarchy to his own
account, especially as in this as in other fields another Spartan, Regent
Pausanias, had pointed the way. It may not be coincidental that King Agis is
said (*ap*. Athen. 543b) to have likened Lysander to a second Pausanias.

   For the pursuance of Lysander's ambitions the institution of the navarchy
offered the ideal vehicle. As Aristotle distastefully noted (*Pol.* 1271a37ff.), this
office was – or at least could be exploited as – 'virtually another kingship'.

Aristotle elsewhere unduly depreciates the potential power of the kingship, as we shall see (Chapter 7), dismissing it as merely a hereditary generalship rather than a full-blown monarchy. But on campaign the king deputed to sole command (after 506) had as free a hand as any individual Spartan official could ever hope to wield. Like a king, the navarch carried out the necessary religious rituals, commanded in person or delegated responsibility, regulated pay and oversaw the sale and distribution of booty, and – subject ultimately to ratification by the home authorities – conducted negotiations with foreign powers and settled the internal affairs of other Greek cities (sources in Rahe 1977, 68-9n.117). This last function is of the most immediate importance for the history of Lysander and Sparta. For it was during his navarchy that Lysander laid the foundations of a personal empire by constructing a clientele of men who owed or would owe their wealth, position and political power in their own states ultimately or proximately to the personal support of Lysander.

There was nothing remarkable in contracting personal relationships across state boundaries. From as early as we have literary evidence (Homer), Greek aristocrats had been linked by such ritualized guest-friendships (*xeniai*) as those we see in the fifth century between Archidamos II and Perikles (Thuc. 2.13.1) or between Lysander's father and a minor north African ruler (DS 14.13.5-6 – hence the name of Lysander's brother Libys, 'the Libyan'). From these private ties had grown the public institution of *proxenia*, whereby a distinguished citizen of state A residing in state A acted as a kind of official *xenos* for citizens of state B who had dealings in or with his state. This was a useful source of royal patronage and a powerful lever for the Spartan kings to manipulate, since it was a peculiarity of Sparta bred of her notorious xenophobia that the kings had the prerogative of appointing the various states' *proxenoi* from among the citizens of Sparta (see further Chapter 13). It was for this prerogative among others that Lysander was later, I believe, to covet the position of king from which he was debarred by an accident of birth. But being navarch offered a not inconsiderable – though not, I think, superior, despite Rahe 1977, 22 – substitute. Lysander, typically, gave it a peculiar twist. As navarch in 407/6 he began deliberately to set up a parallel organization to rival the hereditary clienteles of the two Spartan royal houses, by contracting *xeniai* with men in the Greek cities of the Aegean area who might in the future prove useful to him (DS 13.70.4; Plut. *Lys.* 5.3-5,22.3-4). Thus were sown the seeds of the notorious dekarchies, to which we shall return.

Before Lysander could put any such political projects into effect he had first to defeat Athens militarily, and this despite the Notion victory he was unable to accomplish before the term of his navarchy had expired in 406. His successor, Kallikratidas, was also allegedly a *mothax* by social origin (Aelian,*VH* 12.43). But otherwise he was a man of very different stamp, not merely a less skilful operator than Lysander in all departments but imbued also with such a radically discordant political outlook that it is tempting to see political as well as (or rather than) military motives behind his appointment – specifically, perhaps, the patronage of the Agiad king Pausanias (cf. Rahe 1977, 25; Hamilton 1979b, 38n.53). However, this image of Kallikratidas is in part a deliberate creation of Xenophon and other sources interested either in representing him as a forerunner of the admirable Agesilaos (cf. Ronnet 1981) or merely in denigrating Lysander; so we should be wary of exaggerating the differences between the two men. Still, Kallikratidas' proudly panhellenist reluctance to 'fawn upon the barbarian for silver' (1.6.7) and the factional obstructiveness of the friends of Lysander (1.6.4, with Rahe 1977, 72n.128) certainly combined to hamstring the Spartan war-effort in so far as it depended crucially on Persian aid and thus to prepare the way for Lysander's return as *de facto* commander-in-chief in 405.

His first task was to repair the material and moral damage done by Kallikratidas' disastrous and personally fatal defeat at Arginousai in late summer 406, which had prompted Sparta to treat for a peace that would have left Athens in control of the literally vital Hellespont (cf. Chapter 14). This achieved, he devoted much careful planning (cf. Bommelaer 1981, 83-115) to the decisive victory he finally achieved at Aigospotamoi in the Hellespont late in 405. The precise details of this encounter (see now Strauss 1983), like those of the political settlement Lysander was mainly responsible for imposing on Athens in the spring and summer of 404 (Chapter 14), are disputed beyond the possibility of universal agreement. But two salient points are clear. First, that in both cases deceit was employed, as one would expect of a man said to have freely admitted that 'where the lionskin would not reach it was necessary to stitch on to it the skin of a fox' (Plut. *Mor.* 229b and elsewhere). Second, both battle and settlement were placed by Lysander in the service of his personal aggrandizement. Before considering the wider, geopolitical implications for Sparta of victory in the Athenian War, and the reactions of the Spartan authorities to Lysander's achievements, it will be instructive to examine closely one phenomenon the significance of which does not depend essentially on a precise and accurate chronography: the glorification of Lysander, not least by himself.

Bommelaer (1981, 7-23) engagingly begins his otherwise rather dry study with a catalogue of the sixteen known monuments or dedications of various kinds, all but four made during his lifetime, that commemorated Lysander's triumph over Athens as a highly personal achievement. He continues with the two 'manifestations cultuelles', the four epigrams and the (now fragmentary) paean that were also created for the greater honour and glory of Lysander. From this impressive list two items stand out head and shoulders above the rest, but there is also one striking absentee. On the one hand, there is the so-called 'Navarchs' Monument' at Delphi (Bommelaer no.15), through which Lysander ascribed to himself the equivalent of heroic honours, surpassed only by his actual deification at the hands of his friends and clients on Samos (nos 16-17). On the other, there are no closely similar manifestations or monuments in Lysander's favour known to have been exhibited in Sparta and certainly none officially awarded to him by the Spartan state (a point overlooked by Hamilton 1979a, 87-9). The two Victories (Nikai), each resting on an eagle, dedicated on the Spartan akropolis (no. 6) and the two bronze tripods offered up in the sanctuary of the Graces at Amyklai (no. 5) would seem to be relatively humble and conventionally patriotic trophies rather than symbols of personal aggrandizement. But only in fact at first sight: for it was unprecedented for a

Spartan to erect a memorial of 'his' (not Sparta's) victories at Sparta in his lifetime (von Fritz 1941a, 62).

None the less, it was in the Delphi monument and the Samos deification that Lysander's claim to extraordinary and superhuman status resided. 'Navarchs' Monument' is an inexact but convenient shorthand title for a construction comprising thirty-nine or forty statues, three quarters of which represented admirals, standing on a base nearly eighteen metres long by four and a half deep and at least three high. The other ten statues consisted of six divinities, Lysander, his seer (*mantis*), herald (*kêrux*) and steersman (*kubernêtes*). The centrepiece depicted Poseidon in the act of crowning the victorious Lysander. This intimately close association of Lysander with gods was a strong hint that he was a man of more than merely human status, as we shall see (cf. Zinserling 1965); but it was left to the restored oligarchs of Samos, an island sufficiently removed spatially and spiritually from the navel of the earth and strongly influenced by the orient, to take the unprecedented and qualitatively huge leap of actually worshipping him as a god.

Until quite recently the only evidence for the deification of Lysander had been a statement to that effect by the Samian local historian and pro-Macedonian tyrant of *c.*300, Douris (*FGrHist.* 76F26,71), as reported by Plutarch (*Lys.* 18); and as Douris was generally unreliable and could have had a specific interest in misrepresenting Lysander's honours, scepticism of this statement was perfectly proper. For example, W.W. Tarn (1948, II, 360n.3; cf. Taeger 1957, 161-4,259) considered that the honours mentioned by Douris – sacrifices, altars, paeans – fell within the acceptable bounds of honours deemed appropriate in the fourth century for human benefactors (cf. Arist. *Rhet.* 1361a27). But in 1965 a statue-base was discovered at the Samian Heraion bearing an inscription that left no room for doubting that the Samians' principal national religious festival, the Heraia, had been renamed the Lysandreia for a period of at least four years at some time in the earlier fourth century. Lysander was thereby established as the first known wholly mortal Greek to have received divine, as opposed to heroic (for the differences see Taeger 1957, 259), worship. The only remaining matter for dispute was whether Lysander received this unique accolade in his lifetime or after his death in 395. Plutarch (*Lys.* 18.8) asserts the former, and he has been followed, rightly I believe, by the author of the standard work on the subject of deification as a whole (Habicht 1970, 3-7,243-4). More recently E. Badian (1981, at 33-8) has argued for a posthumous deification, but he ignores the Navarchs' Monument and other certainly lifetime manifestations pointing in the same direction.

A new twist was thus given to the important question of where Lysander stood in the line of politico-religious development culminating in the Hellenistic ruler-cult accorded Alexander and the Successor kings in their lifetimes (cf. Balsdon 1950; Ehrenberg 1974, 61; Badian 1981). For this was a very different matter from the Spartans' familiar custom of calling anyone they specially admired a 'divine man' (Plato, *Meno* 99d; Arist. *EN* 1145a27ff., with Balsdon 1950, 365); and it seemed to ignore the warning of Homer's Apollo to Diomedes that 'Never is the race of immortal gods on a level with men who walk the earth' – a warning that Simonides had thought it worth repeating to Regent Pausanias (*ap.* Aelian, *VH* 9.41, with Huxley 1978,245) and that Xenophon (*Smp.* 1.15) echoed in a professedly philosophical context.

Here it is not so important to look at Lysander's deification and self-heroization prospectively. Rather, we need to understand what political and psychological impact they were meant and are likely to have had at the time (404 in my view), given traditional Greek practice in honouring military victors and Spartan attitudes to the divine. Today we are all too familiar with the politically-inspired cult of personality amounting in some instances to quasi-religious worship even in formally atheistic states (e.g. Tumarkin 1983). In Greece in 405/4 such an attitude was both grossly untraditional and virtually unheralded, although it too was essentially a political rather than a religious or spiritual phenomenon. The starting-point of any discussion should be a remarkable essay by André Aymard (1967, 51-72), which was originally published in 1949 and prompted by horror at what could result from the glorification of the military leader. The essay was ostensibly devoted to the verses of Euripides' *Andromache* (693-8) that reportedly impelled Alexander to murder Black Kleitos at Samarkand in 328, but it ranges far more widely and concentrates in fact on the period with which we are immediately concerned, the late fifth century. For it was only from this period onwards that 'glorifications personnelles' had become significantly frequent.

Homeric heroes had striven aristocratically 'always to be best and surpass the rest', but the Greek aristocrats who listened to the monumental epics in their earliest form tended to be highly envious of each other and so to stress their mutual equality. It was this aristocratic egalitarianism that the Spartans boldly extended in the seventh century to encompass the entire citizen body, commoners as well as nobles, by describing themselves thereafter as Homoioi or 'Peers'. This was a revolutionary departure, but as often the Spartans were simply taking an extreme view of a common Greek attitude. Militarily speaking, although prizes for glorious achievement (*aristeia*) might be awarded to outstandingly valorous individual Spartans (e.g. Hdt. 9.71), the Spartan state collectively claimed the glory of victory and the commanding general had no prescriptive right to *aristeia*.

The Persian Wars, or at least the career or Regent Pausanias, mark the first discernible break in this pattern. In the winter of 480/79 the Spartans had officially honoured Eurybiadas, the notional admiral-in-chief at Salamis, with an olive crown (Hdt. 8.124.2), as if he were an Olympic victor. But Pausanias in 479 was not satisfied with any purely symbolic token of honour that Sparta might bestow upon him for commanding the Greek forces to victory at Plataia. Apart from gratefully accepting his due (and hefty) share of the booty (Hdt. 9.81.2), he made what we might call a Lysandreian gesture. He caused to be added to the official, collective victory-monument erected at Delphi, which simply listed the names of the thirty-one states who had fought on the loyalist side, an arrogant verse epigram celebrating the victory as his own personal achievement (M/L, p.60):

Since as leader of the Greeks he destroyed the army of the Medes,
Pausanias dedicated this memorial to Phoibos.

No wonder Simonides, who knew Sparta and Greek aristocracy generally well, saw fit to remind Pausanias of his mortality. But whereas Lysander's monument was allowed to stand at Delphi, the Spartans hurriedly had this epigram erased, and Pausanias' brief burst of glory was soon swathed in dark shadows. A humbler memorial of his on a less conspicuous site was, however, left undisturbed. The message was clear: such overweening boastfulness (*huperêphania*) was intolerable – as yet.

Between Pausanias, a man apparently born out of his time, and Lysander a further milestone on the road of personal glorification was reached in the career of another Spartan, Brasidas (one of the very few, incidentally, of whom we know the names of both parents – Tellis and Argileonis). Plutarch, who was a priest at Delphi and intimately familiar with the sanctuary, begins his *Lysander* by seeking to dispel a common illusion: the statue of a long-haired, full-bearded warrior standing inside the Treasury of the Akanthians depicts, not Brasidas, but Lysander. He does not say when or why it was erected there, but he does elsewhere allow us to see how this common mistake of identification could be made. For the Treasury was known alternatively as the Treasury of *Brasidas and the Akanthians*, since it had been dedicated in Brasidas' honour by the grateful rulers of Akanthos in Chalkidike out of spoils won while fighting as his allies in 424-2 (Plut. *Lys.* 1.1, *Mor.* 401d; cf. Thuc. 4.84-8).

This signal honour was no doubt accorded Brasidas after his death in 422, just as he was posthumously created founder-hero and duly worshipped as such by the men of Amphipolis (Thuc. 5.11.1). Nevertheless, it was a break with tradition to name the Treasury for Brasidas, an individual, when he had officially been fighting as a representative of Sparta (cf. Hornblower 1982, 283-4). So too it was untraditional for the state of Skione officially to award Brasidas a golden crown in his lifetime (Thuc. 4.121.1 – omitted by Aymard 1967, 63, and consequently by Bommelaer 1981, 208). This was an honour that Athens, for example, seems not to have granted to anyone before 409 (M/L 85.10), and it represents a notable advance on Eurybiadas' token olive wreath.

In his semi-divine cult, his golden crown, and his personalized remembrance at Delphi Brasidas unmistakably points forward to Lysander, and it is not coincidental that Brasidas should have suffered the competitive envy of his peers among Sparta's 'leading men' (*prôtoi andres*: Thuc. 4.108.7), as Lysander was to do after Aigospotamoi and his Athenian settlement. But it was not only to outdo Brasidas that Lysander pitched his self-glorification in such a high key. The 'Navarchs' Monument' was deliberately sited so as to eclipse the adjacent Marathon memorial erected by the Athenians (Fig. 4.1). This was completed between about 480 and 425 and consisted of a base supporting sixteen bronze statues, thirteen of them attributed to Pheidias. Like those of the 'Navarchs' Monument', the Marathon statues represented both the gods, who had willed and facilitated the famous victory, and the mortal chiefly responsible for its achievement, Miltiades. The vital difference was that the statue of Miltiades was a posthumous civic award, whereas Lysander and the other twenty-nine or thirty commanders lived not only to tell the tale of Aigospotamoi but to see themselves enshrined in bronze. Not until 393 did Athens award an honorific statue to one of its living citizens, namely Konon (Chapter 14). Moreover, as we have seen, this was not the only statue of Lysander to be erected at Delphi, and two more were set up elsewhere, one by his loyal Samians at Olympia, the other by the men of Ephesos (Lysander's main Aegean base: Bommelaer 1981, 88) in their famous temple of Artemis (Bommelaer nos 12-13). Portrait statues in the narrow sense of attempts to represent the honorand's facial and bodily features with some fidelity to nature were a thing of the future, partly no doubt for purely artistic reasons (see end of Chapter 16). But these statues of Lysander placed in the two main Panhellenic sanctuaries were a clear augury of that personalized future.

Aymard believed it possible to generalize from the glorification and self-glorification of Lysander to the state of public opinion in Greece at large. Exceptional ('hors série') individuals appear at all times and in all societies, but, he argued, collective mores normally serve as a barrier to the exaltation of such individuals beyond the traditional bounds of social acceptability. The Athenian War, however, broke down that barrier in several ways. It exasperated the partisan struggles (*staseis* – esp. Thuc. 3.82-3) within the cities and so placed a premium on the propaganda value of the individual faction-leaders. Its extended military activity gave a greater weight to the views of the masses, who always tend to be more easily impressed by charismatic leaders. And by disturbing the hierarchies that had hitherto been respected within traditional social and moral frameworks it gave these leaders a heightened consciousness of their value as leaders.

There is considerable truth in this picture painted by Aymard, but he exaggerates the extent to which 'public opinion' (a nebulous concept) shifted definitively away from a collective consciousness towards the recognition of individual military success. Yet more importantly, he fails to observe how restricted in time and space was Lysander's *éclat*. Nowhere, indeed, was it more limited than in his native Sparta, as we shall now see. For at this juncture Lysander's self-promotion must be situated within its proper political context.

Following their decisive victory at Aigospotamoi the Spartans were again faced, as after Plataia and Mykale in 479, with three broad foreign policy options: to withdraw from extended, genuinely military activity overseas and retreat within the Isthmus of Corinth – a 'Fortress Peloponnese' policy; to maintain an active role beyond the Peloponnese in both mainland Greece and the Aegean by in effect broadening the compass of the Peloponnesian League (the organization of which already stretched to the southern borders of Thessaly); or to pursue a strategy of outright imperialism, taking over *mutatis mutandis* where Athens had been obliged to leave off. Each option of course carried with it implications for domestic policy too, although these are less easy to categorize so neatly. It is a moot point, and unprovable on present evidence, whether the first two options were championed by factions headed respectively by Kings Pausanias and Agis (as argued by Hamilton 1979b and David 1981; contrast Thompson 1973). But there is no doubt but that the third option was the one favoured most warmly by Lysander, that he was the leader of a faction of friends and associates both in Sparta and in the Aegean world at large, and that this Lysandreian faction at first captured the heights of Spartan policymaking. The question rather was how Lysander would implement his imperialist programme.

The Greeks may not have had a word for imperialism (see epigraph to this chapter), and all ancient empires differed in their fundamental institutions from those with which the world has been (and is) blessed or cursed in the modern era. But *philotimia* (ambition, competitive love of honour), *polupragmosunê* (activism, meddlesomeness) and *pleonexia* (greed for material aggrandizement) between them come close to covering the semantic range of 'imperialism', at least in its psychological aspect (cf. Wehrli 1968); and it is possible to find a broad, objective definition of the term that will subsume all particular instances, ancient as well as modern. For example, the one recently offered by Ste. Croix (1981, 44) from a Marxist perspective will serve very well:

> *Imperialism*, involving some kind of economic and/or political subjection to a power outside the community, is a special case [of class struggle], in which the exploitation effected by the imperial power (in the form of tribute, for example) or by its individual members, need not necessarily involve direct control of the conditions of production. In such a situation, however, the class struggle within the subject community is very likely to be affected, for example through support given by the imperial power or its agents to the exploiting class or classes within that community, if not by the acquisition by the imperial power or its individual members of control over the conditions of production in the subject community (italics original).

Once it is seen that Spartan policy after 404 – led successively by Lysander, Agis and Agesilaos – satisfies that definition all too well, there is no need to share the doubt expressed by Andrewes (1978, 91) 'about the reality of Spartan imperialism, as distinct from the ambitions of individual Spartans and their followers'. Indeed, as M.I. Finley has observed in a useful synoptic essay on imperialism in the ancient Graeco-Roman world as a whole (1978, 2), even Sparta's domination of the Perioikoi may quite properly be described as 'imperialist'. For Sparta was the quintessential 'conquest-state' (Finley 1983, 61). However, this was of course a different kind of domination from that practised by the Spartans after 404. The attested origins of that go back no further than 413, when following Athens' Sicilian disaster the Spartans calculated that 'they themselves would now dominate in complete security the whole of Hellas' (Thuc. 8.2.4) – a renunciation both of the liberation they had promised in 431 and of the dual hegemony they had been prepared to share with Athens in 425 and 421. Our task therefore is to bring out the salient features of this new mode of imperialism, which was not of course itself monolithic or unchanging.

Sparta's hegemony of the Peloponnnesian League was a form of disguised or indirect imperialism, in that the League's main function from Sparta's viewpoint was to protect her vulnerable economic base in Lakonia and Messenia (Chapters 2 and 13 for the League; Chapter 10 for the economic base). But the Athenian War and its aftermath gave rise to a new form that was at once a product and an irritant of the developing social and economic tensions within Spartan society. In so far as it represented a continuation of the Athenian Empire in its basic geographical, military and financial (but not political or ideological) orientation, this new imperialism is properly associated with the name of Lysander, though he experienced a sharp personal setback in 403/2; and it was terminated abruptly and more or less definitively by the naval battle near Knidos in August 394. The remainder of this chapter will therefore be confined to the decade 404 to 394, even though the justice of Parke's characterization of the entire period down to 371 as 'the Second Spartan Empire' (1930, esp. 71,73) will become plain in later chapters.

Despite Bommelaer (1981, 118), Sparta was not torn in 404 'between the seductions of Athens' imperial heritage and the traditions on which her peculiar equilibrium was founded', for the simple reason that this equilibrium had long since been disrupted by the progress of the Athenian War (Chapter 4). There were now too many influential Spartans with a stake, material as well as ideological, in the maintenance and expansion of Sparta's extra-Peloponnesian empire. There were, however, also leading Spartans who, even if they did not envy or abominate Lysander personally, did fight a rearguard action to prevent any further undermining of the severe economic regimen they ascribed to Lykourgos of hallowed memory (or invention). The issue over which they chose to take up the cudgels first was the private possession of coined money.

According to Dio Chrysostom (74.15 – though he is the only source for this anecdotal variant: Bommelaer 1981, 205n.31), Lysander had said that one tricks children with toys but men with oaths *and money*. Whether or not he in fact said this, money was certainly an integral part of Lysander's scheme for a personalized empire. It was to be the sinews of the Pax Laconica, as it had been the sinews of Sparta's successful war-effort, and Lysander intended to use it as an instrument of foreign and perhaps also of domestic policy. The sums involved at the end of the Athenian War were, as we shall see, far greater than anything experienced by the Spartans hitherto. For the motif of Spartan venality abroad, first attested in a context of 524 (Cartledge 1982, 251n.38), reflected the fact that around 550 the Spartan state had deliberately refused to strike a silver coinage and resolved to retain instead for local monetary purposes a cumbersome system of iron spits (*oboloi*) which functioned chiefly as a store of wealth and standard of value rather than a means of payment or exchange. This did not of course mean that the Spartan state did not handle coined money or that exceptional Spartan individuals had not legally possessed large amounts of precious metal, even if in bullion or other than coined form: it is hard to explain otherwise the fine of fifteen talents levied on King Pleistoanax in 445 (sources in Hill 1951, 344, Index I.7.5) or the threat to fine King Agis 100,000 drachmai (16⅔ talents: Thuc. 5.63.2) in 418. Illegally, too, there had been isolated cases of coined money being deposited for safekeeping beyond the Spartan frontier in Arkadia. But it was not until the closing phase of the Athenian War and its immediate aftermath that the possession of coined money by individual Spartans became sufficiently widespread, obvious and efficacious in Sparta to necessitate a public debate and decision on its legality. There may also have been a discussion as to whether Sparta should herself begin to mint coins (O. Picard *ap.* Bommelaer 1981, 155n.230), but the sources do not happen to mention one.

The sources recording the influx of cash into Sparta at the end of the War agree that it was large, that it was due chiefly to Lysander, and that it had a critically deleterious effect on Spartan power. Their disagreement over the precise amount Lysander either sent home with Gylippos or brought back himself later in 404 is relatively less important; but, as David (1979/80) cogently argued, a figure of between 1500 and 2000 talents seems consonant with the probably somewhat inflated sum of 5000 or more talents reported by the Athenians Andokides (3.29) and Isokrates (8.97) as the total Persian subsidy to Sparta between 412 and 405 (discussed in Pritchett 1974, I, 47). By far the largest portion of this had been donated by Cyrus, especially in 405. Indeed, Cyrus' confidence in Lysander and no doubt his expectation of a handsome future return of benefit were so strong that, when he was summoned to attend his dying father in Media, he uniquely entrusted Lysander with the revenues of his enormous province (2.1.14,3.8; DS 13.104.4; Plut. *Lys.* 9.2).

The Spartans were under no obligation to accept the cash brought to Sparta by Gylippos and Lysander. On the contrary, they were bound by their treaty of 411 (Thuc. 8.58.6) to repay all subsequent Persian subsidy at the end of the War. As it was, they did not even repay the outstanding surplus, thereby exemplifying Samuel Johnson's acid dictum that 'He that brings wealth home is seldom interrogated by what means it was obtained'. This was a considerable triumph for Lysander, who intended the money to be the initial deposit in a newly-opened imperialism account. For Sparta had never seen fit to establish a permanent structure of public finance comparable to that developed by Athens for imperial purposes and had relied instead on *ad hoc* contributions from outside sources to supplement such internal revenues as the state did regularly raise (see generally Andreades 1915; 1933, 40-75; and the commentary on M/L 67). But for some years after 404 the Spartans so broke with this haphazard 'system' of voluntary levies that they were reported to be collecting over 1000 talents a year in tribute (DS 14.10.2; Isok. 12.67-9; Polyb. 6.49.10; cf. Parke 1930, 55-7), even if they did perhaps try to sweeten the pill by calling it a 'contribution' (*sunteleia* – a suggestion of Lotze 1964, 63-4, based mainly on *Ath. Pol.* 39.2). The figure given by Diodoros is not as impossibly high as is often supposed (e.g. Cozzoli 1979, 140-5), since the super-rich oligarchs will have been happier to pay protection money to an imperial power that promoted rather than undermined their local domination (cf. Chapter 11).

However, although it was agreed that the state should continue to handle coined money and levy tribute on its new Aegean empire, a ban on the possession of coined money by individual Spartans was decreed – or, as the traditionalists would have it, reaffirmed in accordance with the ancestral constitution laid down by Lykourgos (esp. Plut. *Lys.* 17.1-6; with David 1981, 5-10). How far this should be interpreted as a reverse for Lysander depends on how far he should be linked with the movement to provide legitimate outlets for the expenditure of private capital in Sparta. My own feeling is that, since Lysander was notoriously impervious to the seductions of personal wealth and could still reasonably expect to channel public funds into the right pockets outside Sparta, this was not much of a setback at all. What he would not have condoned was the peculation of state funds for non-productive purposes; and he must therefore have approved, if indeed he did not engineer, the prosecution and condemnation of Gylippos for raiding the sacks containing the 1000 or 1500 silver talents with the conveyance of which to Sparta Lysander had entrusted him (Hamilton 1979b, 55-7). That incident may in fact have precipitated the debate over the possession of coined money. On the other hand, the prosecution and execution of his henchman Thorax (Poralla 1913, no. 380) under the new or reaffirmed law certainly did constitute an indirect attack on Lysander (Smith 1948, 145-6). But so far as can be seen, this was an isolated case. Besides, the ban was apparently widely flouted in spite of this exemplary punishment (e.g. Xen. *LP* 14.3).

In 404, then, Sparta endowed herself with an essential part of the economic infrastructure for imperialism of the Athenian type. This was, to say the least, a remarkable outcome to a war ostensibly begun and prosecuted to destroy the Athenian Empire and restore freedom and autonomy to Athens' subjects (Prandi 1976); and one sympathizes with those among Sparta's new allies who had piously hailed the destruction of the walls of Athens as the beginning of freedom for Hellas (2.2.23; Plut. *Lys*. 15). For, as Plutarch (*Lys*. 13.8) rather savagely commented, the taste of Spartan rule was harsh and bitter from the outset: not only did Lysander deny the cities the right of self-determination, but he actually installed in power cliques of the most rabid of his oligarchic partisans. The loyalty born of revolutionary fervour that these men exhibited foreshadowed that displayed by the narrow puppet oligarchies established by Sparta at Mantineia in 385 and Phleious in 379 (Chapter 13) and Thebes in 382 (Chapter 14). But whereas the latter were led by aristocrats whose hereditary ties of friendship with leading Spartans stretched back over several generations, the ruling oligarchs of 404 covered a wider social spectrum (including the *novissimi* of *homines*) and owed their exclusive allegiance to their patron Lysander. Both in their composition and in their politics (see generally Cavaignac 1924) these cliques were the very reverse of the 'ancestral' and moderate oligarchic regimes through which Sparta had created and sustained the Peloponnesian League alliance. If modern parallels be sought, it was rather as if Lysander was abandoning Lord Lugard's strategy of indirect rule in British Africa through the accepted emirs and chieftains of a customary society in favour of the present United States' method of ruling Latin America through unstable and far from universally acceptable partisan regimes whose only unifying force is their hatred of communism.

The sources sometimes speak sweepingly of the installation of 'dekarchies', governments or juntas of just ten men, throughout the former Athenian Empire (Rahe 1977, 72n.132,166n.122; Bommelaer 1981, 152n.214). But the dekarchies installed on Samos (2.3.7) and Thasos (Nep. *Lys*. 3.1) are in fact the only ones specifically named, unless we include the Peiraieus Ten (Parke 1930, 52); and the only other regime set up by Lysander the precise size of which is known is the 'triakontarchy' of the Thirty Tyrants at Athens (Chapter 14). However, although it is clear enough that alongside the wholly new dekarchies there continued to exist some broader-based oligarchies, dekarchies were certainly established on the Asiatic mainland as well as the Aegean islands. For under Lysander the cities of Asia Minor were simultaneously allies of Sparta and (since 412/11: Chapter 11) subjects of Persia.

The pertinent features of these regimes were their size and criteria of selection. Never before had oligarchy, literally 'rule of the few', meant rule by so few as ten or even probably thirty. Moreover, these juntas had not apparently been chosen by Lysander solely on the traditional oligarchic criterion of wealth, often enough coupled with high birth. Ability of a sort mattered, but what counted for most was unconditional personal loyalty to Lysander. This will explain the inclusion among the juntas of a fair sprinkling of new men – or, as Cary (1927, 28) less flatteringly describes them, 'the scum that bubbles up in the cauldron of civil war'. Lysander may have sought to dignify his relationship with these partisans by contracting ties of *xenia* with them (Plut. *Lys.* 22.3-4), but this could not disguise the fact that the dekarchies were in current Greek parlance *dunasteiai* – that is, collective tyrannies of non-responsible absolute rulers above the laws (Whibley 1896, 124-6). It would be no surprise if they were the kind of oligarchs who took the bloodcurdling oath cited by Aristotle (*Pol.* 1310a8-11): 'I will bear ill will towards the mass of common people (*dêmos*) and will plot and devise against them all the evil I can.'

Such small groups could only hope to maintain themselves in power without outside assistance if they could convince the bulk of their arms-bearing subjects that their rule was desirable or at least necessary. This they signally failed to do, since they tended to resort to a particularly vicious combination of avarice and bloodthirsty brutality. The behaviour of the Thirty at Athens was presumably paradigmatic in this regard, but the bloodiness at least had been presaged at Miletos early in 405 by that of Lysander himself, who characteristically employed deception in addition (DS 13.104.5; Plut. *Lys.* 8.1-3; note that 'Miletos' in Plut. *Lys.* 19 should be 'Thasos': Bommelaer 1981, 154n.225, 157-8). Thus moderate pro-Spartan oligarchs no less than pro-Athenian democrats were given ample grounds for grievance, and the inevitable corollary of a dekarchy was – again, as exemplified at Athens in 404-3 – a garrison commanded by a Spartan governor known as a harmost (*harmostês* or *harmostêr*, literally a 'fixer').

Some scholars (esp. Parke 1931) are prepared to believe the assertion by an ancient commentator on Pindar that the immediate supervision of all the Perioikoi in Lakonia and Messenia was entrusted to twenty harmosts. In fact, though, the only such harmost whose existence is beyond doubt is the one who had regularly been sent out to control the strategically and economically valuable but vulnerable offshore island of Kythera from some time before 424. Thucydides (4.53.2) calls this official 'Kythêrodikês', but an inscription (*IG* V.1.937) reveals that at least in the fourth century his proper title was harmost (here *harmostêr*). However, the origins of what became under Lysander's direction a co-ordinated system of imperial rule do not lie within Sparta's home territory. They may be detected in central and northern Greece during the first phase of the Athenian War, and, I think, may be attributed pretty firmly to the brain of Brasidas.

It does not really matter whether it was to Herakleia Trachinia (Thuc. 3.93.2; cf. 5.51.2, 52.1) or to Nisaia, the port of Megara (Thuc. 4.69.3), that Sparta first sent out a military governor (*archôn* in Thucydides' generic usage: Parke 1930, 78-9). For it was not until Brasidas between 424 and 422 had won over by force, fraud and diplomacy several of Athens' key allies in Thrace that anything like a system of harmosts (or strictly perhaps proto-harmosts) began to emerge. Thucydides (4.132.3) was struck by how comparatively young these new governors were to be appointed to such important posts (especially in age-worshipping Sparta); and it would probably not be wrong to see them as protégés of Brasidas. But Thucydides is also at pains throughout his account of this northern campaign to distinguish implicitly between the treatment accorded former Athenian allies by Brasidas and that meted out to them by Lysander and his cronies. Brasidas, he says ironically (4.81.3), 'was the first to be sent out [sc. as a kind of area military governor], and since he won the reputation of being thoroughly upright and honourable he left behind the firm expectation that the others would also be of the same clay'. This 'not very subtle intimation of the tyranny of Lysander' (Rawlings 1981, 236-7; cf. Cloché 1943, 106 on Thucydidean irony) is confirmed a few chapters later in the set-piece oration Thucydides (4.85-7) wrote for Brasidas to deliver to the Akanthians. This elaborate and eloquent speech (Brasidas was 'an excellent speaker – for a Spartan': 4.84.2) had a single theme: liberation. But just in case the men of Akanthos were not impressed by the oaths the Spartan authorities had sworn to respect the autonomy of any allies Brasidas should win over from Athens (4.86.1), Brasidas goes on to specify that 'autonomy' will *not* mean the delivery of the Akanthians into the hands of one or other of the rival domestic factions and the consequent political 'enslavement' of the rest (4.86.3-4; rightly interpreted by Cloché 1943, 85). For if he were to behave in this way, the Spartans would not earn honour and glory but reproach.

Which of course is precisely and inevitably what did happen in and after 404, as Thucydides' Athenian speakers addressing the Spartan Assembly in 432 had sagely 'predicted' (1.77.6):

> If, however, you were to destroy us and exercise empire yourselves, you would quickly forfeit the goodwill you have won because of the fear in which we are held. At least you would if you were to act upon similar principles to those you exhibited when for a brief time you exercised the command against the Persians. For the conventions that govern your internal social arrangements are not for export, and in any case each and every one of you who goes abroad observes neither those conventions nor the ones accepted throughout the rest of the Greek world.

Strong words, these, and partly reproducing the conventional rhetorical stereotype of the schizoid Spartans – repressed (Chapter 3) and xenophobic (Chapter 9) at home, tyrannically domineering overseas. However, they are amply borne out, as Thucydides of course knew they would be, by the historian's description of (say) the 'private empire-building' of Pedaritos on Chios in 412 (Thuc. 8.38.3, with A. Andrewes in Gomme 1981, 83-4; Rhodes 1981a, 299) and of other harmosts and commanders (e.g. Astyochos: Cloché 1943, 92-3) elsewhere in the Aegean and approaches to the Black Sea during the last phase of the Athenian War. Even more are they true of the conduct of the Spartan harmosts appointed in and after 405, for which there is a relative abundance of evidence (presented less than admirably by Bockisch 1965, though with a useful table at 233-5; much better by Parke 1930, 51-65, with table at 41).

The latter were positioned on the Bosporos at Byzantion and Chalkedon (a joint appointment at least in the case of Sthenelaos, perhaps a grandson of the well-known Ephor of 432, Sthenelaïdas); in the Thracian Chersonese (Gallipoli peninsula); on the three major islands off the Asiatic coast, Lesbos, Chios and Samos; on Aigina and so perhaps also in the other states restored by Lysander to populations expelled by the Athenians – Melos, Poteidaia, Torone, Skione, Histiaia/Oreos; probably on many other Aegean islands such as Thasos for which there is no specific testimony; and finally in mainland Greece at Athens (Chapter 14) and Epitalion near Elis (Chapter 13). They were formally appointed by and in the first instance responsible to the Ephors. But there is good reason to believe that, like those appointed in Boiotia in the 370s, Phoibidas and Sphodrias (Chapter 14), they were often or even usually nominated by Lysander or one of the kings; the replacement of Derkylidas by Anaxibios in 389 because of Anaxibios' personal connections with members of the Ephorate (4.8.32) was surely exceptional, as Xenophon seems to imply. Despite a couple of rhetorical assertions (3.5.12; Isok. 4.111; but see Lotze 1962, 432-3), it is unlikely in the extreme that Helots or even ex-Helots were appointed harmosts; but the troops they commanded certainly included Neodamodeis (specially liberated Helots: Chapter 10) as well as Peloponnesian League soldiers and assorted mercenaries. The only development that can be detected in the harmost system is the creation of area harmosts in addition to harmosts attached to individual cities (2.4.28; 3.1.3; 4.2.5; 5.2.7, 3.20; Ain. Takt. 27.7, with Parke 1927, 161). This was peculiarly suited to the conditions of Sparta's war in Asia after 400 (Parke 1930, 65-70; Chapter 12), but already in 403 Lysander had received this sort of appointment for Attika (2.4.28) and it was foreshadowed in the roving commission entrusted to Brasidas in the 420s.

Apart from their general brutality and venality, the most striking (in more than one sense) aspect of these harmosts' rule was their unbridled savagery towards democracy or democrats, a trait they shared with their spiritual mentor Lysander (Plut. *Lys.* 19; cf. Isok. 4.113). But no less significant was the effect that their sudden access to liquid capital abroad soon had on Sparta's domestic economy. It may be too strong to speak of a 'noiseless revolution' (as Rahe 1977, 22) in attitudes, but it is plain enough that their newly acquired foreign wealth was put to work at home in a manner that 'the legislator' (*ex hypothesi* Lykourgos) had never intended (see further Chapter 10).

There is a fundamental divergence in our sources concerning the motives of Lysander for establishing this Aegean naval empire based on dekarchies, harmosts, garrisons and tribute. On the Ephoran view (e.g. DS 14.13.1) Lysander was at least initially simply an obedient servant of the Spartan state, dutifully executing the dictates of the home authorities. By contrast Cornelius Nepos (e.g. *Lys.* 1.5) and Plutarch (e.g. *Lys.* 13) are quite clear that it was a personal empire that Lysander held firmly in mind. The latter view, despite Lotze's careful attempt to show that Lysander's behaviour was consistently traditional (Lotze 1964), seems to me preferable, not least in light of the extraordinary 'glorification personnelle' discussed earlier in this chapter. That, too, was apparently the view taken by the Spartan authorities in the second half of 403. At a conjuncture in Spartan domestic politics to be considered more fully later (Chapter 8 and 14) Lysander was recalled from the Hellespont; the colony of former boatswains and steersmen from his victorious fleet that he had settled at the strategically vital site of Sestos in the Hellespont was expelled; and the rug was pulled from under his dekarchies by the Ephors' proclamation that 'all cities should return to their ancestral constitutions' (3.4.2).

The impression given by Xenophon that this proclamation was made nearer 397/6 than 403/2 is grossly misleading and should be firmly resisted (as it is by Andrewes 1971, 206-16). For it presupposes unanimity of the kings in opposition to Lysander, and such unanimity existed only briefly in 403. But the decree could of course lead to contradictory results in foreign policy. On the one hand, the Spartans in the persons of the two kings and the five Ephors used it to deprive Athens temporarily of their longstanding hold on Delos (Tod 99 = *IDélos* 87); on the other, in late summer 403 Pausanias personally effected the restoration of Athens' 'ancestral constitution', namely democracy, and so rid her of the Lysandreian junta (Chapter 14). If it was possible to do this for Sparta's principal defeated enemy, *a fortiori* it should have been so for the other cities of the Spartan empire. True, Pausanias was brought to trial and only narrowly acquitted on a charge of betraying Sparta's interests at Athens. But acquittal was a major victory in the competitive terms of Greek politics, and the board of Ephors which unanimously voted for it (Paus. 3.5.2) could well have been the board which proclaimed the return to 'ancestral constitutions' generally. It would be pleasant to suppose that it was also this board which 'signed' the Delos document, for then we would know all their names.

The abolition of the dekarchies, or at least withdrawal of official Spartan support from this technique of imperial rule, was a major blow to Lysander's influence. The message emanating from Sparta was that the empire was to be maintained through harmosts, garrisons, tribute, a regular succession of navarchs, and perhaps even the despatch of colonists (3.2.8; 4.8.7); but maintained for the greater power and glory of Sparta, not Lysander, and not on Lysander's peculiar political terms. This was far from being the end of Lysander as a political force in Sparta; as Smith (1948) has properly emphasized, he was not overthrown and did not simply go into political eclipse between 402 and 396. But for the time being he was compelled, publicly at least, to hide his personal ambitions behind the mask of loyally supporting others – above all Agesilaos, whom he was instrumental in raising to the Eurypontid throne in 400 (Chapter 7).

Privately, however, it is possible to argue, Lysander dreamed the impossible dream of a future in which he might legitimately aspire to be king himself rather than merely kingmaker or King's Counsel. Unfortunately – but hardly surprisingly in the case of alleged plans that neither came to fruition nor were disclosed by their alleged author – the evidence on this cardinal point is factually and chronologically inconsistent or imprecise (cf. Andrewes 1971, 211; Rahe 1977, 222-5; Hamilton 1979b, 88-9,92-6; Bommelaer 1981, 223-5). The poker-faced Xenophon gives (if he gives anything) merely the barest hint of Lysander's revolutionary plans when in his account of the flare-up between Lysander and Agesilaos at Ephesos in 396 he pregnantly juxtaposes 'Lusandros' and 'king' (*basileus*: 3.4.7 *ad fin.*). For contradictory and mainly undated detail we have to rely principally on Diodoros (14.13) and Plutarch (*Lys.* 24-6), who were partly drawing on the same ultimate source, Ephoros. It is therefore with all due caution that the following reconstruction is presented.

By the summer of 404 Lysander had attained an unprecedented and unparalleled degree of personal power for a Spartan outside the two royal families. But in order to protect and consolidate his influence he needed to occupy permanently an official position in Sparta that carried with it something like what the Romans called *imperium*, the power ultimately of life and death. He had been navarch and could not therefore be so again. By a legal fiction he had been appointed 'Secretary' (*epistoleus*), in effect Vice-Admiral, to the navarch of 405 and reappointed or simply prorogued in 404. Formally, however, this was a subordinate post, and Lysander, who like Sulla (with whom Plutarch paired him) did not have a low opinion of his own worth, might at any time find himself decisively overruled or recalled. He was never, it seems, Ephor, but that post too was annual and non-renewable, besides having the disadvantage of being collegiate. Membership of the Gerousia was by contrast permanent, one of its most attractive features (Chapter 8), but in 404 Lysander was probably almost a decade too young to be eligible. In the summer of 403 he was appointed area harmost for Attika, and it was perhaps just possible to envisage a long career as harmost such as Derkylidas and Panthoidas seem to have enjoyed. But as harmost Lysander found himself embarrassingly trumped by the temporary coalition formed against him by the two kings. The lesson was apparent. The only possible position of the requisite permanency, prestige and (at least abroad) power for a man with ambitions of personal empire was the kingship. Not even a regency would suffice, since 'regents must in the nature of things slip away from the centre of the stage in time' (Hart 1982, 204n.115).

So it was, I believe, that Lysander in 403 (as DS 14.13 suggests) or earlier (cf. Bommelaer 1981, 160,170,221) cast around for a way to open up the kingship to others besides members of the hereditary Agiad and Eurypontid royal houses, or perhaps to substitute for the dual kingship a monarchy of some description. If the funerals of Spartan kings conferred upon them posthumous heroic status (Chapter 16), Lysander was not the one to balk at the idea of extending this charisma to their lifetime. He was indeed 'the man who would be king' (Hamilton 1979b, title of ch.2). Besides, should he have needed any further encouragement towards drawing this conclusion, there was plenty of it to hand.

Neither king had an avowedly legitimate son and heir who was of an age to succeed in his own right, and the one potential candidate for the Eurypontid throne, Agesilaos, was a former *erômenos* of Lysander (Chapter 3) who might not be expected to stand in his way. In addition, 403/2 was apparently a year in which the Ephors might conduct an archaic-seeming eight-yearly skywatching ritual to detect omens unfavourable to the continued rule of the existing kings (Luria 1927, 413-19; Parke 1945; Rahe 1977, 278-9n.145). The origins of this ritual, which is not securely attested before 243/2, are unknown, though there are many parallels for the view that a community might suffer collectively for the sins of a king. However, this opportune conjuncture of favourable circumstances would not alone be enough to legitimate a change in the rules of eligibility for the Spartan thrones. As that legitimacy was grounded ultimately in the divine sanction won from Apollo at Delphi, oracular means were required to undermine it.

Seen in this light, the 'Navarchs' Monument' of 405/4 and Lysander's deification on Samos acquire a new aura. But if they were part of a concerted plan to prepare the Delphic priesthood to recognize Lysander's regal suitability, they were a failure. For Lysander was, reportedly, obliged to resort to bribery (DS 14.13.4-5; Plut. *Lys.* 25.2: Nep. *Lys.* 3.2,3). A man who, as we have seen, could make light of the sanctity of oaths will not have scrupled to take this step, and (despite Smith 1948, 148) there is no incompatibility between Lysander's personal poverty and his ability to spend large sums on bribing oracular officials. However, unlike that of an equally unorthodox and unscrupulous predecessor, King Kleomenes I, Lysander's bribery of Delphi was inefficacious – yet another proof of the entrenched power of the kings, who maintained close contact with Delphi through the Pythioi they appointed (Chapter 4). Perhaps foreseeing this barren outcome, Lysander had covered himself by attempting similarly to suborn two more of the most respected oracular shrines, those of Zeus at Dodona and of Ammon in the Siwah oasis in Libya (a country where he had hereditary connections). But both these attempts too were unsuccessful, and it may indeed have been the denunciation of Lysander at Sparta by an envoy from Siwah (DS 14.13.8) that sealed the fate of his dekarchies.

At this stage, however, it cannot have been clear exactly what plans Lysander had for the kingship. They may in fact never have become clear, at least in public. For both the friends of Lysander and Agesilaos had their different reasons for keeping them dark after Lysander's death at Haliartos in 395 (Chapter 14); and Pausanias, whose immediate condemnation they jointly engineered, will therefore have been unable to gain any reliable information to use as ammunition in the pamphlet he wrote in exile at Tegea in defence of the Laws of Lykourgos (as he understood them: see Chapter 10). Hence the sources' contradictory versions of the plans. Granted that (despite Nepos) he did not wish to abolish the kingship altogether, did he aim to throw it open to all Spartans on an ostensibly meritocratic basis (the Ephoran version: DS 14.13; Plut. *Lys.* 30.4) or just to all 'descendants of Herakles' (Plut. *Lys.* 24-6)? If we must choose, the latter alternative is hugely preferable, since Lysander was himself a Heraklid and, being very far from egalitarian, will not have wished to cast the net too wide. This would, moreover, mark less of a break with tradition, since the kings were already required to take their wives from this supposed descent-group (Plut. *Agis* 11). It is, however, possible that privately what he really wished to do was abolish the dyarchy, so that he could rule perhaps as a kind of constitutional tyrant somewhat on the model of Dionysios I of Syracuse. But one would not expect him to have given public currency to such a notion in, for instance, the speech he commissioned from Kleon of Halikarnassos that Agesilaos allegedly discovered some time after Lysander's death (below).

Lysander's royalist scheming, then, belongs in my view in 404 and 403. But however far his ideas had matured by then, the strength of the reaction against him led by Agis and Pausanias forced him to shelve his plans. He by no means ceased his political activity, since he was probably behind Sparta's cautiously implemented decision to back Cyrus' rebellious bid for the Persian throne (Chapter 11) and certainly behind the accession of Agesilaos in 400. (His alleged and undated embassy to Dionysios, however, may well be fictitious:

Sansone 1981). But it was not until 396 that he was able to return to Asia Minor and renew personal contact with the client oligarchs he had perforce disappointed in 403/2. Any ideas he had of restoring the dekarchies (3.4.2,7) were, however, rapidly aborted by Agesilaos, who had other ideas about the governance of Sparta's empire. Yet despite his demotion in Asia, Lysander was by no means a spent force in Sparta. It was perhaps after his return from Asia that he prosecuted Naukleidas, the corpulent Ephor of 403 who had been prominent in support of Pausanias (2.4.35-6; Agatharchides *ap*. Athen. 550de); and the active role he played in the preliminaries to the Corinthian War (Chapter 14) suggest that it was particularly he and his friends rather than the Spartans at large who 'welcomed the pretext for a campaign against the Thebans' (3.5.5; cf. Bommelaer 1981, 193n.103). All the same, the circumstances of his death, which contrast so starkly with the cool efficiency and precise co-ordination that distinguished his Aigospotamoi campaign, do suggest that he had begun to lose his sureness of touch.

The Spartan defeat at Haliartos was followed by political disequilibrium at home and the conglutination of a menacingly powerful coalition of Sparta's enemies abroad. Agesilaos was hastily recalled from Asia Minor, and though he succeeded in forcing a passage through Thessaly in August 394 (Chapter 12) it was only to learn that in his rear the Spartan fleet, which he had rashly placed under the command of his brother-in-law (cf. Chapter 9), had been crushingly defeated near Knidos by a Persian fleet under Pharnabazus and the expatriate Athenian admiral Konon. This spelled the end of the kind of Spartan empire that Lysander had been largely responsible for creating: harmosts and garrisons were expelled, an Aegean democratic resurgence took place. However, Knidos by no means marked the terminus of Spartan imperialism. The torch lit by Lysander was kept burning brightly by Agesilaos.

We are told that Agesilaos' first thought on discovering the speech written by Kleon of Halikarnassos was to publish it in order to discredit the memory of Lysander and his still strong following in Sparta. But on taking advice from an Ephor or perhaps more plausibly from a fellow-member of the Gerousia, Agesilaos decided instead to suppress it so as not to exaggerate the gulf between himself and Lysander's more ardent devotees. This was a wise decision, entirely worthy of a pupil of the cunning Lysander. For that in truth was what Agesilaos importantly was.

Following the vicissitudes of his former lover's career as closely as he had been able to do over many years had taught Agesilaos what to accept and what to purge from the heritage of Lysander's policies and politics. An imperialist foreign policy might profitably be pursued, but in mainland Greece rather than Asia and under cover of the slogan of liberation and support for 'ancestral' laconophile oligarchies rather than by imposing on allied states excessively narrow and dictatorial regimes of doubtfully respectable clients. Friends and partisans were of course no less indispensable to Agesilaos than they had been to Lysander both at home and abroad, and Agesilaos went to extraordinary lengths to cultivate such political associations (Chapter 9). But they should not be permitted to pay him divine worship or even to erect statues in his honour. Personal politics and power, in other words, should be disguised not flaunted, and the Spartan authorities assiduously flattered not flouted. As for religion, that was indeed an *arcanum imperii*, but orthodoxy was the order of the day.

The manner in which Agesilaos demoted Lysander and nipped his renascent personal empire in the bud in 396 (Chapter 9) showed just how much Agesilaos had already learned from his mentor. Even the canny Lysander seems to have been surprised by the speed of the *démarche*: from kingpin to kingmaker to *roi manqué* in under a decade. Agesilaos was not the king 'to be put almost out of possession' by Lysander's manipulation. Instead, as Bommelaer (1981, 238) has well noted, he insensibly occupied the terrain mapped out by his teacher – but under very different colours. Rather as Augustus progressively realized the monarchical hints and tendencies of Julius Caesar while at every step proclaiming his unswerving fidelity to the old Republican order, so Agesilaos in effect became the chief arbiter of Sparta's destiny behind a smokescreen of humble devotion to the laws of Lykourgos.

7

The Accession of Agesilaos and the Power of the Spartan Throne

It is a miserable state of mind to have few things to desire and many things to fear; and yet that commonly is the case of Kings. (Francis Bacon, Essay XIX 'Of Empire')

That the kings were a persistently disruptive force of a special kind and magnitude in classical Spartan history needs no demonstration. (Finley 1981a, 32)

King Agis II was dead. King Agesilaos II did live long. But in the late summer of 400 (Funke 1980a, 36n.31 for the date, which depends on the chronology of Agis' Elis campaign: Chapter 13) it was not at all clear that Agesilaos would become a king; and since antiquity there have been several influential voices raised in doubt as to whether the kings of Sparta were really kings at all in the proper sense. The aims of this chapter are, first, to discuss how and why Agesilaos succeeded Agis and then to describe and assess the character, functions and power of the Spartan kingship in theory and practice. Fulfilment of these aims is a necessary preliminary to consideration in the next chapters of how major decisions of foreign and domestic policy were taken at Sparta. For in the words of Jack Goody (1966,5), 'An examination of the concomitants of the different modes of transferring high office raises the general question of the "power" of the office and its relation to the structure of the dynasty, the character of the whole governmental system and the organization of the armed force upon which it finally depends'.

I begin by quoting extensively from three chapters of Thucydides (5.15-17) that encapsulate all the salient features of the Spartan kingship. The context is the closing phase of the Ten Years' War. By 422, Thucydides informs his readers, both sides had compelling reasons for making peace, the Spartans perhaps rather more than the Athenians since the latter were holding hostage some 120 Spartan citizens of full status.

It was at this moment, then, that the most energetic policy-makers in each city, Pleistoanax son of Pausanias king of the Spartans and Nikias son of Nikeratos ... redoubled their efforts towards securing a peace. [Nikias' personal motives for pursuing this course are then alleged] As for Pleistoanax, he was being slandered in connection with his restoration, by enemies of his who, whenever Sparta suffered any reverse, continually blamed it on the illegality of that restoration. The accusation they brought against him was that he and his brother Aristokles had bribed the Pythia at Delphi to give the following response to the various official Spartan delegations: Bring back home from abroad the seed of the demigod son of Zeus, or else you will have to plough with a silver ploughshare [? = will experience a dearth]. Pleistoanax had gone into exile at Lykaion because he was deemed to have been bribed to withdraw from Attika, and had built half his house inside the sanctuary of Zeus Lykaios through fear of the Spartans.

So in the end, his enemies alleged, he had induced the Spartans to restore him after nineteen years of exile and to conduct him home with dances and sacrifices like those which had accompanied the establishment of the kings when Sparta was first settled. Pleistoanax was of course angered by this accusation and energetically advocated the conclusion of a peace treaty, calculating that in peacetime no reverse could occur and that with the Spartan hostages returned he would be immune from his enemies' attacks, whereas it was inevitable that the leading men would always be slandered in consequence of any disasters.

Alleged bribery and corruption, both by and of Pleistoanax, involving the Delphic oracle; exile, incontinent flight and the perceived threat of imminent death; residence within a sacred precinct across the Spartan frontier in southern Arkadia; adversary politics co-ordinated by a defined group of enemies and resisted by a brother; direct and intimate connection between foreign and domestic policy strategies – of such turbulent ingredients could the life of a Spartan king be composed in the second half of the fifth century. However, the chequered career of a Pleistoanax (who reigned with an intermission from about 459 to 408) cannot be taken straightforwardly as typical, except in one very important respect: that when the divisions over policy ran high in Sparta, as they did at the time of the exiling of Pleistoanax in 446/5 and after his recall in 427 or 426, the line of demarcation tended to run between the two kings, whether they were acting as the spearheads or merely as the figureheads of the rival political tendencies or groupings.

Two kings. That was the first oddity to strike an outside observer in the fifth century. They were, moreover, full-blooded hereditary kings, not appointive or (ordinarily) elective kings. In anthropological parlance Sparta had preserved a highly determinate system of vertical succession, that is in theory from father to eldest son (Goody 1966; cf. 1976b, 89-90). (The status of porphyrogeniture, the succession of the first son to be born legitimately to a ruling king, is as problematic in Sparta as in Achaemenid Persia and – perhaps – Macedon; in practice it seems never to have been observed, despite Hdt. 7.3.) Consobrinal and fraternal succession did, on the other hand, occur – quite frequently in the latter case; but at least by the fifth century the Spartans believed that this was the result of accident, the non-availability of a son, rather than a fixed design for collateral succession. The truth may of course have been different at an earlier period (cf. Henige 1974, 208).

However that may be, the origins of the Spartan dyarchy are lost in the obscurity of the Greek Dark Age (roughly the eleventh to ninth centuries), during which the site of classical Sparta (officially called Lakedaimon) was settled by Dorian newcomers speaking a dialect of Greek that evolved into

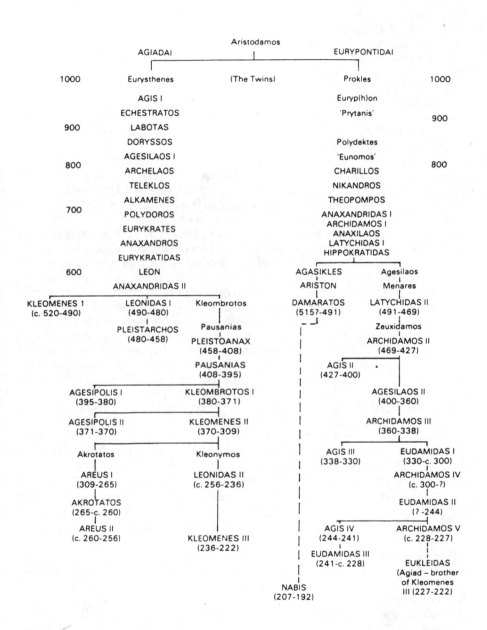

Fig. 7. The Spartan King-lists

classical Doric (Fig. 2) (Cartledge 1979, ch. 7; a different view of the founders in Hooker 1980, 41-5). Herodotus preserves for us what I take to be king-lists (Hdt. 7.204, 8.131.2, with Cartledge 1979, App. 3); these purport to carry the two royal houses back in unbroken father-son succession to the twin sons of Aristodamos, the great-great-grandson of Herakles (Fig. 7). But he also tells us (6.52.1) that 'the Spartans declare, in opposition to the testimony of all the poets, that it was King Aristodamos himself ... who led them to the land they now possess, and not the sons of Aristodamos'. Besides, those twin sons were named Eurysthenes and Prokles, and yet the two royal houses of historical times were called, not Eurysthenidai and Proklidai, but Agiadai and Euryp(h)ontidai, the descendants of Agis and Euryp(h̥)on.

The explanation of these two anomalies is transparently obvious. The Spartans, conscious that they were relatively recent immigrants to the Peloponnese (especially in comparison to their self-styled 'autochthonous' neighbours in Arkadia: 7.1.23), and unsure of the legitimacy of their control of what was in fact spear-won territory, pushed back the settlement of Lakedaimon and the foundation of the Spartan state as far as they dared, as close as possible to the lifetime of their ultimate founder-hero Herakles. Yet the names of the two royal houses stubbornly denounced the falsity of the claim – advanced by implication in the Great Rhetra, accepted of course as true by Pleistoanax, and supported by Aristotle (*Pol.* 1310b38-9) – that the dual kingship was coterminous with the settlement of Lakedaimon. No modern explanation of the dyarchy's origins can be entirely convincing, though I favour the view which connects it with the unification of Sparta's four constituent villages (*kômai*; cf. Appendix II) and regards the Agiad Archelaos and the Eurypontid Charilaos as probably the first *joint* kings somewhere in the first half of the eighth century (cf. Cartledge 1980b, at 98). The functions of the king-lists preserved in Herodotus are rather easier to grasp.

They operated on two overlapping levels. In the first instance they affirmed the determinate, vertical system of succession to high office and specified the limits of eligibility. For the Agiads and Eurypontids were not the only Herakleidai (descendants of Herakles) in Sparta, and there were at least two other Spartan families, the Aigidai (Hdt. 4.149.1) and the Talthybiadai (Hdt. 7.134.1, cf. 6.60), who were not descendants of Herakles and yet were of aristocratic status and (in the latter's case at least) enjoyed hereditary public prerogatives. So the king-lists of the Agiads and Eurypontids acted as a 'mnemonic of social relationships' (Goody/Watt 1963, 309), providing what Malinowski called a genealogical 'charter' of their right to rule.

Secondly, the king-lists asserted the equal legitimacy of the two royal houses in case either one should ever seek to usurp monarchical privilege (as in fact did not happen until the third quarter of the third century). Herodotus (6.51-52), it is true, was informed that the Agiadai were the more honoured of the two because they were the elder house; and he was fed by his Spartan informants a complicated foundation legend according to which the dyarchy had been sanctioned by the Delphic Oracle. But the legend was just that – a legend studded with palpable anachronisms; and in practice, as would be expected in a gerontocracy, the senior of the two joint kings was the one who had reigned longer (Wade-Gery 1925, 567n.2, citing Thuc. 5.24.1 and Tod 99). On the other hand, there was more than just the bias of his informants and the timing of his visit to Sparta (3.55.2, probably soon after the exile of Pleistoanax) to account for his confident statements that Eurysthenes and Prokles had been at odds throughout their adult lives and that 'the houses sprung from their loins have continued the feud to this day' (6.52.8).

Hereditary kingship had more or less disappeared from the Greek world in the course of the eighth century, in so far as it had ever existed (disputed by Drews 1983, but with considerable exaggeration). But if this was precisely when the dyarchy was instituted in Sparta, it seems not unreasonable to link the two phenomena. From the standpoint of Archelaos and Charilaos (or whoever the first joint kings really were) shared rule was better than no rule at all; from the standpoint of their aristocratic but non-royal peers a divided kingship, like a divided consulate at Rome, was a weakened kingship in that each king might be expected to act as a check on the other and the nobility as a whole might hope to exploit the divisions between them for their collective benefit. It was specifically the spectacular enmity between the Agiad Kleomenes I and the Eurypontid Damaratos in the decades on either side of 500 that prompted Herodotus' peculiarly revealing excursus on the Spartan kingship.

Having survived the putative eighth-century crisis, the now joint kingship was soon faced with others. The alleged plotting of a mysterious social group known as Partheniai was somehow linked to the establishment of Sparta's only overseas foundation at Taras (Tarentum in southern Italy) at the very end of the eighth century (Graham 1982, 112-13). The fact (if it is a fact) that in the 520s there was a king (*basileus*: Hdt. 3.136.2) of Taras may suggest an element of royal rivalry in the Partheniai affair. At any rate, it was about 700 that Theopompos the Eurypontid king created the Ephorate as a preservative of the kingship, according to one of the two main Spartan versions of the origins of this office (see further Chapter 8). One reason for believing it is that in the fourth century, when this version is first attested, the Ephorate was more easily seen as the enemy or at least the watchdog of the kingship than as its saviour.

However that may be, the real masterstroke was to secure the inclusion of the kings (here called *archagetai* or 'founder-leaders') in the document known as the Great Rhetra (Plut. *Lyk.* 6, from the lost Aristotelian *Lak. Pol.*). For reasons too complex to discuss here (cf. Cartledge 1980b, 99-106) I believe this to be a genuine document of the first half of the seventh century dressed up in the guise of a Delphic oracle; despite the difficulties the Great Rhetra poses, it seems too austere to plead for 'abstention from making use of it in historical arguments' (Ducat 1983, 204). Now there is no mention of the Ephors here, which is not at all odd if they were not yet specially important and were still effectively controlled by the kings. The kings, however, achieve their place as ex-officio members of the Spartan Senate, the Gerousia, and thus were planned to endure just as long as that august enshrinement of the principle of gerontocracy. It was perhaps at this time that Herodotus' foundation legend involving Delphic sanction for the dyarchy was first created. That would at any rate have been consistent with a Messenian (Helot) domestic servant being credited with an important role in the story, since both the Rhetra and the first conquest of

Messenia were attributed plausibly to the same Theopompos.

By about 650, then, the joint kingship was securely established, and rules of succession had presumably been laid down. But the survival of hereditary kingship involved costs as well as gains both to the individuals concerned and to the Spartan state as a whole. One of Theopompos' co-kings, Polydoros, for example, was reportedly assassinated by an outraged aristocrat for his populist political leanings (on the traditions relating to this king see Marasco 1978). A century later there occurred the first of the several attested cases of dispute over the succession, manifestations which, as Finley (1981a, 32) has well said, 'belong to the courts of tyrants and barbarian monarchs, not to a Greek *polis*'. In the Spartan *polis* the anomaly was the more blatant in so far as the political, social, economic and military package of reforms of which the Rhetra was a central element was imbued with the ideal or at least ideology of equality. Full Spartan citizens described themselves as Homoioi or 'Peers', and although distinctions of birth and wealth were never in fact lacking within the citizen body, their potentially divisive social effect was supposed to be neutralized by the requirements to pass through the *agôgê* and be elected to a common mess (Chapter 3). These communal features of Spartan society were considered by some in antiquity to be among the 'democratic' elements of the Spartan polity (cf. Arist. *Pol.* 1294b19-27).

Here again, though, the kings were different. Although the kings became members of a common mess, they were automatic, hereditary members of a specifically royal mess, or rather of *the* royal mess, since the kings and selected Homoioi messed together apart from the *hoi polloi* (e.g. 5.3.20). And if the system of determinate, vertical succession had always worked in practice as it was intended to do in theory, no kings would have passed through the *agôgê*, since the heirs-apparent in each royal house were specifically exempted from this otherwise universal obligation (Chapter 3). Thus the usual necessary links between successful passage through the *agôgê*, membership of a mess, and full Spartan citizenship were snapped in the case of the kings. In short, properly speaking the kings were not Homoioi.

The analogy with barbarian monarchs drawn by Finley in connection with succession disputes had already been drawn by Herodotus in a different regard. In a natural progression of thought he moves from discussing the origins of the dyarchy to an enumeration of the prerogatives (*gerea*) that the Spartans had accorded their kings. First he lists those granted to them in their lifetime, then he turns to their funerary honours (6.58):

> Horsemen ride around to announce the king's death throughout the territory of the Spartan state, while in the city of Sparta itself women perambulate and bang cauldrons. Whereupon two free people from each household, a man and a woman, are required to don mourning apparel, and heavy punishments are exacted from defaulters. This law of the Spartans concerning their kings is *precisely the same as that of the barbarians of Asia; indeed, most barbarians apply the same regulation to their kings' funerals.*

Herodotus then relates how not only Spartiates but Perioikoi and Helots too must participate in the royal funeral, crying out that the last king to die was the best king yet; and he notes that the funeral was followed by ten days of official mourning during which civic business was suspended. Nor do the barbarian analogies end there: the custom whereby the new king (literally) sets free any Spartiate in debt either to his predecessor or to the public exchequer is said to be shared with the Persians specifically (Hdt. 6.59), and the existence of hereditary professions (heralds, flautists, cooks) is identified with Egyptian practice (Hdt. 6.60; cf. Berthiaume 1976).

The whole passage is thus enormously instructive. For whereas Herodotus on the whole treats Sparta as if it were a normal Greek state, when he deals with the kings' privileges he employs the comparative ethnographic manner typically reserved for non-Greek peoples; and since no other Greek city is deemed to merit exposition of its peculiar customs, the oddity of the Spartan kingship within the wider Greek context is made to stand out in high relief. For present purposes, however, this general peculiarity of the kingship and specifically the singularity of the royal funerary honours (fully discussed in Chapter 16) are less relevant than the gulf placed by their *gerea* between the kings and other Spartans.

The other main source for these royal prerogatives is Xenophon (*LP* 13, 15). But his account of what he calls their *timai* ('honours') is not entirely consistent with or complementary to that of Herodotos, even though Xenophon claims (*Ages.* 1.4; *LP* 15.1) that the kingship 'is the only office that remains today in the form in which it was originally constituted'. In reality, as we shall see, the formal powers of the kingship had been progressively diminished since at least the mid-sixth century. Following the useful distinction of Herodotus and Xenophon, our discussion will be divided between the *gerea* or *timai* accorded in war and peace respectively, and in that order of priority.

(i) War

Herodotus begins (6.56) by noting that the kings were hereditary priests of Zeus Lakedaimonios (Spartan) and Zeus Ouranios (Heavenly Zeus). As high priests, and by virtue of their divine descent, they were qualified to conduct the required sacrifices to Zeus and assorted divinities in Sparta before setting out on campaign, to Zeus and Athena at the Spartan frontier (the uniquely Spartan *diabatêria* ceremony), and to the appointed gods in camp and on the battlefield. They decided how many animals to sacrifice, and – no mean privilege – they received for themselves the skins and chines of all sacrificial beasts. This religious function of the kings is traced back to and made an integral part of the foundation of Sparta both in the Rhetra and in the manner of the recall of Pleistoanax. The existence and continued health of the state, it is implied, were bound up with the existence and continued health of the kingship (cf. Chapter 6 on Lysander's plans to alter the rules of eligibility for the kingship).

The next assertion of Herodotus, however, though formally ambiguous is almost certainly false for his own day and may merely have reflected the ideology of his royalist source (cf. Carlier 1977, 70-5). The kings, he says, could declare war on (or carry war to) any land they wished, and Spartans who attempted to prevent them from exercising this prerogative were liable to fall under a curse. However, earlier (5.75.2) Herodotus had himself recorded that, in consequence of a military fiasco in Attika in about 506 due to a radical division of opinion between Kleomenes and Damaratos, 'a law was passed in Sparta forbidding both kings to go out on the same campaign simultaneously'. Legislation in Sparta was a rarity, and laws were brief and not recorded in writing (Cartledge 1978a, 35). Such a law therefore betokens exceptional concern with, and amounts to a considerable inroads into, royal prerogative. Typically Herodotus does not say by what body the law was passed, nor indeed anything about the procedure of legislation in Sparta. But it seems that it was the Spartan citizen Assembly which took the final decision (see further Chapter 8). Kings who were subject to this degree of control by the citizens are unlikely to have had an unrestricted right to declare war, even if Herodotus should properly be interpreted to imply that they only had this right if both were agreed on the desirability of such a course of action. (The passages that have been cited in support of Hdt. 6.56 all refer to the situation after war has begun: Greenidge 1911, 98 and n.8.) Further restrictions imposed on the commanding king's initiative by the attachment to him of two Ephors and later a board of advisers too (first attested in 479 and 418 respectively) tell in the same sense; and the creation or regularization of the annual navarchy was a further limitation, potentially at least, of the king's freedom of command in war (cf. Chapter 6).

However, for all these limitations it remains true that the king's formal powers were greatest when he was in command of an army beyond the Spartan frontier, rather like those of a Roman *imperator* when he was *militiae* or beyond the sacred boundary of the city of Rome. Aristotle may have downgraded them to the status of mere hereditary generals in comparison with full-blooded kings possessed of extensive or absolute civil as well as military powers (*Pol.* 1285a7, 1271a40-1). But in a military state like Sparta automatic and exclusive access to supreme command of the home and allied armies was no small prerogative and a useful springboard to prestige, influence and patronage (cf. Chapters 9 and 12). On campaign a king even had the power of life and death, and in this as 'in almost every particular the position of the Spartan king in the field bears a striking resemblance to that of the Roman *imperator*' (Greenidge 1911, 99). Xenophon therefore was being misleading, perhaps deliberately so, when he referred to the kings' lifetime honours as being not greatly superior to those of private citizens – unless we should retain the *oikoi* of the manuscripts and so take Xenophon to be contrasting, not their lifetime with their posthumous honours, but their comparative lack of honours *at home* with their great honours abroad. Whatever the correct text of *LP* 15.8, the gap between the kings and private citizens, especially other office-holders, was certainly less pronounced in peacetime. Conversely, for an ambitious and moderately competent king war offered greater scope for personal aggrandizement – a consideration not irrelevant to the reign of Agesilaos.

(ii) Peace

The cardinal text runs as follows (Xen. *LP* 15.7):

The Kings and the Ephors exchange oaths every month, the Ephors swearing on behalf of the *polis*, the King on his own behalf. The form of the oath is that the King swears to be king in accordance with the city's established laws and customs, while the *polis* swears to maintain the kingship free of vexations so long as the King abides by his oath.

The onus was very obviously on the kings to obey the laws, and this together with the regularity of the oath-taking ceremony suggests that the practice was introduced as a consequence of some royal misdemeanour. The leading role allotted to the Ephors therein forbids a date for its introduction much if at all before the mid-sixth century, when one late and unreliable source (Diog. Laert. 1.68.6; with Burn 1960, 207,276) says that Chilon, one of the Seven Sages of ancient Greece, first yoked the Ephorate to the kings in equal harness. It was also about that time that we get our first specific evidence for relations between the Ephors and a king, although it should be noted (as it often is not) that Anaxandridas II refused the initial demand made by the Ephors alone that he divorce an apparently barren wife and only reluctantly complied with the subsequent request, made by the Ephors and Gerousia jointly, that he take a second wife bigamously who would bear a son and Agiad heir, thereby acting in what Herodotus or his informants considered to be 'an utterly un-Spartan manner' (Hdt. 5.39-40, with Cartledge 1981b, 102). Since this led to the disputed succession and controversial reign of Kleomenes I, the mutual oath-taking ceremony was perhaps first introduced after Kleomenes' distinctly suspicious death, allegedly by suicide (Hdt. 6.75, with Harvey 1979).

As we have seen, it was the same Kleomenes who provoked the passage of the law forbidding more than one king to hold a particular foreign command. It was probably also he who, so far as our evidence goes, was the first king to be put on trial in Sparta (Ste. Croix 1972, 351), and certainly it was Kleomenes who engineered the first known deposition of a fellow-king by successfully impugning his legitimacy with the aid of a suitably suborned Delphic priesthood (Hdt. 6.66). The impression is thus very strongly conveyed that the reign of Kleomenes was, after the sea-changes between about 800 and 650, a further watershed in the Spartan kingship. Thereafter the price of the continuing peacetime prerogatives that are shortly to be discussed was a marked diminution of formal political power and initiative. Apart from the oath-taking, this was symbolized by the kings' obligation to comply with a summons by the Ephors if it were repeated thrice (Plut. *Kleom.* 10.5).

Both Herodotus and Xenophon begin with the kings' prerogatives in sacrifice. At all public sacrifices they were entitled to preside, to sit down first to the sacrificial feast, to begin the eating of the meal, and to receive twice as large a portion as the other banqueters. Moreover, just as on campaign they received hides and chines from the sacrificial victims, so in peace they were granted choice pieces (*gera*, the same word as for 'prerogatives' in general) from the animals sacrificed. And in order that the kings should always have a stock of victims readily available, they were permitted to take one piglet from every litter produced should they wish. Nor were these their only economic privileges.

It was mentioned earlier that the kings shared a single mess. This was maintained at public expense (and so known as *hê damosia (skana)*, the public tent) rather than, as was the case with all other *suskania*, by contributions of produce from the members' own estates. A further distinction was that the kings were awarded double the normal rations when they ate in their public tent. This was not – as Xenophon is quick to explain – to enable them to eat twice as much, but so that they might pay honour to special guests. Xenophon himself was presumably honoured in this way by Agesilaos during his sojourns in Sparta (cf. Chapter 5). If, on the other hand, a king elected to eat at home (something strictly forbidden to other Spartans unless they were unavoidably delayed by involvement in a hunt or private sacrifice), they were penalized with half-rations or even, as happened to Agis II apparently in 418 (Plut. *Lyk.* 12.5), no rations at all. The regular membership of the royal mess at home is, unlike that of the commanding king's mess on campaign (Chapter 12), not known beyond the fact that it included the four Pythioi.

Besides being fed at public expense, the kings were also given a *medimnos* (72-3 litres) of barley and a Lakonian quart of wine at each new moon and on every seventh day of the lunar month, partly no doubt for purely religious reasons. But their unique right to possess 'choice' land in the territory of many Perioikic towns seems to have been a secular prerogative, since Xenophon (*LP* 15.3) says this was designed to ensure 'a reasonable competence without excessive wealth'. This was of course special pleading. For they also owned large amounts of Spartan land in the narrow sense, not to mention the 'treasure' for which Herodotus (6.62.2) was significantly prompted to use the good old Homeric word *keimêlion*. As Louis Gernet (as translated in Gordon 1981, 140) remarked, 'The notion of the royal treasure-house, store of riches, ... is founded upon the notion of the protective, powerful sacred objects kept in his safe stronghold by a legendary king or by a high god, lord of all.' In short, the kings were as a rule among the wealthiest of Spartans (cf. Cozzoli 1979, 40-5). Property therefore as well as prestige was at stake in succession disputes such as that involving Agesilaos, as we shall see in more detail later.

Turning from economics to politics, Herodotus mentions just three royal prerogatives. First, it lay with the kings to appoint *proxenoi*, diplomatic representatives for the citizens of other states, from among the Spartan citizens. It has often been noted that this contradicts normal Greek practice, whereby the other states would appoint their own *proxenoi*, but it sorts perfectly with the Spartans' general concern for direct control over all contacts between Spartans and non-Spartans expressed most notoriously in the periodic expulsions of foreigners from Sparta (the *xenêlasiai*: cf. Chapter 13). Given the importance of personal contacts in the conduct of foreign relations, this prerogative was a source of patronage and potential political influence.

Second, Herodotus relates that the kings had judicial prerogatives in only three spheres, implying thereby that originally their judicial competence had been much wider. These were respectively the right to allocate heiresses whose fathers had not provided for their betrothal before they died, to witness male adoptions, and to give judgments concerning public highways. There are unclarity and confusion here. Herodotus has probably misprised the nature of daughter-succession in Sparta, and the kings' alleged right to allocate heiresses (*patrouchoi*, i.e. daughters with no surviving brothers of the same father) was soon to fall into desuetude if indeed it was not already a thing of the past in Herodotus' day (cf. Cartledge 1981b, 97-9). As for the roads, it is unclear whether they were military or civilian, but presumably the former. On the other hand, the statement that the kings had the right merely to witness rather than effect or adjudicate male adoptions seems likely to be correct.

The third royal prerogative in the political sphere is mentioned by Herodotus apropos the Gerousia, though again his meaning is unclear. Thucydides (1.20.3) took him to be saying that the kings each had two votes in the Gerousia and that, when a king was absent from Sparta, these were cast for him by his nearest kinsman, who would thus be in a position to cast three votes including his own. But the likeliest interpretation of Herodotus' ambiguous and possibly corrupt text is that in this circumstance the nearest relative would give just two votes, his own and the king's by proxy. But whatever exactly Herodotus believed or meant to say, the passage does reveal the vital role of kinship in the recruitment and functioning of the Gerousia and indeed implies the potential importance of the body as a deliberative or decision-taking unit (see further Chapter 8). Herodotus might perhaps have added here or elsewhere that the kings might actually sit in judgment on each other, when the Gerousia together with the Ephors functioned as a Supreme Court to hear capital charges. As it is, the trial of Pausanias in 403 provides the earliest evidence for this remarkable procedure.

That more or less exhausts the prerogatives of the kings in peace and war. I have, however, reserved to the end three rather less tangible or material marks of honour. No one, not even an Ephor, might lay hands on a king, a prohibition sanctioned not only by positive law but also by *themis* or divine ordinance (Plut. *Agis* 19.9; cf. 21). Second, all except the Ephors were obliged to stand up in the presence of a king; this was a particularly notable obligation in Sparta, where juniors were otherwise bound to give up their seats in favour of their seniors and rise in their presence (e.g. Hdt. 2.80, noting the Egyptian parallel; or humorously Plut. *Lyk.* 20.15). It was thus a politically calculated reversal of roles for Agesilaos to have made a consistent point of getting off his official seat if an Ephor approached (and to have run, not walked, at the Ephors' first rather than third summons: Plut. *Ages.* 4.5). Third, when the king led out an army, some kind of representation of one of the twin Dioskouroi (Kastor and Polydeukes, brothers of Helen) was taken out with him; for these greatly revered deities served as 'the model and divine guarantee of the Spartan dyarchy' (Carlier 1977, 76n.42).

These three symbolic honours suggest, what Xenophon makes explicit in connection with their funerals (Chapter 16), that the kings of Sparta were regarded in their lifetime too as somewhat above or at least apart from the ordinary mortal estate. It may be an exaggeration to describe the kings as 'men invested with a sanctity as great as that which has ever encompassed a crowned head' (Greenidge 1911, 99-100), but Max Weber (1978, 1285; cf. Taeger 1935, 260; 1957, 33) was absolutely correct to speak of 'family-charismatic kingship' in Sparta. That is to say, in spite of the formal restrictions progressively imposed upon the powers of the kings as Sparta developed as a *polis*, the prerogatives of the kings in our period still bore clear traces of their sources of authority in charisma, 'i.e. actual revelation or grace resting in such a person as a savior, a prophet, or a hero' (Weber 1978, 954; cf. Aymard 1967, 149). This aspect of the Spartan kingship should be kept in the forefront of the mind as we turn to consider the motives and mechanisms of Agesilaos' accession.

Agis II, elder half-brother of Agesilaos, died of illness in the spring of 400, either in Sparta (3.3.1) or in Arkadia en route home from Delphi (Plut. *Lys.* 22.6). Xenophon and Plutarch agree, however, that the dedication to Delphic Apollo of a tithe of the huge booty plundered from the Eleians (Chapter 13) was Agis' last public act. Or rather that it was his last officially recognized public act. For Plutarch – but not, significantly, Xenophon – records that on his deathbed Agis belatedly acknowledged Latychidas as his legitimate son and so heir both to his considerable private fortune and to the Eurypontid throne. Even if Agis really did experience this deathbed conversion, and it was not just a story put about by those friends of his who canvassed furiously on Latychidas' behalf, it proved to be of no avail in the end. The doubts about the paternity of Latychidas were sufficiently strong, the widely suspected identity of his natural father so repugnant to Spartan opinion, and the backing for his rival so influential, that the crown in the contest for the Eurypontid succession was awarded to Agesilaos.

In theory the main point of a determinate vertical system of succession is that there should be no doubt as to the identity and legitimacy of the successor. This ideal gain is supposed to override such costs as the need for a regency in the case of a minority succession. Latychidas, however, was not the first Spartan prince to be involved in a succession dispute nor would he be the last, though he is the only one to have been formally adjudged a bastard (*nothos*), that is not the son of two Spartan parents. Damaratos, who as we shall see was deemed illegitimate retrospectively after reigning for something like a quarter of a century, was not (so far as is known) disinherited; and some nine generations later the usurping 'tyrant' Nabis claimed to be a direct descendant of his.

The first attested succession dispute occurred about 520, in suitably extraordinary circumstances. Anaxandridas II, as we have seen, had preferred bigamy to divorcing an apparently barren wife, who in accordance with traditional Greek male ideology was blamed for Anaxandridas' failure to practise the cardinal Spartan virtue of *teknopoiïa* (reproduction). Since she was a relative of Chilon, he may in fact have had other reasons besides devoted affection for not repudiating her. But in any event he did not neglect her. For after Kleomenes had been born to his second wife, he proceeded to have no less than three sons by the first, Dorieus being followed by Leonidas and Kleombrotos (possibly twins). The name given to Dorieus ('the Dorian') has been interpreted as Anaxandridas' way of indicating his rejection of Chilon's 'Achaian' policy (cf. Forrest 1980, 83); but whether or not so much can legitimately be read into his name, Dorieus grew up to be a young man in a hurry with ambitions beyond the station to which an accident of generative timing had condemned him.

On the death of their father, Dorieus disputed the succession with Kleomenes on the ground – accepted by Herodotus (5.42.1), who was following sources manifestly hostile to Kleomenes – that he was the superior in manly quality (*andragathia*). This could be a reference to the belief – again, shared by

Herodotus (5.42.1; 6.75.1) – that Kleomenes was not quite right in the head; but it could equally mean that Dorieus had performed spectacularly well in the *agôgê*, from which Kleomenes as heir-apparent had been exempted. Either way, however, Dorieus had no substantial case. For not only was Kleomenes the eldest son of Anaxandridas, but he had been born to him after his father had become king and was therefore – if Herodotus' assertion of porphyrogeniture in Sparta (7.3) carries any weight – doubly qualified to succeed.

There is no evidence that the claim of Dorieus to the throne was put to any kind of formal or legal test, unlike that of Latychidas. But in order to prove the illegitimacy of his Eurypontid co-king Damaratos and have him dethroned therefor twenty-five years after his unchallenged accession, Kleomenes needed some extraordinary and extraordinarily powerful sanction. This he naturally sought in the Delphic Oracle, just as it was through the Oracle's good offices that Pleistoanax later secured his restoration; but it took bribery to get the opinion he wanted, again as Pleistoanax was alleged to have been the beneficiary of similar corruption (cf. Zeilhofer 1959, 17-19).

The choice of Delphi was an obvious one. Once the Oracle had achieved panhellenic authority in the course of the eighth century (Rolley 1977, 131-46), Sparta had been quick to establish permanent quasi-diplomatic contacts with Delphi; and the oracle allegedly delivered to Kings Archelaos and Charilaos is by far the earliest of those which the most sceptical of modern scholars are prepared to consider as perhaps genuine (e.g. Fontenrose 1978, 272-3, Q12). The Great Rhetra, which enshrined the kings' privileged position in the Spartan constitution, either was, or was sanctioned by, a Delphic oracle. Moreover, relations between Sparta and Delphi were channelled through the four Pythioi, distinguished men whose appointment – possibly on a hereditary basis – was in the gift of the kings (see beginning of Chapter 4). Hence Kleomenes' reliance on a Delphic oracle, and perhaps too the Spartans' willingness to be convinced of Damaratos' illegitimacy.

We do not, however, know for certain which Spartan body or authority ruled on the legitimacy of Damaratos or that of his distantly related (?second cousin) replacement Latychidas II. But it was pretty clearly not the Assembly, since this lacked judicial powers of any kind (cf. Chapter 8). The likeliest supposition is that it was the same body as that which acted as a court of law in the trials of kings, that is – at least on the one occasion when its composition is specified (Paus. 3.5.2 – the trial of Pausanias in 403) – the Gerousia and Ephors in combination (cf. Ste. Croix 1972, 350-1; Kelly 1975, 42-3; 1981a, 52n.17). These two magisterial organs of state have already been witnessed concerting action regarding the succession in the case of Anaxandridas; and 'Baedeker' Pausanias (3.6.2) specifically states that the succession dispute between Areus (I) and Kleonymos in 309 was resolved by the Gerousia. So when Xenophon (3.3.4; *Ages.* 1.5) says that the decision as between Agesilaos and Latychidas rested with 'the *polis*' as a whole, that need not connote the involvement of the Assembly, which at most may have merely rubber-stamped a decision already taken by the Gerousia and Ephors. For Xenophon had an interest in representing Agesilaos as if he were 'the People's choice', and there are plenty of parallels for a warrior assembly having the right to recognize or acclaim a king, even if recognition was a formality and the choice automatic and predetermined: we need look no further afield than Macedon (cf. Lévy 1978, esp. 218-21).

Xenophon's two accounts of Agesilaos' accession differ significantly from each other in one respect. In the *Agesilaos* he waxes lyrical about the *aretê* of his hero, avering that he was chosen by the *polis* not just on grounds of birth (*genos*) but also because he was considered superior to his rival in *aretê* (moral excellence); and he infers from this choice that Agesilaos had already proved himself worthy to rule before his unheralded accession. The encomiast thus manages to breathe not a word about the politics of the struggle for high office. In the *Hellenika*, however, the memoirist Xenophon not only mentions but attributes the decisive role to the intervention of Lysander, although he does not go so far as to suggest (as does Plut. *Lys.* 25) that it was at Lysander's instigation that Agesilaos put forward his claim to the throne. After indulging himself with a hint of dialogue between the principals Latychidas and Agesilaos, couched for authentic effect in the Doric dialect (cf. Gray 1981), Xenophon introduces their chief supporting witnesses, respectively the oracle-expert (*chrêsmologos*) Diopeithes and Lysander.

From his ample resources Diopeithes produced this timely example (Fontenrose 1978, Q163):

> Boasting Sparta, be careful not to sprout
> a crippled kingship, you are sure-footed;
> unexpected troubles will overtake you,
> the lamentations of the storm of war
> destroyer of mankind (Paus. 3.8.9, trans. P. Levi)

This was not a Delphic oracle, though probably Apolline in origin, and it is noticeable that this succession dispute was not referred to Delphi for resolution. For this Lysander, who was not in good odour with the Delphic priesthood (cf. Chapter 6), probably deserves a great deal of credit. Indeed, the oracle may not even have been taken from a Spartan collection but could have been invented *ad hoc* (?as a variant of the oracle cited at DS 11.50.4 in a context of the 470s), if Diopeithes is the famous Athenian Diopeithes who had earlier pitted his skill with some success against Perikles. But whatever its origin and status, the oracle was an argument nicely calculated to appeal to the most august citizens of 'a state swayed beyond all others by fear of the gods' (Greenidge 1911, 79; see e.g. Hdt. 5.63.2; 6.82; 7.134.2). And Plutarch (*Comp. Ages. Pomp.* 2.2) was not alone in supposing that it was because the Spartans had ignored its literal meaning that they had subsequently had their arms engulfed by a sea of Agesilaos-inspired troubles.

What counted in 400, though, was that the argument had failed to convince the Spartan *polis*. For Lysander stood forward as Agesilaos' champion, and rather as Themistokles had done eighty years before in the face of an overtly defeatist Delphic oracle he gave to this oracle a symbolic interpretation that turned its obvious, literal meaning on its head. The Spartan kingship would go lame, he argued, if a person of improper birth, that is one who was not a lineal descendant of Herakles, should become king. The fact that he did not attempt to rebut the oracle by pointing out that the lameness of Agesilaos was the result of an accident or wound virtually proves that it was congenital (cf. beginning of Chapter 3) and so, according to a widely distributed folk belief, all the more sinister, especially in a king.

Lysander was thereby alleging what Agesilaos had already claimed in Xenophon's set-piece dialogue, that Latychidas was not the natural son of Agis. In this he was much aided by Agis himself, who seems to have been convinced of Latychidas' illegitimacy until his deathbed recantation. The fact that Latychidas had been reared and not exposed was presumably therefore a function of the responsibility in this matter being entrusted in Sparta to the appropriate tribal elders and not to the natural or putative father (cf. Chapter 3). Xenophon, however, writing as always for those who already knew, did not trouble to say who his real father was widely rumoured to be. Thucydides, who austerely excluded such picaresque biographical details, merely hints at his identity (8.12.2, with A. Andrewes in Gomme 1981, 26). Plutarch was less restrained: the adulterous progenitor was Alkibiades.

This was surely the most sensational scandal of the Athenian War and perhaps the greatest domestic scandal of all Spartan history. What is more, the rumour may even have been true (*contra* Luria 1927; Littman 1969; Kelly 1975, 46-9). For Alkibiades was living traitorously at Sparta at what could have been the operative time; his chameleon character and towering ambition were perfectly capable of prompting him both to 'go native' and to exploit in unsporting fashion the (to an Athenian) surprising availability of Spartan wives for extra-marital sex (cf. Cartledge 1981b, 102-4); and Agis' wife Timaia was so far from invoking a supernatural visitation to explain her pregnancy (the technique employed by Damaratos' mother, according to Hdt. 6.63-6; cf. Burkert 1965) that she reportedly gave currency to the rumour by calling Latychidas in private 'Alkibiades' (originally a Spartan name, incidentally: Thuc. 8.6.3). It is true that the Ephors were supposed to ensure that a Spartan king's children were pure in blood (Plat. *Alk.* 1.121), but they could have been bribed or outwitted. As for the claim by Xenophon's Latychidas that Timaia had always maintained that Agis was his natural father, this was clearly self-interested since there was a great deal of property at stake. However, it has to be said that the only remotely credible piece of circumstantial evidence in favour of Alkibiades' paternity concerns the earthquake that caused all the trouble in the first place. For this could be identified with the one independently attested by Thucydides (8.6.5) that occurred in winter 413/2. But against this it must be pointed out that earthquakes were not infrequent in hollow Lakedaimon (cf. Cartledge 1976c), and besides Xenophon and Plutarch report the effect of the earthquake in question with a significant difference that calls into doubt the veracity of the whole story: for Xenophon it was by implication Alkibiades who was driven out into the open from his adulterous bed by the earthquake, for Plutarch it was Agis who thereafter superstitiously refrained from intercourse with Timaia for a period during which Latychidas was conceived (or so Agis calculated).

The evidence against Alkibiades falls well short of proof, therefore, but there seems to be sufficient reason to suppose that, whoever the natural father of Latychidas really was, it was probably not Agis. The role of Lysander in 400, then, was not so much to convince the relevant Spartans of this as to persuade them not to be swayed either by Agis' belated recognition of Latychidas or by the apparent meaning of Diopeithes' oracle. We do not know whether Lysander was, as Thucydides (4.84.2) said of Brasidas, 'an excellent speaker – for a Spartan'. But if the sources are taken at face value, it was anyway not his eloquence but his personal authority that won over the Spartans, much as that of Kleomenes I had convinced an earlier Spartan audience to accept his interpretation of an ambiguous portent (Hdt. 6.82.2).

The intervention of Lysander thus raises a cluster of questions concerning both the development of his and Agesilaos' careers and the character of Spartan politics in the post-war period. What had Lysander been up to since the overturning of his policy towards Athens and his imperial conception as a whole in 403/2 (Chapter 6)? Was his support given to Agesilaos because he hoped to use his former beloved to further his own policy objectives, as he is later said (3.4.2) to have urged the appointment of Agesilaos to the Asiatic command so as to secure the re-establishment of his dekarchies? Did Agis recognize Latychidas at the last moment (if he did) precisely because he anticipated that Lysander would thus seek to direct Spartan policy through a puppet king? And how did Agesilaos regard this vigorous championing of his cause by his one-time lover? Did he welcome it, *faute de mieux*, as the only way of achieving a long-cherished ambition to be king, the realisation of which was now in jeopardy? Or did the initiative, as Plutarch supposed, come rather from Lysander? Certainty is impossible. But one ingredient studiously ignored by Xenophon must be stirred into the brew even at the risk of causing the pot to boil over: Lysander's alleged revolutionary constitutional plans.

If the hypotheses and arguments put forward in Chapter 6 have any plausibility, it is not impossible that in or even before 403 Lysander had conceived the idea of transforming himself from the uncrowned king of Hellas into a (or the) crowned king of Sparta. Specifically, he may have sought to take advantage of a regular state ritual designed to test the validity of the kings' rule in order to challenge the legitimacy of the two royal houses and, with oracular support from Apollo at Delphi, Zeus at Dodona and Ammon at Siwah, throw open the kingship to all 'descendants of Herakles' rather than just descendants of Agis and Euryp(h)on. Ideally, perhaps, he would have wished to become a sole ruler of some description; but as the history of Kleomenes III and Nabis was to show, that sort of constitutional change ought to have implied the espousal of a social and economic revolution for which Lysander betrayed no hint of a taste. However that may be, the combination of Kings Agis and Pausanias against him in 403 proved irresistible, and by 400 the best Lysander could hope to achieve was to act as kingmaker for Agesilaos, which he did with complete success.

As for Agesilaos, even if he had a notion that Lysander had been manoeuvring with an eye to becoming king, that was no reason to abstain from taking advantage of Lysander's support. For Lysander's failures will have been both reassuring and instructive to Agesilaos. Lysander now needed him to be king as much as he needed Lysander's help to become king, and Agesilaos could in time employ the very institutional advantages of the kingship that Lysander craved in order to rid himself of an awkward and embarrassing rival. That at any rate is precisely what Agesilaos did in Asia in 396/5 after apparently submitting docilely to Lysander's direction in foreign policy (Chapter 9).

Once the statutory ten days of public mourning for Agis were over, Agesilaos acceded to the Eurypontid throne to the accompaniment of the traditional dances and sacrifices. But the declaration of the *polis* in favour of Agesilaos did not only exclude Latychidas from the Eurypontid throne; it also debarred him as a bastard from all the rest of what Damaratos had called his *patrôïa gerea* (Hdt. 7.104.2), most conspicuously his paternal inheritance. Agesilaos was therefore publicly adjudged sole heir to Agis' fortune. But instead of keeping it all for himself he gave half of it away to those related to him through his mother's second marriage, who were in reduced circumstances. Xenophon in his encomium (*Ages.* 4.5-6) cites this as an example of Agesilaos' 'justice in money matters' (*hê eis chrêmata dikaiosunê*). But Plutarch (*Ages.* 4.1) was nearer the mark when he says that Agesilaos aimed thereby to win good will and a fine reputation in place of envy and hostility (though Plutarch seems wrongly to have thought that it was to the poor maternal relatives of Latychidas that the half-share was going). Since one of these maternal *homogonoi* of Agesilaos was his half-brother Teleutias (probably son of Eupolia by Theodoros: Poralla 1913, p.159; cf. Lewis 1977, 35), we may go further with confidence and affirm that Agesilaos' apparently disinterested largesse brought him, as it was designed to, energetic supporters among the Spartan elite. Financially, at all events, the 'gift' cost him little or nothing. His father's legacy was sufficient to enable Kyniska (probably Agesilaos' full sister) to race winning horses at Olympia, and she probably inherited less from Archidamos than Agesilaos and had fewer opportunities for increasing her wealth through presents and other such kingly perks as the mysterious 'royal tribute' (*basilikos phoros*: Cozzoli 1979, 54). In other words, this first act of Agesilaos as king was calculated to win him friends and influence people. It shows that from the very outset he had a clear idea of how to begin laying the groundwork of the informal political authority discussed in Chapter 9.

It was later in 400 that the Spartans committed what has been called, no doubt with some exaggeration, 'the greatest error of policy ever made by Sparta' (Cawkwell 1972b, 46). This was the decision to declare war on Persia ostensibly to liberate the Greeks of Asia from the Persian empire. The possible reasons and implications of this decision will be explored in context in Chapter 11. Here it will be enough to state in advance the conclusion that behind it lay the recent accession of Agesilaos. To substantiate that claim, it is necessary first to consider in detail what can be ascertained about the modalities of policymaking and decision-taking in Sparta.

8

Agesilaos and Spartan Policymaking

There is a good deal of cogency in the doctrine that what may be called the Crown at Sparta was not limited; but each of the kings was, and the kings in Sparta were at times not only equal but opposite. (Adcock 1953, 166-7)

Spartan policy, while in general it continued in one direction, did none the less from time to time deviate strangely. (Smith 1953/4, 274)

Someone somewhere in the Greek world at some time before Herodotus published his *Histories* had the blindingly simple but still brilliant perception that all species of political constitution may in theory be subsumed under just three genera: rule by one, rule by some, rule by all. This was an instance of Greek 'scientific' thinking at its best and most fruitful, reducing issues to their basic terms and producing generalizations that account for the greatest possible number of observable, empirically verifiable phenomena. Paradoxically, though, the discovery caused a major headache for those writers in antiquity who had an interest in classifying the *politeia* (conventionally translated 'constitution') of Sparta (cf. Bordes 1982, esp. 280-95). The ensuing mental chaos is most clearly to be seen, again paradoxically, in the *Politics* of Aristotle, who for once found that *ta phainomena*, received opinions, were rather a barrier than a window to enlightenment.

During a sharp critique of the ideal state of Plato's *Laws* Aristotle concedes that one might perhaps approve it if it were being proposed as a more acceptable, practicable model than any more extreme utopia (such as the *Republic*, already rejected by Aristotle). Philosophically, however, it should not be approved, even as a second best:

For in that case one might well prefer the Spartan, or some other constitution with a more aristocratic basis. There are indeed some who say that the best constitution is one composed of a mixture of all types, and who therefore praise the Spartan. Some of these say that it is made up out of oligarchy, monarchy, and democracy: its kingship is monarchy, the authority of its Elders is oligarchy, and yet it is also run democratically through the authority exercised by the Ephors, who come from the people. Others, though, say that the Ephorate is a tyranny, and that the democratic element is to be found in the common meals and the other features of daily life (*Pol.* 1265b31-66a2, trans. T.J. Saunders slightly modified)

Elsewhere (*Pol.* 1294b20-35) Aristotle reveals a deeper split of opinion. The Spartan constitution, he says, is in fact a combination of elements from other 'pure' constitutions, but the mix is so good that, while many label it a democracy, others see it as an oligarchy. The former do so

> because the system has a number of democratic features: first the rearing of the children, under which the sons of the rich are reared in the same way as the sons of the poor and receive an education which the sons of the poor could also receive; then similarly in the next age group, and when they are grown up, the arrangements for feeding in the communal messes are the same for all ... There is also the fact that the people choose the members of the Gerousia and share in the Ephorate, the two most important offices in the state.

On the other hand, there are those who describe the Spartan *politeia* as an oligarchy

> because of its many oligarchical features: the absence of the use of the lot, all offices being elected; the power of few to pronounce binding sentence of death or exile, and many other similar points.

From this second passage Aristotle's own view, that Sparta was a *miktê* or 'mixed' constitution, might seem to be tolerably clear. Not so. For elsewhere in the *Politics* he expresses or assumes two other views, one of these at least with apparently firm conviction. On the one hand, he several times treats Sparta as a species of aristocracy that inclines to oligarchy (*Pol.* 1293b7ff., 1307a34ff., 1316a, 1316b6ff.). On the other hand, in his extended critique of the Spartan *politeia* in Book 2, which follows shortly on that of Plato's ideal states, he states bluntly that the near-tyrannical power of the Ephorate 'has caused further damage to the constitution, for an aristocracy has turned into a democracy' (*Pol.* 1270b17-18).

This contradiction between the 'mixed constitution' view of Book 4 and the 'democracy' view of Book 2 has been variously explained away (Cloché 1943; de Laix 1974). But all that we may confidently assert is that, whatever Aristotle's 'final' classification of the Spartan *politeia* would have been, his assessment of its success as a constitution by the time the *Politics* was being delivered as lectures to his pupils at the Lyceum in the 330s was determinedly negative (*Pol.* 1333b5-34a40). As for helping us to decide whether Sparta was an aristocracy, oligarchy, democracy, 'mixed constitution', or whatever, the *Politics* is a perhaps surprisingly unstraightforward tool. It is not always clear how far Aristotle was addressing the present Sparta, how far the past; there are signs that his first-hand information improved dramatically in the course of composing the different drafts that are rather awkwardly stitched together in the work as it has come down to us; and the principal discussion of the Spartan constitution is in its extant form an unbalanced survey of the main criticisms that could be levelled against it and of the chief points of comparison and contrast that could be drawn with the constitutions of Crete and Carthage rather than a systematic account of its nature and workings. Xenophon's misnamed *Lak. Pol.* obviously does not remedy these defects (cf. Chapter 5); and the Aristotelian *Lak. Pol.* (one of 158 such 'Constitutions' produced at the Lyceum) survives only in the truncated summary by Herakleides Lembos and indirectly through the quite extensive use made of it by Plutarch in his *Lykourgos*.

None the less, the *Politics* passages already quoted or referred to and other related passages do have their value, in two ways in particular. First, they introduce the two partly overlapping and mutually reinforcing aspects of the aptly named Spartan 'mirage' which have jointly ensured that much of the voluminous modern literature on the Spartan constitution is either more or less free invention or intelligent speculation distorted by ancient theorizing: the Lykourgos legend, and the mixed constitution theory. Second, they remind us forcibly that the Greek words conventionally translated as 'constitution' and 'laws' (*politeia, nomoi*) have a much wider reference in Greek, such that it is necessary to avoid making the mistake of drawing too sharp a distinction between legal formalities and the actual functioning of the constitutional machinery.

Some people, Aristotle noted, rejected the constitution under which they happened to live and extolled the Spartan instead. Such a man pre-eminently was Kritias, the oligarch installed by Lysander as head of a puppet junta at Athens in summer 404 (Chapter 14). 'I suppose it is agreed,' Xenophon (2.3.34) makes him say at the rigged trial of his rival oligarch Theramenes, 'that the best constitution is that of Sparta.' As good as his spoken word, Kritias wrote on the Spartan *politeia* both in verse and in prose and thus became the godfather of the Spartan 'mirage', the partly distorted, partly invented image created by and for non-Spartans (with not a little help from their Spartan friends) of what Sparta ideally represented (see further Chapter 22). What appealed above all to Kritias and his kind, and to philosophers of politics too, was the supposed stability and discipline of the Spartan *politeia*, for which an alternative name was significantly *kosmos* or 'order' (Hdt. 1.65.4). *Eukosmia, eutaxia* (discipline) and *eunomia* (orderliness as well as obedience to good laws) were notions that sprang readily to the lips of *bien pensant* oligarchs throughout Greece when they contemplated Sparta, especially to the lips of those who owed part of their education to the Spartan *agôgê* (the *trophimoi xenoi* of 5.3.9) and power in their own states to Sparta's general support for oligarchy. In proportion as *stasis* (civil strife, often outright civil war), the reverse of stability, grew endemic and increasingly fraught in Greece during the fourth century, so the voices raised in favour of Sparta became more insistently shrill.

The Lakonizers (*lakônizontes*), however, could no more agree among themselves on a precise characterization of the Spartan constitution than more critical or dispassionate observers. A popular exit from the impasse was to embrace a version of the 'mixed constitution' theory. According to the two main variants of this conception, the best because most stable constitution *either* combined in a harmonious whole ingredients from each of the three basic constitutional genera *or* it comprised elements from each which mutually acted as checks and balances. The latter is the version to which Aristotle refers and which at one point he apparently espoused. It is uncertain when the theory was first devised in any form, though Thucydides (8.97.2) may imply that it was current before the end of the fifth century; so far as is known, however, it was not applied to Sparta before the fourth. It is, on the other hand, easier to suggest why it was invented and found particularly applicable to Sparta. For the theory sought in effect to ensure 'a balance in the political class struggle' (Ste. Croix 1981, 75) between 'rich' and 'poor' Greek citizens, by allowing these two decisive groups in society a share in the control of the state without affecting the social basis of the two classes, namely their unequal ownership of (especially landed) property. All too often, or so it seemed to the theorists (who were of course leisured property-owners), democracy of any kind involved confiscation of or distraint upon the property of the few rich by the poor majority. How much better it would be, they thought, if democratic egalitarianism were tempered by a judicious admixture of oligarchy, aristocracy and kingship. Needless to say, such theorizing tended to bear as much – or rather as little – fidelity to the realities of Spartan political life as Polybius' notorious attempt to apply it to the constitution of the Roman Middle Republic; and there is a great deal to be said for the cynical opinion of Tacitus (*Ann.* 4.33) that a mixed constitution can hardly be achieved or, if achieved, cannot be lasting. But Aristotle has none the less had his more recent supporters (e.g. Greenidge 1911, 92-107; Michell 1952, 145).

So too there have been scholars prepared to swallow much of what I have called for short the Lykourgos legend, which overlaps with and reinforces the 'mixed constitution' theory in its stress on the supposed absence of *stasis* from Sparta ever since the lawgiving of Lykourgos. Even the Spartans, though, were unsure whether Lykourgos had been a man or a god (Hdt. 1.65.2-3), and his person is probably best left out of account as a no doubt intriguing side-issue. The point worth discussing is whether Classical Sparta really was, as the legend maintained, the paradigm of a state that owed all its most basic economic, social and political institutions to the *nomoi* proposed as a package by a single lawgiver (*nomothetês*).

If these institutions be regarded as creations *ex novo* by 'Lykourgos', then the picture is clearly false. But if they are taken as products of a revolutionary transformation of Spartan society that involved some innovation but also much re-adaptation of previously existing institutions, then the ancient picture (Hdt. 1.65.2-5; Thuc. 1.18.1) of an exceptionally disordered Sparta reduced to order by the application of conscious legislative principles does begin to look very much more plausible. The bulk of the reforms, as I have already suggested (Chapter 2), could have been introduced during the first half of the seventh century. But in the present context it does not matter so much when precisely they were introduced as that they had been introduced long before the time of Aristotle and his fellow theorists. The peculiarity of Sparta's political development was that, whereas for (*ex hypothesi*) the seventh century it was precocious, by the fourth it looked arrested and antiquated. Put differently, in regard to the evolution of her political institutions Sparta's Archaic period (chronologically speaking) was also her 'classical' era (qualitatively speaking). That explains why her *politeia* could not be slotted neatly into the preconceived categories of fifth- and fourth-century political thought (cf. Spahn 1977, 98; and esp. Nippel 1980, 124-31).

This does not of course mean that the Spartan constitution did not alter after the seventh century. There is enough evidence to show that changes in the rules of government were introduced by formal legislation. But Sparta was of set purpose a conservative society, prone to overvalue the past, and so changes deemed inevitable were consciously restricted in scope and content. The Spartans would have understood the Romans' reverence for the *mos maiorum*, the way of the ancestors, and their conservatism helps explain the continued existence of what struck other Greeks as anomalous survivals from an archaic past, such as the kingship. Not even the Spartans, however, were immune to the law that social and economic changes – like those affecting Sparta profoundly in the fifth and fourth centuries (Chapter 10) – inevitably entail alterations in the character of a state's constitution. Indeed, this was especially true of an ancient Greek *polis*, whose *politeia* in a broad sense was its life and soul. It was not, that is to say, merely a dry collection of formal rules, chiefly instructions to officials, but rather it grew, developed, changed with the collective consciousness and life-experience of the citizens, the *politai* or *polis*-people. 'Men are the *polis*', as Thucydides' Nikias put it (Thuc. 7.77.7); and seen in this light the Spartan *agôgê* and common meals were just as important 'constitutionally' as the formal powers of the major components in the Spartan decision-taking process, as Aristotle makes crystal clear.

So much by way of introduction to the strengths and weaknesses of Aristotle's *Politics* as a guide to understanding the Spartan constitution. For matters of substance, above all particular policy decisions, it is obviously necessary to turn also to the historical authors. But here too a preliminary caveat must be entered. Thucydides employed his enforced exile from Athens after 424 fruitfully by seeing what was being done on both sides, especially the Peloponnesian (Thuc. 5.26.5). But in Sparta itself, or in attempting to pump certain Spartan informants, he met a stone wall of silence. Partly no doubt this was because he was an Athenian, partly it was because he was Thucydides. But what he darkly called 'the secrecy of the *politeia*' (Thuc. 5.68.2) was not peculiarly reserved for him. This was the common experience of all but a few privileged foreigners, who either became Spartans by adoption or were trusted lakonizers. Other visitors to Sparta might reasonably expect to be swept up in one of the periodic *xenêlasiai* (expulsions of non-Spartans). As for the privileged, they had either no occasion or (as in the case of Xenophon) no desire to tell all about the secret springs of Spartan policy-making. So we should expect – to borrow a remark of Cassius Dio (53.19.2) on the principate of Augustus – much that happened in Sparta to be kept quiet, much that did not happen to be bruited abroad.

Still, the following analysis of the machinery of decision-making in Sparta and the way in which the principal components meshed together to produce political actions by the state is intended at least to be as complete as possible and, by stressing factors that have not perhaps received their due attention from recent students, explain why and how for most of his reign Agesilaos was able to secure the implementation of the policies he favoured and actively promoted. The present chapter will concentrate on the formal mechanisms, the next on the informal, but neither, needless to say, can be fully understood in isolation from the other.

The four major structural components of the Spartan *politeia* in its political

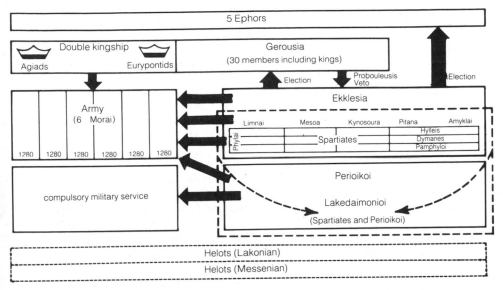

Fig. 8. Policymaking in Sparta: schematic flow-chart

aspect during the 'age of Xenophon' were the kingship, the Gerousia, the Ephorate and the Assembly (Fig. 8). (I leave out of account the lesser civil magistracies and subordinate military commands and simply note the absence of evidence for a defined *cursus honorum* or ladder of offices.) Since I have set out in detail the formal powers of the kings in the previous chapter, it will be enough to repeat here that there was a marked disparity between those they enjoyed in war, which rivalled the panoply available to a Roman *imperator*, and those they might use at home in peacetime – a disparity potentially exacerbated by the fact that both kings might seek to be politically decisive at the same time but in opposite causes, whereas on campaign the command was entrusted to a single king. However, as I shall hope now to demonstrate, the formal restrictions on their domestic powers were the beginning not the end of the story, which may appropriately commence with the Gerousia of which the kings were *ex officio* members.

This was the most senior political body in Sparta in every sense. With just two potential exceptions, the kings, it was quite literally a senate, a body of old men; membership of it was regarded as the highest political honour in Sparta; and, as will be argued below, its corporate powers outweighed those of any other political institution. The one certain qualification for membership for all but the kings was to have attained the age of sixty. That is, the Gerousia was recruited from men who had passed the age of obligatory active military service between their twenty-first and sixtieth years inclusive (e.g. 5.4.13); once recruited, they served for life (cf. Rhodes 1981a, 108, on the Athenian Areiopagos). Modern opinions differ, however, over the important question whether eligibility was also restricted legally to a defined group of privileged, that is aristocratic families (cf.

Ste. Croix 1972, 353-4). Certainly there was an aristocracy in Sparta, and certainly the language of both Xenophon (*LP* 10.1: *kalokagathia*) and Aristotle (*Pol.* 1306a18-19: *dunasteutikê*; see further below) is compatible with the existence of such a limitation. But it cannot be proved, and so it is probably safest to assert only that in practice, *de facto* rather than *de iure*, the Gerontes were drawn from a restricted social group (cf. Bringmann 1980, 472, 483-4).

This can only have intensified a competition for membership that was already intense for other reasons. For besides the kings there were only twenty-eight 'ordinary' members. This number will probably never be satisfactorily explained, but its precise definition marks a stage of political development beyond that visible in the poems of Homer (cf. Finley 1979, 82). Anyhow, a relatively few people, equal in social status, competing for a minute number of places that might be held for life in the most honorific of Spartan political bodies: small wonder that there was fierce canvassing for office involving the use of bribery (Arist. *Pol.* 1271a4-5, 10-12) or that Aristotle's adjective to describe the method of selection should connote manipulation as well as limited eligibility (*dunasteutikê*; cf. Rahe 1980b, 387n.8; Rhodes 1981a, 447-8). Before consideration of any further implications of this adjective let us see how Gerontes were appointed.

All voting in the Spartan Assembly, as Thucydides (1.87.2) was typically careful to remark, was conducted by shouting (*boa*), not by secret ballot (*psêphos*) nor even by the raising of hands (*cheirotonia*). Thus candidates for the Gerousia processed singly before the assembled electorate of all duly qualified citizens, and the relative loudness of the Assembly's favourable shouts was assessed by a select panel of men who were shut up out of sight in a windowless building and were not supposed to know the order in which the candidates appeared. Knowledge of this remarkable procedure is owed proximately to Plutarch (*Lyk.* 26.3-5), but he almost certainly took the details from the lost Aristotelian *Lak. Pol.*

Undoubtedly this was the sort of easily manipulable voting method that would have earned Aristotle's curt dismissal of it as 'childish' (*Pol.* 1271a10). But, as we have seen, he also characterized the method of election as *dunasteutikê*, which implied the further notion of restricted eligibility. Indeed, I would argue that it implied even more. A *dunasteia* (of which this is the feminine adjective) was for Aristotle 'a cabal of "powerful people" (*dunatoi*) acting in an arbitrary and sharply oligarchical manner' (Saunders 1981, 153); or, to put it in terms yet more obnoxious to Greek republican sensibilities, 'a small group which exercised arbitrary authority *without due control of law*' (Jones, A.H.M., 1966, 174n.36; my italics). In one of its forms a *dunasteia* might seek to perpetuate itself by co-option on a hereditary basis. Now the Spartan Gerousia was not strictly a hereditary body. But the system of proxy voting, whereby an absent king's vote might be cast by his nearest relative (Hdt. 6.57.5, discussed in Chapter 7), implies that at least one other member of each royal house could normally be expected to be a member of the Gerousia at any time. Which conveys, I would say, a pretty broad hint as to who might be behind the manipulation of the election procedure. Moreover, Herodotus' disclosure of this system of proxy voting not only reveals that votes in the Gerousia, unlike those in the Assembly, were normally counted but also strongly suggests that it was important for the votes to be counted or at any rate individually registered by some means, especially in the case of a king. In fact, as we shall shortly see, voting in the Gerousia was open.

Let us now turn to consider the contexts in which the Gerousia might be required to make decisions important and controversial enough to demand the counting of heads. The one occasion on which it is known precisely how the vote was split is the trial of King Pausanias in 403 (Paus. 3.5.2). Pausanias was being prosecuted on a capital charge arising out of his conduct of a campaign in Attika (Chapter 14) by a court consisting of the Gerousia sitting with the five Ephors. The implications of this trial for the nature of the Spartan decision-taking process will be examined closely at the end of this chapter; suffice it to say here that the trial is a classic illustration of Xenophon's general statement (*LP* 10.2; cf. Arist. *Pol.* 1270b38-40, 1294b31-4) that the Gerousia was the competent court in capital cases. There was, moreover, no appeal from its verdicts except in the perverted sense that a verdict of 'not guilty' did not necessarily rule out a further trial on precisely the same charge at some later date – as Pausanias learned to his cost in 395. Retrospectively, in other words, and to a smaller extent prospectively, the Gerousia's (and sometimes at least the Ephorate's) control of supreme criminal jurisdiction exercised a powerful influence on the determination and conduct of foreign policy. For a king whose influence in the Gerousia was parlous might have to reckon with the possibility of a major political trial as an almost routine occurrence whenever there were deep divisions over foreign policy, as there were throughout the age of Xenophon. This point is made explicitly in an important passage of the *Hellenika* (6.4.5), where the friends of King Kleombrotos advise him to prosecute the war with Thebes vigorously if he does not wish to be the victim of a successful prosecution; the Battle of Leuktra followed shortly.

If that was the total extent of the Gerousia's formal political power, it would be impressive enough, especially as Sparta was a society imbued with a pronounced, almost exaggerated respect for and deference to old age. But it is possible to argue that the Gerousia was much more than the Spartan Supreme Court, that it was in fact – as Aristotle and Plutarch clearly believed – the kingpin of the Spartan constitution. The case rests on the interpretation placed upon two further powers held by the Gerousia, *nomophulakia* and *probouleusis*.

Together with the Ephorate, the Gerousia had a general supervision of Spartan *nomoi*, laws and customs. Since the positive laws were unwritten (cf. Cartledge 1978a, 35), the interpretation of them was clearly a powerful political weapon, at least potentially so. Moreover, in their *nomophulakia* (guardianship of the *nomoi*) the Gerousia's power is akin to that exercised at Athens by the Areiopagos before and perhaps even after the passage of Solon's reforms in 594. There has been much debate as to what precisely Solon prescribed in this regard (cf. Rhodes 1981a, 315-16); but unlike Rhodes, I incline to the view of those who in his words 'have thought guardianship of the laws to be a power of overriding the assembly if it passed an illegal or otherwise undesirable resolution'.

With hindsight it is apparent that Solon's political (and economic) reforms set Athens on the road to democracy, a system of government in which sovereignty (*kratos*) resided with the People (*dêmos*) meeting in their Assembly (*ekklêsia*) and popular jury-courts (*dikastêria*). In the developed Athenian democracy of the fifth century a cardinal role in decision-making and legislating was played by the procedure of preliminary deliberation or *probouleusis*. No decree or law might legally be passed by the Athenian Assembly without its having been deliberated in advance by a smaller body, the popular Council consisting of 500 members, and presented to the Assembly in the form of a pre-deliberated motion (*probouleuma*). There was no popular Council at Sparta, but *probouleusis* was also a feature of the Classical Spartan constitution, it being the function of the Gerousia. Indeed, since Sparta was one of the first Greek states (if not the first) to give its decision-making and legislative procedures a fixed, defined form, and since the texts which enshrine or apparently presuppose *probouleusis* in Sparta – respectively the Great Rhetra (*ap.* Plut. *Lyk.* 6) and the 'Eunomia' poem of Tyrtaios (fr. 4 West) – may be dated to the first half of the seventh century, it is possible that the technique of *probouleusis* was invented in Sparta and borrowed therefrom by Athens in the person of Solon (cf. Andrewes 1954). On the principle of the economy of hypotheses, moreover, one could argue that it was invented at Sparta to meet the revolutionary situation that prompted the Great Rhetra as a whole (*contra* Sealey 1969).

More scholarly ink has been spilt, often to no good effect, on the fifty-odd words of this corrupt text than on any other similar document of comparable length. This is not the place to increase the pool greatly, especially as I have already added my own few drops (Cartledge 1980b, 99-106; add now Welwei 1979; Bringmann 1980; Ducat 1983, 202-4). So I just print a translation, which is also inevitably an interpretation, and summarise briefly my understanding of the document's context and significance.

> Having established a cult of Syllanian (?) Zeus and Athena, having done the 'tribing and obing', and having established a Gerousia of 30 members including the kings, (1) season in, season out they are to celebrate the festival of Apollo between Babyka and Knakiôn; (2) the Gerousia is both (a) to introduce proposals and (b) to stand aloof; (3) the *damos* is to have power to [in Plutarch's gloss on a badly garbled Doric phrase] 'give a decisive verdict'; (4) but if the *damos* speaks crookedly, the Gerousia and kings are to be removers.

Like the rest of the reform package of which I believe the Rhetra was an integral part (land redistribution, *agôgê*, common messes, hoplite reform), the Rhetra enshrined a mixture of tradition and innovation and was introduced in the first half of the seventh century. Kings, Council of Elders, *damos* (people) – this is the Homeric trinity. But in Homer kings ruled in the full sense: theirs was the sovereignty, the power of final decision. The reactionary Tyrtaios seems to have wanted to preserve this position: 'Let initiative in counsel belong to the god-honoured kings, who have care of the lovely city of Sparta' (trans. Sealey 1969, 257); but the Rhetra enacted otherwise. For in this enigmatic text the kings, who are called by the religious-sounding title 'founder-leaders' (*archagetai*), appear in the main body of the document merely as members of the Gerousia, not in their own right. This clearly marks a retreat from the Homeric situation. In the so-called 'Rider' (Clause 4, above) they do seem to appear independently, but again in close conjunction with and indeed after the Gerousia.

The Gerousia, we learn, was empowered both to introduce proposals and to stand aloof, that is presumably to refuse to introduce proposals. The recipient of their proposals was to be the *damos*, here no doubt used in the sense of the mass of the common people as opposed to the nobility. This *damos* meeting in assembly at unspecified but perhaps regular intervals was empowered to give a decisive verdict, exercising what is described as *kratos*. This was one of the standard words for political sovereignty in Classical Greece, as in *dêmokratia*. But, as the final clause of the Rhetra at once makes plain, the *kratos* of the Spartan *damos* was severely hedged about, so severely in fact that it may only be described as passive or negative. That is to say, although the sorts of decisions that were to be governed by the Rhetra procedure of *probouleusis* were valid only when given the popular assent, the initiative in presenting proposals lay with the Gerousia, which seemingly might also reject any decision that it considered to have been reached improperly. In effect, therefore, according to the Rhetra the Gerousia enjoyed a right of both prospective and retrospective veto. The framing of the document in such vague terms, a characteristically archaic feature, materially corroborated this right.

By speaking just now of 'the sorts of decisions' the Rhetra procedure was to govern I was trying not to prejudge the issue of whether this procedure applied to all public decisions or only to decisions of domestic as opposed to foreign policy. For Aristotle (*Pol.* 1298a24-8, 1298b5-8) indicates that in some states decisions of foreign policy were reached by a different method from that in use for, say, legislation; and Ste. Croix (1972, 127) is inclined to believe that this may have been the case in Sparta. Other scholars, indeed, have thought that the Rhetra procedure as a whole was a dead letter by the fifth century, not to mention those who have condemned the document as a fourth-century forgery. Neither of the two latter views seems cogent to me, and Ste. Croix's doubts as to the applicability of the Rhetra procedure to the making of foreign policy can, as I shall hope to show, be allayed. There is, nevertheless, one major discrepancy between the formal prescriptions of the Rhetra and the situation current in the age of Xenophon, namely the glaring omission from the Rhetra of the Ephorate.

To fill this gap, it has been suggested that the granting of *kratos* to the *damos* implies the existence of popular magistrates who could represent the cause of the *damos* (cf. Nippel 1980, 132). But the fact remains that the Ephors are not explicitly mentioned here. Whatever their status and functions in the seventh century – and their existence by this date need not be doubted (cf. Pareti 1958 (1910a), 117-42) – they probably acquired their eventually formidable bundle of executive and judicial powers gradually and through customary practice rather than by formal constitutional enactment (for the powers cf. Pareti 1958, 142-59, 165-201; and see further below).

The ultimate origins of the Ephorate are uncertain, both because the literary sources naturally give conflicting testimony and because its historical powers, though overwhelmingly secular, include one or two apparently archaic religious functions like the sky-watching ritual noted in Chapter 6. The latter have suggested to some (e.g. Dümmler 1901, II, 213-16) that the office was originally religious, but the secularization of a religious office in this way is hard to account for and to my knowledge unparalleled. Rather, there seems to be something to be said for a fourth-century view (Arist. *Pol.* 1313a25-33; cf. Plat. *Laws* 692a) that the Ephorate was in some sense created by the Eurypontid king Theopompos (somewhere around 700 in our terms). Not only does this contradict the inevitable ascription to Lykourgos (e.g. Hdt. 1.65.5), but it would seem unlikely to have been fabricated on the basis of the then existing balance of formal powers between the kings and the Ephorate (Chapter 7). All anecdotes are probably literally false, but Theopompos' alleged claim to have instituted the Ephorate in order to ensure the continued existence of the kingship (that is, by making a significant concession to the *damos*) could contain an important germ of the truth.

There remained none the less a constant potential for tension and even outright hostility between an individual king or the two kings jointly and an individual board of Ephors, the more so as the Ephorate's powers increased. This should not be confused with the old and rightly discarded view that a permanent struggle between 'the Crown' and 'the Ephorate' was the key to the development of the Spartan constitution. For the Ephorate was no more a uniform and unidirectional force in Spartan politics than the kingship, for several reasons. In the first place, tenure was annual and could almost certainly not be repeated (cf. Westlake 1976); this republican-spirited restriction was perhaps mainly designed to prevent Ephors from limiting the powers unduly of the supreme military and naval commanders. Secondly, after his term of office an ex-Ephor was most likely to find himself once again a *privatus*, an ordinary citizen with no special powers or immunities. So unless he happened anyway to be an Endios or a Naukleidas, a member of the Spartan political and social elite, his future advancement would be heavily jeopardized if he were to incur the enmity of one or other king. It may not be coincidental that we hear no more of Sthenelaïdas after 432 (see below). Then, thirdly, there is the method whereby an Ephor was appointed, which seems to have militated against the office developing an independent, corporate identity.

We do not unfortunately know for certain either the grounds on which a man might put himself forward or be put forward for election as Ephor or the procedure whereby the selection between rival candidates was made. The comment of Aristotle (*Pol.* 1270b10-12) that Ephors were often poor men and *therefore* easily bribed may apply particularly to his own day, when the total number of Spartan full citizens had dropped well below a thousand and the pool of eligible men (men presumably over thirty who had not been Ephor before and held no other incompatible office) had shrunk proportionately (cf. Rhodes 1981b). Nor do his statements that Ephors were drawn at random from all the people, not any smaller section of it (e.g. *Pol.* 1270b10,29; 1294b32), and that the method of appointment was 'exceedingly childish' (*Pol.* 1270b28), decide the issue. It could be that the Ephors were elected in the same manner as the Gerontes, but since there was apparently no canvassing for the Ephorate, it may be that they were somehow nominated or co-opted (perhaps by the Gerousia, as suggested by Momigliano 1963, 152) and that the acclamation by the Assembly was purely formal (cf. Chrimes 1949, 422; the heterodox view advocated in Rahe 1980b that Ephors were selected by lot from a previously elected panel has been adequately refuted by Rhodes 1981b).

However that may be, the one passage that does speak of the 'fixing' of the appointment of an Ephor, that of Lysandros by King Agis IV in 243 (Plut. *Agis* 8-11), cannot straightforwardly be applied to the age of Xenophon, for this was a revolutionary tactic. On the other hand, it does not seem impossible that an influential king would regularly seek to impose himself in some way upon the 'elections' to the Ephorate, and it is at least noticeable that very few Ephors indeed either were or had been or became considerable political figures in their own right (the Ephoral 'Fasti' are set out in Pareti 1958, 212-20). The lesson of the foregoing arguments, that is, is that the very great powers of the office must not be confused with the status (usually, it seems, quite humble) of the office-holders.

Nor should it automatically be supposed that, as the rise of the Ephorate entailed a diminution of the formal powers of the kings and of the nobility as a whole, the Ephors were always by definition representatives or champions of the *damos*, the common people, against the aristocracy led by the kings. The parallel between the Ephorate and the Roman tribunate of the plebs that was drawn in antiquity for this reason is therefore inexact but still instructive. For at different times in the history of the Roman Republic the tribunes could be described as 'slaves of the nobles' as well as seditious populist agitators. Moreover, the Ephorate like the tribunate could be divided against itself; and just as an Octavius or Drusus could be sponsored against a Tiberius or Gaius Gracchus by rival factions within the Roman oligarchy, so the rivalry of kings might extend to securing the necessary majority (cf. 2.3.34) of Ephors for one or other royal cause – by bribery, if we are to believe Aristotle, on more than a few occasions. In short, composed as it was of men who were often undistinguished, whose tenure was annual and not renewable, and who might be sharply divided among themselves in policy and in personal allegiance, the Ephorate as such should not be expected to have provided an institutional power-base for the Spartan *dunatoi* or most influential political figures; nor could it have been able, let alone willing, to pursue a corporate line of policy in domestic or foreign affairs over an extended period.

This does not of course mean that on occasion individual Ephors or boards of Ephors might not turn their powers to political advantage, as we shall see; but I have deliberately set out the limitations on their political role before enumerating the very considerable powers of the office because this seems to me the correct order of priority for explaining the workings of the Spartan machinery of policy-making, at least in the reign of Agesilaos. With the further warning not to mistake delegated administrative powers for independent powers of initiative the Ephors' formal powers in the age of Xenophon may now be rehearsed. Briefly, they fall into three categories – executive, judicial and religious. But since the ancient Greeks knew and wanted to know nothing about the relatively modern doctrine of the 'separation of powers', their executive and judicial powers being equally 'political' in the modern sense; and since religion permeated all Greek life, and nowhere more than in the state 'swayed beyond all others by fear of the gods' (Greenidge 1911, 99), it makes only for confusion and misunderstanding to draw sharp distinctions between the Ephors' powers in these three spheres. The useful discriminations are those between their roles in peace and war, and in foreign and domestic policy.

It was particularly in the sphere of foreign relations that their influence could be felt. They controlled contacts between Spartans and foreigners through their conduct of collective or individual *xenêlasiai*, and they gave or withheld permission for Spartans to reside abroad. It was they who as a rule received foreign embassies, engaged in negotiations in detail with other states, and laid foreign business before both Gerousia and Assembly. Two Ephors accompanied a king on campaign, perhaps to assist in any post-war negotiations, but also to supervise the king's conduct in a general way. They were also entitled to give orders to other overseas commanders, for example the harmosts or political residents in the appointment of whom they also had some say (Chapter 7). It was a decree of the Ephors, moreover, that formally terminated Lysander's dekarchies. Once war had been declared (by the Assembly: below), it was the Ephors who 'called out the ban' – that is, determined the age-groups of the army to be called up, detailed the necessary technicians, and arranged the baggage-train. Finally, through their powers to arrest and (with the Gerousia) try kings, they exercised an important retrospective constraint on the conduct of foreign policy. In short, apart from actually commanding an army in the field, or appointing *proxenoi* and Pythioi, the competence of the Ephors in foreign affairs was comprehensive.

At home they performed the role denoted by their title, that of supervision. On entry into office – perhaps at the first new moon after the autumnal equinox, perhaps at the heliacal rising of Arktouros, but in any event about the end of September or early October by our Julian reckoning (cf. Ste. Croix 1972, App. XII) – the Ephors made two remarkable proclamations: the first was a command to the citizens to shave their moustaches and obey the laws, the second a declaration of war on the Helots. These proclamations symbolize respectively their responsibility for maintaining the Spartan *kosmos* or putatively 'Lykourgan' social regimen and their police function towards the enemy within. They had overall supervision of the *agôgê*, and it was they who chose the three most outstanding recent graduates from the body to serve as leaders and selectors of the elite 300 Hippeis (Chapter 12). This crack force was occasionally involved in terrorist or counter-insurgency measures against the Helots, but that task fell regularly to the Krypteia, which was no doubt also supervised by the Ephors (Chapter 3).

One of the five Ephors gave his name to the Spartan civil year, though it is not known how the eponym was selected; and it was the Ephors who supervised and no doubt also manipulated the Spartan calendar, which like other Greek calendars operated with a complicated luni-solar year necessitating intercalation every nine years. Also semi-religious and semi-political was their eight-yearly star-gazing ritual, which might lead to the trial and deposition of a king. This was just the most colourful of the ways in which they were empowered to control the kings, and of all Spartans the Ephors had least reason to stand in awe of the kings' institutionalized charisma (Chapter 7).

The Ephors' judicial powers were far from confined to the trials of kings. In all capital cases they conducted the *anakrisis* or preliminary hearing to decide whether a case should come to court. Moreover, unfettered by written laws or rules of judicial procedure they judged all civil suits individually, this being the one sphere in which their independent initiative and competence were absolute. In non-capital criminal cases they might impose and exact fines *ad hoc* on all including the kings, and the proceeds were supposed to go to the public treasury of which the Ephors were also the comptrollers. To the same end they supervised the collection of such taxes as the Spartans were grudgingly prepared to pay and of foreign tribute, and they received the proceeds from the sale of war booty. In short, the Ephors were virtually omnicompetent political and judicial executives, and a bare listing of their powers and functions (for source references see e.g. Gilbert 1895, 52-9; Rahe 1980b) makes Aristotle's description of their authority as 'near-tyrannical' (*Pol.* 1270b15) wholly comprehensible if rather misleading.

The Ephors did not only lay business before the Assembly; one of their number, perhaps the eponym, also had the privilege and potential power of presiding over its meetings. These took place 'season in, season out', according to the poetical formula of the Great Rhetra, which may originally have meant once a year but in our period meant once a month at each new moon in connection with a festival of Apollo. ('Apella' was Spartan for a feast of Apollo, not the official designation of the Assembly: Ste. Croix 1972, 346-7; for the meeting-place(s) of the Assembly see Shatzman 1968.) It was presumably then that the kings and Ephors exchanged oaths. Apart from these stated meetings, it was possible for the Ephors to call extraordinary sessions of the Assembly. But the character of the one occasion on which it is recorded that the Spartans held consecutive sessions (Hdt. 7.134, a typically Spartan mix of religion and politics) reminds us forcefully of the institutional and psychological gulf that lay between the Ekklesia of democratic Athens and the Ekklesia of Sparta. (Kelly 1981a, 54-5, has not persuaded me that 6.1.2-18 is an 'instance of prolonged debate … *in the Spartan assembly*' – my emphasis.)

The Rhetra apparently gave *kratos* to the Spartan *damos*, but this was *kratos* of a severely restricted kind. By no stretch of the imagination – except of a highly perverse imagination like that of Isokrates (7.61; cf. Cloché 1933, 139-45; Bordes 1982, 219-25) – could the Spartan polity be described as a *dēmokratia*. True, it was the Assembly that took the final decision on matters of peace and war, in legislation and in (some at any rate) elections; but the Assembly's role was ordinarily confined to rubber-stamping the *probouleumata* of the Gerousia placed before it by the presiding Ephor. The Assembly had no initiative and could only vote on – not (*pace* Butler 1962, 388, 394-5) amend or discuss – the motions placed before it. There was almost certainly no *isēgoria* in the Assembly, that is no right for anyone who wished – as opposed to kings, Gerontes, Ephors and perhaps others specially called by the presiding Ephor – to address the Assembly. When the vote was taken, it was a matter of collective shouting not individual balloting: the notion of one man/one vote was not integral to the procedure (cf. Ste. Croix 1972, 348-9). Once, in 432, the Assembly was asked to divide, but only after the presiding Ephor had claimed – perhaps speciously (see below) – that the shouting was indecisive. Finally, but in no way least, although the Spartan Assembly was open to all full citizens, as at Athens, in Sparta there were both educational and property qualifications for membership as well as a birth criterion. Not only were these oligarchic in spirit but in practice they reduced the size of the Assembly by the end of the age of Xenophon to that of a large council, perhaps one sixth the size of a normal Athenian Assembly meeting at this period.

In case there are still those who are unimpressed by these institutional arguments and would wish to maintain the comparison with Athens by stressing the apparent openness of Spartan government on the grounds that in our main sources, Thucydides and Xenophon, major decisions of policy seem to be taken in the Assembly, I would add three further counter-arguments. The first arises from the character of Spartan society as a whole, in which the habit of deference to those in authority was ingrained from the tenderest age. The Spartans' reverence for seniority has already been noted; but it was exceeded, at least in the case of ordinary Spartans, by their respect for the laws and the human incarnations of those laws, the officials. Add to these the military discipline under which all Spartans constantly lived and the rigidly hierarchical organization of Spartan society, and it becomes hard to conceive of the ordinary Spartan ranker suddenly in the Assembly dropping his mask of deferential conformism to become a floating and independent voter.

The one faintly plausible exception to this rule occurred in 418, but the episode is often misinterpreted. King Agis II had been appointed leader of an expedition the obvious aim of which was to inflict a swingeing military defeat upon Argos. Agis, however, preferred to neutralize and control Argos through diplomacy rather than arms. The Spartans and their allies chafed, but the Spartan army obediently followed Agis home (Thuc. 5.60.2). But once back in Sparta Agis came under increasingly bitter attack, and the Spartans 'were in favour of pulling down the house of Agis immediately and fining him 100,000 drachmai' (Thuc. 5.63.2). Agis managed to avert this fate, but a law (*nomos*) was passed instead, appointing an advisory commission whose permission was required before Agis could again command an army – as he did shortly thereafter to win the (First) Battle of Mantineia. Thucydides' use of *nomos* (probably in fact a resolution specifically applicable to the present campaign under Agis) should mean that a vote was taken in the Spartan Assembly. But that by no means excludes a *probouleuma* to that effect from the Gerousia; and in default of certain evidence to the contrary, it could only have been the Gerousia (or Gerousia *plus* Ephors) who would have tried and sentenced Agis according to the terms mooted (cf. Ste. Croix 1972, 351; Kelly 1981a, 48-9 and n.5). Moreover, despite Agis' conspicuous initial failure to carry out his mission, and even though the Spartans had reportedly been 'carried away by passion in a manner quite unlike themselves', Agis was not only not tried but given the chance to make good his promise to 'atone for his faults by some noble action' (Thuc. 5.63.2-4). So even if we were to allow that ordinary Spartans could 'distinguish the roles of soldier and citizen' (Andrewes 1966, 3), there were insurmountable obstacles to the ability of the Ephors, let alone the Assembly, to coerce a king.

The second further argument against a 'democratic' reading of Assembly decisions reported by Thucydides and Xenophon is derived from a single, incidental reference in the *Hellenika* (3.3.8). During his uniquely valuable account of Kinadon's conspiracy Xenophon uses two technical Spartan terms that appear nowhere else in surviving sources. One of these is 'the so-called Little Ekklesia', a body which the Ephors of 399 on learning of the plot decided not to convene; instead, 'they consulted with some individual members of the Gerousia here and there ...'. Since we cannot know what the Little Ekklesia was or how it functioned, it was rather bold of Glotz (1968, 94) to describe it as 'une des maîtresses pièces du gouvernement spartiate'. But his instinct was, I am sure right, and the existence of a regularly constituted organ of government capable of deciding upon executive action without reference to the full Assembly hardly tells in favour of the view that the Assembly was an important, let alone the most important policymaking body in Sparta. The presumption of Kelly (1981a, 55) that it was 'an emergency session of the ekklesia' is belied both by its title (which must denote size of membership rather than irregularity of meeting) and by Xenophon's association of ideas, expressed in his repetition of the verb *sullegein* (convene), between the Little Ekklesia as a body and individual Gerontes. If I were to guess at its composition, I would say that it was not just the Gerousia under another name (if so, why two names for the same body?), but a body comprising the Gerontes and Ephors *ex officio* and perhaps other leading Spartans, officials and ex-officials, who might be co-opted *ad hoc*.

Thirdly and finally, the operation of the common messes should not be left out of account in any complete analysis of Spartan policymaking. Some ancient theorists, as we saw from the passage of Aristotle quoted at the start of this chapter, took the messes to be a democratic feature of the Spartan *politeia* inasmuch as all Spartans were supposed to mess together as equals. In reality, some messmates were more equal than others (the rich ones had taken to contributing optional wheaten bread in addition to the compulsory barley meal by Xenophon's day: *LP* 5.3), and I strongly suspect that the same was true of some messes as well. We do not know how the messes were recruited, that is, why a man would apply for and be accepted as a member of one mess rather than another – except of course in the case of the royal mess and the presumed mess shared by the Ephors of any given year. But in light of the hierarchical ordering of Spartan society at all stages from a Spartan's earliest youth to his death, it would not be extravagant to postulate that some messes were more desirable socially and more influential politically than others, as the royal mess self-evidently was. Even if, on the other hand, it be supposed that recruitment was in all other instances random rather than hereditary or by special selection, the very principle of messing in small groups none the less contributed powerfully to the un- or anti-democratic character of Spartan society. The opinion-forming role of the mess-system has been noticed by more than one scholar (e.g. Lewis 1977, 34-5); but only Greenidge (1911, 89) has to my knowledge expressly made the due allowance for the way in which it 'fostered the tendency of the Spartans to secrecy and intrigue, and gave them a *penchant* to the oligarchical club and a belief in the efficiency of narrow corporations'. Greenidge rightly noted the connection between this *penchant* and the Lysandreian form of imperialism practised after the Athenian War (Chapter 6). We may add that, when Agesilaos urged his Phleiasian oligarchic partisans in the 380s to form themselves into *sussitia* (messes) and submit themselves to a Spartan-type *agôgê* (5.3.17; see Chapter 13), he was both following faithfully where his master had led and showing himself a true product of his society's mores.

How, then, to return to our starting-point, should the Spartan *politeia* be ultimately characterized? Granted that it was *sui generis* and comprised elements of disparate origin and uneven development whose constitutional status was never given formally written definition, it seems to me that taken overall it is best regarded as a peculiar form of oligarchy. Not just in the trivial sense that a privileged minority with full citizen rights ruled dictatorially over many people, who had either few or no political rights – that was no less true of the Athenian democracy. But in the full-blooded sense that within the *politeuma*, that is the citizen body of Spartiates, the reins of political power lay in the grasp of only a small minority, the social and political elite (references to which are conveniently cited in Ste. Croix 1972, 137). Plutarch was no theoretician and gave contradictory opinions in different works; but in a little-noticed passage (*Dion* 53.4) he hit the mark in observing that in Sparta as in Crete 'it is an oligarchy which is in control of affairs and decides the most important issues'. If a slightly more specific classification is desired, then perhaps that of Glotz (1968, 86) – an oligarchy 'à plusieurs degrès' and 'à forme de pyramide' – will do. This general conclusion may be illustrated rather more sharply by exhibiting in some detail three particularly well documented examples of Spartan policymaking in action.

(i) The decision to declare war on Athens in 432/1

According to Thucydides (1.23.5-6, 88, 118.2), fear of Athens' growing power impelled Sparta to declare war on Athens in 432 as a lesser evil than standing aside while her alliance dissolved under Athenian pressure. This judgment he stated in different ways three times: first in his introduction, then after his version of the Spartan Assembly meeting that took the decision for war, and thirdly after a long account of the Peloponnesian League congress that ratified this decision. But until recently few believed Thucydides or indeed interpreted him correctly. According to modern orthodoxy, allied (especially Corinthian) goading had pricked the sluggish and reluctant Spartans into belated action. That orthodoxy was vigorously challenged and effectively refuted by Ste. Croix (1972, esp. ch. 2; but see already Cloché 1943, 88-91).

However, in cogently upholding the consistency and validity of Thucydides' judgment, according to which the Spartans were slow to go to war *unless* (as here) war was perceived to be the lesser of two unavoidable evils, Ste. Croix found himself obliged to treat the modality of this decision as an exception to what he argued was a general rule of Spartan politics, namely that a strong king might exert a decisive influence on policymaking especially in the absence of concerted opposition led by the other royal family. For Archidamos II, Ste. Croix inferred from Thucydides' presentation of him, was just such a strong king and he opposed war with Athens or at least an immediate declaration of war; while the other king, Pausanias, was a minor ('ruling' only because his father Pleistoanax was in exile) and hardly in a position to mount effective opposition to Archidamos. Yet even so the Spartans declared for war by a very large majority in the Assembly.

In order to explain away this apparent anomaly, Ste. Croix resorted to the suggestion that it was the faction not dominant among the leading Spartans which managed to get the decision transferred from the Archidamos-dominated Gerousia to the war-hungry Assembly; and he conceded to the 'open government' interpretation of Spartan policymaking (with which he was not in general sympathy) that decisions of the Assembly might not be a foregone conclusion since foreign ambassadors might introduce new and impressive arguments. Both this suggestion and this concession are unnecessary and implausible. Nor need we suppose, as Ste. Croix was inclined to do, that in Sparta issues of foreign policy were decided by a different procedure from that applicable to internal issues. For the apparent anomaly disappears once it is accepted that Archidamos, though doubtless in general 'very respected' and at least in some sense 'the leading Spartan of his day' (Ste. Croix 1972, 130, 323), was not as skilled as Agesilaos was to prove to be in bending a majority of the Gerousia and Ephors to this way of thinking on the major foreign policy issue of his epoch.

As Ste. Croix himself points out (1972, 146), not even his son and immediate successor Agis pursued Archidamos' policy of *détente* with Athens; his other son, Agesilaos, was only about twelve or thirteen in 432, but he was shortly to become the beloved of a man whose attitude towards democratic Athens is unlikely ever to have been pacific. If members of the immediate circle of Archidamos were unsympathetic, it would hardly be odd if he was unable to persuade a majority of the Gerousia to his views. And this, if I am right about the machinery of Spartan decision-taking, was Archidamos' crucial political failure. For it was precisely because the majority of the Gerousia was in favour of an immediate declaration of war on Athens in 432 that the Assembly had been asked to vote on the motion (*probouleuma*) that the Athenians had broken the Peace of 445. Had Archidamos been able to persuade a majority of the Gerousia, then the matter might not even have been brought before the Assembly or at any rate the motion would have been differently phrased. Hence, the absence of the Gerousia from Thucydides' detailed account of the debates in the Spartan Assembly, first in open session when foreign ambassadors were invited to speak and then in closed session, is very far from proving that it played no role. Rather, the majority of the Gerontes were of one mind with the mass of ordinary Spartans over the need for war, even if they did not all necessarily share the hotheads' view that victory in a couple of years was a foregone conclusion. As for the fact that the Assembly was, uniquely, asked to divide, this was perhaps merely a device of the presiding Ephor to cow the few waverers and achieve as near total solidarity as was possible. If, on the other hand, the initial shouting really was as close as Sthenelaïdas claimed, this was presumably a tribute to the authority of Archidamos and to the deference such authority traditionally commanded in Sparta. Whatever the truth of this, the Assembly's decision of 432 is perfectly compatible with the interpretation of Spartan policymaking presented earlier in this chapter.

(ii) The trial of King Pausanias in 403

In the century between about 470 and 370 the Eurypontid house had to provide just three kings. During the same period the Agiads had to find six, no less then four of whom were minors when they acceded; between 480 and 432, indeed, the Agiads had an adult king for a total of fifteen years at most. Lack of age and experience was clearly a handicap in building up a close-knit group of supporters among the influential people within and around the Gerousia and no doubt partly explains why it was only the Agiads Pleistoanax and Pausanias, father and son, who were successfully brought to trial and convicted in these years. In 395 Pausanias anticipated his condemnation by flight and survived for at least fifteen years; but he was living under a sentence of death passed partly because of dereliction of military duty at Haliartos (Chapter 14) but also on a charge arising out of his conduct eight years earlier in 'having allowed the *dêmos* of the Athenians to escape when he had them in his power in Peiraieus' (3.5.25).

There was nothing odd to Spartan eyes about bringing – or, as it might seem to us, raking up – the last accusation. Political trials in Greece regularly involved a malicious review of the defendant's entire career, and in Sparta, exceptionally even by Greek standards, a man might be tried twice on the same capital charge. There was, though, a particular point to resuscitating the way Pausanias had treated the Athenian *dêmos* in 403. For that had decisively overthrown the policy of Lysander, and it was for Lysander's death in 395 among other things that Pausanias was being arraigned for a second time. On the *cui bono* argument, therefore, it is morally certain that the trial was concerted by the friends of Agesilaos (then absent on campaign in Asia Minor) with the aid of complaisant Ephors. The plot had been very different in 403.

Then the chief actors involved were the kings Agis and Pausanias and the master general, diplomat and politician Lysander, with Agis shifting from one to the other in a bid to establish his own leading influence and authority. The main sources for the context of the trial are Xenophon, Diodoros (using Ephorus) and Plutarch, but what makes the episode uniquely revealing of the mainsprings of Spartan policymaking is a passage of Pausanias' *Description of Greece* (composed in the second century AD but ultimately perhaps drawn here from a near-contemporary author). This passage (3.5.2) not only specifies the identity of the Supreme Court, namely the Gerousia together with the Ephors, but even details the breakdown of the voting, which must therefore have been open. Fifteen Gerontes, including Agis, voted 'guilty', but the other fourteen Gerontes and all five Ephors effected the acquittal of Pausanias by majority vote.

The context of the trial is examined closely elsewhere in this book (Chapters 6 and 14); here it will be enough to say that, while Agis had initially backed what was essentially Lysander's policy towards Athens after the Athenian War, he had then shifted in favour of Pausanias' anti-Lysander mission to Athens in the summer of 403, only to reverse his position once again and vote against Pausanias at the trial held upon the latter's return from Athens after negotiating a new settlement. As with the position of Sthenelaïdas in 432, there is a chronological complication, for we do not know whether it was the same board of Ephors which both backed Pausanias' mission to Athens by a majority of three to two and then unanimously acquitted him; but the consensus of modern opinion is probably correct in supposing that two boards were involved, those of 404/3 and 403/2 respectively. From the way Agis voted it is pretty clear that it was he who, prompted and abetted no doubt by Lysander and his friends, laid the accusation against Pausanias before the Ephors, and from the way the latter voted that their preliminary decision (*anakrisis*) to bring Pausanias to trial was due to the authority of Agis rather than their belief in the guilt of Pausanias. Further questions arise, however, as to why Agis behaved so inconsistently at first sight, and why he nevertheless failed to persuade a majority of the non-royal Gerontes or a single one of the Ephors to share his final attitude. Conversely, why did half the Gerontes and all the Ephors vote for Pausanias?

Certainty is impossible, and balanced judgment is hindered by the excessive personalization of history to which all the sources were prone, but one or two threads may be securely picked out. First, it is to be noted that, as soon as the two kings agreed on a foreign policy decision, even so influential a Spartan as Lysander found himself automatically overtrumped. However, Pausanias was no doubt also greatly aided by the fact that one of the three Ephors he managed to persuade in the summer of 403 was Naukleidas, an influential man in his own right on whom Lysander later thought it necessary and worthwhile to attempt (unsuccessfully) to wreak vengeance in the courts (Poralla 1913, no. 548). Naukleidas may have already been an enemy of Lysander or a client of Pausanias, but the other two Ephors presumably had to be genuinely persuaded to abandon Lysandreian imperialism and adopt the very different *gnômê* (policy: 2.4.36) of Pausanias.

The shifty behaviour of Agis, however, is not so susceptible of explanation in terms of principled disagreement on policy towards Athens. It is true that in light of his own past record of support for oligarchy at Argos and his subsequent attempt to coerce democratic Elis (Chapter 13) Agis would probably not have been quite so tolerant of democratic government at Athens as Pausanias. But we should also allow for a good deal of personal animus in his prosecution of Pausanias, which arose in general from the traditional rivalry between the royal houses and specifically from Agis' desire to dominate Spartan policymaking. Hence his very temporary *rapprochement* with Pausanias, simply in order to dethrone Lysander, followed by a political prosecution designed to overthrow Pausanias in his turn.

At the trial the Gerousia was split quite literally down the middle. This means that either the membership of this body was then evenly divided between the friends and supporters of Agis and those of Pausanias or there was an unattached group of floating voters whose views on this particular issue of policy and leadership by chance produced an exact division of the votes. The former might seem the easier explanation, but the trial of Sphodrias (below) could be adduced in favour of the latter. Either way, however, it was the votes of the five Ephors that decided the issue, the clearest possible indication of how vital it might be for a king who wished to pursue a vigorous but controversial line of foreign policy to win over the Ephors to his viewpoint. The lesson was not lost on Agesilaos, who succeeded Agis just three years later. Nor should the lesson be lost on us that all this high-level politicking in the autumn and winter of 403 on a supremely important issue of foreign policy took place without any reference whatsoever to the Spartan Assembly.

(iii) The trial of Sphodrias in 378

My final instance of Spartan policymaking in action became a *cause célèbre* in Greece. Not only did it have critical implications for interstate relations in the early 370s (Chapter 14) but it provided the only known instance in all Greek history of a case in which the defendant disobeyed a summons to stand trial on a capital charge and yet was acquitted *in absentia*. For naturally enough failure to answer such a charge was taken as a virtual admission of guilt, as had happened in the case of Pausanias in 395 (3.5.25). Small wonder that many considered the acquittal of Sphodrias to be the most unjust verdict ever reached by a Spartan court (5.4.24).

Sphodrias was a high-ranking Spartan officer who had been appointed harmost of Thespiai in Boiotia. This appointment he probably owed to the patronage of King Kleombrotos, who was also according to one ancient view (DS 15.29.5) behind the action that occasioned Sphodrias' trial. For in about March 378, while a top-level Spartan delegation was actually at Athens conducting negotiations, Sphodrias tried to capture the ungated Peiraieus in a surprise night attack. The result was a fiasco, the three Spartan ambassadors were at once arrested and only released on the assurance that Sphodrias would of course be executed and the policy he had been attempting to effect abjured forthwith.

The Athenians had unusually good reason to accept this assurance. For one of the ambassadors, Etymokles, was not only a member of the Gerousia but also one of those friends of Agesilaos whose role will be considered at length in the next chapter; and it is a near certainty that the embassy had been despatched to Athens at the instigation of Agesilaos, who then dominated Spartan policymaking and was extremely concerned to forestall a *rapprochement* between Athens and the hated Thebes. In other words, the Athenians would reasonably have expected Agesilaos to bring all the force of his massive influence to bear in order to secure the condemnation of Sphodrias, whose witless attack on Athens had jeopardized the balance of power in mainland Greece besides threatening to undermine Agesilaos' authority.

Yet against all the odds Sphodrias was not executed. Nor was he even heavily fined, as had been the Spartan commander who had no less flagrantly violated the Peace of Antalkidas four years earlier but had done so in a manner calculated to appeal to Agesilaos. Sphodrias was actually acquitted – thanks to none other than Agesilaos. The trial, as I said, became a *cause célèbre*. This was partly because of its international ramifications, but also because the outcome was thought to have been influenced decisively by the homosexual relationship between Agesilaos' son Archidamos and Sphodrias' son Kleonymos. Plutarch (*Ages.* 25.10), impressed perhaps by Agesilaos' known homoerotic proclivities, was convinced that the intercession of Archidamos on behalf of his beloved's father had caused Agesilaos' change of heart. Xenophon, however, who was very far from hiding the existence of the pederastic relationship, was nevertheless at pains to stress that Agesilaos had been swayed not by emotion but by his conception of Sparta's best interests. No doubt Xenophon was anxious to clear his patron of what he obviously regarded as a slur on Agesilaos' character, and as so often he was not telling the whole truth; but there is no doubt in my mind that he was nearer the mark than Plutarch.

For present purposes, though, the result of Agesilaos' change of heart matters more than its motivation. But equally as important as the result are the reasons why it was Agesilaos' switch of vote that proved decisive at the trial. In spring 378, we learn from the uniquely well informed Xenophon (5.4.25), the Gerousia was divided into three sections – not two, as it may have been in 403 (above). These three were respectively the friends of Agesilaos (who included Etymokles), the friends of Kleombrotos, and those who were uncommitted to either of the other two groups (*hoi dia mesou*; cf. for the expression Thuc. 8.75.1) but did not necessarily constitute a third 'faction' (*contra* Rice 1975, 120). The friends of Kleombrotos were 'comrades' (*hetairoi*) of Sphodrias and so could be counted on to vote for Sphodrias' acquittal, but Kleombrotos had only recently come to the Agiad throne and so far had achieved nothing that would lead us to expect a majority of the uncommitted to take his side of the argument. Agesilaos, by contrast, had been king for over twenty years, during which he had achieved many successes both in battle and through diplomacy, and one would have expected his *auctoritas* to weigh heavily with the uncommitted (most if not all of whom had been elected to the Gerousia after Agesilaos' accession), quite apart from the merits of the case against Sphodrias in terms of international law and Sparta's interests. In other words, Agesilaos, his friends and the uncommitted should between them have heavily outnumbered Kleombrotos and his friends on the Gerousia – which is precisely the impression given by Xenophon. (Xenophon says nothing of the Ephors, and it is possible that they did not sit with the Gerousia in capital trials involving commoners; but if they did, at least a majority of those of 378 would surely have voted with Agesilaos, since they must have authorized the diplomatic mission of Etymokles and his two fellow-envoys.) On the other hand, as Xenophon makes plain, the decision of Agesilaos to switch his vote entailed a majority in favour of acquittal. This does not necessarily mean that he carried with him most or even any of the uncommitted, but the votes of the latter will have been easily exceeded by the combined votes of Agesilaos, Kleombrotos and their respective friends. As in 403 we see how, when the two kings acted with one accord (however discordant their motivation), they could exercise a decisive influence on the direction of Spartan policy.

The astuteness of Agesilaos' change of vote has rarely been appreciated by modern scholars, though its true significance could have been divined by a careful reading of another work of Xenophon, the *Agesilaos* (esp. 7.3). For Agesilaos constantly sought to turn enemies into friends or at least into unwilling executants of his policies. By acquitting Sphodrias he had placed his fellow-king and a leading member of his circle under a deep personal obligation to himself. His foreign policy was for the time being in tatters; but if the *rapprochement* between Athens and Thebes could not now be prevented, at least Agesilaos had the comfort of knowing that the opposition within the Spartan elite to his policy of aggression towards Thebes had been significantly weakened. Kleombrotos wriggled, but it was he who in 371, fearing the consequence of a political trial if he refused to fight, commanded the defeated army at Leuktra and died there alongside both Sphodrias and Kleonymos. The trial of Sphodrias was a watershed in Spartan and indeed all Greek history. In the context of policymaking at Sparta it reveals as no other episode the extraordinary *de facto* power that a king such as Agesilaos might wield. Above all, it throws a flood of light on the politics of patronage and friendship at Sparta, the subject of the next chapter.

9

All the King's Men: Agesilaos and the Politics of Spartan Patronage

Faithful friends are to kings the truest and safest sceptre. (Xen. *Cyr.* 8.7.13)

There is little friendship in the world, and least of all between equals, which was wont to be magnified. That that is, is between superior and inferior, whose fortunes may comprehend the one the other. (Francis Bacon, *Essay* XLVIII 'Of Followers and Friends')

Politics in a narrower sense than government or social control was a Greek invention, or perhaps both a Greek and an Etrusco-Roman one. On a minimal definition it consists in the taking of decisions in public after the discussion of issues, although the specific manifestations of the available techniques vary enormously from society to society (cf. Finley 1983, esp. 51,83,119). Broadly speaking, the relevant procedures and methods may be divided into two categories, the formal and the informal. In the previous two chapters I have considered respectively the formal aspects of the kings' powers and privileges (see further Chapter 16 for their posthumous honours) and the formal mechanisms whereby the Spartans made decisions of public policy. In the present chapter the object is rather to expose what seem to be the most significant of the less public, even hidden, springs of politics in Sparta under the general rubric of political friendship (cf. for a comparable formal/informal dichotomy Pitt-Rivers 1971, chs 9 and 10). In particular, I shall be concerned to explore the informal means at the disposal of an adroit Spartan king to determine in advance the outcome both of meetings of the Assembly and of major political trials and to ensure as far as was possible or desirable that he or his men had the responsibility for executing those decisions of public policy that he had sponsored or approved.

Several recent students of Sparta in the age of Agesilaos (Rice 1974, 1975; Hamilton 1979b; David 1981), building on an older study of the opposition to Agesilaos' foreign policy between 394 and 371 (Smith 1953/4), have sought to operate with a 'factional' model of Spartan politics. But none of these has tried to show how a faction leader might set about creating and maintaining his faction; and their rigid demarcation of factions, to the leading personnel of which they mechanically ascribe mutually incompatible foreign and domestic policies, has often obscured rather than illumined the realities of Spartan politics in this period, besides being without support in the sources. It is true that Sparta was a notoriously secretive society (esp. Thuc. 5.68.2) and that the evidence for all aspects of Spartan societal organization is generally less than optimal. But in the present context we do at least have the uniquely valuable testimony of Xenophon, who was both subjectively a comrade and objectively a client of Agesilaos. By reading as much between as on the lines of his *Agesilaos* and *Lak. Pol.*, and not forgetting the *Hellenika* and *Cyropaedia*, it is possible to demonstrate how and why Agesilaos achieved his unparalleled sway over Spartan politics through connections of friendship or, more often and more particularly, the dispensation of patronage.

Scholarly opinion on the role of patronage in Spartan society and politics is divided. Some scholars would minimize it to the point of oblivion (e.g. Kelly 1981a, 57n.37). Others have suspected its importance without marshalling all the extensive evidence available (Ste. Croix 1972, e.g. 354; cf. Lewis 1977, 35). Only Rahe (1977) and now Hodkinson (1983, esp. 260-5) have to my knowledge developed anything like the argument of this chapter in their discussions of how political and military leaders were selected at Sparta; and no historian of ancient Sparta – not even those who have adopted a 'factional' model of explanation – has yet adequately tapped the wealth of recent work on economic and political patronage and clientelism by anthropologists, sociologists and political scientists (e.g. Gellner/Waterbury 1977, with a valuable bibliographical essay by J.C. Scott at 483-505; Schmidt et al. 1977; Eisenstadt/Lemarchand 1981). Admittedly, a fair amount of this recent work, especially on the theoretical side, is worse than useless for analysing any system of politics (cf. Finley 1983, ch.2, esp. 35n.25). But the following working hypotheses seem to me solidly based and fruitfully relevant.

The patron-client relationship cannot (*pace* Eisenstadt/Roniger 1980, 48-9) offer a complete and self-sufficient explanation of how a society or a society's political system operates, but it can provide an essential supplementary or interstitial explanation of how some or all of the major components of a social or political network mesh together. Secondly, this kind of relationship acquires especial significance in societies where social groups and power relations are not, on the one hand, ordered exclusively or predominantly by kinship ties nor, on the other hand, by an impersonal and notionally impartial central bureaucracy. Thirdly, the patron-client relationship is a relationship of power, in which the patron has the capacity to command the service or compliance of his clients. For although it is reciprocal (cf. Gouldner 1960; J.C. Scott in Gellner/Waterbury 1977, 26-8) and dyadic (that is, a voluntary agreement between two individuals to exchange favours and help in time of need), the relationship is always asymmetrical or lop-sided in two senses: the patron has more to offer than the client can give in return; and the goods and services they mutually exchange are incommensurable, those a patron offers tending to be solidly material, whereas what he expects from a client has a more symbolic quality – loyalty, honour, prestige and general political support, in a word deference. The positive moral connotations of 'patron' and 'client' should not therefore be accepted at face value but subjected to an empirical assessment of the balance of mutual advantage. Finally, in a political context it is at times of change or crisis that the networks of patron-client relationships tend to coalesce into more or less solidary factions, though such factions (however composed or described) are logically and chronologically posterior to patronage relations in their dyadic form (cf. Nicholas 1965; Wolf 1966; C.H. Landé in Schmidt et al. 1977, xxxii). None the less, what A.H.M. Jones said of patronage in the Later Roman Empire remains true of the concept of patronage as such: it is a 'vague term and seems to cover many different forms of contract, legal or illegal, which prevailed at various periods in various areas' (Jones 1964, 774; cf. in a modern context Chubb 1982, 7). Our task is thus to make precise the material significance of political friendship and patronage in Spartan society and politics in the age of Agesilaos and Xenophon.

As with our study of Spartan policymaking, so our present study may usefully begin with Aristotle. In the *Nicomachean Ethics*, which was composed as a prolegomenon and propaedeutic to the *Politics*, he devotes two whole books (8 and 9) to the functions of friendship within the *polis*, any *polis* (cf. Adkins 1963; Hutter 1979, 102-16). At one level, he observes, friendship (*philia*) is essential to the very existence of the *polis*, since this is the bond which at bottom unites all its full members, the *politai* or citizens. At a less general level, however, and in a stronger sense friendship, according to Aristotle, can and should be analysed into three basic kinds – the utilitarian, the pleasurable, and the morally perfect; and the people who contract friendships may be either equals or unequals morally and socially. In the case of unequals the friendship can – and indeed must, if it is to be at all durable – be proportionate, in the double sense that the inferior party makes up in demonstrations of friendly behaviour for his own deficiency in utility, pleasantness or goodness and that the superior confers an amount of benefit proportionate to the distance separating him from his inferior friend. Of these the most relevant kind of friendship for our purposes is utilitarian friendship, and in particular utilitarian friendship between unequals. But it is perhaps worth remarking that in any event 'personal and emotional elements do not appear to dominate in discussions of the making and breaking of friendships so much as compatibilities of wealth and status, and still more the record of past actions and promises of future actions between the members' (Fisher 1976, 18). Unlike Hutter (1979), therefore, I shall not be primarily or even prominently concerned with the affective and psychodynamic elements of ancient Greek friendship.

Utilitarian friendships between equals may, according to Aristotle, be contracted in either a strong, strictly legal, sense or in an informal, 'moral' sense. But the 'moral' species is so understood by Aristotle that in practice it shades into utilitarian friendship between unequals. For although the gift or other benefit is in this case conferred as if on a friend, yet the donor or benefactor 'expects to recover the equivalent *or more*, because he feels that he has made not a gift but a loan' (*EN* 1162b, my emphasis). The words I have emphasized are crucial. For not only do utilitarian friends love each other solely in so far as they derive some benefit from each other, but each partner to this kind of friendship always wants the better of the bargain. This is why friendships based on utility are highly unstable and never, in Aristotle's censorious view, arouse goodwill – a serious charge, since 'Greek is rich in words for the types of behaviour motivated by goodwill' (Dover 1974, 204n.14). This also explains why utilitarian friends tend to be men of bad moral character who wish to receive rather than confer benefits (of which the benefactor can never supply enough). Specifically, such friendships occur chiefly between people of opposite type – rich and poor, beautiful and ugly, lover and beloved, for example; and they are frequently made between older people and those in early or middle life who are ambitiously pursuing their own advantage. The inferior's attitude is summed up in the rhetorical question 'What is the point of being the friend of an influential man if there is no prospect of enjoying any advantage from it?' (*EN* 1163a) – a classic expression of patronage mentality. On the other side, those who hold wealth, office and power are thought to need friends more than other people do in order to confer benefits upon them and so safeguard and preserve their prosperity. Moreover, people in high places tend to have friends of different sorts – wits for their amusement, and otherwise 'agents who are clever at carrying out their instructions' (*EN* 1158a).

It would be excessive to assert that Agesilaos had no more or less equal friends and that none of his friendships was concluded for purposes of goodness rather than pleasure or advantage. However, if we leave aside Aristotle's moral condemnation of utilitarian friendship (to which he uncharacteristically counterposes an unrealizable ideal type of perfect friendship between moral and social equals), we then need not hesitate to use this account to strip the idealizing veneer from Xenophon's picture of Agesilaos' dealings with his various sorts of friends and comrades. For, as Aristotle concedes (*EN* 1169b) when reality again breaks in upon him, 'in the popular view our friends are those who are useful to us'. Or, to quote a leading authority on ancient Greek popular ethics, 'the whole ancient theory of friendship is based on the assumption that favours will be returned: a man who helps his friend usually does so with the expectation that some return for his favor will be made' (Pearson 1962a,136). Thus the line between friendship and patronage in Classical Greece was thin and easily transgressed.

What, then, of Sparta in particular? The dominant characteristics of this professedly egalitarian society were in fact competitiveness (*philonikia, philotimia*), martial aggressiveness equated with manly virtue (*aretê, andragathia*), and hierarchical subordination whether in terms of age, wealth or birth. Hardly surprisingly, therefore, 'the Equals turned out, in the end, to be meshed in a complex of inequalities', and 'In actual practice the system was filled with tensions and anomie' (Finley 1981a, 29,30). Patronage, I would argue, was one of the more important techniques by which this systematic inegalitarianism was perpetrated and perpetuated; and since few if any Spartans were more equal than the kings in respect of their noble birth, huge personal wealth and institutionalized honours and privileges, it was they who were potentially best placed to exploit such channels of patronage as existed.

These channels served in the first instance, as I have indicated in Chapter 3, as a vital means of recruiting the Spartan elite – through strategies of heirship, patronage of promising youths, pederastic connections and manipulation of entry to common messes. No less competitive, however, was the struggle within the elite to dominate the day-to-day workings of Spartan politics. Sparta fully bears out the generalization ascribed to Darius by Herodotus (3.82.3) that in an oligarchy quarrels and conflicts tend to erupt between the men who are striving to win distinction for themselves. This intestine struggle was sometimes dignified under the title *philotimia*, love of honour in the abstract or of honours in the concrete sense of political office. But contest for honour(s) in a Greek *polis* was also a contest for victory (hence *philonikia*) in a zero-sum game. No one, that is, could win unless someone else lost — and lost badly too. Indeed, the contest was not infrequently fought quite literally to the death or at least exile, which was tantamount to political and social death (cf. Finley 1983, 118). In Sparta this traditional elite struggle for power and influence was greatly intensified and exacerbated as Sparta's direct political and military control was extended beyond the Peloponnese to much of the rest of mainland Greece, to the Aegean and the approaches to the Black Sea, and to the western Asia Minor littoral in the course and aftermath of the Athenian War.

To the victor the (now potentially much increased) spoils; and the victor in Sparta was he who could count on the largest number of the right kind of political friends to be in the right places at the right times and to deliver the political goods. Two passages in Xenophon (*Ages.* 11.13; 5.4.20-33) largely unconsciously and incidentally illustrate, first, the components of the relevant networks of political connections in Sparta and, secondly, the manner in which a Spartan pastmaster of the art went about his business of dispensing patronage. The remainder of this chapter amounts to an extended commentary on these passages, the full significance of which does not seem yet to have been appreciated.

Having skimmed selectively through Agesilaos' public career in the first two chapters of the *Agesilaos*, and having then dealt in a more leisurely and repetitive fashion with his various alleged virtues in the next eight chapters, Xenophon appends a concluding summary 'so that the encomium of his excellence (*aretê*) may be the more easily memorable' (11.1). As one would have expected, Xenophon's conception of *aretê* is very largely traditional, notwithstanding his bows in other works to the more cerebral virtues, and in one respect it is wholly so: without going so far as to define justice or goodness exclusively in these terms, he does nevertheless agree that an essential ingredient of these cardinal virtues was helping one's friends to the greatest possible extent. This theme runs through the final chapter of the *Agesilaos* until just before the climactic coda of the work as a whole Xenophon summarises thus (11.13):

> By his relatives (*suggeneis*) he was described as 'attached to his family' (*philokêdemôn*), by his close associates (*chrômenoi*) as 'unhesitatingly devoted' (*aprophasistos*), by those who served him (*hupourgêsantes*) as 'ever mindful' (*mnêmôn*), by those who were wronged or treated unjustly (*adikoumenoi*) as a 'champion' (*epikouros*), and by those who endured dangers with him (*sugkinduneuontes*) as a 'saviour second only to the gods' (*meta theous sôtêr*).

The last of these five groups of admirers is the least informative and may be dealt with briefly. The colourful language might at first be thought conventionally Greek, but it is in fact peculiarly appropriate in Sparta where any especially admired man was apt to be called 'divine' (*theios*: Arist. *EN* 1145a28; cf.

discussion of the deification of Lysander in Chapter 6). The group in question here could in theory consist of all those who had fought with or under Agesilaos, men whose obedience and affection he had been able to win through personal example and care for their material, spiritual and physical welfare (Xen. *Ages.* 6.4). But in so far as the reference is specifically to Spartan soldiers, it is worth recalling that Agesilaos had himself shared their education and in consequence, if we may believe Plutarch (*Ages.* 1.5, cf. 7.3), had learned what may be paraphrased as 'the common touch' (*to dêmotikon*). This had supposedly advantaged him in his succession dispute with Latychidas and in general had helped make him of all Spartan kings the most in tune with (*euharmostotatos*) his subjects (Plut. *Ages.* 3.5, 1.5). This quality was not unconnected with his exaggerated, almost slavish subservience not only to the laws but also to those currently holding office. It is worth noting here that Agesilaos, unlike many another king, was *azêmios* throughout his very long reign (Xen. *Ages.* 6.8; Plut. *Ages.* 4.2); that is, he never had a public penalty inflicted upon him for any offence. Plutarch's story (*Ages.* 5.4) that the Ephors once fined him for (literally) 'making public citizens private' is, though false in fact, at least apocryphal – as we shall see from the variety of means he successfully employed to bind Spartans through personal obligations to his exclusive interest.

Charity, our saying goes, begins at home. *Charites* (favours), Agesilaos might have said, begin with those who are related by birth or by marriage. The compound adjective *philokêdemôn* is a strikingly rare word and perhaps another peculiarly Spartan usage, although its two individual components are perfectly familiar. From a root meaning of a sensation of failing, deprivation, disaster (cf. Scott 1981, 7-12) *kêdos* in Homer (and later – e.g. Hdt. 6.58.2 of Spartan kings) came to be used specifically for funerals and the cognate *kêdemones* for persons attending to the dead. Since funerals other than those of public dignitaries were particularly an affair of kith and kin, *kêdemones* by an easy transference of meaning acquired the sense of kinsmen like the synonymous *kêdestai*. In Attic at least a *kêdemôn* could be opposed to a *suggenês* in the sense of a relative by marriage as opposed to one by birth, but clearly Xenophon intended no such opposition here. The force of *philo-* is formally ambiguous, since, as Aristotle shrewdly observed (*EN* 1125b14-15), 'people are called lovers of such-and-such in more than one sense'. But it would not be unreasonable, or unfair to Agesilaos, to interpret it as denoting the kind of feelings a man had for his close but unrelated friends rather than the kind of paternal affection that Agesilaos happens to be on record as displaying in private (Plut. *Ages.* 25.11, *Mor.* 213e; Ael. *VH* 12.13) – much to the delight of Dryden.

We are not nearly as well informed about the kindred of Agesilaos as we could wish; there is no scope for the Spartan equivalent of Gelzer's or Syme's seminal prosopographical studies of the Roman nobility. Down to the time of Alexander the Great (336-323) we know the names, and too often only the names, of not many more than 800 historical men and women including Perioikoi and slaves who lived within the confines of the Spartan state.[1] This is

---

[1] The 817 entries in Poralla 1913 include mythological and other fictional personages and some possible doublets; but he missed a score or so of historical persons, and since 1913 getting on for fifty

indeed poverty of evidence. However, upper-class Greek habits of nomenclature lend weight to conjecture, and it is possible to make something of the scraps the sources offer.

When Agesilaos' father Archidamos II died in 427 or 426, his elder half-brother Agis succeeded to the Eurypontid throne as Agis II, but Agesilaos presumably shared in the paternal inheritance (*patrôïa*) along with Kyniska – if indeed she was the full sister rather than half-sister of Agesilaos (certain evidence either way is lacking). The widow of Archidamos and mother of Agesilaos, Eupolia, was young enough to be given in marriage, presumably by her father Melesippidas, to one Theodoros (Poralla 1913, no. 360, if the identification is correct) and to produce by him the far better attested Teleutias. It was towards Teleutias and other unidentifiable *homogonoi* of Eupolia that Agesilaos is first known to have revealed himself as *philokêdemôn*, when he gave to them the inheritance of Agis that fell to him after Latychidas had been adjudged not to be Agis' legitimate son and heir (Chapter 7).

We know no more for certain about this branch of Agesilaos' family, but a coincidence of name makes it plausible to speculate a bit further. For a Plutarchan anecdote (*Mor.* 241de [11] – not [10], as Poralla has it) reveals a Teleutia as being the mother of a Paidaretos who, from the content of the anecdote, must be identical with Thucydides' Pedaritos, a leading Spartan who held high command as harmost in the final phase of the Athenian War (Poralla 1913, no. 599; cf. A. Andrewes in Gomme 1981, 12,69,83-5). Since Pedaritos was of superior birth (Theopompos 115F8), there would be nothing incongruous in his mother's being related, as her name suggests, to Teleutias. The simplest, though not of course necessarily the correct, hypothesis would be to make Teleutia the sister of Theodoros and so the paternal aunt of Teleutias.

If she really was thus closely related to Teleutias, the connection may have a yet wider interest. For Thucydides' Pedaritos was son of a Leon, and a Leon was the father of the Antalkidas (not Antialkidas: see Whitehead 1979) who distinguished himself as ambassador, Ephor and critic of Sparta's policy towards Thebes during the reign of Agesilaos. It is true that Leon ('lion') was a common name in Greece, and it is by no means impossible that it was not one and the same Spartan Leon who in the second half of the fifth century won an Olympic victory, served as one of the three founders (*oikistai*) of Herakleia Trachinia, as envoy to Athens in 420 and as Ephor in 419/8, and succeeded Pedaritos as harmost of Chios in 412/1. But it would be surprising if different Leons had fathered Antalkidas and Pedaritos, and I therefore regard them as brothers (following Poralla 1913, nos 97, 599; Lewis 1977, 35n.65), putatively full brothers. If this chain of interconnecting hypotheses is correct, Teuleutias and Antalkidas were first cousins, and Agesilaos was therefore quite closely related to Antalkidas through his mother (see reconstructed stemma in Fig. 9.1).

Teleutias, like the late Lord Mountbatten within the British royal family, displayed a particular aptitude for naval command. But it was Agesilaos, according to Plutarch (*Ages.* 21.1) who somehow 'arranged' or 'fixed'

---

more are now attested through inscriptions. An augmented edition of Poralla's dissertation by A.S. Bradford is announced [published July 1985, Ares, Chicago].

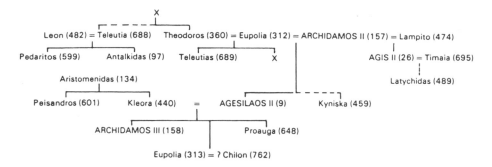

Fig. 9.1. The family of Agesilaos (numbers in brackets after Poralla 1913; broken lines = filiation uncertain)

(*diaprattetai*) his appointment as *nauarchos*, since he (Agesilaos) was by then the most powerful man in the Spartan *polis*. This is presumably a reference to Teleutias' first command, in 391 (4.4.19); for thereafter he could not technically be reappointed *nauarchos* (cf. 2.1.7). But Teleutias was not the first of Agesilaos' kinsmen to receive the supreme naval command through the good offices of the king.

Four years earlier Lysander had been killed at Haliartos and Agesilaos' Agiad co-king Pausanias had been forced into permanent exile under sentence of death. He was succeeded by a son, Agesipolis, who was still too young to command the allied levy at the Battle of the Nemea River in 394 (4.2.9; see Chapter 12). However much faith we place in Plutarch's assertion (*Ages.* 20.7-9) that it was by arranging Agesipolis' pederastic affairs that Agesilaos secured his subservience (and there is no reason to doubt that Agesilaos could act as a pederastic matchmaker, as we shall see), Agesilaos in 395 was so preeminent that he became the first Spartan king to be entrusted with the supreme military command by land and by sea simultaneously (3.4.27-8; Plut. *Ages.* 10.11). The way in which Agesilaos used this unique authorization is hugely revealing of his conception of 'attachment to his family'. For he appointed as *nauarchos* his brother-in-law Peisandros.

One of his motives, no doubt, was to prevent if he could the emergence of a second Lysander to threaten his control of the Asiatic war. But according to the apparently well informed Plutarch he did so because he wanted to do, or return, a favour to his wife Kleora. Aristotle would surely have counted this as a spectacular example of the gynecocracy he deplored at Sparta, where, he said rather sweepingly, many things were managed by women at the time of Sparta's empire (*Pol.* 1269b31). So it is irritating that we know nothing for certain about Kleora apart from her name and those of her brother and children (Poralla 1913, no.440). However, a very plausible correction by Hertzberg (1856, 235n.19a; accepted by Poralla 1913, no.134) of Paus. 3.9.3 would yield the important information that Kleora's father and Agesilaos' father-in-law was Aristomenidas (or Aristomelidas), a member of the Spartan elite with a suitably aristocratic name who was a Boiotian affairs specialist still on active duty in 396.

For his father-in-law could then have provided Agesilaos with an *entrée* to the dominant oligarchic circle of Leontiadas at Thebes, and Agesilaos' appointment of Peisandros could have been the *quid pro quo* for Aristomenidas' support of Agesilaos' controversial Theban policy. The date of Kleora's marriage can only be fixed within fairly broad limits. It should have been not earlier than 420, when Agesilaos was about twenty-five, since Spartan men seem to have married typically in their late twenties; and not later than about 400, since their son Archidamos was certainly over twenty in 378 (below). If Archidamos was their first child and was born soon after the marriage, then the outer limits would be roughly 408 and 400, for Archidamos was almost certainly under thirty in 378 and still relatively young in about 366 (Isok. 6.1). Most probably, therefore, Agesilaos was married before Agis died, and if he was already the father of a legitimate son that will not have harmed his cause in the succession dispute.

Being heir-apparent to the Eurypontid throne Archidamos was spared the rigours of the *agôgê*, although what we are told of his subsequent career suggests that he would have passed through it no less successfully than his father. As it was, other means were necessary to ensure that he would make the right personal connections and in general be prepared to accept the role allotted him by birth. Apart from the homely anecdote (Plut. *Ages.* 25.11) about Agesilaos riding on a hobby-horse to amuse his children, we first meet Archidamos in the charged atmosphere of Sphodrias' trial in 378. We are not explicitly told how Archidamos had come to be the lover (*erastês*) of Sphodrias' son Kleonymos. But if Agesilaos was able to be of service in his boy-hunting to Agesipolis (who had died in 380), it is not difficult to believe that he could have had a hand in making the match. For Sphodrias just happened to be – or rather did not just happen to be – a member of the rival political circle of his co-king Kleombrotos, who was far less subservient to Agesilaos than his older brother had been; and the pederastic relationship between the sons of Agesilaos and Sphodrias gave Agesilaos a line of communication to the heart of the chief focus of political opposition (cf. Cartledge 1981a, 29).

Having, as I believe, taken good care to arrange Archidamos' premarital homosexual love-life, Agesilaos next had to fix a politically suitable marriage for him. Once more we have to call in aid Greek habits of nomenclature to elucidate the bare names of Archidamos' wife and sons that the sources provide. His wife, Deinicha, is otherwise unknown to fame; but in form her name is closest to that of the Deinis who three centuries earlier had dedicated a fine bronze perfume-flask at the Menelaion sanctuary (Catling/Cavanagh 1976, 145-52).[2] His eldest and third sons were named respectively for their step-great-uncle Agis II and paternal grandfather Agesilaos II, but it is the name of the second son, Eudamidas (who in 331 or 330 succeeded Agis III as Eudamidas I) that has a particular interest. For the only other Spartans with that name known from the fourth century are an Ephor (attested by *IG* V.1, 1232) and the commander of a force sent to Olynthos in 382 (5.2.24-5), who may indeed be one and the same man (Poralla 1913, nos 294-5). The commander at any rate we know to have been brother to the Phoibidas who was a protégé of Agesilaos certainly after

___

[2] Now *CAH* III[2] Plate vol. (Cambridge, 1984) no. 321.

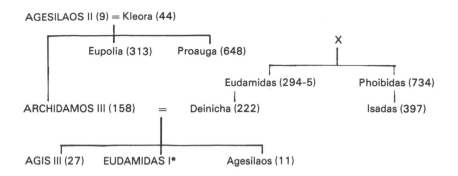

Fig. 9.2. The family of Archidamos (numbers in brackets after Poralla 1913; * omitted by Poralla)

and, I suspect, before his officially unauthorized seizure of the Theban akropolis in 382 (Chapter 14). It is far from illegitimate in these circumstances to speculate that Deinicha was Phoibidas' niece and daughter of his brother Eudamidas, and that King Eudamidas I was therefore named for his maternal grandfather (cf. Cawkwell 1976a, 78n.59; and see hypothetical stemma in Fig. 9.2). Since Eudamidas was killed at Olynthos, Deinicha may also have been an heiress (*patrouchos*) and so doubly attractive as a match for Archidamos some time after 378. Phoibidas, however, had managed to father a son, Isadas, between 381 and his death in 378, and Isadas was rich enough to be fined 1000 drachmai in 362 when still under the age of twenty (Plut. *Ages.* 34.8-11; cf. Poralla 1913, no. 397).

Archidamos was presumably not eligible for election or nomination to any of the official posts such as Hippagretes, Paidonomos or Ephor which ambitious Spartan parents would doubtless have tried to secure for their sons (cf. Finley 1981a, 32-3); that at least would seem to be the implication of Latychidas II's famous jibe to the newly-deposed Damaratos (Hdt. 6.67.2). But Archidamos became automatically a member of the royal mess, and Agesilaos could and did ensure that his son and heir had the chance to win his spurs and taste high military command. It is probably technically false to say (as Hamilton 1982b, 7,10-11) that Archidamos was made regent for his father; but in 371, 368 and 364 he was put in command of mainly Spartan forces in important situations. This sharing of responsibility was of course physically and politically convenient for the old and beleaguered Agesilaos, but it may be too that he was trying to make sure Archidamos did not suffer from the inexperience of leadership that had been his own lot at the time of his succession. Archidamos duly showed his gratitude for this and other favours by carrying the universal Greek ideal of unquestioning filial submission (cf. Dover 1974, 273-5) to the lengths of espousing unreservedly Agesilaos' disastrous foreign policy in the Peloponnese and central Greece. This is the viewpoint he is made by Isokrates to express with un-Spartan eloquence in the oration named after him, the dramatic date of which is about 366 (Isok. 6).

Of the known relations of Agesilaos by birth or marriage that leaves for discussion only his daughters, Eupolia and Proauga (a preferable reading to Prolyta at Plut. *Ages.* 19.10) and his sister or half-sister Kyniska. It is characteristic of our evidence for all Greek history that we should be told so little about his daughters; indeed, it is thanks only to the diligence of Plutarch that we know their names. However, we do learn that one of them was compelled by Agesilaos to ride down to the Hyakinthia festival at Amyklai in the ordinary public car, not in any specially elaborate carriage (Xen. *Ages.* 8.7; Plut. *Ages.* 19.7-8), rather as Agesilaos had himself once deliberately taken an inconspicuous place in the boys' chorus at the Gymnopaidiai festival (Plut. *Mor.* 208de). Moreover, one of the daughters was married to a Chilon at some time before his death in battle in 364 (7.4.23). It is just possible that this Chilon is the Cheilon of Aischines (2.78) who was harmost of Aigina in 395 (if it is correct to identify this Cheilon with the Milon of Hell. Ox. 6.3; 8.1,2). But whether or not these identifications are right, the name of Agesilaos' son-in-law announces that he was a descendant of his namesake, the heroized sage of the mid-sixth century who had appropriately been related to both royal houses.

Also heroized after her death was Kyniska (Paus. 3.15.1; cf. Chapter 16). Her name, meaning 'puppy-dog' or 'whelp', may at first reading appear odd, but in context it was not at all so. For her paternal grandfather or step-grandfather had Kyniskos for a sort of nickname (Hdt. 6.71.1, with Tuplin 1977b); a Kyniskos (presumably a relative: Poralla 1913, no.460) was harmost in the Thracian Chersonese in 400; and the so-called 'Lakonian hound' specially bred for its virtues as a scenter in boar-hunting was one of the two sorts of possession thought peculiarly appropriate to adorn the *oikos* of a Spartiate (Xen. *Ages.* 9.6; cf. *LP* 6.3).

The other possession of this sort was reckoned to be horses – warhorses, that is, as opposed to horses bred for chariot-racing (cf. Plut. *Ages.* 20.1) For the latter, according to Agesilaos at any rate, were not a mark of their owner's *aretê* but merely of his or her wealth and willingness to spend it (cf. Xen. *LP* 7.4). The fact that there were wealthy horse-breeding and horse-racing Spartans in Agesilaos' day – and indeed from at least the mid-sixth century (cf. Ste. Croix 1972, 354-5) – is interesting enough in itself as a contradiction of the ideal myth of egalitarianism. But more immediately relevant is Agesilaos' apparently eccentric attitude. Why did he not seek to emulate such Spartan grandees as Lichas (Poralla 1913, no. 492; cf. now Pouilloux/ Salviat 1983) or his own ancestor Damaratos in breeding horses to carry off the crown in the 'blue ribbon' event at Olympia, the four-horse chariot-race? Why did he entrust the honour and glory of his *oikos* in this peculiarly aristocratic and potentially politically significant type of competition to his sister Kyniska?

A clue may be found in Aristotle's portrait of the *megalopsuchos* man (*EN* 1124b-25a). *Megalopsuchia* for Aristotle is the virtuous condition that lies in the mean between vanity (*chaunotês*) and pusillanimity (*mikropsuchia*) with respect to the feeling or sphere of action of honour (*timê*); and he describes *timê* as 'clearly the greatest external good' and 'the prize of virtue' (*EN* 1123b), indeed 'broadly speaking the goal of political life' (*EN* 1095b). This makes 'magnanimity' an inadequate translation of *megalopsuchia*, especially as Aristotle's depiction of this exclusively upper-class Greek virtue contains many of the hallmarks of the political patron. Thus the *megalopsuchos* man is said to be disposed to confer, but ashamed to receive, benefits; and when he does receive a service, he repays it with interest so as to transform his benefactor into a beneficiary and debtor; he makes a request for aid only with reluctance but eagerly offers to help others; the only person upon whom he can bear to live in dependence is a friend; and so on. In regard to Agesilaos' attitude to horse-racing the relevant trait of Aristotle's *megalopsuchos* man is that he does not enter for popular contests or ones in which others can distinguish themselves. In other words, this conscious abstention of Agesilaos was not, despite Xenophon, dictated by any moral considerations. Rather, Agesilaos was concerned to project the image of being above this kind of sordid, material competition in which other members of the Spartan elite, debarred as they were from other sorts of ostentatious consumption, so passionately indulged. At the same time his abstention reinforced the aura of ordinariness with which he liked to surround himself. Agesilaos with his unrivalled private wealth and alternative sources of honour could well afford to adopt this contemptuous attitude.

The timing of Kyniska's Olympic activity may, however, have a further significance. For if she competed in 396 and 392, this was when Agesilaos was at his most actively 'panhellenist', and the Olympic Games was the Panhellenic festival *par excellence*; indeed, it was in 392 that the Sicilian Sophist Gorgias delivered his famous Olympic Oration. Nor was it insignificant that Kyniska not merely competed but took the olive crown, thereby becoming the first woman (though not the last Spartan woman) to achieve this feat. Following a well established tradition she dedicated a chariot and team in bronze and commissioned a metrical epigram to be inscribed on the group's stone pedestal. The bronzes have not been recovered, but the pedestal and epigram have survived in part (Ebert 1972, no. 33):

> My father and brothers were Spartan kings,
> I won with a team of fast-footed horses,
> and put up this monument: I am Kyniska:
> I say I am the only woman in all Greece to have won this crown
>
> (trans. P. Levi slightly modified)

Agesilaos might well have been suspicious of the tone of this epigram and would undoubtedly have disapproved mightily of the portrait statue of Kyniska also at Olympia ascribed to the hand of the Megarian sculptor Apelles (Paus. 6.1.6; cf. 3.8.1; 5.12.5). But there is no evidence that she – unlike the mysterious aunts of the harmost Lysanoridas who were allegedly executed for political reasons (Theop. 115F240; cf. Poralla 1913, nos 570, 769; missed by Lewis 1977, 34) – caused Agesilaos any political trouble, and her posthumous heroization presumably had his support. Which makes it all the more disappointing that we know absolutely nothing of her marital career. Kyniskos the harmost could have been her son, but he equally might have been more distantly related or owed his name to a political rather than a kinship connection with the family of Agesilaos (cf. Tuplin 1977b, 7-8). It is to such political connections of Agesilaos that I now turn, beginning with those whom Xenophon characterized as *hoi chrômenoi*.

Meaning literally 'those who use (him)', this term, which occurs elsewhere (Plut. *Ages*. 15.8), embraces those otherwise designated as *hetairoi* ('comrades': Xen. *Ages*. 6.4,9.7,11.10), *hoi heautou* ('his own people': Xen. *Ages*. 11.8), or *sunêtheis* ('intimates', 'familiars': Plut. *Ages*. 11.8). In a factional context its semantic range is probably comparable to *hoi peri* X, 'those around/in the circle of X', though that expression happens not to be used of Agesilaos and is once applied to a powerful Spartan Ephor, Xenares, who was also appointed harmost immediately after his term of office (Thuc. 5.46.4; cf. 5.51; Poralla 1913, no. 567). The sphere of reference of *hoi chrômenoi* and its equivalents was narrower than that of *philoi*, though all such intimates would of course also be 'friends'. Xenophon (*Ages*. 6.4) neatly conveys the distinction, and also the strongly contractual connotations of *philia*, when he writes that 'by being zealous on behalf of his *hetairoi* Agesilaos turned them into unhesitatingly devoted (*aprophasistous*) friends'; it is noteworthy, too, that *aprophasistos* was precisely the word Xenophon (*Ages*. 11.13) says that his *chrômenoi* applied to Agesilaos himself.

In Sparta, a sex-segregated, age-graded society where blood-ties were supposed normally to count for less than the bonds uniting fellow-members of a mess or a platoon, and less still than shared membership in the corporate body of Peers, it was natural that comradeship, and specifically military comradeship (apparently the root meaning of *hetaireia*), should have been unusually important (cf. Hutter 1979, 30-4). But it acquired a particular value in the competitive life at the top of the Spartan political heap, and no doubt affective as well as purely instrumental value too (cf. Gouldner 1965, 61). On the other hand, *hetaireiai* such as are known for example at Athens – friendship groupings composed of men equal in age as well as social class (Cavaignac 1924, 289-91; Hutter 1979, 27-8, 36-55) – could not formally exist in Sparta, where the common messes were specifically designed to cut across age-grouping in the interests of promoting trans-generational solidarity. Agesilaos' *chrômenoi*, therefore, will have been a more diverse and fluid group of intimate associates.

Problems of identification, however, are yet more acute for this group than for the kin of Agesilaos. Although references to his 'friends' collectively are too numerous to cite in full (e.g. Xen. *Ages*. 1.17-19; Plut. *Ages*. 5.1-2; *Mor*. 210f; Isok. 5.86-7), only two Spartans are explicitly referred to as such: Lysander (e.g. Plut. *Ages*. 6.5) and Etymokles (5.4.32; Plut. *Ages*. 25.8). (The Nikias of Plut. *Ages*. 13.5 = *Mor*. 209e may or may not be a Spartan; Xenophon was never of course granted Spartan citizenship.) Nevertheless, both Lysander and Etymokles can confidently be counted among the intimates of Agesilaos, and in their very different ways they admirably illustrate all the most salient features of this kind of friendship.

Lysander had been, if not the only, at least the most important *erastês* of Agesilaos (Chapter 3). The cementing of this pederastic relationship may tentatively be ascribed to the influence of Agesilaos' father Archidamos II, and Lysander's much later appointment to the supreme naval command to that of his half-brother Agis II. It was probably usual for Spartan pederastic couples to remain friends when the junior partner attained adulthood, and to become political associates if the partners belonged to the political elite. So Lysander was acting precisely as a *philos* should when he exerted his influence to secure the

Eurypontid throne for his former *erômenos*. But this of course put Agesilaos exceptionally deeply in the debt of Lysander; and if Agesilaos needed persuading by Lysander (cf. 3.4.2: *peithei*) to undertake his Asiatic campaign of 396, the consciousness of this debt should have weighed heavily with him. The sequel, however, suggests that Agesilaos had no intention of fulfilling the aim imputed to Lysander, that of restoring Spartan imperial rule through dekarchies, and this was not least because the dekarchs were friends of Lysander not of Agesilaos. The demise of Lysander is a classic of patronal manipulation.

It was not long after his arrival in Asia with Lysander as the chief of his thirty advisers (*sumbouloi*) that Agesilaos made plain where the power really lay. Plutarch's accounts of this vital episode (*Lys.* 23.5-10; *Ages.* 7-8) are fuller and less favourable to Agesilaos than that of Xenophon (3.4.7-9), and the additional details tally with what we know about inter-patronal disputes in other societies. In the closing phase of the Athenian War the dispenser of patronage throughout the Aegean was Lysander, in the now familiar sense that it was he who secured the plum jobs for his clients and followers. In 396 these men or their agents flocked to Ephesos to press their claim for restoration to power. They were aware that Agesilaos as king and commander wielded the ultimate authority, but they had no personal connections with him – for the simple reason that they were in the main not the kind of traditional landed aristocrats with whom Spartan kings had long been in the habit of contracting *xeniai* or ritualized guest-friendships: for instance, Hegetoridas of Kos with Regent Pausanias (Hdt. 9.76.3), Perikles with Archidamos II (Thuc. 2.13.1; with Lewis 1977, 46-7), or Xenias of Elis with Agis II (Paus. 3.8.4) – all probably inherited relationships. They therefore needed a 'broker', that is a 'manipulator of people and information who brings about communication for profit' (Boissevain 1974, 148), and turned naturally to Lysander. But Agesilaos, by spurning all Lysander's requests and intercessions on his clients' behalf, bankrupted him of the credit he had previously stored up as a man able to 'get things done' (*diaprattesthai*: 3.4.7; cf. Xen. *Ages.* 8.2; Plut. *Ages.* 20.6, 21.1; cf. *prattein*: Plut. *Ages.* 7.1).

The details are instructive. Agesilaos made a habit of rejecting any advice Lysander offered him – a very odd thing to do on the face of it, since Lysander's official function was precisely to advise him. He refused to grant any favours for clients of Lysander, whether it was the clients or Lysander who made the actual request. He dispensed justice (*kriseis*) in favour of those whom Lysander was seeking to destroy and to the detriment of his clients. Whatever the equity of such behaviour, it would serve to establish obligations for the future, when the cities of Asia Minor might be stably run by men indebted to Agesilaos. Finally, rather than appoint or recommend the appointment of Lysander to a harmostship or some other obviously important military-political command, Agesilaos endowed him with the empty though not intrinsically perhaps unflattering title of 'carver' (*Kreodaitês*; cf. perhaps the Athenian *Kôlakretai*, literally 'collectors of hams': Rhodes 1981a, 139-40). Plutarch considered that Agesilaos had carried his feud with Lysander too far, and he would no doubt have included it among those excesses of *philonikia* that were apt to bring difficulties and great dangers to cities (*Ages.* 5.7). But from Agesilaos' point of view it was essential to translate the titular authority vested in him as king on campaign into real personal authority and power, even at the cost of an open clash of honour with one of his most intimate *philoi*. Lysander's true attitude to Agesilaos thereafter is unknown, but in Greek terms his demotion was sufficient grounds for converting him from a *philos* into an *echthros* (political enemy). It was probably fortunate for Agesilaos that Lysander died soon afterwards.

The clash with Lysander occurred on campaign in Asia, and it is doubtful if Agesilaos could have effected his coup quite so painlessly in peacetime at Sparta. But the distinction between a king's powers of patronage at home and abroad should not be drawn too sharply. By 378 and probably long before that Agesilaos was being thronged by suitors in Sparta no less vigorously than Lysander had been at Ephesos in 396, and with much better hope of gaining satisfaction; and the suitors included foreigners and even his Helot domestics as well as Spartan citizens (5.4.28). The picture given here by Xenophon of suitors waiting for Agesilaos to leave his house early in the morning (for his daily dip in the Eurotas) smacks more of Roman patronage practices than anything we are accustomed to find in Greek history; and it is pretty clear that Agesilaos regularly held more formal audiences as well (Xen. *Ages.* 8.2, 9.2; Plut. *Ages.* 4.5, *Mor.* 208cd). But the relevant point to make is that most of the Spartan suitors would probably have belonged to the category labelled *hupourgêsantes* by Xenophon (*Ages.* 11.13) rather than to the *chrômenoi*.

If any of the latter group had a request to make of Agesilaos, it was more likely to be put in the context of hospitality, whether on days of sacrifice when Agesilaos would give a modest feast (Xen. *Ages.* 8.7), or when he used his double royal rations to honour a guest at the royal mess (Xen. *Ages.* 5.1, *LP* 15.4). Such hospitality was of the very essence of the aristocratic Greek lifestyle, but it had never been disinterested hospitality. Rather, it should be regarded as a particular instance of the more general political tactic of giving for a return. In the context of political patronage it was no less important for Agesilaos than it is today for a leading Swat Pathan in building up, maintaining and consolidating a political following (cf. Barth 1965).

By the time of Xenophon, however, a sharp distinction had long since been drawn both formally and informally between gifts that were good, what we might call 'presents', and gifts that were deemed to be bad, that is bribes, even if between these two white-capped polar extremes there was an extensive grey expanse in which one man's 'present' was another man's 'bribe'. Xenophon, naturally, was at pains to deny that Agesilaos' gift-giving was sordidly mercenary and to create an image of it corresponding to the boundless generosity (*poludôria*) of his fictional Cyrus (*Cyr.* 8.2.1-23; cf. Carlier 1978, 153-4). Agesilaos did not sell his favours (*charites*) or perform benefactions in return for pay (*misthos*: *Ages.* 4.4), Xenophon stressed; and although Xenophon had no need or wish to conceal the solidly material element in Agesilaos' *charites*, since material gifts were evaluated as a species of virtuous actions in general, he did deliberately counter any moral objections by redescribing Agesilaos' dispensation of patronage as 'justice in regard to material goods or money matters' (*dikaiosunê eis chrêmata*).

Xenophon's accounts of Agesilaos' generosity are perhaps understandably allusive and unspecific. Agesilaos, he says (*Ages.* 11.8), believed that the generous man (*eleutherios*) ought to use his own goods to help 'his own people' (*hoi heautou*), and he is only slightly more informative in revealing that Agesilaos enabled his 'friends' to get rich quick from the proceeds of selling booty plundered in Asia (*Ages.* 1.17-19). Plutarch, however, is much more lavish of detail. Immediately before the Battle of Koroneia in 394, he notes (*Ages.* 17.5), Agesilaos distributed meat from sacrificial animals to his *philoi*; who these *philoi* were is not stated, but in the previous chapter (16.5-6 = *Mor.* 211e) Agesilaos is said to have shown such solicitude in rescuing Xenokles and Skythes from their Thessalian captivity that they must surely be counted among them. These men were two of the thirty 'advisers' sent out to Agesilaos in Asia in 395; they had each received an important command from him (3.4.20) and then been jointly entrusted with a sensitive diplomatic mission. Another such 'friend' within the Spartan elite was Herippidas, the senior man of the thirty 'advisers' of 395; I am not the first to have noticed that between his harmostship at Herakleia Trachinia in 399 and his disgrace at Thebes in 379/8 he consistently turns up in top posts carrying out policies which Agesilaos was at least closely in sympathy with if he was not actually directing in person (cf. Smith 1953/4, 278n.1).

The meat Agesilaos disbursed at Koroneia was of course a highly practical gift in the circumstances, but its symbolic value was scarcely less exalted. Meat was not part of the regular mess rations in Sparta, which explains why it could appropriately be given as a special reward to the man who brought the news of Sparta's victory at Mantineia in 418 (Plut. *Ages.* 33.8). This also gives particular point to one of Agesilaos' more obviously political gift-giving practices recorded by Plutarch (*Ages.* 4.5; *Mor.* 482d). There was, it seems, no Spartan equivalent of the Roman *cursus honorum* or ladder of political offices and so no office-holding focus precisely comparable to the consulship. But there was one office in Sparta election to which was deemed to be the ultimate (in all senses) accolade, namely the Gerousia (Xen. *Ages.* 10.1-3; Plut. *Lyk.* 26). Both in the *Lykourgos* (5-6) and in the *Agesilaos* (4.2-6) Plutarch represents the Gerousia as the kingpin of the Spartan constitution – rightly in my view (Chapter 8). The power of the Gerousia, Plutarch says, was greater even than that of the Ephors, a fact that Agesilaos recognized by courting the Gerontes rather than confronting them as his predecessors had done. Agesilaos, he continues, would do nothing without their advice, he rushed to see them if summoned and – the main point for our present purposes – he always sent a cloak (*chlaina* – presumably woven by his Helot domestics) and an ox (selected from the extensive herds mentioned in Plat. *Alk.* 1.122c-123a) to each newly-elected member of the Gerousia as a mark of honour (*aristeion*).

In one place (*Mor.* 482c) Plutarch says that this practice caused Agesilaos to be fined, but this is probably just an illegitimate inference from his (also doubtless false) allegation that he was fined for 'turning public citizens into his own private property' (*Ages.* 5.4). In any case these gifts did not mean that all Gerontes elected after 400 were Agesilaos' men, as we shall see. However, what has been nicely called the 'gentle violence' inherent in the gift (Bourdieu 1970, 191ff.) will have had some effect in confirming the loyalty of those for whom Agesilaos had perhaps himself canvassed or appeasing somewhat the hostility of those whose allegiance lay elsewhere. For these were valuable gifts indeed. A sixth-century bronze figurine that very likely depicts a Geron shows him wearing a *chlaina* (Fellmann/Scheyhing 1972, 96 no.46), so perhaps it was a kind of visible symbol of office in a society where dress was otherwise drably uniform (Thuc. 1.6.5). As for the ox, that would go far towards repaying the elected member's debts to his friends and clients. If Agesilaos was never tried and punished by the Gerousia, he owed this exemption to gentle violence of this sort. The one Geron who is known to have been an intimate of Agesilaos is Etymokles; we shall return to him shortly.

Of Xenophon's two remaining categories the *hupourgêsantes* have been mentioned in passing in connection with Agesilaos' daybreak suitors. But we hardly surprisingly lack specific, individuated evidence about these 'servants' of Agesilaos, who must have been ordinary Spartans in the main. Being socially unequal to Agesilaos they may properly be designated clients in the fullest sense, even though they may in fact have been flatteringly referred to as 'friends' in a manner familiar from other patronage societies (e.g. Du Boulay 1974, 219; Eisenstadt/Roniger 1980, 44n.3). To such men Agesilaos would have appeared much as a Melanesian 'big-man' does to his followers: like the biggest banyan tree in the forest, he gives support to more lianas and creepers, provides more food for the birds and better protection for men against sun and rain (Sahlins 1963, 222). Translating that colourful image into Spartan language, we might expect Agesilaos to have helped his clients settle their inheritance disputes, contract pederastic or marital ties, perhaps even to have used his wealth to pay their mess bills or sponsor their sons as *mothakes* through the *agôgê*. Such self-interested 'subsistence crisis insurance' (J.C. Scott's phrase in Gellner/Waterbury 1977, 23) provided by the rich for the poor was conducive to social unanimity (*homonoia*), according to the contemporary philosopher Demokritos (F255 D-K). For their part the clients would have been expected to shout for the right candidates (e.g. Etymokles) in elections to the Gerousia and for the right policies in the Assembly (as they did with disastrous effect in 371 when they howled down Prothoös' opposition to the war-policy of Agesilaos: 6.4.2-3; Plut. *Ages.* 28.6), in addition to paying Agesilaos the more generalized respect and honour that would enhance his prestige.

The last of Xenophon's categories, the *adikoumenoi*, warrants rather more extended treatment. The verb *adikein* had a wide referential range – from 'harm' through 'wrong' to 'act illegally' (cf. Dover 1974, 180-4) – and carried a powerful emotive charge. Its regular occurrence in the context of friendship and enmity would suggest that the *adikoumenoi* in question here – those who were being harmed, wronged or illegally treated – were simply a special category of Agesilaos' friends. However, both Xenophon and Plutarch provide striking evidence which suggests that a broader interpretation is in order and that the relevant passage of Xenophon (*Ages.* 11.13) should be paraphrased something like this: 'those who were indebted to him for taking their side when they found themselves under attack called him their "champion" '.

Men in this category might well include political opponents of Agesilaos, not only friends of his. For according to Xenophon (*Ages.* 7.3), Agesilaos behaved towards his opponents in the *polis* like a father towards disobedient children, abusing them for their errors but honouring them for good conduct and standing by them in disaster (cf. Xen. *Cyr.* 8.2.9 for the paternalism of the quintessential patron Cyrus); while, according to Plutarch (*Ages.* 5.3), he helped his enemies when they were in difficulties and thereby made them friends. Indeed, if we are to believe another claim by Plutarch (*Ages.* 20.6 = *Mor.* 212cd), Agesilaos would arrange for (*diaprattomenos*) his more prominent opponents to be appointed generals and governors and then support them when they were subsequently put on trial for extortion or some other crime. Such a machiavellian tactic does have Roman parallels but seems initially rather unlikely in a Spartan context besides being politically highly risky. However, it is clear that Agesilaos did, for example, arrange (*diepraxato*) through his friends back in Sparta for himself to determine the final settlement at Phleious in 379 (5.3.24) and wholly plausible that he used his influence to secure top appointments and commissions for 'friends' like Teleutias. So perhaps the statement that he could do the same for his opponents should be accepted in the sense that he aimed thereby to trap them into executing his own policies. The cases of Agesipolis at Mantineia in 385 (Chapter 13) and Kleombrotos in Boiotia in 378 and 376 (Chapter 14) come readily to mind, although neither of these was subsequently put on trial.

On the other hand, the more modest claim that Agesilaos would help his enemies in their time of dire need can be substantiated in at least one and possibly two instances. The possible case is that of Phoibidas, whose officially unauthorized seizure of the Theban akropolis in 382 displeased 'the Ephors and most of the citizens' (5.2.32) and led to his trial on a capital charge before the Gerousia (and perhaps the Ephors). Agesilaos defended Phoibidas, or rather his action, on grounds of expediency; and although he was unable to secure his acquittal, he did save Phoibidas' life and perhaps, as Philistos had done for Dionysios I of Syracuse (DS 13.91.4), he paid Phoibidas' large fine (DS 15.20.2) – an example of Agesilaos' 'justice in money matters' that Xenophon would not have cared to dwell on. This behaviour of Agesilaos could in principle be construed as help given to an opponent in difficulty in order to win his friendship, and Xenophon (5.2.28) does his best to distance Phoibidas from Agesilaos by impugning the former's soundness of judgment. However, Phoibidas' action, though flagrantly illegal, was so consonant with Agesilaos' foreign policy that Agesilaos may well not only have defended it retrospectively but actually, as Plutarch (*Ages.* 24.1) alleges, have put Phoibidas up to it. Phoibidas' 'passion for doing something distinguished' is mentioned slightingly by Xenophon, but the phrase so strikingly recalls his earlier disparagement of Herippidas (4.1.21) that I would explain the zeal of both men as typically Spartan ambition being channelled towards gaining credit in the eyes of their mutual patron. Phoibidas, moreover, may have been related to Agesilaos by marriage (above).

In the second case, however, there is not the slightest doubt that it involved a prominent opponent of Agesilaos. In the previous chapter the formal aspects of the trial of Sphodrias were closely examined, since the passage of the *Hellenika* (5.4.20-33) that deals with the immediate circumstances and the outcome of the trial is perhaps the single most informative piece of ancient evidence regarding policymaking in Sparta. I now conclude the present chapter with a similarly detailed examination of the trial's informal modalities with special reference to the dispensation of patronage.

Sphodrias had been appointed harmost of Boiotian Thespiai in 378. By whom, we are not told by Xenophon, who simply reports that King Kleombrotos 'left' Sphodrias there as harmost. But since Agesilaos is also said to have 'left' Sphodrias' successor, Phoibidas, as harmost, it is a reasonable inference that Sphodrias owed his appointment at least to the influence of Kleombrotos. At all events, there is no question about the political allegiance of Sphodrias. The friends of Kleombrotos in the Gerousia were *hetairoi* of Sphodrias (5.4.25), and both Sphodrias and his son were to be found at Leuktra in Kleombrotos' personal suite (*hoi peri (tân) damosian*: 6.4.14; cf. for the expression 4.5.8, 7.4; Xen. *LP* 13.1,7; 15.4-5; further Chapter 12). It was presumably this known personal relationship that gave rise to the blunt assertion in Diodoros (15.29.5, where Sphodrias is miscalled Sphodriades) that Kleombrotos 'persuaded him to seize the Peiraieus without the authorization of the Ephors'. This assertion has been believed (e.g. Rice 1975, 108-9,112-18; following MacDonald 1972); but Xenophon (5.4.20) refers only to the suspicion that Sphodrias had been bribed by the Thebans. This suspicion was apparently endorsed, at least in public, by Agesilaos (5.4.30); and Xenophon was the last person to miss a chance of blackening the name of Kleombrotos. A third possibility is that Sphodrias conceived the idea of capturing the Peiraieus himself with the notion of thereby ingratiating himself with his patron Kleombrotos (cf. Herippidas and possibly Phoibidas above).

What is certain, though, is that, even if the plan had been successfully executed, it would have run directly counter to the policy of Agesilaos. For he was then seeking to prevent through diplomatic means an establishment of harmonious relations between Thebes and Athens. The Spartans tended to send as ambassadors men who had some special connection with or expert knowledge of the state in question (cf. Mosley 1979). But Etymokles, one of the three ambassadors actually in Athens when Sphodrias made his abortive attack, was not only an Athens-expert like his colleague Okyllos (cf. 6.5.33, where they reappear together at Athens a decade later) but a member of the Gerousia and a friend of Agesilaos. His arrest by the Athenians (5.4.22) will have caused Agesilaos no less pain than that of Skythes and Xenokles by the Thessalians in 394 and can only have aggravated his fury at their mutual political opponent Sphodrias.

Such at any rate was the perception of the ambassadors themselves, who asserted in good faith that Sphodrias would soon be executed and were on that account released, and of the luckless Sphodrias, who – advised perhaps by his *hetairoi* in the Gerousia – failed to appear when summonsed to stand trial. The outcome of the trial was thus as good as decided in advance. But as a desperate last resort Sphodrias fell back on an indirect entreaty for clemency to Agesilaos, whose verdict – for the reasons given in Chapter 8 – was literally the critical one. It is possible that Sphodrias, backed no doubt by Kleombrotos, was encouraged to make this entreaty by Agesilaos' past record of support for political opponents in comparably hopeless situations. But it seems more likely that he was pinning his faith on the efficacy of an emotional appeal to Agesilaos the *philokêdemôn*, that is on the grounds of his attachment to his family. For the conveyor of the entreaty, the patronage broker, was to be Agesilaos' son, Archidamos, who was the lover of Sphodrias' eighteen- or nineteen-year-old son Kleonymos (5.4.25).

Plutarch (*Ages*. 25.5) believed that Agesilaos had merely not put an end to this pederastic relationship between his son and the son of a leading political opponent. My own view, as I have already intimated, is that Agesilaos had actively promoted it, precisely because it might yield him some political dividend in the future; though he could not of course have anticipated quite this scenario. Anyway, Kleonymos duly bore the message of entreaty from his father to his lover, whereupon Archidamos – as Xenophon recounts in an excessively sentimental passage (5.4.27; cf. Henry 1967, 160) – wept for his beloved, confided his awe of Agesilaos but agreed nevertheless to beard the lion in his den. Or rather just outside his den. For on at least two successive mornings he waited outside Agesilaos' house but instead of making his plea gave way before a veritable host of suitors – Spartans, Helots and foreigners. Eventually, though, he did screw up the courage to make the intercession, only to receive the expected rebuff. He none the less tried once more, and this time received the ambiguous response from Agesilaos that he would pardon Sphodrias 'if that should turn out honourably for us' (5.4.31). Archidamos naturally enough took this to mean that Sphodrias' fate was sealed, but Agesilaos let it be known through Etymokles that he had changed his mind and would now vote for acquittal.

Agesilaos' professed reason, as reported through Etymokles, was that Sparta could not do without soldiers like Sphodrias, whose career as a *pais* (*sc*. in the *agôgê*), as a *paidiskos* (in the Krypteia?) and as a *hêbôn* (presumably as a member of the Hippeis and perhaps also as an Agathoergos) had been exemplary (5.4.32). Plutarch (*Ages*. 25.10-26.1), mistaking the channel of communication and the tenor of Archidamos' appeal for Agesilaos' motive, ascribed his change of heart to paternal and homoerotic sentiment. But although Agesilaos was willing to commit injustices on his friends' behalf (cf. Plut. *Ages*. 5.1-2) – typical patronal behaviour (e.g. Reina 1959, 45) – he was never prepared to put anyone, let alone an opponent, above what he considered to be the best interests of the Spartan state; and except perhaps in the one case of the appointment of Peisandros, a mistake he did not repeat, he never allowed sentiment to dictate matters of high public policy. *Realpolitik*, as Xenophon indicates, was indeed the real reason why Agesilaos switched his vote.

Xenophon, however, was not telling the whole truth. Sparta did desperately need soldiers of Sphodrias' calibre, it is true, thanks to the drastic decline in citizen manpower to be discussed further in the next chapter; and Agesilaos was said (Xen. *Ages*. 7.3) to have counted it a loss if even a citizen of little worth was destroyed. But Sphodrias was of course no ordinary Spartan soldier. He was a member of the political hierarchy and, yet more to the point, of the opposing royal circle. By granting Sphodrias his life, Agesilaos had conferred upon him the greatest favour (*charis*) possible, one that was almost by definition not repayable in kind (cf. Pearson 1962a, 149; C.H. Landé in Schmidt et al. 1977, xvii). But Agesilaos had done more than this: by acquitting Sphodrias, Agesilaos had enabled him to pursue his political and military career with honour intact. In short, Agesilaos had placed Sphodrias, and to a smaller extent those friends of Kleombrotos who were *hetairoi* of Sphodrias, eternally in his debt. It was thus no accident that both Sphodrias and his son died seven years later at Leuktra carrying out a policy with which Kleombrotos at least was far from wholly in sympathy – the policy of Agesilaos. This was perhaps the most spectacular result of Agesilaos' consistent and consistently successful exploitation of the many and varied sources of patronage available to a king who was willing and able to arrange for political opponents as well as family, friends and clients to act on his behalf.

10

Agesilaos and the Spartan Class Struggle

We suffer for the helot, under the severities and unequal treatment to which he was exposed: but when we think only of the superior order of men in this state ... we are apt to forget, like themselves, that slaves have a title to be treated like men. (Adam Ferguson, *An Essay on the History of Civil Society*, 1767)

It was fear that had knit Spartan society together and guaranteed the stability of the state. But not all Greek states were fortunate enough to have a helot problem. (Arnheim 1977, 121)

The Helot danger was the curse Sparta had brought upon herself, an admirable illustration of the maxim that a people which oppresses another cannot itself be free (Ste. Croix 1972, 292)

The capstone of the edifice ascribed by official Spartan tradition to the lawgiver Lykourgos was the *homonoia* (concord, unanimity) that was supposed to have reigned eternally among the self-styled Homoioi or Peers. As Plutarch tells the story in his 'biography' of the lawgiver (*Lyk.* 8.9), Lykourgos once returned from abroad immediately after a harvest and smilingly remarked to his companions that Lakonia resembled an inheritance recently shared out completely and equally among many brothers. Yet precisely when *homonoia* was entering the Spartan mirage being created for public consumption from the latter part of the fifth century (Chapter 22), the real-world Sparta was being racked by internal dissensions. Disagreements over policy within the Spartan political hierarchy were only to be expected in the course of a lengthy and for long unsuccessful war such as the Athenian War; but on one and possibly two occasions Thucydides also briefly trailed before his readers' goggling eyes some of that dirty domestic linen which the Spartans were extremely anxious to avoid having to wash in public.

By the summer of 424 Sparta's situation as depicted by Thucydides was grim. The previous year a detachment of 420 hoplites had been cut off by the Athenians on the island of Sphakteria in the bay of Pylos (Navarino Bay) in western Messenia. Partly through bad luck, partly by their opponents' clever exploitation of the terrain, the 292 survivors of this detachment including about 120 full Spartan citizens were compelled to surrender and taken as hostages to Athens, where they helped to ensure that Sparta ceased her annual invasions of

160

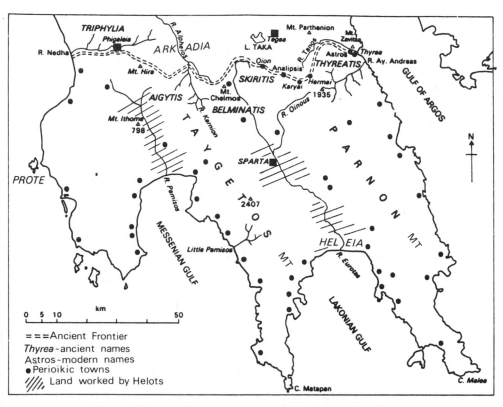

Fig. 10. The populations of Lakedaimôn. After Cartledge 1979

Attika. Hard on the heels of this débâcle the Spartans in 424 lost possession of the island of Kythera off the Lakonian Gulf to the Athenians, who used it as a base for making lightning raids simultaneously upon both of Sparta's economically vital heartlands – the Eurotas and Pamisos valleys worked by the Helots. Fear of a Helot uprising is explicitly given as one of the motivations for the three crisis measures taken by the Spartans in this period: an exemplary massacre of 2000 Helots, the despatch of another 700 Helots as hoplites to a far-distant theatre, and the raising of small forces of cavalry and archers (see Chapter 4). But when Thucydides (4.55.1) says that in 424 the Spartans feared a revolution (*neôteron ti*), his wording does not formally exclude the possibility that the authorities feared an outbreak of civil strife (*stasis*) within the citizen population – the very contingency that the system attributed to Lykourgos was supposedly geared to obviate.

Three years later, at least according to Thucydides (5.34.2), there is no doubt that such *stasis* was perceived to be a major danger. Under the terms of the Peace of Nikias (Thuc. 5.18.7), but not in fact until after a bilateral defensive alliance had been sworn between Sparta and Athens alone (5.24.2), the

Athenians had returned the Sphakteria hostages. Among the 120 or so Spartiates, it transpired, were members of the Spartan political elite whose high status (coupled no doubt with Spartiate *oliganthrôpia*) had led to their being somehow appointed to state offices immediately on their return. But they comported themselves in such a way – mainly perhaps by seeking rather too vigorously to sabotage the precarious entente between Sparta and Athens – that the highest Spartan authorities feared or claimed they feared internal revolution from this quarter (*mê ti ... neôterisôsin*). On this account or pretext they went so far as to deprive the high-ranking returnees of their full citizen rights, visiting them with a species of *atimia* that included a prohibition of their right to buy and sell.

Two clear hints, then, that already by the middle years of the Athenian War the vaunted *homonoia* among the Homoioi was a screen and a sham. With the reign of Agesilaos hints yield place to tangible revolutionary manifestations. Both at the beginning of the reign and towards its end the sources reveal serious cracks in the ideological monolith. Indeed, the cracks became so serious that Agesilaos, the staunch upholder of law and order, was in 371 obliged to suspend the laws for a day and in 370/69 to put a group of Spartiates to death without trial – both measures being unprecedented in Spartan history.

Sparta, in other words, was not quite as abnormal in respect of the absence of *stasis* as the mirage liked to pretend. In fact, one of the leitmotifs of Agesilaos' reign is the contradiction between his avowed maintenance of the 'Lykourgan' status quo in all its basic aspects and his enforced accommodation to the rapidly accelerating change that was to an extent unavoidably undermining it. Nowhere does this contradiction stand out more starkly than in the sphere of society and economy, the subject matter of the present chapter. For the Athenian War and the subsequent policy of aggressive imperialism had brought Sparta for the first time into prolonged and intimate contact with the mainstream of Greek socio-economic development. The clash between the old Spartan ideals and present reality was resounding. Tensions were generated at all levels of society within the Spartan *polis*, and in the persons of Lysander, Pausanias and Kinadon these tensions were sufficiently strong to find their way into Aristotle's *summa politica*, the *Politics*.

Book 5 of that work deals with equality, justice and above all constitutional change – both the reasons why constitutions do or tend to change and the methods whereby such change can be (and ought to be, as Aristotle thought) deflected, halted or prevented. The opening chapter of this Book is, in the words of a recent commentator (Saunders 1981, 295-6), 'a fine example of Aristotle's shrewd analysis. He is here concerned not merely to list what circumstances lead to what changes, but to penetrate to the psychological or intellectual or "ideological" sources of social conflict. These sources he locates in differing notions of distributive justice, which in turn depend on different criteria for measuring the equality and inequality of men'. In this chapter Aristotle gives as examples of factional strife 'the alleged attempt of Lysander to abolish the kingship or of King Pausanias to abolish the Ephorate' (*Pol.* 1301b19-21). He does not further elucidate the motives of Pausanias, but a few chapters later (*Pol.* 1306b33-4) he does give an explanation of why Lysander sought constitutional change: it was because, although he was not at all inferior in *aretê* to the kings (Pausanias, Agis II and perhaps Agesilaos), he was dishonoured by them.

Lysander's alleged machinations have been discussed at length already (Chapter 6). But it is worth dwelling briefly on Pausanias' alleged constitutional proposal, not least because the pamphlet (*logos*) in which it was made is quite likely to have marked 'an important stage in the idealisation of "Lycurgan" Sparta' (David 1979b, 116). Unfortunately, though, both the nature of this pamphlet and the circumstances of its production are deeply obscure. The passage of Strabo (8.5.5, C366) that is our only evidence for its existence is textually corrupt, so that scholars have argued interminably as to whether Pausanias wrote in favour of or in opposition to the 'laws of Lykourgos'. The latest contributor to the debate (David 1979b) prefers the former alternative, and this seems to me the more plausible one *a priori*. Even revolutionaries in ancient Greece tended to couch their projects for radical change in terms of a restoration of the good old 'ancestral constitution' established by a profoundly wise legislator of more or less hoary antiquity. On this view Pausanias would have called for the abolition of the Ephorate on the grounds that it was an unscriptural, post-Lykourgan innovation. This reinterpretation can be tied in to the fact that, whereas in the fifth century the Ephorate was apparently unanimously attributed to Lykourgos, in the fourth century there appears for the first time an alternative attribution – to King Theopompos – that Aristotle (*Pol.* 1313a25-7) could have read in Pausanias' *logos*. If it should seem odd that Pausanias, who wished to establish the kingship more securely against Ephoral control, ascribed the damnable Ephorate to a royal predecessor, it must be remembered that Theopompos was an Eurypontid and not an Agiad like Pausanias. Then again, the ascription may even be true (cf. Chapter 8).

However that may be, it is not known precisely how Pausanias couched his attack on the Ephorate or conducted his defence of the laws of Lykourgos as he understood them. But it is a reasonable guess that one of his trump cards was to quote the Great Rhetra, a document that was deafeningly and gratifyingly silent about the very existence of the Ephors let alone their powers. It could, then, have been from Pausanias' pamphlet that Aristotle or his pupils learned directly or indirectly of the Rhetra, which came to Plutarch (*Lyk.* 6) through the now lost Aristotelian *Lak. Pol.* Another way in which Pausanias' work could have contributed to the idealisation of 'Lykourgan' Sparta has also been suggested by David, namely by the use that may have been made of it for propaganda purposes by the revolutionary third-century kings Agis IV and Kleomenes III. If this suggestion is right, then Pausanias must bear a large part of the responsibility for the horribly confused state of the ancient evidence on Spartan land-tenure, to which we shall shortly return. For the moment, however, it is enough to note that Pausanias felt sufficiently strongly about his trial and exile to indulge in the highly un-Spartan pastime of literary composition. In this he may have either been setting a precedent or following that set by one Thibron, who also wrote admiringly of Lykourgos in a work on the Spartan constitution (Arist. *Pol.* 1333b17-19) and who may well be the similarly exiled Spartan commander of the 390s (cf. Poralla 1913, no. 374).

These splits at the very top of the Spartan governing class involving Pausanias and Lysander were in fact but the surface froth generated by the unrest that was seething at all levels of Spartan society from the bottom up during the reign of Agesilaos. The most disturbing and most fully reported agitation centred around an abortive conspiracy led by a certain Kinadon within a year of Agesilaos' accession. But before looking at that in some detail it is instructive to consider two further outbreaks that are mentioned only by Plutarch (*Ages.* 32.6-12) and have received less scholarly attention than they merit (but see David 1980).

These occurred during one of Sparta's darkest hours, when Epameinondas invaded Lakonia and menaced the settlement of Sparta itself with a massive army drawn from central Greece and the Peloponnese in midwinter 370/69 (see further Chapter 12). To bolster his depleted manpower reserves at a moment when all the Messenian Helots and many of the Perioikoi were in open revolt, Agesilaos resorted to enrolling 6000 Lakonian Helots as hoplites with the prospect of their eventual liberation. Not all of these stood their ground, however, and the very number of the new recruits – over six times as big as the full Spartan citizen levy – inspired terror within the Spartiate ranks. Of this terror two groups sought to take political advantage. The first, who Plutarch says (*Ages.* 32.6) had long been disaffected, numbered some 200. But Agesilaos' intelligence was good and, suspecting some revolutionary design (*neôterismos*), he lulled their suspicions and then aborted their plot by executing some fifteen of them in the night. This was the state's normal method of disposing of Spartan criminals (cf. Hdt. 4.146.2), but Plutarch does not specify the political status of those concerned. In the case of a second, and larger, conspiracy, however, Plutarch is as specific as he could possibly be: the conspirators were Spartiates, full Spartan citizens; and Agesilaos in consultation with the Ephors took what Plutarch calls the unprecedented step of executing them (or their leaders?) without trial despite their status. The fifteen or so executed earlier were presumably therefore of less than full citizen status, and their inferiority could well have been the source of their long disaffection, especially if it had been brought about by degradation from Spartiate status. That at least would be a legitimate inference from Xenophon's remarkably detailed account of the conspiracy promoted by Kinadon thirty years earlier (3.3.4-11; cf. Arist. *Pol.* 1306b34; with Cartledge 1979, 273-5,312-14; David 1979a).

The plot was uncovered some time before late summer 399 (according to the chronology adopted in this book). Agesilaos was conducting a public sacrifice, perhaps to Apollo (cf. Hertzberg 1856, 24), when the seer (*mantis*) reported ill omens that seemed to be saying they were surrounded by enemies. *Manteis* had a no doubt deserved reputation for chicanery in fourth-century Greece (e.g. Ain. Takt. 10.4), but this was a prophecy of things as they were and had been for many years so far as the Spartiates were concerned. The tiny and shrinking citizen body ruled over a vastly more numerous and more or less hostile subject population, and existing structural tensions had been greatly exacerbated by the Athenian War. Now, however, an informer opportunely told the Ephors how Kinadon had tried to recruit him to what was projected as a near-universal anti-Spartiate insurrection. Kinadon had taken the informer to the edge of the Spartan Agora (civic centre) and pointed out that the ratio of non-Spartiates to

Spartiates present was of the order of 100:1. The same point about the numerical inferiority of the Spartiates was graphically impressed upon him as they together travelled the streets of Sparta and visited the landed estates in the rural hinterland. At that stage, however, the conspiracy was more potential than actual, as the informer learned when he was told that thus far there was just a nucleus of trustworthy leaders. But these cadres assured him that the plot promised to be pandemic. For if ever there was mention made of the Spartiates among the Helots, the Neodamodeis, the Hupomeiones or the Perioikoi, no one belonging to these social groups could conceal their anxiety to devour the Spartiates – even raw!

Allowances must obviously be made for a good deal of agit-prop exaggeration here. But it is safe to infer that these were the four most important divisions of the sub-Spartiate inhabitants of the Spartan *polis* and that at least some members of each category might feel thus cannibalistically inclined. Indeed, this uniquely revealing passage exhibits more clearly and economically than any other source the complexity and hierarchical organization of Spartan society, in which the tendency of all Greek states to multiply social categories (cf. Aymard 1967, 287-9) was consciously taken to its extreme limits. But it also does very much more than that. Written with hindsight after Sparta's débâcle at Leuktra and the consequent invasion of Lakonia and Messenia by Epameinondas, it puts its finger on one of the chief symptoms and causes of the Spartan crisis, *oliganthrôpia* or the shortage of Spartiate military manpower. It brilliantly conveys just how precarious and insecurely based was the *archê* (empire) over which Sparta held sway in 399. Above all, though, it illuminates as if by a whole battery of arc-lamps the form and character of the Spartan class struggle.

Class, like slavery, is an explosive subject, and when, as here, the two are interconnected or even interchangeable, the fall-out is likely to be enormous. Except perhaps for a Christian troubled by the negative role of the early Churches, the existence of servile systems in Graeco-Roman antiquity need not disturb a modern scholar's conscience. But 'discussions of different theories of class are often academic substitutes for a real conflict over political orientations' (Bendix/Lipset 1966/7; quoted by Ste. Croix 1981, 31). This is not the place to conduct such a discussion, but the appearance of a massive theoretical and empirical study of class struggle in the ancient Graeco-Roman world as a whole (Ste. Croix 1981) has confirmed my earlier view (Cartledge 1975) that the dominant and decisive contradiction or tension of Spartan society can fruitfully be analysed in terms of a class struggle between the Spartiates and the Helots. The Spartiates, that is to say, extracted the economic surplus that enabled them to live (and sometimes enjoy) their peculiarly military mode of life from and at the expense of the Helots, who were the primary agricultural producers. The Spartiates individually and collectively controlled the conditions of production, above all through their ownership of the land the Helots tilled in the Eurotas and Pamisos valleys. As for the Helots, those of Messenia at least were conscious of their own identity and common interests as a class. Not only were they involved in class struggle in the passive sense that they were systematically exploited, but they also had a precisely political conception of their class struggle, which the Spartiates from their side of the barricades fully reciprocated. Here, then, was class struggle in the purest or completest form known in ancient Greece. Thucydides may have lacked the (or any) theoretical concept of class struggle, but that did not make him any the less confident or correct in identifying relations between the Spartans and the Helots as the motor of Spartan history (e.g. 4.80.2, a generalization provoked by the exemplary massacre of 425/4). Aristotle, on the other hand, did articulate a class struggle theory of political change (cf. Ste. Croix 1981, 69-80) and vividly likened the Helots to 'an enemy constantly sitting in wait for the disasters of the Spartans' (*Pol.* 1269a37-9).

In what follows, though, I shall be considering not only relations between Spartiates and Helots but also relations between Spartiates and Perioikoi and, not least, relations within the Spartan citizen body: the role of women as well as men, of degraded 'Inferiors' as well as citizens of full status. I shall thus be treating the first of the three strands into which M.I. Finley (1981a, 25) schematically divided the structure of 'Classical' (for him *c.*550-371) Sparta: that is, 'the infrastructure of land allotments, helots and perioikoi, with everything that includes with respect to labour, production and circulation'. Unlike Finley, however, I shall be less concerned with this infrastructure as an ideal type than with the 'tensions and anomie' by which, as he points out (cf. further Hodkinson 1983), the system was filled in actual practice. For the age of Xenophon and Agesilaos witnessed profound changes in Spartan society, accelerated though not wholly caused by the Athenian War. It is true that no group or combination of groups of the many malcontents thrown up by this fundamental upheaval succeeded in overturning the system in its entirety. But the effect of their unrest on Spartiate morale must not be overlooked, especially as this demoralization in its turn gave hope to those outside Sparta who resented her leadership, hegemony or overbearing domination. The army that lost the Battle of Leuktra was not merely out-of-date tactically and spearheaded by a dangerously small Spartiate contingent. It was also a demoralized army (cf. Chapter 12). For that, responsibility lies ultimately with the failure of the Spartan social system and with those who sought to perpetuate the system when they would have been better employed in trying to remake it.

First, then, the land allotments. If Spartan social history is as a whole 'an area so rich in uncertainties' (Lotze 1971, 76), the latter cluster most thickly in this corner of the field. To describe the problem of Spartan land-tenure as 'one of the most vexed in the obscure field of Spartan institutions' (Walbank 1957, 628) is therefore saying a great deal. It is not so much or only the scantiness but more importantly the systematically distorted slant of the ancient data that has created this sorry situation. For by ancient standards the economy of ancient Sparta is reported with unusual fullness. But realities have to be descried through the mists of the Spartan mirage. In this instance the chief culprits were Kings Agis IV and Kleomenes III and their propagandists, although they may been drawing on Pausanias to some extent (as we saw above). Agis succeeded in putting into effect one half of the traditional demand of the ancient oppressed: the cancellation of debts (*chreôn apokopê*). Kleomenes later managed the other half, the redivision of land (*gês anadasmos*). But in order to give their revolutionary reforms the desired and necessary gloss of conservatism, they represented their measures as a return to legality, a restoration of the happy situation created by the legislation of Lykourgos (see beginning of this chapter) but long since fallen into desuetude.

This was one of the reasons why Plutarch in writing their *Lives* chose to compare them to the Roman Republican reformers Tiberius and Gaius Gracchus. But since Plutarch, who apart from Aristotle is our main 'authority' on Spartan land-tenure, drew heavily on sources close to Agis and Kleomenes like Phylarchos (cf. Africa 1960, 1961; Gabba 1957), it is not unreasonable to suppose that his account of the supposedly 'Lykourgan' land regulations was decisively contaminated thereby. That at any rate is how I would explain the genesis of the myth that each Spartan citizen was endowed at birth (subject to passing a test of physical and perhaps spiritual fitness) with an equal, indivisible and legally inalienable lot (*klaros*) and that the number of *klaroi* and *ipso facto* of Spartan citizens remained constant at 9000 from the time of the 'Lykourgan' land-division down to the reign of Agis II (cf. Cartledge 1979, 165-70; and on landownership by women Cartledge 1981b, 97-9). To this same myth I would assign the supposed *rhetra* (enactment) moved by the Ephor Epitadeus, which allegedly gave the Spartans something like freedom of testament at some time after the death of Agis II. Aristotle knew of no such *rhetra*, and one's suspicions can only be aroused by the fact that this 'tradition' appears first in Plutarch's *Life* of Agis IV (*Agis* 5) rather than in his *Lykourgos*, in which he certainly used the lost Aristotelian *Lak. Pol.* Despite the arguments of Marasco (1980; following and seeking to correct Cary 1922, 185n.12; 1926, 186-7; and Asheri 1961; 1963, 5-6, 12-13), I see no reason to alter the view expressed in my earlier book (Cartledge 1979, 167-8; cf. 316,318,319). The most that any legislative enactment of this kind is likely to have achieved is retrospectively to have legalized a *de facto* situation, much as Thomas Jefferson's abolition of primogeniture gave legal standing to the existing practice of partible inheritance. Epitadeus, as Forrest (1980, 137) has neatly said, 'if he existed, does not belong to the fourth century or, if he does, did not create the trouble'.

The 'trouble' in question is *oliganthrôpia* (or *oligandria*), a shortage of Spartiate military manpower that was already marked by the first phase of the Athenian War (see Chapter 4). This in its turn was chiefly the result of the increasing concentration of landed properties and not primarily due to any individual natural disaster like the great earthquake of *c.*465 (the argument of Ziehen 1933, followed by Porter 1935 and others, was adequately refuted in advance by Andreades 1931). For as Aristotle observed (*Pol.* 1307a34ff.), 'a further consequence of the fact that all aristocratic constitutions are oligarchic in character is that the notables (*gnôrimoi*) win even greater advantage: for example, at Sparta where landed properties (*ousiai*) keep coming into the hands of the few'. In fact, by Aristotle's day, the third quarter of the fourth century, the situation had reached such a pass that there were appreciably fewer than 1000 full citizens and almost two fifths of the land were in the hands of women (*Pol.* 1270a30-2; 1270a23-5), while by the mid-third century the full citizen complement had declined further to a mere 700 (Plut. *Agis* 5.6) as compared to some 8000 in 480 (Hdt. 7.234.2). Already by the early fourth century, the implied date of Epitadeus' supposed *rhetra*, the figure had fallen to a maximum of

3000 (cf. Cartledge 1979, 280-1). So if the concentration of property was caused mainly by testamentary alienation of land outside the patrilineage, as the Plutarchan tradition would have it, Aristotle was absolutely right to locate the origin of this severe, indeed ultimately catastrophic, defect in the basic structure of the 'Lykourgan' regime of land-tenure rather than some alleged legally enacted (as opposed to customary) modification of it.

There is nevertheless no denying that in this as in so many other aspects of Spartan social and political practice the Athenian War registered a watershed. By bringing significant numbers of elite Spartans into sustained and intimate contact with hitherto unimagined amounts of coined silver and gold, this war accelerated and gave a new twist to a process that had been underway since at least the mid-fifth century. There had of course always been rich and poor Spartans; the evidence for this is unambiguous from the late eighth century onwards. In this respect Sparta was like any other Greek state. What differentiated Sparta, at least from the mid-seventh century, was, in the first place, a self-imposed restraint on the part of the rich whereby their lifestyle in Sparta was rendered not conspicuously different from that of the majority (cf. Thuc. 1.6.5); and, secondly, state interventions in the property-regime in order to try and ensure that all full Spartan citizens should possess the minimum of income necessary to enable them to be equipped as hoplites and to devote themselves full-time to the one manual craft to which no social stigma was ever attached, the craft of soldiering. Hence the imposition of a common, public, barrack-room style of life and the distribution of *klaroi* in newly-conquered Messenia, the two being so linked by the institution of the communal messes that the monthly contribution of a fixed amount of natural produce to a mess was a condition of exercising full citizenship.

From the mid-seventh century Spartan society as a whole was unique. But the history of its property-regime is the history of its progressive 'normalization' (or re-normalization), that is of the progressive triumph of *oikos* (individual household) particularism over the communitarian, Lykourgan ideal – or myth. Thus the Spartan rich who, beside their *klaros*, drew wealth from other landed property and possessed 'treasure' (*keimêlia*: Hdt. 6.62.2) in the shape of movables such as horses, chariots and precious metals, resorted unsurprisingly to the familiar upper-class Greek 'strategies of heirship' (cf. Goody 1976b, ch.7) in an attempt to preserve their and their *oikos*' superior social status. In a 'malthusian' – or 'Hesiodic' (*WD* 376) – way they aimed to limit their male offspring to a single son; and any daughters they sired they would seek to marry off to the sons of other wealthy houses, especially if the daughters happened to be heiresses (*patrouchoi*, that is having no living brothers of the same father; cf. Cartledge 1981b, 98). For in Sparta, unlike contemporary Athens, women could own real property in their own right (though probably subject to male control in many cases). The ancient prerogative of the kings to assign heiresses whose deceased fathers had failed to make provision for their marriages was presumably designed to counteract such alliances, for these would have tended to concentrate landed property in the hands of ever fewer *oikoi*. But this prerogative was a dead letter by the time of Aristotle, if indeed it was not already so in the time of Herodotus (6.57.4), who is our source for its existence (cf. Chapter 7).

Besides, the kings themselves hardly acted in accordance with the spirit of their supposed prerogative, since we know of several cases where they married close consanguineous kin from considerations of property power (cf. Cartledge 1981b, 99). Such in-marriage as practised by the royal houses was probably typical of the Spartan propertied class as a whole and nicely exemplifies the nexus between land, class, kin and marriage (the theme of Goody 1976b).

It was presumably to counteract this 'malthusianism' on the part of the Spartan rich that a dispensation was introduced, perhaps around 500, whereby the father of three sons was exempted from military service, the father of four or more from all public impositions (Arist. *Pol.* 1270a40-b7; cf. Ael. *VH* 6.6). At any rate, had poor Spartans been encouraged by this to go forth and multiply exceedingly, the dispensation would only have fostered the tendency to *oliganthrôpia* that it was designed to halt: for by having and raising several sons a poor father risked their being excluded eventually from the enjoyment of full citizen rights on the grounds that they could not keep up the required mess-contribution (cf. Marasco 1980, 136). On the other hand, there were measures to the same end such as the legal obligation to marry and marry within prescribed age-limits that were aimed at the poor no less than the rich. But all these measures proved to be of no avail against restricted fertility, considerations of social status, and other demographic inhibitions like natural disaster and death in warfare (cf. the low rate of social reproduction of the Roman senatorial aristocracy discussed by K. Hopkins and G.P. Burton in Hopkins 1983, chs 2-3). For, as Aristotle (*Pol.* 1270a39-40) observed with the benefit of hindsight, the way to keep up Spartan citizen numbers would have been to even out the distribution of property ownership rather than encourage brute procreation. Such a radical measure, however, the Spartan rich refused to contemplate, as is symbolized by the Epitadeus story and implied in the prohibition on buying and selling (land) imposed on the Sphakteria returnees (Thuc. 5.34.2; with Gomme 1970, *ad loc.*).

Precisely what a poor Spartan would do when he was in danger of defaulting on his mess-contribution, or what happened to him after he had so defaulted, we are largely left to guess in the absence of direct, explicit evidence. One possible answer was bachelorhood, but this was in most cases highly unsatisfactory, since it was visited with a rich array of social humiliations and punishments (cf. Cartledge 1981b, 95). Another possible strategy was for several brothers to take a single wife (Polyb. 12.6b.8; cf. the wholly exceptional seven brothers of *Anth. Pal.* 7.435), since such adelphic polyandry would tend to reduce the number of heirs and perhaps enable the males of a family to cling on to citizen rights for another generation. But the crisis of the later fifth century clearly demanded untraditional and yet more extreme expedients. It has been supposed, for example, that a poor Spartiate, debarred as he was from trade and manufacture, might go into debt by raising a 'mortgage' from a rich Spartan on the security of the crops or a portion of the crops grown on his *klaros* (cf. Christien 1974). But this legalistic distinction between crops and land seems anachronistic, especially in a society without written laws and with the haziest juristic notions of ownership. A more plausible suggestion is that he might sell his *klaros* (or part thereof) outright in return for the coined money to which rich Spartans were gaining access and that with this cash he might hope to pay for the necessary mess-contributions (cf. Buckler 1977a). This suggestion apparently falls foul of the absolute legal prohibition on selling one's 'ancient portion' (*archaia moira*), that is probably *klaros* land in Messenia; but that prohibition could have been and *in extremis* no doubt was circumvented by a fictitious and fraudulent gift or bequest (cf. Arist. *Pol.* 1270a20-23).

All that is known for certain, however, is that Spartans who were too poor to pay their mess bills lost their full citizen status; and it is virtually certain that they joined the swelling band of Hupomeiones or 'Inferiors' (a title attested only at 3.3.6) along with those who had been degraded for failing to pass through the *agôgê* or get elected to a mess, for cowardice on the battlefield or some other misdemeanour. Some of the 'Inferiors' like Kinadon, who had clearly been degraded for economic reasons, might be specially enrolled in the regular army to make up the numbers (cf. Chapter 12) or employed by the Ephors in counter-insurgency work against potentially rebellious Helots. But even such apparently privileged treatment did not prevent Kinadon from contemplating revolution (or at least the forcible restoration of his full rights); and as a group the Hupomeiones palpably constituted 'an undigested lump within the system' (Finley 1981a, 34). In short, the economic transformations undergone by Sparta in the late fifth and early fourth centuries brought her more into line with many fourth-century Greek cities in which the antagonism between rich and poor citizens became 'the dominant fact of their history' (Mossé 1962, 226).

In Spartan history, however, the dominant fact then, as before and after, was the antagonism between the Spartans and the Helots (cf. for useful reviews of the recent literature Oliva 1981; and Ducat 1983, 205-7; but Manso 1800, Beylage 10, pp.135-55 is still worth consulting). Rather than attempt to cover again (cf. Cartledge 1979, ch. 10) all the many and complex interrelated facets of this fundamental antagonism, I propose to concentrate here on the Spartiates' exploitation of the Helots: that is, to try to determine – inevitably roughly – how far the Spartiates extracted the surplus that enabled them to live as they did at the expense of the Helots without giving any corresponding benefits in return. This topic is far from being, as it may at first seem, narrowly economic. It embraces everything from the size of *klaros* and nature of the crops grown to the reasons why the Helots, almost alone of Greek servile populations, were able as well as willing to revolt quite frequently and, in the case of the Messenians, with ultimate success.

The first point to establish is the legal status of the Helots, not for purely formal reasons but because 'the condition of being a slave in the ancient Greek world, for example, was likely (though far from certain) to result in a more intense degree of exploitation than being a citizen or even a free foreigner' (Ste. Croix 1981, 74). In a broad sense the Helots were of course 'slaves', as is demonstrated most satisfyingly by the Spartans' use in an official document of the most general Greek term for unfreedom, *douleia*, to refer concretely to the Helot class (Thuc. 5.23.3). But they were not *douloi* on exactly the same terms as the slaves in, say, Chios – as Theopompos, a native of that island, appears to have been the first to make explicit in the wake of the liberation of the Messenian Helots (Theop. 115F122; with Vidal-Naquet 1981, 220, 223-48). Whereas the *douloi* of Chios were non-Greeks bought on the market, the Helots and comparable servile populations in Thessaly and elsewhere were enslaved locals. Theopompos believed that all the Helots, Lakonian as well as Messenian, had originally acquired their status through conquest; but an alternative ancient view, no doubt influenced by contemporary fifth-century developments within the Spartan citizen body, held that some of them at least had acquired it through degradation from Spartiate status. Both ancient views on Helot origins have had their modern supporters; but the relevant point is that in the age of Xenophon the Spartans treated the Helots as a conquered enemy, most remarkably and extremely in the Ephors' annual declaration of war upon them (Arist. fr. 538). No doubt this declaration was partly symbolic, being designed to remind the Helots of their unalterable 'otherness' and to renew the legitimacy of their subordination (cf. Ducat 1974). But its practical effect was to give the Spartans an incomparably free hand in dealing with their workforce.

The origins of the *douloi* of Chios helped to determine their status as mere property, chattels who were almost completely at the disposal of their individual masters. It is this rightlessness, combined with their social position as deracinated outsiders torn from ties of kin and community, that distinguishes chattel slaves from all other kinds of forced labourers (of the many studies by M.I. Finley see e.g. Finley 1980, 73-7). But if the Helots were not chattel *douloi*, what sort were they? The ancients gave two answers, neither of them very helpful. They were 'between free men and *douloi*' (Pollux 3.83; with Lotze 1959; Finley 1981a, ch.7). Or they were *douloi* who were 'in a way public' (*tropon tina dêmosioi*: Strabo 8.5.4; cf. Paus. 3.20.6).

The elements of freedom that inspired the first of these formulations presumably included the fact that the Helots were permitted some kind of family life (though it is unlikely that their marriages were recognised at law) and some sort of property rights. Evidence for the latter is far more extensive than for the former. They had a right to retain for their own use whatever produce was left over after the required rent had been paid (below); they perhaps owned or rather possessed some instruments of production (which could be turned into offensive weapons on occasion) and certainly possessed movables such as boats; and by 223 as many as 6000 Lakonian Helots had amassed the 500 drachmai required by Kleomenes III to purchase their freedom (though this is the earliest evidence for Helots handling cash as opposed to other movable property and may reflect changed conditions in Lakonia after the emancipation of the Messenian Helots). However, to classify the Helots as 'between free men and *douloi*' is to make the same sort of mistake as those modern scholars who demarcate Helotage as an 'undeveloped' form of (chattel) slavery. In reality Helotage was a servitude of a different kind.

To the extent that the alternative formulation stresses the communal aspect of Helotage it represents an improvement. For the Helots were treated, as we saw, as members of defeated communities and had war declared on them collectively by the Spartan state. For some purposes, moreover, Helots were at the disposal of all Spartans, regardless of whose *klaros* they happened to be attached to, and they could only be manumitted by 'Act of Parliament', that is by act of the Spartan Assembly. All the same, the qualification 'in a way' public slaves was vital, because it was to an individual Spartiate master, the *klaros*-holder, that the Helots paid their stipulated rent. Besides, a personal relationship might grow up between a Spartiate and 'his' Helots as a result of the Helots' functions as batmen on campaign or servants in the home at Sparta. Even so, the alternative formulation is also inadequate as a classification, since it fails to distinguish Helots sharply enough from chattel slaves or to bring out the peculiarities of their status.

The solution adopted by the author of the most recent synthetic study of unfree labourers in ancient Greece is to group the Helots, along with debt-bondsmen, other Helot-type populations, some Hellenistic *laoi*, and sacred slaves, under the overall label of 'communal servitude'; more particularly the Helots are here characterized as a species of 'intercommunal servitude', viz. 'tributary servitude' (Garlan 1982, ch. 2, esp. 108-16). This makes the necessary break between Helotage and chattel slavery sufficiently sharp, but only at the cost of lumping the Helots with the very dissimilar sacred slaves and of exaggerating their similarity to peoples experiencing imperialist domination. My own preference, therefore, is to describe the Helots as a species of 'serf' (according to the definition reached by a 1956 U.N. Convention, quoted in Ste. Croix 1981, 135), that is as state serfs. It is true that 'serfdom' covers a very considerable range of statuses (cf. Kahrstedt 1919, 285-7, on the differences between 'Hörige' and 'Leibeigen') and that there are important distinctions between Helots and the serfs of mediaeval feudalism (cf. Finley 1981a, 142). But 'state serfs' seems to me to circumvent these objections, besides conveying the importance and the extent of state power exercised by the Spartans over the Helots (cf. Finley 1981a, 132; 266n.34).

A yet harder task than that of juridical – or rather quasi-legalistic – definition is to establish the degree of the Helots' exploitation with any precision at all in the total absence of ancient statistical data. When Kritias expressed the qualitative judgment that within the Spartan state there were to be found both the most free and the most enslaved of people (88B37D-K), he meant that the Spartans so far exploited Helot labour-power that they were themselves released entirely from directly producing the material necessities of life. This ideal division of labour may have become rather less clearcut in the fourth century, when some Hupomeiones may have plied a trade and some Spartiates may even have had to put their hands to the plough (a possible inference from a puzzling remark at Arist. *Pol.* 1264a10-11). But an 'apophthegm' attributed to King Kleomenes I (Plut. *Mor.* 223a), though in itself unhistorical, still captured the essence of the situation in the time of Agesilaos: Homer, according to 'Kleomenes', was the poet of the Spartans, Hesiod the poet of the Helots, since the former had given the necessary directions for warfare, the latter those for agriculture. It remains to discuss, however, whether the amount of rent exacted from the Helots was extortionate, so that the Spartans were indeed 'maintained by the sulky labour of Helot serfs' (Heitland 1921, 75); or whether, as the *Instituta Laconica* ('Ancient Customs of the Spartans') attributed to Plutarch maintained, the 'long-established rent' (*apophora*) was so fixed that the Helots might 'serve gladly because gainfully', while the Spartan *klaros*-holder was constrained by fear of incurring a curse from exacting more than a stipulated maximum amount of produce (Plut. *Mor.* 239de).

The latter passage does not specify the amount of rent, so it could be referring either to a fixed maximum *proportion* of the annual yield or to a fixed absolute maximum *quantity* of produce to be paid regardless of yield. The first alternative appears to have been the case at the time of the Second Messenian War, at least for the Messenian Helots, since Tyrtaios (fr. 6) compares them to 'asses exhausted under great loads: under painful necessity to bring their masters *full half* the fruit their ploughed land produced'. Such a system of *métayage* or *mezzadria* is relatively simple to operate and quite flexible, and it has not always and everywhere been by any means as burdensome as Tyrtaios suggests it was in seventh-century Messenia (cf. Franklin 1971, 43-5; and for a detailed study of a village in Uttar Pradesh, India, see Bliss/Stern 1982, esp. 125-32). But there is no evidence that the system was maintained in Messenia after the Second Messenian War, and the only explicit evidence for the size and nature of the annual *apophora* at a later date indicates that a fixed amount of produce rather than a quota of the yield had to be delivered.

According to this evidence (Plut. *Lyk.* 8.7), the rent amounted to eighty-two *medimnoi* of barley and a 'proportionate' amount of fresh fruits (whatever that may mean). This figure is vulnerable to the doubt raised earlier, as to whether it could be a product of the reforms of Agis and Kleomenes rather than a genuinely 'Lykourgan' figure applicable to the age of Agesilaos. The fact that the rent is reckoned in barley and not wheat is at least consistent with the way that mess rations were fixed in the fourth century (Dikaiarchos fr. 72; cf. Cartledge 1979, 170-1). But beyond that it is not legitimate to go. On the other hand, we may confidently apply the figure to the Kleomenean dispensation. For Kleomenes, who succeeded in dividing up the Spartiate land in Lakonia into some 4000 *klaroi*, would undoubtedly have fixed the *apophora* sufficiently high to guard against a recurrence of the fatal *oliganthrôpia* of Agesilaos' day; and eighty-two *medimnoi* were more than adequate to feed some six or seven adults, not just the *klaros*-holder and his wife of whom Plutarch speaks. The surplus could have gone towards maintaining children or other dependent relatives, including those who had embarked on the revived *agôgê*, and even towards swelling the central store of provisions in case of need to supply an army. Now a family of four receiving one and a half times the average adult rations attested in other parts of Greece would have needed a *klaros* of between eleven and eighteen hectares or 120 and 200 *plethra*, when the food consumed by Helots, biennial rotation of crops, land needed for pasturage and other factors have been taken into account.[1] Since there were, I believe, some 50-75,000 hectares of arable available to the Spartans in the Eurotas valley (allowing for geomorphological changes since antiquity), that would have comfortably allowed for the creation of 4000 *klaroi* ranging between the required eleven and eighteen hectares and not necessarily all equal in surface area.

As for the pre-Kleomenean dispensation, however, almost all is unclear. 'The number of land allotments, the size of the individual allotments, and the

---

[1] I owe this estimate to an unpublished paper of M.H. Jameson, which he has kindly allowed me to use. Far more adventurous, if not perhaps rather rash, is T.J. Figueira, 'Mess contributions and subsistence at Sparta', *TAPA* 114 (1984), 87-109, at 98-100.

number of people who depended on the allotments for support are all unknown and, in my view, unknowable' (Buckler 1977a, 258). Strictly, that is true; but some parameters may be established. The only more or less fixed points of reference are the stipulated mess contribution of one Lakonian *medimnos* of barley-meal a month and the fact that between 480 and 371 the number of Spartans in a position to pay this fell from some 8000 to scarcely more than 1000 (Chapter 4). These together suggest that either the rent was then fixed differently or many more Spartiates had to find the mess contribution from an *apophora* of eighty-two *medimnoi*. Whichever is correct, a valuable passage in Xenophon's account of Kinadon's conspiracy (3.3.5) makes it clear that at any rate on the larger estates in the vicinity of Sparta there lived and worked many more than one Helot family. This together with the reported ratio of seven Helots for every one Spartan sent to Plataia in 479 (Hdt. 9.10.1,28.2,29.1) suggests that the Helots, most of whom lived in Messenia, vastly outnumbered the Spartans; and since the Helots were presumably not subject to the *oliganthrôpia* that blighted the master class, the disproportion between them and the Spartans increased. Absolute figures are no less difficult to come by for the Helots than for the Spartans; but if the modern estimate of 170-200,000 is anywhere near right for the former, we do have a strong hint as to the source of their oppression. For that range of figures would yield a population density something like three to four times as great as the average usually postulated for Greek terrain under pre-industrial conditions. Most Helots, in other words, could have been living at or near the margin of subsistence, notwithstanding any alleged interdiction on the Spartans' exacting more than a stipulated maximum of rent from each *klaros*; such an interdiction is in any case unlikely to have been rigorously observed at a time of crisis when other prohibitions were being flouted at least by rich Spartans.

Not all Helots, however, were necessarily exploited to the same extent; some Helots, like Russian kulaks, may have been exploiting their fellows. That at any rate is a possible explanation of an otherwise enigmatic entry of unknown provenance in the lexicon of Hesychios (5/6c AD) under *monomoïtos*, which is defined as 'leader of Helots' (*heilôtôn archôn*). This person was perhaps the *chef d'entreprise*, the overseer who made sure that the work on the *klaros* was done regularly and properly, particularly where vines were cultivated, who negotiated for equipment, repairs to buildings and so on, and who arranged for the payment of the stipulated rent and for the disposal of the remainder including any surplus for sale outside the *klaros* – all with a sharp eye to personal gain.

Further speculation of a pseudo-quantitative nature would be unprofitable. Enough has been said to suggest very strongly that the lot of at least the ordinary rural Helot was probably not often a happy one economically speaking. Some Helots, however, apart from the putative 'leaders', were better placed than others, in particular those who were selected to serve as batmen on campaign and were thus in a position to develop some kind of personal relationship with their master. Such men were probably mainly Lakonian rather than Messenian Helots and ordinarily employed in domestic rather than agricultural activities. They too are the likeliest candidates for the most-favoured-Helot treatment through which the Spartans aimed both to remedy the lacuna of citizen manpower and, by the multiplication of more or less privileged statuses of ex-Helots, to divide the Helots against themselves.

Regent Pausanias was alleged to have offered Helots not merely their personal freedom but also Spartan citizenship, in furtherance of his political designs in the 470s (Thuc. 1.132.4). If true (as Thucydides firmly asserted with uncharacteristic lack of scepticism), this will have been the first known offer of this type to be made to Helot-type *douloi* (as opposed to chattel slaves). But since the allegation emanated from official Spartan circles, to which Pausanias had been denounced revealingly by Helot informers, it is more likely legitimating propaganda rather than truth unadorned. No such doubt, however, surrounds the offer of freedom (but not citizenship) made by the Spartan authorities in 425 to any Helots who would risk their lives running the blockade of the Sphakteria garrison (Thuc. 4.26.5); as a sweetener 'much silver' was promised into the bargain. At about the same time the Spartans effected the first mass liberation of Helots on record – only to massacre the 2000 or so who had unwisely presented themselves for this award (Thuc. 4.80.2-4). First the carrot, then the stick, then the carrot again: three years later the survivors of those Helots who had been armed as hoplites and sent with Brasidas to Thrace were voted their freedom as a reward and settled together with the Neodamodeis at Lepreon to guard the frontier of Triphylia against disaffected Elis (Thuc. 5.34.1).

Both components of the Lepreon garrison are the first attested examples of their type. But whereas the Spartans only rarely recruited Helots as hoplites thereafter, Neodamodeis became a permanent fixture between 421 and 371. Thucydides' casual reference to 'the Neodamodeis' at Lepreon suggests that by 421 they were a well-known category and that all of them then in existence (?500) were settled at Lepreon. But by the time Kinadon felt he could count on them to support his revolution there were many more than this. Agesilaos in 396 took 2000 'of the Neodamodeis', that is not all of them, with him to Asia (3.4.2). Despite the apparent meaning of their title, 'new members of the *damos*', their status was clearly not on all fours with that of the Homoioi. Though freed from their Helot condition, they could not be elected to a common mess as they had not been through the *agôgê*. The settlement of the first known Neodamodeis at Lepreon suitably reflects their hybrid and marginal status, which threatened to be an embarrassment in the absence of sustained campaigning abroad. After the Athenian War, by contrast, they were tailor-made for the running of Sparta's new oversea empire. After 371 they were no longer needed, since Spartiate *oliganthrôpia* could by then no longer be compensated by this expedient.

Neodamodeis were not the only category of liberated Helots by any means, though they would appear to have constituted the elite of the ex-Helots. According to a writer of the Hellenistic period (Myron *FGrHist*. 106F1), 'the Spartans often freed their *douloi*, calling some Aphetai [Released?], some Adespotoi [Masterless?], some Eruktêres [Curbers?], others again Desposionautai [Master-seamen?], whom they assigned to naval expeditions, and others finally Neodamodeis'. Myron's 'often' probably does not mean that the Spartans often created the members of the various categories but rather that they created a remarkable number of different categories, all most likely between the late fifth and early part of the fourth centuries. Again, the Spartans' aim was surely to divide the Helots as well as to rule an empire. They needed to manumit Helots for military reasons, but they cunningly used the manumission process as a political weapon too, fostering emulous loyalty within the subject class.

Ideological warfare of this kind was a Spartan speciality. 'One of the most striking characteristics of Spartan society,' it has been well noted (Ducat 1978, 30n.86), 'is the effectiveness with which ideological pressure was exerted by the dominant group' – the nobles upon the commons, the men on the women, the adults on the young, the masters on the Helots. In the case of the latter a remarkably illuminating passage of Plutarch (*Lyk.* 28.10) can be called in evidence: 'at the time of the Thebans' invasion of Lakonia [370/69] the captured Helots were invited to sing the poems of Terpandros, Alkman and the Spartan composer Spendon; but they refused, saying that their masters would not permit it.' These prisoners were perhaps among the 6000 Helots who had been specially enrolled with a promise of eventual freedom in order to meet the invasion (above); alternatively, they were Helots working the farms in the Spartan basin. Either way, they were Lakonian not Messenian Helots, for the latter had revolted *en masse* and, in stark contrast to the continued servitude of the great majority of their Lakonian brothers and sisters were soon to become (at least the men among them) citizens of the reborn *polis* of Messene, the political equals of their former masters in Sparta.

Economically speaking the difference between the Lakonian and the Messenian Helots is relatively unimportant, with the exception of the privileged categories mentioned above. It is, moreover, easy to exaggerate the ideological difference between the two geographical groups by ignoring such facts as the participation of Lakonian Helots in the great revolt of the 460s, the flight of Lakonian Helots to the Athenians during the Athenian War, the potential for rebellion that Kinadon saw in them, and Aristotle's comparison of them to an enemy constantly sitting in wait for the Spartans' disasters. It remains true, nevertheless, that the Helot danger, as opposed to the Helot problem, was posed principally by the Messenians. Discussion of why the Messenians, unlike chattel slaves in Classical Greece but in common with the Thessalian Penestai, were not only willing but able to revolt (as opposed to commit individual acts of resistance) is greatly facilitated by a recent attempt to account for the relative scarcity and low intensity of revolts by chattel slaves in the American Old South (Genovese 1979).[2]

Genovese, after comparing and contrasting the experience of chattel slaves in Brazil and the Caribbean, identified eight factors that singly or more especially in combination favoured revolt. Not all can be applied directly to Spartan history, mainly because the Messenians were not irretrievably divided from their masters by race and colour; but Genovese's list of favouring factors does usefully indicate the range and complexity of the relevant variables: psychological independence and cultural estrangement; economic crisis; large slaveholding units; frequent splits within the ruling class; heavy preponderance of blacks over whites; excess of purchased African-born slaves over locally bred

---

[2] A fuller discussion will appear in my 'Rebels and Sambos in Classical Greece: a comparative view', *History of Political Thought* 6.1/2 (1985) = *Festschrift for G.E.M. de Ste. Croix* (Duckworth, London, 1985).

slaves; an autonomous black leadership; and a suitable environment for establishing colonies of runaways.

Mutatis mutandis, all but one of these factors operated in Messenia among the Helots. The exception is the outnumbering of local-born by purchased slaves. For although some Spartans did apparently own chattel slaves, they were few in number and used for conspicuous display in domestic service at Sparta rather than as labourers on Messenian farms. But this exception is crucial. For the existence of family ties not only made flight (the usual escape-route of chattel slaves) an undesirable option for most Messenians but also increased their determination to revolt successfully *in situ*, a determination born of their belief that they were descended from men who had been citizens of the *polis* of Messene before the Spartan conquest. Solidarity arising from shared kinship and community was, moreover, an indispensable factor in co-ordinating revolt. Even so, for an organized Messenian revolt as opposed to sporadic outbreaks of resistance to occur, some major catastrophe like the earthquake of *c*.465 had to provide the occasion and hamper the Spartans' ability to respond; and for a revolt to be successful the combination of a major Spartan military defeat and massive foreign intervention was required. As for the Lakonian Helots, terror mixed judiciously with contempt and differential promotion ensured the continuation of the Spartans' uniquely successful system of economic exploitation in Lakonia for almost two centuries after its demise in Messenia.

Only once do we learn of Perioikoi revolting in company with Helots, when two Messenian communities (Thouria and Aithaia) joined what became a kind of 'nationalist' uprising in the 460s (Thuc. 1.101.2). Otherwise, apart from Kinadon's expectation of Perioikic support and the defection of Perioikoi in northern Lakonia in 370/69, relations were probably peaceable between the Spartans and the Perioikoi. At least, 'the Perioikoi had as much interest in suppressing a Helot revolt as the Spartans themselves' (Freeman 1893, 123n.3), and they could normally be relied upon to act as a kind of early warning device and first line of defence against insurrection. The precise nature of these relations, however, is embarrassingly obscure, for lack of relevant evidence. But taken as a whole they satisfy Ste. Croix's definition of imperialist exploitation (1981, 44), which has been quoted in a different context in Chapter 6.

In a sense Sparta was not 'a power outside the community', since the Perioikic communities lay within the borders of the Spartan state and in military contexts at least the Perioikoi could be described as 'Lakedaimonioi' like the Spartans. But such local autonomy as the Perioikic *poleis* possessed was strictly conditional upon the whim of Sparta, who imposed an obligation of military service upon her Perioikic subjects, mulcted many of the communities of choice lands for the benefit of her kings, probably imposed other financial burdens upon them and more or less forcibly requisitioned various goods and services. Sparta also decisively affected social relations within the Perioikic *poleis*.

Just two passages (5.3.9; Plut. *Kleom.* 10.11) explicitly state what we would anyway have inferred, that there was social differentiation within the Perioikoi. Probably in each of the eighty or so attested communities there was a small ruling class, from whose ranks came the hoplites who from at least the later sixth century were bound to fight with the Spartans even though they had no say in

Spartan policy-making. From a position of numerical parity at Plataia in 479 these hoplites came to outnumber by far the Spartiates in the regular phalanx; and by 425 they were actually brigaded with the Spartiates (cf. Chapter 4 and 12). This ruling elite will also have provided the few named Perioikic admirals, envoys and captains who turn up during and immediately after the Athenian War. The basis of their wealth was no doubt that of all Greek ruling classes, landed property and forced labour, but their labourers will have been chattel slaves not Helots.

It is unlikely that many of the ruling classes will have been sufficiently disaffected in 399 to contemplate joining Kinadon, let alone eating Spartiates raw; though the situation had changed by 370/69, when many of the Perioikoi revolted from Sparta both individually and collectively (7.2.2; Xen. *Ages.* 2.24). But Kinadon is likely to have anticipated a warmer response from the majority of poor Perioikoi. Most of these were peasants, many no doubt indebted to their rich compatriots and some perhaps even reduced to debt-bondage. But in the coastal communities there were also fishermen and traders, and in the major centres, especially those with important sanctuaries attached to them, craftsmen. The role of these craftsmen was vital – for the Spartans rather than the Perioikic communities in some cases. Since Spartiates were legally barred from all banausic activities in the age of Xenophon (cf. Cartledge 1976b), the production and maintenance of arms and armour devolved on Perioikoi, together perhaps with some 'Inferiors' and Helots. The iron that went into the making of military hardware (knives, swords, spits, axes, hatchets and sickles: 3.3.7) and agricultural implements was located on Perioikic territory, and the ore was presumably extracted by Perioikic mining contractors using slave labour. The bronze needed for shields, on the other hand, had to be imported, mainly no doubt through the chief Perioikic town of Gytheion, which appears to have been walled by the 360s at latest. Besides serving as the port of Sparta Gytheion housed the Spartan dockyards (e.g. 1.4.11), which again required imported materials: timber, pitch, papyrus and so forth.

How the exchanges took place between Perioikoi and Spartans is not known; but so far as purchases for military purposes by the Spartan state were concerned, it is surely more appropriate to think in terms of a 'command' rather than 'free market' economy. As for the rich Spartans who exhibited such gusto for chariot-racing inside and outside Lakonia (cf. Chapter 9), they should have been compelled to buy the relevant goods with surplus *naturalia* from their estates, since their 'currency' of iron spits was so valueless that 'even ten minas could not be brought into the house without the knowledge of both masters and Helots – it would require a great deal of space and a wagon to cart it' (Xen. *LP* 7.5). But that of course was only the 'Lykourgan' theory. In practice, the prohibition on the private possession of gold and silver coin was increasingly flouted, despite regular house-to-house searches; and the taste of rich Spartans for 'good things' (*agatha*) not sanctioned by the austere Lykourgan regimen is artfully revealed by Xenophon's seemingly incidental remark (6.5.27) that the invaders of 370/69 destroyed Spartan houses stuffed full of such valuables. Like the contribution of wheaten bread by the rich to their messes over and above the required barley-flour (Xen. *LP* 5.3), this possessive individualism symbolized the dissolution of the Lykourgan order.

It was on this breakdown that Kinadon had sought, prematurely, to capitalize.

His attempt to unite all those below Spartiate status against the Homoioi was therefore a dismal failure. But that it could even be contemplated is a significant comment on the nature and condition of Spartan society and the development of the Spartan class struggle at the outset of Agesilaos' reign. Unfortunately for the future of Sparta's power, as can be seen with hindsight, Agesilaos' triumph over threatened revolution from above (Pausanias and Lysander) and below (Kinadon) reinforced an already conservative disposition that had been tempered in the fire of the *agôgê*. Sparta thus found herself with a staunchly reactionary leader 'at the very moment when the natural evolution of Spartan society, accelerated by twenty-seven years of war, would have merited an attentive re-examination and brand-new solutions' (Bommelaer 1981, 170-1). A comparison with the far-reaching social reforms of Agis IV and Kleomenes III suggests that a reform backed with all Agesilaos' enormous authority might have had some chance of success; and Zierke (1936, 54-9) has argued vehemently that the conclusion of the Peace of Antalkidas in 386 afforded the ideal opportunity to put such a reform into effect. Instead, the reaction of Agesilaos to the aftermath of Leuktra was emblematic of his consistently stolid refusal to countenance radical social change.

Not only had 400 Spartiates died in the battle, over a quarter of the then total of full citizens; but many of the remaining 300 at Leuktra, including some elite Spartiates, had failed to stand their ground (cf. Chapter 12, end). The prescribed penalty for such un-Spartan behaviour (cf. Hammond 1979/80) was reduction to the status of 'tremblers' (*tresantes*), a form of *atimia* or partial disfranchisement (cf. Ehrenberg 1937). But Sparta could not afford any further diminution of the full citizen body, not least because such a largescale disfranchisement might stretch existing social tensions within the Spartan *polis* beyond breaking point. So Agesilaos, being still by far the most influential individual in Sparta, was chosen (presumably by the Gerousia *qua* 'guardian of the laws') to act as *nomothetês* or 'lawgiver'. But rather than seize the chance to rethink the laws and recast the social system Agesilaos decreed, ostrich-like, that the laws should be deemed to sleep for a day (Plut. *Ages.* 30.6; *Mor.* 191c, 214b). 'An astute political stroke', Plutarch elsewhere (*Comp. Ages. Pomp.* 2.3) called it, but it was a sophism that revealed unmistakably that the crisis of Sparta could not be solved within the framework of the social and economic status quo. Zierke's condemnation of Agesilaos for failing to perform his necessary public duty would have seemed preposterous to Xenophon, but on a longer and cooler view it may be regarded as all too cogent. As it was, 'devotion to the laws of Lycurgus numbed the Spartan mind' (Cawkwell 1976a, 84) – and no mind more than that of Agesilaos.

11

Agesilaos and Persia

It was too easy for the Greeks and still is for Greek historians to conceive the Persian king and his subordinates as having nothing to think about except Aegean problems. (Lewis 1958, 397)

The Persian ideal and its aim of 'equals' around a king merged easily for Xenophon with the mirage of Spartan 'gentlemanliness' in Greece itself. (Lane Fox 1980, 132)

Three years after the Kinadon affair Agesilaos was deputed commander of the Spartans' Persian expedition. This enterprise had been decided upon soon after his accession and begun in earnest the following spring (399). No source reveals the attitude of Agesilaos either to the launching or to the initial conduct of the expedition. But it would be a fair inference that he was in favour of the former and unimpressed by the latter. All that Xenophon (3.4.2) says explicitly is that the appointment of Agesilaos to the overall command in 396 was the brainchild of Lysander. Yet the sequel suggests, as Xenophon intended, that from the start Agesilaos had interpreted his mission in a singular and personal way.

For in the pages of Xenophon, more openly in the *Agesilaos* than the *Hellenika*, Agesilaos was the 'Panhellenist' *par excellence*, the Persian-hater (*misopersês*: *Ages.* 7.7; cf. 1.8) whose life's task was to humble the pride of the Great King of Persia in the name of all the Greeks and to cut his mighty empire down to size, beginning in Asia Minor. This interpretation is not without its difficulties, to put it mildly (cf. Perlman 1976, 17-19), but Xenophon was certainly not wrong to draw attention to the Persian factor. This was a major theme of Agesilaos' reign and indeed of all Greek history in the fourth century, when it was 'a constant element in Greek political life, and no city could determine its conduct without taking it into account' (Picard 1980, 299; cf. generally Hornblower 1982). In this chapter I shall first briefly outline the character and development of the Achaemenid Persian Empire down to about 400, so far as the available sources permit, and then look at relations between Persia and Sparta both in that period and more particularly in the age of Agesilaos.[1]

---

[1] Apart from Hallock 1971 (see Bibliography), *The Cambridge History of Iran* II. *The Median and Achaemenian Periods* (1985) unfortunately appeared far too late to be taken into account here.

Within half a century of the conquest of the Persian Empire by Alexander the Great, Demetrios of Phaleron is reported to have scornfully asked (Polyb. 29.21.4): 'Do you suppose that either the Persians and the Persian ruler or the Macedonians and their king ... could ever have believed that at the time when we live the very name of the Persians would have perished utterly – those who were the masters of almost the whole world?' Demetrios of course crowed too soon. Some nine centuries later the Sasanian Khusro II 'Victorious' (AD 591-628) re-established the old Persian Empire in its full extent throughout the Middle East. But only for a generation. In the long view the achievement of the Achaemenid dynasty from Cyrus II (559-530) to Darius III (336-330) still borders on the miraculous. For they ruled for over two centuries an empire that had been acquired essentially within a generation and that encompassed at its maximum some three million square kilometres from Libya to the Jaxartes River, from the Danube to the Oxus (Fig. 11.1).

Nor was it merely the most extensive and most speedily created empire in the ancient Orient. It was also the most heterogeneous. 'Heir and successor', as Rostovtzeff put it (1941, 77), 'of the Sumerian, Babylonian, Egyptian, Hittite, and Assyrian Empires', it 'never formed a natural economic and social unit'. Its political organization therefore had to be 'loose-hung' (Glover 1917, 216), and such unity as it possessed was imparted by the person of the Great King, whose unique power the Greeks rather ruefully acknowledged by referring to him simply as 'King' (*Basileus*). This heterogeneity and looseness are neatly captured in the Achaemenids' surprisingly un-triumphalist imperial style of art (cf. Nylander 1979).

A story in Plutarch's *Life* of Alexander (ch. 65) is revealingly *ben trovato*. On reaching the Punjab, the easternmost limit of the Achaemenid Empire at its greatest extent but by then long since lost to the Persians, Alexander was visited by the Indian sage Calanus, who

> threw on the ground a dry and shrunken piece of oxhide and put his foot on the outer edge: the hide was thus pressed down at one point on the surface, but rose up at others. He walked round the circumference and showed that this was what happened whenever he stepped on the edge. Then finally he put his weight on the centre, whereupon the whole of the hide lay flat and still.

The point of the parable was to impress upon Alexander that he should concentrate the weight of his authority at the centre of his newly won empire, and in theory the advice was sound. But in practice the specific gravity of the individual Achaemenid rulers had varied enormously, and by a nice historical coincidence the crisis of Sparta under Agesilaos was almost exactly coeval with what looked very much like a crisis of the Persian Empire under Arsikas (404-359/8), who was known to the Greeks as Artaxerxes (II) Mnêmôn ('Ever-mindful'). 'Crisis', as we shall see, may be somewhat misleading in this case, but there were two big wrinkles clearly visible at the western edge of the oxhide throughout his reign. One was located in western Anatolia, the other in Egypt, and Agesilaos became directly involved with both in respectively the first and last decades of his rule. This temporal conjunction was strongly felt by Xenophon, who in the 360s or 350s contrasted the present reality of moral and

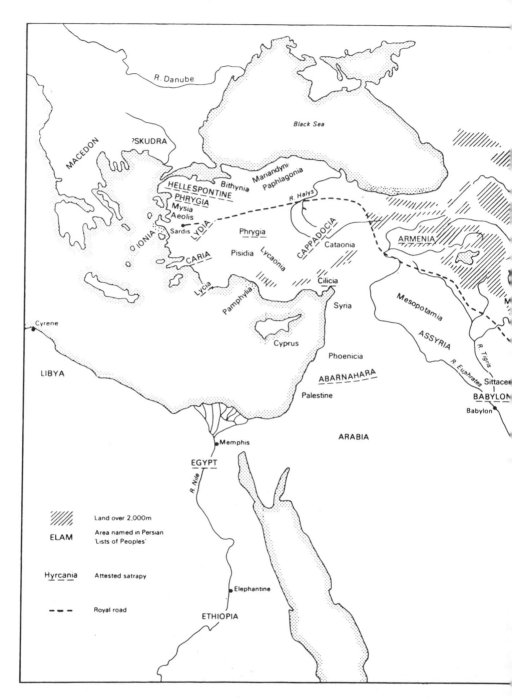

R. Danube

Black Sea

MACEDON

?SKUDRA

Bithynia

Mariandyni
Paphlagonia

HELLESPONTINE

PHRYGIA

R. Halys

Mysia
Aeolis

IONIA

LYDIA

Sardis

Phrygia

CAPPADOCIA

Cataonia

ARMENIA

CARIA

Pisidia

Lycaonia

Lycia

Pamphylia

Cilicia

Syria

Mesopotamia

Cyrene

Cyprus

ASSYRIA

R. Tigris

LIBYA

Phoenicia

ABARNAHARA

Palestine

Sittacer

BABYLON

Babylon

R. Euphrates

ARABIA

Memphis

EGYPT

R. Nile

Elephantine

ETHIOPIA

///// Land over 2,000m

ELAM   Area named in Persian
         'Lists of Peoples'

Hyrcania Attested satrapy

- - -   Royal road

Fig. 11.1. The Persian Empire in the age of Agesilaos. After Talbert

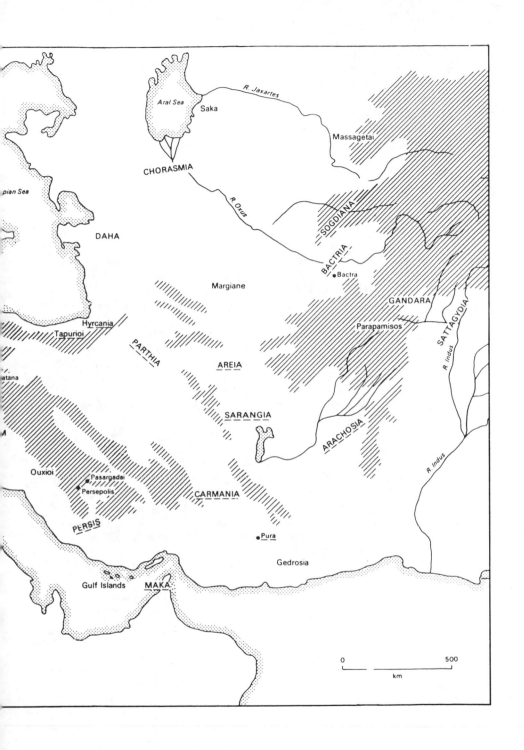

Aral Sea

R. Jaxartes

Saka

pian Sea

Massagetai

CHORASMIA

R. Oxus

DAHA

SOGDIANA

BACTRIA

Bactra

Margiane

GANDARA

Hyrcania

Tapurioi

Parapamisos

SATTAGYDIA

PARTHIA

AREIA

R. Indus

atana

M

SARANGIA

ARACHOSIA

R. Indus

Ouxioi

Pasargadai

Persepolis

CARMANIA

PERSIS

Pura

Gedrosia

Gulf Islands

MAKA

0   500

km

physical decay with the idealized past of both Sparta (*LP* 14) and Persia (*Cyr.* 8.8). However, before we leap to embrace this viewpoint unreservedly it has to be said forcefully that it suffers from the defect common to virtually all our contemporary literary evidence – and not a few of the more recent studies (cf. the protest of Glover 1917, viii and ch.7) – Hellenocentricity.

'Our histories are so deeply impressed by a Hellenic stamp that even careful scholars are not aware of the distortions which they introduce' (Starr 1975, 41). This is of course reprehensible, and Starr's counsel to stand imaginatively 'in Susa or Persepolis, or even in the Persian satrapal centers of Dascylium and Sardis' is in principle admirable. But the counsel is hard to put into effect. For Achaemenid Persia produced no historians in the Greek sense, not even a Xenophon, nor yet many fulsomely propagandistic chronicles of royal achievements in the manner of Darius I's famous trilingual inscription carved in the living rock at Bisutun in Media about 520. What remains on the Persian side are a handful of official inscriptions written in the chancellery language known as Old Persian and a very much larger number of official records on clay, most notably the so-called Persepolis Fortification Tablets written chiefly in Elamite (Hallock 1969, 1971). The latter are vastly more informative and show that 'virtually everyone, even the highest, was on a regular ration-scale ... or salary' (Lewis 1977, 4-5); in other words, that the Achaemenid Empire was as subtly hierarchical and intricately bureaucratic as its great oriental forerunners. From elsewhere than the Iranian heartland come disparate testimonies: the clay archives of the Egibi and Murashu banking dynasties of Babylon; the biblical Books of Esther, Nehemiah, Ezra and Daniel; the papyrus letters of Prince Arsames to the officials of his Egyptian estates; and the papyrus detritus of the Jewish garrison at Egyptian Elephantine. These can inform variously on the economic, political, military and religious arrangements of the Achaemenids. But for the narrative framework even orientalists have to rely on Greek sources (Herodotus, Thucydides, Xenophon, Ktesias and Diodoros above all); and it is in Herodotus (3.89-96) – not the royal archives of Pasargadai, Persepolis, Susa, Ekbatana or Babylon – that the fullest account may be found of the sinews of empire, the tribute in cash and kind levied on its several administrative provinces (*satrapeiai* in Greek transcription). Despite new documentary evidence, it is still true that George Rawlinson in the 1860s 'possessed virtually all the sources even now available for the general narrative' (Olmstead 1948, vii; for the contribution of Greek sources cf. now Briant 1982, 491-506).

Hellenocentricity is thus inevitable up to a point, which involves three main dangers for the historian of Agesilaos and Sparta. The first is the least serious, and this is to follow the lead of Herodotus and Xenophon in over-identifying the Spartan and Persian social and ceremonial systems, especially in respect of royal prerogatives (e.g. Hdt. 6.59) and general educational ideals (Xen. *Cyr. passim*; cf. Arr. *Anab.* 5.4.5). In reality the two societies bore as much, or rather as little, resemblance to each other as Homeric to Bronze Age Mycenae. If individual Spartans managed to establish a close rapport with individual Persians – most notably Lysander and Klearchos with the younger Cyrus, and Antalkidas with Ariobarzanes and Artaxerxes II – that tells us much about practical exigencies and diplomatic skills, nothing about national systems and characters. Agesilaos was not the only Spartan who had precious little understanding of the subtleties of decorum and etiquette called for in dealings with Persian grandees.

The second and more insidious danger of Hellenocentricity is to incline us to share the Greek view that the Persian king took the Greeks as seriously as they took him – and themselves. Fortunately, there is enough evidence to indicate that 'at any given moment the Greek world was only of peripheral importance to the Persian State. Even in Asia Minor the Greeks were after all a small minority' (Momigliano 1979, 41). The expedition of Xerxes, the failure of which cast heroic Greek tradition into a misleading mould of rigidly polar opposition between the slavish Persian Empire and the free Greek world, was an aberration, as unnecessary as it was costly and degrading. It was not repeated. Thereafter diplomacy, often enough 'cheque-book' diplomacy relying heavily on the transfer of gold and silver into the appropriate Greek hands, was the norm, rather than military confrontation. Leading Greeks like the Athenian Kimon and Agesilaos promoted for their own reasons aggressive activity on the mainland of Asia (which the Persian kings always regarded as 'theirs'), but their victories at the Eurymedon and Hermos Rivers respectively did not come close to jeopardizing the stability and integrity of the Empire. Far more serious militarily and economically were 'nationalist' revolts in Egypt, Babylonia, Phoenicia and above all Media; far more destabilizing politically were the recurrent succession struggles and jockeying for position within the nobility at court that were the inevitable consequence of the harem system; and a far more worrying frontier problem than that of Greek Asia Minor was that posed by the nomad-ridden steppe-lands of north-east Iran. In short, the conquest of the Persian Empire from the west by an army that included Greek mainlanders and was commanded by the king of a one-time vassal country was the height of paradox – not the inevitability that Xenophon and Isokrates too simply maintained it would be (but see Cook 1983, 217).

The third and related danger, perhaps most insidious of all, is the temptation to accept at face value our Greek sources' tendentious view of Persian weakness in the reign of Artaxerxes II. 'Debunking Persia was a favourite Panhellenist pastime' (Cawkwell 1979, 366n. *ad* 7.1.38), the proximate source of which was the alleged humiliation of Artaxerxes by the small Greek forces commanded by the younger Cyrus in 401 and Agesilaos between 396 and 394 (6.1.12). To the old slavery/freedom dichotomy was added the new argument from the supposed military weakness of the Persian Empire. The Persians' repeated failure to reconquer Egypt (in revolt since 405) and the satrapal rebellions of the 370s and 360s were further 'proof' of this; and from 380 until his death in 338 Isokrates never ceased to trumpet the need for a Panhellenic war of revenge against Persia that would unite the incessantly warring Greek powers at home and provide new lands for settlement of the landless Greek malcontents in Asia Minor (cf. Fuks 1972). To this end Isokrates proposed a succession of Greek champions – Athens and Sparta, Jason of Pherai, perhaps Agesilaos, Archidamos III, Dionysios of Syracuse, Philip of Macedon – only the last of whom had the capacity as well as the inclination to deliver the 'Panhellenist' goods.

But was the Persian Empire really such a push-over? Was Agesilaos in fact a die-hard Panhellenist Persian-hater? These are the two main dimensions to the question of relations between Sparta and Persia in the reign of Agesilaos that will be explored here. There is no better place to begin the exploration than the expedition of Cyrus the Younger, which involves all the major components of our problems: inter-Greek hostility and Graeco-Persian diplomacy; the condition of the western satrapies; the dynastic politics of the Achaemenid court; and, not least, the character of our sources.

At the Battle of Cunaxa (not far from Nineveh in Assyria) in 401 Cyrus was killed and so defeated in his attempt to wrest the throne from his elder brother Artaxerxes. With Cyrus there fought the young Xenophon, then a stateless Athenian mercenary commander of oligarchic sympathies who much later wrote up his version of the affair. The *Anabasis* is extremely sketchy on the preliminaries to the battle, far fuller on the return march of some 3000 kilometres from Assyria to the Black Sea accomplished by the 'Ten Thousand' (in fact considerably more at the start, appreciably fewer by the end) Greek mercenaries. On the opposite side at Cunaxa in close attendance on Artaxerxes was another Greek émigré, a physician called Ktesias from Knidos in south-west Anatolia. It seems certain that the latter's twenty-three book *Persika* ('Persian History') was published before the *Anabasis*; but unlike that work, the *Persika* survives only in the drastically abbreviated epitome made by the Byzantine patriarch Photios (on whose *Bibliotheca* see generally Wilson 1983, 93-111), in a handful of interpolated additions to Xenophon's *Hellenika*, and in Plutarch's *Life* of Artaxerxes.

Ktesias shared Xenophon's partiality for Sparta (cf. Plut. *Artax.* 13.7). But as a historian of Persia he was even less satisfactory than the Athenian, being essentially a romancer and gossip-monger; and the otherwise unrecorded details of court intrigue that he provided from his apparently privileged position of intimate familiarity should often be treated with a strong measure of suspicious reserve. On the other hand, there is no obviously compelling reason to reject out of hand his information that Cyrus was the favourite of his mother Parysatis. For this would account for Cyrus' meteoric rise to power and command at an early age in the declining years of his father Darius II and help explain the tenacity with which he subsequently refused to accept the succession of his elder brother.

Parysatis was the half-sister as well as wife of Darius, and enormously wealthy in her own right. It was through her influence, according to Ktesias, that the sixteen-year-old Cyrus was sent out west endowed with a supreme command in the closing phase of the Athenian War – in 407, according to the 'low' chronology followed here (cf. Robertson 1980). By then Thucydides' inchoate *History* has failed us for four years, but in a misplaced excursus on the causes of Athens' eventual defeat that appears in the published work as an obituary notice for Perikles Thucydides does note that Cyrus 'provided the Peloponnesians with money for their fleet' (2.65.12). Since both of the satraps of western Asia Minor – Tissaphernes of Lydia, Ionia and Caria, and Pharnabazus of Hellespontine Phrygia – had in their emulous and inconsistent way been doing the same since the Spartan-Persian entente of 412/1, what

Thucydides means is that Cyrus' appointment made the difference. At last Darius had intervened centrally by making his son *karanos* or margrave of 'all those whose mobilization centre is Kastolos' (1.4.3), although neither he nor Parysatis could have predicted just how intimately Cyrus would find himself able to co-operate with Lysander. Here, briefly, is the background.

Sparta had been involved in direct dealings with Persia from the very rise of the Persian Empire under Cyrus II ('the Great') in the mid-sixth century. At first her attitude was consistently hostile, though more in word than in deed until the invasion of Xerxes; and the decision of the deposed king Damaratos to become a trusted (and opulent) vassal of the Persian king was roundly condemned as an act of 'medism' (the Greeks being congenitally incapable, it seems, of distinguishing the Medes from the Persians, although this blurring of identity was at least as crass as a refusal to distinguish between Scotsmen and Irishmen would be today). But after the Persian Wars Athens assumed the mantle of Sparta as leader of the Greeks against Persia; and although Sparta remained formally at war with Persia until 412, this did not prevent the two parties from soliciting mutual aid against the common enemy. From 431 the Spartans were particularly importunate in their demands for Persian cash (Thuc. 2.7.1, 67.1; 4.50), but the strings applied to such aid by both sides were found mutually unacceptable until a happy coincidence of interest and opportunity arose after Athens' disastrous Sicilian expedition (415-413). For two reasons the Spartan-Persian accords of 412/1 and their subsequent fate merit quite extensive examination. In the first place, they perfectly illustrate what was to be Agesilaos' guiding maxim of foreign policy, namely that the interest of Sparta narrowly conceived in predominantly material terms was the supreme law. Secondly, they are the first of a series of Graeco-Persian agreements which involved the historic renunciation of the political independence of the Greek cities of Asia and indeed the recognition of the Asia Minor littoral as a political as well as a geographical frontier.

Some time after Athens had rashly decided to aid the rebellious Persian Amorges, bastard son of a former satrap, Darius entrusted his loyal servant Tissaphernes with a special superior command in the west akin perhaps to those held by Hydarnes (a possible ancestor: Lewis 1977, 83-4) before him and Cyrus soon after. His formal mission was to capture alive or kill Amorges and 'produce the tribute from his province, for which he was in arrears, since he had not been able to raise it from the Greek cities because of the Athenians' (Thuc. 8.5.5). Despite his strongly hellenizing coinage, Tissaphernes was a reputed Greek-hater (Plut. *Alk.* 24.6). Anyway, he interpreted his mission as being to procure the tribute by getting the Greek cities within his sphere to revolt from Athens and to gain the credit for bringing the Spartans into alliance with the Great King (Thuc. 8.6.1) – at the expense of his more genuinely philhellenic rival Pharnabazus. This rivalry was to be an important factor in the King's decision to replace Tissaphernes with Cyrus, but by the summer of 411 Tissaphernes had almost achieved both his objectives by bringing about a series of three agreements with the Spartan commanders on the spot.

All three have been dignified by some modern scholars with the title of treaty and named after the relevant Spartan commander: the Treaty of Chalkideus, of

Therimenes and of Lichas (Thuc. 8.18, 37, 58 = Bengtson 1975, nos 200-202). But such dignity is unwarranted for the first two agreements, and it is not certain – though it is probable (cf. now Lévy 1983, 222 and n.13; 227) – that even the third was ratified in Sparta. At any rate, the first 'treaty' was 'no more than a preliminary working arrangement between the forces on the spot' (A. Andrewes in Gomme 1981, 40). This was fortunate for the credit and credibility of the Spartans, who had ostensibly begun the war against Athens in the name of the freedom of Athens' Greek subjects. For if its terms had been taken literally, Sparta would have signed away at a stroke to Persian suzerainty not only the Asiatic littoral but all of mainland Greece from Boiotia northwards as well. In practice Tissaphernes and Darius were only interested in securing recognition of the King's suzerainty of Asia – including the Greek cities, which he regarded as belonging integrally to (his) Asia – and the Spartans' agreement not to prevent the collection of tribute by the satraps. Not only did the Spartans make these fundamental concessions, but they received nothing very clearcut in return.

It was small wonder that Therimenes was anxious for terms to be renegotiated. But the agreement he reached did not mark a substantial improvement from the Spartan point of view. There is, however, a question whether he committed the Spartans to quite so total a recognition of Persian suzerainty. For by now some Asiatic Greek cities such as Erythrai and (very probably) Miletos had been received into the Spartan alliance, and Sparta therefore had treaty obligations towards them which could and almost inevitably would clash with the King's demands. It has therefore been proposed (cf. A. Andrewes in Gomme 1981, 81-2, 141) that the 'agreement' referred to in a clause of Therimenes' 'treaty' ('if those cities who have made an agreement with the King shall attack the King's territory ...') is an agreement separate from the 'treaty' itself and that the Spartans thereby extracted some Persian guarantees to protect the interests of her new allies. But what these guarantees may have been, we cannot begin to guess, and their practical effect was nil.

No such mitigating provisos can be pleaded in defence of the 'Treaty of Lichas' concluded in the summer of 411. Lichas was an exceptionally wealthy and distinguished Spartan – an Olympic victor in the four-horse chariot-race, *proxenos* of Argos, host to many visiting foreign dignitaries, and perhaps a member of the Gerousia (cf. Pouilloux/Salviat 1983[2]). His despatch to the Aegean theatre with ten advisers argues exceptional Spartan concern over the conduct of relations with Persia. But this was not so much concern for Sparta's reputation among her old and new allies or for the condition of the Greek cities that were now again within reach of Darius' long arm, but concern rather for the regularity and rate of the pay being provided for Sparta's growing Aegean fleet. Even a staunch believer in the substantial genuineness of the Spartans' professed Panhellenism is forced to admit that 'the liberators have conceded Asia to the King' (Lewis 1977, 107). Since this is the only one of the three agreements that has a chance of having been formally ratified in Sparta (among

---

[2] See now my reply in *LCM* 9 (1984), 98-102; 'member of the Gerousia' is a possible translation of *andra geronta* (3.2.21).

other things it alone has a proper introductory formula with both a Persian and a Spartan date), it is worth quoting the relevant clause: 'the King shall be able to do as he pleases with regard to his territory.' Any doubts about the official Spartan understanding of this clause are silenced by Lichas' response to Milesians who were objecting to their rough handling by Tissaphernes: 'the Milesians and all others in the King's territory should within reason act subserviently towards Tissaphernes until the war was satisfactorily concluded' (Thuc. 8.84.4-5). (The verb I have translated 'act subserviently' means literally 'act as slaves' and was perhaps a deliberate echo of official Persian usage.) The Milesians in fact had little choice in the matter, especially as their city lacked a continuous fortified enceinte, and they expressed their bitterness towards Lichas by refusing him the kind of honorific burial that distinguished Spartans who died abroad had been accustomed to receive (see Chapter 16).

Those who seek to exonerate the Spartans from a charge of cynically breaking their promise and betraying the dearly beloved freedom of the Greek cities of Asia make much of the last clause quoted above, pointing out that the agreement was merely a temporary expedient and *faute de mieux*. They add that, as soon as Sparta was decently able, she raised the standard of liberty once more in 400. These objections are fair within a narrow perspective, but ignore the general direction of what has rightly been called Sparta's 'natural' foreign policy of abstention from direct involvement on the Asiatic mainland (cf. Ste. Croix 1972, 96) and in particular the near-identical performance of Sparta in 386. These facts need stressing more strongly than ever in response to the recent attempt by two leading scholars in this field to depict Spartan behaviour in a far more congenial light. A. Andrewes, as we have seen, has argued that in a separate agreement Sparta obtained certain guarantees for their Asiatic Greek allies. He has suggested moreover that these guarantees were not necessarily overridden even by the 'Treaty of Lichas', which the Spartans in any case came close to abrogating soon afterwards by authorizing their commander to transfer his fleet from Tissaphernes to Pharnabazus. D.M. Lewis agrees that the Treaty soon lapsed for all practical purposes, but he goes much further in arguing that the Spartans not only tried to get better terms for the Asiatic Greeks but actually succeeded in winning a treaty to that effect from Darius, the so-called 'Treaty of Boiotios' (Lewis 1977, 124-5).

For what it is worth, his case for this agreement, hitherto unknown to science, is briefly as follows. Dissatisfied not just with the amount and kind of Persian aid (which was not obviously winning them the war) but also with the debatable legal status of the Asiatic Greeks, the Spartans in late 408 sent a delegation headed by one Boiotios to the King. This apparently succeeded in getting through to Darius (perhaps at Babylon, where the court normally resided during the winter months), and on its return to Asia Minor was only too delighted to inform an Athenian embassy then being conducted to Darius by Pharnabazus that 'the Spartans had secured all that they requested from the King; also that Cyrus had been appointed to take command of the whole coastline and to help the Spartans in the war' (1.4.2-3). By 'all' Lewis understands Boiotios to have meant not only improved pay for the fleet but a renegotiation of the territorial clause of the 'Treaty of Lichas', such that the

Greek cities of Asia were to enjoy some form and degree of autonomy under Cyrus.

Several objections to this speculation come to mind (for others cf. Seager/Tuplin 1980, 144n.36). Xenophon's silences are never a decisive argument, but it seems odd that the pro-Spartan Xenophon did not either spell out the nature of Boiotios' agreement in this case or find some other context in which to refer back to it with approbation. A highly suitable context would have been his enormously sympathetic portrayal of Kallikratidas, who in 406 objected violently to having to 'fawn on the barbarian for the sake of money' and promised that 'if he got home safely he would do his best to make peace between Athens and Sparta' (1.6.7); but this attitude seems more understandable in face of the agreement certainly reached by Lichas than that putatively achieved by Boiotios. It seems moreover implausible that Darius, when he was already committing himself directly to the Spartan side by sending down his son with more or less unlimited funds, should also have been willing to concede a renegotiation of the territorial clause.

However that may be, the legal niceties became strictly academic in 407 when Lysander arrived as navarch. For he and Cyrus saw so closely eye-to-eye that the Persian could even entrust Lysander with all his revenues from the cities when he was recalled to his father's deathbed in 405 and made no attempt to reclaim the surplus when the war was over (2.1.14-15; cf. 2.3.8; DS 13.104.4; Plut. *Lys.* 19.2). Lysander, that is to say, with the connivance of Cyrus was able to prepare the way in 407 and 405/4 for absorbing the Greeks of Asia within a new Spartan empire, one where dekarchies, harmosts and garrisons left little scope for genuine autonomy regardless of the attitude or actions of Persia (cf. Chapter 6).

The recall of Cyrus is a timely reminder that his appointment in the first place had belonged more to the sphere of domestic Persian politics than to that of Greek history, whatever Boiotios and his colleagues might have claimed. The appointment had apparently been engineered by his mother with a view to the coming struggle for the Persian succession, which bid fair to be as intense and bloody as the one from which she and Darius had emerged victorious in the Persian 'Year of the Four Emperors' (as Lewis 1977, 73, nicely has it). Cyrus in the event lost the first round of that struggle but never lost the ambition to be Great King; and it was as part of a strategy for a future coup that Parysatis extorted from Artaxerxes II the reappointment of Cyrus to his satrapy in perhaps 404. By then any treaty relations between Sparta and Persia should have lapsed, since it appears that ordinarily such treaties had to be renewed on the accession of a new Persian King. But Cyrus' relationship with Lysander, Lysander's controversial position both in the Aegean and within the Spartan hierarchy, Cyrus' ambition and his rivalry with Tissaphernes together ensured that sooner or later Sparta would be faced with an awkward choice between several options: to fight on in Asia to liberate the Greeks from Persia as well as Athens; to support Cyrus in his bid for the throne in the hope that he would prove more complaisant towards the cities than Tissaphernes; to continue with Lysander's personalized form of imperialism; or to withdraw from the Aegean and *a fortiori* from Asia altogether. Not all of these options were mutually exclusive, however, and in practice Sparta eschewed only the last and wavered inconsistently between the other three.

In 403/2 (as argued in Chapter 6) official Spartan support was withdrawn from Lysander's dekarchies. But the harmost of Byzantion had a garrison at Chalkedon in Asia within the satrapy of Pharnabazus in 400; and Sthenelaos, left by Lysander as harmost of Byzantion and Chalkedon in 405 (2.2.1), may not in fact have been the only harmost retained by Sparta in Asia after the Athenian War. Successful opposition in Sparta to Lysander could have entailed a break with Cyrus. But influenced by the Greek cities' preference for Cyrus over Tissaphernes the Spartans decided to give official though covert support to the young pretender. Not only did they permit him to recruit mercenaries in mainland Greece (and the largest single contingent from neighbouring Arkadia), but they overlooked his appointment of an exiled Spartan, Klearchos, as his second-in-command and in 401 gave him a modicum of military support: the Spartan Cheirisophos was despatched to him with 700 hoplites (probably Peloponnesian mercenaries), and the navarch Samios (or Pythagoras) was ordered up with thirty-five ships.

Cyrus' death at Cunaxa removed a key piece from the board. Thereafter, to judge by the Byzantion harmost's hostile reception of the remnant of Cyrus' Greek mercenaries in 400, the Spartans appear at first to have been adopting a more conciliatory policy towards Artaxerxes. But a few months later, in the late autumn of 400, a decisive initiative was announced that marked a definitive break with the policy of subservience advocated by Lichas and abhorred by Kallikratidas. The Spartans had undertaken to fight both Tissaphernes and Pharnabazus in order to secure the autonomy of the Greeks of Asia (3.1.3; cf. 3.2.12, 4.5; Xen. *Anab.* 7.6.1).

The switch of policy was sudden but not entirely unpredictable (cf. Alkibiades' advice to Tissaphernes, Thuc. 8.46.1; and Lichas' counsel to the Milesians, Thuc. 8.84.4-5). Now that Sparta no longer needed Persian finance to defeat Athens and was released from obligation to Cyrus, she was free to indulge her expressed passion for liberation. Indeed, she was up to a point compelled to do so. On the one hand, she needed to justify her claim to be 'champion of Hellas' – a claim that the Ionian Greeks seem to have cleverly exploited (3.1.3; cf. Bengtson 1969, 206); on the other, the Ionians who were appealing for Spartan aid were probably oligarchs whom either Sparta or Lysander had installed in power in 407 or 405/4 and against whom Tissaphernes was supporting democracies (cf. Lins 1914, 7-8). But over and above these considerations there was, I believe, a further factor pushing Sparta in the same direction, the accession of Agesilaos in late summer 400 (cf. Funke 1980a, 37, for the date).

This had been achieved with the energetic backing of Lysander (Chapter 7). Since it was again Lysander who in 396 vigorously supported the appointment of Agesilaos as supreme commander of the Persian expedition, it is by no means inconceivable that in 400 Lysander had favoured the commencement of hostilities with Persia and had from the start envisaged Agesilaos as a pawn in his strategy of reinstalling his pet dekarchies. But Agesilaos will have had his own reasons for giving his vote on the Gerousia to the enterprise, not least because like the Roman emperor Claudius (the 'conqueror' of Britain) he needed a prestigious military victory to establish his credentials as leader in a peculiarly military state. If Agesilaos was not himself initially appointed to the overall command, this is easily explicable in terms of traditional Spartan caution. No Spartan king had ever before been deputed to campaign specifically on the Asiatic mainland, and the force sent under Thibron in 399 was not exactly equipped to inflict a crushing defeat on either Tissaphernes or Pharnabazus, let alone the two of them in combination (see Chapter 12). Besides, the Kinadon affair would have prevented Agesilaos' departing from Sparta until spring 398 at the earliest.

There is a further hint in Xenophon that this Persian war of the Spartans had more than just the blessing of Agesilaos from the outset. It was the Greek cities of Ionia specifically, not all the Asiatic Greeks, who had preferred Cyrus to Tissaphernes, who had therefore endured Tissaphernes' aggression and had then sent representatives to Sparta requesting aid in 400 (3.1.3). But the representatives are portrayed by Xenophon as asking the Spartans to help 'the Greeks in Asia', not just the Ionian Greeks. This is not the first known occurrence of the phrase; but Herodotus (1.27.1) had used it to contrast the Greeks of the Asiatic mainland with those of the offshore islands, whereas according to the standard fourth-century usage 'the Greeks in Asia' were always contrasted with the Greeks of Old Greece. Since there was no 'natural' unity or solidarity among the Greeks in Asia as a group, some special circumstance was necessary to bring this fourth-century distinction into being, and that circumstance was in practice the conclusion of the King's Peace or Peace of Antalkidas in 386 (cf. Seager/Tuplin 1980, esp. 145). Xenophon's usage of it in the context of 400 was therefore anachronistic, but revealingly so. For it chimed with Agesilaos' propagandistic representation of the whole campaign as a 'Panhellenist' enterprise undertaken to secure 'the freedom of the Greeks in Asia', with himself cast in the role of a second Agamemnon leading the forces of Greek civilisation against the tyrannous barbarian. The Boiotians were not the only contemporaries to see through this propaganda (Chapter 14), and we should not hesitate to follow the Boiotians' lead. The suggestion that 'the freedom of the Greeks of Asia, like other highminded slogans now as later, may have been only a mask for the ugly face of imperialism' (Seager 1977, 184) is surely correct.

The Spartan campaign in Asia Minor between 399 and 394 will be considered in detail from the military standpoint in the next chapter. In the present context, however, it is worth pausing to consider one very enlightening episode, and not only because Xenophon (4.1.29-41; cf. Gray 1981 for a general discussion of dialogue in the *Hellenika*) chose to devote unusual care to it: this is the parley between Agesilaos and Pharnabazus somewhere near the latter's satrapal seat at Daskyleion in early spring 394. The interview was arranged by one Apollophanes, a leading citizen of Greek Kyzikos (about 50 km. north of Daskyleion) who was a longstanding *xenos* (ritualized guest-friend) of the satrap but had also recently contracted a *xenia* with Agesilaos. This is a nice example of Agesilaos' preferred method of conducting diplomacy through such personal contacts (cf. Chapter 13).

Xenophon begins by drawing a dramatic and moralizing contrast between the pomp and finery of the Persian viceroy and the unostentatious simplicity of Agesilaos and his thirty Spartiate advisers, echoing that drawn by Herodotus (9.82) between Regent Pausanias and Mardonius. There follows a dialogue as different in atmosphere from Thucydides' Melian Dialogue as could well be imagined but in its way no less truthful in that it artfully conveys the essential political realities. Pharnabazus, the older man, speaks first – Xenophon did not have to remind his readers of the Spartans' extreme reverence for and deference to seniority.

Pharnabazus begins with an appeal to the Greek aristocratic code, according to which it was the height of morality to help one's friends (cf. Chapter 9). For the Spartans, he points out, are ravaging the domains he inherited from his father (*sc.* Pharnakes: Lewis 1977, 52), even though he unlike Tissaphernes had been unswerving in his support of the Spartan war-effort from 411 onwards. The Spartiates are shamed into silence, and the irony of the situation transpires. At length Agesilaos finds his tongue and points out, what the hellenized Pharnabazus knew perfectly well, that among Greeks not even the sacred tie of *xenia* overrode the claims of patriotism. The Spartans had to act in what they took to be their country's best interests even against a former friend like Pharnabazus (who was now acting as a chattel of their enemy Artaxerxes). But, Agesilaos continues, it was in the Persian's interest to desert his master, for he would thereby both gain his freedom and increase his wealth with Spartan help. This quintessentially Greek notion of political freedom was, it need hardly be said, more attractive to Agesilaos than Pharnabazus (whose loyalty to the Persian crown was unshakeable over a quarter of a century and ultimately rewarded in 388 by marriage to a daughter of Artaxerxes: 5.1.28); so the satrap pledges that, as long as Artaxerxes does not place a superior over him in his province, he will fight Agesilaos to the best of his ability – which of course proved all too adequate at Knidos later in the year. In fact, Pharnabazus' entire career was consistent with Herodotus' judgment (7.238.2) that 'the Persians are of all men known to me the most accustomed to honour valiant warriors'.

That ended the dialogue but not the episode. For after Pharnabazus had ridden away, his teenage son made Agesilaos an offer he had no desire to refuse, an offer of *xenia* which was duly concluded according to the traditional verbal and material rituals. No doubt Agesilaos was not unaffected by the boy's physical charms, but this was a business deal not a love match and motivated by the same diplomatic and perhaps military considerations as prompted him to become the *xenos* of Maussollos (or his father Hekatomnôs) of Caria (Xen. *Ages.* 2.27; with Hornblower 1982, 105n.209, 142 and n.39, 168). Indeed, if there is anything to the view that Agesilaos' grand strategy in Asia Minor was to create a 'buffer zone of rebel satraps' (Seager 1977, 183-4), this was just how a Spartan king like Agesilaos would have set about implementing it. But Agesilaos, as we shall see, was not destined to be the first Spartan to make diplomatic capital out of a *xenia* relationship with a high-ranking Persian.

By August 394 any dreams Sparta or Agesilaos may have entertained of humiliating and preoccupying the Persians, let alone of far-reaching conquest in Asia, were just that: dreams (cf. Xen. *Ages.* 1.7,34,36; 7.5-7). Agesilaos had by then been recalled to Greece to help his countrymen face a formidable coalition of enemies brought about by an explosive combination of Spartan imperialism and Persian 'slush' money (Chapter 14); and the Spartan fleet under the incompetent command of Agesilaos' brother-in-law (cf. Chapter 9) had been severely defeated off Knidos by a mixed Greek and oriental fleet under Pharnabazus and Konon (Chapter 12). Had Xenophon's picture of Sparta the liberator been accurate, this must surely have spelled the end of 'the freedom of the Greeks in Asia'. Very far from it, in fact. For the cities and offshore islands of the east Aegean actually welcomed the victorious fleet of Pharnabazus and Konon as if with a huge sigh of relief, emboldened thereto by the guarantee that their cities would be left both autonomous and free from garrisons (4.8.1-2,5; DS 14.84; Tod 106). Since autonomy on all fours with that enjoyed by mainland Greek states had been on offer from Agesilaos to the Asiatic Greeks (3.4.5), it is clear that freedom from Spartan garrisons was regarded as no less important than liberation from Persian suzerainty. But was it not naive of the leaders of the Greek cities to suppose that Pharnabazus and Tiribazus (successor of Tissaphernes, who had been executed in 395) would genuinely respect their autonomy once the post-Knidos euphoria had ebbed away? It would appear not. Shortly before 386, as a newly published inscription has revealed (Hornblower 1982, 369, M14), the Erythraians asked the Athenians not to hand them over to 'the barbarian', i.e. Persia. The clear implication of this is that 'the Greek cities of the Asia Minor coast did not finally pass to Persia until 386. They were therefore autonomous until then' (Hornblower 1982, 85n.56); a similar picture emerges from an honorific decree (Tod 114) passed by Athens in early 386 in favour of Klazomenai which, though technically an island, was regarded by the Great King as belonging to Asia. For the Persians, though, autonomy was not regarded as incompatible with the payment of tribute (e.g. 3.4.25). But even so some Asiatic Greeks at least thought this was a fair price to pay for liberation from Agesilaos' Sparta.

This is the background against which the negotiations with Persia conducted by Antalkidas on and off between 392/1 (probably) and 386 have to be judged. Already in 393 the enormity of their mistake in breaking with Persia in 400 (cf. Zierke 1936, 32; Cawkwell 1972b, 46) had been brought all too literally home to thinking Spartans. The war in Greece was not going brilliantly, the war at sea had been such a disaster that Konon and Pharnabazus had actually seized – and garrisoned! – part of Sparta's own nuclear territory, the strategically placed island of Kythera (4.8.7-8; cf. Cartledge 1979, 283-4). Once again, as in 412/1, fear and profit dictated an accommodation with Persia, no matter what loss of prestige this might entail in the eyes of the allies, and especially of the Asiatic Greeks. Hence the choice of Antalkidas in 392 as special envoy to Tiribazus at Sardis with the mission of persuading the Great King to renew the old entente with Sparta in return for a Spartan renunciation of involvement in Asia.

Antalkidas appears to have been surprisingly young for this vital mission, but he was of a distinguished family with inherited Persian connections and perhaps (no less relevantly) related by marriage to the Eurypontids (cf. Chapter 9). Whatever precisely his background, the diplomacy of Antalkidas was spectacularly successful with Tiribazus, who crossed his palm with much money and arrested Konon. But neither Tiribazus nor Antalkidas could entirely rid

Artaxerxes of his not unreasonable and wholly understandable view that the Spartans, who had doublecrossed him, were the most shameless and insolent of men (Deinon, *FGrHist.* 690F19, *ap.* Plut. *Artax.* 22.1). As part of a reorganization of the western end of the Persian Empire (in which Caria, for example, became a separate satrapy or sub-satrapy under the native ruler Hekatomnôs, distinct from the satrapy or sub-satrapy of Ionia under Strouthas or Strouses) Tiribazus was deprived of his post. And although Artaxerxes was not averse to promoting a Greek peace through Sparta, who called a conference at Sparta early in 391 with that end in view, Antalkidas was robbed of a strong argument in favour of his view that the Greeks should swear a 'common peace' on the basis of universal autonomy but cede the Greek cities of Asia to the Great King (Andok. 3, esp. 15, 17, 34; with Martin 1944; 1949).

Even Lewis (1977, 144) is obliged to characterize the policy fronted by Antalkidas as a 'Spartan betrayal of panhellenism'. But what did the *soi-disant* 'Panhellenist' Agesilaos think of this reversion to the Spartan position of 412/1? Was he its prime mover, or at least prominent in its support? Or were he and Antalkidas, as Xenophon tried to suggest and Plutarch explicitly stated, at loggerheads over the matter? In a not unimportant sense these questions raise a non-issue, since 'the only passage (Plut. *Ages.* 23.2-4) which asserts Antalkidas' hostility to Agesilaos also attests Agesilaos' acceptance of Antalkidas' policy' (Lewis 1977, 145n.61). But the question remains whether it was indeed the policy of Antalkidas or that of Agesilaos, a question that affects our understanding of policymaking in Sparta.

First, we must discount Plutarch's view that Agesilaos and Antalkidas were bitter personal enemies. That is almost certainly an illegitimate inference from Antalkidas' oft-cited reproof of Agesilaos for his unreasoning aggressiveness toward Thebes in the 370s (Plut. *Ages.* 26.5, etc.; Polyain. 1.16.2). For it is hard to see how Antalkidas could possibly have pursued his long and for the most part highly successful diplomatic career without at least the passive support of Agesilaos. Certainly there is no reason (*pace* Payrau 1961, 29) to believe that the change of policy in 392 could have been sponsored by the other royal house, whose incumbent (Agesipolis) was young, inexperienced, the son of a discredited exile and at any rate later gratifyingly susceptible to the much older man's winning ways (e.g. 5.3.20; Chapter 9). Antalkidas, in short, was Agesilaos' man, a convenient cover for his own failure to bring the King to heel by military means. No doubt Agesilaos would ideally have preferred not to have to resort to negotiation and surrender the liberty (as he understood it) of the Asiatic Greeks. He would perhaps have echoed the words Xenophon (5.1.17) attributes to his step-brother Teleutias in 387, precisely when Antalkidas was actually bargaining with the Great King in person – words which in turn pick up the echo of those of Kallikratidas quoted earlier (1.6.7). But Agesilaos should not thereby be represented, as he is by Cawkwell (1976a, 66-71), as a genuine Panhellenist dragged kicking and screaming to the conference table and itching for revenge upon Artaxerxes from 394 on. If there was one concern that overrode all other individual motivations thereafter, that was his hostility, not to Persia, but to Thebes; and even that was only the most important single plank in his overarching aim to maintain Sparta by any means available as the leading power in mainland Greece (cf. von Stern 1884, 20). Not that Agesilaos' brand of Panhellenism was at all exceptional: in practical terms Panhellenism generally 'served as a tool of propaganda for the hegemonial or imperial rule of a *polis*' (Perlman 1976, 6).

Tiribazus' successor Strouthas was a friend to Athens rather than Sparta (4.8.17), but within four years a renascence of Athens' capacity for implementing her undying hegemonial aspirations had caused Artaxerxes to reconsider his attitude towards Sparta (cf. Chapter 14). The Spartans in the mass and perhaps Agesilaos in particular he no doubt continued to regard as unutterably shameless and insolent, but by Antalkidas he was apparently completely charmed when he received him in audience at Susa in 388. Like his father a score of years earlier, Artaxerxes now decided to give his full backing to Sparta in a war against her Greek enemies, and at the end of 388 he replaced Pharnabazus at Daskyleion with a longstanding *xenos* of Antalkidas, by name Ariobarzanes (5.1.28), and restored Tiribazus to Sardis. With this renewed Persian support, and with additional aid from their Syracusan friend Dionysios I, the Spartans before long were in a position to dictate terms to their defeated Greek opponents – Athens, Thebes, Argos and Corinth above all.

The diplomatic instrument in question carried alternative titles in antiquity, each revealing in its own way. For some it was the 'King's Peace' (e.g. Tod 133.23-4), since formally the Great King had ordered the Greeks to swear to its terms (5.1.35; cf. 6.3.9). This was in line with what appears to have been the usual Persian view that relations with Greeks were regulated by a kind of ultimatum, although it is not insignificant that the King himself also swore oaths (Tod 118 = SV 248.7; *contra* Martin 1944, 19n.6,21n.12,24; 1949, 130,137). For others it was the 'Peace of Antalkidas' (5.1.36; DS 15.5.1,19.1; cf. Martin 1944, 14-17,28-9). If I prefer to use the latter, it is because I believe that Agesilaos got the balance of immediate advantage right when, in rebutting the accusation that the Spartans had shamefully 'medized', he is supposed to have observed that on the contrary it was the Persians who had 'lakonized' – a remark that Plutarch quoted almost as often as Antalkidas' criticism of Agesilaos' later Theban policy (*Ages.* 23.4; *Artax.* 22.4; *Mor.* 213b).

There was, none the less, much substance in the accusation. For by the Peace of 386 Artaxerxes had formally secured universal Greek recognition of his title to Asia, including the Greek *poleis* as well as his own territory (*chôra*), and this recognition materially affected also the offshore islands like Samos which had possessed substantial territories (*peraiai*) on the adjoining Asiatic mainland. The status of the Greek cities as Persian subjects ruled by oligarchies (cf. Hornblower 1982, 107-8) persisted unaltered for over fifty years, until, after the Battle of the Granikos River in 334, Alexander – for reasons of *Realpolitik* rather than ideological preference (cf. Badian 1966) – 'dispossessed the oligarchies and established democracies, allowing every community to enjoy its own laws and customs and discontinue payment of tribute to the Persians' (Arr. *Anab.* 1.18.2). Incorporation in Alexander's empire, though, was to mean only a change of location from the frying-pan of the Achaemenids to the fire of Alexander's Successors.

It has been alleged that, in contrast to the two generations of Athenian

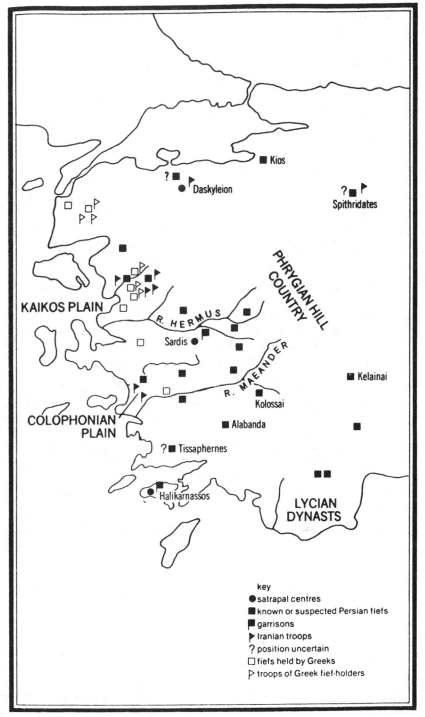

Kios

? ■ Daskyleion

? ■ Spithridates

KAIKOS PLAIN

PHRYGIAN HILL COUNTRY

R. HERMUS

Sardis

R. MAEANDER

Kelainai

Kolossai

COLOPHONIAN PLAIN

Alabanda

? ■ Tissaphernes

Halikarnassos

LYCIAN DYNASTS

key
● satrapal centres
■ known or suspected Persian fiefs
▐ garrisons
▶ Iranian troops
? position uncertain
□ fiefs held by Greeks
▷ troops of Greek fief-holders

Fig. 11.2. The Persian presence in Western Asia Minor. After Cook 1983

hegemony in the fifth century and the decade or so of Spartan rule, this half-century of Persian suzerainty from 386 fostered economic prosperity and urbanization and that under the aegis of the Peace of Antalkidas the hellenization of Asia Minor was able to proceed apace (esp. Starr 1975, 76-99; 1977-78). But this was prosperity for the few, exploitation for the many, as may be seen by a glance at the tombs of Persian grandees at Sardis or near Ephesos and of native dynasts at Xanthos and Halikarnassos, not to mention literary accounts of, for example, the estate of the Persian Asidates in the Kaikos valley (Xen. *Anab.* 7.8) or the huge wealth piled up in Anatolia by the quisling Greek émigré families of the Damaratids and Gongylids (3.1.6; Xen. *Anab.* 2.1.3; 7.8.8,17; cf. Pareti 1961 (1911), 179-91, with a table illustrating their intermarriage) (see Fig. 11.2). In an evocative analogy Tarn (1930, 52) suggested that 'the castle of a Persian probably bore a considerable resemblance to Scott's Branksome Hall', but it may be doubted whether the humble citizen of a Greek *polis* in Asia under Persian domination shared Tarn's romantic vision of such edifices. Moreover, since none of these Persian or Greek nabobs will have been a friend of democracy, we may be sure that the rate of exploitation of the majority in the Greek cities will have been stepped up under cover of Persian hegemony – as it was under the cloak of Spartan hegemony in mainland Greece (Chapter 13). Finally, thanks to the Peace the King was able to tap Greek expertise and manpower, first in pursuit of the reconquest of Egypt and Cyprus, later in the quelling of rebellious satraps (cf. Chapter 15).

Once more, then, the dangers of a Hellenocentric vision are illustrated. So too our sources rather grossly misrepresent, or at least underexpose, the nuts and bolts of the Peace. Xenophon the 'Panhellenist' clearly felt very uneasy about the way Agesilaos promoted it so eagerly, giving his attitude the most favourable possible gloss (Xen. *Ages.* 2.21; see further Chapters 13 and 14). And it is only when Thebes, his and Agesilaos' *bête noire*, became the principal Greek beneficiary of Persian intervention in the early 360s that his account of the mechanics of peacemaking grows noticeably much fuller (7.1.33-40). But he does at least quote verbatim what purports to be the Rescript of Artaxerxes in its official Greek translation (5.1.31; cf. DS 14.110.3):

> Artaxerxes, (Great) King, considers it just that (1) the cities in Asia belong to him, together with, of the islands, Klazomenai and Cyprus; and that (2) the other Greek cities both great and small be left autonomous, excepting only Lemnos and Imbros and Skyros: these should belong to the Athenians as of old. But (3) if either of the two parties does not accept this peace treaty, on these will I make war with the assistance of those who do wish to accept the peace, both on land and by sea, both with ships and money.

However, the various stone or bronze *stelai* on which the terms of the Peace were recorded must surely also have specified the nature of the treaty, its intended duration, the manner of settling disputes, the names of those swearing the oaths, and the means whereby those oaths would be administered. Nor was the text of the Peace literally the same as the Rescript, since the King's right to the Greek cities of Asia, for example, was more fully prescribed. But just how to supply these deficiencies is problematic. One possible method of procedure is to attempt to determine whether known clauses in the various renewals or possible renewals of the Peace – 375/4 (SV 265), 371 (twice: SV 269-70), and possibly 365 (SV 285) – are innovation or survivals from the original; but this is inevitably speculative or 'highly inferential' (Cargill 1981, 8n.3) and leads to contradictory results (e.g. Sinclair 1978, 29-37; contrast Cawkwell 1981a). For what they are worth, Cawkwell's latest published speculations are that the autonomy clause involved a specific guarantee against garrisons in Asia, that there was a demobilization clause and a sanctions clause, but no clause enjoining the restoration of political exiles.

There is also plenty of room for argument as to whether or not the Peace of Antalkidas was in fact called a 'Common Peace' (*koinê eirênê*) from the start, as Diodoros (15.5.1) would suggest it was. The phrase has been restored in a famous Athenian inscription of early 377, the so-called Magna Carta of the Second Athenian League, but this restoration 'has no epigraphical basis' (Cargill 1981, 11; cf. 29-32); and the earliest certain epigraphical use of the phrase belongs to a document conjecturally dated to 362/1 (Tod 145 = SV 292.6). It had, however, appeared already in an Athenian speech of 392/1, that in which Andokides (3.17,34) sought to persuade the Athenians to accept the revised peace terms worked out at the Sparta conference; so it is not impossible that the Peace of Antalkidas was originally labelled a 'Common Peace'.

This terminological uncertainty is not unimportant to the question whether the Peace of Antalkidas and its successors evince the evolution of a genuinely panhellenic sentiment or striving for political unity (cf. Mossé 1962, 455-60; Payrau 1971; Lévy 1976, 155-64). But for the history of Agesilaos and Sparta neither the exact title nor the precise terms of the Peace of 386 count as much as its practical interpretation and implementation (or non-implementation). Rarely can Ambrose Bierce's definition of 'peace' as 'a period of cheating between two periods of fighting' (*A Devil's Dictionary*) have been more apt. For in the next two decades, as first Sparta, then Athens and then Thebes sought to exploit it to develop and consolidate their hegemonies, the Peace became 'the fundamental *shibboleth* of Greek politics' (Cargill 1981, 189 – my emphasis).

The details of the way in which Agesilaos and Sparta put their *ex parte* construction upon the Peace will be explored in later chapters. But it is worth noting here a dissenting Spartan voice crying, alas, in the political wilderness. Not content with composing a tendentious pamphlet on the Spartan constitution (Chapter 10) and intervening on behalf of his clients at Mantineia in 385 (Chapter 13), the exiled Agiad king Pausanias seized the opportunity of his son's death at Olynthos in 380 to make a public demonstration of his opposition to Agesilaos' imperialist policy. He commissioned an expensive funerary monument (*mnâmeion*) from a distinguished Sikyonian sculptor and had it erected symbolically in the great Panhellenic sanctuary of Delphi, the navel of the earth. On the base of the monument he had inscribed the following two hexameter verses (Tod 120):

> Me, as a memorial to his dear son, his father Pausanias dedicated: Hellas with one voice hymns his excellence.

The choice of location and vocabulary was Pausanias' nicely judged way of indicating to the Greek world at large that he considered the Panhellenism of Agesilaos to be bogus – as it surely was.

The Battle of Leuktra in 371, however, upset all Agesilaos' calculations; and although the Peace was renewed after the battle, this was not altogether a replica of either of its predecessors (cf. Cargill 1981, 76-7; cf. 12, 67). Indeed, it is not absolutely certain that Sparta was involved in swearing the oaths, which were taken for the first time at Athens not Sparta. But even if she was (as I believe, following Ryder 1965, 131-3; cf. Osborne 1982, 57-8), the Peace by itself could not deliver what Sparta was now reduced to wanting, namely maintenance of her hegemony in the Peloponnese. Still less could it make good the disastrous territorial losses she suffered in the winter of 370/69.

So long as Sparta had been both chief negotiator and chief executor of the Peace in mainland Greece, there had been no question in practice of the Greeks under Sparta's direct rule in Lakonia and Messenia enjoying genuine autonomy. But in the aftermath of Leuktra not only did the Perioikic towns of northern Lakonia break away temporarily (and in some cases permanently) from Spartan control but the former Helots of the Pamisos valley were reborn as the citizens of the *polis* of (New) Messene. In 368 yet another peace congress was held, but at Delphi this time, and on the initiative of Dionysios of Syracuse as well as Artaxerxes. Both the Persian King and the Syracusan tyrant were prepared to recognize Sparta's claim to all Messenia, but the Thebans, who were then the most powerful state in mainland Greece and had been principally responsible for the rebirth of Messene, not surprisingly were not. Equally naturally, when the Thebans through Pelopidas finally persuaded Artaxerxes to promote a Thebes-led Peace in 367-6, the terms involved the recognition of the autonomy of Messene.

The peace initiative of 368 was certainly abortive. But on balance I am inclined to suppose that Pelopidas' initiative did culminate in the conclusion of a Peace in 365. Whether it did so or not, Artaxerxes had unquestionably renounced the association with Sparta that had been so mutually beneficial in the 380s and 370s. For the first time since 394 Agesilaos was again both willing and – despite his advanced age – able to contemplate undertaking active anti-Persian military service. The opportunity was not long in arising. Beginning in 372 a series of revolts by satraps had disrupted the western reaches of the Persian Empire, and to optimistic 'Panhellenists' it could have seemed 'as if the whole western unit was about to split off, standing on its own from the Aegean to Mesopotamia' (Lane Fox 1980, 122). The reality of this 'crisis', however, was that it was a kind of prolonged and glorified succession struggle brought about by Artaxerxes' failure to observe the due proprieties of the higher Persian nobility's ladder of promotion. The revolting satraps from Datames through Ariobarzanes to Orontes were opting into rather than out of the system, and 'if they were reduced, it was because they sold one another to the King' (Glover 1917, 233; cf. Parke 1933, 110). But for Agesilaos this prolonged unrest offered scope for replenishing Sparta's empty coffers and at the same time reviving – or perhaps creating – the myth of his undying hatred of Persia and all its works.

In about 365 he turned up in the Troad, officially on a diplomatic mission intended no doubt to raise cash from the King's enemies. But he was able in some minor way to support the revolt of Sparta's ally Ariobarzanes and was handsomely rewarded for his efforts both by Ariobarzanes and by Maussollos, satrap of Caria, who was also a *xenos* of his (Xen. *Ages.* 2.26-7). Half a dozen years later he was under arms – for the last time – as a mercenary commander aiding the Egyptian rebellion from Persia, another highly lucrative venture (see in detail Chapter 15). It would, however, give a one-sided picture of this late flurry of misopersic endeavour by Agesilaos if a remarkable letter written to him by Artaxerxes himself were omitted.

The context of the letter is not specified by the sources (Xen. *Ages.* 8.3ff.; Plut. *Ages.* 23.10; *Mor.* 213d), but a good case has been made for placing it in 362 or 361 (Hatzfeld 1946). In 362 the satraps' revolt reached its apogee under the ambiguous leadership of Orontes (cf. for his career Osborne 1982, 61-80). Following what was by now standard procedure, the satraps sought to employ Greek mercenaries to counter the King and his Greek mercenaries; but their request was met – if the relevant inscription is correctly dated – with a strong rebuff by those Greek states which, mainly from mutual exhaustion, had sworn a Common Peace on the battlefield of Mantineia. Since this was the first such Peace to be concluded without the intervention of the Persian Great King, the participants expressed their rejection of the satraps' request for mercenaries in the following stiffly diplomatic terms:

> They are not aware of the existence of any state of war between the King and themselves. If he keeps the Peace and does not embroil the Greeks with each other and does not seek to break the Peace which exists among us by any device or strategem then we will keep peace with the King. But if he makes war against any of our allies or supplies money for breaking the Peace, or moves against the Greeks who share in the Peace, or if anyone from his territory does so, we shall unite to repel him in a manner appropriate to the Peace we now enjoy and to our past deeds … (Tod 145 = SV 292).

Sparta, because the Peace deplorably recognised the autonomy of Messene, was no more a party to it than the Great King. It was therefore in this context that Hatzfeld placed Artaxerxes' letter to Agesilaos offering him both ritualized guest-friendship (*xenia*) and friendship, since he plausibly took Artaxerxes to be seeking the aid of Agesilaos against the rebel satraps. If Agesilaos refused this request, it was not so much for ideological, 'Panhellenist' reasons as because Artaxerxes showed no signs of changing the opinion he had held since 367 on the question of Messene's autonomy. It was perhaps also about this time (rather than 367) that Antalkidas, despairing over the ruins of his *Ostpolitik*, decided to take his own life (Plut. *Artax.* 22.6-7; cf. Buckler 1977b).

In retrospect, Sparta's dealings with Persia in the age of Agesilaos are not particularly savoury, revealing as they do that Sparta 'had nothing good to offer to the Greek states' (Ste. Croix 1972, 161). As for Agesilaos, he did not make his last journeys to Asia Minor and Egypt because he was a good pan-Greek loyalist, but because he was a Spartan patriot and Sparta had gone bankrupt financially, politically, militarily, even perhaps morally. Just like the liberation propaganda under whose banner his father had begun the Athenian War, his own

Panhellenist propaganda was ultimately mere window-dressing. To discover the more solid achievements of Agesilaos, it is necessary to direct attention to a different field of his activity, the field of battle.

12

The Generalship of Agesilaos

War is the father of all and the king of all things; these war has revealed to be gods, the rest mortals – these slaves, these free men. (Herakleitos fr. 53)

Anyone who has taken even the humblest part in a great battle is very well aware that it sometimes becomes impossible to be precise about a major episode after only a few hours. (Bloch, Marc, 1954, 57)

Generalship, it has been said, is essentially a matter of reacting to mistakes – the enemy's, those of one's subordinates, one's own. This negative view would not have appealed to any ancient general, and it is not one that is usually taken by historians called to assess the generalship of an Alexander or a Julius Caesar. But it will serve well enough for Agesilaos, as we shall see. His generalship has been variously assessed by modern writers from a variety of standpoints, but surprisingly only in relation to specific campaigns (especially that in Asia Minor: e.g. Lins 1914). Never has it been scrutinized as a whole within the broad context of the warfare of his day or viewed as it should be from the interrelated vantage points of politics, economics, religion, social organization and so on.[1]

Neglect of Agesilaos' generalship in these terms is surprising for two main reasons. In the first place, war in Classical Greece was not conceived primarily as a painful interruption of peaceful normality but rather as a state of nature. For many citizens of most Greek states and for all full citizens of Sparta war was akin to a way of life (cf. de Romilly 1968, 207-8; Havelock 1972, esp. 61-2; Vermeule 1979, 84). Leadership in the conquest-state of Sparta thus inevitably acquired a military cast, and the fact that Spartan kings were hereditary generals is of more than incidental interest and importance. Secondly, although Agesilaos happened not to be directly involved in two of the major pitched battles of his epoch, his career as general embraced all the possible modes and circumstances of land warfare during the first four decades of the fourth century. He fought on terrain ranging from the plains of Asia Minor, the Nile Delta and Boiotia to the broken, hilly country of the Corinthia and Akarnania. He presided over the pitched battle and the siege, the long march and the defence of an unwalled habitation.

---

[1] This deficiency has been remedied to some extent in an unpublished paper by C.D. Hamilton, which the author kindly let me see in typescript.

He utilized in varying combinations and with considerable success almost all the arms, forces and manoeuvres known to Europe besides introducing exotic addenda from Asia.

In fact, the evidence bearing directly and indirectly upon Agesilaos' generalship as conceived here is so rich, and the issues it raises not just for Spartan history but for the history of Greece as a whole are so fundamental, that it has been found necessary to divide the discussion between two chapters. Their respective subject-matters naturally intersect and overlap with each other. But broadly speaking the present chapter will deal with Agesilaos' command of troops recruited, equipped and trained within the framework of the *polis*, whether or not they happen to be citizens of Sparta and of states allied to her, while the later one (Chapter 15) will be addressed to his command of mercenaries both Greek and non-Greek. This division also reflects the very different circumstances in which he found himself as general at the beginning and at the end of his career. In both chapters the emphasis will be on the changes wrought in strategy and tactics during this militarily transitional era and on the ways in which Agesilaos and Sparta could and did – or rather could not and did not – inspire or react adequately to such changes.

First, then, Agesilaos' generalship must be located within the Spartan military hierarchy. In war there must be leaders, and notwithstanding the ideology of egalitarianism Spartan society was permeated with officially approved and sponsored competitiveness of an appropriately martial character. Competition of course produced losers as well as winners, but even after the social and economic basis of the military system began to fail, there was a sufficient pool of men of the required material to supply the office-holding elite. Thucydides (5.66.4), indeed, said that at the time of the first Battle of Mantineia (418) most of the Spartan contingent in the allied army consisted of officers commanding other officers, so that the responsibility for seeing that orders were carried out was widely shared. This was no doubt something *of* an exaggeration, and Xenophon (*LP* 11.5) was probably technically right to designate only the file-leaders (*prôtostatai*) as *archontes*. But Thucydides was surely correct to single out the Spartan system of subordinate command as a major source of strength on the battlefield. The Spartan custom (*nomos*) of choosing two deputy commanders of a unit (Thuc. 4.38.1; cf. 3.109.1) confirms this point, besides indicating that Spartan officers were expected to set an example by making the supreme sacrifice.

We do not know how a man would become eligible for appointment to the most junior rank of enomotarch or commander of an *enômotia* (cf. Appendix II). But it is an easy guess that he would be the sort of man who had already been singled out from his age-mates for inclusion in the Helot-policing Krypteia (Chapter 3) and then for election to the super-elite corps of 300 known as Hippeis (literally 'cavalrymen', though they fought as hoplites) or 'Youths' (*koroi*: *IG* V.1, 457). Nor is it known for certain how the Hippeis were recruited or how long they served. But a plausible hypothesis would be that they were chosen from among the ten youngest year-classes (20-29) of the militarily active citizens (*emphrouroi*) and that the full-strength of 300 was maintained by competitive election to fill the vacancies created by death, disablement or retirement on reaching the age of thirty (*contra* Cozzoli 1979, 88, who supposes that a Hippeus remained a Hippeus until he retired from active service at sixty). The actual selection was made by the three commanding officers called Hippagretai, who were themselves over thirty and appointed by the Ephors (Xen. *LP* 4.3). Their choice is likely to have fallen mainly on members of the Spartan social and economic elite and perhaps especially on those with whom existing Hippeis had formed pederastic ties when the prospective candidates were in the final stages of the *agôgê*. The point of the anecdote about Pedaritos – who on failing to be selected is said to have rejoiced that Sparta had 300 men better than he (Plut. *Lyk.* 25.6; *Mor.* 191f, 231bc) – must be that, as a man of high birth (cf. Chapter 9) and a future top office-holder (Chapter 6), he would normally have been expected to be chosen.

Membership of the Hippeis was tough in the sense that in real life most disappointed candidates did not adopt Pedaritos' cheerfully philosophical attitude but considered themselves to be at war both with the Hippagretai who had not selected them and with the chosen candidates (Xen. *LP* 4.4; cf. Villard 1981, 304). But the compensations of membership were more than enough to offset this envious aggravation. Apart from performing occasional honorific tasks off the battlefield (e.g. providing an escort for Themistokles in the winter of 480/79: Hdt. 8.124.3), their primary function was to serve as the king's bodyguard in battle (Thuc. 5.72.4; 6.4.14 – emended; Isok. *Ep.* 2.6), somewhat in the manner of Alexander's Macedonian Hypaspists (cf. G.T. Griffith in Hammond/Griffith 1979, 416-17) or the Persian King's so-called 'Immortals'. Their special status was symbolized by their exclusion from the regular organization of the Spartan army in our period into six *morai* (Chapter 4; Appendix II). At Leuktra in 371 the Hippeis probably were killed almost to a man, anticipating the heroic fate of the elite Theban 'Sacred Band' of 300 at Chaironeia in 338. But their sacrifice did not save the life of King Kleombrotos – nor would he have wished it to.

The climactic Battle of Leuktra will provide a fitting coda to this chapter; for the moment it is only the position of Kleombrotos at the apex of the Spartan command structure that concerns me. In his day and for many years before that it was not the kings but the Ephors who formally declared war on Sparta's behalf (*phrouran phainein* in technical parlance) and so placed Sparta in a state of alert (*taga*). The Ephors, too, decided how many year-classes to call out for active duty, how many *morai* to despatch, how large the baggage-train should be and other such preliminary matters of detail. They probably also had some part in the choice of the supreme commander, although the decision apparently had to be ratified by the Assembly of phalangites. However, once the supreme commander had passed beyond the Spartan frontiers with his army it was he not the Ephors who ran the show.

Aristotle (*Pol.* 1285a7-8, 1285b26-8) rather slightingly referred to the Spartan kings as mere hereditary generals; that is, he placed them at the opposite end of the scale of kingship to absolute monarchs. But Aristotle did also realize that *qua* generals they were *autokratores*, capable of making decisions on their own account without reference back to the home authorities at any rate for the duration of the campaign. We may add that a prescriptive right to the supreme command of citizen and allied armies in a militarized state like Sparta was potentially a passport to undying fame abroad and enormous political influence at home. This potential was greatly increased in *c*.506 following the passage of a law enjoining that only one king should be in command of a given army at a time (Hdt. 5.75.2). For although the aim of the law was to promote military efficiency, its unintended consequences were the creation of yet another focus for competition between the traditionally hostile royal houses (cf. Hdt. 6.52.8) and of another standing opportunity for the more astute of the two kings to increase his political leverage.

It is irritating therefore that Herodotus and Xenophon, who set out quite fully the prerogatives on campaign of the kings (cf. Chapter 7), fail to make clear the grounds on which one king rather than the other would be given a particular command. However, since Agesilaos is twice recorded by Xenophon (5.2.3; 5.4.13) as abjuring a command on specious pretexts, there was undoubtedly a political art to acceptance or refusal. Another relevant factor was the prospect of booty, the king's personal share of which could be as high as one third (Polyb. 2.62.1, with Pritchett 1974, I, 76-7,84; the profits of generals are further discussed at Pritchett 1974, II, 126-32). Nor do Herodotus or Xenophon specify the mechanisms whereby the top jobs other than that of supreme commander were allocated, but there is good reason for suspecting royal patronage in at least some instances (cf. Chapter 9) and the same may hold good right down to the level of the enomotarchs.

These aspects of the king's commanding role well illustrate the intimate connection between the military function in Sparta and the character of the Spartan political hierarchy. Turning to the more narrowly military aspects we find by contrast that the king's role was rather severely restricted by the stolid, almost ritualistic character of hoplite fighting down to the Athenian War (cf. Cartledge 1977,12-17); indeed, it is only a slight and pardonable exaggeration to say that it was 'nearly exhausted with the choosing of a battle-ground to suit the phalanx' (Snodgrass 1967, 62). Since the hoplite general, unlike the Duke of Plazatoro, led his troops from the front of the mêlée and had no mechanical means of communicating detailed instructions beyond his immediate entourage, his primary function had been to maintain the morale of his troops at the highest possible pitch by reassurances of divine favour, by personal example, even by sheer deception if need be. Napoleon is said to have evaluated the moral to the physical in warfare in the ratio of three to one, and (as has been said of the English at Agincourt, but with equal relevance to Agesilaos' Sparta) 'the presence of the king would also have provided what present-day soldiers call a "moral factor" of great importance. The personal bond between leader and follower lies at the root of all explanations of what does and does not happen in battle: and that bond is always strongest in martial societies' (Keegan 1978, 114). A suggestive list of comparisons between the Spartan and Zulu military systems (Ferguson 1918) fully bears that out, and the bond will presumably have been reinforced in the case of kings like Agesilaos who had gone through the *agôgê*. The strong element of soldier in Agesilaos contributed significantly to his make-up as general.

However, during the course of the Athenian War a transformation occurred. Although the importance of the morale aspect of generalship diminished not at all, its technical aspect changed out of all recognition. Regent Pausanias in 479 had been required to command the largest and most heterogeneous army of Greek hoplites yet assembled and he commanded it well given his inexperience. But it cannot be said that he did much more than keep morale high and allow his crack Spartan troops to deliver the knockout blow at the appropriate moment. But by the time that Agis II tried to do something out of the ordinary on the point of engagement at Mantineia in 418 (and failed) it had become apparent that generalship was no less of an art than leadership in politics and equally subject to theoretical analysis. Agis was saved by Spartan drill and toughness, but the future lay with men like Brasidas and Lysander, who exemplified the trend towards a greater professionalism and specialization in command. The closing phase of the Athenian War in particular 'brought before men's notice the real meaning of generalship, as opposed to the mere disposition and command of troops in battle' (Hunter 1927, xxix).

This change of emphasis has been described by a good judge as 'perhaps the most important single matter in the history of ancient warfare' (Tarn 1930, 37). Agesilaos knew how to profit from it. One aspect of his generalship brings this out more sharply than all the rest put together – what Xenophon (*Ages.* 6.4-7) called his *sophia* or know-how. In old-style hoplite warfare surprise was at a discount, and not just because of what Clausewitz called 'the frictions engendered by the whole [military] apparatus' (quoted by Howard 1983, 186) that tended to frustrate any initial advantages it secured. For surprise contradicted the agonistic, almost chivalric character of hoplite warfare. The Athenian War, however, witnessed a change in the ethos of warfare (cf. Vidal-Naquet 1981, 140-1), and it became a mark of the good general to employ deceiving 'stratagems' or ruses. On this score Agesilaos earned high praise from the compilers of casebooks of such devices in the early Roman Imperial period. Most of Frontinus' examples are Roman, but among the Greek ones Sparta figures prominently and of the twenty he cites nine are attributed to Agesilaos. The Greek Polyainos went even further. For him Agesilaos was the central character, and his thirty-three *exempla* extend over his entire career as general.

Sophia, however, was just one of the many qualities that Xenophon postulated of the ideal general whose composite portrait he paints in his many works (cf. Wood 1964; Carlier 1978, 136). This paragon should know and discipline himself so as to be able to assume many different roles (*Mem.* 3.1.6-7). He should set an example of industriousness, respect for law, cheerfulness, and dignity; and should live in a simple and moderate style (*Ages.* 5.3,7.2). He should take great thought for the welfare of his troops (4.5.4, 5.1.14-16; *Anab.* 7.6.41) and treat his subordinates as friends in order to secure their affection and admiration (*Hiero* 1.33). To get the best out of his men, he should make a discriminating use of rewards and punishments, hitting a paternalist mean between the excessive severity of a Klearchos (*Anab.* 2.6.9-14) and the excessive leniency of a Proxenos (*Anab.* 2.6.20) and provoking their spirit of competition through incentive bonuses in the form of prizes for games (3.4.16; *Hipp.* 1.25-6; *Cyr.* 2.1.22-4). To raise morale, he should possess persuasive rhetorical powers (*Anab. passim*, e.g. 3.1). More technically, he should be the master of forward planning (*Hipp.* 4.6, 5.9-15, 6.3; *Cyr.* 1.6.27-42) and an encyclopaedia of wiles and strategems (*Cyr.* 1.6.27,38). It is very noticeable from this list that Xenophon's ideal general was more of an artist than a scientist in warfare. For Xenophon was torn between the novelty of contemporary experience and reflection, including his own, and tradition, but on the whole he opted for tradition (cf. Garlan 1972, 170). Agesilaos, as we shall see in some detail shortly, garnered a comparable wealth of experience but was even less inclined to subject it to critical reflection or make it the basis for innovation.

First, though, a word of caution concerning the evidence. It is difficult enough to reconstruct in depth the Battle of the Somme, which took place only seventy years ago, despite the great variety of official and personal testimonies available, the certain knowledge of the local topography, and perhaps above all the disinterested desire to learn the objective truth (cf. Keegan 1978, 281-2). *A fortiori* the possibility of reconstructing any ancient battle, for knowledge of whose details we depend often enough on writers who were not in any sense professional soldiers, is slight to the point of non-existence (cf. Whatley 1964). The most that can be attempted is to fill in the main lines of strategy (operations in plan) and tactics (operations in action) with broad brush-strokes, and to place a campaign or battle within the general history of the art of war and the history of the Greek and Persian worlds. Or, to borrow a formulation of Michael Howard (1983, 195-7), we can and should write ancient military history in width and context but not in depth. These limitations are particularly in evidence with regard to the first of Agesilaos' campaigns, since the two main sources by their profound and probably irreconcilable differences manage to illustrate most of the deficiencies of all the ancient testimony.

(i) The Persian Expedition, 396-4

Towards the beginning and right at the end of his long reign Agesilaos commanded Greek and non-Greek troops against the forces of the Great King on the western fringes of his Empire. But the circumstances differed so greatly that the campaigns are treated in different chapters of the present book. In Chapter 11 the political and diplomatic background to Agesilaos' first involvement on the Asiatic landmass was considered, together with the wider implications and consequences of the campaign. Here the Persian expedition will be examined from a more narrowly military standpoint.

The land battles of the Persian Wars of 480-79 had been fought in mainland Greece on battlefields of the Greeks' own choosing. They had resulted in a decisive victory of the Greek spear over the Asiatic bow. Arrows, whether fired from the ground or from horseback, could temporarily disrupt, harass and alarm a disciplined and co-ordinated body of infantrymen; but in the circumstances of 480-79 they could not by themselves defeat it. No more could the famed Asiatic cavalrymen overcome the hoplite phalanx, although they were far better equipped and trained and seated on sturdier horses than most if not all of their Greek counterparts. In Asia the situation was different. Here infantry, apart from the 10,000 royal lifeguards known to the Greeks as the Immortals, was an underdeveloped arm of Persian warfare. The nature of the terrain with its wide plains and adequate horse-fodder, combined with the socio-economic structure of Persian imperial society, fostered an equestrian aristocracy. Even the Greeks of Asia, although they had followed their mainland brethren in adopting the hoplite phalanx, were more used in practice to siege warfare and naval warfare than the typical set-piece hoplite engagement, as the campaigning of the so-called Ionian Revolt (499-4) well exemplifies. However, experience in mainland Greece and – if the detailed evidence from Mesopotamian clay documents may be generalized to western Asia as a whole – an apparently marked deterioration in the quasi-feudal cavalry levies in Asia had taught at least some Persians in the fifth century the value of Greek hoplites employed on a mercenary basis in conjunction with the traditional cavalry (cf. Rahe 1980a). The attempted coup of Cyrus the Younger may be accommodated to this schema of a virtual revolution in military tactics. For Cyrus made his unprecedentedly large force of Greek mercenary hoplites (Roy 1967; Perlman 1976-7) the core of his army.

It would be a mistake, however, to exaggerate the extent to which the balance of effectiveness and emphasis had shifted in favour of Greek hoplites in Asiatic warfare as a result of Cyrus' expedition. Agesilaos may have been encouraged in his dreams of Asiatic conquest by the prowess of the Greeks at Cunaxa in 401 and by their ability to cut a path home from the heartland of the Persian Empire, which reinforced his contempt for 'barbarians'. But the Greeks had not after all won the battle, and the Persians' attempts to prevent their return were only halfhearted. Moreover, it did not take Agesilaos long after his arrival on the spot in 396 to realize that, if he was to defeat his Persian adversaries in a more or less formal encounter, his cavalry would have to be improved rapidly and dramatically in both quantity and quality.

This perception of Agesilaos puts the Spartan war effort of the previous three years in a rather sorry light. Sparta had declared war on the Great King, she said, to secure the lives, property and political freedom and autonomy of the Asiatic Greeks against interference and encroachment by Pharnabazus and Tissaphernes, the King's vicegerents in the west. Yet if the Spartans' aim was to deter the satraps by inflicting a serious defeat on them or mustering a sufficient show of force to make a peace treaty stick, they had provided their commanders with palpably inadequate forces and supply-systems.

The war was at first conducted solely on land by the area harmost Thibron. Several fortified cities of the Troad ruled by Greek quisling dynasts had come over to him voluntarily, and he had stormed some weak cities (3.1.7), but he had failed in his one assault on a strongly fortified Persian position. This, however, was not why he was replaced in the autumn of 399, but because he was accused (and later found guilty and exiled) of allowing his troops to plunder lands belonging to friends of Sparta's allies. Before his recall to Sparta – at least according to the irreconcilably different account of Diodoros (14.36) – he conducted some operations in Tissaphernes' Caria from his base at Ephesos. The timing is uncertain, but the chief strategic point of such an operation would seem to have been to gain control of the only area of western Asia Minor that could serve as a base for a Persian fleet in the Aegean. But again, if that was the objective, neither Thibron nor any other Spartan commander could have hoped to secure it without the siege-train necessary to storm Miletos, Halikarnassos or Kaunos.

Thibron's replacement was the cunning Derkylidas, a man with a general fondness for overseas service (4.3.2) and previous experience of command in Asia as harmost of Abydos in 407 (3.1.9), besides a burning personal hatred of Pharnabazus. There is reason to think that he was one of Agesilaos' friends (below). He now commanded some 12,000 men: 4000 or so Peloponnesian League allies, 1000 Neodamodeis (the only Lakedaimonian contingent), some 5000 of Cyrus' Greek mercenaries now commanded by Xenophon, 2000 troops locally raised among the Asiatic Greeks, and a paltry 300 Athenian cavalry. The deficiency of good light-armed and cavalry is glaring, not to mention the continued lack of a siege-train. But Derkylidas cannily exploited the mutual antagonisms and rivalries of Pharnabazus and Tissaphernes and of the Greek quisling potentates within Pharnabazus' satrapy of Hellespontine Phrygia by attacking Aiolis (for the limits of which see Lewis 1977, 127n.123). By a combination of propaganda and military competence reminiscent of Brasidas in Thrace he secured the voluntary submission of six Greek towns. Kebren, however, was more resistant, and it is hard not to interpret the four days of unfavourable omens in terms of Derkylidas' inability to conduct a proper assault rather than of genuine piety. When Skepsis and Gergis had surrendered virtually without a blow, again through bluff rather than siegecraft, Derkylidas had enough cash (perhaps 350 talents: Ste. Croix 1981, 558n.7) to maintain his 8000 Neodamodeis, Asiatics and Cyreians for nearly a year without troubling his Asiatic allies for funds – so great was the surplus wealth piled up by the successive Greek under-satraps Zenis, his widow Mania and their son-in-law Meidias.

For the rest of the campaigning season Derkylidas garrisoned the newly 'liberated' cities. But in winter 399/8, rather than fight on with no hope of significant military success and burden the cities by billeting his soldiers on them, Derkylidas concluded a truce with Pharnabazus (3.2.1; perhaps for eight months: DS 14.38). Xenophon puts Derkylidas' feat of 'capturing' the nine cities in eight days in the best possible military light (3.2.7; but note his animus towards Thibron, perhaps an enemy of Agesilaos – 4.8.22) and says Pharnabazus made the truce because he felt threatened by this Aiolian *epiteichismos* (fortification of points within his own territory). More likely it was a smokescreen to camouflage the build-up of a large Persian fleet for use behind the Spartans' backs. That at any rate was the motive for the renewal of the truce by Pharnabazus and Tissaphernes jointly in summer 397 (3.2.20) and probably for the earlier renewal by Pharnabazus in spring 398 (3.2.6,9).

During the truce Derkylidas at first plundered Bithynia to the north-east of Pharnabazus' satrapal seat at Daskyleion. This was hardly the best way to further the anti-Persian cause, since the Bithynians – like the neighbouring Mysians (3.1.13; Xen. *Anab.* 1.6.7; 1.9.14 etc.) and Paphlagonians (Xen. *Anab.* 5.6.6) – were not the sort of tame subjects Persia naturally preferred. So it was not entirely surprising that the new Ephors of 398/7 should have sent out a three-man commission to 'get a general view of the situation in Asia' (3.2.6). The commission met Derkylidas at Lampsakos on the Hellespont and told him that his command had been extended. In light of the Persian build-up it is probably not irrelevant that two of the commissioners (Arakos and Antisthenes) had experience of naval command (the third, Naubates, has a naval name but is otherwise unknown); but Xenophon does not deign to mention the Spartan fleet until a context of 397 (3.2.12). It is in Diodoros (14.39) and other sources that we read of Pharnabazus' ultimately successful lobbying of Artaxerxes for funds and to the Oxyrhynchos Historian that we must look for the kind of detail one would expect of a competent naval historian.

Nor does Xenophon bring out the wider significance of Derkylidas' two other projects during the time of truce: the protection of the Thracian Chersonese (Gallipoli peninsula) and the siege of Atarneus. The former was achieved within a few months by restoring a basically earthen wall built across the neck of the peninsula originally in the sixth century (Hdt. 6.39). Good land for agriculture and pasturage was thereby made safe for the eleven towns within its protection against Thracian incursion. But not only for them. 'Lakedaimonian' colonists were also sent out (3.2.8; cf. 4.8.5). This was a neat way of disposing of the kind of obstreperous Hupomeiones and Perioikoi who had been willing to lend an ear to Kinadon the previous year (Chapter 10) as well as undercutting Athenian influence in an area so important to Athens' grain supply.

The objective of the siege of Atarneus was to evict a nest of pro-Athenian democratic exiles displaced from Chios either in 412 or in 409 who were making a handsome profit from plunder. For their activity was a challenge to Sparta's claim to be 'liberating' the area, and Atarneus was also a convenient supply-depot for any further campaigning in Pharnabazus' satrapy. The siege was protracted for eight months (3.2.11), but with the proceeds of eventual victory Derkylidas is said (Isok. 4.144) to have hired as many as 3000 mercenary peltasts. This figure may well be exaggerated (cf. Anderson 1970, 303n.33), but they are in any event the first peltasts recorded in Spartan service in Asia. Perhaps Derkylidas had come to appreciate their special qualities (see further below, section ii) in Bithynia the previous winter (3.2.3-4).

By now, early 397, Sparta had been in a state of truce with Persia for well over a year. Yet again ambassadors were despatched to Sparta by the Greeks of Ionia to demand action against Tissaphernes, and the Ephors instructed Derkylidas and the navarch Pharax to mount a combined land-sea operation against Caria. But Tissaphernes, co-operating at last with Pharnabazus, anticipated them and garrisoned Caria's strong points before returning to the territory of Ephesos. Here they confronted Derkylidas' pursuing force in battle array, but rather than seize the opportunity to win an outright victory in a set-piece encounter they negotiated for yet another truce. The terms amounted to a virtual abdication of Sparta's war aims, and it is unlikely that they were ratified in Sparta.

Even so Derkylidas does not appear to have been held responsible for what can only be described, militarily speaking, as two wasted years of almost fruitless antagonism towards the Persian Empire. In 396 Derkylidas turns up again as one of three commissioners sent by Agesilaos to conclude (yet another) truce with Tissaphernes (3.4.6), and in 394 it was he who conveyed to Agesilaos at Amphipolis the glad tidings of a Spartan victory at the Nemea River (4.3.1-2; see further below). It looks very much as though Derkylidas was Agesilaos' man, and he may well be imagined as lending support in autumn 397 to the view propounded by the much more influential Lysander that Agesilaos should personally take command in Asia with a greatly enlarged force.

Lysander's initiative was occasioned by belated intelligence of the size of the Persian naval build-up (3.4.1; Xen. *Ages*. 1.6; Plut. *Ages*. 6.1). No doubt the figure of 300 Phoenician ships was a 'paper' figure thought appropriate for a fleet worthy of the Persian King (cf. Cawkwell 1968, 3). But this fleet was undoubtedly considerably larger and more real than the 147 ships at Aspendos with which Tissaphernes had made much play in 411 (Thuc. 8.81.3, 87.3 etc.). With such a fleet, which was placed under Pharnabazus, the Persians could not only cut Sparta's communications and so undermine her Asiatic venture but also wrest from Sparta her Aegean empire. Moreover, the presence of Konon, one of the two Athenian admirals to have escaped from the Aigospotamoi débâcle in 405, was an earnest of future offensive possibilities directed at Sparta in mainland Greece as well as her Asiatic harmosts and garrisons. Even so, it seems that Agesilaos committed two cardinal strategic errors before setting foot on Asiatic soil.

First, he did not clearly formulate a strategy that was either attainable with the resources available or adequate to the need to meet force with force by land and by sea. The sincerity of his anti-Persian zeal, at any rate to begin with, need not be doubted, and posing as a second Agamemnon was perhaps the kind of histrionic gesture required to lift the great 'panhellenist' enterprise out of the doldrums. But in so far as his propaganda gave the impression that a decisive victory over Persia might be won, this was a wholly insensitive and misleading posture. Not the least reason for this was that Agesilaos apparently neglected entirely what Sir Julian Corbett once called 'the delicate interactions of land and sea factors'. Secondly, as even Isokrates was able to perceive with the benefit of hindsight (Isok. 4.153; 5.87-8), Agesilaos failed to make sure of his rear before departing for Asia – in sharp and instructive contrast to Alexander the Great in 336-5. His mistake was to disregard the clear ultimatum delivered to Sparta by the Boiotian Confederacy. This did not merely, like Corinth and Athens, refuse to contribute troops to the 'panhellenic' expedition, but actually sent cavalry to overthrow the altars on which Agesilaos, Agamemnon-like, was conducting the pre-embarkation sacrifice at Aulis (3.4.3; 3.5.5; 7.1.34). This was in the eyes of the pious Agesilaos a sacrilege for which he never forgave the Confederacy – or more particularly the Thebans (5.1.33).

As in 400/399 the Spartans in 396 again sent no hoplites from the regular establishment of Spartiate and Perioikic *morai*. But they did send thirty Spartiates including most prominently Lysander (references and general discussion in Pritchett 1974, II, 36-8). The intended functions of this board are not entirely clear. During the Athenian War Spartan commanders who were judged to have performed unsatisfactorily had different sizes of boards of 'advisers' (*sumbouloi*) foisted upon them (Thuc. 2.85.1; 3.69.1; 5.63.4; 8.39.2). But Derkylidas was not regarded as having failed, and Agesilaos had no previous experience of command whatsoever. It seems therefore that this board of thirty was intended to act somewhat as Agesilaos' General Staff – something unprecedented in the history of Greek generalship. In warfare conducted in Greece by the *morai* the Spartan king was closely attended by 'those about (the) public (tent)' (*hoi peri <tân> damosian* [*sc. skanan*]: 4.5.8; 6.4.14; Xen. *LP* 13.7).

This expression is often translated 'staff', but misleadingly so. For this heterogeneous body comprised the king's regular messmates in Sparta, three kinds of specialists (seers, doctors, flautists), and volunteers like Xenophon, who presumably first met Agesilaos at Ephesos in 396 (cf. Chapter 5). But the thirty Spartiates seconded to Agesilaos in 396 and their successors of 395 were a very different animal. They were available for diplomatic missions (4.1.5-6, 11,13) and specific military details (3.4.20) as required. So far as we can judge, none of these men was an active political opponent of Agesilaos, but they did regrettably carry with them to Asia all the high-level tension, jealousy and ambition that characterized political life within the Spartan elite at home (3.4.8; 4.1.23).

Under Agesilaos' command there were in addition to the troops he inherited from Derkylidas 2000 more Neodamodeis – or rather 2000 more 'of the Neodamodeis': Xenophon's partitive genitive (3.4.2) indicates that, thanks to Persian money and imperial tribute, Sparta had been able to arm great numbers of these ex-Helots (cf. Chapter 10). He brought over also 6000 Peloponnesian League soldiers, making a total under his command in excess of 15,000 men (Lins 1914, 16). But the deficiency in siege-equipment and cavalry was not made good.

Anticipating Philip of Macedon, Agesilaos announced that his overall aim was to conquer Asia, that is the Persian Empire, in revenge for the Persian invasion of Greece in 480-79 (Xen. *Ages.* 1.8); such a declaration of 'just war' (cf. Andok. 3.13) was more or less obligatory, and possibly good for morale. More precisely he aimed to secure autonomy for the Greek cities of Asia on a par with that enjoyed by those in mainland Greece. By this he meant freedom from garrisons and tribute but not necessarily – or even probably – freedom from Spartan interference in their internal political affairs (cf. Thuc. 1.19). Like Lysander, Agesilaos was no friend to democracy; but he does seem to have drawn the line at his mentor's penchant for dekarchies, preferring instead 'ancestral' oligarchies controlled by men personally bound to him as patron. On this issue of policy, and more generally on the question of authority, influence and patronage (cf. Chapter 9), Agesilaos and Lysander quarrelled, until Agesilaos found a neat way of removing Lysander from G.H.Q. by giving him an important diplomatic mission – to exploit internal dissension between Pharnabazus and one of his leading subordinates.

Agesilaos had now won his independence without having to resort to the string of judicial murders that disfigured Alexander's Asiatic expedition. He put it to good use in his inaugural campaign. After first concluding a truce that Tissaphernes honoured only in the breach Agesilaos attacked the satrapy of Pharnabazus. In this he was aided by intelligence gleaned from Spithridates, a rebel Persian of apparently illustrious descent who had held an under-satrapal appointment from Pharnabazus; it was Lysander who had seduced Spithridates from his natural allegiance. Agesilaos first achieved an unmolested passage northwards from Ephesos by a ruse that he was to employ on at least two other occasions, feinting in a direction opposite to that which he intended to take (cf. 4.5.3,5; 5.4.49). With Tissaphernes and his newly reinforced army kicking their heels in the Maiandros (Meander) plain, Agesilaos marched on Hellespontine Phrygia with the six months' provisions he had been allocated by the Spartan authorities (3.4.3). En route north he gained further troops from the Greek cities, whose internal unrest he somehow managed to quell for the moment (3.4.12; Xen. *Ages.* 1.37; cf. 3.4.7), and acquired huge amounts of booty into the bargain. He probably followed the main coastal route as far as the Gulf of Atramyttion but then, instead of cutting off sharply to the east as he was to do in autumn 395, he proceeded north-east towards Daskyleion. Somewhere in its vicinity a cavalry encounter occurred, which revealed one of Agesilaos' two main tactical lacunae, his lack of good cavalry (3.4.13-14).

In Greece, with the exception of Thessaly, Macedon and Boiotia, cavalry were allotted only a very subsidiary role. Reconnaissance, ravaging crops or protecting them, pursuit of an enemy or the covering of a flight, harassment of an infantry line with missiles – these were the kind of tasks cavalry were expected to perform. Anything, virtually, other than a front-line role as shock troops in pitched battle. This was not really surprising since peasant farming – the economic basis of hoplite warfare – and the cavalry principle tend to be antipathetic. Nor was it odd that Greek horses were small and unshod and that their riders used neither saddle nor stirrups but relied on knee-pressure to keep their seat (Anderson 1961, 15-39, 140-54). Sparta's experience with cavalry, or rather lack of it, was therefore no unconquerable handicap in mainland Greece. It was only in 424, at least in the Athenian War, that Sparta first regularly raised a troop of horse (Thuc. 4.55) and that only for strictly limited local use and recruited in all probability from second-class Spartan citizens and Perioikoi (cf. 4.5.16; 6.4.11).

Whatever his other limitations, however, Agesilaos had the tactical sense to realize quickly that 'without an adequate force of cavalry he would be unable to campaign in the plains, and so he decided that he must acquire such a force rather than have to fight a campaign as if he were always on the run' (3.4.15; cf. Xen. *Ages.* 1.23-4; *Cyr.* 4.3.3ff.). He also, it seems, knew how to steal leaves from the book of his enemy. For the principle whereby rich Asiatic Greeks might 'contract out' their obligation to serve as cavalrymen recalls the quasi-feudal way in which the Persians allocated 'horse-land' to colonists of various nationalities on condition that they or their 'retainers' enlisted as and when required in the cavalry (cf. Lane Fox 1973, 157-60). It is apparently to this stiffening of Spartan cavalry with mercenary horsemen that Xenophon refers with approval in the *Hipparchicus* (9.3-4).

In the early spring of 395 these new recruits were brought together with the rest of Agesilaos' forces at Ephesos and introduced to a training programme for which Xenophon has nothing but praise. For him a combination of piety with sound military training was very heaven, and he singles out in particular Agesilaos' emphasis on competitions with prizes as incentives for the best trained and equipped troops of various kinds (hoplites, cavalrymen, peltasts, archers), an emphasis shared by Xenophon's Cyrus the Great (*Cyr.* 1.2.12, 1.6.18, 2.1.22, 6.2.6, 8.2.26), and the stimulus given to the production of armaments – in a memorable phrase Ephesos is said to have become a 'workshop of war' (*polemou ergastêrion*: 3.4.17). Everything may indeed have been 'full of good hopes' (3.5.18); but hopes for what? No great and lasting benefit was to accrue from these admirably energetic preparations.

The first of Agesilaos' two campaigns in Asia Minor in 395 is bedevilled by a discordance between our main sources that is remarkable even in the spotty annals of ancient military historiography. It is agreed that the campaign of spring and early summer culminated in some sort of battle somewhere in the vicinity of Sardis and that the result was a significant victory for Agesilaos over Tissaphernes. Otherwise there is disagreement all the way between Xenophon (3.4.20-25), on the one hand, and the Oxyrhynchos Historian (11-12) supplemented by Diodoros (14.80), on the other. The situation is complicated further by the incomplete preservation of the Oxyrhynchos Historian's account and by the fact that Diodoros was an inefficient compiler who was probably immediately dependent on the rhetorical and imprecise Ephorus (cf. Chapter 5). In the circumstances scholars have unsurprisingly run the gamut of possible responses – from complete acceptance or rejection of Xenophon or the Oxyrhynchos Historian, through attempted reconciliation of the two, to agnosticism (e.g. Dugas 1910; Lins 1914, 19-34; Nellen 1972; Bonamente 1973, 142ff.; Anderson 1974a; Kelly 1975, 82-94; Gray 1979). My own (no doubt prejudiced) preference for the Oxyrhynchos Historian must be received as it is offered, with all due caution.

On an unprejudiced reading the two major discrepancies concern the route taken northwards from Ephesos by Agesilaos and the circumstances and location in which his troops came to blows with those of Tissaphernes. According to Xenophon, Agesilaos took the 'shorter route' from Ephesos to Sardis after successfully repeating the trick of a feint towards Caria. Whether or not one believes that this ruse is likely to have been attempted and attempted successfully twice, Xenophon is certainly meaning to indicate a different route from that given by Diodoros. By specifying that Agesilaos went 'by Sipylos' and so by the Kara Bel pass (cf. Hdt. 2.106), Diodoros is implying that in some sense Agesilaos made a detour. The fact that the Kara Bel route and the route through Mt Tmolos are roughly the same length is beside the point: Xenophon's march is straightforward, Diodoros' somewhat complex. The best objective argument in favour of the latter is that it offered better prospects of booty.

Different routes logically mean different points at which Agesilaos first made contact with Tissaphernes' forces, and the rival traditions do clearly disagree on this. It is not, unfortunately, so easy to state where, how and why they differ on the site and the character of the one formal encounter they each describe. It is, for example, just possible to argue that the authors are in fact describing two different battles and to suggest reasons why each omitted one of them – Xenophon because he felt that a more or less pitched battle did Agesilaos more credit, the Oxyrhynchos Historian because the papyrus is incomplete. On the other hand, the fact that the result of their very different battles is given as identical (the capture of Tissaphernes' camp with much booty) is a strong presumption in favour of there having been only the one battle. But if so, which are we to choose?

There seem to me two main reasons for preferring that of the Oxyrhynchos Historian. The first is a consequence of my preference for his route, which yields a battle-site in the Hermos plain below Sardis; whereas Xenophon's explicit reference to the Paktolos (3.4.22) should mean that he envisaged a site further west. Secondly, Agesilaos' employment of the tactic of ambuscade (repeated in autumn 395, but with a significant variation) is wholly consistent both with the overall cast of Agesilaos' generalship and with the objective circumstances in which he found himself (numerical inferiority, unfamiliar terrain, untried cavalry and peltasts). Xenophon's set-piece engagement entered on more or less equal terms redounds more to the credit of Agesilaos, but is *ipso facto* suspect; so too is the coincidence between Xenophon's version of Agesilaos' battle-plan and his own previous experience with the Ten Thousand (*Anab.* 3.4.1-5).

This does not of course mean that all Xenophon's information concerning the campaign as a whole or even the battle in particular should be jettisoned. His stress on the way Agesilaos paid attention to the spiritual and psychological as well as material welfare of his troops explains their morale and *élan*; and the information that Agesilaos reorganized the high command by appointing five of his thirty-strong General Staff to specific posts (including two cavalry commanders in recognition of the increased importance of this arm) speaks for Agesilaos' ability to adapt traditional Spartan methods to an alien environment. As for the evolution of the battle itself, Xenophon (3.4.23; *Ages.* 1.31) is very likely right that, in accordance with Spartan practice, Agesilaos had organized his hoplites into age-groups; Brasidas after all had been able to do the same with his far more 'scratch' army (Thuc. 4.125.3).

According to Xenophon, Tissaphernes was in Sardis during the battle, but the Oxyrhynchos Historian's picture of Tissaphernes retreating to Sardis in disarray after the battle is intrinsically more plausible at any rate. They agree, uniquely, that Agesilaos next took the Persian camp and huge amounts of booty, but on what happened thereafter disagreement is as fierce as ever. Xenophon, indeed, gives two different versions. In his encomium (*Ages.* 1.33) he speaks of a proclamation (*kêrugma*) issued by Agesilaos to Tissaphernes' non-Persian subjects (and perhaps to his Persian subordinates too) to come and join him in the fight for 'Asia'. But in the supposedly more objective *Hellenika* (3.4.24-5) he passes straight from the capture of the camp and booty to the execution of Tissaphernes and the negotiations between his successor, Tithraustes, and Agesilaos that resulted in the latter's late summer/autumn campaign against Pharnabazus. Xenophon has at least reported the events that had significant issue, but it is to the credit of the Oxyrhynchos Historian (12.3-4) that he records in detail how and why Agesilaos returned shortly to Ephesos before embarking on his Phrygian Long March. One curiosity might perhaps be mentioned here. Among the booty in Tissaphernes' camp Agesilaos had acquired several baggage-camels, which he eventually took back with him all the way to Boiotia (3.4.24), presumably because he found them useful rather than for their rarity value.

Tissaphernes was succeeded at Sardis by Tithraustes, probably the chiliarch or Grand Vizier of the entire Empire (cf. Cook 1983, 218-19). This appointment, together with the reinforcements that had readily been granted earlier to Tissaphernes (3.4.6,11), suggest that a close personal interest was being taken in these western events by Artaxerxes, whose anger with the Spartans at this juncture knew no bounds. But Tithraustes proved no more able or willing than Tissaphernes to co-operate with Pharnabazus. Instead, he concluded a six-month truce with Agesilaos and gave him the considerable sum of thirty talents as an inducement to pass through the lower satrapy without plundering it and on into that of Pharnabazus, who had perhaps already succeeded to Tissaphernes' superior command of the land and sea campaign (4.1.37; 4.8.3,6; cf. 3.2.13).

The discrepancies between the two main accounts of this second campaign of 395 are not so marked in point of detail but they do diverge greatly in selection and emphasis – again to the discredit of Xenophon, for whom the 'glorification of Agesilaus is the central motive' (Grenfell/Hunt 1908, 239) and whose penchant for telling pretty tales while neglecting military essentials fails to disguise the ineffectual outcome of this extensive promenade through Asia Minor (cf. Bruce 1967, 134). To cut a long story short, Agesilaos marched up the coast from Ephesos, turned sharply eastwards at the Gulf of Atramyttion, passed through the plain of Apia, made an unexplained side-trip into the highlands of dissident Mysia before descending to the valley of the Tembris, failed to capture the stronghold of Leontôn Kephalai (not certainly identified), proceeded thence – perhaps along the Susa-Sardis Royal Road – to Gordion, which he also failed to storm, marched on as far east as the Halys River before returning west along the Sangarios valley to the environs of Daskyleion, where yet again he failed to capture a stronghold (Miletou Teichos), before disbanding his troops in Mysia and repairing to camp at Thebe. No one could deny that he had covered an immense amount of ground, but what else had he achieved?

All along he had plundered mercilessly. It is this campaign that most justifies the rather damning comment that Agesilaos treated the Persian Empire as if it were a Peloponnesian country town that could be brought to its knees by the traditional (but even in Greece somewhat outmoded) strategy of ravaging (cf. Anderson 1970, 6-7,9). His two diplomatic initiatives brought no decisive advantages: Spithridates soon deserted Agesilaos with his Paphlagonian troops, and even Xenophon does not conceal the fruitlessness of Agesilaos' interview with Pharnabazus (see in detail Chapter 11). Agesilaos' three encounters with strongly fortified positions had painfully exposed his inadequacy in this department: as Xenophon (*Cyr.* 6.1.16) made his Cyrus pronounce, unless one fortifies bases in the country one overruns and captures enemy strongholds, one resembles sailors who no more 'take' the waters they sail over than the waters that lie ahead. Only an Isokrates (4.144) could have made the ludicrous claim that Agesilaos had 'conquered practically all Asia this side of the Halys'. As for the future, the plan attributed to him by the Oxyrhynchos Historian (22.4) of invading Cappadocia in spring 394 was based on a misconception of Asia Minor as a kind of triangle whose apex was formed by a comparatively narrow isthmus joining Sinope to the Gulf of Issos. The even more grandiose plans of Asiatic conquest ascribed to him by Xenophon (4.1.41; *Ages.* 1.36) are simply a bad joke.

But it was at sea rather than on land that the limitations of Agesilaos as a strategist were most fatally revealed. For even though it was the Persian naval build-up that had caused the Spartans to take their Persian War more seriously and despatch Agesilaos (3.4.1), his response was both too late and too little. In the summer or autumn of 396 Konon deprived Sparta of the key base of Rhodes

(*Hell. Ox.* 15; DS 14.79.6; with Funke 1980b) and captured the grain-ships donated to Sparta by the Egyptian rebel ruler Nepherites I (DS 14.79.7); and when Agesilaos engineered an unprecedented joint command by both land and sea in the summer of 395 (3.4.27; Plut. *Ages.* 10.9-10), he entrusted an inadequate fleet of (eventually) 120 ships to the incompetent command of his brother-in-law Peisandros (cf. Chapter 9). The price of Agesilaos' neglect was paid in the catastrophic defeat off Knidos in August 394, which spelled the end of Sparta's Aegean empire (Isok. 5.63-4. 9.56, 12.56; cf. Chapter 6) and left her with just a toehold in Asia at Abydos. But by then Agesilaos was safely back in central Greece.

Three years later, following the diplomatic failure of 392/1 (Chapter 11), Sparta did renew the war in Asia, no doubt at Agesilaos' urging. But a succession of commanders made little or no headway against the pro-Athenian Strouthas (or Strouses), the first satrap of 'Ionia' and a military plenipotentiary (Tod 113; cf. Lewis 1977, 118n.75; Hornblower 1982, 19n.109, 37-8); and when in 389/8 no fewer than a dozen Spartan harmosts were killed in battle at Abydos (4.8.39), Sparta sensibly threw in the strigil. Artaxerxes was now to be wooed determinedly as a potential friend and ally rather than warred against as the oppressor of Greek liberties. This belated recognition that the last decade of hostilities had been counterproductive bore fruit in the Peace of Antalkidas.

(ii) The Corinthian War, 394-386 (Fig. 12.1)

News of Knidos reached Agesilaos on 14 August 394. The eclipse of the sun that permits so precise a chronological determination gladdens the heart of the modern historian but was taken as an inauspicious divine sign by the pious Xenophon and presumably most Spartans (cf. Hdt. 9.10.2). Quite rightly from the morale point of view Agesilaos turned the defeat into a victory for public consumption (cf. 1.6.36-7 for an earlier Spartan use of this device), thereby keeping up the momentum derived from news of a Spartan victory in the north-east Peloponnese (below) and from Agesilaos' own considerable triumph over the master cavalrymen of Thessaly near Narthakion. But if he were to achieve his immediate strategic objectives and expunge the humiliation of being recalled to Greece by something more concrete than a witticism about the 10,000 'archers' that had driven him from Asia (Plut. *Ages.* 15. 8), he needed a big victory over the coalition headed by Boiotia, Athens, Argos and Corinth. So once over the Boiotian frontier and into the territory of Koroneia, Agesilaos distributed meat to numbers of people in his army quite literally to 'beef them up', and prepared the stage for his one set-piece battle on Greek soil and the only basically hoplite set-piece battle he ever fought.

His strategic objectives were twofold. First he had to convey safely to Sparta the huge booty he had garnered in Asia, minus the obligatory 'tithe' to Apollo at Delphi (cf. Pritchett 1974, I, 93-100, esp. 96). This plunder was the major success of his Asiatic campaign, and Sparta, deprived now of imperial tribute, desperately needed funds to counter those flowing to her enemies from Persian sources. Secondly, Agesilaos aimed to restore Sparta's controlling influence in north-central Greece. This influence had been steadily consolidated since the

Fig. 12.1. The Corinthian War, 395-386 (major battle sites underlined). After J.B. Salmon, *Wealthy Corinth: a history of the city to 338 B.C.* (Oxford 1984).

early part of the Athenian War and more especially in its aftermath, but had been shattered by the defeat at Haliartos in 395 (cf. Chapter 14). Hence the need for Agesilaos to fight his way through at Narthakion.

To help him achieve these objectives, Agesilaos had under his immediate command the following 'Lakedaimonian' troops: a *mora* that had crossed the Corinthian Gulf by sea, since the enemy controlled the Isthmus – this was probably under the command of Gylis (cf. 4.3.21); half of the *mora* that since the summer of 395 had been garrisoning Orchomenos after its defection from the Boiotian Confederacy (cf. 3.5.6); and those of the 3000 Neodamodeis sent to Asia (3.1.4, 3.4.2) who had not been either killed or left behind on garrison duty under the area harmost Euxenos. He also had mercenary hoplites – both those who had been selected by competitive review in the Thracian Chersonese on Agesilaos' way back to Greece and the remainder of the Cyreians – whom he placed under one of his most trusted lieutenants, Herippidas. Then there were soldiers from the Greek cities of Ionia, Aiolis and the Hellespontine region, while in Boiotia itself Agesilaos had been joined by hoplites from Orchomenos, whom he placed in a position of honour and responsibility on the extreme left of his line, and from his Phokian allies. Xenophon remarks that Agesilaos had many more peltasts than his opponents and about the same number of cavalry, but in the event neither of these groups contributed much to the outcome. Ranged against Agesilaos were Boiotians, Athenians, Argives, and Corinthians, together with Ainianians, Euboians and Lokrians from both W. and E. Lokris. No source gives figures, but the totals on either side were probably of the order of 15-20,000, and Xenophon (*Ages.* 2.7,9) expressly says that both in numbers and in preparation they were evenly matched. This deserves some credence, since he was a participant in the battle (Plut. *Ages.* 18.2; cf. Anderson 1970, 78).

Both in the *Agesilaos* (2.9) and in the *Hellenika* (4.3.16) Xenophon describes the Battle of Koroneia as unique in his time. The details are of course as unrecoverable as those of any ancient battle. But since Koroneia certainly was not the biggest or most decisive battle of his age, and not necessarily the bloodiest (*contra* Hertzberg 1856, 9), Xenophon is probably rightly taken to be referring to its evolution – 'a double battle, a sort of knock-out championship for military excellence' (Cawkwell 1979, 204n.) – and to the heroic role of Agesilaos. What matters in the present context, however, is whether and to what extent and in what manner Agesilaos controlled the battle, and this can be best brought out by casting a brief backward glance at the Battle of the Nemea River fought earlier that same summer.

This was a major conflict into which all parties threw their utmost endeavour. The Spartans probably contributed five out of their six mixed Spartiate-Perioikic *morai* and 6000 out of their total hoplite effective of some 10,000 (cf. Cozzoli 1979, 82; Cartledge 1979, 280-1). Their force as a whole, which was under the command of Aristodamos (acting as regent for Pausanias' under-age son Agesipolis), numbered some 22,500 as against their opponents' 24,000 (cf. Pritchett 1969, 74), making this the largest inter-Greek battle yet fought. It was also the first major such pitched battle since Mantineia (418). But whereas that could well be described as one of the last examples of 'the waste of mere hammer-and-tongs fighting' (Tarn 1930, 22), the Battle of the Nemea River marked new departures. Two features deserve special mention. On the anti-Spartan side it was a matter for discussion how deep the phalanx should be drawn up. True, this was partly because the Confederates were very recently allied and fielding an untried joint army. But the important point is that depth of phalanx was now a subject on which there could be more than one opinion (cf. generally Pritchett 1974, I, 134-43). The Thebans, by aligning their men 'altogether deep' (4.2.18), showed that the twenty-five ranks they had deployed at Delion in 424 (Thuc. 4.93) was not a nine-days wonder but the result of a conscious decision to shift from what in eighteenth-century terms would have been called *l'ordre mince* to *l'ordre profonde*. On the Spartan side the traditional and almost 'natural' tendency of the hoplite phalanx to move rightwards in the advance as the flank men sought to place their unshielded sides beyond reach of their opposite numbers (well exemplified at Mantineia: Thuc. 5.71) was transformed into a conscious manoeuvre. By deliberately outflanking the enemy and then wheeling back to the left the Spartans could 'roll up' their opponents' line. Manoeuvring of this sort was facilitated by the lightening of hoplite equipment that had been in progress during the fifth century and accelerated under pressure from the development of peltast fighting.

Koroneia, by comparison, seems on the whole more traditional in its evolution. Both armies placed their best troops on their respective right wings in time-honoured fashion (cf. Pritchett 1974, II, 190-207), with the Spartan king commanding as usual (Xen. *LP* 13.6) from the right; and the first round of the battle was settled, as was customary, on the wings. Despite signs of improvement in their hoplite efficiency in the recent past, the Argives simply refused to face the Lakedaimonians opposite them and headed back posthaste to the shelter of Mt Helikon. On the other wings the Thebans, presumably using their deepened line, smashed through the traitorous (as they saw them) Orchomenians.

If there was any anomaly in this first phase, it was that Herippidas and his mercenaries broke ranks just before the point of engagement. It was a similar excess of enthusiasm (engendered throughout the army by Agesilaos, according to Xen. *Ages.* 2.8) that led some of these mercenaries to crown Agesilaos with the victor's garlands before the battle was in fact won. For just as they were doing so came that news the Thebans had carried the fight to the baggage-train, thereby jeopardizing the booty that Agesilaos was determined to convey safely to Sparta. Battle was therefore renewed by Agesilaos, but in a manner that not even Xenophon could forbear to reprimand.

On learning of the Theban breakthrough, Agesilaos had at once countermarched his Lakedaimonian contingent (after the manner described somewhat unclearly at Xen. *LP* 11.8) in a superb demonstration of Spartan drill. But instead of drawing the contingent up so as to be able to take the Thebans in flank or rear as they retired to Mt Helikon (as the Spartans had done to their retreating opponents at the Nemea River: 4.2.22), Agesilaos led it head-on against them. Despite his great numerical superiority one can only suppose that he adopted this much more risky course because of his hatred of the Thebans rather than out of any cool tactical consideration, although he may also have been influenced by some misplaced 'chivalric' notion of battle as a school of prowess. Xenophon approved his bravery but condemned his tactical sense. In these circumstances it is most unlikely that Agesilaos did in fact open his ranks to let the Thebans pass through (as the late military writers would have it). Xenophon's description of a 'hammer-and-tongs' encounter with shield crashing upon shield rings far more true.

This also means that our final judgement on Agesilaos' generalship at Koroneia should be far less laudatory than that of either Frontinus (*Strat.* 2.6.6) or Polyainos (2.1.19). There is no reason to doubt Agesilaos' exemplary personal bravery (cf. Xen. *Ages.* 6.2); the wounds he received here were neither his first nor his last, although we do not know whether he could boast like Alexander (Arr. *Anab.* 7.10.2) that only his back was not wound-scarred. (The fact that such wounds healed is not surprising, since wounds from edged weapons were rarely fatal so long as bleeding was not severe and no dirt was carried into them [cf. Keegan 1978, 268]; but as we shall see, the doctors in the Spartan king's regular entourage – Xen. *LP* 13.7 – were as likely to aggravate as to heal injuries.) Nor need we doubt the piety of Agesilaos; Xenophon concludes his fuller account in the *Agesilaos* by emphasizing how he spared the lives of some eighty of the enemy who had taken sanctuary in a temple (of Athena Itonia: Plut. *Ages.* 19.2). But of his character and talents as a general our opinion must be that 'he had done nothing but place his men where the enemy would have to fight them or run away' (Anderson 1970, 153). Moreover, of the two strategic objectives mentioned earlier he had achieved only one. Sparta's position north of the Isthmus of Corinth had not been restored to what it had been before Haliartos. On the other hand, he did secure the Asiatic booty, huge as it was. If he did literally dedicate one tenth of it at Delphi, the total amassed was not less than 1000 talents (4.3.21; Plut. *Ages.* 19.4) and possibly getting on for 2000 (Xen. *Ages.* 1.34).

During the active phase of the Corinthian War Agesilaos took the field at the head of an army on three further occasions, the first in 391. By then the Spartans had begun to recover some of the confidence lost following the Knidos disaster and the ensuing occupation and ravaging of her own territory by Konon. Plutarch (*Ages.* 19-20) gives Agesilaos the credit for restoring Spartan morale by insisting, in the wake of the alleged revelations concerning Lysander (Chapter 6), on maintaining the strict Spartan regimen; and it was presumably Agesilaos who organized the relief forces (*boêtheia*) for the defence of Spartan territory against Konon's coastal marauding (4.8.7; for a similar situation in 424 cf. Thuc. 4.55). Once Sparta had won the extremely sanguinary Battle of the Long Walls of Corinth in 392 (4.4.6-13; contrast DS 14.86), and the peace negotiations of 392/1 had proved abortive (Chapter 11), Agesilaos can only have been delighted to lead a Lakedaimonian and allied army against the Argives and Corinthians (4.4.19, 4.7.5; Xen. *Ages.* 2.17), especially as these were now closely united politically (cf. Chapter 13).

Ravaging, as we have seen, was a darling strategy of Agesilaos. But even so it is extremely doubtful whether he really did ravage all of the Argives' territory, as Xenophon maintained (cf. generally Hanson 1980, esp. ch.4). For had that been so, it is difficult to see how Agesipolis, commanding for the first time in 388, could have thought he might outstrip Agesilaos 'like an athlete competing in the pentathlon' (4.7.5). No doubt he did much damage, though, and it may have been in 391 as well as 388 that the Argives were obliged to buy wheat from Sparta's allies, the Mantineians – a typical instance of Greek private enterprise which the Mantineians' *hêgemôn* later chose to regard as a *casus belli* (5.2.2; cf. Chapter 13). The remainder of Agesilaos' campaign of 391 is of a piece with that of 390.

After the two major set-piece battles of 394 the Corinthian War had settled down to a game of position and attrition. With the vast influx of Persian money that accrued to the Confederates through Konon's good offices in 393 they were able to establish a permanent 'Foreign Legion' of mercenaries in the Corinthia under the Athenian Iphikrates, and until the Battle of the Long Walls they clearly had the upper hand. That battle, however, temporarily swung the balance in the Spartans' favour. In addition to their garrison at Sikyon they were now able to garrison Sidous, Krommyon and Epieikeia. Indeed, they may also have captured and garrisoned Corinth's port of Lechaion on the Corinthian Gulf at this time (4.4.17; Andok. 3.18-20; DS 14.86); but if so, they appear to have lost it again before the campaigning season of 391. That would have given extra point to Agesilaos' march from the Argolid over the pass of Tenea to Corinth. But what is particularly noteworthy about Agesilaos' Corinthian activities in 391 is that he appears at last to have learned the need for combined land-sea operations.

In 392 the Spartans (and probably Agesilaos in particular) had been guilty of precisely the error they had committed before Knidos. By appointing Herippidas as (perhaps temporary) navarch in succession to the dead Podanemos and his wounded deputy Pollis they had appointed an unsuitable and inexperienced admiral. But in 391, and expressly thanks to Agesilaos (Plut. *Ages*. 21.1), his uterine half-brother Teleutias received the supreme naval command. Between them and together Agesilaos and Teleutias captured the (rebuilt) Long Walls linking Corinth and Lechaion and the enemy's ships and dockyards (*neôria*: 4.4.19), which can only mean that they took Lechaion itself.

Xenophon (*Ages*. 2.17) speaks of Agesilaos in 391 as having unbarred the gates of the Peloponnese. But he was of course forgetting the small matter of Corinth, which with its Argive garrison held the key to the lock on those gates, and it was precisely to achieve that objective that Agesilaos set out once again in May/June 390 at the time of the Isthmian Games (cf. A. Andrewes in Gomme 1981, 23). His first target was Peiraion, which comprised most if not all of the Perachora peninsula (cf. Wiseman 1978, 32-3). This was partly because Peiraion contained a significant proportion of Corinth's food-supply in both crops and animals (this uncharacteristic dependence on meat testifies to the success of the ravaging of crops being conducted from Sidous, Krommyon and Epieikeia), and partly because the Boiotians from Kreusis were supplying Corinth through Peiraion. But his principal aim was doubtless to root out Iphikrates and his mercenaries from their Peiraion base.

As in Asia, Agesilaos once again feinted to march in one direction (in this case directly at Corinth itself, so as to draw away Iphikrates to defend Corinth against the all too common threat of betrayal from within) and in fact took another – to Peiraion. *En route* he sent a *mora* on ahead to occupy the heights of Mt Loutraki (ancient Aigiplanktos?), and when these men became cold and dispirited took the trouble to send fire up to them in earthenware pots. Peiraion fell to Agesilaos without a struggle, and the *mora* captured another fort at Oinoe (modern Vrokastro). Agesilaos then combined profit with political expediency by handing over those responsible for the massacre of extreme pro-Spartan oligarchs in 392 to their exiled opponents for summary justice and selling the remaining men and women, free and slave, into slavery.

This was a fine haul, but the real objective – the liberation of Corinth from its Argive allegiance and garrison – was destined to elude Agesilaos for another four years. For in the very flush of his Peiraion success Agesilaos received news of 'the disaster (*pathos*) of the *mora* at Lechaion' (4.5.7). This disaster should perhaps be placed third after the defeat at Hysiai in the seventh century (cf. Cartledge 1979, 126) and the Sphakteria débâcle of 425 in the very short list of Spartan military failures up to that time. The relatives of the Spartan dead may have rejoiced back in Sparta, as Spartan ethics required (4.5.10; cf. 6.4.16 – after

Leuktra). But with the exception of Lechaion the *pathos* cost Sparta all the gains of the past two years: Sidous, Krommyon, Epieikeia, Peiraion, Oinoe. The gates of the Peloponnese were again entirely barred to Sparta, and the Boiotians suddenly lost interest in treating for peace.

Militarily, the great significance of the *pathos* is that it was a spectacular victory of peltasts (necessarily aided and abetted by hoplites) over hoplites. Not long before this the Spartans had laughed at the Mantineians for being afraid of the peltast 'bogeymen' (4.4.17). Now they were laughing on the other side of their faces (cf. 4.5.12,18). Briefly, this is what had happened. The Lechaion garrison, an understrength *mora* of 600 commanded perhaps by Bias (Plut. *Mor.* 219c), was returning to base – after escorting the men of Amyklai, who had been released from duty as normal to attend the Hyakinthia back home, to within a few kilometres of Sikyon – when it was ambushed by Iphikrates and his mercenary peltasts (see generally Pritchett 1974, II, 117-25). These men were perhaps mainly Greeks rather than Thracians or native Asiatics, who had been raised in the Hellespontine region or further south in Asia (cf. Parke 1933, 50-1 – seeing the nucleus in 4.8.7; Best 1969, 86; Anderson 1970, 121). Since Iphikrates had apparently not yet introduced the changes in equipment for which his name became celebrated (e.g. 'Iphikratid' boots), the tactical efficiency of this Foreign Legion (*to xenikon*) must have been due rather to his ferocious discipline (Front. *Strat.* 3.12.2) and intelligent handling (cf. Hunter 1927, xxxi). Above all the latter, since according to his famous anatomical simile (Plut. *Pelop.* 2.1), the general was the 'head' of an army – a dictum Napoleon was to echo.

However, the quality of the raw material was also crucial. For the increased mobility of the lighter-armed peltasts suited them for use in difficult terrain and for ambushes, blocking armies on the march or preventing hoplites from ravaging crops; and this style of fighting demanded a quicker-witted, more self-reliant soldierly type than was absolutely necessary in hoplite warfare. Rightly has it been said that peltasts became 'the arm truly representative of Greek professionalism' (Delbrück 1975, 151). Inevitably the Spartans employed mercenary peltasts on occasion but generally without exploiting their peculiar virtues (cf. Chapter 15). It was one of the ironies of the *pathos* of 390 that Agesilaos was something of an exception to this rule. However, although he was not directly implicated in the disaster, he must bear the brunt of the responsibility for not providing sufficient competent cavalry both to escort the Amyklaians and to cover the return to base of the Lechaion *mora*. He had failed to heed the lesson of 423, when Brasidas' hoplites were mauled by Thracian peltasts after being left unprotected by Perdikkas' Macedonian cavalry (Thuc. 4.127-8).

Just how many of the (at least) 250 Lakedaimonians killed in the *pathos* were full Spartan citizens is not made clear by Xenophon (4.5.14,17). But the manner in which he draws attention to citizen deaths in the *Hellenika* (e.g. 4.3.23) indicates one of the major constraints on Sparta's prosecution of the Corinthian War. None the less in 389, as a welcome diversion from their failure to force the issue at the Isthmus, the Spartans did respond positively to a request from their Achaian allies for help against the Akarnanians which the Achaians were careful to couple with a threat to secede from the Peloponnesian League. Agesilaos was despatched with two *morai* and appropriate numbers of allied troops. The Achaians, as the aggrieved party (they wanted to secure their garrison in occupied Kalydon in Aitolia: cf. Kelly 1978b, 138-41), went in full force. This Akarnanian campaign (4.6) is a perfect microcosm of the strengths and weaknesses of Agesilaos as a field commander.

With the exception of Oiniadai the Akarnanians had been among the staunchest of Athens' allies during the Athenian War, and since the death of Lysander at Haliartos they had been in effect part of the anti-Spartan alliance (cf. DS 14.82.3). Culturally, however, they were still living in what seemed to the sophisticated Athenian Thucydides to be the 'Stone Age' (Thuc. 1.5.3), even if they had compensated for this to some extent by striking a flourishing coinage to pay a standing federal army based on the 'capital' of Stratos. The Achaians, who occupied the largely unproductive coastal strip on the southern shore of the Corinthian Gulf to west of Sikyon, were only slightly more advanced politically and militarily; they had been admitted to the Peloponnesian League, as a group, only during the course of the Athenian War (cf. Chapter 13). We should not therefore expect to find here the more progressive developments in contemporary Greek warfare, except in so far as the terrain ruled out the pitched hoplite battle and dictated the use of light-armed in addition to hoplites.

Nor do we find them. Agesilaos' sole strategy was – not unexpectedly – the ravaging of crops, which he pursued methodically and singlemindedly. Surprise was again part of his armoury as general. It took the form of a day's march of forty kilometres into the interior to a position by a lake where the Akarnanians had fondly supposed their cattle, horses, other animals, and slaves would all be quite secure. The lake was presumably Lake Trichonas, and it is tempting to associate the sixty-five graves of this period recently excavated on its south side with a skirmish between Agesilaos' troops and Akarnanian peltasts. This was won by the latter with no casualties, but that was the extent of their success in the field. Their attempt to ambush Agesilaos with peltasts and slingers as he was leading his army up from the surrounds of the lake through a narrow mountain defile misfired badly, whatever the precise details (contrast 4.6.8-10 with Xen. *Ages.* 2.20). All the more credit must be given to Agesilaos' determined and skilful generalship in these circumstances (cf. Holladay 1982, 98), when the fate of another Spartan-led force at the hands of peltasts in that same year in the mountains behind Abydos is compared (4.8.37-9; cf. Ain. Takt. 1.2, 15.7 on the need for a general to be prepared for such a contingency).

Agesilaos next continued his ravaging of trees and crops, but the Achaians significantly were not satisfied by that. Clearly, they had heard that towns might now be taken quite quickly by assault. Reluctantly, Agesilaos mounted regular assaults on some Akarnanian fortified positions but, as in Asia in autumn 395, without result. The Achaians were mortified and thought ill of Agesilaos as he marched east through Aitolia to Lokris and then crossed perforce from what is now Antirhion to Rhion, rather than take the nearer crossing from Kalydon, to avoid the Athenian ships at Oiniadai. But in the event Agesilaos' strategy proved triumphantly suited to Akarnanian conditions. All he had to do in spring 388 was threaten another invasion, and the Akarnanians were forced into alliance with Sparta (4.7.1; Xen. *Ages.* 2.20) – though not for very long.

That virtually concluded Agesilaos' militarily active role in the Corinthian War. For the last campaign in mainland Greece, against Argos, was led by Agesipolis in 388, and the War was decided, like the Athenian War, at sea in the Hellespont (cf. Chapter 14). But in 387/6 he did persuade the Ephors to order some sort of mobilization against the Boiotian Confederacy, which was unwilling to accept the dissolution of the Confederacy as a condition of peace, and he had got as far as Tegea before the Thebans backed down (5.1.33). The mere threat of similar force was enough to secure Argive and Corinthian compliance with the peace terms arranged by Sparta and Persia (Chapter 11).

(iii) The Siege of Phleious, 381-379 (Fig. 12.2)

Under cover of the 'autonomy' clause of the Peace of Antalkidas, to which a variety of inconsistent interpretations was given at need, Sparta ruthlessly pursued Agesilaos' narrow conception of the state's best interests (cf. 5.2.32), at first in the Peloponnese, then in Boiotia, and finally as far north as Chalkidike. The two kings, as law and custom enjoined, spearheaded the Spartan assault, but more than ever before (so far as the evidence goes) the question of which king should take which command became a matter of political finesse.

Agesilaos in the event so outmanoeuvred his much younger and greatly less experienced colleague and messmate (cf. 5.3.20) that Agesipolis was not only pressured into taking on the politically sensitive and personally embarrassing mission of disciplining Mantineia in 385 but also for two years forced to yield the far more prestigious command in Chalkidike to nominees of Agesilaos. As P. Carlier (1977, 83n.66) has rightly noted, it was 'l'habileté suprême' for a popular king to accept only those commands which promised glory and profit, leaving others for his colleague. But it should be added that both at Mantineia and in Chalkidike Agesipolis was ensnared into carrying out a policy for which his sympathy was appreciably less than wholehearted. No wonder Agesilaos mourned his early death.

Agesipolis' siege of Mantineia proved to be a curtain-raiser to that of Phleious conducted by Agesilaos, and it is greatly to the credit of Agesipolis that he managed it expeditiously. In a sense he had to do so, because the Corinthian War had placed undue strain on the manpower and resources of both Sparta and her Peloponnesian League allies. But it was none the less good generalship to realize so quickly the waste that would be involved in traditional ravaging and circumvallation strategy, and a brilliant stroke of intuition and presumably a considerable feat of engineering to dam the Ophis in order to undermine the mudbrick house- and city-walls. (Xenophon calls the Ophis a large river, but the topography has since altered and no such river flows here at any time of the year: A. Andrewes in Gomme 1981, 458.) Two sources speak of a pitched battle, but for once there is good reason to respect the silence of Xenophon (cf. Buckler 1980a). All the same Xenophon had no interest in magnifying Agesipolis' achievement, since his speed contrasts favourably with the twenty months it took Agesilaos to reduce Phleious (5.3.25), twice as long as had been anticipated (5.3.21).

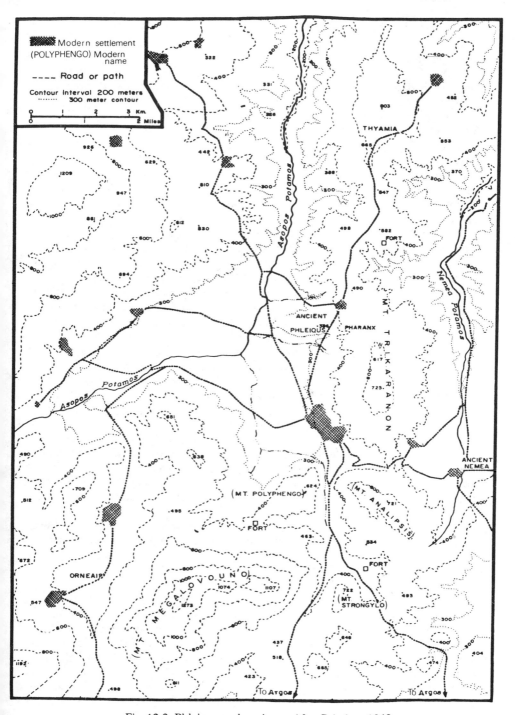

Fig. 12.2. Phleious and environs. After Pritchett 1969

Phleious occupied a site of great strategic importance to Sparta. For it lay on a thoroughfare from Arkadia to Nemea, Kleonai and Corinth, and commanded the route from Stymphalos to the Argive plain (Fig. 12.2). This location explains why its broad plain regularly served as a muster-station for Peloponnesian League armies (references in Pritchett 1969, 96n.5) and also why it was a matter of the utmost gravity when (democratic) Phleious displayed both political and military dissidence towards Sparta in the late 390s. In 390, however, Phleious was sufficiently unnerved by Iphikrates' peltasts to request a Spartan garrison and under its influence remained overtly loyal for the rest of the Corinthian War. Neither then, however, nor under the terms of the Peace of Antalkidas was a group of influential oligarchic exiles restored. But in about 384 Sparta, inspired clearly by Agesilaos, demanded their restoration and Phleious, not uninfluenced by the fate of Mantineia in 385, complied.

They did so mainly because they feared that, if they were to resist and the Spartans were to send an army to enforce their request, a dissident group within the city would open the gates. Such dissident, indeed revolutionary groups, Xenophon (5.2.9) comments, were to be found in most cities; and this remark is entirely borne out by the one surviving portion of a contemporary military treatise by Aineias of Stymphalos. This is much preoccupied with the means whereby a besieged city may guard against precisely this contingency of betrayal from within (e.g. 1.3,4,6; 5.1; 11; 22.7; cf. Ste. Croix 1981, 609n.57). For 'it is assumed that force will not be applied till fraud has failed' (Hunter 1927, xxxii). Which makes it all the more remarkable that, when trouble again flared in 381 between the restored exiles and the established democratic regime and the Spartans did indeed lay siege to Phleious, the city was not in fact betrayed from within – despite the presence of an actively pro-Spartan 'peace party' led by Prokles, a personal friend of Agesilaos (cf. Chapter 13).

The siege began in late summer or early autumn 381, in the following circumstances. In accordance with a recent Peloponnesian League decision, but also because they wished to ingratiate themselves with Agesipolis, the Phleiasians had sent a large sum of money in lieu of troops as their contribution to the League campaign against Olynthos. But under a misapprehension that Sparta would never send both kings out on campaign at once they also started to get tough with the exiles restored in 384. It was on the latter's behalf and with the encouragement of Prokles' faction that Agesilaos was despatched to Phleious by a board of Ephors more in sympathy with his outlook than their predecessors (5.3.13; contrast 5.2.32).

It is a nice comment on Sparta's shortage of funds and the reputation of Spartans abroad for venality that the Phleiasians thought they could bribe Agesilaos not to invade Phleiasia. But this was not Asia, and Agesilaos had no alternative target. So when the Phleiasians refused again (as in the late 390s) to hand over their akropolis, mindful no doubt of the fate of Thebes the previous year (Chapter 14), Agesilaos invested the city with a wall and settled down to starve them into submission in the traditional manner. Agesilaos, however, was not faced simply with a military problem. 'Many' Spartans (5.3.16), presumably including some of the political elite, were antipathetic to the whole enterprise. To win them round, or at least silence them, he devised a solution that was characteristic at once of his ingenuity and of his deep conservatism. He advised the exiles, together with any friends or relatives they could get to join them, to form themselves into private messes and train themselves up to a suitably Spartan condition. Whether or not Agesilaos was aware of it, this private-enterprise mess-system was a throwback to a discarded aristocratic mode of social organization attested in seventh-century Tiryns, for example. But it had the necessary contemporary effect. Wavering Spartans were swayed to the view that these pseudo-Spartan messmates were 'just the sort of fellow-soldiers they needed' (5.3.17). In view of Spartiate *oliganthrôpia*, Agesilaos must have also been delighted by the addition of more than a thousand well equipped and motivated allies.

The besieged Phleiasians, however, were not to be cowed so easily. By issuing half-rations and somehow preventing black-marketeering, they forced Agesilaos to spent two winters camped outside their city. A certain Delphion organized a picked force of 300 (modelled on the Spartan Hippeis?) to act both as an internal watchdog against subversion and as an occasional sally-force against the circumvallation. Agesilaos, for his part, seems to have done nothing to speed the end of the siege, despite the great transformation that had occurred in the besieger's art within the past generation. Indeed, his conduct of the siege of Phleious seems to have been even less venturesome and imaginative than the Spartans' siege of Plataia in the Athenian War (Chapter 4). Only after twenty months were the Phleiasians compelled to submit and to receive the garrison (and constitutional subversion) they had so defiantly resisted.

(iv) Agesilaos in Boiotia, 378 and 377 (Fig. 12.3)

By the end of the campaigning season of 379 Sparta could look back on six years of unbroken military success in implementing Agesilaos' hard-line interpretation of the Peace of Antalkidas. But in winter 379/8 the tide began to run the other way when Thebes was liberated from direct Spartan rule. Since the seizure of the Theban akropolis in 382 was probably the brainchild of Agesilaos (cf. Chapters 9 and 14), one might have supposed that Agesilaos would be the obvious choice to lead the expedition mobilized early in 378 to restore Spartan control. But using an even more obviously specious excuse than in 385, the speciosity of which even Xenophon was prepared to expose (5.4.13), Agesilaos stood down in favour of Kleombrotos. He had succeeded to the Agiad throne on the death of his brother Agesipolis at Olynthos in 380.

The way in which Xenophon describes the choice of Kleombrotos (5.4.14) suggests that, as in 382, a non-royal commander could have been selected. This corroborates the inference that Agesilaos' refusal had been calculated to involve his newly acceded co-king in a policy with which he was not in sympathy. But if this is so, the ploy does not seem to have been entirely successful, for Kleombrotos was made of sterner stuff than Agesipolis and was prepared to play Agesilaos at his own game. He did succeed with the aid of peltasts in penetrating Boiotia early in 378, but he made no attempt on Thebes. Instead, he simply reinforced or otherwise encouraged Sparta's existing garrisons (Plataia, Thespiai, Kynoskephalai: 5.4.15; cf. 5.4.10; Isok. 14.13,18). Moreover, as

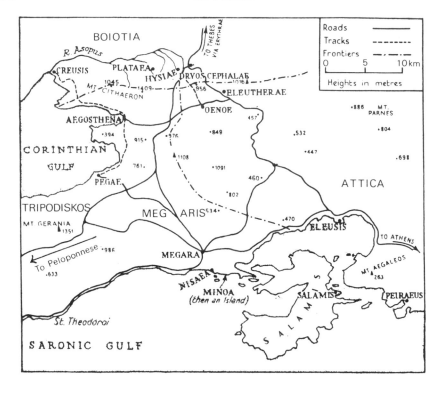

Fig. 12.3. The Boiotian Campaigns of Agesilaos, 378-377 (routes from the Peloponnese to Megaris and Boiotia). After N.G.L. Hammond, *A History of Greece to 322 B.C.*, 2nd edn (Oxford 1967).

harmost of Thespiai he left behind Sphodrias with a third of the allied troops and cash to hire mercenaries. Whatever view is taken of Kleombrotos' involvement in Sphodrias' subsequent attack on Athens (cf. Chapters 8,9 and 14), there can be no doubting that Sphodrias was Kleombrotos' man. Since he probably also owed his appointment as harmost to Kleombrotos, it seems clear that Kleombrotos was using Sphodrias as a tool in his opposition to Agesilaos' Boiotian policy. Once Sphodrias' raid had wrecked any prospects of Athens' co-operation with Sparta against Thebes, Agesilaos was doubly anxious to assume the Boiotian command in person. So far from feeling constrained by his earlier alleged scruple (that he was beyond military age), he now remarked sardonically on accepting his appointment that he would never oppose any state resolution (5.4.35).

Both in 378 (summer) and 377 (spring) Agesilaos led allied expeditions into Boiotia, but only after a second and more far-reaching alteration in the running of the Peloponnesian League (discussed further in Chapter 13). The alliance was now divided into ten regional groups; but if Diodoros' figures for Agesilaos' 378 campaign are correct (DS 15.32.1, wrongly attributed to 377/6), the

Lakedaimonians constituted almost a quarter of the total force on that occasion (about 4500 out of more than 18,000) although they accounted for only one of the ten groups. Apart from hoplites Agesilaos had with him 1500 cavalry and an unstated number of peltasts (presumably the mercenaries he 'borrowed' from Arkadian Kleitor: 5.4.37; cf. Best 1969, 98-9).

Agesilaos' first move in 378 was to order the mercenaries to occupy the Kithairon pass in advance, a tactic he repeated using the garrison at Thespiai in 377. Later Agesilaos and his entourage were to make a great deal of Kleombrotos' failure to force a passage over Kithairon in 376 (5.4.59; 6.4.5); but it is clear from Xenophon that in 378 and 377 the Thebans and their Athenian allies were less concerned to block Agesilaos' passage over Kithairon than to prevent his ravaging the most valuable agricultural land in Thebes' territory. To this end they had dug a trench and constructed a palisade (cf. Anderson 1970, 132-4); traces of the earthworks are still visible today. On both campaigns, however, although Agesilaos came nowhere near his major objective of re-establishing Spartan control of Thebes, he did succeed in penetrating the stockade by dint of guileful stratagems. In 378, using a ploy reminiscent of Lysander's trick at Aigospotamoi, he advanced his army through at first light without allowing his men to take their customary breakfast (5.4.41) – a considerable sacrifice, it would appear (cf. 4.5.8). In 377 he yet once more pulled off the ruse of the feint march (cf. 3.4.12, 20-1; 4.5.3), and instead of taking the direct route from Thespiai to Thebes he cut off south-eastwards towards Erythrai and by forced marching got behind the stockade at Skolos in half the usual time (5.4.47-9).

The ravaging of Theban territory that these devices made possible did have the desired effect on Thebes' grain production (5.4.56). But in other respects these expeditions of Agesilaos were if anything counterproductive, not least from the morale point of view. Sparta's allies became progressively more demoralized and unwilling to continue the devastation, and it is in this context that Plutarch sets the famous anecdote (*Ages.* 26.6-9 etc.) of Agesilaos separating the men (i.e. the full-time professional soldiers of the Lakedaimonians) from the boys (i.e. most of the allies who were not full-timers) in order to still the complaint that the few Spartans were dictating to a vastly greater number of unduly subordinated allies. Here too Plutarch places Antalkidas' complaint that Agesilaos was teaching the Boiotians how to fight (*Ages.* 26.3 etc.). Morale also suffered from a tactic employed by the Athenian Chabrias, probably using hoplites rather than peltasts (Best 1969, 109-10; *contra* Parke 1933, 77), which deterred Agesilaos from attacking (DS 15.32-3; Nep. *Chabr.* 1; cf. Anderson 1970, 89, 295n.15; Buckler 1972).

Nor was it only morale that was lost on the Spartan side. In 378 an encounter to the west of Thebes resulted in quite heavy loss of life among the peltasts and cavalry (one of whom was the only named Perioikos in the *Hellenika*, Eudikos: 5.4.39). It is not inconceivable that the tombstone of the Lakedaimonian Hip(p)okles at Thespiai (*IG* VII.1904; cf. DS 15.52.5) is to be associated with this engagement. In 377 the Thebans felt they had done sufficiently well in an encounter near Potniai to the south-east of Thebes to erect a battlefield trophy (5.4.50-3; DS 15.34.1-2; cf. Pritchett 1979, 246-75, at 269). Moreover, after

Agesilaos' withdrawal in 378 Phoibidas, Sphodrias' replacement as harmost of Thespiai, got himself killed through incompetent management of peltasts.

In short, although Sparta still retained garrisoned bases ringing Thebes at Orchomenos, Thespiai, Plataia and Tanagra, and although Thebes was temporarily reduced to a state of near-famine, Agesilaos had made no progress towards achieving his ultimate political objective. Indeed, rather the reverse. Violent civil disorder (*stasis*) had broken out at Thespiai in 377, indicating that despite the withdrawal of democratic elements to Thebes in 378 (5.4.46) there still remained a nucleus of anti-Spartan feeling (5.4.55). And Sparta's allies had begun to lose the political will to follow Sparta's lead in this direction, as they made plain both in Boiotia (above) and in 376 in Sparta at a Peloponnesian League congress which decided to redirect the main war effort against Athens (5.4.60).

From summer 377 to late 370 Agesilaos was *hors de combat* owing chiefly to a serious leg injury that had been aggravated by incompetent medical attention (5.4.58). Xenophon (*Ages.* 2.23) was technically correct to say that the reverses (*sphalmata*) Sparta suffered during this period could not be attributed to Agesilaos' leadership. But they were all a direct consequence of his anti-Theban aggressive policies, and there is more than a grain of truth in Antalkidas' view that Agesilaos was partly responsible for the military prowess displayed by the Thebans at Tegyra in 375 and, fatally for Sparta, Leuktra in 371.

(v) **Agesilaos' Defences of Sparta, 370/69 and 362** (Fig. 12.4)

After his seven-year lay-off Agesilaos next took the field with an army towards the very end of 370 in Arkadia; this was well beyond the normal campaigning season, although the prevalence of mercenary service was blurring that old distinction, and a response to a crisis. His army consisted of Lakedaimonians only (Xen. *Ages.* 2.23), both because of the need for speed and surprise and because of the thorough disarray of the Peloponnesian League. Agesilaos personally was under considerable pressure to make some kind of military demonstration in Arkadia, in order to bolster such pro-Spartan feeling as subsisted after the formation of the Arkadian League (Chapter 13) and to silence those domestic critics who, remembering the 'lame kingship' oracle (Plut. *Ages.* 30.1; cf. Chapter 7), were blaming him above all for the Leuktra débâcle and its aftermath. But although Agesilaos did capture the border town of Eutaia and brilliantly executed one of those complicated marching manoeuvres that only men trained in Spartan drill could (6.5.12,18-19), his Arkadian foray had as its main result an appeal by the Arkadians, Argives and Eleians first to Athens, who rejected it out of hand, and then to the Boiotian Confederacy for an immediate invasion of Lakonia and Messenia (DS 15.62.3-5). Xenophon omits the appeal and represents 'the Thebans' (meaning the Boiotian Confederacy) as reluctant invaders. But the size (over 30,000 men), co-ordination and effectiveness of the multi-state force determinedly commanded by Epameinondas speak otherwise (6.5.23; Xen. *Ages.* 2.24; cf. Cozzoli 1979, 170-216).

Sparta was already desperately short of citizen military manpower. More than

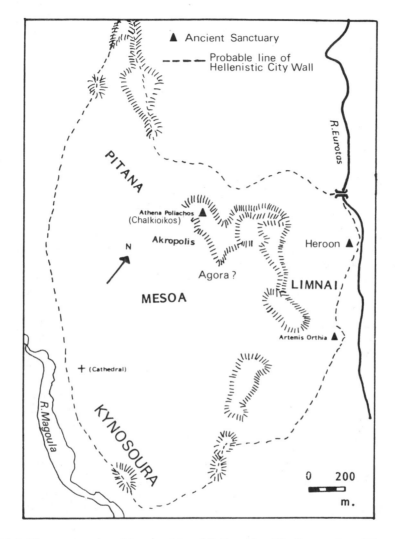

Fig. 12.4. The topography of Sparta. After J.F. Lazenby, *The Spartan Army* (Warminster 1985)

half of the Spartiates present at Leuktra had been killed, representing a loss of over a quarter of the total available. The strategic position of Agesilaos as commander of the defence forces was further compromised by the defection of some of the Perioikoi of northern Lakonia, including the men of Skiritis who in happier days had made a special contribution to the regular Lakedaimonian army (Thuc. 5.68.3; DS 15.32.1; Xen. *LP* 12.3,13.6). This is not to mention the final, successful revolt of the Messenian Helots (Xen. *Ages.* 2.24). Points of entry into Lakonia were garrisoned, probably chiefly with Neodamodeis, at Leuktron above Maleatis, Oion in Skiritis, and somewhere on the route from the Thyreatis (cf. Cartledge 1979, 297); but all were stormed with ease, and the separate groups of invaders united somewhere just north of Sparta in preparation for assault on the central place itself. Here the size of the defending force had been dramatically increased by arming as hoplites large numbers of still loyal Lakonian Helots, with a promise of freedom if they – and Sparta – survived the assault (6.5.29; DS 15.65.6 – in a later context). But this emergency measure is said to have sown alarm among the few hundred Spartiates, who were anyway disturbed by disaffection not only among the Hupomeiones and Perioikoi but even within the Spartiate ranks (cf. Chapter 10). The timely arrival of reinforcements from half a dozen loyal Peloponnesian League allies and of mercenary peltasts from Arkadian Orchomenos did something to allay their fears – but not apparently those of their wives, sisters and daughters, who in marked contrast to their reaction to the Lechaion and Leuktra disasters were unhinged by seeing the smoke rising from destroyed land and property (especially no doubt their own).

Probably about a decade later Aineias of Stymphalos (the 'Tactician') devoted a treatise to siegecraft, as we have seen. The typical town he had in mind was girdled by a fortification wall, which had become *de rigueur* for towns of any size or importance by the second quarter of the fourth century (e.g. Mantineia and Phleious, above). Agesilaos, however, was defending a city that in its antique way was entirely unfortified. If fortifications are 'une image fidèle de la cité grecque' (Garlan 1968, 259, citing Martin 1951, 545), that is no less true of their absence at Sparta. For Sparta was a garrison-town 'in the most specific sense ... which despised walls, precisely because it was the permanent open military camp of the Spartans' (Weber 1978, 1221; cf. 1360). The best therefore that Agesilaos could do was dispose pickets at salient points around the perimeter of habitation, for example on the hill of Issorion (modern Klaraki), and hope by cunning placement of his hoplites outside the perimeter to deter or prevent Epameinondas from penetrating it.

This objective he attained initially by stationing most of his hoplites to north-east of the town in the sanctuary of Athena Alea (6.5.23), but only because Nature in the shape of climate and topography lent her vital support. The Eurotas was heavily swollen by melted snow and was bitterly cold, for it was deep midwinter. Epameinondas therefore kept to the left bank until south of Sparta and crossed at a point opposite Amyklai (the fifth constituent village of Sparta, which had naturally been abandoned), before again moving north as far as a horse-race track in the immediate environs of central Sparta. But here he was ambushed by a force of 300 of the younger Spartan hoplites and thereupon withdrew to continue the invasion further south and west. It was perhaps in this or the later attack upon Sparta that a certain Ainesias met his death and so qualified for a named tombstone (*IG* V.1, 703; cf. Plut. *Lyk.* 27.3; with Cartledge 1978a, 35 and n.71).

In his encomium Xenophon (*Ages.* 2.24) naturally claims that it was Agesilaos who had kept Sparta inviolate. This judgment is supported by Plutarch (*Ages.* 33.2), who is at any rate right to be sceptical of Theopompos' story (115F323) that Agesilaos had bribed the Theban commanders to retreat. But although Agesilaos did show great energy, control and good tactical sense, it is seriously to be questioned whether Epameinondas had ever intended capturing, let alone destroying Sparta. Precisely the same doubt is provoked by the second occasion on which an army led by Epameinondas found itself at the gates (metaphorically speaking) of Sparta in May/June 362. Was Epameinondas really again pursuing a *Niederwerfungsstrategie* or rather an *Ermattungsstrategie* (to put it in the vocabulary of German military historians)?

The case for 370/69 is not perhaps proven, or provable (but see Polyain. 2.2.5). But for 362 it seems to me that Roloff (1903, 7-10, 12-41) has comprehensively disproved the thesis of Bauer (1890) that Epameinondas marks the transition in this regard from the *ancien* to the *nouveau régime* in Greek warfare – to a strategy, that is, of totally destructive warfare as realized by Philip and Alexander of Macedon. Rather, Epameinondas' invasion of Lakonia and march on Sparta in 362 should be regarded as a diversionary tactic. It was designed to prevent the Spartans from being present to aid their Mantineian allies in anything like full force and at the same moment to gain time for Epameinondas' own Messenian and Argive allies to be able to make their contribution to the decisive battle he was preparing in the 'cockpit of the Peloponnesos' (Pritchett 1969, 37). This view involves, not implausibly, rejection of Polybios' statement that the Spartans were at Mantineia in full force under Agesilaos (9.8.2,6) in favour of Xenophon's version, and disregard of the wholly modern speculation that Epameinondas' march on Sparta was designed to liberate the Lakonian Helots as he had earlier liberated the Messenians.

Turning to details, we find that in early summer 362 Epameinondas led an army across the Isthmus for the fourth time. His aim was to heal a deep rift that had arisen within the Arkadian League and thus make clear that stability in the Peloponnese depended on the maintenance of some form of Theban hegemony (cf. Chapter 14). Opponents of this notion within and outside the Arkadian League had secured guarantees of military support from both Sparta and Athens, and it was now just a question of when, where and on what terms the 'show-down' pitched battle would be fought. In the event it was fought at Mantineia at the time of the cereal harvest on terms decided by Epameinondas. But in order to achieve this, he had had to pursue the diversionary tactic of forced marches to and from Sparta. His rapid advance to Tegea pre-empted the possibility of the Spartan and Athenian forces uniting in Lakonia; his further push from Tegea to Sparta (no doubt by the same route *via* Karyai and Sellasia that he had used in 370/69) compelled Agesilaos, who had already reached Pellana *via* the easier route up the Eurotas valley, to split his force. He sent on in advance to Mantineia his cavalry and three of the twelve *lochoi* (a *mora* and a half), while he himself returned to Sparta with the remainder.

It may seem remarkable that Agesilaos at the age of eighty-two had been entrusted with command of Sparta's levy. But Bardylis I of Dardania, a slightly older contemporary of his, was killed in battle in 358 aged about ninety, and in a more recent epoch the Marshal Duc de Villars became in the words of Voltaire 'at the age of eighty-two generalissimo of the armies of France, Spain and Sardinia, an officer full of daring and self-confidence'. The energy displayed by

Agesilaos in returning to Sparta before Epameinondas arrived was not at all inferior to theirs (though the inactivity of the Agiad Kleomenes II throughout his sixty-year reign must remain one of the minor puzzles of Spartan history).

Even so, Epameinondas did succeed in becoming the first enemy to penetrate Sparta proper as opposed to its suburbs. But here he was impeded by the old-fashioned (cf. Arist. *Pol.* 1330b27-32), higgledy-piggledy layout of Sparta's streets and, if we may believe Xenophon and Plutarch, resisted heroically by Spartans who fulfilled the prediction (6.5.29) that they would fight best in their own country. Xenophon (7.5.12-13) privileges the heroism of a band of less than one hundred men led by Agesilaos' son Archidamos, whose military experience (including command: first at 6.4.18) was by now considerable. Plutarch (*Ages.* 34.8-11) singles out rather an individual feat accomplished by the heroically nude son of Phoibidas, although he does also give credit to the overall leadership of Agesilaos (*Ages.* 34.5-6). Implicitly both Xenophon and Plutarch felt the need for some supramundane explanation of Sparta's seemingly miraculous preservation. Such a belief rests on a misunderstanding of Epameinondas' purpose.

(vi) The Battle of Leuktra, 371 (Fig. 12.5)

When Epameinondas' troops retreated before Archidamos and his small band, Xenophon eagerly seized another opportunity to denigrate the Thebans' soliderly qualities, referring scornfully to 'these Thebans, these fire-breathers, these conquerors of the Spartans' (7.5.10; cf. 4.2.18, 6.5.24). Diodoros, too, though he had no reason to share Xenophon's vitriolic personal animosity towards Thebes, once spoke of their 'Leuktric airs' (16.58.3). But neither Xenophon nor Diodoros, who with Plutarch (cf. Buckler 1980b) are our principal sources for the Battle of Leuktra, can disguise the fact that Leuktra really was a decisive victory. Decisive not just for the soldiers immediately involved, but also in the senses that the result was absolutely clearcut and that it caused 'a real shift in the direction of human affairs away from the battlefield' (Keegan 1978, 342). To risk all on a decisive battle can be to throw away in as many hours advantages accumulated over many years. But it was part of the 'genius' of Epameinondas, what Napoleon called 'the inexplicable measure of a great commander', to have been able to calculate the risks so nicely, not once but twice. Leuktra, however, rather than Mantineia, was Epameinondas' masterpiece, and his handling both of the preliminaries and of the battle itself throws into relief – and into the shade – much of what has been written above about the generalship of Agesilaos.

The immediate background to the battle is the exclusion, just twenty days before, of Thebes and her revived Boiotian Confederacy from the renewed (first) Peace of 371. This was Agesilaos' doing, and it was equally his idea that Kleombrotos (he himself still being physically incapacitated) should take a Peloponnesian League army from Phokis into neighbouring Boiotia to try conclusions with the hated Thebans. Not some demon (*daimonion*: 6.4.3) but Agesilaos was the guiding spirit – or evil genius – of the affair. Nor is Xenophon better at describing the battle than he is at explaining why it was fought.

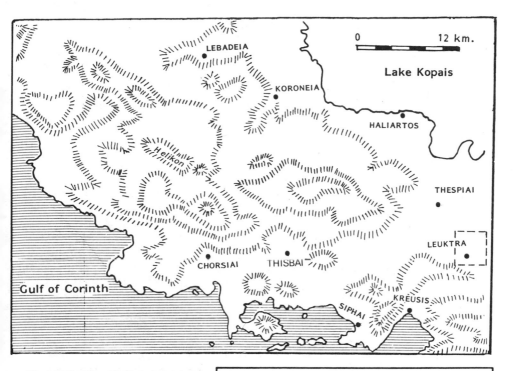

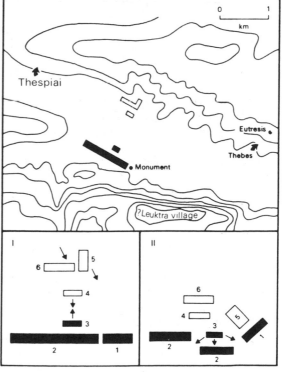

Fig. 12.5. The Battle of Leuktra, 371. *Above*: the site. After Lazenby. *Right*: a possible reconstruction by C.J. Tuplin. 1. Spartans 2. Peloponnesians 3. Spartan cavalry 4. Boiotian cavalry 5. Sacred Band 6. Other Boiotians. After Talbert.

Diodoros relapses into his set-piece battle routine. The best description from the Boiotian side is to be found appropriately in the Boiotian Plutarch. But even so the precise details are as ever unrecoverable.

Kleombrotos began the campaign more than competently, in July or early August. The tortuous route by which he led his army to Leuktra in the territory of Thespiai was intended to secure his communications with the Peloponnese and, if possible, catch Epameinondas off his guard. In both objectives he succeeded more or less. Kleombrotos' subsequent generalship has been severely criticized by historians and polemicists from Xenophon to G.L. Cawkwell. But to argue that defective generalship is a sufficient explanation of his defeat is viciously reductionist. It is true that he had never before fought a major pitched battle, and that he lacked the calm tranquillity and unshakeably clear-headed self-confidence that can be the foundation of the morale of an entire army. But there were also excellent reasons, beyond the control of Kleombrotos, why this should have been so.

The last major pitched battle involving Sparta had been fought twenty-three years previously, before Kleombrotos was old enough to have participated. Since then Spartiate *oliganthrôpia* had bitten ever more deeply, so that at Leuktra Sparta could throw no more than 700 Spartiates into the fray out of a total Spartiate military population of some 1200 to 1500. Sparta's military prestige had been tarnished by the Boiotian events of 378 and 377 and more especially by the severe defeat of Sparta's Orchomenos garrison at Tegyra in 375 (below). Morale within the Peloponnesian League army had sunk ever lower since the late 380s, when allies were permitted to commute men for cash (Chapter 13), so that it comes as little surprise to learn – from Xenophon (6.4.15) of all people – that some of the allies at Leuktra were not actually displeased by the result.

Then there is the question of the relative numerical strength and fighting quality of the two sides. Kleombrotos' army as a whole outnumbered that of Epameinondas appreciably, perhaps some 10 or 11,000 men as against 6 or 7,000. But his Lakedaimonian contingent (Spartiates, Perioikoi, perhaps some Hupomeiones) was certainly not much larger and perhaps smaller than the specifically Theban hoplite force commanded by Pelopidas. Had the battle followed the usual Greek pattern and both right wings been victorious, there could then have been no numerical incentive for Kleombrotos to emulate Agesilaos' tactics in the second phase at Koroneia in 394. Moreover, Kleombrotos' Lakedaimonians were no longer unquestionably superior in quality to their Theban counterparts. The latter had long been the best fighters in Boiotia: consider the terror they had inspired in the Thespian hoplites in 378 (5.4.45). But the Battle of Tegyra was an earnest of yet greater achievements to come.

Xenophon typically makes no direct (but see perhaps 6.4.10) reference to it. Plutarch's account (*Pelop.* 16-17) may be based ultimately on that of the near-contemporary Kallisthenes (124F11,18). From the hoplite standpoint the battle is chiefly noteworthy for the role played by the Sacred Band (*hieros lochos*) commanded by Pelopidas. This force of 150 homosexual couples was apparently formed by Gorgidas in 378; it was an excellent notion to combine the idea of an elite force with the longstanding institution of homosexuality and a sure sign that military matters were being thought about hard in Thebes. Pelopidas saw the value of concentrating it as a shock force and used it as such successfully for the first time at Tegyra. Tegyra, however, was also apparently the first Greek battle in which cavalry was used as an integral part of a plan of attack rather than allotted a merely ancillary role (cf. Pritchett 1982, 119).

That is a pretty formidable list of objective reasons why Kleombrotos' morale need not have been at the highest pitch before the battle began. Subjectively, too, he was not the best man for the Spartans to have had in this place at this time. For it seems quite plain that his heart was not in the campaign as a whole and that if he had had a free choice he would not have fought the Boiotians at all, for political rather than military reasons. What made him go through with the battle was fear of the consequences if he did not, whether they were the sort of punishments with which Agis had been threatened in 418 or, more likely, exile under sentence of death as his father had suffered in 395.

Looked at from the other side, the factors enumerated above help explain why Epameinondas was prepared for the Boiotians to be excluded from the Peace in 371 in the certain knowledge that Sparta would move quickly to attack them and the confident belief that they could win. To assert flatly that 'Sparta should have won the battle of Leuctra' (Cawkwell 1976a, 82) is to miss this crucial point. I write of course with the benefit of hindsight but not, I think, anachronistic judgment. Epameinondas was a great enough general to be able, like Themistokles (Thuc. 1.138.3), both to act appropriately to meet immediate circumstances and to forecast the future more reliably than others. At any rate, his forecast was more accurate than that of the three of his fellow Boiotian generals who opposed an immediate engagement with Kleombrotos; and that it was more accurate was due in no small measure to his own endeavours. For after the battleground had been staked out he outgeneralled Kleombrotos all along the line, beginning with the morale factor.

There is more than usually good reason for us, like some contemporaries (6.4.7-8), to suspect the authenticity of a whole spate of 'portents' that were rumoured to have occurred opportunely immediately before the battle. For the philosophical Epameinondas is less likely to have scrupled to fabricate them than a true believer like Agesilaos. Doubtless they had the desired effect on the morale of the respective sides. Kleombrotos' religious stance is unknown, and he may well have been capable of the kind of hard-headed pragmatism that his elder brother had displayed in face of an earthquake in the Argolid in 388 (4.7.2-5). But despite Xenophon's silence, it is unthinkable that he would have omitted the customary pre-battle sacrifice (evidence collected in Pritchett 1974, I, 114). Rather, Xenophon's failure to mention it is part and parcel of his theological view that the gods were willing the impending disaster (6.4.3, 8,23; cf. 5.4.1, further discussed in Chapter 21).

There is, on the other hand, every reason to accept Xenophon's testimony that Kleombrotos and his entourage went into battle slightly tipsy. 'Dutch' courage seems to be a universal phenomenon from, for instance, the English at Agincourt (cf. Keegan 1978, 115) to the fierce Yanomamo people of the Brazilian jungle today (cf. Harris 1978, 45). But, despite Xenophon's innuendo, wine does not explain Kleombrotos' defeat. That ensued because Epameinondas had brought his enemies to battle on his own terms, compelling them to fight by his rules, not theirs.

Epameinondas' first successful manoeuvre was to use his efficient cavalry against the low-grade Spartan cavalry in order to prevent Kleombrotos from advancing his hoplite line as he would have wished. It is not clear whether Kleombrotos was in fact attempting some such outflanking movement as had been successfully executed at the Nemea River; but whatever manoeuvre he was trying was hopelessly disrupted by his own cavalry, which was pressed back upon the Spartan line in confusion by their Theban counterparts. Epameinondas next put into operation his tactic of indirect approach, deliberately refusing his right wing and advancing obliquely with his left in such a way that the phalanx could be described as 'slanted' (*loxê*: DS 15.55.2). Now Kleombrotos was going by the book and was commanding from the right wing, the strongest element of his army. Epameinondas, however, had stationed himself and his crack hoplites (including the Sacred Band under Pelopidas, though it is not certain where they were exactly at the beginning of the battle) on his left wing, directly opposite Kleombrotos.

Although Regent Pausanias had perhaps contemplated winning Plataia from the left wing (Hdt. 9.46.3) and Teleutias in 381 had commanded from the left for topographical reasons outside the walls of Olynthos (5.2.40), this is the first recorded occasion on which the left had been privileged over the right wing in a regular hoplite pitched battle in open country. Such a reversal of priorities does certainly represent a 'paradigm shift' in Greek military thinking. But (*pace* Vidal-Naquet 1981, esp. 113, 117) there is no need to invoke Pythagorean doctrine to account for Epameinondas' decision nor indeed to suppose that the decision was wholly or mainly ideological in this philosophical sense. What Epameinondas aimed to do was win the battle as quickly and cleanly as possible by obliterating at a stroke its prime movers, that is the Spartans, while at the same time inflicting as few casualties as possible on Sparta's allies whose goodwill he hoped to secure in favour of his projected post-battle settlement. (Contrast the Nemea River battle, in which only eight Lakedaimonians lost their lives – but at the cost of deliberately sacrificing allied lives.)

To this end Epameinondas obeyed what has been called 'the first rule of war' (Tarn 1930, 70), namely the concentration of force at the decisive point of the battle. The Chevalier Jean du Teil (one of Napoleon's teachers) and the Prussian military analyst von Clausewitz were both particularly insistent on this rule, but it can rarely have been observed to such good effect as at Leuktra in 371. Epameinondas was by no means the first Theban hoplite commander willingly to sacrifice width of front for weight in depth, but so far as the evidence goes he more than doubled the deepest hoplite formation thitherto employed (see generally Pritchett 1974, I, 134-43). For his 4000 or so Theban hoplites were mustered not less than fifty ranks deep, according to Xenophon (6.4.12). Opposite them Kleombrotos' Lakedaimonians, already thrown into confusion by their own cavalry, were lined up only twelve deep. Thus when the Theban hoplites with the Sacred Band somehow in the van crashed into them, their formation was so disrupted that they could not demonstrate what Xenophon considered a peculiarly Spartan ability to 'campaign in battle with any troops at hand when the line gets into confusion' (Xen. *LP* 11.7; cf. Plut. *Pelop.* 23.3-4).

The Lakedaimonians, or at least the Spartiates in the immediate vicinity of their king including the 300 Hippeis, fought bravely, especially when there was a danger that the enemy might get possession of the mortally wounded Kleombrotos as the Persians had captured (and mutilated) the corpse of Leonidas at Thermopylai (Hdt. 7.225.1; cf. generally Paus. 9.13.10). But within the deliberately narrowed 'killing zone' no less than 400 of the 700 full Spartan citizens involved were slain, together with some 600 of the other Lakedaimonian troops in the four *morai* present. However, if it is right that the 400 Spartiates killed embraced all the Hippeis and that the Hippeis were not included in the regular establishment of the *morai*, then only one quarter of the 400 Spartiates in the *morai* died at Leuktra. This at first sight surprisingly low proportion is wholly compatible with Plutarch's information (*Ages.* 30.6) that there had been many 'tremblers' (*tresantes*) at Leuktra, including some of the Spartan elite (cf. Chapter 10, end). If so many were anxious to save their skins rather than achieve, Leonidas-like, 'la belle mort' or death in battle on behalf of their *patris* (cf. Loraux 1977), this does rather suggest a serious lowering of morale among the Spartiates. However that may be, Sparta collapsed after Leuktra – like Prussia after the defeat of 1806 and France after that of 1870 – for reasons that were deeply social rather than military in the narrowest and most superficial sense (cf. Howard 1983, 197). There could be no sharper illustration of a dictum whose truth and relevance should by now be apparent, that 'battle is the warp to the weft of a whole social fabric' (Keegan 1978, 61).

13

Agesilaos and the Peloponnesian League

Much that [Xenophon] tells us of Elis, let us say, or Phleious or Sicyon, is perhaps in itself of little significance in the world's history; these were small and unimportant places, but they stood in close relations with a great power, and everything that illuminates Sparta's methods at this period [404-357] is of value to the historian who wishes to understand the world's course. (Glover 1917, 372)

Sparta in truth, by her conquest of Olynthos, betrayed the Greeks of Thrace to the Macedonian King, just as she had already, by the Peace of Antalkidas, betrayed the Greeks of Asia to the Persian King. (Freeman 1893, 149)

Neither in Asia Minor in 396-4 nor in various parts of central Greece between 394 and 389 nor yet in Boiotia in 378-7 could Agesilaos so deploy his generalship as to compel the enemies of Sparta to fulfil his political will. But if he could not win the Persian, Corinthian or Boiotian Wars by military means alone, he certainly was able to win the peace – initially at least – by a mixture of diplomacy and military might. Under cover of the Peace of Antalkidas (Chapter 11) Agesilaos imposed his conception of 'good sense' (*sôphrosunê*: cf. Xen. *Ages.* 7.3) in mainland Greece as far north as Thrace to such a degree that Plutarch's reference (*Ages.* 40.3) to his 'being accounted leader and king of practically all Hellas' applies most nearly to the latter half of the 380s.

In his encomium of Agesilaos Xenophon naturally enough preferred not to represent his foreign policy from 386 onwards in terms of impersonal coercion and illegitimate when not flagrantly illegal interpretation of the Peace's autonomy clause. Instead, loyally echoing his patron, he chose the moralizing language of friendship to characterize Agesilaos' motivation. Rather than speak of the forcible disaggregation of Corinth and Argos against the will of most Corinthians and Argives, of the similarly resented overthrow of democratic government in Phleious after a twenty-month siege, and of the unsuccessful attempts to renew the illegal occupation and permanent garrisoning of (now democratic) Thebes, Xenophon somewhat apologetically alleges that in all cases Agesilaos was motivated solely by a spirit of comradeliness (*philetairia*: Xen. *Ages.* 2.21-2; cf. Dümmler 1901, I, 273). Specifically, Agesilaos desired to restore his exiled friends to power in Corinth, Phleious and Thebes. In the same way Agesilaos' disastrous intervention in Arkadia late in 370 is portrayed, not as an attempt to break up the newly-formed Arkadian League, but as a rescue-mission on behalf of his friends and ritualized guest-friends (*xenoi*) in Tegea (Xen. *Ages.* 2.23).

Objectively, as we shall see in this and the next chapter,[1] Sparta's actions in this period constituted gross violations of the autonomy of Corinth, Argos, Thebes and Tegea, not to mention Mantineia and Olynthos (where the *philetairia* motive could not be invoked so readily or at all). But, to be fair to Xenophon's historiographical pretensions, he does at least drop a hint of this in the *Agesilaos* in connection with Phleious and he does on several occasions in the *Hellenika* make quite clear what the objective grounds for complaint against Agesilaos' politics were. Indeed, it is precisely in this dissonance or outright conflict between the *Agesilaos* and *Hellenika* that Xenophon's peculiar value as a source for these episodes can be located. It would be wrong, moreover, to accuse Agesilaos and Xenophon of mere humbug and hypocrisy, of trying to draw an acceptably moral veil over the unacceptable face of Spartan imperialism. For to a Greek aristocrat the bond of comradeship could rank as high as any family tie, both affectively and instrumentally – indeed, higher to a Spartan aristocrat brought up in a society whose institutions and expressed ideology were designed to exalt the values of the community to the detriment of those of any narrower kinship grouping (cf. Chapter 9). It is only to be expected that the manipulation of friendship-alliances of one sort or another was of the essence of political life for members of the Spartan political hierarchy.

Earlier (Chapter 9) I tried to show how such friendship-alliances, ranging from close ties of comradeship at one extreme to asymmetrical patronage relations at the other, could explain what lay behind the formal mechanisms of public decision-making within the Spartan citizen body. My main object here is to demonstrate how Agesilaos sought to re-adapt one kind of friendship-alliance, the ancient pre- and trans-*polis* tie of *xenia*, to the purpose of transforming the Peloponnesian League into an instrument for the imperialist domination of virtually all mainland Greece. In other words, just as friendship was the hidden lubricant of Spartan domestic politics, so it was friendship that silently greased the wheels of the Peloponnesian League in the age of Agesilaos. However, as readers of this book will not by now be amazed to discover, Agesilaos' aim was characteristically reactionary. By 400 *xeniai* in the Greek world generally had long since ceased to coincide neatly with diplomatic relations between *poleis*, a fact that Xenophon (4.1.34) disingenuously makes Agesilaos himself point out to the non-Greek Pharnabazus (cf. Chapter 11). But what Agesilaos was trying to do was reinstate that congruence in all important respects for the sake of Spartan hegemony. Xenophon's attempt to blind his readers to this reactionary aspect of Agesilaos' foreign policy has achieved considerable success in recent times, but it deserves and will get in this study a less sympathetic reception.

By the last quarter of the fifth century at latest Sparta was notorious throughout Greece, especially in contrast to Athens, for her phobia of *xenoi* or foreigners. This xenophobia she carried to the remarkable and in a sense

---

[1] Thebes and/or the Boiotian Confederacy were also at various times and under varying conditions members of the Peloponnesian League, as was Athens. But their status as powers of the first rank makes it necessary to give Sparta's relationship with these states a separate treatment in Chapter 14.

un-Greek lengths of conducting systematic *xenêlasiai*, 'expulsions of foreigners' (Thuc. 2.39.1; cf. 1.144.2; with Gomme *ad locc.* for further references). It is not known when the Spartans first introduced this version of an Alien Act, although the earliest attested instance seems to be that affecting the Samian Maiandrios in about 517 (Hdt. 3.148; Plut. *Mor.* 224ab). But Spartan tradition inevitably attributed the practice to Lykourgos, who was also supposed to have prohibited Spartans from living permanently abroad and to have allowed into Sparta only those whose activities would not threaten the Spartan *kosmos* or *diaita* and provoke civil dissension (esp. Plut. *Lyk.* 27.6-7; cf. 9.5). Certainly, the phobia was deepseated, as a linguistic mannerism recorded by Herodotus (9.11.2, 55.2) amply reveals. Whether or not language shapes as well as reflects mentality, it speaks worlds that the Spartans were the only Greeks who elided the crucial distinction between non-Spartans who were Greek and non-Spartans who were not (elsewhere called *barbaroi*), by calling both groups indiscriminately *xenoi* and thereby devaluing that term in its collective application.

Not all non-Spartans, however, had been equally unwelcome in Sparta at all times since 'Lykourgos'. Nor did the Spartans devalue the term *xenoi* in all contexts. The meetings of Telemachos and Menelaos at Sparta in Homer's *Odyssey*, whatever *we* may think of its historicity, was not just a fairytale encounter but conformed in essentials to a pattern of relationships between aristocrats of different *poleis* that the Spartans no less than other Greeks dignified with the title of *xeniai*. *Xenia* is usually translated into English by some such periphrasis as 'guest-friendship'. But no single term can in fact capture all the nuances, and it can be misleading to single out the aspect of mutual hospitality from all the rest.[2] 'Ritualized guest-friendship' is admittedly clumsy, but it does at least convey the idea that the contracting of this relationship involved participation in a quasi-religious set of rituals the totality of which could almost be said to constitute a *rite de passage* conferring a new social status on the participants. In its original conception, as the use of *xenos* to mean both 'host' and 'guest' implies (cf. Latin *hostis*, French *hôte*), this was a reciprocal relationship of perfect symmetry between social equals; and since to begin with it was the preserve of aristocrats, the tie tended naturally to be a hereditary one (although lineal descendants of the original contracting parties might never have occasion to meet or might even be ignorant of each other's very existence). Thus the elaboration of *xenia* as an institution marked the beginnings of interstate relations between the aristocratically governed *poleis* of early Greece by providing a mechanism for automatically allocating the outlander a place within the norms of an alien society (cf. Pitt-Rivers 1968, 15). 'The stranger who had a *xenos* in a foreign land ... had an effective substitute for kinsmen, a protector, representative and ally' (Finley 1979, 102).

Aristotle (*Pol.* 1270a34-9) boldly asserted that in the time of 'the ancient kings' Sparta had kept up her military effective by being notably more generous in conferring her citizenship on foreigners than she was in the historical period (cf. Kelly 1979, 98n.3). This should not be taken too seriously, since all Greek

[2] For this point and much else on this important but neglected topic I am indebted to Dr G. Herman, whose doctoral thesis 'Ritualised Friendship and the Greek City' I was privileged to examine.

states were more or less parsimonious in extending this unique privilege before the Hellenistic era. But there is no reason to doubt that distinguished aristocratic foreigners were regular visitors to Sparta from early times, whether their visit was occasioned by some public festival like the Gymnopaidiai (Xen. *Mem.* 1.2.61; Plut. *Kim.* 10.6, *Ages.* 29.3) or some affair of state or some private business they had to transact with their Spartan *xenoi*. Since the visitors in question were typically members of ruling aristocracies or tyrannies down to the fifth century, the personal and private relationship of *xenia* shaded easily into a relationship of friendship and perhaps military co-operation between their respective states (cf. Cartledge 1982, 258-9, for a probably seventh-century instance involving Sparta and Samos). The treaties of the Classical period and later still used the aristocratic language of friendship and enmity to describe impersonal relations of military alliance (cf. Ste. Croix 1972, 298-9).

The formalities of Greek diplomacy 'developed and grew up about the person of the herald' (Mosley 1973, 88), who became invested with a quasi-religious sacrosanctity to help him perform his function. It was wholly understandable, therefore, that in Sparta the profession of herald (*kêrux*) should be hereditary (Hdt. 6.60; cf. Berthiaume 1976) and hereditary within the aristocratic family claiming descent from Agamemnon's herald Talthybios, who was worshipped in Sparta as a hero (Hdt. 7.134.1; Paus. 3.12.7). But the name of the Talthybiad who brought to Sparta news of victory in the 'Tearless Battle' of 368 (7.1.32) is eloquent of the development in diplomacy that inevitably accompanied the development of the *polis*: Damoteles was performing (*teleô*) a public and communal function with religious overtones on behalf of the Spartan *damos* (people) as a whole.

By Damoteles' day, too, the day-to-day conduct of diplomatic business had long since been in the hands, not of individual ruling aristocrats, but of the Ephors, who were appointed from and perhaps by the whole *damos* (Chapter 8). Moreover, Sparta's permanent relations with other states no longer depended solely on the existence of individual *xeniai* between Spartan aristocrats and aristocrats in those states but were mediated by the public office of *proxenos* held by a distinguished citizen who (etymologically) substituted for a *xenos* or acted in the interests of foreigners (cf. Kienast 1973, 581-7). That is, a citizen of state A (say Sparta) resident in state A acted as *proxenos* or diplomatic representative for the citizens of state B (say Athens), whether he represented them collectively in such matters as treaty negotiations or individually in, for example, suits arising out of alleged breaches of contract. Such a system of 'consular' representation anticipated that developed by the Venetians in more recent times. It is first attested in the later seventh century and cannot have been instituted much before that (cf. Wallace 1970; Walbank 1978, 2-8; and generally Gschnitzer 1973). *Proxenia*, as might be expected from its origins in *xenia*, was often hereditary, and the men selected to hold the office would already have private *xenia* relationships with leading citizens of the state for which they were acting as *proxenoi*.

Sparta moved with the rest of Greece in the fact that she appointed *proxenoi*, but because of her xenophobia she did so in a peculiar and possibly unique way. Ordinarily it was the prerogative of state B to appoint its own *proxenos* or more than one *proxenoi* in state A. But in Sparta it was one of the ancient privileges (*gerea*) of the kings to appoint *proxenoi* from among the citizens (*astoi*). It is true that Herodotus (6.57.2) does not say the kings were privileged to appoint 'the' or 'all' *proxenoi*, but his formulation does not entail that none of the *proxenoi* they appointed was in any sense a political appointee (*contra* Mosley 1971b). The kings, in other words, 'placed a kind of liturgic obligation on prominent Spartans to look after certain foreigners' (Wallace 1970, 198). This useful regal privilege was somewhat akin to that of being entitled to appoint, on a hereditary basis, two Pythioi each, these being distinguished Spartans who shared the royal mess in Sparta and acted as permanent ambassadors to Pythian Apollo's oracular shrine at Delphi (Hdt. 6.57.2,4; cf. Cartledge 1978a, 30).

If the kings in the age of Agesilaos were intimately involved both in individual *xeniai* and in appointing *proxenoi*, how, it may be asked, had the formal responsibility for the day-to-day conduct of foreign affairs including diplomacy come to devolve upon the Ephors? The straight answer is that we do not know. But there is one development in Sparta's interstate relations in the appropriate period that provides a highly likely occasion for such a devolution to have occurred. That development was the growth of numerous individual alliances between Sparta and other *poleis*, at first within the Peloponnese only, into what we call the Peloponnesian League by about the end of the sixth century (see Chapter 2 for an account of the League as it stood in about 445).

The origins of this rather loose League, the first Greek multi-state organization whose membership was political rather than ethnic or religious in character, are strictly irrecoverable, but 'the most satisfactory account would appear to be that which grounds the extension of Spartan influence in a policy of suppressing tyrannies and restoring exile aristocracies with which she entered into agreements of friendship and mutual defence' (Cawkwell 1976a, 71; cf. Figueira 1981, 14-16). More specifically, the Spartans agreed to support these more or less broadly based oligarchies (perhaps called *isokratiai*: Hdt. 5.92a), in return for their support in case of Helot unrest or uprising. With some of the leading members of these regimes one or other of the Spartan kings might already have had ties of *xenia*, but not necessarily with all, and there will surely have been cases where the kings' traditional mutual enmity did not make such royal *xeniai* the best instrument for dealing with these oligarchies as a whole. In such cases the quintessentially *polis* institution of the Ephorate might more usefully represent the *polis* of Sparta, just as it was the Ephors who swore on behalf of the *polis* to uphold the rights of the kings so long as the kings obeyed the laws of the *polis* (Xen. *LP* 15.7). The *quid pro quo* for the kings so far as their role in foreign relations was concerned was the maintenance (or perhaps creation) of their privilege of creating *proxenoi*.[3] This gave them as it were a 'hot line' to Sparta's oligarchic allies as well as a means of influencing foreign policy determination within the Spartan political hierarchy. At the same time of course they were free to preserve their existing *xeniai* or create new ones as circumstances arose.

---

[3] One of the earliest attested is Gorgos, *proxenos* of Elis *c*.500; his name recalls that of the Agiad Gorgo, daughter of Kleomenes I and wife of Leonidas.

Diplomacy among the Greeks generally was notoriously underdeveloped or even backward (cf. Adcock 1924, esp. 92; Adcock/Mosley 1975; Hunt 1982, 7). But Sparta was an exception to this rule, partly because she normally preferred diplomacy to war as a result of her Helot danger (Thuc. 1.118.2; with Ste. Croix 1972, 95), partly because for this same reason she was the centre of a loose-hung but still exceptionally complex by Greek standards web of alliance. It is not until the late fifth and early fourth centuries that we get any detailed insights into the workings of Spartan diplomacy (cf. Mosley 1979; and for a useful list of embassies Kienast 1973, 619-28), but what is immediately noticeable is its relative professionalism. 'Beneath a cloak of Laconic bluntness and conservative propriety Spartan diplomacy was crafty, tortuous and selfish' (Adcock 1948, 5). The practice of employing men with personal connections of *xenia* as ambassadors to a particular state is just one example of Sparta's diplomatic finesse. Already in about 506 the co-ordination of the allied expedition against Athens reveals an exceptional degree of diplomatic organization, as does the ensuing meeting of the first recorded Peloponnesian League Congress. But that expedition has another point of interest for our purposes. For it was the first to be mounted by Sparta not just in favour of oligarchy but against a form of regime that was later known as 'democracy' but apparently called at the time *isonomia*, equality under the laws (cf. Ostwald 1969). Not only did the fledgling Athenian democracy survive the onslaught, but as early as 493 it tried to export its revolutionary form of government to Aigina, which was probably (*pace* Figueira 1981) a member of the Peloponnesian League. These were danger-signals as far as Sparta's preferred method of controlling her alliance through tame oligarchies was concerned. Moreover, the situation at Athens in 506 and probably Aigina in 493 foreshadowed in all essentials the condition of all the major Peloponnesian League states with which Agesilaos had to deal, the condition of *stasis*.

Stasis, literally a process of standing, came to mean especially the condition of civil strife that all too often spilled over into outright and bloody civil war. Thucydides (3.82.1) concluded his celebrated description and analysis of the horrific outbreak on Kerkyra (Corfu) in 427 by lamenting that thereafter practically the whole of the Hellenic world was similarly convulsed by *stasis*. This passage moved David Hume to make two telling observations in his essay 'Of the Populousness of Ancient Nations' (1742). 'The utmost energy of the nervous style of Thucydides, and the copiousness and expression of the Greek language, seem to sink under that historian, when he attempts to describe the disorders which arose from faction throughout all the Grecian commonwealths. You would imagine that he still labours with a thought greater than he can find words to communicate.' In a footnote he adds: 'The country in Europe wherein I have observed the factions to be most violent, and party hatred the strongest, is Ireland.' Four constant elements in the *stasis* that disfigured the Classical epoch of Greek history may be identified (cf. Lintott 1982): class conflict between those whom the Greeks both popularly and 'scientifically' labelled 'the rich' and 'the poor' citizens (cf. Ste. Croix 1981, 69-80); struggles for power within 'the rich', who were also appropriately named 'the powerful' (*dunatoi*), less objectively 'the best' (*aristoi, beltistoi*); struggle for control of the *politeia*, a word that meant more to a Greek citizen than our rather colourless 'constitution', at its most emotive coming near to 'way of life'; and finally intervention by foreign powers, whether Greek or non-Greek.

All four of these elements were present in some degree in the series of case studies to which the remainder of this chapter will be devoted. These examples of Sparta's relations with her Peloponnesian League allies in the age of Agesilaos illustrate singly and in combination both Sparta's changing and increasingly onerous demands upon these allies and Agesilaos' personal conception of the uses to which the alliance should be put. What is remarkable is not that the Peloponnesian League came to an end in the mid-360s but that it should have persisted as an active force in Greek interstate politics for so long.

(i) Elis

It is just possible that it was with Elis in north-west Peloponnese rather than with Arkadian Tegea that Sparta concluded the first of the alliances that culminated in the establishment of the Peloponnesian League. This would have been some time in the second quarter of the sixth century when Elis with Spartan aid was restored to control of the Olympic Games at the expense of their local rivals, the men of Pisa, whose economic and political development the Eleians managed to retard thereafter (cf. 3.2.31). But long before this the Spartans had established a special relationship with the sanctuary of Olympia, where they consulted the oracle of Zeus as a state and competed individually (and with great success) in the quadrennial Games. The importance of Olympia to the pious Spartans helps explain why Elis was permitted to pursue an aggressively independent foreign and domestic policy for so long without suffering Spartan reprisals, even though her territorial claims to the borderland of Triphylia between Eleia and Messenia variously trespassed on the pretended rights both of Sparta and of Sparta's allies in Arkadia.

As it was, it was not until early in the Athenian War that the Spartans formally charged the Eleians with infringing the autonomy of the Triphylian towns and not until that War was over that Sparta used the charge as pretext for a full-scale Peloponnesian League attack. By then Sparta had a long shopping-list of grievances against Elis, and King Agis personally was still smarting from the humiliations he had been forced to undergo. By 470 – or even 500 (cf. O'Neil 1981, 340) – Elis had become a democracy, one of the only two (with Mantineia) that Sparta is known to have tolerated within the Peloponnesian League in the fifth century (cf. Ste. Croix 1972, 98 and n.25). In the 460s Elis had united with the bulk of the Arkadian towns and with democratic Argos in military opposition to Sparta, presumably in order to escape the clause of her treaty that bound her to have the same friends and enemies as Sparta and so restricted her freedom of action in Triphylia. The rebels were soundly defeated, but Elis was not subsequently compelled to give up her democracy or pull down her city wall. Indeed, she was able to get away with not only conducting further aggression in Triphylia (Hdt. 4.148.4; perhaps in the 440s) but even acquiring control of half of the territory of Lepreon before the Athenian War (Thuc. 5.32.2).

Early in that War, however, Sparta did hand down the unwelcome arbitral judgment that Elis was infringing the autonomy of the Lepreates and must restore their land (Thuc. 5.31.4; cf. Piccirilli 1976, 129-31; Ostwald 1982, 5, 28). Soon after the Peace of Nikias (421), which the Eleians refused to acknowledge on the grounds that it broke Sparta's pre-war agreement that her allies should retain after the War what they had possessed at its outbreak (Thuc. 5.32.5), Sparta garrisoned Lepreon with liberated Helots (Thuc. 5.34.1; cf. Chapter 10). But by then the Eleians had revolted from Sparta, allying themselves first with Corinth, Mantineia and Argos, and later (after Corinth had returned to the Spartan fold) with Athens too (Thuc. 5.47). In the following, Olympic year of 420 they exploited their presidency of the Games to ban Spartans from participating and to insult Sparta publicly in the person of the distinguished Lichas, who among much else was *proxenos* of Argos (Thuc. 5.49-50, 76.3; 3.2.21); Sparta was perhaps still excluded in 404. Some time later, perhaps in 414 or 413 when the Spartans judged that they might legitimately renew aggression upon Athens directly (Thuc. 7.18.3), Agis was sent in obedience to an oracle to sacrifice to Zeus at Olympia on behalf of the Peloponnesian alliance. But the Eleians debarred him on the pretext that 'it was an ancient and established principle that Greeks should not consult the oracle with regard to a war waged against Greeks' (3.2.22). This was a nice hit at Delphi's support for Sparta in 432/1 (Thuc. 1.118.3), but they had somehow managed to forget the alleged principle by 388 when no such obstacle was placed in the way of Agesipolis (4.7.2). Finally, to add injury to insult, the Eleian democratic leader Thrasydaios subscribed two talents to the cause of the Athenian democratic exiles in 404/3 (Plut. *Mor.* 835f) at a time when Elis was refusing to settle the arrears of payment claimed by Sparta for expenses incurred in the Athenian War (DS 14.17.5).

Thus the record of Elis as an ally of Sparta was chequered, to say the least. But the real reasons why between 402 and 400 – on the chronology I follow (cf. Funke 1980a, 32n.16; *contra* Kelly 1975, 21-41) – Elis had to bear the brunt of a Spartan-led military offensive had more to do with Sparta's internal politics and general foreign policy at the time and with the depressed economic condition of parts of the Peloponnese after a long and debilitating war. For the expedition proved to be 'a kind of process for restocking the whole Peloponnese' (3.2.26; cf. 5.2.19). It was conducted when Sparta was approaching the peak of her imperialist expansiveness, directly ruling most of the former Athenian Empire (Chapter 6) and covertly supporting the Younger Cyrus' attempted palace revolution (Chapter 11). As for Agis, apart from wishing to revenge himself upon the *damos* of Elis (like Kleomenes I upon the *dêmos* of Athens in *c.*506), he needed a successful command to compensate for his failure to convict his co-king Pausanias on a capital charge arising out of his settlement at Athens (cf. Chapters 8 and 14). Agis clearly did not believe that Pausanias had employed the best method of handling the internal affairs of a disaffected subordinate ally. Indeed, his campaign against Elis points up as sharply as one could wish the diametrically opposed constructions that might be placed upon the weasel-word *autonomia*.

Like Sir Isaiah Berlin's 'liberty', *autonomia* was really two concepts, not one. Positively, as its etymology would suggest, it meant the right of a state to live according to its own political norms, to make its own laws and to conduct legal justice as it wished – in other words, to have the *politeia* it freely chose for itself (cf. Ste. Croix 1972, 98-9). Since in practice such internal freedom was conditional upon *eleutheria*, a state's freedom to conduct its foreign relations as it preferred, the two tended to shade into each other and could be used interchangeably (e.g. 6.3.8). Negatively, *autonomia* could (but need not) connote freedom from any or all of the following: compulsory tribute enforced by a hegemonial power (e.g. Thuc. 1.19, 139.1; 5.31.4; contrast 5.18.5) as opposed to voluntary contributions (e.g. M/L 67); harmosts (6.3.18) or the exercise of magisterial power in one's own state by any official of another state (6.5.4); a foreign garrison (5.1.34,36; DS 15.20.3); and the occupation, control or alienation by whatever means of one state's territory by another state (Thuc. 5.32.2,79.1; 3.2.30). The scope for divergent interpretations or persuasive definitions of this loaded concept was therefore distressingly wide (cf. generally Ostwald 1982). But in one respect at least there can be no doubting that Pausanias' treatment of Athens in 403 ran very much counter to the general trend of Spartan policy towards her subordinate allies. For although Sparta consistently proclaimed her absolute belief in the principle of autonomy, and may even have had the principle enshrined verbally in her individual treaties with her Peloponnesian League allies (as she did in her treaty of 418/7 with Argos: Thuc. 5.77.5,79.1; with Ostwald 1982, 5-6), she 'lavished great care on ensuring that her allies should be governed oligarchically in accordance solely with her own convenience' (Thuc. 1.19; cf. 144.2). *Autonomia*, that is to say, belonged to the language of power-politics, being 'a concession which [major powers] extend to states less powerful than themselves' (Ostwald 1982, 8).

In a fundamental article discussing the character of the Athenian Empire Ste. Croix (1954/5, 20n.5) listed the principal occasions on which Sparta intervened militarily either to replace a democracy with an oligarchy or an oligarchy with an even narrower and so more 'convenient', that is loyal and easy to control, oligarchy. Two of these occasions will be considered fully later in this chapter. But Agis' expedition against Elis should, I believe, be added to the list, even though constitutional interference was not an announced objective and the peace terms (unlike those for Mantineia in 385 and Phleious in 379) did not include the enforced termination of democracy at Elis. Two main arguments may be advanced in support of this view.

In the first place, there is the one word chosen by Xenophon (3.2.23) to summarize what he with technical propriety calls 'the resolution of the Ephors and Assembly (*ekklêsia*)'. The word, *sôphronisai*, could have a purely moral meaning, something like 'to make the Eleians come to their senses (or see reason)'; and indeed, according to Xenophon, the Spartan ultimatum insisted that it was right (*dikaion*) for the Eleians to grant autonomy to the outlying communities (*perioikides poleis*) in Pisatis to the north and Triphylia to the south of the Alpheios River (cf. Niese 1910, 3-19; Gschnitzer 1958, 7-17). However, by Xenophon's day *sôphrosunê* in a political context had acquired a peculiarly oligarchic connotation. One of the nicest examples of this usage is a passage of Thucydides (8.64.5) in which the historian without any obvious irony characterises the revolted allies of Athens who had overthrown their democratic governments and become oligarchies as 'having received *sôphrosunê*'.

The second argument emerges from Xenophon's brief and allusive narrative (3.2.23-9).[4] The first campaign (summer 402) was aborted following an earthquake that the superstitious Agis (cf. Thuc. 3.89.1; and the story of the alleged paternity of Latychidas: Chapter 7) interpreted as a sign of divine displeasure. But the allies were again called out by the Ephors in the same (civil) year (probably spring 401), and all except the Boiotians and Corinthians duly followed where Sparta led. Elis was not in a state of active *stasis*; indeed, the invasion had united most Eleians solidly behind the democratic leader Thrasydaios. But, 'as one will find in most cities' (to borrow a remark Xenophon made in another context, 5.2.9), there was a faction led by the fabulously wealthy Xenias which wanted what the Greeks euphemistically called 'newer things' (*neôtera pragmata*), that is revolutionary change – in this case from democracy to oligarchy. Xenias and his faction were eager to get the credit for bringing Elis back into alignment with Sparta, who – as Xenophon did not need to spell out – would then support this 'convenient' faction as the legitimate oligarchic government of Elis. But what Xenophon could and should have mentioned (as he does in a parallel case later, 5.3.13) is that the pro-Spartan would-be oligarchic leader was both a *xenos* of Agis and a *proxenos* of the Spartans (Paus. 3.8.4). The fact that he and his comrades were not then in exile, the usual lot of the more extreme opponents of existing regimes (cf. Balogh 1943; Seibert 1979), is probably a tribute to the moderation of Thrasydaios as well as to the deep-rooted stability of this long-established democracy; but that is no reason for not suspecting collusion between Agis and Xenias before the expedition was voted by the Spartan Assembly. Confirmation, if it be needed, may be derived from the sequel. When the attempt by Xenias' men to massacre Thrasydaios and other leading democrats misfired badly and the oligarchs were forced into exile, Agis installed them together with a harmost and garrison at nearby Epitalion. The clear implication is that they would be restored when Elis was eventually compelled to bow before the repeated ravaging of her territory – as she was in 400.

It is to be presumed that the exiles were indeed restored, perhaps as a condition of the imposed settlement, with an eye to their future utility to Sparta; this had happened at Athens in 404 (Chapter 14). But Xenophon's silence about the political aspects of the settlement leaves us in the dark. However, it does not appear that *sôphrosunê* in the sense of oligarchic government was forced on the Eleians (cf. Perlman 1964, 74-5) – unlike the Phleiasians in 379. No doubt Sparta represented this abstention as respect for *autonomia*, and King Pausanias may have advocated the settlement on precisely those grounds. But this was also a prudent concession to the strength of anti-Spartan feeling mustered under the banner of democracy. Instead, Sparta was content to require Elis to pull down her city-wall (cf. Paus. 3.8.5), disband her trireme fleet (DS 14.34.1) and of course relinquish all claims to the 'perioikic cities'. Now that Elis was deprived of her mini-empire and effectively insulated from other potentially or actually

---

[4] Diodoros (14.17.6-12) has a circumstantial account, irreconcilable with that of Xenophon, of a campaign led by Pausanias not Agis. If this is not simply a combination of fantasy and mistaken identity (as at 14.97.5 and 15.82.6,83.1-2), it could belong in spring 402.

dissident Spartan allies by a sanitary cordon of solidly pro-Spartan regimes, Sparta could afford the 'generous' act of permitting Elis to retain her presidency of the Olympic shrine and Games – in the fervent hope that there would be no repetition of her humiliating exclusion in 420.

Another of Xenophon's silences is also noteworthy. One of the communities 'liberated' from Elis in 400 was Triphylian Skillous; and it was because the second Peace of 371 forced Elis (again) to recognize formally the autonomy of the Marganians, Skillountians and (other) Triphylians that Elis revolted from Sparta once more (6.5.2). But in connection with the 400 settlement Xenophon fails to mention Skillous, and this must be for a very personal reason. For it was here that less than a decade later he was granted a magnificent estate by the Spartans, doubtless through the good offices of Agesilaos, and here that he stayed until the Eleians' successful reclamation of the area in 371 necessitated his departure (cf. Chapter 5). The explanation of his silence about Skillous in 400, and indeed his very scanty information on Eleian affairs thereafter until an oligarchic Elis rejoined the Spartan camp in the mid-360s, is surely that the Eleian democracy liked this cuckoo in their nest as little as Xenophon liked that regime.

For Xenophon's connections and sympathies were with the Xenias-es of his world, not the Thrasydaios-es, with the men who 'had the best interests of the Peloponnese at heart' (7.4.35; cf. 7.5.1) and who, for example, at the Peloponnesian League Congress of 383/2 said what the Spartans wanted to hear when asked 'to give what each considered to be the best advice for the Peloponnese as a whole' (5.2.20). If Xenophon was a Spartan by adoption, he was as much if not more an adopted Peloponnesian. This was not, however, merely a matter of private sentiment. Rather, Xenophon formed part of the network of 'best men' through whom Agesilaos sought to control Peloponnesian affairs on an oligarchic basis in what Agesilaos took to be Sparta's interest (cf. Cawkwell 1976a, 71-4). As an exile from Athens, Xenophon could not of course have played a role in this network comparable to that of, say, Agesilaos' *xenos* Prokles of Phleious (7.1.1-11; cf. 5.3.13). But if there is any truth to the report that Xenophon was created a *proxenos* of the Spartans (Diog. Laert. 2.51), and if this was not a purely honorific title, the likeliest function that he in common with other *proxenoi* would have performed was that of diplomacy (cf. Mosley 1971a, 432). Not of course public, interstate diplomacy, but private, informal, secret diplomacy between Agesilaos and his Peloponnesian protégés. Such a roving brief for gathering political intelligence in a world without mass media would have been invaluable. His estate near Olympia was admirably placed for a clearing-house of information.

Whatever the merits of that speculation, Xenophon certainly did make his contribution to another of Agesilaos' techniques for binding the alliance more closely to Sparta and to himself, by sending his two sons to be put through the Spartan *agôgê* (cf. Chapter 5). We do not know whether Agesilaos invented this technique, which could be interpreted on one level as a response to Spartiate *oliganthrôpia*. But it was typical of him to combine ideology and pragmatism in this way, recalling as it does Rome's practice with the children of client-kings or the Soviet Union's establishment of cadre schools for young communists from other countries. By 381 such *agôgê*-trained foreigners were sufficiently numerous to have acquired a collective title (*trophimoi xenoi*, literally 'nurtured foreigners') and to make a substantial contribution as volunteers to Agesipolis' Olynthos campaign of that year (5.3.9; cf. Plat. *Protag.* 342bc).

After the settlement of 400 we hear precious litle of Elis' relations with Sparta. The fact that she fought on the Spartan side in the Corinthian War (4.2.16 – thereby falsifying the 'Theban' prediction of 3.5.12) must have been partly due to Sparta's relative leniency, and as late as 373 (6.2.3) Elis was still fulfilling the military obligations of her alliance to Sparta. In 371, however, after Leuktra, Elis' simmering resentment at being deprived of what she considered her 'perioikic cities' led her to secede from the Peloponnesian League. As in 421, she refused to swear to a Peace sponsored by Sparta, in this case the second Peace of 371 (6.5.2). Elis was instrumental also in persuading the Thebans to lead the massive invasions of Lakonia and Messenia in winter 370/69 (Chapter 14) and played an important part in the invasion itself (DS 15.62-3, 64.6ff.; 6.5.19,23; cf. Chapter 12). In 369 Elis was still in the anti-Spartan camp (7.1.18; 7.2.5), but between then and 365 *stasis* had apparently resulted in the establishment of a pro-Spartan oligarchy (7.4.13,15). This was partly because of a territorial dispute with the democratic Arkadian League, which indirectly led to protracted war (including fighting actually within the sacred precinct at Olympia in 364) and a fatal split within the Arkadian League (7.4.12-35). The oligarchic regime survived these vicissitudes, maintained its alliance with Sparta even after the effective end of the Peloponnesian League in 365, and fought on the Spartan side at Mantineia in 362 (7.5.1,18). But the alliance she concluded thereafter with Athens, the Mantineian-led rump of the Arkadian League and Phleious (Tod 144=SV 290; new readings in *SEG* 29.90) did not include a thoroughly debilitated and diplomatically isolated Sparta.

(ii) Corinth[5]

In 432 the Corinthians had been particularly active in pressing the Spartans to begin the Athenian War, alleging (falsely) that Athens had broken the terms of the Thirty Years' Peace (cf. Chapter 2). In this they were at one with the Spartans. But in 402/1, as we saw in passing above, Corinth was at odds with Sparta (*dusmenês*: 3.2.25). To put it more precisely, dominant opinion within the exceedingly long-lived and apparently stable Corinthian oligarchy had once again swung against its Spartan *hêgemôn*, as it had on a number of previous and scarcely less important occasions from the late sixth century on (cf. Cartledge 1979, 301). To go no farther back than 421, the Corinthians like the Eleians had refused to swear to the Peace of Nikias and by careful manoeuvring had managed to prise apart the *rapprochement* between Sparta and Athens, which they disliked not least because since about 460 (Thuc. 1.103.4; cf. Ste. Croix 1972, 212-13) they had entertained a great, though intermittent, hatred for the Athenians.

---

[5] J.B. Salmon, *Wealthy Corinth. A History of the City to 338 B.C.* (Oxford, 1984) ch. 24, which appeared too late for consideration here, offers some very different views; but see my review in *CR* n.s. 35 (1985), 115-17.

The original cause of that hatred was the defection to Athens of Megara, the neighbour and longstanding rival of Corinth who had nevertheless until then preferred co-existence with Corinth within the Peloponnesian League to outright subservience to Athens. After the return of Megara to the Peloponnesian fold in 446 she never again made a clean break with Sparta, despite three years of democratic government in the early part of the Athenian War and subsequent spasms of defiance (cf. generally Legon 1981). So Corinth's reasons for hating Athens after 446 had less to do with Megara than with the general decline in her economic, military and political power that Athens was chiefly responsible for.

This hatred surfaced most spectacularly at Sparta in 404 at the meetings of the Spartan Assembly and the Peloponnesian League Congress (typically not distinguished by Xenophon) held to decide what treatment to mete out to the now at last defeated Athens. The Spartans and the majority of the allies agreed to disarm Athens and enrol her as a subordinate member of the Peloponnesian League, but many allies including the Corinthians were of the view that Athens should suffer the fate she had herself inflicted on Skione and other states and be wiped off the face of the earth (2.2.19-20; Andok. 3.21; Plut. *Lys.* 15). Sparta claimed to have been moved to spare Athens by sentiment, but the Corinthians (rightly – see Chapter 14) suspected her of harbouring less high-flown motives of *Realpolitik*. Whereupon they, like the Boiotians, adopted a posture of outright opposition to all Spartan directives, giving sanctuary to at least one democratic exile from Athens in 404/3 (Aisch. 2.178), and consistently refusing to contribute troops to League expeditions against Athens in 403, Elis in 402/1, and Persia in 399 (probably) and 396 (cf. Ste. Croix 1972, 342-5).

In this policy the Corinthians were led by Timolaos, who – like Euphron of Sikyon in the 360s (7.1.44) – allegedly changed his coat from being a rabid Lakonizer to becoming an equally rabid anti-Spartan (Hell. Ox. 7.3). In 396 or 395 he compounded the felony in the eyes of Sparta by accepting Persian money to help organize a revolt against Sparta and thus necessitate the recall of Agesilaos (3.5.1; cf. Chapter 12). Although the money was the occasion rather than the cause (so, rightly, Hell. Ox. 7.2), precisely such a revolt was engineered in the second half of 395 by a quadruple alliance of Corinth, Argos, Athens and the Boiotians (minus Orchomenos) assisted by sundry other central and northern Greek states.

Corinth's attitude to Athens at the meetings in Sparta of 404 can be explained partly by the fact that the balance of economic benefit from the Athenian War seemed to her – or more especially to Corinth's ruling class – to have been tipped most unfairly in favour of Sparta. The progressively more high-handed attitude of Sparta towards the Peloponnesian League as a whole in the years following 404 (cf. Kahrstedt 1922, 92-6, 291-4) was particularly galling to Corinth as the single most important ally apart from the Boiotians (thanks to her strategic location athwart the Isthmus). If there had been truth to Corinth's claim in 421 that the Spartans were conniving at the 'enslavement' of the Peloponnese, there was yet more substance to the claim of Elis in 402 that it was the Greeks as a whole whom the Spartans were now enslaving (DS 14.17.6). This claim the Corinthians endorsed (3.5.25), and Timolaos and his associates would doubtless have expressed the same sort of complaints about powerlessness and lack of consultation against their *hêgemôn* as the Mytilenaians had against theirs (Athens) in 428 – ironically enough to the Spartans (Thuc. 3.9-14).

Foreign relations, however, and domestic politics were inevitably too closely interlinked in Corinth as elsewhere for the one not to have an important effect on the other. Not all Corinthian oligarchs were always necessarily pro-Spartan, as the behaviour of Timolaos amply illustrates, but all those Corinthians who remained actively pro-Spartan after 404 and especially after 395 were almost by definition extreme oligarchs. They included men like the resilient Pasimelos, who was certainly one of those who 'had the best interests of the Peloponnese at heart', almost certainly one of Xenophon's major sources of information for Corinthian events of the 390s, and very likely a member of Agesilaos' Peloponnesian circle (4.4.6; cf. Cawkwell 1979, 209n.). Since such men could now be represented as unpatriotic, and since the course of the Corinthian War involved ever closer political co-operation between Corinth and democratic Argos, the way was steadily paved for one of the more remarkable political experiments of Classical Greece, the union of Corinth and Argos.

Since our principal detailed source is Xenophon (4.4.1-6;cf. DS 14.92), our knowledge of this development is unfortunately obscured both by bias and by technical, especially chronological imprecision. The two main features are, however, tolerably clear: that the union was born amid a particularly bloody episode of *stasis*, something which Corinth had apparently never suffered before, and that the Corinthians who most favoured the union preferred the absorption of the *polis* of Corinth into an enlarged 'Argos' to the forcible reimposition on a nominally 'autonomous' Corinth of a 'conveniently' pro-Spartan extreme oligarchy led by Pasimelos and his kind.

There had been examples of common citizenship in genuinely federal states in Greece, such as the Boiotian and Chalkidian confederacies; but the separate identity of the constituent member-states was not in principle reduced thereby (cf. Chapter 14). There had also been isolated cases of *isopoliteia*, the legal entitlement of citizens of state A to exercise the citizen rights of and in state B and *vice versa*, for example between Athens and the Samian democracy in 405 (M/L 94; cf. Gawantka 1975, 178-97). But never before 392 or 389 – depending on whether one adopts the chronology of Tuplin 1982 or Griffith 1950 – had two adjoining *poleis* torn up their mutual boundary-stones and merged their identities to create a single *polis*. Had the example of Corinth and Argos been followed to its logical conclusion, Aristotle would have had no cause to lament the notorious failure of the Greeks to unite politically in the enjoyment of a single *politeia*; but then he would have had no cause or opportunity to write the *Politics* either, for that work is premised on the ideal notion of the irreducibly separate identities of the myriad *poleis* that collectively comprised the politically vague concept of 'Hellas'.

Looked at more parochially, the union has two main points of interest: the effect of any constitutional change on those Corinthians who fell within the operative definition of citizenship in the new, enlarged *polis*; and the effect of the union on geopolitical relations within the Peloponnesian League. As Aristotle sagely observed (*Pol.* 1306a9ff.), 'an oligarchy which is of one mind within itself is not easily destroyed from within'. That requisite *homonoia* was fatally disturbed by the Athenian War and the subsequent behaviour of Sparta. For the first time in Corinth's history we hear explicitly (if DS 14.86.1 is correctly emended to read *dêmokratias*) of an influential group of Corinthians who desired some form of democracy, though their earlier existence seems to be implied by the Oxyrhynchos Historian (7.3). Whether Timolaos was one of these is a separate question, and perhaps it is more likely that he was not. For in order to break the grip of 'good order' (*eunomia*: 4.4.6), that is oligarchy, and so fulfil the essential precondition of political union as opposed to mere military alliance with Argos, it was judged that a massacre of the leading oligarchic ultras was also necessary together with the installation on Akrokorinthos of an Argive garrison.

The purge of the oligarchs was timed to coincide with a religious festival, a device no less familiar in the modern than in the ancient world but particularly repugnant to the pious Xenophon, who pointedly described the staunchly pro-Spartan Tegean oligarch Stasippos as 'the sort of man who was averse to killing many of his fellow-citizens' (6.5.9). The purge succeeded in achieving its immediate objectives, but this was at the cost of producing an influential cell of highly embittered oligarchs who gained the full military and diplomatic backing of Agesilaos' Sparta. It was ostensibly on their behalf that Agesilaos, fired up by *philetairia*, insisted in 386 on the dissolution of the union and the restoration of the exiles to power in the recreated Corinthian oligarchy. Only then would he agree to the Peace of Antalkidas (Xen. *Ages.* 2.21). His initial show of opposition to the Peace was not of course made because he was genuinely some kind of 'Panhellenist' who objected on principle to any concordat between Sparta and the King of Persia (cf. Chapter 11). The Peace suited his conception of Sparta's interests only too well. But in order for the Peace to perform the function envisaged by Agesilaos, that of atomizing Sparta's subordinate allies and enemies so that she might the more easily rule them, Corinth had first to be disaggregated from Argos and reconstituted as an oligarchic *polis* before she could be admitted to the framework of the Peace. It was now the turn of the democrats to eat the bitter fruits of exile – at Argos naturally (DS 15.40.3). As for the rest of the Corinthian citizenry, they were, according to Xenophon's information (5.1.34), 'happy to receive back again those who had been exiles before'. This is sheer 'humbug' (Griffith 1950, 254n.55) – unless by 'citizens' Xenophon meant the few rich Corinthians whose property qualified them to exercise full citizen rights.

Besides his general concern to establish 'convenient' oligarchies led by his comrades throughout the Spartan sphere Agesilaos had a pressing geopolitical reason for wanting to break the union. So long as Corinth (and preferably Megara too) was a loyal ally, passage through the Isthmus could be more or less regulated to suit Sparta, other things being equal. In order to keep Corinth loyal, it was useful for Sparta to be able to stand forth as her champion against the aggressive intent of Argos, Sparta's natural rival for hegemony of the Peloponnese; this argument worked equally well for other states within the reach of Argos like Epidauros, Troizen, Phleious and Mantineia (cf. Grundy 1908, 84-5; Carlier 1977, 74n.46). In times of Spartan weakness (such as the later 460s or 421-418) these neat lines of demarcation became somewhat blurred. But as long as Sparta was able to prop up 'convenient' oligarchies or refrain from antagonizing unduly the few democracies she perforce tolerated within the Peloponnesian League, there was little risk of the system breaking down altogether. The union of Corinth and Argos threatened precisely that. Hence its forcible dissolution as a condition of their being admitted to the Peace of 386.

The restored Corinthian oligarchs led by Pasimelos served Sparta well, proving to be 'extremely reliable' (5.3.27) right down to 366/5 (6.2.3; 6.4.18; 6.5.29; 7.1.18-19,40; 7.2.2). In that year, however, exhausted by the repeated passage of armies through their ravaged territory, the Corinthians once again took the initiative within the League in opposing Spartan policy. They did not wish to become part of the Boiotian alliance; but, as they told the Spartans at the meeting in Sparta that perhaps provided the dramatic occasion for Isokrates' *Archidamos* oration, they saw no purpose or profit in continuing to fight the Boiotians either (7.4.8). In so declaring they were speaking for most of the remaining Peloponnesian League allies, and in seeking their *hêgemôn's* permission to make a separate peace with the Boiotians the Corinthians were observing to the end the letter of their treaty with Sparta. Yet even so Xenophon (and no doubt Agesilaos) counted their action as a 'revolt' (7.2.2). Presumably this was chiefly because the Corinthians thereby recognized the autonomy of New Messene, something the Spartans under Agesilaos and then Archidamos stubbornly refused to do (7.1.27; 7.4.9; DS 15.89.1-2; Plut. *Ages*. 35.3; Polyb. 4.33.8-9). To all intents and purposes that was the end of the Peloponnesian League. Documentary proof in the shape of a treaty between Messene and Sikyon in autumn 365 (SV 285a = *SEG* 29.405) is soon to hand. But it is the composition of the respective alliances at the time of the Battle of Mantineia in 362 (7.5.1-5) that most graphically displays the irretrievable break-up of that handy instrument of Spartan domination.

(iii) Mantineia and Tegea

The political history of Arkadia and of Sparta's determination that 'Arkadia' should remain merely a geographical expression revolves around the ill-documented histories of Mantineia and Tegea. These were the two most powerful states in the region, both lying on its eastern flank. Since Arkadia's geographical situation made its control vital to Sparta's military and economic security, Sparta had decided to try to keep it weak politically through a determined divide-and-rule policy that was aimed above all at dividing Mantineia from Tegea. With just one or possibly two exceptions (the 460s and perhaps the late 490s) this policy succeeded remarkably well for almost two hundred years. Indeed, during the Athenian War the Mantineians and Tegeans actually came to blows (Thuc. 4.134), and in the period of unrest following the Peace of Nikias Tegea refused to join an anti-Spartan axis precisely because it included Mantineia.

But this policy had some costs as well as this major benefit for Sparta. If the two remained under the same Peloponnesian League umbrella for so long, this was largely because Sparta was obliged to allow Mantineia an unusual degree of separate development and genuine autonomy. When Mantineia became a democracy about 470 (cf. Andrewes 1952; Forrest 1960; but see O'Neil 1981, 337), Sparta if anything had to be even more circumspect in her dealings for fear of pushing Mantineia into the arms of democratic Argos. There were, however, limits to Sparta's toleration. It was one thing if Mantineia and Tegea cultivated their own alliances within and outside Arkadia and even fought each other with them. It was quite another when Mantineia's 'empire' (*archê*: Thuc. 5.69.1,81.1) in south-west Arkadia (Mainalia, Eutresia, Parrhasia) seemed to the Spartans to be threatening their own domestic security, as it did in the late 420s. The building and garrisoning of a fort at Kypsele in Parrhasia were interpreted by the Spartans as a hostile act, and in 421 they were happy to respond to one group of Parrhasians' request for aid, masking their intervention under the slogan of 'autonomy' for all Parrhasians from Mantineia (Thuc. 5.33).[6] Small wonder that the latter seized the opportunity to join the anti-Spartan coalition (Argos, Elis, Athens and Mantineia) that fought but lost the Battle of Mantineia in 418.

Sparta's resounding victory here prompted a bout of successful pro-oligarchic interventions in Achaia, Sikyon and even Argos (Thuc. 5.81.2,82.1). But with Mantineia – as with the still more important Boiotians in 420 (Thuc. 5.39.3 etc.) – Sparta chose to conclude a separate and more tolerant agreement, a truce that was to last for thirty years (Thuc. 5.81.1; 5.2.2). The precise nature of this agreement is unknown, and its very existence has both puzzled those scholars who do believe there was a formal organization that we call the Peloponnesian League (e.g. A. Andrewes in Gomme 1970, 148) and confirmed in their disbelief those who do not. But there is really no need for puzzlement. The oligarchy imposed on Argos was highly unstable and in fact very soon overthrown, although the Spartans did not of course relax their support for the oligarchs (Hell. Ox. 7.2). So the Spartans had to take precautions against a future *rapprochement* between Mantineia and Argos. On the other hand, they would not tolerate a repetition of the Mantineian 'empire' on their own borders. So while the agreement compelled Mantineia to renounce that, she was left genuinely autonomous in the enjoyment of her wall and her democracy – and perhaps given an express guarantee to that effect. For reasons that will emerge the hand of King Pleistoanax, who had held one of his very few commands when he intervened in Parrhasia in 421, may surely be detected behind this reasonable accommodation that formally governed relations between Sparta and Mantineia until very nearly the end of the Corinthian War.

During that War, however, like the Eleians during the Athenian War, the Mantineians chalked up a number of 'black marks' against their name. In the sight of dominant opinion-formers like Agesilaos these amounted to 'being disloyal' (5.2.1-2; cf. 5.1.29). They had sent and presumably sold grain to Argos, whose land the Spartans had twice ravaged severely (4.4.19; 4.7.5-7; Xen. *Ages.* 2.17). They had more than once declined to contribute their stipulated contingent to Peloponnesian League armies, invoking – like the Phleiasians (4.2.16) – the existence of a sacred truce (*ekecheiria*); although this

---

[6] The mention of Sellasia in a new inscription from Argos of probably about this date (Mitsos 1983, line 14) hints at Argive machinations (cf. Cartledge 1979, 253).

was probably a legitimate grounds for exemption (cf. Thuc. 5.30.3; with Ste. Croix 1972, 120), the Spartans took it as a mere pretext. Moreover, when they had served they had done so reluctantly (cf. 5.2.7) and poorly, being unreasonably fearful of Iphikrates' peltasts (4.4.17; cf. Chapter 12) and unseasonably delighted by the Spartans' disaster near Lechaion in 390 (4.5.18; cf. Plut. *Ages.* 22.8). The Spartans therefore decided to punish the Mantineians and prevent them from being disloyal again, and there is no doubt (as there was in the case of Elis) that the major means of achieving these ends was envisaged by the Spartans as the abolition of democracy.

The proud symbol of Mantineia's independence was her city-wall. This had originally been built when Mantineia's constituent villages (four or five of them: cf. Hodkinson/Hodkinson 1981, 261-5, 246-56) were synoecized (literally 'housed together') to form one centralized political community with a civic centre (*agora*), council-chamber and the other defining physical characteristics of a Greek *polis*. The date of the synoecism is disputed (cf. Hodkinson/Hodkinson 1981, 256-61); but it had indisputably been a fact of Mantineian life for at least three quarters of a century when the Spartans in 385 demanded that the Mantineians should pull their city-wall down. This demand was in line with their general distaste for such constructions within their alliance (Sparta itself being wall-less; cf. Chapter 12), but it was only a preliminary to their far more radical ultimate objective. Perceiving this, the Mantineians prepared to withstand a long siege.

Xenophon not unexpectedly presents the affair as if it were a purely internal quarrel between Sparta and Mantineia, *hêgemôn* and subordinate ally. But in Diodoros, who records it shortly after the denunciatory, anti-Spartan preface to his fifteenth Book, it is but one episode in the saga of Sparta's exploitation of the Peace of Antalkidas. Unfortunately for Mantineia the Athenians chose to interpret the Peace in such a way as to rule out their aiding her, and the sources who credit the Thebans with sending aid are guilty of fiction (cf. Buckler 1980a). The sober truth was that Mantineia was left to face alone a Spartan (and presumably Peloponnesian: *contra* Hack 1978, 217-18n.21) offensive that was ideological as well as purely military. For after concluding the siege expeditiously (cf. Chapter 12) the Spartans did not only compel the Mantineians to pull down their wall and abolish their democracy but went to the extraordinary lengths of 'dioikizing' their *polis*, that is breaking it up into its original four or five villages. Xenophon, who was deeply in sympathy with this programme, could not be a more valuable witness both for the details and for the underlying 'philosophy'.

In 385, it appears, the Mantineian citizen-body was divided politically in two different ways. There was, first, an ideological division between the 'best men', that is the oligarchs, who desired revolutionary change, and the vast majority who favoured the existing democratic *politeia*. Secondly, there was a division in respect of foreign policy between, on one hand, the oligarchs, who apparently favoured Sparta to a man (as one would expect in such a situation), and, on the other, two groups of democrats, of which one was pursuing a pro-Argos line and the other was hoping in a utopian way to be able to adopt an independent stance. Agesilaos would have known that the oligarchs would support the coming

Spartan intervention whichever of the two kings was appointed to lead it, and he would not have wished to unite the democrats in solidary opposition to a notorious foe of democracy (cf. Chapter 12). By claiming exemption on the spurious ground that 'the city of the Mantineians' (that is, the probably democratic *polis* of Mantineia) had performed signal service for his father against the revolted Messenians seventy or eighty years previously, Agesilaos was really seeking to embarrass his much younger, less influential, and emulous co-king Agesipolis.

For whereas Agesilaos' hereditary ties of friendship (6.5.4) were to be found among the oligarchs (note the Mantineian father and son both called Kyniskos, recalling the Eurypontid Kyniska: cf. Tuplin 1977b, 8-10; further Chapter 9), the hereditary connections of Agesipolis lay with the Mantineian democratic leaders (*prostatai tou dêmou*), perhaps specifically with those who were pro-Argos (*argolizontes*). Agesipolis' grandfather, Pleistoanax, was very likely responsible for the thirty-year truce concluded with Mantineia in *c.*417, as was suggested above, while his father, Pausanias, was so intimately connected to the democratic leaders of 385 that he actually came from his Tegean exile to Mantineia to intercede with his son for their lives as patron on behalf of his clients. This does not of course mean that Pausanias was in any sense a democrat but rather that he, unlike Agesilaos (and probably Agis before him), was prepared not merely to tolerate but actively to co-operate with long-established, stable democracies within the Peloponnesian League; compare his attitude to the restoration of democracy in 403 at Athens, then a subject-ally of Sparta (Chapter 14). Whether Agesipolis shared his father's view then or later is not certainly known, but he did bow to Pausanias' request and allow sixty of the democratic leaders to go into exile rather than be executed; some of these at least made their way to Athens (*IG* ii² 33.7-8; cf. Osborne 1982, 51-2). However, as Agesilaos had no doubt calculated, this act of clemency made Agesipolis highly unpopular not just with the Mantineian oligarchs but also with his own Spartan troops. The latter, if Xenophon (5.2.6) may be believed, so hated the democratic leaders that only the iron Spartan discipline restrained them from massacring them as they went into exile.

This single spark of clemency in any case did not mitigate the savagery of the settlement as a whole over which Agesipolis was obliged to preside. For the majority of Mantineians were hardly surprisingly not best pleased at being deprived of political power, and indeed of full political rights, and at having to pull down their homes and rebuild new ones in the now separately reconstituted villages. The wealthy landowners (*hoi echontes tas ousias*), by contrast, saw matters very differently: 'they now lived nearer to their estates, and they had also got rid of all the trouble they had had with the demagogues, since their government was now run on aristocratic lines' (5.2.7 – one of Xenophon's only two uses of the abusive term *dêmagôgoi*). It has rightly been commented that 'In this paragraph Xenophon expounds the secret of Spartan power in the Peloponnese, *viz.* prevention of urbanization, and support of and from the landed aristocracy' (Cawkwell 1979, 259-60n.; cf. 1976a, 72-3). What ought to be added is that, whereas this had been a 'natural' policy in the sixth century as Sparta built up her power through the development of the Peloponnesian League, in 385 in the case of a deep-rooted democracy like Mantineia it was a policy of outright reaction – besides being a clear violation of the autonomy clause of the Peace of Antalkidas (DS 15.5.1).

Moreover, it is not sufficiently appreciated that the *dioikismos* coupled with the abolition of democracy will have significantly worsened the economic condition of the poor Mantineian peasants on their 1-2 hectare farms in this overwhelmingly agrarian society (cf. Hodkinson/Hodkinson 1981, esp. 290-1, for the Mantineian political economy). For in the absence of the legal safeguards provided by a democratic constitution – even a relatively moderate one such as that of Mantineia seems to have been (cf. Arist. *Pol.* 1318b27-32) – 'those possessing the landed properties' could once more reduce them to the condition of exploited clients burdened with debt and compulsory labour service (cf. Scott 1977, esp. 38n.7; Ste. Croix 1981, Index s.v. 'democracy ... important role in protecting poor against exploitation and oppression'). In his *Archidamos* (6.67) Isokrates virtually gives the game played by the *beltistoi* away. Referring to the outbreak of *stasis* throughout the Peloponnese after Leuktra and the subsequent invasion of Lakonia and Messenia, 'Archidamos' comments in his biased way on relations between rich and poor: 'social intercourse between them has so far broken down that the landed property-owners would rather cast their possessions into the sea than help the needy, while the poor prefer to tear away the property of the rich by force rather than receive it through a chance find.' The good old economic order, in other words, that had been guaranteed by Spartan hegemony, was temporarily in total disarray.

Once divided into their villages, the Mantineians provided their stipulated (hoplite) contingents to Peloponnesian League armies far more readily than heretofore (5.2.8,37) – just as the Theban oligarchic junta installed and propped up by Sparta in 382 'gave the Spartans even more help than they were asked to give' (5.2.36, cf. 27; see Chapter 14). This enthusiastic loyalty persisted up to and immediately after the Battle of Leuktra, at which time, Xenophon (6.4.18) pointedly comments, the Mantineians were aristocratically governed and the pro-Spartan oligarchic faction led by Stasippos were still alive to govern Tegea. But within eighteen months Mantineia had been resynoecized; democracy and the democratic exiles had been restored; and despite – or because of – the personal intervention of Agesilaos, work had begun on rebuilding the wall destroyed in 385 (6.5.3-5; cf. Underhill 1900, 255); Elis contributed the large sum of three talents towards its cost, rather as Thrasydaios had contributed two talents towards the return of the Athenian democratic exiles in 403 (above).

Worse was yet to come from Agesilaos' point of view. With Mantineian aid Stasippos and 800 fellow-adherents of Tegea's 'ancestral constitution' were exiled. Tegea, which had 'hitherto served as a kind of Lacedaemonian outpost' (David 1981, 84), became a democracy. Finally – horror of horrors – these two states combined successfully for the first time ever to establish a Pan-Arkadian Federation (*koinon*; cf. Freeman 1893, 154-62; Larsen 1968, 180-95). This was almost pan-Arkadian in fact as well as name. Orchomenos stood aloof through hatred of Mantineia (6.5.11), and it was presumably the descendants of Agis II's clients (cf. Paus. 3.8.8) who kept Heraia loyal to Sparta. But the remainder created a workable federal machinery, political and military, centred on a new federal capital at Megalopolis. This was completed in 368 and incorporated no less than forty communities on Sparta's northern border (cf. Bury 1898; Roy 1971, 597-8,590-1). Xenophon characteristically omitted its foundation but could not conceal its existence (7.5.5).

If anything was needed to strengthen the wings of this fledgling federal state, it was a Spartan invasion led by Agesilaos to restore his exiled friends and *xenoi* to power in Tegea. This duly occurred, even though it was approaching midwinter and so well past the normal campaigning season of 370 (6.5.10-21; Xen. *Ages.* 2.23). By showing the flag and ravaging, Agesilaos considered that he had 'done something to restore Spartan morale' (6.5.21; cf. Plut. *Ages.* 30.7). His lasting achievement was to precipitate Epameinondas' first invasion of the Peloponnese and more especially Lakonia and Messenia. Sparta's refusal to countenance the autonomy of New Messene led to the cessation of the Peloponnesian League, but the fragile integument of the Arkadian League was also soon rent asunder by tensions between Mantineia and Tegea, pro-Thebans and pro-Spartans, democrats and oligarchs (cf. Thompson 1983a). The paradoxical outcome was that a democratic Tegea fought under Epameinondas at Mantineia in 362 against an oligarchic, pro-Spartan Mantineia. The confederacy was thus dismantled, but an attempt to desynoecize the ex-federal capital of Megalopolis in 361 was a failure (DS 15.94.1-3) and Megalopolis survived to block Sparta's easiest route of military access to Messenia (cf. Cartledge 1979, 118,187) – a permanent bone in the throat of the Spartans like, say, Krak des Chevaliers in that of the Muslims of the Levant.

(iv) Phleious (see Fig. 12.2)

We hear explicitly of no domestic opposition at Sparta to the forcible interventions in the internal affairs of Elis, Corinth and Mantineia; rather the contrary, in the case of Mantineia. But with regard to Sparta's hard line towards Phleious after the Corinthian War Xenophon speaks revealingly with two voices, thereby reflecting the strong division of contemporary opinion within Sparta itself. In the *Agesilaos* (2.21) Xenophon says that his hero had opposed the Peace of Antalkidas until he had compelled Corinth and Thebes to restore the Lakonizers they had expelled. In the same way, Xenophon continues, Agesilaos later restored the Phleiasians who had been exiled in the same, pro-Spartan cause. 'Possibly some,' he comments, 'may censure these actions on other grounds, but at least it is clear that they were motivated by *philetairia.*' What those 'other grounds' might be Xenophon delicately passes over as matter unfit for an encomium. But in the *Hellenika* the veil slips sufficiently for us to get an inkling of the kind of foreign policy that Sparta might have adopted towards Phleious had the dominant role in Spartan policymaking not been played by Agesilaos.

Phleious, given its crucial strategic location (cf. Chapter 12), had probably been allied to Sparta since the third quarter of the sixth century and a member of the Peloponnesian League proper from its inception. The hostility of neighbouring Argos helped keep Phleious loyal to Sparta throughout the fifth century. But some time before 394 (4.2.16) or at latest 391 (4.4.15) Phleious had become the third known democracy within the Peloponnesian League (5.2.10; 5.3.16,21; cf. Legon 1967, 326-8; *contra* Thompson 1970, esp. 230n.20) and a less 'convenient' ally. Phleious, like Mantineia, was availing herself of her strategic importance to snatch this constitutional advantage; but, as so often happened in a political revolution like this, a group of extreme oligarchs found themselves forced into exile. Naturally, they appealed to Sparta to restore them, although it would appear from Xenophon's phraseology (4.4.15; contrast 5.2.9) that they had been exiled more for their opposition to democracy than for their pro-Spartan attitude. Equally naturally, the Phleiasians feared that the Spartans would attempt to restore them by force and, utterly reasonably in light of the experience of the shortlived Megarian democracy in 424 (Thuc. 4.71), therefore refused on one or more occasions in or before 391 to admit a Spartan garrison (4.4.15).

For this refusal and for invoking the 'gods and heroes' exemption from contributing to a League army by declaring a sacred truce (4.2.16; see above for Mantineia) the Phleiasians could be charged with being disloyal to Sparta during the Corinthian War (cf. 5.2.1). But it was not as easy for Agesilaos to use these acts of disloyalty as *casus belli* against Phleious as it was in the case of Mantineia. For in 390 the Phleiasians had after all admitted, indeed requested, a Spartan garrison (to enable them to resist Iphikrates' peltasts) and perhaps also a Spartan harmost (cf. Parke 1930, 64), and in 388 Phleious had again served as a muster-station for the Peloponnesian League army (4.7.3). Indeed, Phleious was so well behaved between 390 and 386 that in 386 the Spartans restored to the Phleiasians 'their city and their laws just as they had been when they took the place over' (4.4.15). That formulation of Xenophon is richly eloquent of Sparta's normal procedure in such cases, but more specifically of course it points the enormous contrast between Sparta's treatment of democratic Phleious before and after the Peace of Antalkidas.

There was, it would seem, no clause in that Peace that required the restoration of political exiles (cf. Cawkwell 1981a, 80-3). But when the exiled oligarchic ultras from Phleious saw how Sparta had dealt with Mantineia's democracy, they judged the moment opportune to renew their appeal to Sparta to restore them, pointing out that it was only after they had been exiled that Phleious had been a disloyal ally. Thucydides' Nikias (6.12.1) had rightly observed in 415 that exiles were the kind of people whose interest it was to lie cleverly at the expense of their neighbours, and Machiavelli was shrewdly to note that exiles are men whose minds are distorted by their wishes. But what the Phleiasian exiles had to say was good enough for the Spartan Ephors of (probably) 384, who – perhaps acting on their own account and without taking the matter to the Spartan Assembly (cf. Mosley 1979, 196) – recommended rather than ordered Phleious to restore them.

This scrupulous regard for legality contrasts strongly with the sequel, but there were, I think, several reasons why Sparta exceptionally respected the autonomy of democratic Phleious as long as she did, apart from the city's strategic importance. It appears that there was a less extreme oligarchic faction within Phleious which, although it of course wanted a change back to oligarchy (5.2.9), was nevertheless more prepared to work with the democracy than those oligarchs who had been exiled. Secondly, there was no pro-Argos faction within the Phleiasian democratic leadership, as there was at Mantineia. Finally, the democratic leaders on the whole conducted a prudently moderate policy and were able to carry the Phleiasian Assembly with them. Thus in *c*.384 they accommodatingly put the Ephors' request to the vote, and the citizenry voted not only to recall the exiles but also to restore to them all property to which their title was indisputable, to compensate from public funds those who had bought any of the property in question, and to try all disputed cases of ownership in the courts (5.2.10). In practice, however, restoration of the *status quo ante* proved a far more ticklish matter.

If the practical problems were anything like those caused by Alexander the Great's notorious Exiles Decree of 324 (cf. Tod 201-2 = Heisserer 1980, chs 5,8), it is hardly surprising that the wrangling was still going on in 381. But by then the issues were not merely pragmatic but ideological. The returned Phleiasian exiles probably wanted the Spartans to be called in as arbitrators (as they had been called in by the Lepreates in the 420s, above). But this request was refused by the Phleiasian democratic leaders, who also went out of their way to establish or maintain good relations with Agesipolis (5.3.10) by making a prompt and handsome donation to his Olynthos campaign of 381 – a move that might serve to weaken the case of those in Sparta like Agesilaos who were looking for a pretext to intervene and overthrow the democracy. In this they were mistaken. When the restored exiles again came to Sparta to plead in person for Spartan intervention, 'it seemed to the Ephors that the Phleiasians were indeed acting outrageously and they ordered mobilization' (5.3.13).

There were two reasons for this change of heart, both directly connected with Agesilaos. In the first place, the relationship between Agesipolis and the Phleiasian democratic leaders was beginning to look – or could be made to look – like that between Pausanias and the Mantineian 'demagogues'. Secondly, the restored exiles now enjoyed the active support not only of their relatives and political friends as before (cf. 5.2.9) but also of the more moderate group of oligarchs, some of whom accompanied them to Sparta to make the case for immediate Spartan intervention. Their case was reinforced – at least in the eyes of those Spartans who considered they had a case – by the fine levied on these dissidents or traitors by their home government (5.3.11-12). But the reason why the personnel involved in this plea was such an important, indeed the decisive, factor in the matter only emerges now at this late stage of Xenophon's thoroughly disingenuous narrative. Agesilaos, he reports (5.3.13), was 'by no means unhappy' with the Ephors' decision (a palpable litotes), since 'the faction led by Podanemos, who were at that time among the restored exiles, were *xenoi* of his father Archidamos, while the faction of Prokles son of Hipponikos were his own *xenoi*'. Podanemos ('swift as the wind') was a name in current use at Sparta (4.8.10). But it was the presence in Sparta of Prokles, a man with whom Agesilaos personally had contracted a *xenia* rather than a *xenos* he had inherited from his father, that carried the day with the Ephors and so paved the way for Agesilaos to lead an army against Phleious.[7] It is not, I think, irrelevant that

---

[7] With his marvellously Spartan name and impeccably aristocratic patronymic Prokles is just the sort of man one might expect to be a *trophimos* foreigner in Sparta.

Prokles was a relatively moderate oligarch: the example of Lysander had taught Agesilaos to avoid connections with rabidly extreme oligarchs. But that of course in no way alters the fact that Agesilaos was acting on behalf of a small minority of Phleiasians to overthrow by force a democratic government approved and actively supported by the great majority.

Without further ado, that is without even the pretence that he was punishing a disloyal ally or a state that had infringed the Peace of Antalkidas, Agesilaos led his troops across the Spartan frontier through Arkadia past loyal Tegea and Mantineia to join the other allied contingents in the territory of Phleious (cf. 5.3.25). Seeing what had happened to Thebes the previous year (Chapter 14), the Phleiasian democracy refused to hand over their akropolis and settled down to a long siege (5.3.14-15). It is at this juncture that Xenophon reveals what were the 'other grounds' for censure of Agesilaos' behaviour. 'There were many Spartans who said that for the sake of a few men they were incurring the hatred of a city of more than 5000 men' (5.3.16) – a citizen body more than three times as big as Sparta's and indeed among the larger ones in Greece (cf. Finley 1983, 59).

That 'many' Spartans should have been so openly hostile to Agesilaos may seem at first glance surprising, but it should be recalled that in 382 'the Ephors and most of the [Spartan] citizens' had been unhappy with the publicly unauthorized (and blatantly illegal) seizure of the Theban akropolis – an action that Agesilaos had at the very least condoned (5.2.32). Whereas Agesipolis at Mantineia had shown clemency to the democratic leaders in the teeth of his troops' desire to tear them apart, Agesilaos now had somehow to convince his troops that they ought to want to tear the Phleiasian democratic leaders to pieces. To this end he devised a brilliant stratagem much to his reactionary taste (see Chapter 12); and after an unexpectedly prolonged, twenty-month siege he finally brought the Phleiasians to terms.

Agesipolis was by now dead, but the Phleiasian democratic government seems to have hoped to receive a sympathetic hearing in Sparta by appealing to the home authorities over Agesilaos' head. This hope proved illusory. For Agesilaos pulled patronal strings with his friends (*philoi*) in Sparta and through them 'arranged' (*diepraxato*) for the fate of Phleious to be left entirely in his hands (5.3.24; cf. Chapter 9). Pausanias had been entrusted with the settlement of Athens in 403, but that was after a vote of the Spartan Assembly and the assignation to him of a board of fifteen Spartans (2.4.38); together they had agreed to the restoration of democracy in a tributary Athens deprived of Eleusis. Agesilaos, however, had no intention of allowing the majority of Phleiasian citizens to have the form of *politeia* they wished. Instead, he adopted the Lysandreian device employed at Athens in 404 and established a commission with full powers to draw up the future constitution – except that, in contrast to 404, there was to be no pseudo-democratic charade of electing the commissioners, a Spartan garrison was in Phleious from the start, and the commissioners were to have the power of decreeing death or exile (5.3.25). The statement of Diodoros (15.19.3) that the Phleiasians were compelled to be subservient to the Spartans is not at all too strong.

The composition of the commission was another of Agesilaos' masterstrokes: fifty men from the restored exiles, fifty men from those 'at home' (few or none of whom, naturally, will have been ideological democrats). In other words, the oligarchic ultras like Podanemos were to be restrained by the more moderate oligarchs like Agesilaos' friend Prokles, and the sort of split within the ranks of the oligarchs that must have preceded the expulsion of the ultras in the first place was to be avoided for the future. *Mutatis mutandis*, this was probably the kind of solution to *stasis* that Agesilaos enforced on Boiotian Thespiai a couple of years later (5.4.55). It should be needless to say that the solution was an oligarchic one (but see Lintott 1982, 225). Nor does it take much imagination to suppose that those whom the commissioners judged worthy of death or exile (7.2.5; 7.4.11) were leading democrats.

Thereafter oligarchic Phleious was Sparta's good and faithful servant right down to the effective end of the Peloponnesian League in 365, apart from one brief interlude when democratic exiles managed to re-establish themselves amid considerable bloodshed probably soon after Leuktra (DS 15.40.5). Indeed, the fidelity of Phleious was so conspicuous and so morally admirable in Xenophon's book that he devoted a whole chapter to the city's exploits between 370 and 366 on the revealing (of Xenophon's mentality) grounds that 'if a state which is only a small one has performed many fine actions then it is all the more right and proper to expatiate upon them' (7.2.1). The fact that the leading light of this regime was Prokles, a noted friend of Agesilaos and of Sparta (6.5.45) and after Leuktra a champion of the dual hegemony thesis (of joint Spartan and Athenian hegemony of Greece) to which Xenophon himself subscribed (6.5.38-48; 7.1.1-11), is not irrelevant to Xenophon's moral commendation. Nor ought we to be surprised (as was Legon 1967, 336-7) by the loyalty of Phleious to Sparta: the 'citizens' who unitedly and determinedly resisted the assaults of Argos and the Arkadian League in the early 360s (7.2.8-9) were only those with full citizen rights who satisfied the probably moderate (hoplite census?) property qualification for membership of the *politeuma* (cf. Ste. Croix 1981, 296 and 608n.49).

On the other hand, it would not be unreasonable to infer from the space Xenophon accords to Phleious that her fidelity was by now the exception rather than the rule. Agesilaos' 'severe policy' (Cawkwell 1976a, 76-7) had worked temporarily here and elsewhere, but it required a strong Spartan military machine to back it up. The Battle of Leuktra exposed the incompatibility of Agesilaos' hard line of pro-oligarchic intervention with this fact of military life. In 365 the Phleiasians no less than the Corinthians 'revolted' from Sparta and made peace with Thebes (7.4.11; cf. 7.2.2), and some time after the Battle of Mantineia in 362 a now once more democratic Phleious was party to an eternal alliance with Athens and her Second Athenian League (Tod 144=*SEG* 29.90, lines 29-30). Moreover, the explicit guarantee that all parties would undertake to preserve each other's existing constitutions was an implicit critique of Spartan interventionism. So much for the fidelity of Phleious, and for Agesilaos' 'severe policy'.

(v) Olynthos (Fig. 13)

Readers who are in any case unhappy with the second word of the title 'Peloponnesian League' will hardly be mollified by my extension of the title in

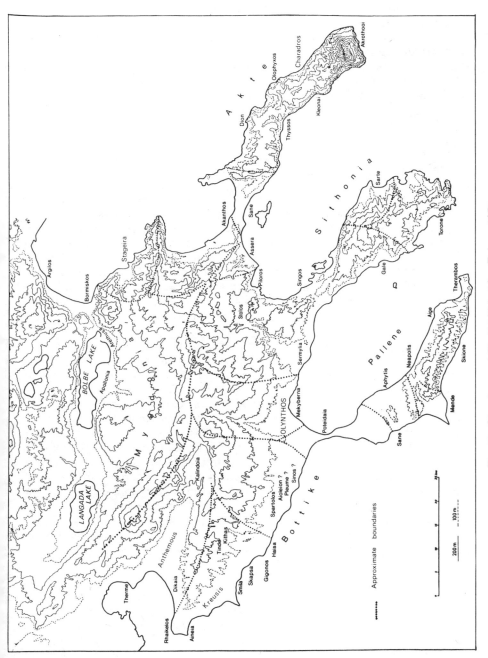

Fig. 13. Olynthos and Chalkidikê. After Zahrnt 1971

space to include Olynthos and other cities of the Chalkidike peninsula of northern Greece. But in 379 Sparta conferred or imposed upon these cities precisely the same form of alliance as those she had contracted with the other members of the Peloponnesian League, most of whom were indeed situated within the Peloponnese. There was, however, a crucial difference in the manner whereby the alliances were concluded. Whereas the formation of the League had been prompted chiefly by an essentially defensive policy of containing the Helots, the subordination of Olynthos was the culmination of a frankly imperialist *Nordpolitik* that was all of a piece with Sparta's behaviour elsewhere in Aegean Greece, the islands and Asia Minor in the wake of her victory in the Athenian War. Since this *Nordpolitik* crucially affected Thebes and her conception of Boiotian interests, Sparta's forcible reduction of Olynthos to the status of subject-ally after a long and costly campaign forms a natural bridge to the subject-matter of the next chapter. It also affords the opportunity of placing Sparta's use of the Peloponnesian League in a wider, Hellenic perspective.

Archaeologically, thanks to Philip of Macedon's destruction of the site in 348, Classical Olynthos is uniquely well documented. We know more about the urban development of Olynthos in the eighty or so years between its enlargement through the absorption of neighbouring coastal settlements (*anoikismos*) in 432 and its destruction than about that of any other comparable site in this period. The written sources are, by contrast, sparse, scattered, episodic, fragmentary, and ambiguous. In fact, for our 'knowledge' of the political history of Olynthos in the early fourth century we are heavily dependent on a single passage of Xenophon (5.2.12-19); what is worse, the passage is a speech, composed of course by Xenophon and put in the mouth of a leading opponent of Olynthos. With great caution I begin with a sketch of the background to Sparta's intervention in Chalkidian affairs in 382.

In 432 Olynthos, actively encouraged by Perdikkas II king of Macedon, broke away from her Athenian alliance and at the same time increased her size, power and security by *anoikismos* (above). This enlarged Olynthos at once became the most important state among 'the Chalkidians in the direction of Thrace', as the inhabitants of the three-pronged Chalkidike peninsula and its immediate hinterland were known. But both the literary sources and contemporary coinage attest the existence of some kind of unitary state of 'the Chalkidians', which was centred on Olynthos. Precisely what state-form 'the Chalkidians' enjoyed is a matter of unresolvable dispute (cf. Larsen 1968, 175-80; Zahrnt 1971, 49-79); but whatever it was, it certainly survived Athens' attempt, which had the agreement of Sparta, to dissolve it under the terms of the Peace of Nikias in 421 (Thuc. 5.18.5-6).

Sparta's complaisance accorded with her general hostility to supra-*polis* combinations but contradicted her professed championing of *autonomia* and so amounted to a betrayal of the Chalkidians. For between 424 and 422 Brasidas had won great acclaim in the area for seeming genuinely to practise that respect for *autonomia* which Sparta as a rule merely preached (cf. Cartledge 1979, 247). Akanthos, indeed, went so far as to dedicate a 'treasury' at Delphi in the joint names of the Akanthians and Brasidas (Chapter 6), while Skione honoured Brasidas with a golden crown as if he were a local man who had carried off the prize in one of the major Games (Thuc. 4.121.1). This act of betrayal, however, was not unpredictable. Brasidas had received only lukewarm support from home, he was now in any case dead, and his northern campaign had more than served its purpose by not only bringing Athens to the negotiating table at rather less of an advantage than she might otherwise have been but also depriving Athens (permanently, as it transpired) of her control of the key strategic site of Amphipolis. The Corinthians made this betrayal a ground for their temporary disloyalty from Sparta. But with hindsight the Chalkidians could probably count themselves fortunate that the Spartan presence had not lasted longer. The proto-harmosts installed by Brasidas (Chapter 6) did not augur well for the future of 'autonomy' hereabouts.

After 421 Chalkidike and the northern Aegean seaboard ceased to be a storm-centre of the Athenian War, and virtually nothing is known of Olynthos and the Chalkidians until 393/2. But one of the few pieces of information, if correct, is remarkably interesting. For they are said to have joined the anti-Spartan coalition in the Corinthian War (Isaios 5.46; cf. DS 14.82.3). The notice of Isaios has been rejected on both palaeographical and historical grounds (cf. Zahrnt 1971, 81n.3); but Diodoros could have been drawing ultimately on the contemporary Oxyrhynchos Historian (Xenophon's silence is no obstacle), and Sparta's intervention in Thessaly between 404 and 395 (Chapter 14) and Lysander's in Chalkidike gave Olynthos good reason to fear that, if Sparta won the Corinthian War, she might well redirect her attention to Chalkidike in her new, imperialist manner.

However that may be, in 393/2 Amyntas III of Macedon was driven from his throne and kingdom by an Illyrian invasion and ceded to the Olynthians (rather than the Chalkidians) some land on the border between what had been his and what was still their territories (DS 14.92.3). No doubt this was for temporary safekeeping only, and the Olynthians appear to have returned it without demur when Amyntas was restored with Thessalian aid in or about 391; that at any rate is a plausible interpretation of a fragmentary inscription from Olynthos recording a fifty-year defensive alliance between Amyntas and the Chalkidians (Tod 111; cf. N.G.L. Hammond in Hammond/Griffith 1979, 172-3; Zahrnt 1971, 81-2,122-7). Some eight years later, however, another Illyrian invasion and another temporary cession of borderland by Amyntas ended in tears.

Not only did the alliance break down but the Olynthians actually seized Amyntas' capital of Pella (DS 15.19.2; Isok. 6.46; cf. Hammond/Griffith 1979, 174-6). Or rather not the Olynthians, but the newly constituted *Bundesstaat* or federal state (*sustêma*: Polyb. 9.28.2) of 'the Chalkidians' led by Olynthos (cf. Zahrnt 1971, 83-8). Very little indeed is known about the structure of this state. But like the Boiotian Confederacy, on which it may have been modelled (another argument for Olynthos' participation in the Corinthian War?), it appears to have been a true federal state with common citizenship (5.2.18), common laws (5.2.14), and common coinage. Citizens possessed the private rights of intermarriage and full legal title to real property throughout the federal territory (5.2.19), but full political rights were perhaps reserved, as in Boiotia, to the 8000 (a possible emendation of the impossible '800' of 5.2.14) who possessed a minimum property qualification (the hoplite census?). The prerogative of the

Confederacy was foreign policy, and there were of course federal magistrates, although it so happens that their existence is not positively attested until 356 (Tod 158). This was twenty or so years after the federal state had been reconstituted following its dismemberment by Sparta in 379.

The Chalkidian Confederacy appears not to have yet been formed at the time of the Peace of Antalkidas (*contra* Larsen 1968, 75-80), and its establishment obviously offended against Sparta's deeply anti-federalist instincts. But it was not so much because the Chalkidians were a federal state that Agesilaos wished to dissolve it as because he envisaged its dissolution as part of a wider geopolitical strategy for extending Sparta's hegemony to virtually all mainland Greece and so (not incidentally) destroying the power of Thebes and the Boiotian Confederacy north of the Isthmus for ever. However, as patron of the Peace of Antalkidas Agesilaos needed a suitable pretext for intervention in Chalkidike, and in late 383 or early 382 one conveniently dropped into his lap in the shape of an appeal from two of the member states of the Chalkidian Confederacy, Akanthos and Apollonia (perhaps to be distinguished from Apollonia in Mygdonia). Hence the speech written by Xenophon (5.2.12-19) referred to above.

Olynthos and the Chalkidians had probably not been directly involved in swearing the oaths of the Peace of Antalkidas. But since the Peace applied in principle to all Greek states, the representatives from Akanthos and Apollonia could in that sense legitimately appeal to Sparta to enforce the autonomy clause (cf. Seager 1974, 41). So what they claimed was that the federal state was a sham, being in reality an instrument of Olynthos' imperialist designs, and that the terms of federation had not been freely offered and received but enforced 'at the point of the sword' (Freeman 1893, 152); rather than be 'Chalkidians' they wanted to become again citizens of their own independent *poleis* enjoying their 'ancestral constitutions' (5.2.14; cf. Lewis 1977, 112n.34). To this principled argument they added two of a more immediately practical nature. The Olynthians intended, they said, to expand eastwards with a view to seizing the gold (and silver) mines of Mt Pangaion (5.2.17). This suggestion has rightly been dismissed as 'deliberately alarmist' (G.T. Griffith in Hammond/Griffith 1979, 231n.2). But their earlier reference to current negotiations between Olynthos, Thebes and Athens (5.2.15; cf. 5.2.34) not only had substance but implied a potentially far more serious threat to Sparta.

Nevertheless, the fundamental question remains whether it really was, as Xenophon would have his readers believe, this appeal of Akanthos and Apollonia that motivated the decision to intervene taken by Sparta and – though Xenophon (5.2.37; cf. Ste. Croix 1972, 112n.60, 341) fails to make the distinction explicit – ratified by the Peloponnesian League Congress. For Diodoros (15.19.2-3) preserves a radically different version of the affair. His guiding theme in the early part of his fifteenth Book is how Sparta led by the 'interventionist' Agesilaos (*drastikos*: 15.19.4) interpreted the Peace of Antalkidas in an imperialist way. In his account it was not the 'subjects' of Olynthos in Chalkidike but King Amyntas of Macedon who made the decisive appeal. For although it was in Sparta's interest to keep Macedon divided and weak (cf. 5.2.40), the extension of Olynthian control to Pella was not a tolerable way of achieving that end. Xenophon's silence about Amyntas (though he drops a hint at 5.2.38) is wholly explicable by the fact that he was not a party to the Peace of Antalkidas and so offered no scope to Sparta for intervening under cover of guaranteeing its terms. On the other hand, Sparta's concern to prevent further Olynthian expansion by disbanding the Chalkidian Confederacy can only have been heightened by the embassies sent to Olynthos by Thebes and Athens with a view to securing alliances: here the accounts of Diodoros and Xenophon usefully complement each other.

That Agesilaos was indeed the prime mover of the Olynthian campaign, as Diodoros seems to imply, may be inferred both from the cool seizure of the Theban akropolis by a part of the Peloponnesian League force on its way to Chalkidike (5.2.25-36; cf. Chapter 14) and from the identity of the first three Spartan commanders appointed – the brothers Eudamidas and Phoibidas and Agesilaos' half-brother Teleutias (cf. Chapter 9 and Fig. 9.1). If the campaign was completed by Agesipolis and Polybiadas (probably son of the Naukleidas who had been a prominent opponent of Lysander: Chapter 6), that was merely the *quid pro quo* for Agesilaos' being given free rein at Phleious (cf. Rice 1974, 178; David 1981, 28). In any case, as at Mantineia in 385, Agesilaos had again contrived that the opposing royal house should implement a policy with which they were probably out of sympathy.

The details of the long, arduous and costly fighting over three years need not concern us here (cf. Hammond/Griffith 1979, 177-8; Zahrnt 1971, 91-7). But both before and after the campaign Sparta was compelled to introduce changes in the organization of the Peloponnesian League for the first time on record since the League's inception. The first of these innovatory measures was clearly taken on the advice of the leading Lakonizers in the Peloponnese, who wished to safeguard their positions of power and influence at home by forestalling or at least minimizing any hostility towards Sparta that might arise from the obligation to participate in such a far-flung, imperialistic campaign – if indeed disaffection had not already been engendered by the Mantineia affair of 385 (cf. Smith 1953/4, 76n.9). For in 382 it was agreed that an allied state's stipulated contribution in manpower might be commuted to a contribution in cash according to an agreed scale of equivalences for hoplites (three Aiginetan obols each) and cavalrymen (four times the rate of a hoplite), and that fines were to be levied on states that defaulted (5.2.21). Economically speaking, the cash raised by this anticipation of Plantagenet scutage would have enabled Sparta to buy mercenaries (cf. Chapter 15), although the only state known to have availed itself of this option for the Olynthos campaign is Phleious (5.3.10), which had special reasons for doing so. But the system may also have benefited the poorest allied hoplites, who like the peasant soldiers in the lowest census class in Republican Rome were liable to suffer most from a long campaign away from their small farms. If it prevented them from being forced below the hoplite census, that may also have kept them from the embrace of the anti-Spartan revolutionaries who were allegedly to be found in most Peloponnesian League cities (cf. 5.2.9).

The allies, however, were not alone in experiencing manpower difficulties of one kind or another at this time. In 381, after suffering particularly heavy losses (though exaggerated by DS 15.21.2), the Spartans unprecedentedly made use of volunteers to reinforce their 'Lakedaimonian' contingent, drawing upon men of inferior Spartan status (who could, just, be described as Lakedaimonian) and *trophimoi* foreigners (who could not), as well as high-status Perioikoi whose role as volunteers rather than conscripts is particularly remarkable (5.3.9). Presumably it was also considerations of manpower-distribution throughout the alliance that lay at the bottom of the second attested reorganization of the Peloponnesian League less than five years after the first (DS 15.31.1-3).

One of the main reasons for separating this reorganization from that of 382 is that it presupposes the enrolment of the Olynthians and other, now 'autonomous' Chalkidian states in the Peloponnesian League. This had not been effected until 379, on the usual terms of subject-alliance to Sparta (5.3.27; cf. 5.4.54). Indeed, the list of allies given here by Diodoros (15.31.2) is the best evidence we have for the membership of what we call the Peloponnesian League (as distinct from the wider Spartan alliance: cf. Chapter 2) at any time in its history (for some of the allies of Sparta that the list excludes cf. Cozzoli 1979, 151-2). In 378 (Diodoros' absolute chronology is as often a couple of years adrift) the Peloponnesian League proper was thus divided into ten geographically grouped units:

1. Lakedaimonians
2. and 3. Arkadians
4. Eleians
5. Achaians
6. Corinthians and Megarians
7. Sikyonians, Phleiasians, and the inhabitants of the Akte peninsula
8. Akarnanians
9. Phokians and Lokrians
10. Olynthians and other Chalkidians 'in the direction of Thrace'.

The units were apparently called *merê*, literally 'parts' or 'divisions', the same term as had been used for the 'wards' of the Boiotian Confederacy that Sparta had disbanded in 386 (Chapter 14). Presumably, like those 'wards', the new 'divisions' of the Peloponnesian League were meant to be roughly equal in numbers of troops (cf. 6.1.1). That gave the League a paper strength of well in excess of 25,000 men, significantly more than the number actually fielded at the Nemea River in 394 (Chapter 12).

Precisely what the aim of this reorganization was is unclear. If it was improved military efficiency in the field, then it is hard to see why the commutation system was not discontinued (cf. 6.2.16). Diodoros, however, believed that Sparta's motive was to still allied complaints about her heavy-handedness (*barutês*), which was causing them to look favourably towards Athens. But even if the reorganization did emphasize the disproportionate share of the military burden that Sparta was shouldering, that did nothing to halt allied dissatisfaction with Spartan leadership – precisely on the grounds that a few Spartans were dictating to many allies (see Chapter 12). By 375 the Olynthians had again re-established some form of Chalkidian Confederacy and besides defected from the Peloponnesian League to join the Second Athenian

League (SV 250; cf. Zahrnt 1971, 98, 125-7; Tod 123.101 of early 377 includes 'the Chalkidians of Thrace', which may or not be the Confederacy). By 371 dissatisfaction among the still notionally loyal allies had reached such a pitch that some of them were not even displeased by the result of the Battle of Leuktra (6.4.15; cf. 6.4.24).

I conclude this chapter with two observations of more general import. They both concern the complete loss of any remaining genuine autonomy by all the *poleis* of mainland Greece in the wake of the Macedonian conquest effected by Philip II, son of Amyntas III. First, so far as Sparta's treatment of Olynthos goes, hindsight amply justifies this ringing judgment: 'There can be no doubt that, seen from a general Hellenic point of view, the dissolution of the Olynthian confederacy was one of the most calamitous events in Grecian history' (Freeman 1893, 149). For it removed the one likely obstacle to the expansion of Macedonian power under Philip in northern Greece. The Confederacy was revived in some form, as we have seen, but it did not recover its former strength or anything approaching it until the late 350s, by which time it was too late to stop Philip (cf. Hammond/Griffith 1979, 296-328).

Secondly, when Philip in 338/7 established the sensitive and supple diplomatic-cum-military instrument for ruling over Greece that we call the League of Corinth, he deliberately left a now internally debilitated and territorially much leaner Sparta in her self-willed but hardly splendid isolation outside this Hellenic framework. The reasoning behind this decision, which may have been anticipated somewhat by Epameinondas (who like Philip had invaded Lakonia, mulcted Sparta of territory but left Sparta itself standing: Chapter 12), cannot be better expressed than in the words of G.T. Griffith (in Hammond/Griffith 1979, 619):

> While Sparta survived, she took first place in the attentions of Argos, Arcadia, and Messene, and she concentrated their minds wonderfully. A risk, no doubt, to leave Sparta free and embittered; ready to work with Persia, no doubt, in the coming Persian war. But a risk evidently which he preferred to take, following the instinct which told him that most of the Greeks would co-operate with him best if they had something on their minds, something to suggest to them that he and they might be necessary to each other still.

The lukewarm support received by Agis III when he attempted to lead a revolt against Macedon in 331 or 330 (cf. Ste. Croix 1972, 164-6) confirmed that the instinct of Philip (and his son Alexander the Great: cf. Arr. *Anab.* 1.16.7 – the inspiration of C.P. Cavafy's poem 'In the Year 200 B.C.') had been right. It was entirely fitting that Agis should have died near Megalopolis.

14

Agesilaos and the Fateful Triangle: Sparta, Thebes, Athens

The obstinacy of monarchs is not as that of other men. (Lytton Strachey, *Queen Victoria*)

The political history of Boeotia is ..., in an indirect way, one of the most important portions of the political history of Greece. (Freeman 1893, 120)

The special significance of Thebes and Athens in the age of Agesilaos lies in their triangular relationship with Sparta. It was in the interests of each to keep the other two at each other's throats or at least sufficiently preoccupied with each other to allow space and time for the third party to pursue its own hegemonial ambitions. For a period in the 370s the Thessalian dynast Jason of Pherai threatened to disrupt this cosy triangular pattern; but he was assassinated in 370, and it was left to another northern Greek dynast, Philip II of Macedon, to penetrate south of Thermopylai with an army and at Chaironeia in Boiotia in 338 win the battle that gave him the suzerainty of mainland Greece. By contrast, the (second) Battle of Mantineia in 362 had confirmed that none of the big three central and southern Greek powers had the strength to achieve this position of authority.

Sparta and Thebes were land-based and indeed largely land-locked powers. For the former the land battles of Leuktra and Mantineia, for the latter that of Chaironeia ultimately decided their hegemonial fate. But the Athenians, as Agesilaos' *xenos* Prokles of Phleious (cf. Chapter 13) is supposed to have observed at Athens in 369, were a sea-power: 'for you salvation depends upon the sea' (7.1.6; cf. Graefe 1935, 263). Nor was this merely in a military sense: 'For most of you the means of life come from the sea' (7.1.4). Prokles did not mean that most Athenian citizens attending the Assembly were professional sailors, traders or fishermen, but rather that the mass of poor Athenians were more or less dependent for their very survival on the regular annual importation of wheat from the northern shores of the Black Sea (supplemented as necessary by less substantial and more occasional supplies from places like Cyprus, Egypt and Cyrenaica or exceptional persons such as the Persian satrap Orontes).[1] In the

[1] See P.D.A. Garnsey, 'Grain for Athens', forthcoming in *Crux. Essays in Greek History presented to G.E.M. de Ste. Croix on his 75th birthday* (London, 1985) = *History of Political Thought* 6.1/2 (1985).

fourth century, when the Athenians' naval strength was constantly stretched up to or beyond their financial capacity to man, equip and pay for large and efficient fleets (cf. Mossé 1962, 316n.2; Ste. Croix 1981, 607n.37), this dependence is made absolutely plain in several key speeches of Demosthenes, for example (18.87; 20.31; but cf. Ober 1978), or in the laws Athens passed both to facilitate the trade and to ensure fairness in the distribution of the grain (cf. Rhodes 1981a, 577-9). But for much of the fifth century, following the creation of a large trireme fleet in the later 480s, it had been masked by Athenian naval power. Until, that is, 'the disaster in the Hellespont' (Lys. 16.4) – the catastrophic defeat of the Athenian fleet in 405 that gave Lysander command of the narrows and so a lethal grip on Athens' jugular vein (cf. Bommelaer 1981, 103-15; Strauss 1983). The pattern was repeated in 387 (below) and 340, but for the moment it is the aftermath of Aigospotamoi that is of concern.

In March/April 404, when the Athenians were finally starved by Lysander's blockade into unconditional surrender, Sparta was faced with two operable choices: to inflict upon Athens the kind of physical destruction or even annihilation that Athens had herself wreaked upon the people of Melos, Histiaia, Skione, Torone, Aigina, and other states (cf. 2.2.3); or to permit Athens to survive but wholly demilitarized and utterly subservient to the dictates of Sparta and (very secondarily) Sparta's Peloponnesian League allies. Sparta chose the latter option, for two main reasons, though she professed yet a third motive in public. First, the dominant voice in Sparta was that of Lysander, who then still enjoyed the confidence and support of King Agis II (cf. Hamilton 1979b, 52). It was Lysander's settled policy to assume Athens' role as leader of an Aegean empire and indeed to extend that empire into central and northern Greece. His preferred technique of imperial rule was through puppet juntas of his personal clients known generically as 'dekarchies', ten-man rules (cf. Chapter 6). Since these extremely narrow oligarchies or collective tyrannies were inherently unstable, they regularly required bolstering with a garrison commanded by a Spartan harmost. If Sparta's peace terms for Athens made no explicit and defined constitutional provision, this was because a gradualist approach was required in order to win round or at least mollify those large numbers of relatively prosperous Athenians who had a healthy distaste for extreme oligarchy after their experiences of 411 and to humour those influential Spartans and allies who mistrusted or openly disapproved of Lysander and Lysandreian imperialism.

The second main reason why Sparta chose to preserve an etiolated and hamstrung Athens as a satellite state was a matter of geopolitics. Many of Sparta's allies at the Peloponnesian League Congress held in Sparta to decide Athens' fate were of the opinion that Athens should be extirpated. But the grievances of two allies in particular stood out, both for their intensity and because of the importance of the allies in question. The possible reasons why Corinth took this view have already been canvassed (Chapter 13). It was, however, the attitude (2.2.19, 3.5.8, 6.5.36; Andok. 3.21; Isok. 14.31) and more especially the growing power of Thebes that determined the Spartans' decision to keep Athens alive. Polyainos (1.45.5) happens to state this explicitly, but Xenophon (2.3.41, 2.4.30) clearly implies as much elsewhere. What the Spartans feared in effect was that with Athens annihilated Thebes would step into her shoes in central Greece, thereby both threatening Sparta's communications by land with her northern Greek allies and dependencies and acting as a rival pole of attraction for actual and potential malcontents within the Peloponnesian League (especially Corinth and Megara). Ironically, Sparta herself was not a little responsible for making Thebes thus formidable.

The power-base of Thebes was regional, not confined to her immediate *polis*-territory. It lay in the relatively fertile and strategically crucial 3000 or so square kilometres of Boiotia in central Greece (on the topography cf. Buck 1979, 1-31; Buckler 1980c, 4-14). There had apparently been a Boiotian politico-military federation of some description since the last quarter of the sixth century, built upon a sense of 'ethnic' solidarity expressed in the Pamboiotia or All-Boiotia festival and symbolized by a common coinage (cf. Buck 1979, 107-20). But this exaggerated rather than prevented the rivalry between the Boiotian states whose economic and geographical situations rendered them naturally the two most powerful, Thebes in the south-east and Orchomenos in the north-west separated by Lake Kopaïs (not then drained). Nor was the federation itself a universally attractive proposition within Boiotia. Plataia (almost due south of Thebes) was jealous of her independence and fearful of being engulfed in the Theban maw. So in 519 (if the date extrapolated from Thuc. 3.68.5 may be trusted) she turned her back on the federation and sought the security of an alliance with Athens. The expression 'an Attic neighbour' became proverbial for a bad neighbour (for the context that provoked it cf. Griffith 1978, 140 and n.40); and Thebes and Athens, like many neighbouring Greek states, already had territorial disputes over Eleutherai and Oropos. So in agreeing to ally herself with Plataia Athens knew full well what implications this would have for short-term and longer-term relations with Thebes (cf. Thuc. 4.92.4). But according to Herodotus (6.108.3), the suggestion for the alliance had come from the Spartan king Kleomenes I, here pursuing Sparta's customary divide-and-rule policy (cf. Ste. Croix 1972, 167-8).

One result was that it was not until 427/6 that a Boiotian federation embraced all Boiotia, and even then this was only because in that year the Thebans physically destroyed Plataia. For 'the freedom of Boiotia from external interference demanded either the adherence of Plataia to the federal government or its destruction' (Buckler 1980c, 12). The Athenian response was to grant the Plataian survivors the sensational privilege of Athenian citizenship (cf. Osborne 1982, 1-16). In 427/6, however, unlike 519, the Spartans actively supported the action of their Theban allies, just as at some time between 447 and 431 they had made an exception in Boiotia's favour to their rule of not allying with federations (cf. Ste. Croix 1972, 123-4,335-7) and in 431 had condoned Thebes' illegal attack on Plataia in peacetime. The reason for Sparta's *volte-face*, which required her also to overlook Thebes' open and vigorous medism during the Persian Wars of 480-79 (Hdt. 7.122; 9.40,67-8, 86-8; cf. Demand 1982, 20-7), is straightforward: fear of the growth of Athenian power.

The one major land battle of the so-called First Peloponnesian War (*c*.460-45) had been fought on Boiotian soil at Tanagra in 458 or 457 (Hill 1951, 342, I.5.7). The result had been a narrow Spartan victory; but only a couple of months later Athens was able for the first (and last) time to bring all Boiotia with the possible exception of Thebes under her sway, apparently through the medium of friendly democracies in some cities (cf. Buck 1970). This land-empire of Athens in central Greece proved to be a strategic error and was never repeated. The resilient generation that in 459 had carried Athenian arms simultaneously to Phoenicia, Cyprus, Egypt, Halieis, Aigina and Megara (*IG* i³ 1147 = M/L 33) had overreached itself, and in 447 Boiotia was liberated from Athenian control. Whether the original Boiotian federation had survived the Persian Wars or not is unclear, but the period of Athenian occupation necessitated a fresh start thereafter. It had also convinced the Spartans that the Boiotians, especially the Thebans, required their unequivocal backing against the Athenian menace. Hence their exceptional toleration of the new Boiotian Confederacy that was founded in 447 or 446.

As the decade of Athenian domination had again demonstrated all too blatantly, the Boiotians were pastmasters of the Hellenic art of political disunion; Perikles, indeed, is said to have likened them to holm-oaks whose tops crash together in the wind and so act as their own executioners. Political unification was therefore a condition of Boiotia's – and Thebes' – playing a major role on the wider Greek stage, and after 447 Thebes set about achieving unity with a will, not shrinking from emasculating or even annihilating any Boiotian state that stood in the way of her domination of a united Boiotia. Whatever the relative positions of Thebes and Orchomenos at the time of the foundation of the Confederacy (contrast Larsen 1960 with Dull 1977), it was unquestionably Thebes who had come to dominate the organization by 404.

That much we would have known from Xenophon, Diodoros, Plutarch and Pausanias and could have predicted from Thucydides (whose narrative breaks off in 411). But thanks to the chance find of the fourth-century Oxyrhynchos Historian (Chapter 5) we have a much deeper insight into how and why Theban power had grown to such an alarming (as the Spartans viewed it) eminence. The best chapter of his work as preserved outlines the innovative constitutional arrangements of the Confederacy as they stood in 395 before the Spartan-inspired secession of Orchomenos, and we may be tolerably sure that in essentials this is how they had stood in 447 or 446. The chapter is not entirely self-explanatory (cf. Bruce 1967, 102-9,157-64; Larsen 1968, 26-40,175-8). But it does certainly enlighten the obscurity of Thucydides' accurate but unexplained references to 'the Boiotians', and it exposes Xenophon's tendentious silence about the whole organization: with rare exceptions (e.g. 4.5.6,9) Xenophon uses 'the Thebans' when he means 'the Boiotian Confederacy' (e.g. 3.5.4-24) and he barely acknowledges the existence of the latter – in retrospect (5.2.16). Moreover, the chapter demonstrates that we are dealing with a true federal state (cf. Walbank 1976/77), not a series of bilateral relationships between a *hêgemôn* and its subject-allies as in the Peloponnesian League. It was unfortunate for G.F. Hertzberg that his admirable *Agesilaos* (cf. Appendix I) was published half a century before the 'Hellenika Oxyrhynchia' was made available to the scholarly world as *P.Oxy.* 842 (cf. Grenfell/Hunt 1908; Bruce 1967; Breitenbach 1970).

The anonymous historian makes a threefold distinction regarding the institutions of Boiotia. He distinguishes first between federal and local institutions and then, among the local units, between *poleis* and *chôria* –

independent and satellite states or 'cities' and 'villages'. Local organization to some extent provided the model for the Boiotia-wide federal administrative set-up. There were eleven *poleis* but considerably more than eleven individual, nucleated settlements. For the largest *poleis* – Thebes, Orchomenos, Thespiai – incorporated smaller, satellite communities: for instance, Eutresis and Thisbai were merged in the *polis* of Thespiai, perhaps by an act of *sumpoliteia*, that is by the granting of Thespian citizenship to the other two (on the ancient federal terminology cf. Stanton 1982, though his own use of 'federal' is unacceptably loose).

Citizenship within each *polis* was of two grades, the criterion of differentiation being the ownership of real property. Only those who satisfied the minimum property qualification which probably corresponded to the ability to equip and maintain oneself as a hoplite (cf. Ste. Croix 1972, 35n.65), were eligible for election to the local deliberative, executive and judicial organ, the Boule or Council. Such men possessed full or active citizen rights, whereas the lower-grade, second-class citizens possessed only partial or passive rights. It is even conceivable that the second-class citizens could not vote in elections, but most scholars believe that their disability consisted rather in their ineligibility for office on the Council. Aristotle later noted that Thebes had once had a law banning from office those who had participated in commercial exchange (*agora*) within the previous decade (*Pol.* 1278a25-6) and that membership of the *politeuma* (i.e. possession of full citizen rights) at Thebes was only granted to those former manual workers who had not laboured at their menial occupation for a stated period (*Pol.* 1321a29-30). It is not clear whether Aristotle was referring to two laws or one nor whether both applied to the period of Boiotian history under consideration here; but it would not be unreasonable to infer that at Thebes the great majority of local Councillors in 395 were well-to-do landed proprietors. The local Councils varied in size from *polis* to *polis* depending on population. Presumably to spread the load of business, each Council was split into four sections such that only a quarter of the Councillors would be in permanent session at any one time. Major decisions were taken by majority vote of all Councillors at plenary sessions.

For federal purposes the eleven *poleis* (including the incorporated satellites) were grouped in eleven wards or districts (*merê*). Each ward contributed the same number of troops (1000 hoplites, 100 cavalrymen) to the federal army, which suggests that they were roughly equal at least in the number of qualified citizens of hoplite status or above. Contributions to and disbursements from the federal treasury were also equally distributed among the wards, as were the costs and benefits of federal justice. Each ward sent sixty representatives to the federal Boule, which (it is assumed from Thuc. 5.38.2) functioned on broadly the same lines as the local Councils. Finally, each ward provided one of the eleven Boiotarchs, literally 'leaders of the Boiotians', who were elected probably by those citizens of the federal state who qualified locally as first-class citizens (for the use of double ethnics in Boiotia cf. *IG* ii² 2a.2,9-10, with Walbank 1982b,263-4). The Boiotarchs, who like the Spartan Ephors took decisions among themselves by majority vote, formed the federal executive: they levied troops, commanded in the field and played an important role in diplomacy; they may also have exercised a probouleutic function in relation to the Federal Boule. In short, the Boiotian Confederacy was a genuinely representative system, although strictly it represented only the propertied minority of Boiotian citizens. The expression that Thucydides (3.62.3) puts into the mouth of his Theban speakers at Plataia in 427 – *oligarchia isonomos* (literally 'equally distributed oligarchy') – captures its political essence.

Such proportional representation might seem wholly fair, but it masked a real inequality of power among the constituent Boiotian polities. For it was not the case that one *polis* (including any satellites) made up one ward. The actual distribution of wards in 395 (before the defection of Orchomenos) was as follows: Thebes and incorporated satellites – 4; Orchomenos (with Hysiai) – 2; Thespiai (with Eutresis and Thisbai) – 2; Tanagra – 1; Haliartos, Lebadeia, Koroneia – 1 (between the three); Akraiphia, Kopai, Chaironeia – 1 (between the three). In other words, Thebes and her satellites contributed 240 out of the 660 federal Councillors, just over thirty-six per cent. of the total, which was surely sufficient to ensure a majority on most major issues, and four out of the eleven Boiotarchs. Moreover, the federal Boule met on the Kadmeia (akropolis) of Thebes, and it was presumably also there that the federal treasury and lawcourt were located; and between 447 and 386 Thebes alone coined money.

By 395, therefore, the prepotence of Thebes within the Confederacy was patent. It had been no less so in 404, and it was the Athenian War that had brought this about. In 431 the *polis*-territory of Thebes had been doubled in size by the political incorporation of smaller, unwalled communities as far afield as Aulis on the east coast of Boiotia (Hell. Ox. 16.3, 17.3; cf. Hornblower 1982, 82). Either then or in 427/6, after the elimination of Plataia, Thebes' ward-quota was increased correspondingly from two to four. In 424 Chaironeia had been a satellite of Orchomenos (Thuc. 4.76.3), in 395 she was independent (though still minor). The Battle of Delion in 424 was not only a Theban victory over Athens but a defeat for democratic tendencies within Boiotia. In 423 Thebes used the accusation of 'Atticism' (pro-Athenian sympathies) as a pretext to dismantle the wall of Thespiai (Thuc. 4.133.1); nine years later she helped suppress an abortive democratic uprising in the same city (Thuc. 6.95.2).

In 427 the Spartans had backed Thebes against Plataia because 'they considered the Thebans were useful to them' (Thuc. 3.68.4; cf. 3.52.4,53.4,56.3-7). Their utility was less apparent in 421 when the Thebans refused to swear to the Peace of Nikias, and it was a mark of Spartan weakness that in 420 Sparta granted the Boiotians a more equal alliance within the Peloponnesian League (Thuc. 5.39.3, cf. 40.1,42.2,44.1,3,46.2,4). In 419, notwithstanding, Thebes had the temerity to drive the Spartan harmost from Herakleia Trachinia and garrison it herself, whereupon the Spartans 'began to be angry' (Thuc. 5.52.1; cf. DS 12.77.4). Though summoned (Thuc. 5.64.4), the Boiotians failed to appear at the Battle of Mantineia (418), but a meeting of the two parties in 415 (Thuc. 6.61.2) seems to have patched up relations sufficiently for the Boiotians to lend aid to the Spartan capture and fortification of the Athenian fort of Dekeleia in 413. But this was hardly disinterested aid. During the so-called Dekeleian War of 413-404 the Thebans in particular made a handsome profit out of slaves and other war-booty acquired from Attika, including even the timber and tiles from Athenian country-houses (Hell. Ox. 17.4-5; cf. generally Thuc. 7.27.2-28; and for the tithe of booty, Parke 1932). The dramatic date of one of Xenophon's Socratic dialogues – ?407 (*Mem.* 3.5.2) – suggests that this increase in wealth had encouraged Thebes' desire for extending her power in Boiotia.

This, then, was the Thebes that dominated the Boiotian Confederacy and wanted Athens destroyed in 404. She was no longer just one ally of Sparta among many or even, like Mantineia (Chapter 13), a relatively privileged ally, but a power in the land and a potential rival of Sparta (cf. Nep. *Pelop.* 1.3). Hence, as argued above, Sparta's refusal to destroy Athens. But hence also the reason which Sparta professed to her Peloponnesian League allies for that refusal, namely that she 'would not enslave [quite literally – for the meaning of *andrapodizein* cf. Ducrey 1968, 23-6] a Greek city which had performed such a signal service at the time of Greece's supreme danger' (2.2.20; cf. 6.3.13; 6.5.36; Andok. 1.142; Justin 5.8.4-5). For this reference to Athens' role in the Persian Wars of 480-479 was not merely a fine 'Panhellenist' declaration of faith nor even a concession to those in Sparta who still hankered for the Kimonian 'dual hegemony' thesis of shared Spartan-Athenian hegemony of Greece. It was specifically calculated to remind the assembled allies, whose states had formed the backbone of resistance to Xerxes' invasion, of Thebes' treachery to the Greek cause and so to undermine Thebes' support within the Congress.

Sparta in any event had her way, and the terms actually imposed on Athens after negotiations that are as obscure to us as they were to the Athenian Assembly were as follows: (1) The walls of Peiraieus (the port of Athens and virtually a second city since its remodelling in the mid-fifth century) were to be razed, as were the three 'legs' or Long Walls connecting the city of Athens to Peiraieus and to Phaleron; (2) Athens' navy was to be destroyed except for twelve ships to be used for coastal patrol only; (3) thus demilitarized, Athens was to become a subordinate member of the Peloponnesian League, having the same friends and enemies as Sparta and following Sparta whithersoever she might lead; (4) as such, in line with Sparta's general insistence on 'autonomy' (cf. Chapter 13), Athens was to withdraw from all other cities and keep to her own territory; (5) Athens was herself to be autonomous, but political exiles – that is, oligarchic exiles – had to be restored to full rights; and (6) the 'ancestral constitution' was to be restored. Modern scholarship is virtually unanimous in accepting the first five of these provisions (esp. 2.2.20; Plut. *Lys.* 14 – purporting to quote a *dogma* of the Ephors in its original Doric). But the sixth provision has been widely rejected as anachronistic.

The rejection is based not least on the fact that the earliest writer to mention it is the author of an *Athenaiôn Politeia* produced within Aristotle's Lyceum in the 330s and 320s who was following source(s) by no means unsympathetic to the ensuing establishment of a bloodstained, pro-Spartan oligarchic junta (*Ath. Pol.* 34.3; cf. DS 14.3.2; Justin 5.8.5). But despite the author's oligarchic bias, which is palpable in his account of the oligarchic counter-revolution at Athens in 411 (*Ath. Pol.* 29-34.1; cf. A. Andrewes in Gomme 1981, 212-51; Rhodes 1981a, 362-415), there are reasons for believing his categorical assertion that Sparta imposed such a constitutional provision on Athens in 404. It is entirely in line with Sparta's general attitude to the political arrangements of her subject-allies (cf. Thuc. 1.19); Sparta was in a position to dictate what terms she pleased; and the phrase 'ancestral constitution' (*patrios politeia*) was sufficiently vague and yet sufficiently in vogue to appeal to all shades of Athenian political opinion to right of the existing radical democracy – from exiles like Aristoteles (a member of the extreme oligarchy of the 400 that ruled Athens briefly in 411) and of course Kritias, through professedly moderate oligarchs like Theramenes (e.g. 2.3.48; and esp. *Ath. Pol.* 34.3, which manages to avoid mentioning that he became a leading light in the Thirty as he had been of the 400), to those like Thucydides (8.97.2) who considered that the genuinely moderate oligarchy of the '5000' which succeeded the 400 was the best form of government that he at least had ever known of at Athens.

It was Theramenes who acted as Athens' chief negotiator, and, although the detailed and circumstantial evidence against him piled up by Lysias is the reverse of disinterested, it is hard to stifle the suspicion that Theramenes was not entirely surprised by the constitutional change that shortly ensued. In late spring or early summer 404, on the pretext that the walls had not been demolished within the prescribed time-limit (Lys. 12.74; DS 14.3.6; Plut. *Lys.* 15.2), Lysander sailed in to Athens and at a packed meeting of the Assembly secured the appointment of a board of thirty men who, like their extreme oligarchic forerunners of 411, were notionally to act as a legislative commission. But since the process of reviewing, refining and harmonizing Athens' democratic code of laws had been set in motion five years before, this new board was clearly intended to perform some other function. In point of fact, the Thirty seized power for themselves, constituting what the Greeks called a *dunasteia* or non-responsible autocracy, and thoroughly earned their later sobriquet of 'The Thirty Tyrants'. Apart from going through the motions of establishing a tame Council (of 500?) and a (savagely reduced) citizen-body of 3000 propertied supporters, they to all intents and purposes ruled by dictatorial fiat, taking care to disarm all those not on the roll of the 3000. This development was not at all uncongenial to Lysander, who may indeed have nominated one third of the Thirty and certainly counted personal adherents of his among their number. For in its basic principles this 'triakontarchy' (so labelled at 6.3.8) differed only in size from the dekarchies through which Lysander ruled his highly personal Aegean empire (Chapter 6).

Such a regime was scarcely 'ancestral'. Yet until its sudden, unexpected demise after less than a year in power, the Spartan authorities backed it to the hilt. When the Thirty found themselves unable to impose their version of law and order on a population long accustomed to democratic self-rule, their request for a garrison commanded by a Spartan harmost was at once met (2.3.13-14; DS 14.4.3-4; Plut. *Lys.* 15.6; Justin 5.8.11). When their use of this garrison to further the proscription of rich resident aliens (*metoikoi*, metics) as well as die-hard Athenian democrats led to hundreds of murders and a significant exodus of political exiles, the Spartans violated the autonomy of their other allies by forbidding them to harbour the exiles. When a band of exiles forced its way back to the staunchly democratic Peiraieus and won a battle that ended the rule of the Thirty and the life of their leader Kritias, the Spartans rallied at once to the support of the Thirty's oligarchic successors: they loaned them 100 talents to hire mercenaries and appointed Lysander as harmost for Athens to reimpose oligarchic good order in co-operation with his brother Libys the then navarch or Admiral of the Fleet. Only now did King Pausanias unpredictably reverse the trend of Spartan policy towards Athens since Aigospotamoi by sanctioning the restoration of democratic government, but even he made one large concession to the survivors of the Thirty the implications of which were not reassuring to the handful of democracies within Sparta's Peloponnesian League alliance.

Those are the bare bones of the episode (cf. in detail Rahe 1977, 97-105,190-223; Bommelaer 1981, 138-62; Rhodes 1981a,415-82 – with a comparative table of sources at 416-19; Krentz 1982). Two aspects require closer examination here: the lakonizing character of the Thirty's regime; and the effect of the junta's behaviour on the Boiotians and other Peloponnesian League members. Kritias was, on papyrus at least, a devoted Lakonophile. We do not know whether he was a 'keen competitor in physical prowess' (4.8.18) like the lakonizing flautist Thersandros and indeed his own young relative Plato, but he did write essays both in prose and in verse in praise of the Spartan way of life (88B6-9, 32-7 Diels-Kranz); and according to Xenophon (2.3.34), he considered it to be generally recognized that the Spartan *politeia* was the best there was (cf. beginning of Chapter 8). But Kritias was no Peloponnesian gentleman-farmer nor yet an adopted Peloponnesian with pretensions to sophistication like his fellow Athenian and pro-Spartan oligarch Xenophon. Kritias was an urbane Athenian intellectual capable of entertaining highly unorthodox religious sentiments and sponsoring highly controversial political initiatives that would have been anathema to even the most open-minded Spartan. The Lakonism of Kritias, in other words, was to some extent a pose assumed for an occasion that demanded wholehearted Spartan support (cf. Usher 1979). The five 'Ephors' including Kritias who had been appointed by the oligarchic clubs (*hetaireiai*) and were alleged to have nominated ten of the Thirty (Lys. 12.43-7) should therefore be regarded as pure Madison Avenue, not an earnest of Kritias' intention to model his regime on that of Sparta; once the Thirty had been installed, the 'Ephors' are not heard of again. Similarly, the number thirty was only accidentally identical to that of the Spartan Gerousia, not chosen deliberately to ape it. For although aspects of the Gerousia were characteristic of a *dunasteia* (cf. Chapter 8), the Gerousia did not by itself constitute the government of Sparta – unlike the Thirty at Athens in 404/3. In short, the Thirty ought not to be interpreted as one component of a grand design by Lysander to reconstruct his new empire literally on the Spartan political model, nor should Kritias be thought to have been so slavish in his Lakonism (cf. Lévy 1976, 197-203, at 201; *contra* Krentz 1982; Whitehead, forthcoming[2]).

The conduct of the Thirty was for long actively abetted by the Spartan state, but elsewhere in Sparta's sphere of influence the reaction was very different. The decree issued by Sparta forbidding her allies to harbour Athenian exiles was openly flouted by Thebes, Corinth, and Megara and contravened in spirit by Elis (cf. Funke 1980a, 47n.3). The Thebans, indeed, went so far as to pass a

[2] See Whitehead 1982/83 in Bibliography.

counter-decree to the effect that any Theban *not* assisting the refugees would be liable to punishment (DS 14.6.3). This is the first tangible evidence that a sea-change was taking place in the balance of power between the contending factions within Thebes and the Boiotian Confederacy at large. There was as yet no possibility of the Boiotians standing up militarily to the Spartans. But from the second half of 404 onwards they adopted a series of measures consistently in opposition to Sparta's will that culminated in the outbreak of the Corinthian War in late summer 395.

Heading this opposition was the anti-Spartan faction at Thebes led by Hismenias (or Ismenias: for the former spelling cf. Buckler 1980c, 281n.2). What tipped the balance away from his chief opponent Leontiadas was Sparta's decision to preserve a puppet Athens as watchdog over Boiotian expansionism. Anti-Spartan feeling will then have been aggravated by Sparta's refusal to share the spoils of war equitably (3.5.5). Finally, Sparta's intervention in Thessaly against Archelaos of Macedon – if this is correctly dated to mid-404 (cf. Andrewes 1971, 218; *contra* Funke 1980a, 39ff. and n.42) – will have confirmed the anti-Spartans' worst fears, especially if Lysander's voyage to Chalkidike is to be connected with the Thessalian intervention. For Sparta's *Nordpolitik* had as much bearing on the Boiotians' decision to go to war in 395 as Sparta's Aegean imperialism had on that of Athens or her expedition to coerce Elis on those taken by Corinth and Argos.

Immediately, in 404/3, it was the assistance given by the Thebans to Thrasyboulos and some seventy other exiles towards the seizure of the Athenian frontier-fort of Phyle that sounded the death-knell of the Thirty's regime. Thrasyboulos was the ideal leader of the democratic Resistance, a competent general with an unspotted record of democratic loyalty not carried to ideological excess. Attractive to all shades of democratic opinion opposed to the Thirty, his presence was doubtless as reassuring to oligarchic Thebans like Hismenias as it may have seemed later to Pausanias. Under his leadership a decisive defeat was inflicted on the Thirty in Peiraieus. All but two of the surviving members of the junta fled to Eleusis, a bolt-hole that had been carefully prepared by a massacre of unco-operative locals. From there they sent an urgent request for help to Sparta, which produced Lysander and Libys and much money. But hard on their heels came Pausanias at the head of a Peloponnesian League army – minus only the Boiotians and Corinthians (2.4.30, 5.2.33), who expected him to be as firm as Lysander with the democrats and no doubt interpreted his appointment in terms of Spartan domestic politicking rather than as heralding a fundamental change of Spartan policy.

As it turned out, this expectation was falsified nearly as completely as it could be. Rather than forcibly restore a narrow oligarchic junta, Pausanias reconciled – or at least knocked together the heads of – extreme oligarchs and democrats and those in between who had supported or opposed the Thirty and their successors from a mixture of ideological and material motives; and he retired the League army on the understanding that Athens would continue to be a member of the Peloponnesian League but a more genuinely autonomous one in that some form of democratic government would be restored. However, in case there is a temptation to espouse uncritically the accusation of his enemies in

Sparta, that he had let the Athenian democrats go when he had them in his power (3.5.25; cf. Chapter 8), it should not be overlooked that Pausanias did also make a not insignificant concession to oligarchic opinion. He recognized the Thirty's purged bolt-hole at Eleusis as an autonomous and largely separate *polis*, to which Athenian oligarchic sympathizers might withdraw in the enjoyment of full local citizen-rights (2.4.40; *Ath. Pol.* 39.1). Whatever Pausanias' motives were for tolerating this Eleusinian statelet, he had in effect turned the clock of Athens' political development back some three centuries and carried out a desynoecism (*dioikismos*) of the Athenian *polis* – even if it was an infinitely less radical one than that imposed by his son Agesipolis on Mantineia in 385 (Chapter 13). The schism was not healed until 401/0.

Pausanias' settlement of Athens in 403 and the subsequent vindication of it through his acquittal on a charge brought probably by his co-king Agis have been examined earlier in the contexts of Spartan imperialism (Chapter 6) and policymaking (Chapter 8). The questions why Pausanias went to such trouble to oppose Lysander's policy towards Athens and why he was able to persuade (probably) two successive boards of Ephors to his way of thinking remain to be answered. The dominant ancient view was that Pausanias had acted out of jealousy of Lysander (2.4.29-37; DS 14.33.6; Plut. *Lys.* 21.4-7), and this has been echoed by most modern writers (e.g. Hertzberg 1856, 13). It is at least a more plausible motive than pity for the democratic exiles (Justin 5.10.7; cf. Lys. 18.10-12), since Pausanias had obviously made up his mind before he left Sparta and so before he could hear their no doubt moving appeals outside the city of Athens. Jealousy, however, should not be accepted as a sufficient explanation (cf. Colin 1933, 71ff.).

No doubt Pausanias was jealous of Lysander. Competitive envy was fostered as a structural feature of Spartan society, and both Pausanias and Agis (who temporarily sided with Pausanias against Lysander) had even more reason to be jealous of Lysander than the leading Spartans of the late 420s had had for being envious of Brasidas (Thuc. 4.108.7) or Damaratos of Kleomenes I (Hdt. 6.61.1). But if jealousy were to be a satisfyingly complete explanation of Pausanias' behaviour in 403, then he ought by his policy to have somehow outdone Lysander – which was hardly the case. Whereas Lysander had effectively subjugated the old enemy by devising an extreme version of Sparta's normal technique of controlling her subject-allies through 'convenient' oligarchies, Pausanias had permitted the hated *dêmos* of Athens to regain the *kratos* (sovereign power) of their state and so made it harder for Sparta to control Athens' every move. In addition to and over and above jealousy, therefore, we must allow for a good deal of principled ideology or realistic pragmatism or a combination of the two.

There are no reasons for supposing that Pausanias was 'soft on', let alone a supporter of, democracy as such. In exile at oligarchic Tegea after 395 he wrote a pamphlet somehow defending the ancestral constitution of Sparta, the so-called laws of Lykourgos (Chapter 10). That constitution was not democratic (cf. Chapter 8). On the other hand, the pamphlet may suggest how principle entered Pausanias' calculations at Athens in 403 – in the form of a genuine respect for and toleration of the *autonomia* of Sparta's subject-allies including each ally's 'ancestral constitution'. There was room for argument over the ultimate progenitor of the Athenian *politeia* as it had stood before the rule of the Thirty, but no question but that the 'ancestral constitution' was a form of democracy. It is not coincidental that the other known case where Pausanias decisively countered the dominant thrust of Spartan foreign policy was at Mantineia in 385, when he successfully interceded with his son Agesipolis for the lives of sixty leading democrats (Chapter 13). By then Mantineia had probably been a democracy for almost as long as Athens had in 403.

This attitude of live-and-let-live, however, need not have been and almost certainly was not purely conditioned by high-minded principle. Pausanias seems to have been a Spartan traditionalist (cf. Plut. *Mor.* 230f) alarmed at the effect that the aggressive imperialism pursued by Agis and Lysander (and later Agesilaos) was having and would continue to have on the Spartan *kosmos* or way of life. If he had been able to establish his authority permanently within the Spartan political hierarchy, it is not inconceivable that he would have favoured a 'Little Peloponnesian' (or even 'Little Spartan') foreign policy of avoiding direct military entanglements in central Greece or beyond and maintaining the Peloponnesian alliance through active support for long-established moderate oligarchies, toleration of a handful of democracies, and irredentist hostility to Argos. Some corroboration of this hypothesis may be found in the peace initiatives towards Athens that followed his accession in 408; they suggest that in this respect he had inherited the views of his father Pleistoanax (cf. Ste. Croix 1972, 197-9, esp. 198).

Both ideological and pragmatic reasons can therefore plausibly be suggested to account for Pausanias' desire to overturn Lysander's post-war settlement of Athens. But it is a separate question why he was able to persuade a majority of the Ephors of 404/3 and all the Ephors of (probably) 403/2 to his *gnômê*. The answer to that lies in a broader consideration of interstate relations within the Peloponnesian League alliance. Many allies, not just the Boiotians and Corinthians, had wanted Athens destroyed in 404, motivated principally by revenge no doubt. They got no satisfaction. Then there was alarmingly widespread defiance of the Spartan *diktat* not to harbour Athenian exiles, involving Megara as well as Thebes and Corinth. Sparta's authority with her allies was not what it might be (cf. DS 14.33.6). But the real danger signal was set off when Lysander's settlement, so far from serving to cow and check the Boiotians, began to give rise to active and effective co-operation between the Thebans and the Athenian democratic Resistance. If this co-operation were to cease and Thebes and Athens were to revert to their 'natural' mutual enmity, then it had better be Sparta and not Thebes that restored democratic government to Athens and reaped a harvest of gratitude from an impoverished and still virtually defenceless population. When looked at in these terms Pausanias' settlement seems virtually demanded by the exigencies of the situation rather than a 'sell-out'; and the recognition of a separate, ultra-oligarchic statelet at Eleusis was a useful sop to those in Sparta who hankered for the eventual reimposition of extreme oligarchy on all Athens. That Pausanias succeeded in his major practical objective was made clear in 402 when Thebes, taking advantage of Sparta's preoccupation with Elis, annexed in a most unneighbourly spirit the borderland of Oropos over which Athens and Thebes had contended for many years (DS 14.17.3; cf. Rhodes 1981a,610-11).

Under the aegis of Pausanias the warring Athenians achieved a reconciliation (*dialuseis, diallagai*) sanctioned by oaths (*horkoi*) whereby they might live in peace (*eirênê*) with each other. A general amnesty was declared, the first recorded anywhere in the world, for all except members of the various extreme oligarchic cliques that had ruled in 404/3. Despite obvious tensions (still tangible in 382: Lys. 26.2) and several political trials which breached the amnesty in spirit and probably also in the letter, all contemporary commentators agree that on the whole the restored democracy honoured its pledges with extraordinary fidelity (cf. Rhodes 1981a, 471-2).[3] Gratitude to Pausanias and the Spartans was tangibly – and prudently – expressed in the honorific tomb constructed for fourteen Spartans who had died during Pausanias' expedition (cf. Cartledge 1979, 270-1), and the huge sum loaned by Sparta to the oligarchs in the City was punctiliously repaid in full (cf. Ste. Croix 1981, 606n.34). But though weak and inevitably largely subservient, the restored democracy was from the start not merely a Spartan catspaw, partly because the tolerant Pausanias survived the trial he had to face on his return to Sparta, partly because Sparta had other preoccupations in these years. When the less than radically democratic Phormisios in 403/2 proposed, with Spartan backing, that Athenian citizenship should be restricted to those who owned land in Attika (thereby excluding wealthy men whose assets were held in movable form, but more especially some thousands of poor, urban-dwelling and radically democratic citizens), the proposal was firmly rejected (Lys. 34; Dion. Hal. *Lys.* 32-3; cf. Perlman 1968, 262n.51; Rhodes 1981a,432-3,472).

Citizenship, it is clear, was the burning issue of the immediate post-restoration period at Athens – not surprisingly, given Athens' impotence in foreign affairs. Thrasyboulos wished to reward with the citizenship those non-Athenians (slaves or freedmen as well as freeborn metics) who had joined him 'from Peiraieus' (*Ath. Pol.* 40.2; Plut. *Mor.* 835f); but Archinos prevailed against him to begin with, by playing on nervous fears that the privileges of Athenian citizenship, however reduced they might be by comparison with the good old days of Athenian empire, might yet be diluted through over-generous dissemination. Perikles' citizenship law of 451 was re-enacted to reaffirm the principle of status-differentiation by descent (cf. Davies 1977/8), and this principle was vigorously enforced in the orphans' law of Theozotides (cf. Stroud 1971). It is true that in 403/2 the extraordinary block grant of Athenian citizenship made to all Samians in 405 was inscribed (or re-inscribed) on stone, perhaps when Sparta withdrew her support from Lysander's dekarchies, one of which had been installed on Samos (Chapter 6). But the honours decreed for the Samian Poses and his sons that were inscribed on the same stele offer them the hospitality that was accorded to foreigners (Tod 97.23,34; cf. Osborne 1982, 25-6). In 403/2, then, the *status quo ante* 404 had been reaffirmed so far as the citizenship was concerned. But in 401, presumably after the Eleusis statelet had been

---

[3] In what follows I have benefited greatly from the researches of my pupil, Dr S.C. Todd, though he should not be taken to endorse what I have written to the letter.

reincorporated into the *polis* of Athens during Sparta's continued preoccupation with Elis, the Athenians had a fit of remorse and retrospective generosity towards those non-citizens who had played a conspicuous part in the restoration of democracy. Between seventy and ninety of the honorands whose names were inscribed on a massive stele received the citizenship, it appears, and the rest (between 850 and 870) equality in taxation (*isoteleia*) with citizens (Osborne 1981, D6; 1982, 26-43).[4]

Turning from domestic to foreign affairs we find the restored Athenian democracy a pale wraith by comparison with her former imperial self. No tribute, no fleet to speak of, no Long Walls, no land abroad owned by the state or by individual Athenians, no revenue from the silver-mines, no jobs for the big boys as governors, inspectors, tribute-collectors or other imperial functionaries, few jobs for the little men as rowers, dockers, ship's carpenters or other tradesmen, no guaranteed low-cost grain-supply, no magnetic attraction of all sorts of goods to the Peiraieus or flow of tax-revenue therefrom; and so on. No wonder, therefore, that Athens was also powerless to prevent the Thebans from grabbing Oropos or to resist Sparta's demands for troops against Elis in 402/1 (3.2.25). The wonder was that Athens recovered her nerve so quickly.

The reunification of the Athenian state in 401 was both a sign of and a boost to her growing self-confidence. In 400 when Sparta again requested troops, this time for the Persian expedition (Chapter 12), Athens cheekily sent 300 cavalrymen (3.1.4), the kind of Athenians who had shown rather too much zeal in defending the Spartan-backed junta against the democratic Resistance. Two years or so later Konon, one of the two Athenian admirals who had managed to escape from the Aigospotamoi disaster, was summoned from his Cypriot exile to command the anti-Spartan fleet being prepared under the overall direction of Pharnabazus, satrap of Hellespontine Phrygia (cf. Chapter 12). This appointment the Athenians somewhat irrationally took as a compliment to themselves, and from 398 it is possible to document a strand of Athenian opinion that favoured active co-operation with Persia against Sparta. In 395 that strand became the dominant one in Athenian counsels, but it was only translated into military deeds through the prompting of Athens' unreliable neighbours in Boiotia.

Unlike debilitated Athens, the Boiotians had disobeyed Sparta's order to contribute troops to the Elis expedition (3.2.25) and had used some of their considerable forces to snatch Oropos instead. Such behaviour was not congenial to Sparta, but rather than confront the Boiotians directly she decided in 400 or 399 to reassert (cf. 1.2.18) her presence in Trachis and Thessaly.[5] The idea was to prevent Boiotian expansion northwards and provide a base for possible future intervention in Boiotia itself, but in retrospect this decision was almost as grave

---

[4] In an article published after this chapter was written it has been argued that *all* the listed honorands received the citizenship: D. Whitehead, 'A thousand new Athenians', *LCM* 9.1 (Jan. 1984), 8-10. This view is attractive.

[5] This is possibly the dramatic date of Pseudo-Herodes, *Peri Politeias*: see Funke 1980a, 39ff. and n.42; *contra* Ste. Croix 1972, 35n.65 (summer 404); Kelly 1975, 16,64 (404/3). This speech, which purports to be an appeal for Spartan aid by a Thessalian oligarch, is of course a much later rhetorical exercise: Russell 1983, 111.

an error as the decision taken at roughly the same time to declare war on Persia (Chapter 11). It is hard to resist the suspicion that Agesilaos and Lysander were implicated in both initiatives.

Sparta founded only one 'colony' (*apoikia*) in the sense of a wholly separate and independent new *polis*, namely Taras in South Italy at the very end of the eighth century (cf. Cartledge 1982, 243-4). Quite different in kind was Sparta's foundation in 426 of the colony (in something like our sense) of Herakleia Trachinia or 'in Trachis' (cf. Graham 1983, 206-8). For this was intended to be an outpost of empire settled by some 10,000 Doric-speakers including Spartiates and Perioikoi under the leadership of three distinguished Spartans, one of whom may have been the father of Antalkidas and Pedaritos (Thuc. 3.92-3; DS 12.59.3-5). This surprisingly large foundation was supposed to have been made in response to entreaties from the Trachinians, who were being pressed by the men of Oita, and from the people of Doris, the alleged mother-country of all Dorians: hence the composition of the settlers. But it incidentally provided a solution to land-hunger (cf. Bockisch 1967, 312, 315n.27); and it was chiefly envisaged by the Spartans as a strategically important base for launching attacks on northern Euboia and ensuring Sparta's communications with Athens' disaffected allies in Chalkidike. It had, moreover, a more general potential for supporting Spartan imperial expansion in northern Greece (cf. Andrewes 1978, 96-7). The mind of Brasidas can be detected (cf. Gomme 1956, 395), but it was probably not just a coincidence that Agis had succeeded his father on the Eurypontid throne the previous year. For in winter 413/2 Agis, then based at Dekeleia in northern Attika, conducted a punitive expedition not only against the Oitaians (thereby presumably restoring Spartan control of Herakleia) but also against the Achaians of Phthiotis and other subjects of the Thessalians hereabouts (Thuc. 8.3.1). Agis at least, it seems, 'entertained plans to subject certain areas of central and northern Greece to a control tighter than that which they [the Spartans] exercised over their Peloponnesian allies' (Andrewes 1978, 97-8; cf. Westlake 1938, 35-8). In view of this, Sparta's intervention in Thessaly after the Athenian War (probably mooted by Agis, who died before he could put it into effect) marked no new departure.

The Boiotians, and in particular the Thebans, had never been too keen on Herakleia Trachinia. In 419 they actually drove the Spartan harmost out and occupied the place themselves (Thuc. 5.52), greatly to the delight of the Ainianians, Dolopians, Malians and some Thessalians who had also resented the foundation from the outset (Thuc. 3.93, 5.51; cf. 1.2.18). Thucydides blamed the harsh administration of successive harmosts for Herakleia's ineffectiveness, and this was no doubt a contributory factor. But the Boiotians' occupation was a pre-emptive strike in anticipation of an Athenian attempt to do likewise at a time of Spartan weakness. In 400 or 399, however, Sparta was on the crest of an imperialistic wave and determined to reimpose herself on Herakleia Trachinia (DS 14.38.3-5, 82.7; Polyain. 2.21).

The fact that the harmost deputed to carry out this task was Herippidas lends weight to the conjecture that the policy was sponsored by Agesilaos (cf. Chapter 9). But Herippidas' conception of good order was hardly calculated to render Herakleia a secure possession or allay Theban unease. 'This man,' wrote David

Hume, 'not provoked by any opposition, not inflamed by party rage, knew no better expedient than immediately putting to death about 500 of the citizens.' We might compare the action of a contemporary harmost at Byzantion in selling into slavery at least 400 of Cyrus' former mercenaries at the recruitment of whom Sparta had connived (Xen. *Anab.* 7.1.36, 7.2.6; cf. Glover 1917, 260). It was perhaps also at this time that Sparta, with the aid of their *proxenos*, managed to install a garrison at Pharsalos, the southernmost of the four major Thessalian cities (cf. 6.1.4; DS 14.82.6). If so, it must be accounted one of the most serious of Xenophon's many historiographical lapses that he made but a single explicit reference (7.1.28) to the fact that Boiotia could be – or feel – threatened from Thessaly and that he did not make it until a context of the early 360s when Sparta and Athens were allied against Thebes, who was then the dominant power in mainland Greece and herself pursuing an imperialist strategy. For there is every reason for thinking that all this Spartan activity in central Greece in *c.*400 'must have a bearing on the vexed question of the causes of the Corinthian War' (Andrewes 1971, 223).

In practice that war did not break out until the second half of 395. For four conditions had to be satisfied before such a war could be embarked upon by the enemies of Sparta (whose dominance by land and sea in Aegean Greece was still unquestionable in 400). First, Sparta must continue to pursue, or at least give grounds for thinking that she might at any time adopt again, an aggressively interventionist foreign policy; she would thereby play into the hands of the anti-Spartan factions within the most powerful Peloponnesian League states and of those democratic leaders at Argos who most resented Sparta's support for their oligarchic opponents (cf. Hell. Ox. 7.2). Secondly, Sparta must none the less show sufficient signs of military weakness or internal political and social disunity to give hope that a determined display of force might persuade her to desist at least from extra-Peloponnesian imperialism. Thirdly, the enemies of Sparta must feel that they possessed the material and moral means to wage a predictably protracted struggle. Finally, the Boiotians and the Athenians must overcome their little local differences to pursue in common their mutual interest in nullifying Spartan influence in central Greece. No ancient source brings all these conditions together within an explanatory framework. There is not even a Thucydides to distinguish between publicly professed grievances and real motives for going to war. Thus the origins of the Corinthian War is one of the most important and yet one of the most obscure problems in the history of Classical Greece (cf. Perlman 1964; Lehmann 1978a,1978b; Hamilton 1979b, 182-208; Hornblower 1983, ch. 14).

In 404 Sparta had decided to carry on more or less where Athens had left off. Support was withdrawn from Lysander's juntas of personal clients in (probably) 403/2 (cf. Chapter 6), but the empire continued to be governed through harmosts and garrisons and the fleet to be financed from tribute as well as individual goodwill contributions. In mainland Greece Sparta expanded into Thessaly, took a hard line with Elis, and reasserted control of Herakleia Trachinia. In all this the balance of benefit was heavily tipped in Sparta's favour and the profits of empire were not shared with the allies. Outside mainland Greece Sparta had aided Dionysios of Syracuse in his seizure of a dictatorship and maintained her connections with him thereafter (Chapter 15). But what seems to have occasioned the greatest alarm was Sparta's intervention on the Asiatic mainland from 399. There was no chance that Sparta would defeat Artaxerxes in any decisive sense (cf. Chapter 12), but her Persian War did extend the harmost system and yield huge funds in the form of booty which could be used to further Spartan imperialism in mainland Greece. So when Agesilaos assumed command in 396 with the support of Lysander, the Athenians refused for the first time to contribute troops to a Spartan expedition, the Corinthians again refused to do so, and the Boiotians not only did that but also moved from passive to active resistance to Sparta by obstructing Agesilaos' sacrifice at Boiotian Aulis (3.5.5; 7.1.34).

Spartan imperialism, however, both resulted from and exacerbated internal social, economic and political tensions and divisions (cf. Chapter 10). *Olig-anthrôpia*, the decline of Spartiate manpower, had already been a source of grave concern in the 420s, when it was decided to compensate for it somewhat by liberating some thousands of Helots for military purposes. These Neodamodeis were just the sort of troops to do garrison duty under a harmost in Sparta's growing empire, and Agesilaos took 2000 of them to Asia in 396. But while these promotions had military advantages and also served to divide the Helots against themselves, they did nothing to minimize the gulf between the diminishing number of increasingly rich Spartiates and the ever more numerous men of inferior status. The abortive conspiracy of Kinadon in 399 neatly exposes this spreading cancer within the Spartan body politic. As for high politics, Pausanias is conspicuous by his near-total absence from all our main accounts of Spartan history between his acquittal in 403 and his condemnation for failure in Boiotia in 395. But absence does not mean approval, and the opposition of Boiotia, Athens and (probably) Corinth to Agesilaos and Lysander in 396 is likely to have aroused in him the same kind of response as in 404-3. His failure to co-ordinate the Spartan attack on Haliartos in 395 with Lysander is unlikely to have a purely operational explanation (cf. Bommelaer 1981, 196).

The material and morale factor in the outbreak of the Corinthian War is bound up with the progress of Sparta's Asiatic campaign. In 398/7 Konon was appointed vice-admiral of a Persian fleet under Pharnabazus, largely on the recommend-ation of his friend Euagoras I, the Persian vassal king of Cypriot Salamis, who had been awarded Athenian citizenship a decade or so earlier (cf. Osborne 1982, 21-4). In summer or autumn 396 Konon achieved the most significant result of his naval campaign to date, the defection of Sparta's main southern Aegean base of Rhodes. It was probably some time after this that Pharnabazus (Hell. Ox. 7.5; Polyain. 1.48.3; *contra* 3.5.1 – Tissaphernes) despatched a Rhodian agent, Timok-rates, to distribute money to the leading anti-Spartan politicians in Boiotia, Athens, Corinth and Argos and in the process put these men into touch with each other (if they were not so already). This money did not cause the Corinthian War (Hell. Ox. 7.2-3; *pace* 3.5.1-2), but it will have been a powerful argument to deploy for men who had long been awaiting a suitable moment to take their states into war. It will have helped convince those who were still suffering the effects of the Athenian War and silence those who were unwilling to make any personal financial sacrifice in the anti-Spartan cause.

The Athenian recipients of this Persian money were Kephalos, a die-hard foe of Sparta, and the more flexible Epikrates. It was presumably at their instigation that in 398/7 the Athenians began to mend the fences broken by the Theban seizure of Oropos by passing honorific decrees in favour of two leading Boiotians (*IG* ii² 2*a-b*, dated epigraphically; but Walbank 1982b, 274, puts them in 383/2). They too are likely to have been behind an official though naturally secret Athenian embassy to Artaxerxes in 397/6, which was intercepted with fatal consequences on its way home by the Spartan navarch Pharax (Hell. Ox. 7.1; Isaios 11.8; cf. Seager 1967, 95-6). No objections are known to have been raised at Athens, for a reason that became apparent in 396. Demainetos had then set off from Athens, without public authorization but in a state trireme, to make contact with Konon. But Thrasyboulos and others persuaded the Assembly that it would be folly to risk war with Sparta by such a provocation and alerted the Spartan harmost on Aigina. The harmost seems to have failed to stop Demainetos, but the very fact that Sparta controlled 'the eyesore of the Peiraieus' (as Perikles had called Aigina) was sufficient corroboration of Thrasyboulos' caution. Yet in late summer 395 it was none other than Thrasyboulos who proposed accepting the Boiotians' request for an alliance against Sparta that committed Athens to instant military action in Boiotia. What had brought Thrasyboulos into line with Kephalos and Epikrates? Partly the prospect of Persian funds opened up by the continuing success of Konon, partly no doubt gratitude for Theban aid to the democratic Resistance in 404/3, but mainly an alarming growth of Spartan power and influence in central Greece at the expense of Thebes above all in the first instance.

It is not certain when Hismenias' anti-Spartan faction gained an insuperable ascendancy within Thebes and the Boiotian Confederacy as a whole (contrast Perlman 1964, 65-6, with Funke 1980a, 47). But the Confederacy's decision to scatter Agesilaos' Aulis sacrifice as 'contrary to the customs and ordinances of the Boiotians' (Plut. *Ages*. 6.10) surely gives the *terminus ante quem*. The rise of Hismenias meant the fall of Leontiadas and so the failure of Agesilaos' preferred technique of exerting Spartan control over her allies through personal connections with oligarchic leaders. For Leontiadas was almost certainly son of the Eurymachos who was prominent in attacking Plataia in 431 (Thuc. 2.2.3; 2.5.7); and the man whom Agesilaos had sent as ambassador to Thebes in 397/6 with a request for troops had been one of the Spartan judges appointed by Agesilaos' father to decide the fate of Plataia in 427 (Paus. 3.9.3), besides being *proxenos* of the Thebans and probably Agesilaos' own father-in-law (cf. Chapter 9). The Boiotians' behaviour towards Agesilaos at Aulis was therefore a double rebuff and insult to the king, personal as well as political. From it stemmed his unreasoning hatred of Thebes (as a state: he did not hate all Thebans of course), a feeling that was given more scope for expression than was conducive to Sparta's best interests (5.1.33; Plut. *Ages*. 22.1,23.3-7,26.2-3).

The Spartans, however, still had powerful cards to play in the preliminaries to a war that must have looked as inevitable to them as the coming Athenian War had appeared to the Athenians in 433. In about May of 395 the Boiotians had refused to submit to arbitration a dispute between their allies in Lokris (East, according to 3.5.3; West, according to Hell. Ox. 18.2) and the Spartans' allies in

Phokis (Hell. Ox. 18.4). The Athenians allegedly showed goodwill to the Boiotians by sending an embassy to Sparta requesting her not to go to war (Paus. 3.9.11). But the Spartan response to Boiotian provocation, encouraged perhaps by Agesilaos' victory near Sardis and certainly with the blessing of Agesilaos, was to appoint Lysander and Pausanias to a joint command against Boiotia. There had been a Spartan garrison at Pharsalos since at least 399 and control of Herakleia Trachinia had been reasserted for about as long. The respective commanders will have been alerted well in advance of July 395 when Lysander was sent by the Ephors to Phokis with orders to collect the forces of the Phokians, Oitaians, Herakleians, Malians, Ainianians and Thessalians and to come with them to Haliartos there to await Pausanias and the forces of the Peloponnesian League (3.5.6; DS 14.82.5-6).

Lysander duly gathered the appointed forces, but hardly less significant was his spectacular diplomatic success in persuading the people of Orchomenos to revolt from the Boiotian Confederacy (outside which, thanks largely to a Spartan garrison, Orchomenos remained until after the Battle of Leuktra). In other words, between the Aulis incident of 396 and the Ephors' mobilization order to Lysander in high summer 395 the Spartans had been very active in behind-the-scenes diplomacy in Boiotia, reverting to their old tactic of divide-and-rule. If, as the sources suggest, the anti-Spartan politicians in Thebes had to employ a ruse involving their Lokrian allies in order to precipitate the war with Sparta, this was no doubt because Sparta had been intriguing with the Orchomenian members of the federal Council to prevent an outright declaration of aggressive war on Sparta by the Confederacy.

Shortly before Lysander reached Haliartos the Athenians, on the proposal of Thrasyboulos, concluded a perpetual defensive alliance with the Boiotians (minus Orchomenos and of course Plataia). The surviving stele (Tod 101 = SV 223) embodies Athens' 'definite and deliberate acceptance of war against Sparta' (Hamilton 1979b, 206), for Lysander was already in Boiotia when the alliance was concluded. The fact that it was Thrasyboulos, not Kephalos or Epikrates, who made the proposal exposes for what it is the low-grade calumny of the Oxyrhynchos Historian (7.2), who ascribed Athens' entry into the war to a clique of warmongering demagogues anxious to 'enrich themselves at public expense'. Xenophon was for once nearer the truth when he made the Boiotian ambassadors to Athens remark that all Athenians notoriously wanted to recover their empire (3.5.10). No doubt their speech as a whole (3.5.8-15) is a heterogeneous cocktail of truths, half-truths and demonstrable falsehoods, but empire (*archê*) was indeed something that all Athenians, not just the starveling mob, would wish to regain.

Archê, however, did not mean the same in Athens as in Sparta. Four strands at least must be distinguished. First, there were the ambitions of the Athenian governing class, whether traditional or newly-politicised, to be satisfied. Despite *Ath. Pol.* 24.3 (cf. Rhodes 1981a, *ad loc.*), there had probably not been as many as 700 imperial posts even at the height of Athens' fifth-century Empire; but there had still been enough to make empire a lucrative source of additional income for many rich Athenians. It was presumably also such men who had managed to acquire the quite remarkable amounts of foreign property detailed on the so-called 'Attic Stelai' of 414 (*IG* i³ 421,426 = M/L 79; cf. Davies 1981, 55ff.). Their natural successors of the 390s turn up in the speeches of Lysias (27.4; 28.6;19.28-9) and Andokides (3.15).

A second strand concerns more particularly the Athenian 'poor', that is those of sub-hoplite status or barely hoplite status. For some 10,000 of these, it has been estimated, the fifth-century Empire had provided land abroad in colonies (new independent settlements: e.g. M/L 49) or in cleruchies where Athenians either settled without forfeiting their Athenian citizenship or drew rents from the labour of the local population (cf. Brunt 1966; Gauthier 1966, 1973). So too it was principally the Athenian poor who benefited from the third strand in *archê*, the grain-supply. The chain linking the compulsion to secure up to one half of Athens' annual grain requirements from abroad to the need for raw materials such as timber to build the fleet that would protect the grain-supply was inextricable: hence Athenian 'raw materials' imperialism.

Finally, and more nebulously, Athenian imperialism of the fifth century had contained a more genuinely panhellenist element than anything the Spartans could muster in favour of their empire. Whatever her faults, and they were many, imperial Athens had after all kept the Asiatic Greeks free from non-Greek control for over two generations. Under the Spartan dispensation, by contrast, they had first been handed back to Persian suzerainty in 412/1 (Chapter 11) and were now (395) being rescued from Persian control solely – it could plausibly be argued – to further Sparta's plans for subjugating the entire Greek world east of the Adriatic (while her ally, Dionysios I of Syracuse, was bringing Greek Sicily and South Italy under his sway). This 'panhellenist' strand in the Athenian desire for *archê* became fully visible in 393 and notably prominent in the peace negotiations of (probably) 392/1.

The Corinthian War had begun badly for Sparta with Lysander's defeat and death at Haliartos followed by the trial and exile of Pausanias. The Boiotians had then overturned Sparta's control of central Greece and southern Thessaly, and Argos and Corinth had joined with them and the Athenians to form a quadruple alliance to which several other former allies of Sparta defected (cf. Accame 1951, 53-63). Sparta's position was retrieved somewhat by victories in the two major land-battles of the war, both in 394, but these were more than offset by the naval defeat off Knidos, which curtailed Sparta's pretensions to maritime hegemony and even led to the occupation in 393 of part of her home territory (Kythera). Athens was the chief beneficiary of this development. With the money Pharnabazus channelled to the anti-Spartans through Konon the walls that Athens had begun to rebuild in 395 or 394 could be finished off more smartly (in both senses). Once again Athens could develop a useful fleet and entertain more realistically the old dream of re-establishing an *archê* of some description. The Boiotians, however, had sustained heavy losses, and the pendulum will have begun to swing back towards Leontiadas at Thebes. The Corinthians, too, were suffering from being the central focus of the war by land and experiencing the continual ravaging or occupation of their territory. The Argives had probably suffered less than the Boiotians and Corinthians but had gained less from the war than the Athenians.

It was with mixed feelings, therefore, that representatives from the four main opponents of Sparta followed Antalkidas to Sardis in 392, and it was perhaps fortunate for the unity of the Quadruple Alliance that Artaxerxes (unlike Tiribazus) was not yet prepared to settle on Sparta's preferred terms (cf. Chapter 11). But by the time the Spartans called a further peace conference at Sparta in the winter of 392/1 the terms for peace had been significantly altered, apparently with the concurrence of the Great King (cf. Philochoros 328F149). The concessions that Sparta had earlier felt no need or desire to make are revealed in Andokides' speech to the Athenian Assembly in favour of the new deal: to the Thebans retention intact of the Boiotian Confederacy as then constituted (Andok. 3.13,20), to the Athenians retention of their recently replanted cleruchies on the islands of Lemnos, Imbros and Skyros (Andok. 3.12,14) – so vital for safeguarding the grain route (cf. Rhodes 1981a, 686-7,694-5; Graham 1983, 184-9). But there were to be no concessions to the Corinthians and Argives, who were now closely united and perhaps fully integrated (cf. Chapter 13); so their ability to continue their martial opposition to Sparta hung on the attitude of the Athenians and Boiotians. The latter were now prepared to make peace: Leontiadas was presumably again in the ascendant at Thebes, and he had Sparta's Orchomenos garrison to back him up. But the Athenians – unlike Andokides and his fellow envoys to Sparta – were not. Knidos and its aftermath encouraged the Athenians to believe that their best hope for restoring *archê* was by continuing the war against Sparta with the backing of Tiribazus' successor, the pro-Athenian Strouthas or Strouses.

The peace negotiations of 392/1 thus failed. But the Boiotians did not recover their appetite for the war until Iphikrates' peltasts destroyed half a Spartan regiment near Lechaion in 390 (Chapter 12). Indeed, Boiotian ambassadors were actually treating for peace with Agesilaos through Pharax, the Theban *proxenos* at Sparta, when news of the Lechaion disaster arrived (4.5.6-9). Neither side, however, showed any sign of being able to win the war outright by land. It took startling developments in the war at sea between 391 and 388 to break the deadlock. Briefly, Athens through Thrasyboulos above all and with the aid of a now anti-Persian Euagoras (cf. Costa 1974) began to recreate what to Artaxerxes and Sparta looked suspiciously like her fifth-century Empire. Strouthas was therefore replaced by Tiribazus, Pharnabazus by a *xenos* of Antalkidas, and an alliance made by Artaxerxes with Sparta through Antalkidas, who as navarch in 388/7 was also aided by Syracusan ships. Athens' war ended in 387 when Antalkidas emulated Lysander in closing the Hellespont. Athens' allies made a show of resisting the peace terms worked out between Persia and Sparta, but Agesilaos was able to insist on the separation of Argos and Corinth, the dismemberment of the Boiotian Confederacy and the restoration of pro-Spartan exiles at Thebes and Corinth before the terms of the Peace of Antalkidas were sworn. If Athens was permitted to retain Lemnos, Imbros and Skyros, this was to drive a wedge between Athens and Thebes. Agesilaos' real quarrel was not with Athens.

Or so he thought – wrongly, as it proved. For just as Sparta's aggressive imperialism after 404 had in 395 thrown up an anti-Spartan alliance inspired by Thebes, so her similar behaviour after 386 generated in 378 an anti-Spartan alliance headed by Athens; in both alliances the 'natural' enemies, Athens and

Thebes, were to be found co-operating, uneasily to be sure. How had Athens come to assume a potentially hegemonial position once more? What had brought Thebes and Athens together again?

As pointed out earlier, *archê* of some form was in a sense a necessity not a luxury for Athens. But after her defeat in the Athenian War there was little she could do to re-establish her Aegean connections other than pass or reaffirm honorific decrees in favour of the leading pro-Athenian politicians in strategically vital cities like Abydos, Byzantion and Thasos (*IG* ii^2 49,76; Tod 98). In the wake of Knidos, however, Athens became bolder and made at least two or three individual grants of Athenian citizenship (to citizens of Rhodes, Thasos and Klazomenai: Osborne 1982, D7-8; Walbank 1983), besides honouring Euagoras as 'a Greek conferring benefits on Greece' (Hornblower 1982, 294 and n.3, referring to Lewis/Stroud 1979, whose text supersedes Tod 109) and showering unprecedented honours on her favourite son Konon (cf. Tod 128).

Konon's career was cut short in 392, but his mantle was assumed by Thrasyboulos, who wore it with considerable distinction (cf. Seager 1967; Cawkwell 1976b). Between 390 and 389 he renewed Athenian alliances with Thasos, the Thracian Odrysoi, and Byzantion, getting the Thasians to agree to pay a five per cent tax on their seaborne trade and re-establishing the ten per cent tax levied at Byzantion on goods passing through the Bosporos (4.8.27; cf. 1.1.22, 3.5.10). These imposts were necessary to finance Athens' fleet and need not have been seen as oppressive. For an honorific decree passed by Athens in favour of Klazomenai in 387, though providing for payment of the same five per cent tax as the Thasians paid, specifically affirms the freedom of Klazomenai as meaning freedom from a garrison and governor (Tod 114; cf. Konon's manifesto after Knidos: 4.8.1-2,5). Significantly, a recently discovered decree passed by Erythrai at about the same time (*SEG* 26.1282) confirms that at least the democracies in Asiatic Greece which had owed their liberation from Sparta to Konon or Thrasyboulos regarded Persia not Athens as the threat to their autonomy (cf. Hornblower 1982, 108). On the other hand, the automatic assumption in Athens' treaty with Thasos (*IG* ii^2 24*b*. 3-6) that Athenian jurisdiction extended throughout her alliance is a sure, if only semi-conscious, sign of '*archê*-mentality' in a harsher, imperialistic sense (Griffith 1978, 129-30), and it is probably right to see Thrasyboulos as 'a full-blooded would-be restorer of the fifth-century empire' (Cawkwell 1976b, 270). That may explain why *en route* to Rhodes Thrasyboulos was murdered at Aspendos by locals enraged by his soldiers' freebooting.

In 387/6 Athens lost control of the Hellespont to Antalkidas, much to the chagrin of Kephalos (Tod 116.6-22; cf. Pritchett 1974, II, 9) and the majority of poor Athenians. Permission to retain Lemnos, Imbros and Skyros under the terms of the Peace of Antalkidas was poor compensation for the prospects that had seemed to be opening up under Thrasyboulos and his successor as general Agyrrhios, the politician who had proposed the introduction of Assembly pay in the 390s. Once again, as after 404, Athens was reduced to diplomatic manoeuvring. In 386/5 she gave a form of diplomatic recognition to the new king of the Odrysoi, whose situation towards the Hellespont made his friendship desirable (Tod 117; cf. Sinclair 1978, 47-9). In 384 she concluded a defensive alliance with Chios and in 383/2 was interested in making an alliance with Olynthos and the Chalkidians (5.2.15). With hindsight the Chios alliance can be seen as a sort of blueprint for the alliances that constituted the Second Athenian League, but first the Olynthos negotiations require consideration since they reintroduce the main theme of this chapter – the Sparta-Thebes-Athens triangle.

Agesilaos had successfully insisted that the Boiotian Confederacy be dismantled before Thebes and the other Boiotian cities were admitted to the Peace of Antalkidas as atomized units. He had also enforced the restoration of exiles to Thebes, and it would not be over-ambitious to speculate that among their number was Leontiadas, who could well have found it prudent to retire to Orchomenos after the failure of the peace initiatives of 392-0. However, by breaking up the Confederacy Agesilaos had deprived Leontiadas and his sort of a powerful argument in favour of the Spartan connection, since they could no longer claim that Theban hegemony of Boiotia had Sparta's (admittedly grudging) assent. Hismenias, on the other hand, could point to the break-up of the Confederacy as triumphant justification of his opposition to Sparta since 404. Under the circumstances it would have been natural for him and his faction to become not just anti-Spartan but to a degree pro-Athenian, and it is an indication both of this orientation and of the growing ascendancy of Hismenias within Thebes that both Athens and Thebes should have been conducting negotiations at Olynthos in 383/2. But any prospect of a new anti-Spartan axis was temporarily interrupted in 382 when Phoibidas seized and garrisoned the Theban akropolis and entrusted the government to a puppet *dunasteia* led (of course) by Leontiadas. Hismenias was 'tried' and executed, ostensibly for leading the Thebans to break their oaths as Peloponnesian League allies – hence the composition of the 'court': three judges from Sparta, one each from the other allied states (cf. Cawkwell 1973, 53n.3) – and for having 'barbarized', that is treasonously taken money from Persia to embroil 'Greece' in war (5.2.35-6). But his principal colleague, Androkleidas, and 300 other Thebans of his persuasion escaped and were given official and honourable sanctuary at Athens, like the Athenians' *proxenos* at Orchomenos, some of the Mantineians exiled by Agesipolis in 385, some pro-Athenian Thasians who apparently had again (as in 411) found themselves the victims of a pro-Spartan coup, and sundry other political refugees (*IG* ii² 33,37; cf. Osborne 1982, 49-50, 52; Walbank 1982b).

There can be no doubt but that the inspiration behind this remarkable *démarche* was Agesilaos. Xenophon was no friend to Thebes, since for most of his adult life its leaders did not 'have the best interests of the Peloponnese at heart' (7.4.35; 7.5.1; cf. Cawkwell 1972a, 256). Yet even Xenophon virtually makes an outright criticism of Agesilaos for his attitude to the seizure of Thebes. Unlike Plutarch (*Ages.* 24.1; cf. DS 15.20.2), Xenophon does not baldly assert that Agesilaos authorised Phoibidas' action, which he represents as a last-minute private arrangement between Phoibidas and Leontiadas (5.2.25-7), and he is careful to cast aspersions on Phoibidas' suitability as a commander (5.2.28). But he makes it unambiguously clear that it was Agesilaos' support for Phoibidas (whose life he saved: Chapter 9) and Leontiadas which prevailed over the initial opposition of 'the Ephors and most of the citizens' and persuaded them to retain the garrison; he reveals that Agesilaos was prepared to 'turn the state upside down' in order to restore his Theban *hetairoi* when they in their turn were exiled in 379/8 (5.4.13; Xen. *Ages.* 2.22 – where the reading should be *lakônizontôn* not *Lakedaimoniôn*); and he records that Agesilaos left Phoibidas as harmost of Thespiai in 378 (5.4.41; cf. Chapter 12). Yet despite Agesilaos' unswerving commitment to this military 'solution' of the Theban problem, Xenophon makes no secret of the fact that he regards Leontiadas' regime as a collective tyranny (5.4.1,13; cf. 6.3.8 and in general 2.4.38), and he goes so far as to attribute Sparta's ultimate demise as a great power to divine retribution for impiously seizing the Kadmeia in contravention of the oaths she had sworn under the terms of the Peace of Antalkidas to leave all Greek cities autonomous (5.4.1, 6.4.3; cf. 6.3.11). For once Xenophon seems not to have been taken in by Agesilaos' spurious Panhellenism, invoked here to justify the execution of Hismenias.

None the less, as Cawkwell (1979, 279n.) has well observed, 'There seems to be a curious dichotomy in Xenophon's mind: Sparta was punished for her wrongful acts, but Agesilaus, who was largely responsible for them, is shielded from censure and remained for Xenophon "a completely good man" (*Ages.* 1.1)'. However, Cawkwell himself (1976a) is surely less than convincing when he defends Agesilaos' 'severe policy' as conducive to Sparta's best interests. For his overriding objective ought to have been to foster the mutual antipathy of Thebes and Athens in order to nullify any plans that either might have for confronting Sparta and, above all, confronting Sparta jointly. As the aftermaths of Thebes' liberation in 379/8 and her victory at Leuktra in 371 were amply to show, there was a powerful anti-Theban lobby in Athens. But that lobby could hardly hope to make much headway if Sparta did not merely condone but actively promoted military interventions in the internal affairs of autonomous and independent states and propped up regimes at the furthest pole from Athens' own radical brand of democracy. The installation of an oligarchic *dunasteia* backed by a garrison (perhaps two *morai* commanded respectively by Arkissos and Agesilaos' man Herippidas under the harmost Lysanoridas: von Stern 1884, 58-9n.1) was virtually calculated to dispel any jubilation the Athenians felt at the humiliation of Thebes by reminding them of Athens' own similar fate in 404-3. It was not merely out of sentiment, therefore, that Athens sheltered the Theban exiles in 382-379, lent assistance towards the liberation of Thebes in 379/8, made an alliance with Thebes in 378 and sent Thrasyboulos of Kollytos, one of the Phyle and Peiraieus men of 403, as ambassador to Thebes early in 377 (Tod 123.72-8).

By early 377, however, the international standing of Athens had been transformed by the foundation of the Second Athenian League, which appears to have occurred before the middle of 378. Xenophon did not mention, let alone describe, this momentous development, though he does refer much later to the League as a going concern (6.3.19; cf. perhaps 6.2.1; 6.5.2; 7.1.15). Diodoros, on the other hand, excels his usual self in the fullness and seeming accuracy of his detail (DS 15.28.2-4, 29.5-8) – apart from the chronology, agreement on which among modern scholars is probably impossible. Two points about the origins of the League are sufficiently clear: that the seeds of it may be detected in the bilateral alliance of 384 between Athens and Chios, and that the abortive raid on the Peiraieus by the Spartan harmost of Thespiai early in 378 overcame any remaining Athenian resistance to co-operation with Thebes or doubts about the legitimacy, legality or practical wisdom of the League.

The Chians had been founder-members of Athens' first sea-league, the so-called Delian League which rapidly fulfilled its inherent potential for becoming an Athenian Empire. Exceptionally, they had retained both their fleet and their oligarchic constitution until 412, when they revolted. Thucydides admiringly commented (8.24.2) that 'after the Spartans the Chians are the only people I am aware of who have remained sensible in prosperity and who have increased the security of their state in proportion as it grew more powerful'; but his view would have altered after the Battle of Knidos. Alienated by Spartan oppression (Isok. 8.98), the Chians not only revolted from Sparta to Konon (DS 14.84.3) but probably also – like the Knidians (cf. Arist. *Pol.* 1305b12ff.) – went democratic. The terms of their alliance with Athens in 384 made it plain, chiefly for the benefit of Sparta and lakonizing Chian oligarchs (like the father of the historian Theopompos: cf. Hornblower 1982, 131 and n.205), that this was an agreement between democracies. The trend visible in Athens' relations with Byzantion, Klazomenai and Erythrai between 390 and 387 was continued.

The constitutional aspect of the alliance, however, was less important than the scrupulosity with which the terms avoided contravening the Peace of Antalkidas and thereby insinuated that Sparta was in breach – as she had been at Mantineia in 385 (Chapter 13) and probably also Thasos in the same year (cf. Osborne 1982, 52-3). The allies aimed to preserve 'the P[eace and the frien] dship and the oaths and [the existing agreement]s, which (the) Kin[g] an[d (the) Athenians and] Lakedaimonians and the othe[r Greeks] swore' (Tod 118 = SV 248.9-12). The alliance is described as a *summachia*, but it was intended as and could only be purely defensive, whatever its Athenian promoter, Kephalos, might have wished. Not until the liberation of Thebes in the winter of 379/8 did the balance of naval and military power decisively tilt away from Sparta to Athens and Thebes respectively.

This shift was not totally unheralded or unexpected, as a superficial reading of Xenophon (5.3.27; cf. Isok. 4.128; 15.57; DS 15.23.3-5) might suggest. For after pointing out that by 379 Sparta had established her *archê* firmly to all outward appearances, he proceeds straight to his damning comment on the impiety of Sparta's seizure of the Kadmeia by which he explained the demise of that *archê* (5.4.1). This is typical of his allusive manner. On the surface, perhaps, everything in Sparta's extensive garden was lovely, but the soil was producing weeds that were eventually to choke the blooms – *oliganthrôpia*, internal opposition to Agesilaos' foreign policy, allied reluctance to serve personally in Peloponnesian League expeditions. If 'the full military might of Sparta' (Cawkwell 1976a, 80) was unable to resubjugate Thebes after the liberation, this was because it was little compared to what it had been in 431 or even 394.

The epic tale of the recovery of Thebes by exiles led by Pelopidas is no concern of ours (5.4.2-12; Plut. *Pelop.* 8-13, *Mor.* 597-8; cf. von Stern 1884, 44-62; Rice 1975, 96-103). But one unromantic detail is significant. The Spartan harmost, seeing that the Theban cavalry and hoplites had responded enthusiastically to the liberators' call to arms, sent for help to Plataia and Thespiai (5.4.10). Thus covertly does Xenophon betray the resurrection of Plataia from the ashes of 427/6 at some time after the Peace of Antalkidas (Paus. 9.1.4; Isok. 4.109; 14.51; cf. Hack 1978, 216 and n.17). If the Spartans had effected it before their occupation of Thebes in 382, this would further account for Thebes' anti-Spartan activity in 383/2; if after, it makes even more understandable the welcome accorded the liberators by the arms-bearing section of the Theban population. For these were the men who had held full citizen rights under the Boiotian Confederacy and, whatever their other internal disagreements might have been, they were agreed that the Confederacy was a Good Thing and that the non-existence of Plataia was conducive to Thebes' domination of the Confederacy. Leontiadas, on the other hand, had of course had to forswear any attempt to reconstitute the Confederacy (5.2.34; cf. 5.2.16) as a condition of Sparta's – that is, Agesilaos' – support for his regime.

The situation and attitude of Leontiadas were comparable to those of the extreme Athenian oligarchs in 411. Ideally, the latter would have liked to keep the Empire, or at least the fleet and the fortifications of Athens. But if the only way that they could cling on to power at Athens and save their skins was with Spartan support, and if Sparta's conditions for support included the abandonment of all three, then so be it (Thuc. 8.91.3). The upshot was the identification of oligarchy with treachery at Athens and a resurgence of democratic feeling among the men of moderate means. At Thebes in the late 380s there was no democratic tradition to revive, but the liberators had spent several years at Athens, from where the identification of oligarchy with treason and democracy with freedom will have been easier to make; and for the immediate future the fortunes of liberated Thebes were found to be closely intertwined with those of Athens. It was not entirely surprising, therefore, that the renascent Thebes and Boiotian Confederacy of the 370s should have been reconstituted on democratic lines.

Full diplomatic and military *rapprochement* with Athens, however, proved to be far from straightforward. The imprecisions and uncertainties of our sources (especially chronological) mean that the steps whereby it was achieved during the first half of 378 cannot be firmly reconstructed. It seems that the Athenians, prompted by Kephalos, had given official military support to the liberation but that Kleombrotos' invasion of Boiotia had occasioned second thoughts (cf. Cawkwell 1973, 56ff; *contra* von Stern 1884, 59-60n.1). The expedition of Kleombrotos, however, proved such a failure that Agesilaos feared it might speed rather than retard Athens' *rapprochement* with Thebes, especially as the liberation had encouraged Athens to seek further alliances of the kind she already enjoyed with Chios. Hence the despatch post-haste of a three-man embassy to Athens led by Agesilaos' political friend and fellow-member of the Gerousia, Etymokles (cf. Chapter 9).

One of the other two ambassadors was Okyllos, and the kind of line taken in 378 can probably be inferred from the line taken by Etymokles and Okyllos at Athens in 369, by which time Thebes was infinitely more powerful: 'If you and we could be of one mind, Athenians, there is every reason to hope that together

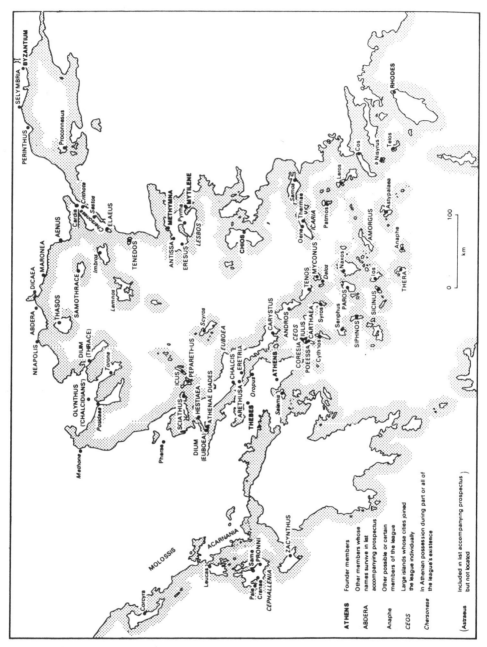

Fig. 14. The Second Athenian League. After Talbert

we could, as the old saying has it, decimate the Thebans' (6.5.35). Despite their suspicion or rather fear of the Thebans, the Athenians remained chary of unstinted co-operation with Sparta even in 369; so in February or March 378 such an appeal is likely to have struck still less of a chord. In any case, any sympathy for co-operation or at least peaceful coexistence with Sparta that the leading anti-Theban Kallistratos might have hoped to exploit was killed by Sphodrias' invasion of Attika at the very moment the ambassadors were in Athens. Either now or after Sphodrias' monstrously unjust acquittal the Athenians voted that the Spartans had definitely broken the Peace of Antalkidas (DS 15.29.7; cf. 5.4.34) and so began to place themselves on a war-footing (cf. Cawkwell 1981a, 74-6).

The aetiology of Sphodrias' horribly abortive incursion will never be known (cf. Chapters 8 and 9 for detailed discussions of his political trial). Plausible arguments can be made for believing that Sphodrias had been bribed by the Thebans (5.4.20,30; cf. Cargill 1981, 59), put up to it by Kleombrotos (DS 15.29.5; cf. Rice 1975, 112-18), or inspired by ambitious rivalry with Phoibidas (cf. Hertzberg 1856, 336n.28). But whatever caused the raid, it destroyed the pacific policy of Agesilaos, who wanted Athens to stand idly by while he forcibly resubjugated Thebes, and it chiefly benefited those politicians in Thebes who advocated an anti-Spartan alliance with Athens. Any initial hesitation that the new Theban democratic regime may have felt about joining the infant Second Athenian League, which appears to have been in existence before the end of the archon-year 379/8, will have been reduced or overcome by the military and political onslaught unleashed by Agesilaos in the summer of 378. The Thebans had declared their intention of restoring a Boiotian Confederacy by electing four Theban Boiotarchs early in 378 (Plut. *Pelop.* 13.1,14.2: cf. *Ages.* 24.6; cf. Buckler 1979, 56). But it was as 'the Thebans' not as leaders of 'the Boiotians' that they joined the Second Athenian League.

This organization was a remarkable attempt to adapt the 'hegemonic symmachy' formula of the fifth century, which had left behind an odour of imperialism, to the 'autonomy' formula enshrined in the Peace of Antalkidas. Getting on for a year after it was founded a prospectus was published – technically a decree proposed by Aristoteles (mentioned only by DS 15.28.2) – to attract new members (*IG* ii² 43 = Tod 123 = SV 257: picture in Sealey 1977, 413; text, translation and commentary in Cargill 1981, 14-47). Names of members, fifty-eight or fifty-nine in all (Fig. 14), were added to the stone at different times and by at least half a dozen masons down to 375. Only these, it has been plausibly argued, were members of the League – as distinct from allies of Athens and the League or bilateral allies of Athens. But since the stone has not survived complete, and as the text is not entirely undamaged, there is still room for argument over the status of some allies, most notably Kerkyra. For although Kerkyra's name does not appear on the prospectus stone, the stele recording her membership of the League has survived (Tod 127 = SV 263). The simplest hypothesis is that Kerkyra's name was inscribed on the prospectus stone but is now lost (cf. Cawkwell 1981b, 42). But in that case Athens would later have been guilty of transgressing a crucial article of the prospectus by interfering with Kerkyra's autonomy (Ain. Takt. 11.13-15; cf. 5.4.64). This is a nice illustration of the difficulties of interpretation that even a relatively well preserved document can produce.

For our purposes the most important section of the prospectus is that which specifies the intended pool from which allies are to be attracted and spells out the meaning of freedom and autonomy for prospective allies (lines 15 to 31). The alliance was to be open to any Greeks or non-Greeks of the mainland or islands except those who belonged to the Great King of Persia; in practice republics, fractions of republics, confederacies and monarchs all joined. As for autonomy, this is to mean self-government in accordance with the constitution preferred by the ally; freedom from garrison, governor and tribute; and prohibition of Athenian public or private ownership of land in the ally's territory. In short: no imperialism of the Spartan variety as displayed since 404 and more especially 386 (cf. Hamilton 1980); no revival of the anti-Persian aggression by Athens of 390-387; and, above all, no return to the unpopular features of the fifth-century Athenian Empire, pre-eminently the Athenian ownership or occupation of allied land.

The latter was a cardinal point to advertise since about four fifths of the certainly identifiable members of the League had also been in the fifth-century Empire; it was, moreover, specified – a major concession – that cases of alleged infringement would be tried solely by the allies (lines 35 to 46; cf. Cargill 1981, 122-3,146). These were to send representatives to a congress (*sunedrion*) that would sit permanently in Athens, in which Athens herself would have no seat. The prospectus is, however, disappointingly silent about the modalities of decision-making by the League as a whole, and documentary evidence of other sorts is neither as full nor as clear on these as could be wished. Modern debate has centred understandably on the extent to which Athens lived up to her pledges or rather the extent to which she breached them in spirit if not in the letter – for example, by collecting what was tantamount to tribute (*phoros*) but designated as *suntaxis* ('contribution'). But as serious in practical terms as any technical or moral infringements of the prospectus by Athens was the growing divergence of interests between the *hêgemôn* and its more important allies. This could be a ground for disaffection or even revolt no less than any specific abuses by Athens.

The first state to show such disaffection arising out of a divergent perception of its real immediate interests was, predictably, Thebes. Just before the names began to be added to the prospectus stone the decree of Aristoteles ends with a clause providing for the despatch of a three-man embassy to Thebes 'to persuade the Thebans to whatever good they can'. What had prompted this embassy is not stated, but in view of the timing (February-March 377) it is most likely that just before the new campaigning season the Athenians wished politely but firmly to remind their Theban allies of their other than narrowly Boiotian responsibilities and obligations. If Athens was to help defend Thebes against the next, imminent invasion of Boiotia by Agesilaos, then Thebes must make her contribution to ridding the Aegean of Spartan influence and presence, not least on Aigina, which since Lysander had restored the expelled islanders in 404 had been a Spartan base threatening communications with Athens by sea.

There is evidence, as we shall see, that Thebes complied. But her Boiotian preoccupation was wholly explicable. For in response to Thebes' declaration of intent to restore a Boiotian Confederacy (which like the government of Thebes herself was likely to be run on democratic lines) Agesilaos in 378 had extended the Lysandreian formula applied to Thebes in 382 to other Boiotian cities including Thespiai, Orchomenos, Tanagra and the reborn Plataia. Xenophon alludes to this development in a characteristically prejudiced way, long after it had actually occurred. After recounting Agesilaos' expedition into Boiotia of summer/autumn 378 (Chapter 12) and the death of Phoibidas, harmost of Thespiai, in winter 378/7, Xenophon writes a sentence whose metaphorical language means roughly: 'After this the ambitions of the Thebans were rekindled' (5.4.46). This is probably a sly allusion to the refoundation in embryo of the Boiotian Confederacy (cf. Buckler 1979; 1980c, 15-45); but he continues: 'They sent out forces against Thespiai and the other neighbouring cities (*perioikides poleis*)'. By using *perioikides*, a term that could connote political subordination (cf. Chapters 10, 12 and 13), Xenophon suggests that in the view of the Thebans these cities were not potential members of an egalitarian Boiotian Confederacy but rather objects of Theban acquisitive aggression. He has succeeded in pulling the wool over the eyes of Freeman (1893, 139), but the reason for his biased introduction becomes apparent immediately afterwards. 'From these cities the *dêmos* had withdrawn and taken refuge in Thebes, since in all of them *dunasteiai* had been established, as in Thebes.' In other words, after the liberation of Thebes and the fiasco of Sphodrias' invasion of Attika Agesilaos and his man Phoibidas had imposed narrow oligarchies on the other main cities of Boiotia and compelled those members of the democratic factions who had not been killed to go into exile at now democratic Thebes (cf. Hack 1978, 216 and n.16; Buckler 1980c, 19-20). This puts the supposed imperialism of Thebes into perspective and explains why, when she had succeeded in re-establishing a Boiotian Confederacy, its decision-making body was a primary democratic assembly not an oligarchic council (hence *damos* in *IG* VII.2407; DS 15.80.2, 16.25.1). The interests of Thebes, therefore, were significantly different from those of Athens and the majority of states attracted by Athens' terms of alliance under the umbrella of the Second Athenian League.

The first four years of the League's existence were years of almost unmitigated success. In Chabrias, Timotheos (son of Konon) and Iphikrates Athens possessed more than passable admirals, in Kallistratos something of a financial wizard. It was Kallistratos who reorganized the system whereby wealthy Athenians paid levies on capital for war purposes (*eisphorai*: Polyb. 2.62; Dem. 22.44; cf. Ste. Croix 1953) and he who was credited with coining the innocuous-sounding 'contribution' label for what were more or less compulsory contributions. In 377 the League fleet was unable to prevent the Spartan harmost of Oreos/Histiaia in north Euboia from intercepting two triremes bearing Thessalian wheat to hungry Thebes (5.4.56-7). But in 376 the tide turned emphatically against Sparta.

The Peloponnesian League expedition of that summer against Thebes had been abortive, and the three previous invasions of Boiotia had failed to bring Thebes to her knees. So in the summer of 376 the Peloponnesians decided to transfer their attentions to Athens and to try conclusions by sea. This was a somewhat bold decision in that Sparta and her allies had allowed their fleet to run down since 386 (cf. Sinclair 1978, 45-7; *contra* Kelly 1975, 164-72). But the aim was to starve Athens into submission by controlling the waters around the islands of Aigina, Keos and Andros so that the grain destined for the Peiraieus could get no further than Geraistos in north Euboia (5.4.60-1). Again, although the plan was sound in principle, the Peloponnesians were disadvantaged by the fact that Andros, the four cities of Keos and all the Euboians except Oreos/Histiaia were already members of the Second Athenian League. Presumably the scheme was the brainchild of Kleombrotos and supported by Antalkidas, who were taking advantage of the temporary indisposition and discrediting of Agesilaos.

Politically, therefore, Chabrias' smashing victory off Naxos in September 376 (5.4.61; DS 15.34-5) must have given Agesilaos some grim satisfaction. But militarily, diplomatically and economically it was a major disaster for the Spartan alliance. Some kind of Spartan naval presence was maintained on Aigina (6.2.1), but in 375 Timotheos could cruise around the Peloponnese in a manner uncomfortably reminiscent of the good old days of Tolmides in the 450s (cf. Cartledge 1979, 228-9), bring Kerkyra under Athenian control, and round his voyage off with another decisive victory at Alyzeia in Akarnania near the island of Leukas (5.4.65-6). Both victories brought a flood of new members of the Second Athenian League, the most pleasing of which to Athens were those in the northern Aegean, Thracian Chersonese and Bosporos regions. As for the Thebans, they in 375 were revelling in their second consecutive year free from Spartan invasion of Boiotia, 'boldly conducting campaigns against the neighbouring (*perioikides*) cities and taking them in hand again' (5.4.63). In other, more neutral words, they were adding the finishing touches to the refoundation of the Boiotian Confederacy on its new, democratic model. Later in 375, according to Xenophon (6.1.1), the process was completed, although the status of Orchomenos, Thespiai and Plataia is murky (cf. Buckler 1979, 56; Gray 1980, 309-11).

The Athenians no doubt were less than totally happy with the growth of Theban power that their alliance had fostered. But, as in early 377, what seems to have upset them most, at least officially, was the Thebans' failure to make the required *quid pro quo* by paying their fair share of the costs of League expeditions (cf. 6.2.1). On the other hand, the supposed exhaustion of the Athenian rich by repeated *eisphora*-payments deserves less sympathy than Xenophon (6.2.1) would suggest: given the amounts actually raised in this way, it seems clear that there was considerable under-declaration of taxable capital wealth.

But if the Athenians had cause for disquiet in regard to Thebes, the Spartans had cause for alarm. Not only did their Orchomenos garrison get mauled by Pelopidas' cavalry and Sacred Band in 375 (Chapter 12) but the Boiotians – as they may now properly be called – invaded the territory of the Spartans' allies in Phokis (6.1.1; cf. Gray 1980, 309). So grave was this threat perceived to be that a Peloponnesian League force was despatched to Phokis under Kleombrotos; and when the Spartans' *proxenos* at Pharsalos appealed for Spartan help against Jason of Pherai, the Spartans decided that they could not either redeploy Kleombrotos' force or raise a further army to prevent Jason from uniting

Thessaly under his control. In this way was the *Nordpolitik* they had pursued largely successfully since the end of the Athenian War rudely interrupted.

Both the Athenians and the Spartans, therefore, now had reasons for finding a renewal of peace attractive. It was most opportune that in the autumn of 375 a royal rescript arrived from Artaxerxes enjoining a remaking of the Peace of Antalkidas so that he might recruit Greek mercenaries to combat internal rebellion (DS 15.38.1). Opportune but not, surely, serendipitous. Xenophon would have been the last person to mention any Spartan embassy that might have winged its way to Artaxerxes in the wake of the Battle of Naxos. But that is probably what happened (cf. Cawkwell 1963, 90; Gray 1980, 315). However, not only the immediate antecedents but also the date and nature of the Peace of 375/4 are highly controversial. On balance, I accept the arguments for placing it in the second half of 375 and interpreting it as being in its basic articles a remaking of the now practically defunct Peace of Antalkidas (cf. Cawkwell 1963, 88-91; Buckler 1971; Gray 1980, 307-15; Cawkwell 1981a). There were, however, two major *de facto* differences.

First, the Peace of 375/4 was like that of 446/5 in that it was essentially concluded between two blocks of allies led respectively, though in very different circumstances, by Sparta and Athens. Indeed, so great was the Athenians' joy, mixed no doubt with relief, that their hegemony at sea was being recognized formally by Sparta (Philochoros, *FGrHist.* 328F151; Nep. *Tim.* 2.3) that they inaugurated a festival of Peace (*SEG* 29.88; cf. Hamdorf 1964, 53-5, 110, T433; Cawkwell 1981b, 43). Given the recent threat to the daily bread of many Athenians, it would not be unreasonable to suppose that it was the child Ploutos (Wealth) rather than the lady Eirene (Peace) who most fully embodied their aspirations as they contemplated Kephisodotos' officially commissioned statue-group.

The second major difference concerns the position of Thebes. Diodoros, it is generally agreed, has seriously confused the Peace of 375/4 with that of 372/1 and is therefore wrong to allege that the Thebans were excluded from the former. On the other hand, it would be surprising if the Thebans had been prepared to swear to the Peace under precisely the same conditions as had been imposed on them by Agesilaos in 386. For they had only just reconstituted a Boiotian Confederacy, and the Spartans, as the Battle of Tegyra in spring 375 had confirmed, were unable to compel them militarily to disband it. Technically speaking, the Thebans presumably swore to the Peace as just one ally among the sixty or so in Athens' Second League. But the Thebans cannot have considered that *eo ipso* they were abolishing their Confederacy. Either formally or informally 'the Thebans' was taken by them to stand for 'the Boiotians'. The Athenians and Spartans will not have liked this, and it is significant that the Athenians never changed 'the Thebans' to 'the Boiotians' on the prospectus stone of the Second Athenian League. But in the immediate term Sparta and Athens were too preoccupied with each other to be able to contemplate united opposition to Thebes. For the situation after the conclusion of the Peace of 375/4 rapidly became one of 'common anarchy' (DS 15.45.1) rather than common peace, and the Peace broke down over differences between Athens and Sparta in western Greece.

Again, there are chronological difficulties of reconstruction; and both sides had grounds for complaint to hurl at each other (cf. Gray 1980, 315-26). But the root cause of the renewed fighting seems to have been that the Athenians, fired by their recent naval and diplomatic successes, were no longer willing to allow the Spartans a monopoly in the exploitation of *stasis* to enforce their ideological interpretation of the Peace's autonomy clause. Neither side, however, had the financial capacity or manpower to wage a protracted naval war. Wealthy Athenians were reluctant not only to pay *eisphorai* but also to perform the compulsory duty (*leitourgia*) of *trierarchia*, that is equipping the triremes to which they were notionally allotted as captains. 'Contributions' were now introduced, or stepped up, to maintain bases at key points and pay crews who were not readily available in the desired quantity or quality. The installation of a garrison on Kephallenia was technically a breach of the prospectus. In short, the Second Athenian League was beginning to run out of steam. As for the Spartans, their Peloponnesian League allies could muster only small fleets and preferred to contribute cash rather than serve in person, according to the commutation system agreed in 382 (Chapter 13). They themselves, with isolated exceptions like Lysander and Teleutias, had a poor record of commanding mercenaries, especially at sea (cf. Chapter 15); but in Mnasippos they failed to maintain even that inadequate standard. To the usual insensitive brutality of the typical Spartan commander he added the vices of meanness and incompetence, with the result that in 372 the war in the west took the nastiest possible turn for the Spartans. As in 393 they were again faced with a direct naval threat to their own home territory, and from a commander, Iphikrates, who was the peer of Konon (6.2.9,33; cf. 6.4.1).

So as in 375 both Sparta and Athens, not to mention their respective allies on the whole, were powerfully motivated to renew the peace. Now, however, over and above their unhappy experience of expensive but ineffectual fighting in 374 and 373, there was a further factor which did not merely counsel peaceful coexistence but suggested the desirability of a more active co-operation in the foreseeable future. That factor was Thebes, whose restless dynamism both political and military was not be halted by anything so insubstantial as a form of words. By the beginning of 371 the Thebans had absorbed both Plataia and Thespiai within their Confederacy (leaving Orchomenos as the only 'holdout') and were again menacing Phokis. It is true that they still maintained to outward appearances their membership of the Second Athenian League: there were Boiotian ships in Timotheos' fleet in 373 (*IG* ii² 1607.50,155; Ps.-Dem. 49.14,21); and it was a Theban who happened to be presiding over the allied *sunedrion* which in 373/2 regulated the affairs of Paros after a revolt or internal disturbances on that island (SV 268; cf. Cargill 1981, 163-4; Cawkwell 1981b, 50-1). But the Thebans' destruction of Plataia probably in 373 (6.3.1; Isok. 14; DS 15.46.4-6; Paus. 9.1.3) reinforced anti-Theban prejudice and fears in Athens; and even if the growth of Theban power had by no means extinguished similar feelings about Sparta, whose brand of anti-democratic imperialism was intensely distasteful to such leading politicians as Autokles, it was possible for Kallistratos to win a majority of the Athenian Assembly to the idea of making a further peace early in 371. Like its three predecessors, the peace conference was held in Sparta.

After his serious disablement in 377 (5.4.58; 6.4.18) Agesilaos did not command in the field for seven years. But apart from those adopted in 376, it is hard to see how his policies could have differed substantially from those Sparta and her allies put into effect between 375 and 372. Anyhow, at the peace conference of 372/1 Agesilaos contrived to purloin the limelight, and the likely re-employment of Antalkidas in shuttle diplomacy with Artaxerxes (cf. 6.3.12;Dion.Hal. *Lys.* 12) argues that the role Agesilaos played in Sparta had been carefully rehearsed and stage-managed. For Athens and Sparta were now sufficiently united by their shared suspicion of Thebes for Agesilaos to contemplate using the conference to isolate the Boiotian Confederacy from the cover provided by the Second Athenian League.

The issue turned on a name, but the name masked matter of the most substantial solidity: was 'the Thebans' to be allowed to do duty for 'the Boiotians' on the roll of oath-takers, as 'the Spartans' was for her Peloponnesian League alliance as a whole? Or was Thebes again to take the oath merely as one of the allies of Athens who – unlike those of Sparta – were permitted to swear separately city by city? The sources report the issue differently (6.3.19; Plut. *Ages.* 27.5-28.3; Nep. *Epam.* 6.4; Paus. 9.13.2; cf. von Stern 1884, 127-9; Freeman 1893, 137n.4), and Xenophon entirely suppresses the role of Epameinondas, who was for the first time publicly impressing his indelible mark on Greek history as the guiding spirit of Theban policy (cf. von Stern 1884, 64n.1). But the heart of the matter seems to have been that, to Agesilaos' demand for in effect the dissolution of the Boiotian Confederacy, Epameinondas made the counter-demand for Sparta to give autonomy to the Perioikic *poleis* of Lakonia and Messenia. In other words, in the view of Epameinondas 'the Thebans' stood for the single Boiotian federal state no less than 'the Spartans' (in fact 'the Lakedaimonians') stood for the single Spartan state. The parallelism was not really exact, but the message was clear: Epameinondas was not going to countenance the same renunciation of the Boiotian Confederacy that Agesilaos had enforced before the swearing of the Peace of Antalkidas. Agesilaos now thought he had the Thebans where he wanted them, isolated and vulnerable; for by excluding themselves from the framework of the Peace of 372/1 the Thebans had both seceded from the Second Athenian League and placed themselves in a state of war with Sparta. Epameinondas, however, as I have already suggested (Chapter 12), was taking a calculated risk, and the aftermath proved his calculations correct.

Sparta's allies in Phokis, again feeling threatened by the Boiotians, once more appealed for Spartan aid, and as in 375 the Spartans despatched Kleombrotos at the head of a Peloponnesian League army (cf. Smith 1953/4, 284n.6; Gray 1980, 310). But since the Boiotians did not in fact invade Phokis on this occasion, there was a question what action if any Kleombrotos should take. A certain Prothöos (not otherwise attested) was of the view that the Spartans should recall Kleombrotos and genuinely honour the oaths they had just sworn by performing a truly peaceful and panhellenist activity, namely sponsoring the raising of funds to rebuild the temple of Apollo at Delphi that had been gutted by earthquake or/and fire in 373 (cf. Tod 140). Prothöos, whom Xenophon (6.4.2-3) seems to include among 'the home authorities' (*ta oikoi telê*), may have been a member of

the Gerousia or one of the four Pythioi. But his words were not music to the ears
of the Spartan Assembly, which by then numbered no more than 1500 and by a
large majority voted for the hawkishly anti-Theban policy of Agesilaos (cf. Plut.
Ages. 28.6). For Prothöos, they thought, was talking drivel. Thus Kleombrotos
was ordered to attack the Thebans unless they agreed to Agesilaos'
interpretation of the autonomy clause, which they still did not (DS 15.51.3-4),
and battle was joined at Leuktra (Chapter 12).

The Boiotians' victory stunned the Spartans (6.4.16) and, scarcely less, the
Athenians (6.4.19-20), however unsurprising it may have been to Epameinondas
and Pelopidas. But Jason, dynast of Pherai and recently appointed *tagos*
(supreme leader) of the Thessalian federation (6.1.18-19), kept his head, secure
in the knowledge that he was the greatest power in northern – or even all
(6.4.28) – Greece. The Boiotians, with whom he had been allied since 376 or
375, summoned Jason to Leuktra with a view to finishing the Spartans off. But
Jason adroitly dissuaded them from this course while at the same time appearing
to be doing a favour to the Spartans, whose retreat was cut off (cf. Cary 1922,
186-8). His true motives, however, transpired when on his return to Thessaly he
destroyed the fortifications of Herakleia Trachinia. The latter had reverted to
Spartan control and fought on the Spartan side at Leuktra: Jason terminated
Sparta's remaining pretensions to northern Greek influence. But his action also
pre-empted any Theban attempt to use Herakleia as a forward base for
operations against Thessaly (6.4.27; cf. 6.4.9). He had, in short, 'left the door
open to Central Greece' (Parke 1933, 103), but before he could pass through it to
execute any of his 'great designs' (6.4.31) he was assassinated in 370. Never
again did a united Thessaly look like becoming a major Greek power in its own
right.

However, the thinking behind Jason's guileful behaviour at Leuktra merits
the closest attention. Xenophon (6.4.25) was surely right to suggest that 'perhaps
he was acting thus with the aim of keeping them [*sc.* the Thebans and the
Spartans] at loggerheads so that each might be dependent on him'. That was
precisely the kind of policy that Agesilaos ought to have pursued towards Thebes
and Athens rather than twice throwing them into each others' arms so that first
the Athenians (during the Corinthian War) and then the Thebans (after 379)
were able to grow powerful to the detriment of Sparta's long-term interests. But
if Agesilaos had not the nous to perceive this, in Philip of Macedon, who became
the first foreigner to lead the Thessalian federation on his way to securing
dominion over all Greece, Jason found a true disciple.

None the less, as Ste. Croix (1972, 163) has carefully put it, 'even Leuctra
need not have spelt the end of Sparta's hegemony *in the Peloponnese*' (italics in the
original). To bring that about, it took the concurrent operation of four further
factors: Spartiate *oliganthrôpia*; the irredentist passion of the Messenian Helots to
become 'the Messenians', citizens of the autonomous *polis* of Messene; an
unbendingly imperialist attitude on the part of Sparta towards her
Peloponnesian League allies, especially those in Arkadia; and the relentless
hostility to Thebes perpetuated by Agesilaos above all. Since the first three of
these factors have been considered earlier (Chapters 4, 10 and 13), the
remainder of this chapter will outline how 'the curse of the Kadmeia' (as

Xenophon might have said) reduced Sparta to the status of a second-grade power within a decade of the Battle of Leuktra.

The period from Leuktra to (Second) Mantineia – July/August 371 to June/July 362 on the chronology of Buckler (1980c, 233-61) – is conventionally known as 'The Theban Hegemony'. But although the Thebans at the head of their Boiotian Confederacy and far-flung alliance were the single most powerful force in mainland Greece, it would be more appropriate – at least in English (cf. Buckler 1982a, 80-4, for a discussion of the ancient terminology) – to speak of the Theban 'ascendancy'. For, whatever the Thebans' intentions, their domination of mainland Greece never attained the level of dominion achieved by Sparta or by Philip of Macedon. To pursue all the ramifications of this ascendancy, in northern as well as central and southern Greece and even briefly in the Aegean, would exceed the scope of this book; so too it would be inappropriate to trace the evolution in this period of the Second Athenian League, now minus 'the Thebans' but soon to be allied to Sparta. But it may be possible to illustrate how, by the time a Common Peace was sworn on the battlefield of Mantineia in 362, the major Greek powers had attained a balance not of strength but of weakness.

Following Leuktra the Athenians assumed the role hitherto played by Sparta in sponsoring a renewal of the Peace sworn earlier in 371. The terms of the Peace as reported by our only source Xenophon (6.5.1-3) have a 'very "Athenian" slant' (Osborne 1982, 58-9; cf. Cargill 1981, 12,67,76-7,191). So Athenian, indeed, does this Peace appear that it has even been questioned whether the Spartans participated in swearing the oaths. But it is more likely than not that they did, as Xenophon seems to imply elsewhere (6.5.5,36; cf. Ryder 1965, 71-3); although it is also possible that the Athenians insisted on Sparta's allies swearing separately like their own allies (cf. Roy 1973, 136-7). Xenophon's silence about Spartan participation may therefore be a tacit reflection of the fact that, in contrast to 375, the Spartans were now playing second fiddle to Athens. However that may be, the Peace of Athens can be seen in retrospect as the penultimate step on the road to a full alliance between Sparta and Athens and their respective allies. The seal was set upon that *entente*, though not without misgivings on the Athenian side (6.5.35-6), after Epameinondas' first, devastatingly successful invasion of the Peloponnese – and in particular Lakonia and Messenia – in 370/69 (Chapter 12).

The immediate origins of that invasion may be traced to the refusal of Elis to swear to the Peace of Athens. For it was the Eleians who, with the now politically united Arkadians and with the Argives, appealed in late 370 first to the Athenians and then to the Thebans to invade (cf. Chapter 13). The Athenians refused because they now saw Thebes as a greater threat to them than Sparta and, sensibly, wished to avoid doing anything that might conceivably lead to a renewed alliance between Sparta and Thebes. But the Thebans under Epameinondas grasped this long-awaited opportunity with both hands and not only liberated Messene and several Perioikic communities from Sparta but also prised from Athens some of her League allies and incorporated them in their own widespread alliance (6.5.23).

In the summer of 369, after Sparta and Athens had allied and he had survived a malicious political prosecution on a technicality, Epameinondas led a second invasion of the Peloponnese. Inconclusive militarily, this was interesting politically in two ways. In central and southern Peloponnese it furthered the construction of Megalopolis as the federal Arkadian capital (Chapter 13) and helped consolidate the infant Messenian state. But in northern Peloponnese, along the southern shore of the Corinthian Gulf, it gave rise to contradictory political developments. In Achaia the oligarchic regimes remained loyal to Sparta, but in neighbouring Sikyon the once strongly pro-Spartan and oligarchic Euphron established a revolutionary, populist dictatorship (7.1.44-6; cf. Griffin 1982, 70-4). When he naturally turned to Thebes for support, he received a Theban governor and garrison (7.2.11). This might suggest that Thebes had decided upon an interventionist, pro-democratic or at least anti-oligarchic policy; but when the Achaians were brought into the Theban alliance in 367 or 366, Epameinondas insisted that the oligarchs should remain in power. Shortly afterwards, however, his policy was reversed, and Theban governors were sent to preside over the introduction of democracy – with unfortunate results (7.1.42-3). In other words, one reason why the Thebans did not give their new alliance any institutionalized form comparable to Sparta's Peloponnesian League or Athens' Second League was deep political disagreement, whether ideological or pragmatic, within Boiotia. This failure was also one reason why the Theban ascendancy was so shortlived (cf. Buckler 1980c, 220-7).

On the other hand, the absence of any constricting institutional framework did allow Thebes potentially a greater flexibility of response to developments as they occurred. As was by now well known, the greatest flexibility of all was required in dealings with Persia. The first attempt at a renewal of the Peace of Athens was originated through Ariobarzanes, satrap of Great Phrygia and *xenos* of Antalkidas, and his Greek agent Philiskos of Abydos (Chapters 11 and 15). But this attempt foundered on the King's preparedness to recognize that Messene belonged to Sparta, a recognition that Thebes could hardly countenance. The other major sponsor was Dionysios of Syracuse, a long-standing ally of Sparta (references in Hicks/Hill 1901, p.215; cf. Chapter 15). Now at last, softened by Athens' alliance with Sparta, Dionysios was prepared to forgive and forget what Athens had tried to do to Syracuse and to his patron Hermokrates in the late fifth century; and twenty-five years after Athens' first attempt to secure his friendship and military aid (Tod 108) he and two of his sons were granted Athenian citizenship (Osborne 1982, 57-9). Within a year he was allied to Athens (Tod 136 = SV 280), thanks perhaps to the good offices of Sparta, since there were Spartan envoys in Athens at about the same time as the alliance was concluded (Tod 135). But any hopes the Athenians entertained of the kind of naval assistance Dionysios had afforded Sparta at the Hellespont in 387 (5.1.28) were dashed by his death, upon which Syracuse relapsed into the sort of factional strife that had given birth to his tyranny almost forty years earlier (cf. Lintott 1982, 206ff.).

This was indeed a disappointment. For in 368 the Athenians, perceiving that the Spartans and Thebans were either preoccupied with each other or at least constituted no naval threat, had decided to reopen the campaign for Amphipolis, of which they had been robbed by Brasidas in 424 (Aisch. 2.26-8; Dem. 23.149;

cf. 7.1.36). In this they had been encouraged by the recognition of their claim by Amyntas III of Macedon, who had been their ally since 375 (Tod 129 = SV 264). But the decision proved to be a monumental blunder, both militarily and diplomatically. Athens never in fact regained Amphipolis and although, through Timotheos between 365 and 362, she temporarily recovered all the Thracian Chersonese (cf. Buckler 1980c, 167-8), her persistent endeavours to re-establish some form of *archê* in the northern Aegean and Hellespont both were economically ruinous and eased the path to dominion of Amyntas' son Philip. Diplomatically, the decision was no less injurious to Athens, as two surviving Athenian decrees in honour of Mytilene on Lesbos graphically reveal; the first was passed in 369/8, the second in early 367, and both were inscribed on the same stele (Tod 131; cf. Cargill 1981, 144-5). The first, proposed significantly by Kallistratos, sought to reassure Mytilene, a founder-member of the Second Athenian League, that Athens had indeed been fighting for the liberty of the Greeks between 378 and 371. The Mytilenaians, in other words, seeing first Athens' *rapprochement* with Sparta and then her redirection of aggressive attention away from Sparta to the northern Aegean, had questioned the sincerity of Athens' professions in the prospectus of the League to which Mytilene clearly still subscribed. Despite the flattering formulae of the two decrees, the imperfect tenses of Kallistratos' proposal make it clear that for Athens the Spartan danger was a thing of the past. It was this divergence of interests between Athens and important allies that fatally undermined the solidarity and effectiveness of the League, although it remained in existence until 338/7 when Philip dictated its dissolution.

The cleruchy on Samos that Athens established in 366 or 365 as 'a microcosm of Athens itself' (Hicks/Hill 1901, p.227) was a further step on the same road. Indeed, it was perhaps the single most important factor in the outbreak of a major revolt within the League, the so-called Social War of 357-5 instigated by the revolt of Rhodes, Byzantion and Chios (cf. Griffith 1978, 139-41; Hornblower 1982, 197ff., 208,213,234; *contra* Cargill 1981, 148-9). For although Samos was not a member of the League, and although Timotheos could claim that he had acted to rid the island of a Persian garrison, the cleruchy and its reinforcements did displace practically all the native population, pro-Athenian democrats no less than medizing oligarchs. The fear and suspicion that this caused within and outside the League encouraged Epameinondas to embark on an Aegean *periplous* (circumnavigation) in probably 364, which is almost certainly to be associated with the revolts from the League of Keos (Tod 142 = SV 289) and perhaps of Naxos (*IG* ii^2 179) and Byzantion too (Tod 160.11, with commentary) in the later 360s (DS 15.78-9; cf. Cawkwell 1972a, 270-3). In short, in the 360s as opposed to the 460s Athens might have been better advised to eschew the more aggressive forms of imperialist expansion, however necessary some kind of *archê* was, and find ways of feeding surplus Athenian mouths through a quieter and financially sounder domestic and foreign policy.

No doubt, too, as after 392 this naval activity of Athens greatly influenced Artaxerxes, who in 367 was won away from Athens to Thebes by Pelopidas (7.1.33-40). It will have been easier to persuade Artaxerxes to cut his ties with Sparta, since that would also have meant cutting his losses; but the probable absence of Antalkidas from the Spartan embassy to Susa and his replacement by Euthykles, who was then beginning an even longer career as a specialist in Persian diplomacy (cf. Mosley 1972a), can only have facilitated Pelopidas' task. The Peace of Thebes (SV 285), which after initial failure in 367 possibly did ensue in 366/5 (cf. Chapter 11), was far more disastrous for Sparta than Athens. For it signalled the failure of the 'Spartano-Boiotian War' (DS 15.76.3) declared at Agesilaos' urging after the first Peace of 371, the end of the Peloponnesian League (Chapter 13), and the widespread diplomatic recognition of the autonomy of New Messene. What made matters even more dispiriting for Sparta was that Athens, her supposed ally, had taken out diplomatic insurance by allying immediately beforehand with the Arkadians (SV 284; cf. Cawkwell 1972a, 269n.4; Cargill 1981, 93).

For the Thebans, however, the Peace did not bring the kind of *archê* of Greece that the Spartans had achieved by exploiting the Peace of Antalkidas and that the Thebans – at least according to the prejudiced Xenophon (7.1.33; cf. 6.5.38) – had always sought but never quite attained. No doubt there were many Thebans who did want this, but their vision was not apparently shared by Epameinondas and Pelopidas. The aim of the latter seems rather to have been first and foremost the preservation of the new Boiotian Confederacy, the *sine qua non* of Theban power. This required constant surveillance and preventive action in Thessaly, the Aegean and the Peloponnese but not the construction of a formalized imperial framework. However, the evidence for Boiotian internal politics in the 360s is desperately poor (cf. Buckler 1980c, 130-50), and the rare glimpses it affords of furious political struggles (such as those which produced the trials of Epameinondas and Pelopidas: Buckler 1978b; 1980c,138-45) usually do not permit us to identify the issues with any confidence. One exception to this generalization is the destruction in 364 of Orchomenos (incorporated at last in the Confederacy in 370), an action that Epameinondas had resolutely opposed (DS 15.79.3). But it was carried out in the absence both of him and of Pelopidas, who was needlessly killed at Kynoskephalai in Thessaly in that same year (cf. Buckler 1980c, 175-82). Such internal dissension helps explain why the Battle of Mantineia in 362 (Chapters 12 and 13) resulted in a victory that the Thebans were unable to exploit. The Common Peace sworn on the battlefield without either Persian or Spartan initiative or participation (SV 292) was the first Peace that was more than a mask for the hegemonial pretensions of Sparta, Athens or Thebes.

In conclusion, the burden of this chapter has been found to be the failure of Sparta – that is of Agesilaos, in so far as he was able to dominate Spartan counsels – to appreciate the balance of power principle. It has recently been claimed that Demosthenes' speech on behalf of the Megalopolitans delivered in the later 350s is, as a theoretical statement of that principle, 'a landmark in the history of political thought' (Hornblower 1982, 210); and that may well be so. But it was a principle already well understood in practice by Jason, by the Athenians, and – in my view most relevantly – by King Pausanias of Sparta with regard to the crucial triangular relationship between Sparta, Thebes and Athens. Without necessarily endorsing the contrast drawn by Paul Veyne (in his 1976 inaugural lecture at the Collège de France) between the 'Greek solution' to interstate relations (mutual recognition and the search for a balance of power) and the 'Roman solution' (conquest of the entire human horizon to its very limits), I would submit that a modest appreciation and application of this principle by Agesilaos would have served Sparta's interests more durably than the aggressiveness towards Thebes that reached its paroxysm in the seizure of the Kadmeia in 382. If a parallel be sought, Hitler's attitude to Soviet Russia comes to mind: in both cases the policy pursued was obsessive, decisive and ultimately disastrous.

15

Agesilaos the Mercenary

Experience has shown that only princes and armed republics achieve solid success, and that mercenaries bring nothing but loss. (Machiavelli, *The Prince*)

These in the day when heaven was falling,
  The hour when earth's foundations fled,
Followed their mercenary calling
  And took their wages and are dead
                    (A.E. Housman, *Epitaph on an Army of Mercenaries*)

Citizen hoplites willingly gave their lives in the service of their *patris*, but mercenary soldiers fought merely for a living and, so far from seeking an honourable death, feared death more than dishonour (Arist. *EN* 1116b15-24). Those at any rate were the conventional collective representations, ideal types to which there were notable exceptions on both sides. It remains true, none the less, that the principle of the citizen militia and that of mercenary service were antipathetic. Yet by the time Xenophon came to write the *Lak. Pol.* 'commanders of mercenary contingents' (*xenôn stratiarchoi: LP* 13.4; cf. 12.3) were perfectly regular and unremarkable participants in the sacrifices offered by a Spartan king on campaign; and when Agesilaos was forced by Epameinondas to return to defend Sparta shortly before the Battle of Mantineia in 362 (Chapter 12), Xenophon (7.5.10) records that he had sent on the mercenary force (*to xenikon*) to Mantineia as if that were the most natural thing in the world. Mercenaries, that is to say, had become so integral a part of the Greek way of warfare by the second quarter of the fourth century that even Sparta, pioneer and *doyenne* of the citizen militia, was obliged to clasp this viper to her bosom. In the present chapter I shall trace the process whereby this relative separation of *civilia* and *militaria* (Lengauer 1979 makes it rather too absolute) had evolved, discuss selectively Sparta's utilization of mercenaries in the late fifth and early fourth centuries, and analyse more closely Agesilaos' two spells as a mercenary commander in order to compare and contrast him with his contemporaries.

Mercenaries, as the two epigraphs to this chapter illustrate, arouse strong feelings (I could have quoted from Hugh MacDiarmid's sharp rejoinder to Housman). This makes definition without moral evaluation awkward. French, however, unlike English, has a useful word 'mercenariat', a back-formation on the model of 'salariat' (and 'proletariat'). This term is used to pick out the situation in which mercenaries are sufficiently numerous as a proportion of all soldiers to exercise an appreciable, if not determining influence on a society's mode of warfare and, by extension, in many cases on its social organization (cf. Aymard 1967, 487-98; Garlan 1972, 67-74). Just such a social situation can be detected in the Greek world by the end of the fifth century, and within a century mercenaries had moved from the periphery to constitute the essential core of the armies of the Hellenistic territorial monarchies (cf. Griffith 1935).

Mercenary service is by its nature a function of supply and demand. In this instance it seems clear that at least initially the supply of men able and willing to serve as mercenaries outstripped and perhaps therefore stimulated the demand for their labour power. This, however, was a novel situation, as a rapid review of mercenary service in Greece from early times will make plain. There were probably some Greeks serving somewhere as mercenaries at all periods so long as there was even a minimal demand, for the type of rootless and adventurous individual required seems to be more or less constant in societies of any complexity. But the earliest Greek mercenaries on record do not happen to belong to this sub-species of the genus. The 'Kerethite' mercenaries whom King David employed in the early tenth century were probably Greek-speaking Cretans (*II Sam.* 20.23; *I Kings* 1.38; cf. Momigliano 1975, 75). If later evidence is a sure guide, they were most likely specialist archers, recruited – like the slingers of the Balearic islands – for their peculiar skill in one branch of warfare. Cretan mercenary archers may even have been employed by Sparta during the First Messenian War of the late eighth century (Paus. 4.8.3,12; 4.10.1; cf. Cartledge 1979, 118-19).

Isolated individuals and ethnic specialists do not constitute a 'mercenariat'. That situation was more closely approached in the seventh and sixth centuries, but on the 'barbarian' fringes of the dramatically expanded Greek world rather than in the Greek heartland. In Greece small numbers of probably locally recruited mercenaries propped up several tyrannies, but they were far outweighed by those mainly Asiatic Greek mercenaries who, equipped more or less fully as hoplites though not necessarily fighting in phalanx formation, found ready employment as front-line fighters and garrison troops all round the eastern Mediterranean in Anatolia, Syria and Egypt. Clearly, they were employed because of their superior arms, armour and fighting quality. What is not so clear is how wide was the social net from which they were trawled by the rival oriental potentates. The relevant poems of Archilochos and Alkaios and the proud use of patronymics on the famous Abu Simbel graffiti (Boardman 1980, figs 134-5) suggest upper-class adventurers temporarily uprooted from their *polis* matrix. On the other hand, the wide dispersal of their places of employment and the numbers presumably involved indicate a broader social catchment. So too does the temporal conjunction of this mercenary phenomenon with colonization and tyranny – both symptoms of social disequilibrium. Whatever their social origins, it is probably safe to say of these Archaic mercenaries that they represent the first appearance of a widespread system of hired labour in the ancient world as a whole (cf. Ste. Croix 1981, 24-5), and it is at least an intriguing possibility that their employment may have prompted the Lydian monarchy to invent a primitive form of coinage as a 'ready means of paying mercenary soldiers' (Boardman 1980, 101; following the speculations of Cook/Woodhead 1958).

The Greek mercenaries of the Archaic period, in other words, perfectly exemplify the reciprocal interaction of social and military phenomena. But, with the exception of Sicily (eccentric both geographically and historically) in the late sixth and early fifth centuries, Greeks had not been used extensively as mercenaries within the Greek world itself, and it would be premature to speak of the existence of a 'mercenariat'. The Athenian War altered that, irreversibly, as it changed so much else, for two main reasons: first, the duration of the war, and, secondly, the distances of the theatres of fighting from the cities involved in the conflict. Together these factors placed an enormous and too often unbearable economic burden on peasant militiamen. A subsidiary contributory factor was that the War became total, not just in the sense that entire populations were implicated but also because the fighting was no longer confined to semi-ritualized set-piece combats on agreed terrain. Topographical considerations thus demanded a more flexible response by the protagonist states and the development of new styles of warrior and warfare. The fighting at sea, moreover, that bulked so large in the concluding phase of the War placed a premium on mercenary sailors besides leading to decisive Persian intervention and influence on the War's final outcome (cf. Chapter 11).

It would be wrong, however, to claim that the War by itself produced the pool of surplus manpower available for mercenary service during and especially after it. Already at the time of Xerxes' invasion of Greece in 480 some Arkadians had come to offer him their aid after he had forced the pass of Thermopylai; this was not because they were spectacularly unpatriotic or particularly keen to be on the then winning side, but simply because though able-bodied and anxious to be active (*energoi*) they lacked *bios*, the necessities of life (Hdt. 8.26.1). Two aspects of this offer have a relevance to our more immediate concerns. First, the place of origin of these men, Arkadia. By the end of the fifth century this barren land of acorn-eaters (*balanêphagoi*: Hdt. 1.66.2) was one of the two principal mercenary-producing regions of Greece, the other being Achaia (cf. Griffith 1935, 237-8, for the essential references). Secondly, the economic compulsion to mercenary service. Despite an axe-grinding passage of Xenophon (*Anab.* 6.4.8), which contrives to suggest that the men who enrolled as mercenaries under the banner of Cyrus the Younger in 401 did so out of lofty idealism, it is perfectly clear from contemporary perceptions (however exaggerated) of their mentality and behaviour and from what we know of their typically low and precarious remuneration that – like their mediaeval counterparts (cf. Howard 1976, 18,25,37) – the great majority of mercenaries in our period were driven to take such risk-ridden employment *faute de mieux*. In the eyes of a rich and *bien pensant* landowner like Isokrates, who delivered himself of many a diatribe in their regard (e.g. 4.146,168; 5.55,120-3; 8.24, 43-6; *Epist.* 9.8-10; cf. Perlman 1976-7, 252-4), such men were simply 'the common enemies of mankind'.

What caused so many thousands of men to be critically short of *bios* is far more difficult to determine on the available evidence, but, again, the Herodotus passage is a salutary warning not to place too much weight on the devastation and dislocation caused by the Athenian War. For except in 418 Arkadia was not one of the principal theatres of fighting. Among possible causal factors, therefore, one might think of demographic pressure, created by or coupled with inflexible systems of land-tenure; inability to maintain or increase production in a land where Poverty (*penia*) was a naturalized citizen (cf. Hdt. 7.102.1, 8.111.3); closure of external outlets for agricultural surplus or of external sources of supply in case of shortfalls; political upheavals involving exile (a form of social death in Classical Greece). These were the kinds of issues underlying what looks very much like a quite general socio-economic crisis aggravated by and in turn aggravating a uniquely prolonged and 'international' war. Whether the total economic 'cake' was diminishing or rather the share of it that was being allocated to the poor is a separate and unanswerable question. Nor should this apparent socio-economic crisis be automatically identified as 'the crisis of the *polis*' (despite the many contributions to Welskopf 1974).

By the end of the fifth century, then, there was a reserve army of potential mercenaries. But it required the operation in conjunction of three further factors to realize their potential in Greek interstate warfare from the early fourth century onwards. The first was a change in the character of Greek warfare; the second the fissiparous condition of the Persian Empire; the third the availability of cash to pay the mercenaries. The change in the character of Greek warfare can be shortly summarized in the one word, professionalism. Not all professional soldiers are mercenaries, but all mercenaries are professional soldiers in the twofold sense that war is both their way of life and the sole source of their livelihood (cf. Aymard 1967, 487; Mockler 1969, 17). The Spartans, on this definition, were professionals but not mercenaries, and indeed they were the only true professional soldiers among the protagonists at the start of the Athenian War. That war fatally exposed the limits of the citizen militia; and since other states could not instantly develop for themselves a Spartan way of life, the best they could hope to achieve with their own citizen manpower was some approximation to Spartan technique in such matters as drill or training or the creation of elite corps. For the rest it was easier to turn to mercenaries in order to fill the gaps in their personnel or specialist troops. Indeed, even Sparta on occasion preferred this solution, though for political as well as military reasons, as in the case of Brasidas' Thracian expedition of 424-2. As a commander, too, Brasidas in some way foreshadowed the mercenary generals of the fourth century, both in his skill as a tactician and in his relative – but no more than relative (cf. Aymard 1967, 66) – independence from the home authorities.

The condition of the Persian Empire was relevant in two respects. On the one hand, the death of Darius II in 405/4 meant, not 'Long live the king!', but that the struggle for the throne was open. This was not by any means the first succession struggle within the Achaemenid dynasty nor even perhaps the first to involve Greek mercenaries. But the struggle between Artaxerxes (as the Greeks transliterated his throne-name) and Cyrus the Younger entailed the raising of the largest Greek mercenary force yet collected under one banner – a force perhaps three or four times as big as the total number of mercenaries serving at any one time during the Athenian War. On the other hand, satrapal independence from the central government in the Iranian heartland of the Empire had been steadily growing in the second half of the fifth century, and it became normal for satraps on the western fringes to surround themselves with a bodyguard of Greek hoplite mercenaries or, if they contemplated actual resistance to the central government, some more substantial force of such soldiers (cf. Rahe 1980a, 87-9). In a sense, these two developments came together or overlapped in the person of Cyrus, who before going into open revolt a couple of years after his elder brother's accession had been created a sort of super-satrap over the western provinces through his mother's good offices (cf. Chapter 11).

Mercenaries by definition need pay. Our word 'soldiers' (ultimately from Latin *solidus*) bears silent witness to this perhaps lamentable fact of military life. Hence the third factor in the 'mercenariat' equation at the end of the fifth century: the prospect, which did not always coincide with the reality, of pay without end from the seemingly inexhaustible coffers of Persian and other oriental (or at any rate 'barbarian') dynasts of one kind or another. A Greek *polis* – if we except imperial Athens and her significantly mercenary fleet (cf. Thuc. 1.121.2-3,143.1-2) or the Syracuse of Dionysios I – could not hope to compete. 'Pay', however, is a misnomer or at least an oversimplified term. For in addition to a *per diem* cash payment a mercenary's contract might stipulate the provision of any or all of the following: rations, expenses, a clothing or arms allowance, special markets, and exceptional gratuities – not to mention a share of any booty acquired and sold. Xenophon's *Anabasis* suggests that the organization of mercenary service was already fairly sophisticated by 400 (cf. Pritchett 1974, I, 3-54 – military pay and provisioning; 53-92 – booty). However, so far at least as the ordinary rank-and-file mercenary was concerned, mercenary service was not typically the high road to El Dorado, even if he lived to enjoy such fruits as he had reaped along the way. To repeat, it was need rather than greed that had forced him on to this path in the first place.

So much for the creation of a 'mercenariat' in the Greek world by the end of the fifth century. If we turn to consider the role of Sparta in this evolution, we find that apart from Brasidas and more distantly Gylippos (who had overall command of mercenaries raised by the Syracusans, not himself: Thuc. 7.48.5) she not surprisingly contributed nothing of significance. In the final phase of the Athenian War, of course, a series of Spartan navarchs and above all Lysander did command large numbers of mercenary sailors paid with Persian funds (cf. Chapters 6 and 11). But in principle this was nothing new, since Athens' Empire had not been won or maintained solely by the horny hands and brawny arms of Athenian citizen rowers. Far more interesting is the list of Lakedaimonians who commanded mercenary soldiers on land or who served themselves as mercenaries in the last half dozen years of the fifth century.

At the head of the list of commanders in chronological order comes Dexippos, not a Spartan but a Perioikos (Xen. *Anab.* 5.1.15). He first turns up in 406 at Akragas in southern Sicily commanding 1000 mercenaries in the fight to keep the eastern two thirds of Sicily Greek in face of a massive Carthaginian thrust from the west that had begun in 409 (Fig. 15.1). Diodoros (13.85.3-4), relying explicitly on the fourth/third-century Sicilian historian Timaios of Taur-omenion, relates that before his appointment by the Akragantines Dexippos had been living at Gela and was in high repute because of his Lakedaimonian origins

Fig. 15.1. Sicily in the age of Dionysios I. After Talbert

(*patris*). Later he is said to have been thought to be something of a military expert (DS 13.87.5). There could be few better illustrations of the extent to which Perioikoi had become assimilated to the Spartan military establishment (cf. Thuc. 8.22.1), but regrettably Diodoros gives no hint as to how and why Dexippos had come to be in Gela initially. If he was merely a 'free lance', offering his services to the highest bidder, it is odd that subsequently Dionysios, during his resourceful rise to the tyranny, sent him packing back to Greece in case Dexippos should frustrate his devious plans rather than simply do away with him on the spot. It looks as if Dexippos' presence at Gela was really part of an official Spartan policy of sending (limited) aid to the Sicilian Greeks with a view to receiving reciprocal aid in the war against Athens. At any rate, the Spartans certainly did send official support to Dionysios in 404 to shore up his tottering tyranny in the person of Aretas (alternatively spelt Aristos or Aristas: DS 14.10.2-3,70.3; cf. Sansone 1981). (The alleged mission of Lysander to Dionysios, which might conceivably be placed in roughly this context, may be simply an anecdotal invention.) If the hypothesis about Dexippos is right, it finds a natural explanation as a response to the Athenians' attempt to elicit Carthaginian aid (attested in an inscription of probably the first half of 406, M/L 92, precisely when Dexippos was at Gela and Akragas).

The hypothesis is at least consistent with our next evidence for Dexippos, since he appears in Asia Minor among the survivors of Cyrus' great mercenary force. Xenophon (*Anab.* 5.1.15; 6.1.32; 6.6.9-33) clearly disliked the man, but the picture he paints of an unscrupulous opportunist does not contradict the vignette of Diodoros (esp. 13.87.4-5, 93). More to the point, it reveals that, whatever the circumstances in which Dexippos had joined Cyrus, he enjoyed favoured status in the eyes of two of the most powerful Spartans in the area, Anaxibios the navarch and Kleandros the harmost of Byzantion. The inference I would draw is that Dexippos had been sent as part of Sparta's covert but none the less official contribution of 700 men, mostly no doubt non-Lakedaimonian mercenaries (cf. Roy 1967, 300), under the command of the Spartiate Cheirisophos (Xen. *Anab.* 1.2.4-5). This was certainly true of his fellow-Perioikos Neon from Messenian Asine, who was Cheirisophos' understudy and perhaps officially designated *hupostratêgos* (but see Roy 1967, 289 and n.12, 300n.58).

However, although the Spartans were at that time 'the masters of Greece' (Xen. *Anab.* 6.6.9; cf. 6.6.12,13; 7.1.28), and Cyrus could not have gathered so vast a mercenary army had they chosen to prevent his principal officers from recruiting, Cheirisophos was not the overall leader of Cyrus' Greek mercenaries. That job was given in effect to another Spartiate, the hard man Klearchos. Again, though, this appointment required Spartan compliance – or connivance. For Klearchos, though formerly high up in the Spartan political hierarchy, was in 402 an exile under sentence of death (cf. Pritchett 1974, II, 356-7); and he had been exiled, moreover, for behaving despotically as harmost of the enormously sensitive city of Byzantion, the gateway to the Black Sea and Asia Minor (for his career see Poralla 1913, no. 425; Hofstetter 1978, no. 178). (His position was utterly different from that of another Spartan exile, Drakontios, who had been exiled as a boy for manslaughtering a playmate during the *agôgê* and had therefore joined Cyrus as an ordinary soldier of fortune: Xen. *Anab.*

4.8.25-6; 6.6.30; as had another Lakedaimonian by the name of Leonymos or Kleonymos: *Anab.* 4.1.18.) In other words, Sparta was eating her cake and having it: while posing as the liberator of the Greeks from Athenian tyranny she had been constrained to take much money from Persia, herself no stranger to despotism over Greeks, and now she was both repaying a debt to the man most responsible for channelling that decisive Persian money, at minimum cost in terms of cash and citizen manpower, and at the same time notionally pursuing a consistent policy of liberating the Greeks (cf. Chapter 11). Besides, by conducting a war against Artaxerxes in effect by proxy, Sparta was obviating the danger of the mercenaries being turned against Spartan power in the Aegean by their immediate commanders.

The political and military significance of the 'Ten Thousand' or 'Cyreians', as these mercenaries came collectively to be known, has already been explored (Chapters 11 and 12). Their chief function, so far as mercenary service in general and Sparta's employment of mercenaries in particular are concerned, was to make the use of mercenaries not merely tolerable but almost respectable in Greece as well as Asia. This was partly because, despite the commercialization of violence that they embodied and the conversion of warfare into a *technê* or full-time craft that they symbolized, they did not widen the gulf between *civilia* and *militaria* quite as far as could have been anticipated. It has often struck readers of the *Anabasis* that the 'Ten Thousand' were a sort of mobile *polis* during their return march to Greek civilization in 400. Perhaps Xenophon had an interest in exaggerating this aspect of their conduct. But he does not extenuate the terror they inspired in the residents of the settled *poleis* along the southern shore of the Black Sea (cf. the similar effect on fourteenth-century Italy of the nearly 10,000-strong 'Great Company' of mercenaries: Howard 1976, 25); and more than one of the leaders of the Cyreians found the transition back to the world of the *polis* smooth and straightforward. Indeed, the remnant of the Cyreians passed *en bloc* and without apparent strain from no fixed employment to the highly civic employ of the Spartans in 399. There they firmly remained until Agesilaos had completed his stint in Asia and indeed thereafter, since they passed the test of quality Agesilaos set for all mercenaries and their commanders (4.2.5) and accompanied him back to Greece in 394 (Chapter 12). Under Herippidas, who had commanded them since 395 (3.4.20), they fought at Koroneia, though not to the satisfaction of Xenophon at any rate (4.3.17); and it seems that some of them were still in Spartan service in the Corinthia several years later (Polyain. 3.9.45).

After the great adventure of the Cyreians in 401-400 the 'mercenariat' spread like an oil-stain (the simile of Aymard 1967, 494) or (as Isokrates might have said) like locusts over the face of the earth – from Sicily to the Black Sea and the furthest limits of the Persian Empire. In the 320s Alexander and his imperial governors may have employed between them something approaching 100,000 mercenaries (cf. Griffith 1935, 39). Grand totals are harder to come by for earlier periods, but the careful and still standard study of Parke (1933) suggests the following minima at three points in the first half of the fourth century: in 399 some 40,000, about half of whom were active in eastern Sicily under Dionysios; in 366 20,000 or so, about half of them in Greece; and in 353 at least 20,000 with more than half of these being employed in Greece thanks to the Phokians' monetization of Delphian treasure for the purpose of waging the Third Sacred War (356-46). Sparta made her relatively small but not wholly insignificant contribution to these figures, both as an employer and as a provider of mercenaries. This early experience stood her in good stead for the time towards the end of the fourth century when Tainaron – the southernmost point of Lakonia, easily defensible and conveniently situated for traffic both east and west – became a flourishing mercenary mart (cf. Griffith 1935, 259-60).

Sparta as provider of mercenaries? The idea may at first blush seem preposterous, especially as Sparta had herself been tapping for military purposes all classes and statuses of the population within her borders since the mid-420s (cf. Chapter 4). Yet in 398 and 397 Sparta permitted Dionysios of Syracuse to recruit mercenaries from within the Spartan state, and in 396 the survivors of these levies were settled permanently with land-grants as citizens of Leontinoi in eastern Sicily (DS 14.44.2,58.1,78.2-3; cf. generally Davies 1978, 203-8). No doubt as in 406 Sparta was anxious to gain military and especially naval support from Dionysios in return for Spartan 'aid'. But it was one thing to send him Spartan 'advisers' like Aretas (above), Aristoteles in 396 (DS 14.78.1) and Aristomenes sometime after 397 (Polyain. 2.31.1), or even a squadron of ships under a Spartan admiral (Pharax in 396: DS 14.63.4, 70; cf. perhaps Theop. 115F192). It was quite another to dispose in this manner of several hundreds and perhaps thousands of ordinary Lakedaimonian soldiers. Diodoros' explanation is that the Spartans were aiming to further their empire thereby; but it is far more plausible that, as in 424 but even more so in the immediate aftermath of Kinadon's abortive conspiracy (Chapter 10), Sparta wished to disembarrass herself of actual or potential malcontents – Inferiors, Neodamodeis, Perioikoi and perhaps even, if Dionysios' recruiting sergeants would have them, Helots (Dionysios was already employing Messenian rebels driven out of Kephallenia and Naupaktos by Sparta in 401 or 400: DS 14.34.2-3). A similar thought presumably lay behind the despatch by Sparta of 'Lakedaimonians' to settle in the Thracian Chersonese in 398 (3.2.8; 4.8.5), although these colonists could also directly further Sparta's imperial ambitions (cf. Chapter 12).

To illustrate Sparta's role as employer of mercenaries it will be enough to select a few salient examples. First, the so-called 'Derkylideioi' ('the men of Derkylidas') who make their solitary appearance under the colours of Agesilaos on the long march of autumn 395 (Hell. Ox. 21.1; cf. Chapter 12). Commentators are unsure whether this is simply an alternative name for the Cyreians (Parke 1933, 44) or not (Bruce 1967, 134) and disagree over the identity of their original recruiter (cf. Anderson 1970, 303-4n.33). But the most significant point is the form of their name or nickname, for this indicates a special relationship of belonging between the men and their supreme commander. Brasidas' 700 Helots acquired the no doubt unofficial tag 'Brasideioi' (Thuc. 5.67.1,71.3,72.3), and Brasidas achieved relative independence from the Spartan authorities at home (but would have liked more). Derkylidas was noted not only for his cunning but also for his preference for living abroad (4.3.2). No doubt this was partly because he did not relish the indignities heaped on confirmed bachelors and childless men like himself in philoprogenitive Sparta (cf. Cartledge 1981b, 95), but such a man was of course more likely to develop over time a personal bond with his troops. Even though there is no sign in Derkylidas' case that he thought of using his troops to pursue his own rather than Sparta's ends, it was precisely this kind of relationship that made it psychologically and materially possible for charismatic commanders of mercenaries to establish personal dictatorships – like those of Timophanes at Corinth, Euphron at Sikyon and Klearchos at Herakleia Pontikê, to name but three.

All Sparta's overall commanders in Asia – Thibron, Derkylidas, Agesilaos, Thibron again, Diphridas, Anaxibios – employed mercenaries in the war against Artaxerxes II, and none more successfully than Agesilaos (cf. Best 1969, 81,83,85,114). The Spartan office of the booty-sellers (*laphuropôlai*) is first attested in 395 (4.1.26; cf. Xen. *LP* 13.11; other passages cited in Pritchett 1974, I, 90), and they were an indispensable link in the chain for providing mercenaries with their pay and maintenance. It remains true, nevertheless, that on the whole 'the Spartans for long proved at best very indifferent leaders of mercenaries' (Parke 1933, 44; cf. 48). Their mediocrity was particularly conspicuous in light of the virtuosity of the Athenian Iphikrates, who followed up his stunning success near Lechaion in 390 (Chapter 12) with a yet more decisive use of mercenary peltasts (modified hoplites geared to greater mobility) near Abydos in 389 (4.8.34-9).

Even so, it was not until 382 that Sparta finally bowed to the inevitable and took very seriously indeed the raising of a mercenary army. Partly because her Peloponnesian League allies were feeling the strain on their citizen manpower, partly because they resented what they saw as Sparta's high-handed and selfish treatment of them, the Spartans were compelled to agree to allow them to commute men for cash as their stipulated contribution to an allied expedition (5.2.21; cf. Chapter 13). With the cash Sparta could hire mercenaries. Since it was also in the late 380s in the campaign against his revolted vassal Euagoras of Cyprus that Artaxerxes is first reported to have employed Greek mercenaries on a large scale (cf. for the later situation Xen. *Cyr.* 8.8.26; with Best 1969, 137-9), it seems that by then the pool of potential mercenaries in Greek lands was becoming a lake. In about 380, too, in his *Panegyric Oration* Isokrates first gave published vent to his pet version of 'Panhellenism', namely the conquest of some part of the western Persian Empire to provide land for a new Greek emigration – of the dreaded mercenary hordes.

Sparta's deployment of the cash raised within the Peloponnesian League by an anticipation of 'scutage' was of indifferent value in both Chalkidike against Olynthos (5.3.10) and in Boiotia against Thebes (e.g. 5.4.15). The gains made by competent commanders of mercenaries like Agesilaos (who commandeered the mercenaries in the pay of Arkadian Kleitor in 378: 5.4.36-7) were cancelled out by literally fatal blunders in using mercenaries for hot pursuit committed by Tlemonidas and Teleutias before Olynthos and by Phoibidas in Boiotia (5.3.3-6; 5.4.43-5; cf. the likewise fatal blunder of Polytropos in Arkadia in 370: 6.5.13-14). But the most spectacular failure was that of Mnasippos on Kerkyra in 373.

The Peace of 375 had been essentially a renewal of the Peace of Antalkidas in form (cf. Chapter 11). Its occasion, however, had been Artaxerxes' pressing need for yet more Greek mercenaries in his unavailing struggle to recover Egypt (DS 15.38.1). Even so there were still plenty of mercenaries on hand for Mnasippos to take more than 1500 to Kerkyra, as fighting with Athens was renewed (6.2.5). Moreover, since most allies had preferred to send money rather than men for this overseas expedition (6.2.16), Mnasippos was not unduly pressed for cash. Yet not only did Mnasippos get two months in arrears with the pay of those mercenaries whom he had not already (through overconfidence) discharged, but he also kept the remainder short of even their necessary day-to-day supplies of food. Not unreasonably their captains (*lochagoi*) remonstrated with him, but Mnasippos – perhaps over-conditioned by the *agôgê* or thinking he was dealing with Helots – simply struck one of them with a stick and another of them with the spiked butt-end of his spear (cf. the bullying tactics of Polydamidas at Mende in 423, Thuc. 4.130.4 – though he may not have been a Spartan). The result was that all Mnasippos' troops went into battle with their morale very low, the worst possible state of mind for men in their situation, as Xenophon (6.2.19) sagely remarks. Mnasippos duly followed Tlemonidas and Co. to his death, his force was routed and the defeat was made more complete by the utter failure to execute one of those wheeling movements for which Spartan drill was supposed to be famous. It is unfair, no doubt, to compare small with great; but it is hard to resist putting Mnasippos alongside Jason, tyrant of Thessalian Pherai and *tagos* of all Thessaly, who was then the most considerable military leader in Greece and particularly noted as the commander of perhaps over 5000 highly disciplined and trained mercenary infantry and cavalry (6.1.4-6; 6.4.28; cf. Parke 1933, 100-4; Westlake 1935, esp. ch.6; Mandel 1980). It was not surprising that Jason should have been Isokrates' second choice, after Athens and Sparta jointly, to lead the glorious 'Panhellenist' crusade against Persia.

Both at Leuktra in 371 (6.4.9) and, as was seen at the beginning of this chapter, at Mantineia in 362 Sparta had a mercenary force. But in neither battle did they make a significant contribution to the course of the fighting, even though Hiaron, the Spartan in command of the mercenaries at Leuktra, was deemed worthy of the posthumous honour of statues at both Olympia and Delphi (Poralla 1913, no.384; cf. Parke 1933, 87). Far more important to Sparta were the mercenaries in her employ between these major battles; for with Spartan citizen manpower at an all-time low ebb and the Peloponnesian League a thing of the past by 365 (cf. Chapter 13), Sparta required either mercenaries or new allies if she were to retrieve her lost *polis* territory and hegemonial position. Since new allies were distinctly thin on the ground, the burden was bound to fall on mercenaries. Three instances of their use by Sparta in this period are particularly informative in their different ways.

In midwinter 370/69, when Sparta town was under direct attack by Epameinondas (Chapter 12), Sparta had a band of mercenaries from Arkadian Orchomenos to aid in the defence (6.5.29). More interesting, however, is the presence in the Spartan camp of one Symmachos of Thasos (Polyain. 2.1.27), for he is the first known non-Spartan commander of mercenaries in Spartan service. Secondly, in 369 and 368 Sparta opportunely received by sea two contingents of mercenaries donated by their long-standing ally Dionysios of Syracuse (7.1.20,28); these were a belated prestation for the help Sparta had given him, including mercenaries and commanders of mercenaries, during the first crucial decade of his long reign (405-367). The first of these contingents was large enough to fill more than twenty triremes (over 4000 men) and consisted of both cavalry and infantry. But even more notable than its size was its ethnic composition, Celts and Iberians (the first Celts known to have fought as mercenaries in Greece). The composition of the second contingent is not specified; but since Agesilaos' son Archidamos used these men to storm Perioikic Karyai on the former Spartan frontier, it would not be unreasonable to infer that it was they who had brought over from Sicily the newfangled arrow-firing catapults that reportedly so dismayed Archidamos (cf. Chapter 4).

My third instance has yet more significant implications for international relations and provides the immediate background to Agesilaos' first spell as a mercenary commander in foreign service. In spring or early summer 368 Philiskos of Abydos arrived in mainland Greece, as Timokrates of Rhodes had done nearly thirty years earlier, bearing gifts from a Persian satrap (Ariobarzanes, *xenos* of Antalkidas). This time, however, the money was to be spent on behalf of, not against, Sparta; and it was to be spent on buying mercenaries, not politicians (7.1.27; cf. perhaps 7.1.41; DS 15.70.2). It is a reasonable surmise that Antalkidas was a member of the Spartan embassy to the peace conference called by Philiskos at Delphi (cf. Buckler 1980c, 103), but not even the skills of Antalkidas could possibly persuade the Thebans to embrace a peace in which Sparta's claim to Messene was to be formally recognized. The peace talks collapsed, but it was probably Antalkidas who negotiated a formal alliance between Sparta and Ariobarzanes somewhere between 368 and 366. The ensuing Peace of Thebes – if such a Peace really was concluded in 366/5 (cf. Chapter 11) – had the backing of Artaxerxes for the Theban recognition of the autonomy of New Messene. This was of course anathema to Agesilaos and those who shared the outlook admirably captured in Isokrates' epideictic oration named after its putative speaker, Archidamos (below). It was therefore opportune that Ariobarzanes' adhesion to the second phase of the Satraps' Revolt against Artaxerxes (cf. Hornblower 1982, 171, 173-4, 198) provided Agesilaos with a wonderful chance to kill three birds with a single projectile: that is, to repay Ariobarzanes' gift of 368, to restore Sparta's bankrupt finances, and to revive his crusade against the Persian devils.

At some point between 366 and 364 (cf. Osborne 1975, 307) Agesilaos set off for the Troad (Fig. 15.2), where Ariobarzanes was under siege from the still loyal Autophradates. Officially he had been sent by Sparta as an ambassador (Xen. *Ages.* 2.26), just as he had been sent to Mantineia in 370 in that ostensible capacity (6.5.3). In reality he had gone to Ariobarzanes with an eye to the main chance, and even Xenophon could not resist pointing out that the success of his mission took a military, not a diplomatic, form. Whatever exactly it was that Agesilaos did for Ariobarzanes (Xenophon, our only source, does not elaborate), he did it virtually as a hired agent, and Ariobarzanes rewarded him handsomely. So too did the Egyptian Tachôs (a necessary emendation of the *tacheôs* of the MSS), although it is not entirely clear what his political status was

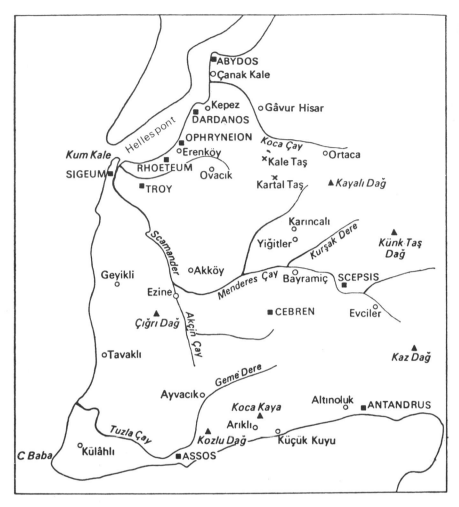

Fig. 15.2. The Troad. After J.M. Cook, *The Troad* (Oxford 1973)

at that time (cf. Kienitz 1953, 95). Another benefactor, rather more puzzlingly, was Maussollos, satrap or quasi-satrap of Caria.

Maussollos is said by Xenophon (*Ages.* 2.27) to be a *xenos* of Agesilaos of some considerable standing, so perhaps their *xenia* was hereditary and had been contracted in the later 390s between Agesilaos and Maussollos's father Hekatomnôs, the first native dynast of a province of the Persian Empire. But this personal tie cannot by itself explain why Maussollos sided (temporarily, in the event) with the enemies of Artaxerxes. Perhaps, as Hornblower (1982, 174, 201-2) has suggested, Maussollos was involved in a shady deal with Agesilaos: money for Sparta in return for the chance to recruit mercenaries in the Peloponnese. (Hornblower's further suggestion, 261n.300, that Agesilaos may

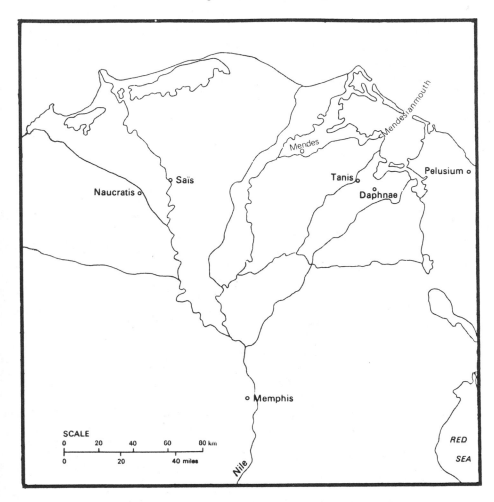

Fig. 15.3. The Nile Delta. After *The Cambridge Ancient History*, 2nd edn, III.3 (1982)

have given Maussollos the idea for his mausoleum is of course sheer fantasy; though, as we shall see in Chapter 16, there was an element of the orient in a Spartan king's funerary honours.) Given the parlous condition of Spartan public finance at all times (cf. Chapter 4), but especially after the effective dissolution of the Peloponnesian League in 365 (Chapter 13), it was presumably the eastern money Agesilaos received from Ariobarzanes, Tachôs and Maussollos that paid for the mercenary force sent by Sparta to fight at Mantineia in 362.

That battle, however, did nothing to abate Sparta's crying need for cash to pay mercenaries to fight the good fight for Messenia; if anything, it aggravated it. At the same time the result of (Second) Mantineia prompted the temporarily united Greeks (minus Sparta: Chapter 11) to present a common front of obstruction to the revolted satraps' request for Greek mercenaries. Even Athens declined Tachôs' plea for assistance in Egypt in 362/1, leaving Chabrias to go to his aid in a private capacity (Hicks/Hill 1901, no.121). All the more reason, therefore, for Agesilaos to become active once more in the anti-Persian cause and spurn the overtures of Artaxerxes (Chapter 11). So in 360 (probably; cf. Kienitz 1953, 175-7) at the age of about eighty-four he was despatched by Sparta to the Nile Delta (Fig. 15.3) to help Tachôs resist Artaxerxes' latest attempt to put an end to Egypt's now forty-five years-long rebellion.

Again, as in *c.*365, Sparta and Agesilaos in particular could claim to be repaying a debt, since an earlier rebel Pharaoh, Nepherites I, had sent him material assistance towards his Persian expedition of 396, including grain and probably shipbuilding timber (DS 14.79.4,7; cf. Kienitz 1953, 79-80; Meiggs 1983, 59); and Tachôs himself had given him cash – no doubt with an eye to the future return of benefit. Again, Agesilaos and his mouthpiece Xenophon (*Ages.* 2.29) could represent this endeavour as another episode in the saga of Agesilaos' 'Panhellenist' liberation-seeking on behalf of the Greeks of Asia, especially if it was after his service with Ariobarzanes that Isokrates (*Ep.* 9.11; with Speusippos *Ep. Phil.* 13) had made Agesilaos his third candidate for the leadership of the great Panhellenist crusade. Yet again, however, the true motivation was more sordidly materialistic, indeed mercenary in both a figurative and the literal sense, namely Sparta's need for cash (Plut. *Ages.* 36.2,37.8-11 – perhaps from Theopompos; cf. Tigerstedt 1974, 525n.964). Nor could Xenophon on this occasion hide the fact that Agesilaos was being hired as a commander of mercenaries, since this forms an essential ingredient in his exculpation of Agesilaos' treacherous behaviour towards Tachôs (Xen. *Ages.* 2.28,30). The other sources (fully discussed in Cloché 1919-20, esp. 1920, 101-11) could afford to be more impartial.

Agesilaos did not sail to Egypt alone but with 1000 hoplites (DS 15.92.2) and thirty Spartiate 'advisers' (*sumbouloi*: Plut. *Ages.* 36.6). The identity of the hoplites is uncertain, but they were probably mercenaries (cf. Plut. *Ages.* 36.6, *Mor.* 214d) rather than, say, Neodamodeis (this category of liberated Helots is last definitely attested in 370/69: 6.5.24). The number may, however, have included some *déclassé* Spartans deprived of full citizenship by the loss of their *klaroi* in liberated Messenia. The presence of the advisers (cf. Chapter 12 for earlier uses of this technique) indicates the gravity with which the Spartan authorities viewed Agesilaos' mission. But it also makes plain that, whatever justification there may be for calling mercenary generals like Chabrias 'condottieri', there is none whatsoever in the case of Agesilaos (cf. Pritchett 1974, II, 34-116, esp. 44-5, 89-90). A few years after Agesilaos' Egyptian mission the ambassadors of a mercenary army could be spoken of as though they were on a par with those sent by a *polis* (Ain. Takt. 10.11), but Sparta at least had no intention of allowing any mercenary army in her employ to get out of hand or escape the reach of her long arm. For once, Sparta seems to have been an exception to a trend affecting the Greek world generally; for as a rule 'mercenaries helped to fragment the cohesion of traditional society' and 'mercenary commanders tended to emancipate themselves from the city' (Davies 1978, 198, 201-2).

In Egypt the resistance to Persian imperialism was complicated in a familiar way by dissension between rival native resistance leaders. Tachôs was ousted by his nephew or cousin, who ruled as Nektanebis II, and fled to Artaxerxes. Agesilaos, however, foxy as always, had cleverly ingratiated himself already with Nektanebis and thereby outwitted Chabrias, the commander of Tachôs' fleet (and something of a financial ace: cf. Will 1960). He then engineered approval of his change of front from the Spartan home authorities, rather as he had arranged for them to delegate to him responsibility for the settlement of Phleious in 379 (Chapter 13). Agesilaos' rewards from Nektanebis for this betrayal of Tachôs and for his subsequent help in repelling another Egyptian pretender were substantial gifts (*dôreai*) for himself and 230 silver talents for the Spartan war-chest (Plut. *Ages.* 40.1). This was a small sum by comparison with the surplus from Cyrus' subsidy and additional booty that Lysander had conveyed to Sparta in 404 (Chapter 6) or the booty realized by Agesilaos in Asia and safely brought back to Sparta in 394 (Chapter 12). Nevertheless it was sufficient to pay something like 5000 mercenaries for approaching a year. However, before Agesilaos could hand the money over in person he died on the north coast of Africa, and it was as an embalmed corpse that he made his last terrestrial journey from the Harbour of Menelaos in Cyrenaica to the Eurypontid burial ground in Sparta (Chapter 16).

Agesilaos was not the last Spartan to serve in a mercenary capacity in the defence of free Egypt: Gastron and Lamias followed in his footsteps, perhaps around 350 (Poralla 1913, nos 181,472; cf. Parke 1933, 112n.5, 165). Nor was he the last Spartan to act as a mercenary commander in the service of a foreign power; perhaps Xanthippos, general of the Carthaginians in the First Punic War, was the most celebrated of his successors in this line. But more directly relevant and more illuminating for our purposes than any of these is the career of Agesilaos' son and successor on the Eurypontid throne, Archidamos III (cf. Hamilton 1982b,c).

A suitably deferential and dutiful son (5.4.25-31) and a brave warrior by repute (7.5.12-13), Archidamos was thought worthy to command Spartan and allied and mercenary forces in the lifetime of his father (6.4.18, 7.1.28, 7.4.20). He was also, unfortunately, typically Spartan and Agesilaos-like in his narrow conservatism of outlook in foreign policy. Throughout his reign (360/59-338) he unswervingly pursued the trail marked out by Agesilaos in the spirit of the *persona* attributed to him by Isokrates (in the *Archidamos*, the dramatic date of which is *c.*366, although it may have been composed a decade or so later: cf. Harding 1973). But his irredentist passion for the great idea of restoring Sparta's direct rule of Messenia and her hegemony in the Peloponnese and beyond came to naught. Both in 346 and in 338/7 (see end of Chapter 13) Philip of Macedon could afford to leave Sparta in isolation outside the diplomatic framework in order to gain the favour of Sparta's chief enemies in the Peloponnese (Argos, Megalopolis, Messene), on the principle that my enemy's enemy is my friend.

History may never repeat itself exactly, but it was a neat twist of Klio to end the career of Archidamos in a manner so similar to that of Agesilaos. Having exhausted Sparta's slender reserves in supplying money to the side that lost the Third Sacred War, Archidamos in 342 took the opportunity to raise funds abroad rather than join a developing and genuinely Panhellenist coalition against Philip at home. After first pausing to rescue the supposedly Spartan colony of Lyktos on Crete from the mercenaries employed by neighbouring Knossos, he made his way to southern Italy to fight as a mercenary general in the pay of Sparta's only true overseas colony, Taras, against the native Lucanians and Messapians. No doubt the story that Archidamos expired on the same day as the Battle of Chaironeia was fought is too good to be true. But it does perfectly symbolize the powerlessness and futility of Spartan foreign policy in this era. It was a sign of the times, too, that Archidamos was honoured with a portrait statue at Olympia, a version of which may be preserved in a herm from Herculaneum now in Naples (Paus. 6.4.9; cf. 6.15.7; Naples Museo Nazionale, inv. 6156). Agesilaos would have been scandalized, as we shall see (end of Chapter 16).

16

The Death and Burial of Agesilaos: Geras
Thanontôn

Great fame it is
To share the lot of those equal to gods
In life, and thereafter in death
        (Sophokles, *Antigone* 836-8)

A. I dare say a man grows weak when he reaches your age, daddo?
B. Oh, musha, he does, my heart. Did you never hear how the life of a man is divided? Twenty years a-growing, twenty years in blossom, twenty years a-stooping and twenty years declining ...
        (Maurice O'Sullivan, *Twenty Years A-Growing*)

Shakespeare's Richard II was anxious to talk of graves, worms and epitaphs and to tell sad stories of the death of kings. But had Agesilaos been a citizen of Plato's utopian Republic, the stories told about his death would have been far from sad. For he would have qualified for posthumous honours on all three of the prescribed counts, having died on active service, after an unusually distinguished life, and in old age (Plat. *Rep.* 468e-469b). In the sink of Lykourgos it was enough, as we shall see, that Agesilaos died a king. But Plato's ideal criteria are by no means irrelevant to Agesilaos and Sparta.

Taking these in reverse order, we saw that he died at the age of about eighty-four. This was four years over the limit set for a man's mortal span by the Psalmist (Psalm XC, verse 10) or that envisaged on the Blasket Islands early this century (see epigraph). But it was no less than twenty-four years beyond the officially determined frontier of 'old age' in Sparta, when a man became a time-expired veteran (*aphrouros*; cf. 5.4.13) and, provided he satisfied the relevant criteria (cf. Chapter 8), became eligible for election as a Gerôn (literally 'old man') or member of the Spartan Gerousia. His longevity was a considerable asset in a gerontocratic society for which the etymological derivation of *geras* (a gift, service or reward, or entitlement to same) from *gêras* ('old age') had lost none of its living force. Moreover, despite the generalization attributed to Atossa, daughter of Cyrus the Great and wife of Darius I, by Herodotus (3.134.3), the wits (*phrenes*) of Agesilaos had not apparently been dulled by old age. Agesilaos, in other words, was a survivor. He had triumphed over a

congenital lameness to pass with credit through the *agôgê*; he had suffered
war-wounds, most conspicuously at Koroneia in 394 (Chapter 12); and he had
survived – despite the ministrations of his Syracusan physician (perhaps the
egregious Menekrates of Plut. *Ages.* 21.10 etc.) – a potentially fatal rupture of a
vein in his good leg that had incapacitated him for half a dozen years in the 370s.
He belonged, in short, to 'a highly selected assemblage, men who possessed both
great luck and great toughness, physiological and psychological' (Finley 1981b,
161).

As for the distinction of his life, there is no need to do more than repeat
Theopompos' view, prejudiced though it is, that he was 'by common consent the
greatest and most illustrious man of his time' (Theop. 115F321, *ap.* Plut. *Ages.*
10.10; cf. 36.2). Finally, therefore, the circumstances of his death. No doubt
Agesilaos would much have preferred to emulate Leonidas and Kleombrotos by
dying in battle and thereby achieving what was reckoned both by Spartans
(since Tyrtaios fr. 9.23-4 in the seventh century) and by Lakonizers in other
states (e.g. 4.4.6) as *the* 'belle mort', the death that confirmed the positive aspects
of life (cf. Loraux 1977). At least he would have wanted to rival Agesipolis, who
died of a fever at Olynthos while conducting a campaign of imperial
aggrandisement (Chapter 13). But as it was, 'the frightening *kêr* that got [him]
by lot when [he] was born' (Homer *Il.* 23.78-9) had other ideas; and Agesilaos
died apparently of natural causes on the Libyan coast during his return from
fund-raising as a mercenary general (Chapter 15). The only consolation was
that he died at 'the Harbour of Menelaos'.

None the less, Agesilaos' Spartiate advisers automatically set in motion the
elaborate, costly, almost un-Greek funerary procedures that were reserved for a
Spartan king no matter how he died. The details of these quite extraordinary
burial honours are intrinsically diverting and challenging. But I shall be less
concerned to describe the mortuary rites than to bring out the social and
political functions they fulfilled, the assumptions they presupposed, and in
general the ways in which they celebrated life in the Spartan state. For, as
Hartog (1982, 143) has eloquently expressed it, 'à qui sait voir, ils [sc. the
funerary rites] disent long sur la vie de la tribu, de l'ethnie, ou de la société; à
qui sait entendre, ils permettent de reconstituer le système de représentations du
groupe auquel appartient celui ou celle dont on célèbre les funérailles'.
Interpretation of this nature would of course be tricky enough even if we
possessed detailed and explicit accounts by participant observers of Spartan
society, or by Spartans. In default of these my suggestions should be received in
the cautious spirit in which they are offered, although I have tried to make the
best possible use of the wealth of recent comparative anthropological and
historical studies in this field (e.g Humphreys/King 1981; Whaley 1981;
Bloch/Parry 1982).

For the details of the obsequies our main source is again that 'ethnographic'
passage of Herodotus (6.56-60) on which we drew heavily in discussing the
powers and privileges of the Spartan kings in their lifetime (Chapter 7). Only
Schaefer (1957) has to my knowledge done anything like justice to this passage
in the present funerary context, but even he leaves much to be said. The relevant
bit of the Herodotus passage (6.58) is not as full and frank as one could wish, but

its overall purport is at least clear. Although the rites followed the basic format common to all Greek societies – this indeed was an essential ingredient of 'Greekness' (*to Hellēnikon*: Hdt. 8.144.2) – their elaboration was a Spartan peculiarity and put him in mind of royal burial customs he had encountered among non-Greek peoples.

We shall return to Herodotus' construction of the rites at several points. Initially, it seems legitimate to infer that, as elsewhere in the Greek world, the funeral of a Spartan king was a three-act drama: a *prothesis* or wake followed by the cortège (*ekphora*) to the tomb, where the burial was performed to the accompaniment of sacrifices and ritual lamentation. In detail the rites (*gerea*, plural form of *geras*, of Homeric and perhaps ultimately Bronze Age provenance) took the following form in the fifth and fourth centuries.

First, horsemen were despatched to spread news of the king's death throughout the whole of the very extensive Spartan state. This was because every free household, Perioikic as well as Spartiate, was obliged to provide two mourners – one male, one female – for the funeral in Sparta, the penalty for failing to do so being a stiff fine. This custom, Herodotus comments, the Spartans shared with most of the non-Greeks of Asia, though he perhaps had in mind more particularly the Persians (cf. 6.59) and Scythians (cf. 4.71; with Hartog 1982, 150-2). Helots, too, were obligated to attend the funeral, presumably representatives from each of the Helot families working the domains of the deceased king together with perhaps a token couple from each of the other *klaroi* (on which several Helot families worked: 3.3.5). Already in the time of Tyrtaios (*ap.* Paus. 4.4.15) Helots had been bound to mourn the master of the *klaros* to which they were tied. While the dispatch-riders were visiting all quarters of Lakonia and Messenia, in Sparta itself married women (*gunaikes*), no doubt the wives, mothers, daughters and sisters of Spartiates, began going the rounds of the town banging portable bronze kettles (*lebētes*).

It will have taken at least three to four days from the time a king's death was announced before the 'many thousands' of male and female Spartiates, Perioikoi and Helots could all have assembled at Sparta for the funeral. During this period the *prothesis* will have been in progress, probably a public 'lying-in-state' with the body resting on a richly caparisoned catafalque (*klinē estrōmenē*) rather than the private, indoor ceremony practised elsewhere in Greece by Herodotus' day even for the rich and powerful. We cannot say, however, where the *prothesis* will have occurred, whether at the king's house (no palaces in Sparta) or in some public arena such as the Agora (cf. Hartog 1982, 151).

Then came the *ekphora*, the formal procession from the place of *prothesis* to the graveside. Herodotus does not refer to, let alone describe, an ordinary Spartan royal *ekphora*, but he does remark that in the case of a king who died in battle abroad the Spartans 'carry out in procession' an image (*eidōlon*) of him, clearly as a substitute for his unavailable cadaver. This remark is not certainly false, but it is not true either of at any rate two fourth-century kings who died away from Sparta though not in battle. Perhaps Herodotus was simply generalizing from the singular fate of Leonidas, to meet whose exceptional and unprecedented case the Spartans may have passed a special law to this effect (cf. Schaefer 1957, 224). For despite the truly Homeric efforts of his picked Spartan comrades, the corpse of Leonidas had not been recovered during the Battle of Thermopylai, and it had subsequently been mutilated on the vengeful orders of Xerxes (Hdt. 7.225.1,238.1; cf. generally on mutilation of this nature Thomas 1980, 109-11). In the circumstances the best that could be done was to bury immediately with full honours some sort of simulacrum of Leonidas. Forty years later, however, the Spartans retrieved what they took to be the remains of Leonidas from Thermopylai and ceremonially reburied them in Sparta (Paus. 3.14.1; cf. Connor 1979). It is not known why the delay was so long, but this rite of secondary burial undoubtedly corroborates the obvious implication of the earlier *eidôlon*, namely that the presence of the king's corpse was an integral and indispensable element in his funeral.

As we shall see, the transfer of Leonidas' presumed relics was also a peculiarly appropriate mode of reburial for a Spartan king. But the cases of Agesipolis in 380 and Agesilaos in 360/59 suggest rather that, unless prevented by circumstances beyond their control, the Spartans would normally arrange for the body of a king who died abroad (though not of course in exile, like Pausanias) to be brought back to Sparta at once to receive the last rite, as Plutarch states (*Ages.* 40.4; cf. Paus. 9.13.10). To this end the corpse was swiftly embalmed – or at least encased in a preservative substance. Honey, it seems, was ideal (5.3.19 – Agesipolis) , but for lack of that wax was used for Agesilaos (Plut. *Ages.* 40.4; Nep. *Ages.* 8.7; *contra* DS 15.93.6; cf. generally Helbig 1884, 41-2; Sacco 1978, 77-81). Had Herodotus known of this custom, he would surely have mentioned it, since he himself reported the current use of both substances for forestalling corporeal putrefaction in the Orient, honey by the Babylonians (Hdt. 1.98), wax by the Persians and Scythians (Hdt. 1.40.2, 4.71.1). As the Assyrians are known to have returned the body of Sargon, who had died abroad in battle, to Assur in 705 for burial, it may be ultimately from Mesopotamia that the Spartans derived the practice of 'embalming'. On the other hand, the exceptionally long delays between the death and burial of Homer's Hektor (*Il.* 24.785-9) and Achilles (*Od.* 24.63-5) should also, if taken literally, imply some form of artificial preservation of the corpse. In all these cases, at any rate, it was clearly important for the body to look well in death, a near-universal notion that was expressed for the Spartans by Tyrtaios (cf. Humphreys 1983, 145).

Elsewhere in the time of Herodotus we hear of stringent regulations designed to ensure complete silence during the *ekphora*. This may have been true of royal funerals in Sparta too, but quite possibly it was during this stage of the proceedings as well as at the graveside that the mourning men and women cried out in unison (as the occasion demanded) that the dead king had been the best yet, violently beating their foreheads the while and indulging in unrestrained and perhaps somewhat un-Greek lamentation (*oimôgê* – a word Herodotus otherwise uses only in Persian contexts: 3.66.1, 8.99.2, 9.24).

The actual burial Herodotus merely touches on in a couple of words, but of two features of it we may be certain. The first is that the grave was situated within not outside the settlement of Sparta. For unlike virtually all other Greeks the Spartans permitted burial within the bounds of habitation, indeed even in close proximity to sanctuaries, in defiance of the usual Greek pollution taboo (Plut. *Lyk.* 27.1; cf. Parker 1983, 71). Strictly, this was not intramural burial, since Sparta had no city-walls until the second century. Thus the royal graves of the Eurypontids lay in the village of Limnai close to a sanctuary of Diktynna (Paus. 3.12.8), while those of the Agiads were situated in Pitana near a shrine of Asklepios (Paus. 3.12.8). The primary interment of the Agiad Regent Pausanias, who narrowly escaped being thrown into the Kaiadas (a burial pit reserved for criminals), may have been made in Pitana; but on the instructions of the Delphic Oracle he was later given a secondary burial at the spot where he died on the Akropolis close by the sanctuary of Athena Chalkioikos (Thuc. 1.134.2). This was wholly exceptional.

Secondly, we may be sure that rich offerings, including above all animal sacrifices, will have been made at the moment of burial. Very few graves of any kind or period have been discovered, let alone excavated, in Sparta; but the earthen tumulus covering a group of four graves datable to the late seventh century proved on recent excavation to be full of animal remains (Christou 1964). This mound provokes and may support a speculation about the form of a Spartan king's tomb, on which we have no positive evidence. For on comparative grounds, both Homeric and archaeological (cf. Garland 1982, 74; Hammond 1982, esp. 115; Humphreys 1983, 90-1), a tumulus would have provided a wholly appropriate funerary monument for a Spartan king. Nor do we have any positive evidence concerning the burial rite, whether cremation or inhumation, or the presence or absence of grave-goods. If it were legitimate to apply what evidence we have for ordinary Spartans (Plut. *Lyk.* 27), it might be suggested that Spartan kings were inhumed with just their scarlet military cloak (*phoinikis*) and were laid on a simple 'bed' of olive leaves. But that inference is likely to be wholly illegitimate. Apart from the un-Greekness of a Spartan royal funeral, the most immediate impression it would have made on a contemporary observer is of the staggering difference in treatment between that accorded a king and that permitted to all other Spartans.

It would be equally rash, therefore, to suggest that the period of private mourning for a Spartan king was restricted to eleven days as it was for a commoner. All we are explicitly told is that after the burial public business (Assemblies, elections) was suspended for ten days (Hdt. 6.58.3) until 'the days had been purified' (3.3.1). Subsequently, no doubt, the king's tomb would receive the customary annual commemoration in the shape of a communal feast (cf. Hdt. 4.26), unless there was some special reason why he should be paid additional honours such as the games later held jointly for Regent Pausanias and Leonidas (see below).

So much for the details: what of their interpretation? That of Herodotus is interesting, revealing and plausible as far as it goes, but it is also one-sided. It is the view of a much travelled and remarkably objective (esp. 3.38; cf. Kluckhohn 1961, 29-30) outsider who has considerable familiarity with non-Greek burial customs. It is fortunate, therefore, that the view is on record of another sympathetic non-Spartan observer, a participant observer of Spartan society. Xenophon twice touches on the import of a Spartan royal funeral. Of the burial of Agis II he comments that it was 'of a grandeur that seemed to exceed what a mere mortal man could claim or expect' (3.3.1). This ambiguous and not necessarily approbatory formula is clarified in the *Lak. Pol.* (15.8-9). First he says, disingenuously or at least inexactly, that the honours paid to the kings in their lifetime were not greatly superior to those bestowed upon private individuals (*idiôtai*); but, he continues, on their death they are honoured as *hêrôës*, that is granted a status somewhere between that of men and that of the immortal gods. It is clear from Xenophon's sentence construction that he is not being merely metaphorical. What he is saying, therefore, is that at their death Spartan kings were translated formally to a status eternally superior to that of their erstwhile 'peers'. Scholars who think little of the Spartan kingship will find this extraordinary, but it is all of a piece with the kind of charismatic kingship that I have sought to reconstruct (esp. Chapter 7). What is more, it helps explain those features of the mortuary rites that are odd both by ordinary Greek and by ordinary Spartan standards.

To establish the fact of posthumous heroic status is the easy part. To give this exceptional mark of honour a history, to account for its origins and development, and to specify the type of heroization involved are far harder tasks. A comparison of the development of Spartan burial customs with those of other Greek states can take us some of the way. Evidence is patchy and as usual fullest for Athens, but it does seem possible to detect with assurance a fairly widespread tendency for Archaic *poleis* of the seventh and sixth centuries to legislate (not necessarily with successful effect, of course) in order to curb extravagance both in the cost and in the duration of funeral ceremonies. The tendency may be documented into the Classical fifth and fourth centuries and beyond (cf. Alexiou 1974, 14-23; Humphreys 1983, 85ff.). The motivation of this legislation seems originally to have been threefold: to restrict the encroachment of death on life and on the community, to reinforce the nascent central authority of the *polis*, and to reduce the threats to public order that were all too prone to arise from the hysteria generated and sustained above all by women at lavish funerals. From the two latter points of view the legislation was clearly directed against the rich, specifically against the bastions of localized power represented by the old aristocratic families; so to call the legislation 'sumptuary' would not be strictly accurate (cf. Jevons 1895).

Spartan legislation in this regard was inevitably attributed *en bloc* to Lykourgos, though it could not in fact have all been passed at one go. As so often, it represented an extreme version of a general Greek phenomenon. Not only were grave-goods kept to a bare minimum and the period of mourning restricted, but there was also a prohibition on named tombstones for all except two categories of Spartan dead, men killed in battle (e.g. the Hippokles who died in Boiotia in the early 370s: Chapter 14) and women who died in childbed (a probable reading of Plut. *Lyk.* 27.3; cf. Cartledge 1978a, 31 and n.39, 35 and n.71). Thus just as the Spartan rich 'were the first to ... lead a life that was as much as possible like the life of the ordinary people (*damos*)' (Thuc. 1.6.5), so in death they were no longer to be distinguished because of their wealth from the other Homoioi or 'Peers'. From some of this legislation, however, a conspicuous, even triumphant exception was made for the Spartan kings, as we have seen. Before trying to explain why, it is worth dwelling further on a feature of their funerals that brings out the exceptional character of their obsequies peculiarly well and has also a particular relevance to Agesilaos.

If a Spartan who was not a king died abroad (which in almost every case would mean while on campaign), he was buried on the spot, no matter how high his rank. At least, this was the case for the second half of the sixth century onwards, despite the traditional ancient interpretation of the famous exhortation to departing Spartan warriors to return home either with their shield or, if dead, upon it (Plut. *Mor.* 241f; cf. 235a; with Hammond 1979/80). We might instance the fine tombs of Archias on Samos (cf. Cartledge 1982, 250-1 and n.40), of Anchimol(i)os at Alopeke in Attika (seen by Herodotus, 5.63.4), of Brasidas at Amphipolis (Thuc. 5.11), and of the several Spartiates specially honoured with burial in the Kerameikos by the restored Athenian democracy (cf. Cartledge 1979, 270-1). On a humbler plane we could cite the tomb of Hippokles at Thespiai attested only by an inscription (*IG* VII. 1904; see above) or those at Argos referred to allusively in an anecdote (Plut. *Ages.* 31.8; *Mor.* 233c). The one glaring exception to this rule of *honorific* burial abroad is Lichas, whom the Milesians refused to bury where (and no doubt how) the Spartans present wished (Thuc. 8.84.5). A partial exception to the rule of on-the-spot burial after 550 is Lysander, who though killed at Haliartos was buried in the nearby territory of friendly Panopeus (Plut. *Lys.* 29; *contra* Paus. 9.33.1). In his case, though, it is legitimate to suspect the machinations of Lysander's friends, who may have been aiming to secure for their leader a burial commensurate with his regal aspirations (cf. Chapter 6).

For the contrast between these extra-Spartan burials and the elaborate arrangements made to recover the remains of Leonidas, Agesipolis and Agesilaos for burial in Sparta is complete and striking. If we combine this with all the other features of their burial rites that were unique to Spartan kings, we cannot hope (despite Schaefer 1957, 223; cf. 225) to explain their uniquely privileged treatment as a mere 'survival' from the good old pre-'Lykourgan' days due to the Spartans' exaggerated reverence for ancestral custom in this sensitive cultural sphere. For what needs explaining is why the kings alone were exempted from the regulations that applied to all other rich and aristocratic Spartans. We are faced, in other words, with a problem parallel to that of the exemption of the heirs-apparent from the otherwise universal obligation to pass through the *agôgê* (Chapter 3). The answer, I suggest, lies in what we – but not the Spartans – would call the area of religion, more precisely the sphere of symbolic representation.

Whatever compromises the institution of the dual kingship enjoined on the Agiads and Eurypontids with respect to the exercise of formal political power, neither royal house was willing to compromise one iota over their shared direct descent from the deified hero Herakles: they were 'the seed of the demigod son of Zeus', in the words of a Delphic injunction (Thuc. 5.16.2; cf. Chapter 7). But whereas aristocrats elsewhere in Greece (with some exceptions, e.g. on Aigina), and indeed other aristocratic families in Sparta, had proved unable to maintain the automatic and exclusive linkage between superhuman descent and political function, the two Spartan royal houses succeeded in convincing all Spartiates of the essential connection between the well-being of the Spartan state and the continued existence of the dual kingship: a brilliant illustration, perhaps, of Herodotus' dictum (5.63.2) that the Spartans 'valued the things of the gods more highly than the things of men'. This connection is referred to obliquely by Xenophon (*Ages.* 1.4), when he says that it is appropriate to praise together the *patris* (country) and *genos* (descent) of Agesilaos, and it was made explicit in the Ephors' eight-yearly sky-watching exercise (Chapter 7). Of course the connection could have its costs as well as benefits for the kings: hence the trouble over the 'lame kingship' oracle that nearly dashed Agesilaos' chance of the succession and that surfaced uncomfortably for Agesilaos in the aftermath of Leuktra. But on the whole the continued successful assertion that the dual kingship was part of the divinely ordained regime – an assertion first explicitly attested in Tyrtaios (fr. 4 West) – served the Agiads and Eurypontids and indeed Sparta well for many centuries. This special relationship, I believe, explains why the kings were exempted from the otherwise universal prohibition on elaborate funerals. It does not by itself, however, explain why their bodies were thought so vital an element in the funeral rites nor why they came to be worshipped as heroes after their death.

Lysander, we noted (Chapter 6), had received not merely heroic cult after his death but divine cult in his lifetime; but this is not a parallel case, since the explanation is overridingly secular and political and the cult was Samian not Spartan. Far closer is the case of Brasidas, for he was paid posthumous heroic cult by the Amphipolitans as if he, and not the Athenian Hagnon, had been the true founder (*oikistês*) of their city (Thuc. 5.11). Indeed, but for the blatantly political motive for severing the emotional cord that normally bound a daughter-city to her metropolis (cf. Graham 1983), this cult of Brasidas as a founder-hero would, I submit, offer an almost exact parallel to the kind of heroic funerary honours paid to a Spartan king. For it was as putatively lineal descendants of the alleged founder of Sparta, Aristodamos (Hdt. 6.52.1), himself directly descended from Herakles, that the kings could legitimately be referred to in the Great Rhetra as *archagetai* or (literally) 'first leaders', i.e. founders (cf. Jeffery 1961b; and note the application of this honorific term to Euphron, tyrant of Sikyon in the early 360s: 7.3.12); and the passage from Thucydides in which Pleistoanax is described as 'seed of the demi-god son of Zeus' also mentions 'the dances and sacrifices [the Spartans] had used originally for the institution of their kings at the time of the foundation of Sparta'.

It is not possible to pinpoint when this conception of the Spartan kings as founder-heroes first attained the status of a dogma, but the outer chronological termini can be determined reasonably firmly. The upper terminus may be set at about 750. For the validity of the conception was underwritten, like much else in Spartan public life, by the Delphic Oracle (cf. Zeilhofer 1959), and Delphi did not achieve its uniquely authoritative status in the Greek world (and *a fortiori* become linked by a special relationship to Sparta) much if at all before 750 (cf. Rolley 1977, 131-46). The lower terminus is given by the Great Rhetra, also connected with Delphi, which I would date somewhere in the second quarter of the seventh century (cf. Cartledge 1980b). If I were to choose a context between 750 and 650 for this seminal innovation, then I would be inclined to attribute it to the united hand of Kings Theopompos and Polydoros and regard it as part and parcel of the radical transformation of Spartan society that occurred towards the mid-seventh century (cf. Chapter 2).

The number of times we have had occasion to refer to Tyrtaios in this chapter is therefore probably not coincidental (cf. Fuqua 1981). For he was articulating a conception of death and a conception of royalty that the Spartans were expected to find mutually consistent. If that inference is correct, it is tempting to go one step further back and find the immediate inspiration for the heroic conception of Spartan kingship in Homer. For in the lifetime of Theopompos and Polydoros, and perhaps at the instigation of one or both of them, the Spartans had erected a sizeable shrine to Menelaos, surely the most famous of all the hero-kings of Sparta (cf. Catling 1976). In a sense this was but a local Spartan variant on a then widespread theme, the veneration of past heroes and heroization of recently dead aristocratic champions (cf. Coldstream 1976). But apart from the Spartans' need to bolster their claim to Lakonia and (recently conquered) Messenia by annexing the Homeric Menelaos, the shrine also acquired a particular relevance to the joint kingship. For it was here, according to Alkman (fr. 7 – writing a couple of generations, perhaps, after Theopompos and Polydoros), that the twin Dioskouroi, brothers of Menelaos' wife Helen, were supposed to live on underground; and the Dioskouroi, representations of whom accompanied the kings on campaign (Hdt. 5.75.2), were 'the model and divine guarantee of the Spartan dyarchy' (Carlier 1977, 76n.42). In light of this association it is therefore very striking that both Menelaos and the Dioskouroi represent something new in the Homeric conception of the afterlife. For in the *Odyssey* (4.561-5 and 11.300-4 respectively) they belong to 'a very thin, recent layer of belief, not integrated with the remaining funerary ideology, according to which a few selected people connected with the gods escape death and gain some sort of immortality' (C. Sourvinou-Inwood in Whaley 1981, 20).

Thereafter Sparta and Spartan history are riddled with heroes and hero-shrines of the most diverse kinds (cf. Stibbe 1978, 7-8). Two categories of hero are of particular relevance to the Spartan kingship, though they represent heroes of different type. First, there are those leading real-life Spartans like the Ephor and sage Chilon whose graves were marked by stone reliefs bearing characteristically heroic depictions (cf. Andronikos 1956; Schaefer 1957, 227n.20). However precisely the iconography of these reliefs should be interpreted, such stelai would have been wholly appropriate for Spartan kings, and we happen to know that Chilon, who was related by marriage to both royal houses towards the middle of the sixth century was worshipped as a hero after his death (Paus. 3.16.4; cf. Stibbe 1978, 9 and – for the stele inscribed with his name – fig. 3). Secondly, there were talismanic figures of myth like Orestes son of Agamemnon. His remains (or rather 'his' remains: the bones may in fact have belonged to a prehistoric animal!) were translated from Tegea to a hero-shrine in Sparta about 550 to serve the needs of Spartan foreign policy (cf. Cartledge 1979, 138,139,158); the fact that it was thought necessary to bring the bones to Sparta indicates a belief in the potency of a hero's presence. This secondary burial, so reminiscent *mutatis mutandis* of the movement of saints' relics during the Middle Ages, offered a precedent for the transfer a century later from Thermopylai of the remains of Leonidas, the Spartan hero *par excellence* (cf. Connor 1979). In his honour, too, as an additional mark of respect, the Spartans instituted annual games in which Spartans alone might compete (*IG* V.1, 660;

Paus. 3.14.1; cf. Schaefer 1957, 225 and n.10,226 and n.15; Connor 1979, 24n.14).

The essential function, then, of the elaborate ritual of a Spartan royal funeral was religious. It symbolized, indeed created the honorand's posthumous status as a hero of more than merely mortal nature and thus naturally complemented and continued the charismatic status he had enjoyed in his lifetime. For the kings this was a remarkable *rite de passage* (cf. Van Gennep 1960, esp. 146-65), culminating in their reincorporation in the community of the living as objects of worship. For the Spartan population at large the transmogrification of the king was – or was thought to be – scarcely less beneficial. If it is true generally that 'c'est avant tout la conservation du mort important qui assure symboliquement la pérennité du groupe' (Thomas 1980, 151), then the victory over social discontinuity was won with especial aplomb through the treatment of dead Spartan kings. For as *daimones* (a sort of 'fairy godfathers': e.g. Alkman 5 fr. 2 i 13; cf. West 1978, 151) and more particularly as heroes they might be expected both to protect the community and to enhance the promotion of crop fertility; the latter function, to judge from the sacrifice to Demeter that terminated mourning in ordinary Spartan funeral rites (Plut. *Lyk.* 27.1), was associated with all burials in Sparta (cf. Alexiou 1974, 9; more cautiously Humphreys 1983, 160-1).

However, this literally vital religious function was by no means the only one served by the ritual of a royal funeral. This also had important political and social dimensions. Xenophon could not have witnessed the funeral of Agis II, but he could have been present at those of Agesipolis and Kleombrotos, and he almost certainly came specially to Sparta to pay his last respects to his beloved patron Agesilaos. Yet in the *Agesilaos* (11.16) he makes the barest mention of Agesilaos' death, the return of his body to Sparta and his royal funeral (*basilikê taphê*), while in the *Hellenika* he chose to comment only on the quality of the funeral of Agis. The reason for this selective frankness may be inferred from the context of the latter, namely the succession dispute between Agesilaos and Latychidas. The elaborate mortuary rites of a Spartan king, that is to say, ideally served to establish and express the legitimacy of the hereditary kingship as the exclusive preserve of the Agiad and Eurypontid houses. No other 'descendants of Herakles' or other Spartan aristocrats need apply. In this respect the funeral played the same sort of role as the preservation and presentation of king-lists (cf. Cartledge 1979, 341-6). But it has to be added that, unlike the funerary ritual employed for Thai kings, the format of the death rites did not in itself help to resolve disputes over the succession in Sparta, and such disputes could not be formally resolved until after the statutory ten days' suspension of public business following the burial was completed.

This legitimating function of the mortuary beliefs and practices was far from unique to the Spartan kingship. Compare, for instance, the funerals of Philip V and the other Capetian kings of France which 'dramatically promoted the ends of dynasticism' and were 'a testimony to ... the lasting capacities of dynasty' (Brown 1980, 284; cf. on Capetian royal succession generally Lewis 1982). But this function is most clearly expressed in cases where, as in Sparta, the dead kings are transformed into a 'transcendent and eternal force' (Bloch/Parry 1982, 41). As a subsidiary aspect of this function a comparative observation made by Goody (1976b, 9; cf. Hopkins 1983, 221) may be relevant: 'where funerals redistribute the dead man's property, they will be more elaborate than where a holder divests himself of his property during his lifetime.' Though not true of rich Spartans generally, this was obviously true of the funeral of a Spartan king, where a great deal of property was at stake, and notoriously so of Agis' funeral; in default of a son and heir who was publicly recognized as legitimate, all his property was adjudged to his nearest male kinsman and royal successor Agesilaos.

If a royal funeral legitimated the hereditary kingship within the closed body of the Spartan aristocracy, it also served the as it were 'externally' legitimating function of helping to maintain the unity of the Spartan state by periodically refocussing attention on the central place. Sparta was one of those societies in which 'the person of the king, alive and dead, represents the prosperity and perpetuity of the political order' (Huntington/Metcalf 1979, 154). In other systems of kingship – those of the Southern Bantu or the Franks, to take two very dissimilar examples – succession to the throne may be hereditary but yet result in fission, the establishment of several petty kingships in what had been a single more or less unified kingdom (cf. Goody 1966, e.g. 6-7, 29). The Spartans, by contrast, succeeded in both institutionalising a dual kingship and maintaining for several centuries the territorial integrity of what by Greek standards was a uniquely vast and disparate *polis*. Part of the explanation for this success lies in the comparative restriction of the formal powers of the individual kings and of the kingship, at least within Lakonia and Messenia. But the role of the kingship as a politically integrative agent was expressed as concretely and forcefully as could be in the compulsory massed concourse of thousands at a royal funeral in Sparta. The congregation represented all sections of the population, who participated as if they were all members of the dead king's household. This form of paternalistic symbolism (cf. Maurice Bloch in Humphreys/King 1981, 141-2) sorts easily with the etymological connection between *kêdos* ('funeral', as in Hdt. 6.58.2) and *kêdestai* ('relatives'; cf. Chapter 9). Political unity and solidarity, however, increasingly became desiderata within the Spartan state rather than realities, and the funeral an increasingly ineffectual way of attempting spasmodically to paper over the cracks. Such cracks in the social fabric became blatant at the time of Kinadon's abortive conspiracy (Chapter 10), and it would have been symbolically as well as physically apt if it was at Agis' funeral that Kinadon conceived his notion of uniting all the subordinate classes and statuses against the Spartiate master class.

Finally, there are those aspects of a Spartan royal funeral that were probably common to some degree and in some form to all Greek funerals. 'A good funeral,' it has been claimed (Vermeule 1979, 3), 'has always been a lot of fun, a reunion stirring open emotions.' No doubt a certain amount of extraordinary potation and copulation was indulged in at or as a by-product of a Spartan royal funeral; but gaiety and release will have been tempered by grief and fear. Grief will naturally have come most easily to the dead king's nearest and dearest, for whom attendance at the obsequies may have been something like taking a tranquilliser or consulting a psychiatrist today (cf. Le Roy Ladurie 1973, 394). But fear will have been the more general emotion. For quite apart from any purely private and irrational fears experienced by individual participants (cf. Huntington/Metcalf 1979, 196-7), death was thought by the fifth century to entail pollution for all (cf. Parker 1983, ch.2). Hence the apotropaic beating of cauldrons by married women, who in many ancient societies were required to take the lead in publicly mourning the dead and in Greece as elsewhere (cf. Bloch/Parry 1982, 24) were particularly associated with the pollution of the corpse; only secondarily may this 'purposeful noisiness' have symbolized the liminal status of the corpse between the living and the dead (cf. Huntington/Metcalf 1979, 46-52). Hence, too, the suspension of public business until the days had been purified; again, it was only secondarily that this *iustitium* served to increase the honour of the dead king.

But over and above the fear of pollution there had developed a yet greater fear that, unless properly buried, the dead person would inevitably return from the grave to haunt the living as a revenant; this fear is remarkably lively in modern Greece and indeed elsewhere (Blum/Blum 1970, Index s.v. 'revenants'; Van Gennep 1960, 160-1). Since funerals are always conducted principally for the benefit of the living, it was this reassuring apotropaic effect that dominated the Greeks' collective mentality in our period. It would not therefore be wholly irresponsible to doubt whether the legislative efforts of 'Lykourgos' really did succeed (if indeed they were chiefly intended) to stiffen the moral fibre of the Spartans in face of the terrors of death. To the latter the macabre humour of the Mexican Day of the Dead is perhaps a more effective antidote than the close physical contact with death ensured by 'intramural' burial.

Most of this chapter has been about Spartan royal funerals in general, but I close as I began with the death or rather the posthumous commemoration of Agesilaos in particular. If Schaefer is right (1957, esp. 228-9, 230-3), the *eidôlon* borne in Leonidas' original funeral cortège was a life-size and lifelike effigy of some kind rather than a doll or mask (such as those discussed in Thomas 1980, 48-50). It could therefore be somehow relevant to the complicated question of the origins of Greek portrait sculpture. It seems, however, that Regent Pausanias was the first Spartan king to be honoured with a posthumous 'portrait' in stone (cf. Dörig 1980, 92-3) and Lysander the first Spartan to be so portrayed in his lifetime (cf. Bielefeld 1964). Agesilaos, however, would have no truck with this kind of personality cult. It was memorials of his character (*psuchê*) and not of his body that he wished to leave behind for posterity (Xen. *Ages.* 11.7; cf. Plut. *Ages.* 2.4; *Mor.* 191d,210d,215a). An unkind critic might suggest that he really took this view because his small, unimposing and deformed body would have been hard to render in suitably majestic fashion at a time when portraits were becoming genuinely representational. But in his defence it should be pointed out that his attitude to portrait sculpture places him squarely within a Spartan tradition extending back over some three centuries to Tyrtaios (esp. fr. 9.32; cf. Mourlon-Beernaert 1961; Fuqua 1981). It is thus on all fours with his consistent attempt to project an image of himself as the quintessential good Spartan citizen.

However, if not in stone or bronze then he would have to be commemorated through the medium of words. That is the true local significance of Xenophon's *Agesilaos*, a prose eulogy that continued and yet developed the native Spartan tradition of composing encomiastic poetry hymning the illustrious dead (Plut.

Lyk. 21.2). Xenophon's version of Agesilaos' self-image will be further considered in the final chapter of this book as part of a general review of Agesilaos' place within the distorted reflections of ancient Sparta handed down since the age of Xenophon and Agesilaos.

PART THREE

Narrative

17

The Spartan Empire, 404-394

The period from 404 to 360, of which a selective narrative account from the Spartan viewpoint is given in this and the three following chapters, has been characterized generally as 'The decline of the Greek Polis-world' (Bengtson 1977, 253-91) and in specifically Spartan terms as 'The policy of the Strong Hand and End' (Berve 1966, 173-207).[1] Decline, power-politics, *finis*: few would cavil at this choice of categories to encapsulate Sparta's experience during this half-century. But the paradox it embodies is worth underlining. Sparta's most comprehensive military victory engendered or precipitated the downfall of what had long been accounted the model Greek military state.

So too the extent of Sparta's fall from grace and power should be emphasized. In 400, Xenophon would later nostalgically recall, the word of a Spartan commander or governor was virtually law throughout the Aegean Greek world. By 360 Sparta had been stripped not only of her Aegean empire, not only of her far more deeply rooted Peloponnesian hegemony, but even of half her own nuclear *polis* territory. Here in Messenia the former Helots had achieved in addition to their personal freedom the rights of citizenship in their own *polis* of Messene, and as 'the Messenians' they were actually allied to some of Sparta's former Peloponnesian League allies – the League itself, one of the major functions of which had been to help Sparta repress the Helots, being a thing of the past since 365. Between them Argos and two new foundations of the early 360s, Messene and Megalopolis, now hemmed Sparta into the south-east Peloponnese, a last bastion or enclave from which she would be unable to break out decisively for over a century. In short, the peripeteia of Sparta in the four and a half decades between the fall of Athens and the death of Agesilaos was as complete as it well could be. *Why* this should have happened we shall attempt to explain later (Chapter 21). For the moment our object is to outline *how*.

Sparta was grouped by the grand systematizer A.J. Toynbee in his highly heterogeneous, multinational company of 'arrested civilizations' along with the Polynesians, Eskimos, Nomads and Osmanlis. In reality, though, Sparta had no divine dispensation from the immutable law of change to which all human

---

[1] Readers are referred to the Chronological Table and reminded that the absolute dating of this period is often controversial, although the sequence of events in the various areas of the world of Agesilaos is normally quite secure. Citations of ancient sources and modern bibliography may be found in the relevant introductory or thematic sections and are not repeated here in the narrative section. Perhaps it should also be added that these narrative chapters are in no way meant to contribute to what has been dubiously hailed as 'the revival of narrative'.

societies are subject, and the Sparta that eventually won the Athenian War in 404 was very different – politically, economically, socially, militarily – from the Sparta that had begun it in 431. For Sparta had defeated Athens at sea, not on land, through the agency of largely mercenary sailors rather than her own citizen and allied hoplites. She owed her victory essentially to Persian money, notwithstanding the contradiction between Persian aid and Sparta's heavily advertized claim to be fighting for the liberty of all Hellenes; and she had won, finally, under the leadership of Lysander, a man who was not simply not a king nor even a member of the Gerousia (Spartan Senate) but of doubtful social origins and technically speaking not in supreme command of the Spartan forces at the time. Even so, it was again Lysander who set his seal on the manner in which Sparta exploited her paradoxical victory.

In autumn 405 Lysander had destroyed all but a handful of Athens' active warfleet at Aigospotamoi ('Goat's Rivers') in the Hellespont (modern Dardanelles). Athens' wheat-supply from the northern shore of the Black Sea being cut off, and with no immediate prospect of remedying the shortfall of cereals from other potential overseas sources (Cyprus, Egypt, Sicily), it was only a matter of time before Athens was forced to capitulate through the sort of mass starvation that the city was not to experience again until the Nazi occupation. Lysander did his best to shorten that interval by concentrating Athenian citizens and people of Athenian origin in Athens and its port city of Peiraieus. He also grabbed the chance offered by the temporary absence of his friend and benefactor Cyrus the Younger (younger son of the dying Persian Great King Darius II and Parysatis) to instal exceedingly narrow partisan regimes of fanatical oligarchs known generically as dekarchies ('ten-man rules') on the Aegean coast of Turkey and the major Aegean islands such as Thasos. The loyalty of these regimes was in the first instance to Lysander not Sparta.

This was the background against which Athens surrendered in early spring 404 and Sparta had to decide Athens' fate. Many of Sparta's inner circle of allies, the members of the so-called Peloponnesian League, were inclined to the harsh view that Athens should be made a desert and that that should be called a peace. But the leaders of opinion in Sparta were agreed that Athens should be spared, though demilitarized and diplomatically isolated, and their view prevailed first over the Spartan Assembly and then over the majority of Peloponnesian League delegates or representatives at a meeting in Sparta of the League congress. Reasons for holding this view differed, however. Men like the Agiad King Pausanias might genuinely have believed Sparta's officially expressed motive, namely that Sparta could not annihilate a city that had done so much to preserve Hellas during the Persian Wars of 480-479. But even the philo-Spartan Xenophon (author of the only surviving more or less continuous narrative account of the period under consideration here) allows us to perceive that Sparta's real reason for preserving Athens was rather less than altruistic. For Athens was to serve as a watchdog of Spartan interests in central Greece against the two allies who had spoken most vehemently in favour of Athens' destruction and who were the most aggrieved by the way in which Sparta appeared to them to be turning a joint victory to her sectional advantage: Corinth and (especially) the Boiotian Confederacy dominated by Thebes.

Naturally, the Spartan most warmly supporting the idea of a puppet Athens was Lysander, who at this juncture still enjoyed the co-operation of the Eurypontid King Agis II (the older half-brother of Agesilaos). Formally, Sparta's peace terms had not imposed any particular form of government on Athens. But Lysander had in mind a variation on the dekarchies already established or in process of being established elsewhere; and on the pretext that Athens had not destroyed her Long Walls linking Athens to Peiraieus and the fortifications of Peiraieus itself within the stipulated time-limit, he was able to intervene directly at Athens in the summer of 404. Through a mixture of deceit and terror he brought about the installation of a narrow oligarchy of thirty men, who were to be abetted by a commission of ten in the Peiraieus. As a political ideal, Sparta had long exercised a curious fascination over frustrated Athenian would-be oligarchs: now was the chance for the maverick intellectual Kritias (a relative of Plato), the supple Theramenes and their colleagues to knock some properly Spartan 'good sense' (*sôphrosunê*) and 'good order' (*eunomia*) into the unruly Athenian masses who so stubbornly clung to their democratic ideology. However, the resistance they expected and encountered soon prompted the junta to apply for a Spartan garrison, and their request was swiftly met by the dispatch of 700 men (perhaps of the elite class of ex-Helots specially liberated for military service called Neodamôdeis) under a Harmost or military governor.

Thus controlled Athens was but one cog in a machinery of Spartan empire that extended directly as far north as Byzantion at the gateway to the Black Sea and that had connections as far east as the Persian administrative capital of Susa (through Cyrus, who was at any rate preferable in the eyes of both the Asiatic Greeks and the Spartans to the new King Artaxerxes II's loyal henchman Tissaphernes, former viceroy of Lydia, Ionia and Caria) and as far west as Syracuse in Sicily (through Dionysios I, who was considerably indebted to Sparta for helping him maintain the tyranny he had usurped in 405 in face of a massive Carthaginian attack on Greek Sicily). It is not known in any detail how this new Spartan empire was run, but it was certainly no less and it was very likely more dictatorial and exploitative than its Athenian predecessor. A contemporary playwright likened Sparta's decision to step into the imperialist shoes she had yanked from the feet of Athens to the pouring of vinegar by tavern-women into the sweet wine of liberty. Yet the running of an overseas empire of this kind caused as many social, economic and political problems for Sparta as it did for her unfortunate subjects; and the very fact that Sparta had acquired an empire was sufficient to alienate – or alienate still further – the sympathies of some of Sparta's more prominent and powerful Peloponnesian League allies. Sparta has been charged, unfairly, with failing to grasp the opportunity to create a federal United States of Greece in and after 404. A justifiable charge would be that she exploited her victory over Athens extremely selfishly and shortsightedly, monopolizing the material perquisites of empire and paying little or no heed to the sensibilities of either subjects or allies.

It was the latter who first raised their heads in overt opposition at Thebes, Corinth, Megara and Elis by resisting Sparta's *diktat* that exiled opponents of the Athenian junta of the Thirty should not be harboured. Indeed, the Thebans at the presumed instigation of Hismenias, who was now commencing his two decades of remarkably successful opposition to Spartan policies, went so far as to pass a counter-decree penalizing any Thebans who did *not* give them sanctuary. It was from Thebes, too, and with Theban connivance and assistance, that a band of Athenian exiles under Thrasyboulos set out in midwinter 404/3 to do battle with the Thirty.

Out of deference to their Spartan suzerain and constrained by the shortage of funds that had encouraged them to rob and kill wealthy residents of Attika regardless of their political opinions, the Thirty had left unguarded the chain of forts along Athens' frontier with Boiotia. Too late did they react to the seizure of one of these, Phyle, and Thrasyboulos with a swelling body of followers was able to take advantage of the inclement seasonal weather to make his way to the Peiraieus, the heart of the democratic Resistance. There he fought and won the Battle of Mounychia early in 403, causing the deaths of Kritias and another relative of Plato, Charmides (one of the Peiraieus Ten commissioners), and precipitating the downfall of the Thirty. As a precaution the latter had prepared for themselves with characteristic brutality a retreat at Eleusis, the nearest point in Attika to the Peloponnese; and it was to this bunker that most of the surviving remnant of the Thirty now fled, while the government of Athens was assumed by another oligarchic clique.

Both sets of oligarchs appealed to Sparta for further support, which came in an unusual form. Rather than call out the Peloponnesian League levy, the enthusiasm if not the loyalty of which was seriously in question, the Spartans appointed Lysander as harmost for Attika. To enable him to hire mercenaries, of which the Athenian War had thrown up a plentiful supply, they entrusted him with the large sum of 100 talents out of the 1500-2000 talents of booty and tribute that Lysander had been responsible for bringing to Sparta in 404. Lysander's brother Libys, the current *nauarchos* or Admiral of the Fleet, was ordered to co-operate with him by blockading the Peiraieus.

Since installing the Thirty in the summer of 404 Lysander had been notably active and on the whole notably successful. He had finally defeated after a siege Athens' staunchest ally, democratic Samos, and had predictably established a dekarchy of his partisans guaranteed by a garrison and harmost (Thorax, whose name means 'breastplate', a firm adherent of his). Less predictably, the restored oligarchy had voted Lysander divine honours, an unprecedented award for a living mortal, and Thorax had been executed by the Spartans, ostensibly for peculating public funds but partly also as a warning to Lysander not to overreach himself. But although a ban on the private possession of coined money by Spartans was in consequence of the Thorax affair imposed (or re-imposed), the Spartan state decided to continue to use coin (minted elsewhere of course, since Sparta did not strike coins before the third century and made do locally with a 'currency' of iron spits) for public, imperialist purposes. Thus fortified, Lysander persisted in gratifying his will to power (rather than material greed, from which he was conspicuously free) by interventions in the northern Aegean and north-west Asia Minor. If he was recalled to Sparta in 403 at the insistence of Sparta's former benefactor Pharnabazus, Persian satrap of Hellespontine Phrygia and rival of Tissaphernes, that was a matter of prudence on Sparta's part and not the prelude to Lysander's political disgrace as a similar recall had been for Regent Pausanias in 478.

Perhaps, though, the Gerousia and Ephors did not expect Lysander to be quite so doggedly one-dimensional in his political outlook or so loyal to his clients among the Thirty when they appointed him harmost for Attika. For not long after he had made it clear that he intended simply to reinstate what was left of the junta, King Pausanias was able to persuade a majority of the Ephors and – no less importantly – King Agis that he should be sent at the head of a Peloponnesian League army to restore a different sort of Spartan control over Athens. The Corinthians and Boiotians professed to be unable to discern the distinction between Lysander and Pausanias and refused to contribute their quota of troops. But after a sharp encounter in the Peiraieus Pausanias was able to show the two contending Athenian camps – 'the men from Peiraieus' (roughly the democrats) and 'the men of the City' (broadly the oligarchs) – just where the real power over their destinies resided. Under Pausanias' aegis and with the approval of the Spartan authorities (Gerousia and Ephors) a General Amnesty for all except the members and agents of the extreme oligarchic cliques was declared and sworn, democracy was restored for most Athenians, but the unity of the *polis* of Athens was now sundered after some three centuries by Sparta's recognition of the Thirty's Eleusis bunker as a separate (and rabidly oligarchic) statelet.

This was a wise and statesmanlike settlement, not at all to be reduced to a matter of Pausanias' personal jealousy of Lysander as Xenophon and other ancient (and too many modern) commentators would have it. For Athens was now no less defenceless than she had been at the time of the original peace settlement of 404 and was yet further impoverished by the Thirty's depredations and hamstrung by extreme civil dissensions arising out of the Thirty's brief year or so of blood-drenched misgovernment. Moreover, Pausanias had snapped the 'unnatural' bond tying democratic Athenians to Sparta's oligarchically governed allies Corinth and Boiotia in opposition to Spartan imperialism, besides appearing genuinely to be honouring Sparta's repeated pledge to respect the autonomy of even the most subject of her subject-allies. When the Boiotians seized the disputed borderland of Oropos from Athens in 402, the politic nature of Pausanias' settlement transpired.

The friends of Lysander in Sparta, however, were beside themselves with fury at Pausanias, and in Agis they found a champion of their cause. In his case jealousy rather than policy does seem to have been the motive that prompted him to vote – and perhaps instigate the criminal proceedings – against Pausanias at his capital trial held on his return from Athens. The precise charge is unknown, but the burden of the accusation clearly was that Pausanias had been excessively lenient towards democrats and democracy. Eight years later that charge could be repeated and made to stick, but in late 403 Pausanias was acquitted by majority vote of the Spartan Supreme Court: fifteen Gerontes including Agis voted 'guilty', the other fourteen Gerontes and all five Ephors 'Not Guilty'. The retrospective bearing on public policymaking of major political trials in Sparta could hardly be more graphically illustrated.

It is a separate and formally unanswerable question whether the opposition of Pausanias to Lysander over the treatment of Athens was part of a principled

opposition to Lysandreian imperialism in general, on the moral ground that
absolute power was actually corrupting those Spartans (harmosts, navarchs, and
their subordinate officers) who were entrusted with its exercise abroad. The most
that can be affirmed is that in the enforced leisure of his exile after 395 Pausanias
composed a tract in which he apparently defended his understanding of the
constitution prescribed by 'Lykourgos' (a largely if not wholly mythical early
Spartan lawgiver) against the usurpations of power-hungry and venal Ephors. All
the same, it is probably not accidental that between 403 and 395 (when in the
absence of Agesilaos he was appointed to joint command with Lysander of
Sparta's attack on Boiotia) Pausanias was conspicuous by his absence from the
fray in Sparta's most frenetically active phase of imperialist expansionism. The
stage was thus left to the kings of the Eurypontid royal house, successively Agis
and Agesilaos.

With Athens temporarily resubjugated, it was thought necessary to discipline
those allies who since spring 404 had shown a regrettable willingness to oppose
Spartan wishes with regard to Athens. Since they were not yet ready to take on
Corinth and Boiotia directly, the Spartans aimed their punitive anger first at little
Elis, with whom they had been at odds on and off since the Persian Wars. Agis,
who had personally been humiliated by the Eleians and who burned to retrieve
the severe political defeat he had suffered by the acquittal of Pausanias, was far
from reluctant to lead the attack in 402. Even the ire of Agis, however, was
overbalanced by his typically Spartan superstitious dread of earthquakes, which
he thought betokened the displeasure of Poseidon. So it was not until 401 that the
Peloponnesian League campaign began in earnest – once again without Boiotian
or Corinthian participation.

Lysander's influence had been eclipsed in 403 when and because the two kings
had transiently coalesced against him. But although it was probably in 403/2 that
Sparta withdrew official support from the dekarchies and perhaps then too that
Lysander failed in successive attempts to suborn oracular blessing for a revolutionary change in the terms of eligibility for the Spartan kingship, he was by no
means a spent political force in Sparta, not least because Agis will have found him
a useful ally against Pausanias. Thus Sparta's decision in 402 covertly and rather
insubstantially to back Cyrus in his attempted coup against Artaxerxes bears the
hallmark of Lysandreian thinking. Not only was Lysander personally friendly
with and deeply in the debt of Cyrus, but the forcible replacement of Artaxerxes by
Cyrus and the resultant power vacuum in western Asia Minor (where Cyrus had
resumed his superior satrapal command in 404 or 403, thanks to Parysatis and
greatly to the chagrin of Tissaphernes) would offer Lysander scope for recreating
something like the personal network of empire that he had achieved in 405-4. Nor
will Lysander have been displeased by Cyrus' appointment of Klearchos as chief
recruiting and commanding officer of the Greek mercenaries on whom Cyrus was
relying for victory; for Klearchos was a man in the Lysandreian mould whom the
Spartans had recalled from his harmostship of Byzantion in 402 in the same
anti-Lysandreian spirit in which they had withdrawn support from Lysander's
dekarchies. If, on the other hand, Cyrus should fail in his risky venture, Sparta
would not be irretrievably compromised in the eyes of Artaxerxes, whose father
had been a good friend to Sparta when it mattered in 408/7.

In the event Cyrus did fail, being killed and so defeated on the battlefield of Cunaxa north of Babylon in summer 401. So much, it might have been thought, for Lysander's – or Sparta's – pretensions to imperial control in Asia as well as the Aegean proper and in the approaches to the Black Sea. Yet late in 400, as the culmination of a chronologically fortuitous conjunction of events and of a period of frantically unstable policy-making in respect of the Persian question, Sparta declared war on Artaxerxes in the name of the liberty of the Asiatic Greeks. Behind this fateful decision, which embroiled Sparta on the Asiatic mainland for a largely fruitless decade and distracted her from a sounder policy of retrenchment closer to home, lay two major developments: an extraordinary display of successful imperial expansion in mainland Greece; and the accession of Agesilaos.

Early in 400 Agis had eventually 'brought the Eleians to their senses', that is inflicted severe economic losses upon them and mulcted them of their *perioikis* or mini-empire in Triphylia and environs. He had not apparently stripped them of their democratic constitution, but he had borrowed another of Lysander's techniques of imperial rule by establishing a Spartan harmost at Epitalion with a garrison in 401. This is the only harmostship known to have been created by Sparta in the Peloponnese at any time, although the practice was imitated by Sparta's enemies Pharnabazus and Konon on the Spartan island of Kythera in 393 and by the Thebans at Sikyon and Tegea in the 360s. No more, however, is heard of the Epitalion harmost after he had done his job of bringing Elis to terms, and thereafter Sparta formally speaking ruled her Peloponnesian subjects in the traditional way, through 'convenient' oligarchies (with a couple of exceptions), even if her attitude towards them grew steadily more imperialistic. Elis remained an overtly loyal member of the Peloponnesian League until 371.

About the same time as Elis was disciplined Sparta saw to another piece of outstanding Peloponnesian business. Two generations earlier Sparta's enemy within, the Helots (especially those of Messenia) had risen in a great revolt. Perhaps conscious of an earlier act of sacrilege towards Helots suppliants, the Spartans in about 460 permitted the surviving Messenian Helot rebels to go free, provided that they never set foot in the Peloponnese again. The Athenians, then openly hostile to the Spartans, cunningly helped these Messenian exiles to resettle at Naupaktos at the mouth of the Corinthian Gulf. From there they more than repaid the Athenian kindness by their aid to Athenian fleets during the Athenian (or Peloponnesian) War and by the crucial role they played in the seizure and garrisoning of Pylos in Messenia in 425. Eventually in 409 the Spartans extricated this dagger from their vitals by recapturing Pylos, and the Messenians withdrew to Naupaktos and the island of Kephallenia. In about 400 with the aid of treachery from inside the Spartans saw to the removal of the Messenian ex-Helots from Naupaktos and Kephallenia, from where they took ship to Sicily and North Africa. But it was not to be long before they and their descendants returned in triumph to the motherland of Messene.

After concluding the settlement with Elis Agis returned to central Greece after an interval of four years in order to fulfil the customary pious obligation to dedicate a tithe of the spoils of war to Apollo at Delphi in Phokis. It would not be unreasonable to suppose that he combined policy with his piety. For later in 400

Sparta became involved once more in an area of central Greece not far north of Delphi where Agis had been notably active in the winter of 413/2. Through Herippidas Sparta now regained control of her military colony of Herakleia in Trachis not far from Thermopylai (founded in 426 but bitterly resented both by the immediately local population and, scarcely less, by the Boiotians). By then Agis was dead, and Herippidas was at any rate later a particular associate of Agesilaos. But the policy is consistent with Agis' aggressively imperialist posture at the end of his life. At about the same time, too, Sparta was drawn yet further north into the complicated affairs of Thessaly, then a loose federation dominated by the 'baronial' families of the three major (and rival) centres of Larissa, Pherai and Pharsalos. To counteract the intervention of the unusually successful Macedonian king Archelaos at Larissa in northern Thessaly, it appears that Sparta was asked to contribute a garrison to the defence of Pharsalos, the most southerly of the major centres. Simultaneously Sparta established close relations with Lykophron, dynast of Pherai to the east, who had pretensions to a hegemony over all Thessaly. In short, Sparta now dominated the entire area from the northern border of Boiotia to the southern border of Achaia Phthiotis, a remarkable extension of imperial ambition and a menace most particularly to Sparta's disaffected ally the Boiotian Confederacy.

It was therefore when Sparta was in expansionist mood that Agis died in the summer of 400 and was succeeded by Agesilaos (II) after a sharp and prolonged wrangle over the succession. In this Lysander played a prominent part by persuading the Gerousia to prefer the claims of his former beloved to those of Agis' belatedly recognized teenage son Latychidas. Coincidentally in that same summer Tissaphernes returned to the Asia Minor coast with his satrapal powers renewed by a grateful Artaxerxes. He promptly sought to realize the titular authority over the Greek cities of Asia ceded by Sparta to Persia in 412/1 by besieging Kyme in Aiolis, but the Ionian Greeks collectively appealed for protection to the only possible Greek source of it, Sparta, despite her poor track record as a defender of the Hellenic faith.

Sparta was no friend of Artaxerxes or Tissaphernes, but it was another matter entirely to declare war openly on Persia. Not only could this be construed legitimately as the height of ingratitude for services rendered in the Athenian War, but it could also lead to extensive campaigning on the continent of Asia in conditions for which Sparta was militarily ill-equipped. On the other hand, there was a sense in which Sparta *had* to accede to the Greeks' request for aid, in order both to repair the damage caused by her previous cession of them to Persian suzerainty and to make good her present claim to be champion of Hellas. Moreover, Lysander and Agesilaos each had their reasons for favouring such an enterprise, the former to rebuild his power-network in the Aegean, the latter to win the kind of glory that his natal station and perhaps his physical disability (congenital lameness in one leg) had so far denied him. Thibron was thus despatched late in 400 as area harmost for western Asia Minor to command Sparta's war-effort against the oriental despotism of Artaxerxes' Persia embodied by Pharnabazus and Tissaphernes.

It would have been remarkable if Agesilaos had been sent at the outset instead of the non-royal (though doubtless elite) Thibron. No Spartan king, indeed no Spartan commander, had ever campaigned specifically and exclusively on the continent of Asia, though both Regent Pausanias and King Latychidas II had done so marginally. But even had Agesilaos burned to succeed Thibron when he was recalled in disgrace in autumn 399, there was a special obstacle to his doing so: the conspiracy hatched by one Kinadon some time before late summer of that year. The conspiracy proved abortive, thanks largely to the smooth functioning of Sparta's normal procedures for internal surveillance. But in this movement of the under-classes of Spartan society there surfaced briefly all the accumulated tensions, jealousies and hatreds engendered and exacerbated by the Athenian War and by Sparta's development of an Aegean empire. To judge from this affair, the wonder is not that Sparta collapsed as a great power after 371 but that she had ever assumed the position of Aegean dominance she held in 400.

The ringleader, Kinadon, is otherwise unknown to fame. He was by birth of Spartiate origin but had apparently been degraded from full Spartiate political status by poverty, that is by inability to meet his monthly mess-bills (paid in produce from Helot-worked allotments). Such men will have resented most keenly their exclusion from the fruits of empire. The other three major categories of plotters – or alleged plotters – were Perioikoi (personally free but disfranchised subjects of Sparta living within the borders of Lakonia and Messenia), the elite ex-Helot Neodamodeis already mentioned, and inevitably the Helots themselves. Not all individual members of these groups were as anxious to devour the Spartiates raw as Kinadon and his few close associates liked to pretend. But the conspiracy does perfectly capture the contradiction between the tiny and shrinking number of Spartiates (less than 3000 at this date, not much more than a thousand a quarter of a century later) and their many times more numerous subjects within the *polis* of Lakedaimon (as Sparta was officially called) – not to mention the perhaps three to four million souls in the Spartan empire as a whole. If the conspiracy was aborted so easily and secretly – but for Xenophon's intimacy with Agesilaos, we would surely never have heard of it – that was because the Spartan state was in a sense entirely organized for counter-insurgency and had long since mastered the art of dividing and ruling by multiplying social statuses and sub-statuses among the subordinate classes and applying judiciously the carrot and the stick as and when appropriate.

Thibron's campaign in Asia had begun satisfactorily enough, and after incorporating the remnant (?5000) of Cyrus' Greek mercenaries now led by Xenophon he had some 12,000 troops under his overall command. However, to the two structural deficiencies – in cavalry and siege-equipment – that were to mar Sparta's chances of lasting success for most of the Asiatic campaign as a whole (399-391) Thibron unfortunately added an alarming deficiency of tact. It was one thing to try to live off the country in the traditional Greek hoplite manner (rather than make elaborate, costly and insecure arrangements for long lines of supply by sea), but quite another to live off the country of one's allies at their expense. For allowing his troops to plunder the territory of Sparta's allies Thibron was recalled and replaced by the far cannier Derkylidas, another close associate of Agesilaos but one who allegedly had a distressingly un-Spartan fondness for spending long periods on service overseas far away from the officially imposed austerities and public humiliations of a bachelor Spartan life.

Derkylidas began more spectacularly well than had Thibron, prising a sort of sub-satrapy of Greek cities in the Troad from the grasp of Pharnabazus under cover of a truce with Tissaphernes. But by the end of 399 he was in a state of truce with both satraps and in spring 398 was only too happy to renew the truce with them in order to busy himself with staking Sparta's claim to hegemony of the Thracian Chersonese (Gallipoli peninsula) by rebuilding a wall across its neck that had originally been constructed by an Athenian dynasty in the later sixth century. Within the wall's protection there were now settled what can only be described as colonists from Sparta's own home territory. It is not known whether these settlers were degraded Spartiates, Perioikoi or liberated Helots, but it is hard to resist the notion that Sparta was not unwilling to disembarrass herself by this expedient of malcontents in the wake of the Kinadon affair. A similar motive could lie behind Sparta's granting permission to her friend and ally Dionysios of Syracuse to recruit mercenaries from the same geographical source in both 398 and 397.

Derkylidas next turned his attention to Atarneus in Aiolis, which had for several years been a nest of democratic, anti-Spartan exiles from the island-state of Chios. But the siege of Atarneus took him many months and was not concluded until spring or early summer 397. Pharnabazus had not been inactive in the interim. Seeing that Sparta could win no decisive victory in Asia over either him or Tissaphernes and that on the other hand he could only defeat Sparta decisively at sea, thereby cutting her communications with mainland Greece and forcing the recall of her troops, he had applied successfully to Artaxerxes for permission and funds to raise a substantial fleet. To this end he was warmly supported by Euagoras, vassal ruler of Cypriot Salamis, and it was through the good offices of Euagoras that his guest and friend Konon (one of the two Athenian admirals to escape the carnage of Aigospotamoi) was promoted to a position equivalent to vice-admiral under Pharnabazus of the proposed fleet. By concluding, together with Tissaphernes, a further armistice with Derkylidas in early summer 397, the wily satrap bought even more time for the build-up of his fleet in Cyprus and Phoenicia, and it was not until late 397 or early 396 that the Spartans back home were belatedly apprised of this substantial threat.

At the prompting of Lysander and Agesilaos Sparta decided to step up the Asiatic campaign by appointing Agesilaos to an unprecedented (and his first) command in Asia and by calling for increased contributions of men from her Peloponnesian League allies. Not unpredictably, Boiotia and Corinth refused, thus maintaining their consistent opposition to Spartan policy since 404. No doubt they regarded the Spartan initiative less as the 'Panhellenic' war of liberation against Persia advertized by Agesilaos than as a way of tightening further Sparta's imperial grip on mainland Greece. More interestingly and revealingly, Athens too refused to make a contribution. True, Athens had not merely been a Spartan catspaw since the restoration of democracy in 403: she had resisted Sparta's desire for a restriction of the Athenian franchise to solid landowners in 403, had paid back Sparta's loan to the oligarchs to demonstrate her independence, had reincorporated Eleusis and made large-scale grants of citizenship to active resistance fighters in 401, had sent only a token force of unwanted (because tainted with oligarchy) cavalrymen to Thibron in 399 and had tried to open negotiations with Artaxerxes in 397. But not before 396 had she openly refused to meet her military obligations as a subject-ally of Sparta. For the moment, though, Athens' opposition was only potentially a worry to Sparta. For by controlling what Perikles had aptly called the 'eyesore of Peiraieus', the island of Aigina, through a harmost and by using it as a naval base, Sparta was able effectively to dominate shipping into and out of Athens, an Athens that in any case had no warfleet to speak of and inadequate defensive fortifications.

Much more immediately significant, therefore, was the opposition of Boiotia, which was manifested in a peculiarly humiliating and aggravating way towards Agesilaos in person. A century earlier, during the Persian Wars, a Spartan envoy to the tyrant of Syracuse had claimed that Agamemnon would groan aloud if he knew that Spartans were agreeing to share the hegemony of Greece with Gelon. Agesilaos too in 396 decided to exploit Sparta's supposed heritage from Agamemnon and imitate his sacrificing at Aulis in Boiotian territory before sailing for Asia Minor. The Boiotarchs (the eleven elected chief executives of the then Boiotian Confederacy), especially the four Theban ones, had other ideas and sent horsemen literally to break up Agesilaos' sacrifice. That, they implied, was all they thought of Agesilaos' self-proclaimed Panhellenism, and behind this implication there lurked a threat of further resistance to Sparta in Greece. Agesilaos, anxious to take up his Asiatic command, chose to ignore the threat, but he interpreted the disruption of his pious and heroic sacrifice as personally as could possibly be imagined. This was the origin of his great hatred for the state of Thebes, despite his family connections with prominent Thebans through his father-in-law. At the time, perhaps, he did not also interpret the Boiotian effrontery as an inauspicious omen for the outcome of his Asiatic campaign. But when it was again the Boiotians who were most responsible for his recall to Greece in 394, such a supernatural construction will have recommended itself forcefully to his naturally superstitious disposition. His passionate and unremitting loathing of Thebes was not good for the health of Spartan foreign relations.

Nevertheless, in spite of the opposition of Boiotia, Corinth and Athens, and in spite of his lack of good cavalry and siege-equipment, Agesilaos was much the most successful of Sparta's commanders in Asia. He adapted far better than the rest to unfamiliar conditions of topography and manpower-resources, perhaps because he was not burdened by inherited traditions of command in mainland Greece; he displayed a strategic skill that occasionally bordered on brilliance; and he established his authority over what looks like a pioneering use of a General Staff from the very outset of his command by displacing Lysander both physically and figuratively. Thus both in 396 and 395 he inflicted great damage on the satrapy of Pharnabazus, not excluding his private 'paradise' (estates) at Daskyleion, and in 395 he defeated Tissaphernes in battle near Sardis so comprehensively that Artaxerxes was moved to arrange the execution of Tissaphernes and his replacement by the Grand Vizier of the entire Persian Empire, Tithraustes. At sea, however, Agesilaos failed and failed disastrously, chiefly through his neglect of this vital element.

It was the build-up of a Persian fleet (mainly Phoenician) under Pharnabazus and Konon with the aid of Euagoras that had prompted the appointment of Agesilaos in the first place. But Agesilaos did nothing to prevent Konon from bringing about the revolt of Rhodes, Sparta's main naval base hereabouts, in the summer or autumn of 396, and Konon was also able to intercept supplies sent to Agesilaos by Sparta's Egyptian ally Nepherites I (Egypt had been in revolt from Persia since 404 and was to remain so until 343). In 395, when Agesilaos' success on land led the Spartan home authorities rashly to entrust him unprecedentedly with the supreme command by sea as well as by land, Agesilaos committed a fatal error of nepotism in appointing his no doubt brave but totally inexperienced and (as it proved) fatally incompetent brother-in-law Peisandros as his *locum tenens* at sea.

The revolt of Rhodes was, in retrospect, the turning-point not just of Sparta's Asiatic venture but also of Sparta's imperial progress in mainland Greece. Towards the end of 396 Pharnabazus despatched to Greece a Rhodian agent bearing gifts of cash and promises of more to come to the leading anti-Spartan politicians in Thebes, Corinth, Athens and Argos. These were not strictly bribes (though the Greek word *dôron* did service for both 'gift' and 'bribe'), since the politicians in question needed no persuading that Sparta ought to be resisted militarily. They were rather inducements to these men and their respective citizenries to turn from passive to active opposition. Even so, it was Sparta who made the first aggressive moves in what was to prove a decade of war by launching a two-pronged pre-emptive strike against Boiotia in or about August 395, using as a pretext Boiotia's support for her (West?) Lokrian allies in their quarrel with Sparta's allies in Phokis.

Lysander had been demoted by Agesilaos at Ephesos in the summer of 396 and sent off to perform useful service in detaching the Paphlagonians from Pharnabazus through the good offices of a high-ranking Persian subordinate of the satrap. He had returned to Sparta later that year and perhaps then brought a prosecution against the Ephor who had been most instrumental in undermining his policy towards Athens in 403. Probably, too, he had not abandoned his revolutionary plans to make himself eligible for the Spartan kingship. But although he was obviously at odds with Agesilaos on the question of which of them was to direct Spartan policy, he saw eye-to-eye with him on the policy to be adopted towards Boiotia. Lysander was as surely behind his own appointment to a joint command in Boiotia with Pausanias in late summer 395 as he had been behind the appointment of Agesilaos to the Asiatic command in 396.

The oddity of Lysander's collaborating with his former – and presumably present – opponent Pausanias is easily explained. Only a Spartan king could lead out the full Peloponnesian League levy, and with Agesilaos being in Asia Minor Pausanias was the only available king. Pausanias' subsequent conduct, however, strongly suggests that he was out of sympathy with the aims and objectives of Lysander in central Greece as well as Sparta, while the conduct of the latter implies that he was all too eager to capitalize on the absence of Agesilaos and the reluctance of Pausanias. For after collecting together an impressive force of Sparta's allies and dependencies in central Greece and effecting the considerable coup of severing Thebes' great rival Orchomenos from the Boiotian Confederacy, Lysander failed to wait for Pausanias as planned and plunged to his death in a headlong assault on Haliartos. Pausanias arrived shortly afterwards and, rather than fight on, concluded a truce with the Boiotians and their new Athenian allies in order to recover the bodies of the Spartan dead including Lysander (who was later buried outside Boiotian territory at Panopeus in Phokis). However, the friends of Lysander and Agesilaos, for once making common cause, were powerful enough to secure against Pausanias a sentence of death. This he obviated by going into permanent exile in Arkadia, from where he was reduced to largely symbolic acts of defiance towards the quickly established domination of Spartan counsels by Agesilaos.

The Battle of Haliartos is often seen as the first action of the so-called Corinthian War. It is perhaps better regarded as the last, that is the first unsuccessful, instance of the imperialist policy that Sparta had steadfastly pursued in Greece and the Aegean since the conclusion of the Athenian War. The failure of Sparta's smash-and-grab raid on Boiotia emboldened Corinth and Argos to combine forces with Athens and Boiotia (minus Orchomenos, where Sparta placed a garrison). It is the cementing of this Quadruple Alliance, to which other states in central and perhaps also northern Greece were soon attracted, that marks the beginning of the Corinthian War proper. It also signals the utter failure of Spartan foreign policy since the Athenian War.

The course of the Corinthian War is the subject of the following narrative chapter. But it remains to conclude here the story of Sparta's decade of aggressive imperialism since the defeat of Athens, by returning to the war at sea in the southern Aegean. The revolt of Rhodes from Sparta in 396 was consolidated in 395 by a democratic revolution. Peisandros nevertheless threw considerable energy into developing a fleet to match that of Pharnabazus and Konon, and by the summer of 394 he was in command of some 120 ships. This fleet was appreciably larger than either side had been able to muster in one place in the closing phase of the Athenian War (with the exception of the Battle of Arginousai in 406), but still it was inadequate both in quantity and in quality. The Persian satrap and the expatriate Athenian admiral between them crushed Peisandros off Knidos in early August 394 shortly before the solar eclipse of 14 August. This was the greatest Persian victory over Greeks since Athens' disaster in Egypt in 454.

Sparta did maintain a presence in Asia Minor until 389, but her trans-Aegean empire with its paraphernalia of harmosts, garrisons, narrow oligarchies, tribute in cash and kind, and obligatory military service was a thing of the past. Agesilaos, it is true, had not reimposed dekarchies in 396, as Lysander had wished. But he was no less committed to a policy of supporting oligarchy and opposing ideologically and pragmatically all manifestations of democracy. The force of the political reaction against Sparta after Knidos along the Aegean shoreline of Asia is largely to be explained by this oligarchic partisanship, and Agesilaos would have been well advised to heed the lesson for the future.

18

The Corinthian War, 395-386

Down to and including 432, as Thucydides rightly observed, Sparta had been slow to go to war unless she had felt that no other tolerable option was open to her. In 395, according to Xenophon, the Spartan authorities positively welcomed the chance to go to war with Thebes, although it could hardly be claimed that Sparta had no other workable choice. It was in fact more particularly Lysander, Agesilaos and their supporters in high places who were so anxious to try conclusions with Thebes – or rather the Boiotian Confederacy. But it remains true that a change in the attitude of Sparta's political hierarchy as a whole to wars of aggression can be detected betwen 432 and 395. Imperialism, whether it took the form of acting as Hellenic policeman or of directly controlling and exploiting yet more Greek subjects, was now the order of the day, and probably almost all top ranking Spartiates were committed to it for private as well as public political and economic reasons.

The Battle of Haliartos, however, administered a sharp shock to Sparta's imperial system and ambitions, especially as her allies had not performed well in the field. In its aftermath, during the autumn and winter of 395/4, the Boiotians, Athenians, and Lokrians soon attracted allies in Argos, Corinth, Euboia, Akarnania, most of Thessaly and perhaps even Chalkidike. The Spartan garrison was expelled from Pharsalos, Sparta was again deprived of her control over Herakleia Trachinia (recently reimposed by Herippidas with typical Spartan heavyhandedness), and the four leading anti-Spartan confederates – Boiotia (except Orchomenos), Athens, Corinth and Argos – established a General Headquarters at Corinth, which dominated the Isthmus and so made it awkward for Sparta to reach her remaining allies in central Greece where most of her enemies were concentrated. Indeed, so strong did the confederates' position appear that the idea actually occurred to some of them that the war might be taken into Sparta's own backyard, her *polis* territory of Lakonia and Messenia, there to exploit the kind of tensions implied by the abortive conspiracy of Kinadon and to nullify Sparta's normal advantage of a protective shield of Peloponnesian League allies. In such circumstances it was hardly surprising that the Ephors should have recalled Agesilaos post-haste from Asia, the message to that effect reaching him in early spring 394. The man they sent to convey these sorry tidings was Epikydidas, who turns up later with Agesilaos in Boiotia and was no doubt *persona grata* with the disappointed king.

Agesilaos, who had wintered near Daskyleion and just conducted a fruitless interview with Pharnabazus, professed to be utterly chagrined by his recall, on the grounds that he was on the point of launching a major strike into the heart of the Persian Empire and challenging Artaxerxes for his very realm. But the Battle of Knidos later in 394 exposed the hollowness of such spuriously Panhellenist boasting. On the other hand, the boast did have another point. By exaggerating the extent of his personal sacrifice he underlined his unswerving obedience to Spartan officialdom, a pose that he studiedly maintained throughout his reign rather as the Roman Emperors in the words of Gibbon 'humbly professed themselves the accountable ministers of the Senate, whose supreme decrees they dictated and obeyed'. Agesilaos' parting quip, to the effect that he was being driven from Asia by Persian money and not Persian arms, was no doubt good for the self-esteem and self-confidence of himself and the troops he selected to accompany him back to Greece (including Xenophon and other survivors from the Greek mercenary force recruited by Cyrus of Persia in 402/1). But its implication that the anti-Spartan confederates in Greece needed to be bribed to fight Sparta missed the mark by a long way, and it is probable that Agesilaos, who had been absent from Greece for two years, underestimated both their determination and their organization. Derkylidas, however, had been keeping an eye on things from Sparta for the past couple of years and was better placed to appreciate the full significance of the news he brought to the returning Agesilaos at Amphipolis. This was that Sparta had won an important victory in enemy territory by the Nemea River in about June 394 with the loss of only eight Spartiate (or Lakedaimonian) hoplites.

Since Pausanias was in exile at Tegea under sentence of death and his elder son Agesipolis was too young, the command of the Peloponnesian League army that fought the Battle of the Nemea River was entrusted to Agesipolis' guardian Aristodamos. The Spartan authorities may have been slow to react to Persia's naval build-up from 398/7, but they were appositely swift to anticipate a possible threat of the invasion of Lakonia by the confederates in early summer 394. Neither Arkadia nor Elis was overtly hostile to Sparta now, as they were when Lakonia was actually invaded in 370/69; but to judge from the way Sparta's allies fought at the Nemea River Sparta was surely wise not to take any chances on their loyalty and to seize the initiative by invading the Corinthia. The ensuing battle was the largest battle hitherto fought between Greeks, involving approximately 50,000 men all told. Despite signs of tactical cogitation and innovation on the confederate side, the battle was ultimately won because the Lakedaimonian (i.e. Spartan and Perioikic) hoplites were better able to capitalize on their routing of the Argive hoplites opposite them than the Thebans were after they had defeated the opposed – and as they saw it, traitorous – Orchomenians. But if only eight Lakedaimonians were killed, that was partly at least because their allies were deliberately left to bear the brunt of the casualties.

From Amphipolis Agesilaos, still following the route taken by Xerxes of Persia in 480, continued to make excellent speed in spite of the huge booty with which he and his picked forces were laden and which it was one of his main objectives to convey safely to Sparta. (The money acquired from Persia in the closing phase of the Athenian War had by now been spent, imperial tribute was drying up, and the Peloponnesian League – unlike the Boiotian Confederacy – had no permanent central reserve fund.) Since most of Thessaly had been lost to Sparta in the wake of Haliartos, Agesilaos was obliged to fight his way through to Boiotia; and it gave him justifiable pride and pleasure to achieve the breakthrough by a cavalry victory at Narthakion over a mainly Pharsalian force, as the Thessalians were accounted the finest cavalrymen in Greece. After entering Boiotia, however, the second piece of news he received en route home to Sparta was far less cheerful than the first: Sparta's fleet had been wiped out off Knidos. Xenophon saw a portent in the solar eclipse of 14 August, but Agesilaos skilfully turned the Knidos disaster into a victory for the troops' consumption. With their morale thus brightened Agesilaos' tried army prepared for the battle that would certainly decide whether Agesilaos was to convey his Asiatic booty safely and might even reverse the strategic position of the two sides in central Greece.

The Battle of Koroneia was the only major pitched battle that Agesilaos fought on Greek soil, and even his devoted friend and client Xenophon (who by participating fought against his own Athenian fellow-countrymen) could not conceal his professional view that the generalship of Agesilaos was not as secure as it might have been. Technically, the outcome was a win for the Spartan side, and Agesilaos did carve a path through to Sparta (by dint of a sea-crossing over the Corinthian Gulf) with his booty – minus the obligatory tithe dedicated to Sparta's friend Apollo at Delphi. But Sparta did not recover central Greece as a result (though Orchomenos and Phokis were secured), and one of Agesilaos' principal subordinate officers at Koroneia, the Spartiate Gylis, was subsequently killed in Lokris while failing to achieve more. The solar eclipse had indeed proved to portend no very bright future for Sparta in the Corinthian War.

Yet worse was to come, however. For in 393 Pharnabazus and Konon were sufficiently confident of their political and military position in Asia Minor to contemplate a reversal of the situation of the past six years: in early spring they took the war back from Asia to Europe and more specifically from the territory of the Great King of Persia to the territory of Sparta herself. Kythera, a small island lying off the easternmost of the three southern prongs of Peloponnese, was captured and garrisoned, and from this handy base raids were made on Spartan soil both in Lakonia and in Messenia. When in 413 the Athenian general Demosthenes had established a fortified position on the mainland not far north of Kythera, this had encouraged many Helots to desert; presumably a similar tactic was yet more successful in 393, half a dozen years after Kinadon's conspiracy. Something akin to the panic that gripped Sparta in 425 and 424 after the occupation of Pylos in Messenia and of Kythera no doubt seized her again – but that was not something Xenophon cared to dwell on.

As if Konon had not already done enough to revenge himself for Athens' and his débâcle at Aigospotamoi, he now proceeded from Kythera to Athens, where he persuaded Pharnabazus to make a further, far heftier financial contribution to the anti-Spartan cause. The money made available was spent by the confederates in two main ways: on completing the rebuilding of Athens' fortifications (the Peiraieus and the two Long Walls linking Peiraieus to the upper city) which had been begun tentatively in 395/4; and on financing a force of mercenary peltasts (a Thracian type of infantrymen originally, more lightly armed and more mobile than hoplites) to be stationed permanently in the Corinthia and placed at first under the command of the Athenian Iphikrates. The fact that Sparta was unable to prevent or even seriously disrupt either of these major developments testifies to her relative impotence. As for the Athenians, they had every reason to shower their favourite son Konon with all sorts of honours, including a public statue in their Agora – the first such award to a living citizen. At the same time they passed a decree in favour of Euagoras of Cypriot Salamis, who had accompanied Konon to Athens, and took the opportunity to stress, somewhat spuriously, the Panhellenist quality of his and Athens' resistance to Sparta by honouring him as a Greek conferring benefits on all Greece.

A *leitmotif* of Greek history since early in the Athenian War had been *stasis*, that is civil strife or – all too frequently – outright, no-holds-barred civil war. This *stasis* arose fundamentally from internal, socio-economic divisions within citizen bodies that stemmed from the (often grossly) unequal ownership of landed property by 'rich' and 'poor' citizens. But it might be exacerbated, or at least complicated, by external relations between *poleis*. Broadly speaking, Sparta had long since come to be recognized as standing for oligarchy, the rule of the rich few, and Athens for democracy, the rule of the poor majority; and ideological oligarchs and democrats in other states tended to look to Sparta and Athens respectively to help them in their bitter struggles with their domestic political opponents. The bait for the two 'superpowers' was the prospect of securing a grateful and loyal ally by a successful intervention. From 404 Athens for a decade was in no position to intervene in the internal affairs of any other state, let alone impose a pro-Athenian democracy, even if she had wanted to. But the revolt of Rhodes from Sparta in 396, followed by an internal democratic revolution in 395, neatly illustrated the correlation between democracy and opposition to Sparta and foreshadowed the situation created by Sparta's defeat off Knidos – a situation in which Athens might again seriously contemplate rebuilding something of her lost empire on democratic lines. In practice she was unable to do so until 390/89, under the leadership of Thrasyboulos. But the Knidos battle, the subsequent seizure of Spartan territory by Konon and Pharnabazus, and the sudden accession of Persian funds to Athens and the other anti-Spartan confederates gave democrats throughout the Aegean world the confidence to raise their heads in overt opposition to Sparta's now crumbling system of oligarchically based empire. In mainland Greece the first major instance of this anti-Spartan, democratic resurgence occurred in Corinth.

Corinth was a founder-member of the Peloponnesian League. Indeed, until her defection in 395/4 she was (apart from her very temporary defection in 421-0) the most important of Sparta's League allies with the possible exception of Boiotia. Since the mid-sixth century Corinth had been ruled by an oligarchy of apparently outstanding stability and political skill. The oligarchs had never feared to challenge or provoke Sparta when they felt that a policy Sparta was advocating was not in Corinth's best interests, and on several occasions, beginning as early as about 504, they had managed to obstruct or abort a Spartan policy with which they violently disagreed. By 404, however, the Corinthian oligarchic regime was deeply split, and the anti-Spartans led by

Timolaos held the whip hand over the pro-Spartan loyalists thereafter until in 395/4 they took Corinth into the anti-Spartan alliance that fought the Corinthian War.

In 420, by contrast, Corinth had refused to join an anti-Spartan axis because it would have placed her under the immediate leadership of her near neighbour and long-standing enemy, Argos. Argos, by then a democracy, had never relinquished her claim to the hegemony of the Peloponnese of which, as she saw it, she had been unjustly robbed by Sparta. Sparta's geopolitical interests in northern Peloponnese were therefore served by fostering the natural ideological antagonism between Argos on the one hand and on the other hand Corinth and the other *poleis* in the area such as Phleious and Epidauros. So inept, however, had been Sparta's handling of intra-Peloponnesian affairs since 404 that Argos and Corinth did not merely lie down together in an anti-Spartan military alliance from 395/4 but in 392 (or 389) actually consummated something like a political marriage – the so-called Union of Corinth and Argos.

Bloodshed, inevitably, was a necessary preliminary. At a Corinthian festival in March 392 there was a massacre of many of the most extreme pro-Spartan oligarchs. Theoretically, this could have been conducted by and on behalf of the more moderate and now anti-Spartan oligarchs within the Corinthian ruling class, but it seems that such men now found themselves – as so often happens in such emergencies – outflanked on the left. For the Corinthians and Argives proceeded to tear up the boundary-stones separating their respective *poleis* and either at once or after an interval of about three years merged to form a new, single *polis*. Argos, the larger and more powerful of the two original entities, understandably gave political shape and colour to the resulting state, which appears to have been run somehow on democratic lines. Sparta was still able in the summer of 392 to win a particularly bloody encounter at the Long Walls that linked Corinth to her port of Lechaion on the Corinthian Gulf, and in 391 Agesilaos in conjunction with his stepbrother Teleutias actually captured and garrisoned Lechaion itself. But an Argive garrison on Akrokorinthos, together with Iphikrates' Foreign Legion of mercenaries, ensured the solidity of the Union, and Sparta's long-standing geopolitical strategy for controlling the Isthmus region was in ruins.

In short, by the summer of 392 Sparta can only have regretted the eagerness with which she had muscled in on Boiotian affairs three years before. She had, it is true, won two pitched battles on land, but neither had been decisive for the hegemony of mainland Greece. At sea she had comprehensively lost a major encounter, the result of which had answered in the negative the question whether Sparta could maintain an empire in western Asia Minor and the offshore islands. Part of her own home territory had been occupied and garrisoned in 393, and her enemies had received a substantial transfusion of Persian funds, which they had put to good use; and now Corinth, formerly her principal Peloponnesian ally, was in close political association with Sparta's chief Peloponnesian rival, Argos. It was predictable in the circumstances that the thoughts of Sparta's political hierarchy (not excluding Agesilaos) should have turned towards a peace settlement and in the direction of the only power that might, paradoxically, guarantee Sparta's hegemony of mainland Greece – Persia.

Sparta, that is to say, reverted in the summer and autumn of 392 to the politics of 412/1 and sought to renew the Spartano-Persian accords whereby Sparta had been enabled eventually to win the Athenian War. This time, of course, besides again agreeing to cede all Asia including the Greek *poleis* to the Persian Great King, Sparta had to swear not to resuscitate the imperial ambitions of 404 and following. In return Persia would withdraw support from Sparta's Greek enemies and lend her backing to the kind of postwar settlement in Greece that Sparta required. On these terms the Spartan negotiator Antalkidas, a man with inherited family connections among the Persian aristocracy, reached agreement with Tiribazus, who had succeeded Tithraustes in the Sardis satrapy. Konon, who had done more than any other individual Greek to destroy Sparta's Aegean empire and jeopardize her hegemony of mainland Greece, was opportunely clapped in custody by Tiribazus, who also made Antalkidas a handsome donative.

That, however, was the extent of the Spartan's success. For although Tiribazus may have been deaf to the counter-arguments put by representatives of the Boiotians, Athenians, Argives and Corinthians, his suzerain Artaxerxes was not. In his eyes the Spartans were the most shameless of mankind, and, although he naturally welcomed Sparta's readiness to yield to his control the Greek cities of Asia, he saw no reason why he should contribute to the aggrandisement of Sparta in mainland Greece. Tiribazus was therefore replaced as part of a reorganization of the western satrapies under which Strouthas (or Strouses, as he is called in a contemporary document from Miletos) received charge of Ionia and the native dynast Hekatomnôs charge of Caria (including notionally such Greek cities as Halikarnassos and Knidos), while Pharnabazus was retained for the time being as satrap of Hellespontine Phrygia. The ideas of Panhellenic solidarity expressed by the Sicilian Sophist and orator Gorgias in his famous set-piece oration at Olympia in late summer 392 thus had no chance of being put into effect, so long as both sides to the Corinthian War could see solid material advantages in collaborating with Persia against their fellow-Greeks rather than *vice versa*.

Sparta, however, did not by any means abandon hope of securing a peace in Greece with Persian backing and duly modified the terms she offered to her principal Greek enemies, though without reneging on her willingness to abandon the Greeks of Asia to Persia. Our chief witness to the transactions at the peace conference convened in Sparta early in 391 is unfortunately far from unimpeachable, but without Andokides' speech *On the Peace* we could not even begin to unravel the remarkably tangled issues. Under the 'common peace' proposed by Sparta – 'common' in the sense that in principle it was to be binding upon all Greek states – no concessions were made to Argos or Corinth, because the basis of the peace was to be 'autonomy' for all *poleis* great and small and autonomy as interpreted by Sparta was deemed incompatible with a political association such as the Union of Corinth and Argos. But the Boiotian Confederacy was to be permitted to continue in existence, save only that the autonomy from it of Orchomenos was to be recognized, and the Athenians were to be allowed to retain control of three islands vital to their wheat-supply – Lemnos, Imbros and Skyros (which they had apparently reoccupied in 393). Such a peace was clearly more acceptable to Artaxerxes (though not to

Agesilaos), but it was rejected by all Sparta's main enemies except Boiotia. Indeed, Andokides was sentenced to death for favouring the peace. Less parochially, the Corinthian War resumed. If Artaxerxes three years later returned to more or less the terms agreed in autumn 392 between Tiribazus and Antalkidas, that was because by then Athens seemed to be proving a far more dangerous adversary of Persia in Asia than Sparta had ever been.

To begin with, however, the resumed war went the way of Sparta, at least in Greece and the Aegean. Thibron, reappointed as overall commander of Sparta's war in Asia, was killed, but Lechaion was captured and garrisoned (as we have seen), Knidos and Samos returned to the Spartan fold, and there were promising signs of a revulsion of oligarchic-led feeling towards Sparta on Rhodes. These advances, though, were definitely halted in 390, when Teleutias' successes on either side of the Aegean were more than counteracted by the naval expedition of Thrasyboulos and by Sparta's irretrievable reverse on land near Lechaion.

Taking the latter first, we find that in 390 Agesilaos followed up his successful ravaging of the Argolid and operations in the Corinthia in 391 with a determined campaign to rout out Iphikrates and his peltasts who had been doing much both to safeguard the Union of Corinth and Argos and to harass Sparta's Peloponnesian League allies in the vicinity. All prospered at first. Agesilaos seized Oinoe and Peiraion, taking much booty and completing the encirclement of Corinth with a ring of fortified positions. But as the Spartan garrison of 600 men was returning to Lechaion in July or August, after escorting the Spartans of Amyklai village (who had been released as was customary to celebrate the Hyakinthia festival at home) towards Sikyon, it was ambushed and decimated by the peltasts of Iphikrates supported by hoplites under another Athenian, Kallias. So severe was this blow to Sparta's morale and prestige as leader that the Boiotians abandoned their rekindled thoughts of peacemaking, the confederates relieved Corinth by retaking Sidous, Krommyon, Peiraion and Oinoe in the Corinthia, and disaffected allies within the Peloponnesian League like Mantineia had their resentment of Sparta powerfully reinforced. Sparta did retain Lechaion, and the Phleiasians were frightened out of their dissident posture into requesting a Spartan garrison. But Sparta now had no hope of winning the Corinthian War on land in the Corinthia. The most she could achieve on land thereafter was effected competently by Agesilaos, on behalf of Sparta's Achaian allies, in Akarnania in 389/8; but that was essentially a sideshow.

At sea the picture was scarcely rosier. Athenian shipping continued to be hampered by Sparta's control of Aigina, but Thrasyboulos was still able to voyage into the Aegean in the summer of 390 with ships built from Persian money – Athens' first sizeable fleet since Aigospotamoi. Ostensibly his mission was to secure Athens' links with Rhodes, but he had far fatter fish to fry, as is made plain by the alliance possibly now concluded between Athens, Euagoras of Salamis (now in revolt from his Persian overlord) and Akoris (also spelled Hakoris and Achoris), who had succeeded Sparta's ally Nepherites as ruler of revolted Egypt in 394 or thereabouts. Persia, in other words, and not only Sparta was now also Athens' proclaimed opponent – the logical consequence of Sparta's attempted peacemaking with Persian backing in 392/1. It was ironical that

Persia should herself have contributed decisively to this *démarche*.

For Athens naval empire of some kind was in a sense a necessity rather than an optional luxury. If she were to feed her unusually highly urbanized population she required constant access to external supplies of grain, especially wheat. But naval empire of any sort demanded large and regular amounts of cash to finance the building of ships and ancillary expenses. Hence the need for cash contributions or tribute from her Greek allies and for friendly relations with non-Greek powers who might threaten her strategic interests. Thrasyboulos was therefore pursuing Athens' 'natural' foreign policy in bringing back into alliance Byzantion and Chalkedon, re-establishing the ten percent toll on goods passing through the Bosporos, recovering Thasos and parts of the Thracian Chersonese and of Lesbos, and renewing alliance with Thracian kings. His efforts at sea were materially complemented on the Asiatic mainland by Iphikrates. He had been recalled under a cloud from Corinth in 389 and given the task of removing the Spartan threat to Athenian interests posed by the area harmost Anaxibios on the southern side of the Hellespont. This he accomplished by ambushing Anaxibios near Abydos and killing him and no less than twelve other Spartan harmosts. That terminated Sparta's rather lacklustre involvement on the Asiatic mainland, and the way was clear for what proved to be the decisive *rapprochement* between Sparta and Persia.

Thrasyboulos was killed later in 389 at Aspendos in Pamphylia while making his way at last to Rhodes; he was succeeded amid major domestic recriminations by Agyrrhios, the politician who had been responsible for introducing Assembly pay at Athens in the later 390s. But it was Thrasyboulos who had brought the Corinthian War to its penultimate stage by destroying the last vestiges of Artaxerxes' resistance to full co-operation with Sparta against her Greek enemies. For Thrasyboulos had not just greatly improved the economic and political position of Athens at Sparta's expense. In fostering democratic revolutions at Byzantion and Klazomenai and in speaking the language of control rather than equal alliance at Thasos (and elsewhere no doubt), he had come suspiciously close to commencing the re-creation of Athens' fifth-century Aegean empire, from which Persia had suffered no less than Sparta. The stage was thus set for a further Spartan attempt to win Artaxerxes round to the kind of peace terms Sparta wanted in Greece, and Antalkidas was therefore appointed both navarch and ambassador in early summer 388: as ambassador, so that he might treat with Artaxerxes in person at Susa; as navarch, in order to profit from the hoped-for Persian aid by repeating Lysander's feat of gaining control of the Hellespont.

All went according to plan. Artaxerxes was utterly charmed by Antalkidas, replaced the too pro-Athenian Strouthas with Tiribazus and the too anti-Spartan Pharnabazus with Ariobarzanes, a family connection of Antalkidas, and channelled funds into the provision of a suitable fleet. With this and with further ships lent by Sparta's grateful ally in the west, Dionysios of Syracuse (who was still not prepared to forget how Athens had behaved towards Syracuse and his friend Hermokrates over twenty years previously), Antalkidas had little difficulty in 387 in defeating an Athenian fleet, the commanders of which were perhaps rather too easily deceived by a stratagem. Since their Black Sea wheat-supply was now cut off once again, the Athenians were in no position to refuse the peace terms offered them by Persia and Sparta in 387/6.

Back on the Greek mainland there had been a military stalemate since 390. But it was a stalemate from which Sparta's enemies were suffering on balance rather more than Sparta. Already in 390, as mentioned, the Boiotians had been interested in peace. Apart from Sparta's disaster near Lechaion in that year, nothing had happened since then to make them desperately anxious to continue the war at any cost. As for the Corinthians, the constant ravaging of the Corinthia during the first five years of the War, the Spartan occupation of Lechaion since 391, the Argive garrison on Akrokorinthos since 392 – these had taken their toll. Argos had suffered less, but her territory too had been severely ravaged by Agesilaos in 391 and by Agesipolis in 388, forcing her to get wheat from Sparta's ally Mantineia on the second occasion.

That was the position on the confederate side. By 387 Sparta had recovered somewhat from the shock of the Lechaion disaster and was happily placed at sea in the Hellespontine region. On the other hand, it was a strain on her already overstretched manpower and financial resources to maintain garrisons in Lechaion, Phleious and Orchomenos. She was, moreover, finding it hard to preserve absolute discipline and loyalty throughout her alliance, as the willingness of Mantineia to make wheat available to Argos and the refusal of contingents on occasions by both Phleious and Mantineia plainly indicate. Thus it was that by 387/6 all major parties to the Corinthian War had overriding reasons to cease hostilities. The question rather was on what terms they would settle.

19

Peace of Antalkidas to Battle of Leuktra, 386-371

Antalkidas in 388/7 had won Artaxerxes round to Sparta's (including Agesilaos') way of thinking about Greek problems and given Athens no choice in 387 but to accept whatever peace terms Artaxerxes and Sparta should dictate. In 387/6 it was left to Agesilaos to compel Sparta's other leading Greek enemies to accede to the proposed peace on his terms. These included, as non-negotiable priorities, the disintegration of the Boiotian Confederacy, the disaggregation of the Union of Corinth and Argos and the restoration to Thebes and Corinth of extreme pro-Spartan oligarchic exiles who were personal friends or clients of Agesilaos.

The Thebans predictably resisted an interpretation of 'autonomy' that meant the so-called autonomy of the other Boiotian cities from Thebes, since they did not count the Boiotian Confederacy as *ipso facto* infringing their autonomy in the first place. But Agesilaos was placed in command of a Peloponnesian League levy and had reached Tegea before the Thebans perforce abandoned their demand to swear to the proposed peace in the name of Boiotia as a whole. From this humiliation of the Thebes he hated Agesilaos derived some vengeful compensation for the injurious insult he had sustained at Theban hands in 396 at Aulis. So far as Argos and Corinth were concerned, a mere threat of force from Agesilaos was enough to persuade the Argives to withdraw their garrison from Akrokorinthos and so prepare the way for a resumption of power by the restored oligarchic rulers of a once again separate Corinth. After these essential preliminaries had been completed to his satisfaction Agesilaos was ready to preside over the swearing of oaths of peace in Sparta in 386.

The ensuing Peace, to which all Greek states were notionally parties, bore alternative titles in antiquity: the 'Peace of the King', because Artaxerxes II of Persia formally speaking had dictated the essentials of the agreement in the shape of a royal rescript; or the 'Peace of (literally 'called after') Antalkidas', since he was the principal Greek negotiator. Both titles are apt in their own way. Through this diplomatic instrument Artaxerxes achieved by the stroke of a stylus the formal suzerainty of Greece that Xerxes had failed to secure by a massive invasion a century earlier and the real sovereignty over the Greeks of Asia (now for the first time collectively thus described) that Xerxes had lost as a consequence of that failure. On the other hand, in mainland Greece Sparta rather than Persia was the real immediate beneficiary of the Peace. As Agesilaos is supposed to have remarked in response to an accusation of treachery to the Greek cause, it was not so much the case that the Spartans had 'medized' as that the Persians had 'lakonized'. Whether or not the Spartans were officially designated 'guarantors' of the Peace on Persia's behalf (*prostatai* could mean simply 'champions'), they were certainly its most ardent Greek supporters.

Whichever title is preferred, the Peace contained three principal provisions. (Other possible clauses are more or less controversial, because the only available sources, all Greek, are regrettably imprecise or even contradictory.) First, the Greek cities of 'Asia' (which for the purposes of the Act was deemed to include the islands of Klazomenai and Cyprus) were to belong henceforth to the Great King. In practice, Artaxerxes was made to fight for another half dozen years before his philhellenic rebel vassal Euagoras was brought to heel, and the Greek cities of the Asiatic mainland were given some respite from Persian political, economic and cultural demands by the revolts of various western Asiatic satraps (provincial governors or viceroys) between 372 and 360. But Persian rule of the Asiatic Greeks persisted none the less until they were liberated by Alexander the Great in 334 – liberated, that is, from the convenient quisling oligarchic regimes through which Persia like Sparta preferred to control her subjects indirectly. The major offshore islands – Lesbos, Chios, Samos, and Rhodes – also had to wait till then to recover their important territories on the adjoining Asiatic mainland.

Second, all Greek cities outside Asia, both great and small, were to be 'autonomous', except that Athens exceptionally was to retain possession of the islands of Lemnos, Imbros and Skyros. Autonomy, as we have noted in the case of the Boiotian Confederacy, was an ambiguous concept in principle. One man's autonomy was another's political subjection – or 'slavery', as the Greeks emotively said. Sparta through Agesilaos interpreted the term negatively to mean an absolute prohibition on political entities embracing more than one *polis* (apart from the Peloponnesian League, needless to add) and a general opposition to *poleis* which interpreted autonomy in a manner Sparta found uncongenial, that is by choosing democracy in preference to oligarchy as their form of government. The one-sidedness of Sparta's interpretation can be simply demonstrated: on etymological grounds the Greek term *autonomia* meant literally the right of a state to choose its own laws and customs.

However, Sparta's interpretation of the autonomy clause prevailed in practice and gave her plenty of scope for intervening in the internal affairs of her enemies or disaffected allies under cover of the third principal provision of the Peace. This prescribed that the King (or his agents) would make war on any Greek state not abiding by either of the two preceding clauses. The first such Spartan intervention that is documented in any detail was directed against Mantineia in (probably) 385.

Relations between Sparta and her Peloponnesian League ally Mantineia had reached such a low ebb during the Corinthian War that in 390 Agesilaos withdrew his army from the Corinthia through the territory of Mantineia *by night* so as to deny the Mantineians the pleasure of crowing over the humiliation of the Spartans inflicted by Iphikrates and his peltasts near Lechaion. Thwarted here, the Mantineians amply succeeded in infuriating their *hêgemôn* (leader of the essentially military Peloponnesian League) in other ways – by refusing on supposedly religious grounds to contribute contingents when required, by fighting poorly when they did provide contingents, and by supplying Argos with grain in 388 as they had perhaps already done in 391. There were three main reasons why Mantineia was both willing and able to manifest such opposition to Sparta during a major war: she was a democracy in the acutely sensitive region of eastern Arkadia; there was within the democratic leadership a powerful pro-Argive lobby; and Sparta could not afford a repetition of the situation of 420-418 when Mantineia had seceded from the Peloponnesian League to join an anti-Spartan axis with Argos, Athens and Elis. However, once a special, thirty-year treaty concluded between Sparta and Mantineia in 418/7 had expired and the Corinthian War was over, the day of reckoning for Mantineia was not long postponed. For as she had taught Elis between 402 and 400, the new imperialist Sparta of the post-Athenian War era would not tolerate such Peloponnesian disloyalty any longer than she absolutely had to.

Agesilaos cleverly declined the command against Mantineia in 385 on the specious ground that Mantineia had helped his father Archidamos II to put down a Messenian Helot revolt in the 460s. He thereby ensnared his younger and suggestible co-king Agesipolis into doing his own dirty work. And dirty it was. Sparta did not merely replace Mantineia's democracy with a narrow pro-Spartan oligarchy of rich landowners, but she also carried Agesilaos' policy of *polis*-atomization to the absurd lengths of breaking up the unified, centralized *polis* of Mantineia into its (four or five) original villages. This was the height – or depth – of reaction. The only, small compensation for this political butchery was that sixty leading democrats were permitted ungraciously to go into exile (some at Athens) instead of being personally butchered. But that was no thanks to Agesilaos. It took a dramatic intervention by the exiled ex-King Pausanias, who came from Tegea to intercede successfully on their behalf with his son Agesipolis. For these men were probably connected to him in the way that the oligarchic exiles restored to Corinth and Thebes in the previous year were linked by personal ties of ritualized friendship (*xenia*) to Agesilaos. Agesilaos' connections in Mantineia, of course, were with the democrats' opponents, who now were brought to power and demonstrated their grateful loyalty by contributing troops to Peloponnesian levies far more enthusiastically than their predecessors. This was fortunate in a way for Sparta, as she was to call on them with monotonous frequency in the next decade until the Peace was renewed in 375.

It was perhaps not only on land that Sparta in 385 was active in restoring what she considered to be the proper balance of power in Aegean Greece. For it may have been in that year that Sparta somehow intervened on the island of Thasos to restore a pro-Spartan oligarchy and so undo the work of Thrasyboulos; at any rate, Thasian democratic exiles turn up at Athens a couple of years later in company with the Mantineian democrats mentioned above. Such an intervention at Thasos would have been designed to remind the Athenians that, even if they had perhaps come off quite lightly under the terms of the Peace, they could not presume on Spartan goodwill. For Athens' former allies Euagoras and Akoris were still in revolt from Artaxerxes, and Sparta was doing Persia as well as herself a favour by policing the Aegean in this way. As in 404, Athens was therefore again compelled to rely on diplomacy to rebuild her influence in this sphere. Apart from harbouring anti-Spartan refugees from Thasos she renewed diplomatic relations with a Thracian king in 386/5 and in 384 concluded a defensive alliance with the island-state of Chios. The stress laid in the wording of this treaty on strict fidelity to the autonomy clause of the Peace of Antalkidas and on the fact that this was an alliance between democracies represented a symbolic challenge to both Sparta and Persia. But it was to be another eight years before that optimistic symbolism could be translated into the practical reality of successful military confrontation with Sparta. It goes without saying that the message of Lysias' speech at Olympia in 384 (probably), urging the Greeks to combine to liberate Sicily from the tyranny of Sparta's ally Dionysios and Asiatic Greece from the despotism of the Persian king, fell on stony ground.

For the next five years, indeed, Sparta's power appeared to grow to a height not far short of that attained in and after 404, under cover of the Peace and at the expense of her fellow-Greeks. Three episodes stand out. In order of significance they are the occupation of Thebes, together with the imposition of direct Spartan military control of all Boiotia; the break-up of the Chalkidian federation led by Olynthos; and the imposition of an oligarchy on formerly democratic Phleious. Chronologically, though, the Phleious episode came first, since it formed a natural sequel to the 'disciplining' of another Peloponnesian League ally, Mantineia (above). For in about 384 some pro-Spartan oligarchic exiles including men linked hereditarily by ties of *xenia* to Agesilaos applied for and received Spartan backing for their restoration to city and property.

It appears that there was no clause enjoining the restoration of political exiles in the Peace of Antalkidas. Agesilaos had taken care to get his friends restored to Corinth and Thebes *before* those cities swore to the Peace. So in 384 Sparta could not legally demand of supposedly autonomous and allied Phleious that the exiles be restored. She could only request it. In any case Sparta's attitude towards Phleious was rather softer than towards Mantineia, since despite her other provocations Phleious had at least asked for a Spartan garrison in 390 (under duress, it is true, from the peltasts of Iphikrates). That garrison was not used by Sparta as a means of restoring the exiled oligarchs, and Xenophon noted with due emphasis that Sparta had not taken advantage of her military control of Phleious to alter her (democratic) constitution before the garrison was withdrawn in 386. In 384, therefore, the Phleiasians expressed willingness to accede to Sparta's request to restore the exiles.

By 381, however, Sparta's line on Phleious had visibly hardened under the influence of Agesilaos. For, as was only to be expected in such cases, the restoration of the formerly wealthy exiles to their extensive landed property had proved more complicated in practice than in theory, and the exiles had complained to Sparta that their rights had not been respected. Since, moreover, the Phleiasians had compromised themselves further in the eyes of Agesilaos by going out of their way to ingratiate themselves with Agesipolis (by sending him a large sum of money towards the expenses of his campaign against Olynthos), Agesilaos now secured command of a Peloponnesian League levy to restore 'good order' at Phleious, that is to reinstate his friends and hand over the government of Phleious to them and to the less extreme Phleiasian oligarchs. Legal justification for such an imposition was there none. But in the flush of what he considered to be Sparta's triumph in Boiotia in 382 Agesilaos clearly felt that he could wield the big stick with impunity. The resistance of Phleious proved far fiercer and more prolonged than he had anticipated, but after a largely unimaginative siege of twenty months Agesilaos forced a capitulation through starvation. Like Pausanias at Athens in 403, Agesilaos at Phleious in 379 was entrusted by the Spartan home authorities with arranging the terms of the political settlement. The difference between the two kings was that, whereas Pausanias had in a sense genuinely respected the autonomy of Athens, Agesilaos chose to ride roughshod over the wishes of the majority of Phleiasian citizens and imposed an oligarchy under a screen of legality reminiscent of the way that Lysander had imposed the Thirty on Athens in 404.

The campaign which Agesipolis was conducting in 381 had been decided upon by Sparta and the Peloponnesian League in the winter of 383/2. In 383 three more appellants had applied for political aid to Sparta following the success of the Phleiasian exiles: Amyntas III, who had been king of Macedon with interruptions since 393/2, and the Chalkidian cities of Akanthos and Apollonia. All three shared a common foe, Olynthos, who it was alleged had respectively robbed Amyntas of part of his rightful kingdom and Akanthos and Apollonia of their autonomy. Xenophon contrives virtually to conceal altogether the appeal of Amyntas and spotlights that of the Chalkidian cities, for the obvious reason that only the latter gave Sparta the chance to invest her fundamentally selfish intervention in Chalkidike with a spuriously legal pretext arising out of the terms of the Peace of Antalkidas. But the Peloponnesian League campaign is better interpreted as a logical development of the Corinthian War and as part of Sparta's imperialist strategy for controlling all mainland Greece that that War had temporarily interrupted. For not only had Olynthos, it seems, fought on the side of the confederates but she was now in 383 involved in negotiations for alliance with both Thebes and Athens. Moreover, the land-route to Chalkidike would take the Spartans past their military colony of Herakleia Trachinia and give them the opportunity to reinstate the presence in Thessaly that had been rudely ousted in 395/4.

The commanders chosen for 382 – the brothers Eudamidas and Phoibidas, and Agesilaos' half-brother Teleutias – were quite possibly all three related to Agesilaos. Their identity suggests strongly that the guiding inspiration behind the whole project was Agesilaos, who had his reasons for not departing so far from Sparta and the Peloponnese to take the command in person. The representatives of the Peloponnesian League allies who voted in favour of Sparta's projected campaign reportedly did so enthusiastically, as if they had been hand-picked by Agesilaos for their known reliability. This was one of the results of Sparta's exemplary treatment of Mantineia a couple of years earlier. On the other hand, the fact that now for the first time on record a change in the obligations of League members was formally introduced indicates that by no means all the citizens of the states they represented, not even all the hoplites, saw matters in quite the same enthusiastic, pro-Spartan way. For in 382 it was agreed that personal service by League members might be commuted for a cash-payment on a recognized scale of equivalences. With the money raised thereby the by now ubiquitous mercenaries might be hired as substitutes for, rather than additions to, the citizen militiamen. This is an important surface indication of a deeper economic and political malaise within the Peloponnesian League.

The Olynthos campaign was spread over four campaigning seasons and brought serious reverses to the Spartan side. Teleutias was killed in battle in 381 and his successor Agesipolis suffered grave losses before himself dying of a fever in 380. If Agesilaos was genuinely grieved by the death of the latter, this was partly because he could not have hoped for a more complaisant and malleable partner in crime. In 379, however, Olynthos was eventually subdued, the Chalkidian federation was dissolved, and the Chalkidian cities were admitted, individually (for that was how Sparta understood 'autonomy'), to the Peloponnesian League, which thus achieved its maximum geographical spread. Apart from Sparta, though, the principal beneficiaries of this development were not the Peloponnesians but Amyntas and – though Sparta cannot be blamed for not foreseeing this – his mighty son the future Philip II.

Thus was the high-water mark of Spartan imperial expansion reached. For latterly Sparta had not only brought military force to bear upon Phleious and Olynthos. In 382 Phoibidas, while ostensibly en route to join his brother in the far north, made a detour to Thebes, seized and garrisoned the Kadmeia (akropolis), and placed the garrison at the disposal of a narrow oligarchy (what the Greeks called a *dunasteia*, hence our 'dynasty') led by a long-standing client of Sparta, Leontiadas. His political enemy Hismenias, who had instigated Theban and Boiotian opposition to Sparta since 404, was now executed for disloyalty to the Peloponnesian League and – utterly unconvincingly – for betraying 'Hellas' to Persia; his trial before a kangaroo court of Peloponnesian League judges was the first of a series of travesties of justice for which Agesilaos' Sparta became notorious in the years on either side of 380. But one of Hismenias' close political associates and some 300 others (including a certain Pelopidas) who shared their views on Sparta escaped to the sanctuary of Athens, where they joined the Mantineian and Thasian refugees already mentioned.

It was perhaps now, if not already soon after the Peace was sworn, that Sparta resurrected Plataia forty odd years after its destruction by Thebes with Spartan connivance in 427/6. Thebes was thus docked of perhaps half her territory to add to the insult of Spartan military occupation. To set the seal on her domination of Boiotia – a domination more thorough than that achieved by Athens between 457 and 447 – Sparta extended her harmost-system to most of the principal 'autonomous' cities of Boiotia in tandem with the imposition of *dunasteiai* on the Theban model. To an impartial observer there could have seemed little difference between Lysander's Aegean empire of 405/4 and following and Sparta's hegemony of Boiotia between 382 and 379. It is not known for certain that Agesilaos put Phoibidas up to the seizure of Thebes, but he certainly was decisive in defending the result of that action on the grounds that it was congruent with Sparta's best interests. Agesilaos must therefore stand convicted of a flagrant breach of the Peace of which he himself was one of the foremost advocates and which he still claimed to champion elsewhere.

Legality, however, tends to count for less in human affairs than power. Where Agesilaos went seriously wrong was in overestimating the power of Sparta. In

380 Isokrates, a conservative Athenian pamphleteer, advocated a 'Panhellenic' expedition against Persia that was to be led jointly by Sparta and Athens. But this was spitting into the wind. Not only had Persia been recently strengthened by her recovery of Cyprus, but Sparta – as Xenophon could see with hindsight, but Isokrates could not at the time – was much less strong than she appeared superficially to be. For military as well as political reasons Sparta was unable either to prevent or to reverse the liberation of Thebes that was achieved in the winter of 379/8, and that crack in the imperial monolith had yawned into a fissure by the time Sparta was decisively defeated in battle at Leuktra in 371.

The three Spartan commanders of the 1500-strong garrison in Thebes who allowed Pelopidas and other exiles to inveigle themselves into the city and wrest control of it from Leontiadas were guilty of criminal negligence. Herippidas, abandoned at last by his patron Agesilaos, was executed at Corinth, while Lysanoridas and Arkissos were fined heavily (as Phoibidas had been in 382) and exiled (as Phoibidas was not). Agesilaos, however, was all too conscious by now that his rigidly hard line on Thebes and Boiotia was far from universally popular in the highest Spartan circles, not least because it had again induced Athens to co-operate, however halfheartedly, with Thebes. So rather than assume the command against Thebes himself and thereby incur the charge of promoting collective tyranny there, he made way for a reluctant Kleombrotos, who had succeeded his older brother on the Agiad throne in 380. When Kleombrotos failed to recover Thebes in January or February 378, Agesilaos' thoughts turned to diplomacy in a bid to prevent the fluctuating and patchy sympathy for Thebes at Athens from being translated into a formal anti-Spartan alliance. However, just when a top-level Spartan delegation (including Etymokles, a friend of Agesilaos who was also a fellow-member of the Gerousia) was actually in Athens, its best efforts at suasion were utterly undermined by the man whom Kleombrotos had left as harmost of Boiotian Thespiai.

Whether it was Kleombrotos or indeed anyone or any state that bribed or otherwise induced Sphodrias to undertake his extremely risky venture, it is quite clear that his attempt to emulate Phoibidas' capture of Thebes by seizing the ungated Peiraieus misfired horribly. Agesilaos' diplomacy was in tatters. Yet even so Agesilaos, believing that the damage done to Sparta's relations with Athens was not immediately reparable and wishing to salvage something from the wreckage, secured the acquittal of Sphodrias, despite the latter's failure to appear at his trial. Agesilaos thus put Sphodrias' patron Kleombrotos, who was proving a more obdurate opponent than either his brother or his father had been, heavily in his debt, and it was no accident that Kleombrotos should have died along with Sphodrias on the battlefield of Leuktra in a fatally unsuccessful attempt to carry out the Theban policy of Agesilaos.

Soon after the monstrously unjust acquittal of Sphodrias Athens and Thebes duly allied bilaterally. Sparta, they agreed, had flagrantly breached the Peace of Antalkidas. But of far greater international moment was the fact that already by midsummer 378 (it would appear) Athens and Thebes were part of a wider anti-Spartan defensive alliance, the so-called Second Athenian League. The germ of the League idea can be traced as far back as the alliance between Athens and Chios in 384. Chios, like four of the other five founder-members of the new League (Mytilene, Methymna, Rhodes and Byzantion), had been a member of Athens' earlier sea-league, the 'Delian League' (a modern name) of the fifth century. But it was the inclusion of Thebes, formerly a member of Sparta's Peloponnesian League but now a democracy and potentially the greatest land-based power in Greece after Sparta, that held out hope of fulfilment of the League's principal aim. This was to resist Spartan imperialism both on land and at sea strictly within the terms of the Peace that Sparta was judged to have broken. It was as 'the Thebans' that Pelopidas, Epameinondas and Gorgidas brought their state into alliance with Athens, and the Athenians seem never to have altered the terms of the alliance in this respect. Yet already in 378 soon after the liberation from Sparta the Thebans had declared their intention of refounding the Boiotian Confederacy dismantled in 386 on new, democratic lines; and by 375 it is fair to talk again of 'Boiotia' rather than simply 'Thebes' as the power-unit with which Sparta and (increasingly) Athens had to reckon.

Initially the Second Athenian League as such played little or no military role, since Spartan aggression in the summer and autumn of 378 was confined to land-operations in Boiotia directed by Agesilaos against the territory of Thebes. But early in 377, after Agesilaos had failed in his major objective and the members of the new League had had time to agree the working details of their relationship, Athens published a decree (proposed by one Aristoteles) designed to attract a wider membership. Since the alliance was to be directed against Sparta, the decree emphasized that it would eschew anything remotely resembling Spartan imperialism since 404. On the other hand, most potential members had already belonged to the Delian League, which had quickly grown into an Athenian empire; so the Athenian Assembly was also at pains to stress that the terms of the new alliance would proscribe the most unpopular features of that earlier empire, above all the ownership of allied land by Athens or individual Athenians. The decree did not spell out in detail how allied decisions would be reached and implemented nor how allied campaigns would be financed ('tribute' was another of the most unpopular aspects of the fifth-century empire). But potential allies will have been reassured both by the prospective establishment of a permanent Congress of allied representatives with judicial powers at Athens and by the Athenians' decision not to levy compulsory tribute or any other taxes.[1]

The prospectus thus summarized did not immediately bear fruit on a wide scale, mainly because in 377 Sparta under Agesilaos again decided to concentrate her energies on land against Thebes. But on the island of Euboia, where Sparta had established a harmost and garrison in the northern settlement of Oreos (originally Histiaia) perhaps in 379, the benefits of membership seemed immediately attractive. The other four Euboian cities therefore joined the Second Athenian League in summer 377, thereby providing the alliance with a base for patrolling the Cyclades. The importance of this facility soon became clear. For in 376 a fourth successive Peloponnesian League expedition against Thebes – led this time by Kleombrotos, since Agesilaos had sustained a

---

[1] An ironical chronological coincidence is perhaps worth noting in passing: it was in 377 that Maussollos, who was to blunt the effectiveness of the League in the 350s, succeeded his father as satrap of Caria.

crippling injury in his good leg on his way back to Sparta in 377 – proved even less successful than its predecessors, and the members of the Peloponnesian League, already dissatisfied with Spartan leadership in 377, decided to transfer their attentions away from Agesilaos' *bête noire* and to try conclusions with Athens at sea.

This turned out to be a serious miscalculation. In September 376 a largely Athenian fleet under Chabrias comprehensively defeated a Peloponnesian fleet off Naxos, Athens' first major victory at sea since the latter part of the Athenian War. In 375 the Athenian alliance followed this up with successful expeditions to the north Aegean under Chabrias again and round the Peloponnese to north-west Greece under Timotheos son of Konon who won a second important naval victory off Alyzeia in Akarnania. These successes prompted large accessions of new allies to the Second Athenian League, until the total approached sixty.

Thebes had played no significant part in these naval developments – hardly surprisingly, given that she would always be principally a land-oriented state. Besides, her immediate objectives were to fend off the Spartan incursions of her territory and to reconstitute the Boiotian Confederacy under her leadership. There was no danger of reconquest in either 378 or 377; indeed, in 378/7 after Agesilaos had retired, the Thebans defeated, killed and so revenged themselves upon Phoibidas, whom Agesilaos had left behind as harmost of Thespiai in succession to Sphodrias. However, the territory of Thebes, which was still reduced to its pre-427 proportions by the resurrection of Plataia, had been severely ravaged for two seasons in a row, and by the autumn of 377 Thebes was suffering something approaching a famine. It was therefore more than a light relief to her when the Spartan harmost of Oreos, who had intercepted and confiscated two triremes full of Thessalian wheat purchased by Thebes, was caught off his guard by his Theban prisoners. Oreos was thus caused to revolt from Sparta and the grain-route by sea from Thessaly to Boiotia secured.

By this means the Thebans endured the winter and spring of 377/6. Being thereafter untroubled by Spartan invasion in either 376 or 375, they put this unaccustomed freedom to profitable use in recovering all Boiotia except Orchomenos, Thespiai and Plataia. This success they owed partly to politic diplomacy: the restored Boiotian Confederacy was run on attractively moderate democratic lines. But yet more important was the military factor. Under Gorgidas, who reputedly founded the elite hoplite force of 150 Theban homosexual pairs known as the Sacred Band in 378, and Pelopidas, who employed it in conjunction with cavalry to inflict a portentous defeat on Sparta's Orchomenos garrison at Tegyra in 375, the Boiotians were becoming a major military force on land. From defence they were emboldened to switch to attack, most naturally against their old enemies – and Sparta's faithful allies – the neighbouring Phokians. King Kleombrotos was swiftly despatched to Phokis with two thirds of Sparta's regular hoplite establishment (the majority of which had long been provided by Perioikoi) and corresponding numbers of allied troops. There he watched events during the summer of 375.

It was at this juncture that the northern question, left in abeyance since 379, was again forced upon Sparta's attention. Thessalian politics after the Peace of

Antalkidas are shrouded in obscurity, but it would be reasonable to suppose that Sparta had reasserted her control of Herakleia Trachinia at least by 382, when she undertook her campaign against Olynthos. It seems too that she had used Herakleia as a base from which to intervene again in Thessalian affairs – but this time on the side of the dynast of Pharsalos, not of the dynast of Pherai. For Jason of Pherai had abandoned Lykophron's allegiance to Sparta, and Sparta's cause in Thessaly was represented chiefly by Polydamas of Pharsalos. In summer 375 Polydamas appealed to Sparta to intervene militarily in order to prevent Jason from making himself master of a united Thessaly and a subordinate Pharsalos.

If Sparta again summoned a Peloponnesian League Congress in 375, she will have found the allies in a very much less charitable mood than in 376, let alone 382. As subsequent events were to show, the allies were still prepared (just) to carry the fight to central Greece against Thebes and to resist Athens' ventures in western waters. But intervention in Thessaly would have smacked too much of aggressive Spartan imperialism, especially as the allies apparently had little comprehension of the potential threat posed by a powerful leader of a united Thessaly such as Jason. In any event, Sparta pre-empted the need for an allied decision by turning down Polydamas' request on her own account. Her military manpower, she had calculated, was stretched to the limit as it was, what with watching the Boiotians in central Greece and preparing to resist attacks on her own *polis* territory by land or sea. Jason was thereby permitted to do what he might well have been able to do anyway, that is assume control of all Thessaly as *tagos* (supreme leader of a Thessalian federation) and conclude alliances with both Athens and Boiotia.

To such a pass had once mighty Sparta been brought by among other things the misguided Boiotian policy of Agesilaos. When a rescript arrived opportunely – and probably not coincidentally – from Artaxerxes in autumn 375, it was seized upon by Sparta with unbecoming alacrity. For Artaxerxes, wishing to recruit Greek mercenaries for yet another attempt to recover Egypt, was enjoining a renewal of the Peace of Antalkidas. The Athenians, too, had powerful reasons for making peace: they needed a respite from the heavy demands on finance and manpower made by the naval campaigns of the past two years, and they were highly suspicious of the intentions of their notional ally Thebes, whose resurgence had been too swift and too complete for Athenian comfort. When Sparta indicated that she was willing in effect to recognize Athens' hegemony of the sea, provided that the Athenian alliance recognized Sparta's by land, the ground was suitably prepared. A renewal of the Peace on the same basis of autonomy for all cities was sworn in Sparta in autumn 375. The Thebans will not have been best pleased at having to swear as a simple – and single – member of the Second Athenian League, but they were not yet in a position to take their passionate desire to be recognized as leaders of the Boiotians to the lengths of outright military opposition to both Sparta and Athens.

Precisely how Agesilaos and the Spartans reacted to the conclusion of peace is unknown. But the joy mixed with relief felt by the Athenians was unbounded. Many of the new members were now formally admitted to the Second Athenian

League, a festival of Peace was inaugurated at Athens, a statue-group depicting the lady Peace holding in her arms the infant Wealth was publicly commissioned, and individual honorific statues of Timotheos and Konon were ordered to be erected on the Athenian akropolis. The sweet taste of peace was soon soured, however. For on his return from the west the very same Timotheos tactlessly restored some pro-Athenian democratic exiles to their native Zakynthos, and Sparta chose to interpret his action as an infringement of the Peace's autonomy clause. Three Spartan naval commanders were sent in quick succession to do battle for Zakynthos and for Kerkyra (from which some pro-Spartans had been ejected) in 374 and 373. Dionysios of Syracuse, perhaps sensing a renewal of Athenian interest in Sicily, was again moved to send help to his Spartan ally.

It was not, however, Sparta that profited from all this naval endeavour in north-western waters, but rather Athens and, indirectly, Thebes. Mnasippos proved to be a more than usually incompetent and insensitive Spartan commander of mercenaries, and in Iphikrates he found himself matched against virtually the best that Athens could produce. So total, indeed, was Mnasippos' failure in 373 to secure Kerkyra for Sparta that in 372 Iphikrates was poised to carry out the threat of attacking Lakonia or Messenia from the sea that Sparta had been anticipating in 375.

Athens in the latter part of the 370s was by no means exclusively preoccupied with western matters. In fact Iphikrates had been chosen to succeed Timotheos only after the latter had been rather too extensively active in Thessaly, Macedon and Thrace for a commander appointed to go to the defence of Kerkyra. Thebes, too, was a major concern for the Athenians much nearer to hand. Some time between 378 and 373 Athens snatched back the perennially disputed borderland of Oropos, but the Theban response was far more devastating, ideologically as well as pragmatically. In 373/2 Thebes again annihilated Plataia and about the same time destroyed the fortifications of Thespiai. When Thebes had wiped out Plataia previously, in 427/6, Athens had made a unique block grant of Athenian citizenship to the survivors, much to the annoyance no doubt of Sparta who was then aiding and abetting Thebes. But now in 373/2 Thebes' action had the effect of bringing Athens and Sparta closer together in opposition to Thebes, a sentiment that Isokrates sought to foster in his Plataian Oration.

In 372, therefore, both Athens and Sparta were strongly motivated to renew the Peace, Sparta if anything more so than Athens. Artaxerxes too now had a further reason for wanting Greek mercenaries, in that the man he had appointed to recover Egypt had gone into revolt himself – against Artaxerxes. The Persian king was thus cordially disposed in advance to the plea for his aid conveyed once more by Antalkidas in 372/1. Urgency in the conclusion of peace was enjoined by the Thebans when they again invaded Phokis, in the spring or early summer of 371. So in June a fourth Peace conference was convened in Sparta to agree a second renewal of the Peace of 386.

Xenophon's account of this conference is viciously incomplete. He not only fails to mention that Epameinondas was the Boiotians' chief spokesman but he also omits the crucial altercation between Epameinondas and Agesilaos (president of the conference) over the operative definition of 'autonomy'. When it was clear that, as in 386, Agesilaos insisted on taking autonomy for all cities to mean the dismantling of the reconstituted Boiotian Confederacy, Epameinondas asked why it should not equally be taken to mean autonomy for the Perioikic *poleis* of Lakonia and Messenia from Sparta. For in the Boiotians' view 'the Boiotians' stood for an integral political unit every bit as much as 'the Lakedaimonians'. That much we can read on and between the lines of Diodoros and Plutarch. What no ancient source so much as hints is that Epameinondas was defying Agesilaos in full awareness of the almost certain consequences – exclusion of Thebes from the Peace followed by a Spartan attack on Boiotia. For earlier in 371 Kleombrotos had again been sent to the aid of Phokis and was handily poised for an offensive.

When twenty days later the Thebans were still adamantly refusing to 'leave the Boiotian cities autonomous', Kleombrotos was ordered to invade Boiotia at the urging of Agesilaos. A lone Spartan voice, that of Prothoös, is recorded as having had the will to speak out against a policy fervently supported by a citizen-body that had by then shrunk to little over a thousand men of full status. But the Spartan Assembly as a whole thought he was talking rubbish. A pity, because a few days later Epameinondas through his brilliantly innovative but clearly long premeditated tactics inflicted a devastating defeat on Kleombrotos at Leuktra in Thespian territory, crushing the head of the serpent (the Spartan contingent) while sparing the body and tail (Sparta's allies) as far as he could. This was wise policy as well as brilliant generalship, since many allies (as even Xenophon does not forbear to mention) were not displeased with the result.

At Leuktra Sparta lost over a quarter of her full citizen manpower (some 400 men) as well as the first king known to have died in battle since Leonidas was killed at Thermopylai (in a rather more glorious cause). Yet more Spartiates would have been demoted from full citizen status after the battle, had the full rigour of Spartan law been brought to bear upon those survivors who had striven perhaps rather too officiously to keep themselves alive. But Agesilaos, who was chosen as an emergency measure to interpret the law, decreed that the relevant legislation should be deemed to sleep for the day – a necessary but hollow gesture signifying both material impotence and spiritual bankruptcy.

The fact that these survivors had not already been killed or at least taken captive was paradoxically due, not to Epameinondas, but to Jason of Pherai. Jason, who was at the same time an ally of the Boiotians and titular representative of the Spartans in Pherai, advised his ally to spare the Spartans for the time being; and Agesilaos' son Archidamos was able to meet the survivors in the Megarid and convoy them the rest of the way home. However, Jason did not give his advice in the interests of either the Boiotians or the Spartans. On his way back to Thessaly he destroyed the fortifications of Herakleia Trachinia, an insult to Sparta but also a threat to Thebes. For he thereby left himself with a clear run through the Spercheios valley into Boiotia should he wish to realize his military potential to become leader of all mainland Greece. Only his assassination in 370, perhaps, prevented that consummation.

Back in Sparta the dire prophecies of the dangers of a lame kingship that had been uttered against Agesilaos during the succession wrangle of 400 were now bitterly recalled. As for Agesilaos, the septuagenarian king was left to muse on the fact that, thanks partly to his own efforts, he presided uneasily over a bruised and battered state which at his accession had been the undisputed 'leader of the Greeks'. *Sic transit gloria.*

20

Leuktra to (Second) Mantineia, 371-362

The Battle of Leuktra, in the informed view of Aristotle, was the 'single blow' that, in conjunction with her chronic shortage of military manpower (now less than a thousand full Spartan citizens), destroyed Sparta. Yet it took over a year for the potential created by this truly decisive battle to be realized by Sparta's enemies. There were several reasons for the delayed reaction, psychological factors being perhaps no less important than the political and military ones. For the power of Sparta had been a constant, a given, in the Greek interstate equation for well-nigh two centuries, and it took time for the idea to be grasped that Sparta was no longer invincible, that a new order might be created in mainland Greece. In the event, it was the Boiotians led by Thebes who profited most from their own military victory, and the period covered in this final chapter of narrative is often labelled conventionally 'the Theban hegemony'. However, 'hegemony' implies a tighter control of mainland Greece than Thebes achieved or perhaps sought; and she was not in a position to challenge for hegemony of the sea, where Athens remained the chief Greek force from 376 to 322. 'Ascendancy' therefore is preferable to 'hegemony', so long as it is appreciated that the ascendancy was both very transitory and highly volatile. In terms of interstate relations a good case could be made for regarding the 360s as the most confused and confusing decade in the history of Classical Greece.

The first significant reaction to the Boiotians' victory at Leuktra that is on record, apart from Jason's, was the stony silence with which the news was greeted in Athens. However bitterly the Athenians misliked Sparta's fondness for promoting oligarchy and remembered Sparta's imperialistic treatment of themselves in 404/3, the growth of Theban power was now a much more potent source of fear; and in Sparta and her Peloponnesian League they saw ironically the only viable counterweight. It was on the initiative of the Athenians, therefore, that the Peace of Antalkidas or King's Peace was renewed for a third time in autumn 371, the peace conference being held in Athens not Sparta as heretofore.

Much is obscure about the details of the negotiations, but the protocol that ensued is fairly clearcut. Taking up where they had left off in June, Athens and Sparta continued the process of mutual *rapprochement* that had been interrupted – chiefly to the benefit of the Boiotians – between 374 and 372. The Boiotians were technically covered by the terms of the Peace of Athens, but Sparta, even with the support of Athens' Second League, was in no position to repeat her disastrous attempt to dismantle the Boiotian Confederacy by force in the name of 'autonomy' for all cities great and small. The only state to participate in the conference that explicitly refused to swear to uphold the agreed terms was Elis, who reasserted her claim (dormant since 400) to control her 'perioikic' settlements in the lower Alpheios valley and thus broke not only the general Peace but also her treaty with Sparta, her nominal *hêgemôn* in the Peloponnesian League. Elis wanted the rest of Triphylia back as well. But the Triphylians had other ideas, and the implications of their resistance to incorporation by Elis were to have an important bearing on Peloponnesian politics throughout the next decade. For the moment, though, Elis like many other Peloponnesian states was too preoccupied with internal dissension to effect any major territorial adjustments without substantial outside support.

For now that the cat (Sparta) had had her claws removed or at least blunted, the Peloponnesian mice began to play a very nasty game of settling old political scores or trying to achieve the overthrow of existing regimes by force or fraud. *Stasis*, that is civil strife, of one kind or another is attested in the years following 371 in Corinth, Sikyon, Argos, Phleious, Elis, Achaia (especially Pellene) and the Arkadian towns of Phigaleia, Tegea and Mantineia. From the Spartan viewpoint by far the most significant developments occurred initially in the spring and summer of 370 at Mantineia and Tegea. First, Mantineia was re-synoecized on a democratic basis and rebuilt (with Eleian aid) the walls she had been compelled by Sparta to destroy in 385. Agesilaos was despatched with the status of ambassador to talk the Mantineians out of these anti-Spartan measures, but persuasion did not sit upon his lips – not least because his intimate personal connections were with the ousted oligarchs. Only a (King) Pausanias might perhaps have made some impact, but he was now presumably dead; and in any case not even he could have resisted the next major setback suffered by Sparta in Arkadia. This took the form of a democratic, anti-Spartan revolution in Tegea accompanied by the death or exile of almost a thousand fervidly pro-Spartan oligarchic partisans. The ground was thus cleared for what can only be called a diplomatic catastrophe for Sparta, greater in the post-Leuktra circumstances even than the Union of Corinth and Argos during the Corinthian War.

Under the leadership of Mantineia (represented most notably by Lykomedes) almost all the Arkadians – and all the most important of them – united to form an Arkadian federation. When 'the Arkadians', now a political rather than merely a geographical concept, allied to Argos and Elis, Sparta found herself confronted by a solid block of enemies lying between her own nuclear territory and her vital allies about the Isthmus. This was something that the confederates of 395-386 (and, for that matter, those of 420-418) had never been able to achieve. For although Mantineia had been disaffected (to the point of outright revolt on the former occasion), the loyalty of Tegea to Sparta had not wavered so far as is known.

Sparta in 370 clearly had to try and consolidate what support remained to her in Arkadia. Agesilaos for his part burned to restore his oligarchic friends to power in Tegea, as he had done for his Corinthian and Theban friends in 386 and his Phleiasian friends in 379. For the first time in seven years he took the field at the head of an army, and it is a fair measure of his and Sparta's desperation that he did so in the winter of late 370, well after the end of the normal hoplite campaigning season. Defenceless Eutaia, which lay just over the Spartan border, he took with ease, but that hollow triumph was the limit of his military success. Diplomatically speaking, the intervention of Agesilaos merely piled Pelion on the Ossa of Sparta's woes. For the Arkadians, together with their Argive and Eleian allies, were moved to appeal for outside support in order to put an end to such Spartan interference once and for all. The ambassadors went first to Athens, but the Athenians were so far from wishing to deliver the *coup de grâce* to Sparta that a few months later they were actually in formal alliance with her. From Athens the Peloponnesians turned next to Thebes.

This was a very different Thebes from the state that had led an almost purely Boiotian army to victory at Leuktra. Some time in the summer of 370 Jason of Pherai, dynast of all Thessaly and Thebes' unreliable ally, had been assassinated. The Boiotian Confederacy, which now again included Orchomenos for the first time since her defection in 395, had become the centre of a web of alliance enfolding Phokis (formerly staunch allies of Sparta and enemies of Boiotia), Lokris, Akarnania, Malis, Trachis and Euboia. Epameinondas and Pelopidas dominated Theban counsels, as they were mostly to do for the next six years; and Epameinondas, strategically the more sensitive of the two, was quick to urge and secure a positive response to the Arkadian, Argive and Eleian appeal. What the anti-Spartan Corinthian leader Timolaos had over-optimistically projected in 395/4 became a reality in midwinter 370/69 – the first ever invasion of Lakonia and Messenia by land since the so-called 'invasion' by Dorian immigrants in about the tenth century BC.

The Boiotian-led invasion was effected along four routes of ingress by altogether something of the order of 30,000 troops. The success with which Epameinondas co-ordinated this massive operation contrasts vividly with the failure of the Athenians in Boiotia in 424 and of the Spartans also in Boiotia in 395 to concert just two separate invading forces. He was of course greatly helped by large-scale defections among the Perioikoi of northern Lakonia (e.g. the men of Karyai), but once he had reached Sparta town the opposition became stiffer. Epameinondas had probably never intended to capture, let alone destroy Sparta itself, since it was in the Boiotians' interests to leave the Arkadians, Argives and Eleians with something to worry about close to home. But it is doubtful whether he could have carried Sparta in any case, despite the town's lack of man-made defences. For a River Eurotas seasonably swollen with winter snow, combined with support from the still loyal Perioikoi and Peloponnesian League allies (Corinth, Phleious and Epidauros to the fore among them) and from mercenaries, would probably have enabled Agesilaos and his few hundred Spartiates to resist even an all-out assault.

None the less, by threatening Sparta directly Epameinondas did raise the heat under a cauldron of social tensions that had been simmering within the Spartan polity since the suppression of Kinadon's conspiracy in 399. Given the rundown of Sparta's empire and finances since 379, Sparta had not been able to maintain the numbers of Neodamodeis attested for the 390s. In fact, the last certain mention of Neodamodeis in the sources concerns one of the garrisons posted, unsuccessfully, to resist Epameinondas' invasion. Instead, therefore, Sparta resorted in 370/69 to an older expedient of arming unliberated Helots against a promise of eventual freedom if they fought well in the defence of Sparta. However, it was one thing to arm 700 Helots and send them a long way out of the country on an aggressive mission, as Sparta had done experimentally in 424. Quite different was the effect of this sudden massive enrolment of 6000 Helots for service in beleaguered Sparta – more than six times the number of full Spartan citizens, against whom some of the new recruits seemed as eager to turn their weapons as against the invaders. This spread considerable unease among the Spartiates, so much so that some of them clearly felt that accommodation with Epameinondas was a much better policy than resistance to the death. Scarcely less worrying for Agesilaos was the disloyalty of a group of 'Inferior', that is socially and politically degraded, Spartans who had long been disaffected and now saw their chance to strike back at the tiny and shrinking elite from which they had been excluded and extruded.

The cunning of Agesilaos, however, matched the situation, and both 'conspiracies' were suppressed. From Sparta Epameinondas processed as far south in Lakonia as Perioikic Gytheion, Sparta's port and naval arsenal, which unlike Sparta was apparently fortified (as it probably had been since the Athenian Tolmides burned the shipyards here in about 456). Perhaps Epameinondas captured Gytheion; but if he did not, this was because he was unwilling to spend more than a few days in laying siege to it. For he had already exceeded the temporal limit of his command, which expired around the time of the winter solstice, and he had a far, far greater objective in immediate view than the capture of Sparta's port. From Gytheion he retraced his steps up the Eurotas valley past Sparta and took the easiest way for an army from Lakonia into Messenia *via* the south-west Arkadian plain (soon to be called the plain of Megalopolis after a major new city-foundation for which Epameinondas was to claim, with much justice, the credit).

In Messenia it seems that the Perioikoi had remained uniformly loyal to Sparta. The Helots, it is almost superfluous to record, had revolted to a man, woman and child. Epameinondas' role was to set the seal on this revolt (by no means the first, thought it was the first to be utterly successful) by supervising the creation or re-creation of the *polis* of Messene. He drew up the citizen-register, summoning expatriate Messenians from as far afield as Sicily, south Italy and north Africa. He laid the economic basis of citizenship by dividing up the city's extensive and remarkably fertile land into suitably sized lots. Finally, the capstone of his achievement, he supervised the construction *ex nihilo* of a massively fortified central settlement on the west side of Mount Ithome. Sparta was thus deprived definitively of the better half of her directly owned *polis* territory, a loss that proved irreparable – and irreparably deleterious to her status as a great power – despite the irredentist passion of Agesilaos and his son and successor Archidamos III (*c.* 359-338).

Apart from her Peloponnesian League allies Sparta had predictably appealed also to Athens in her time of trouble, and not less predictably Athens had responded positively. But although Iphikrates was sent to block the Isthmus, where both Corinth and Megara were still loyal to Sparta, Epameinondas managed to get the central Greek component of his army safely home early in

369. He was himself nevertheless prosecuted by a political opponent on his return to Thebes for exceeding the statutory time-limit of his office, but he was acquitted and appropriately re-elected Boiotarch. Fortified by this vote of confidence in his long-standing collaborator, Pelopidas began to emulate Epameinondas' Peloponnesian success in the areas to north of Boiotia where Spartan power had once posed a serious threat and obstacle to Theban ambitions – Thessaly and Macedon. The Thessalian confederation was reorganized and an alliance was struck between Boiotia and Alexander II of Macedon, who not long before had succeeded to the throne of his father Amyntas III. From 369 until his death Pelopidas confined his attention to the northern sphere, while Epameinondas was chiefly preoccupied with Peloponnesian affairs. This sensible division of labour no doubt helped to preserve their uniquely amicable partnership.

Sparta meanwhile in early summer 369 formalized her relationship with Athens by concluding the by now customary defensive alliance. These two states had allied similarly half a century before, but now it was a question not of the dual hegemony of Aegean Greece but of a rather feeble resistance to a third and greater Greek power. Even so, in July of 369 Epameinondas led a second successful invasion of the Peloponnese, detaching Achaian Pellene and Sikyon from their Spartan allegiance despite the aid sent to Sparta by Dionysios of Syracuse in the shape of some 2000 Gaulish and Iberian mercenaries. This invasion also made it possible for the Arkadians to start in earnest the construction of a new federal capital. It had to be a new city in any case, to prevent friction between Mantineia and Tegea – rather as Washington, D.C., became the federal capital of the United States instead of either New York City or Philadelphia. But to this negative consideration was added a powerful positive motive, the need to place a permanent barrier in the way of Sparta's inevitable attempts to recolonize Messenia. Hence the creation of the double city of Megalopolis ('The Great City') in south-west Arkadia, part federal capital, part new *polis*. The *polis* element was formed by the amalgamation of no less than forty village communities, mainly Arkadian of course but also embracing some in Triphylia, Kynouria (alternatively known as the Thyreatis) and north-central Lakonia (Aigytis, Skiritis) at the expense of Elis, Argos and Sparta respectively. Epameinondas, if his epitaph can be relied on, had more than a hand in this monstrous construction, which as a *polis* long outlived its ephemeral function as capital of a cohesive federal state.

No more than in 370 could Sparta in 369 really afford to sit idly by while Arkadia was thus strengthened against her. On the other hand, she was still not sufficiently organized, equipped and confident to go onto the attack. Indeed, twice in 369 the Arkadians made punitive raids on what remained of Sparta's territory – against Messenian Asine and Lakonian Pellana. However, the arrival late in 369 of Philiskos of Abydos, agent of Sparta's friend Ariobarzanes, offered Sparta better prospects. Ariobarzanes was perhaps already meditating revolt against Artaxerxes II, but ostensibly he was still acting in the interests of his master, who as ever had a pressing need for a constant stream of Greek mercenaries to carry out his programme of recovering Egypt for the Persian Empire. But the peace conference called by Philiskos at Delphi in the spring or summer of 368 was not a success, mainly because Artaxerxes and Dionysios were prepared in the interests of Sparta to interpret the autonomy clause as *not* applying to Messene, whereas the Thebans naturally could not possibly accept this construction.

After this diplomatic failure the Boiotian alliance under Pelopidas concentrated its efforts on Thessaly, where Alexander of Pherai – a quite formidable successor to Jason – had concluded an alliance with Athens. Pelopidas suffered the indignity of capture by Alexander and was not released until 367 by an expedition led by Epameinondas. As for the Athenians, in 368 they resuscitated their atavistic desire to recover Amphipolis in Thrace (lost to them in 424) in a concrete way by appointing Iphikrates as general for Amphipolis. Indeed, they pursued their Amphipolis programme with such singleminded energy that major allies in their Second League such as Mytilene were moved to question whether the original, anti-Spartan motivation and purpose of the League were not now defunct. It was this divergence of interests between Athens and her allies in the League that was as responsible as any other factor for diluting the cohesion and effectiveness of the organization.

Sparta, on the other hand, in 368 was at last in a position thanks to Persian money to try to retrieve what she could in Arkadia, above all to prevent the completion of Megalopolis. She was further fortified by a second force of mercenaries sent by Dionysios, who in June of this year at last accepted an honorific grant of Athenian citizenship now that Athens was allied to his long-standing ally Sparta. With these mercenaries Archidamos, deputizing for his now 75-year-old father Agesilaos, had his revenge for the treachery for Perioikic Karyai in 370. He took the place by storm and killed all prisoners. From Karyai he proceeded westwards to ravage Parrhasia and thence to the south of the plain of Megalopolis. Here he fought a battle against a force of Arkadians, Messenians (Messene had doubtless been allied to Arkadia since its foundation) and Argives. The result was a victory for Archidamos and his mainly mercenary army, Sparta's first significant win on land in the Peloponnese or anywhere else since the Battle of the Long Walls of Corinth in 392. Yet Archidamos failed to prevent the completion of Megalopolis, and it is a fair measure of the Spartans' material impotence and pyschological debility that they should have raised such a hue and cry over the encounter, naming it the 'Tearless Battle' since not a single Spartan had been killed. Even more revealing perhaps were the tears of relief shed by Agesilaos, his fellow Gerontes and the Ephors of the day when they heard the news.

No less lachrymose for Agesilaos was the major diplomatic proceeding of the following year, 367. After his rescue from Thessaly a somewhat chastened Pelopidas was deputed to treat with rather than oppose Artaxerxes, with a view to Boiotia's replacing Sparta as Persia's 'champion' of a renewed Peace in Greece. At Susa in summer 367 the preliminary peace conference proved a triumph for Pelopidas: Artaxerxes was convinced that the Boiotian alliance offered him a better future than the Sparta-Athens axis. Under the terms of the proposed peace Messene was to be autonomous from Sparta, Amphipolis to be autonomous from Athens, who was also to lay up her ships. Elis, too, got what she had been refused by the terms of the second Peace of 371, namely recognition of her claim to control her 'perioikoi' in Triphylia.

It was at once clear that the Boiotians could only secure final adherence to these terms by force or threat of same. For Sparta, at least when led by Agesilaos and Archidamos (in whose mouth Isokrates placed a fictitious but eloquent exposé of this viewpoint), would never accept the autonomy of Messene; Athens was committed to recovering Amphipolis; and the Arkadians under Lykomedes had no intention of relinquishing the Triphylians to Elis nor indeed, more generally, of conceding hegemony to Boiotia. In the circumstances the peace conference at Thebes in winter 367/6 was no less inevitably a failure than that held at Delphi in 368. Epameinondas therefore for a third time took an army across the Isthmus into the Peloponnese in spring 366. It was during the year or so following this invasion that the greatest upheavals thus far occurred within the diplomatic constellations on either side of the Aegean.

Epameinondas won the rest of Achaia (in addition to Pellene) from Sparta for the Boiotian alliance and decided not to tamper with Achaia's internal governmental arrangements. This was wise, as the oligarchic rulers of other states within Sparta's moribund Peloponnesian League were already inclining towards an accommodation with Boiotia to avoid the economic and other costs of constant campaigning. Epameinondas, however, was overruled, and democratic regimes were installed in Achaia with Boiotian military backing. But these new regimes proved remarkably fragile, and the formerly moderate oligarchic exiles both achieved their forcible restoration and espoused the Spartan cause with redoubled vigour. This gain for Sparta, though, was more than cancelled out by the behaviour towards her of her notional ally Athens in 366.

Athens' attention since 368, as we have seen, had been in any case concentrated on the Aegean, specifically on regaining Amphipolis. She was further distracted from the affairs and concerns of Sparta when the Thebans, through the good offices of the Eretrian Themison, recovered the perennially contentious frontier-land of Oropos. So when Lykomedes led an Arkadian delegation to Athens in autumn 366, with a view to concluding an anti-Theban alliance, Athens agreed – even though that meant she was allying with Sparta's most formidable Peloponnesian enemy. Lykomedes died immediately thereafter, and Xenophon typically detected the hand of God in this welcome occurrence for Sparta. But the Athenian-Arkadian alliance also precipitated a development to which Sparta could give no welcome at all. The Boiotians had never abandoned hope of translating the rescript they had received from Artaxerxes in 367 into diplomatic reality. In the winter and spring of 366/5 they came as near to achieving this as they were able. Whether or not a formal Peace was now concluded at Thebes, it is certainly the case that Corinth, the *'enfant terrible* of Spartan foreign politics' (G.B. Grundy), led most of Sparta's remaining Peloponnesian League allies in swearing a peace with the Boiotians. That 'revolt' (as Xenophon and Sparta saw it) marked the end for all practical purposes of the Peloponnesian League as such. An era had passed.

Agesilaos was perhaps not in Greece to witness the demise of an instrument of policy that had served Sparta's geopolitical interests brilliantly and almost uninterruptedly for a century and a half. For Ariobarzanes had at length gone into open revolt against Artaxerxes, perhaps in 367, and made an alliance with Sparta; and it was within the framework of this alliance that Agesilaos was despatched probably in 365 to perform what service he could for Ariobarzanes. Agesilaos' formal title was ambassador rather than military commander, but he somehow relieved the siege of Assos in the Troad by Autophradates, the still loyal satrap of Lydia. For this and other aid he was richly rewarded by Ariobarzanes. At the same time he received subsidies from both Tachôs, perhaps now co-regent of revolted Egypt, and Maussollos, satrap of Caria, who perhaps had it in mind to revolt from Artaxerxes using mercenaries procured for him through the good offices of Agesilaos; that at any rate was how such ritualized friendships (*xeniai*) were expected to operate. Agesilaos had thus achieved the objective of his Anatolian trip: he had raised cash to buy more mercenaries to fight for Sparta's reconquest of Messenia. However pointless that might seem to us in retrospect, it obviously did not seem so to Agesilaos then (or ever).

Perhaps before Agesilaos returned home from Asia another several boatloads of mercenaries arrived from Sicily for Sparta in spring 365. This consignment had been sent by Dionysios II, son and successor of Dionysios I (who had died early in 367 shortly after making alliance with Athens and – the *quid pro quo* no doubt – winning the dramatic prize for tragedy at the Athenian Lenaia festival). With these fresh mercenaries Sparta regained Sellasia, the nearest Perioikic town to Sparta, and perhaps Pellana in the Belminatis to the north-west too. It had been through the Belminatis that the Eleians had invaded Lakonia in 370/69. But in 365, so far from combining with their supposed allies in Arkadia to re-liberate Pellana, the Eleians rejoined the Spartan alliance (not of course any longer the Peloponnesian League). Two related reasons account for a turnabout that was particularly remarkable in that Elis' refusal to swear the second Peace of 371 had started the chain-reaction culminating in the invasion of Lakonia: first, a change of regime from democracy to oligarchy at Elis (perhaps after the oligarchic restoration in Achaia) and, second, the beginnings of a split within the Arkadian federation that became thoroughly visible in 364.

Elis had always resented bitterly the inclusion of Triphylia within the new Arkadian state. But now there were some Arkadians who were less concerned to defend their conception of 'Arkadia' to the last ditch than to root out Theban influence from the Peloponnese. If that meant a *rapprochement* of Arkadia with Sparta to add to the alliance concluded with Athens in autumn 366, then so be it. It is not the least of the paradoxes involved that the Arkadians who thought along these lines were to be found in Mantineia, which had suffered greatly from Sparta when she was still a major power, whereas the ruling democratic element in Tegea remained staunchly pro-Theban.

It was thus at the invitation of an again allied Elis that Archidamos in spring 364 took the field against the dominant, pro-Theban Arkadians. He was particularly glad to accept the invitation as the Arkadians in 365 had liberated two more of Sparta's few remaining Perioikic subjects in Messenia, Koryphasion (Pylos) and Kyparissia (also on the west coast). Archidamos' principal aim, it would appear, was to re-establish Sparta's control of Aigytis, that part of Sparta's former borderland which dominated the passage from south-west Arkadia into Messenia. He took and garrisoned Kromnos, one of the forty communities that had been incorporated in Megalopolis, and then threatened Megalopolis itself. But he was beaten in battle by the Arkadians and their allies, including troops from Boiotia, Argos, and Messene – but not Athens who was not prepared to collaborate actively with the hated Thebans. In this engagement Agesilaos' son-in-law Chilon – whose name conjures up memories of Sparta's days of greatness – was killed. Once Archidamos had retired towards Sparta, the Arkadians besieged the Kromnos garrison; and in his vain attempt to relieve it, Archidamos was wounded and several leading Spartiates killed. More than a hundred Spartiates and Perioikoi from the garrison were captured and (I assume) killed – a loss of citizen manpower that, though absolutely small, Sparta could not afford.

There were Boiotian troops in the Peloponnese in 364, as we have seen. But the preoccupations of the Theban leadership in that year lay elsewhere, improvidently as it was to prove. Pelopidas once again intervened in Thessaly against Alexander of Pherai, only to be killed at Kynoskephalai in July. Epameinondas for the first (and last) time abandoned the land for the sea in an attempt to counter Athens' growing influence in the Aegean and at the Hellespont. For Timotheos, like Agesilaos, had been sent to aid the revolt of Ariobarzanes and in 365 successfully concluded a ten-month siege of Samos, expelling a Persian garrison and establishing a substantial settlement of Athenians on the island. He had next, as successor to Iphikrates, turned his mind to recovering the Thracian Chersonese to some purpose. In his unfamiliar role of admiral Epameinondas promoted the defection from the Second Athenian League of Byzantion, Naxos and Keos and no doubt stimulated discontent elsewhere within the alliance. On the other hand, he achieved little or nothing of lasting value for Boiotia at sea and the cost of this naval expedition seems to have been found a deterrent to further such endeavour. Moreover, while both Pelopidas and Epameinondas were absent from Thebes, less astute Theban politicians seized the opportunity to satisfy what looks to have been a widespread desire for revenge on Orchomenos. That unfortunate city thus suffered the fate of Plataia: annihilation.

None the less, it was in the Peloponnese, not Thessaly or the Aegean, that the fate of Thebes' labile ascendancy was to be decided. The signal for the beginning of its end was given in the late summer of 364, when fighting broke out, not involving Thebes directly, actually in the Altis or sacred precinct at Olympia during a celebration of the quadrennial Games. This had nearly happened in 420 when Elis as president had excluded Sparta from the Games for political reasons. But in 364 the sanctuary was under the control of the anti-Spartan Arkadians and the Eleians' deadly local rivals the men of Pisa. So Elis marched on Olympia, but the Arkadians and Pisatans held her off with Argive and Athenian support and after the interruption completed the normal five-day programme.

In the following spring of 363 tensions within the Arkadian federation between democrats and oligarchs and between Mantineia and Tegea reached breaking-point. The actual occasion of the break was a difference of opinion, partly pragmatic, partly ideological, between the Mantineia-led oligarchs and the Tegea-led democrats over the use (or abuse) for secular, military purposes of sacred moneys held at Olympia. Until 364 the still united Arkadians had managed to maintain a large standing army of 5000 hoplites paid for from federal funds. When these funds dried up, there was a choice, formally speaking, between keeping up a greatly reduced standing force or reverting to the time-honoured hoplite citizen militia of self-supporting soldiers. But since the latter would by definition come from the wealthier section of society, the ideological complexion of the federal army would inevitably alter in a more oligarchic direction. When, therefore, the Mantineian oligarchs accused the Tegea-led democrats of misappropriating sacred moneys, they were indirectly advocating a change of ideological orientation for the Arkadian federation towards traditionally pro-oligarchic Sparta. However much the Tegea-led Arkadians might have preferred to conduct an entirely independent policy, there was only one direction in which they could look to counter this cleverly disguised appeal to most ordinary Arkadians' conservative sense of religious propriety. That direction was towards Thebes. Thus by the summer of 363 Tegea and Megalopolis were still – in a sense yet more firmly – in the Theban camp, while the Mantineia-led oligarchical Arkadians had forged links with Sparta and through Sparta with Elis, Achaia and Athens. The scene was set for the *dénouement* of 362.

The precise details of the incident that precipitated the decisive battle are relatively unimportant. For the record Elis and the (Tegea-led) Arkadians made a truce which the Theban governor of Tegea broke. The Mantineian faction appealed with Elis and the Achaians to Sparta and Athens, the Tegean faction to Boiotia. Epameinondas persuaded the Boiotian alliance that the Theban governor of Tegea must be supported and for the fourth time he invaded the Peloponnese, on this occasion to forestall the snapping of the Messene-Arkadia-Argos diplomatic chain that he had so patiently constructed in order to shackle the Spartans into the south-east Peloponnese. So as to gain time for his Argive and Messenian allies to come to the appointed battleground of Mantineia, Epameinondas launched a lightning raid through Tegea, Karyai and Sellasia on Sparta. Agesilaos, now in his eighty-second year or thereabouts, was already at Pellana when he was informed of Epameinondas' brilliant feint. He was able to get back to defend Sparta with Archidamos, but the shrewd Theban had ensured that his Peloponnesian allies would be with him at Mantineia whereas Sparta could not be there in full force. Thus it was that the Boiotians, Euboians, Thessalians, Lokrians, Malians, Ainianians, Argives, Messenians and Tegea-led Arkadians did battle against Sparta (advance force only), Athens, Achaia, Elis and the Mantineia-led Arkadians in the plain of Mantineia around harvest-time in 362.

Like Leuktra, the result was a clearcut victory for the Boiotian side, but it was decisive in a different sense from its predecessor. Leuktra had decided that Sparta was no longer to be a great power of any kind. (Second) Mantineia decided that Thebes would no longer be the single greatest power in mainland Greece. Epameinondas had died in the battle, and Thebes' material and moral base could not support any further extensive campaigning of the kind she had conducted over the past decade. Moreover, the battle had induced a sort of mental exhaustion in (almost) all the participants, who with one exception swore a Common Peace (perhaps the first to be so called) actually on the battlefield. The basic terms were those that had become almost monotonously familiar since 392/1, but this was the first Peace to be concluded without the intervention of Persia. So too it was the first indisputably concluded Peace not to be sworn to by Sparta (the one exception mentioned above), since Agesilaos would still not permit Sparta's name to be put to a protocol that recognized the autonomy of Messene.

The narrative story of this book is not quite finished. In 361/0, when the revolt against Artaxerxes by his satraps was at its peak under the leadership of Orontes, Sparta responded positively to a request for assistance from Tachôs. Agesilaos was appointed commander and assigned a staff of thirty Spartiates – for all the world as though this were 396 and not 361/0. In spring 360 he sailed for Egypt with a thousand hoplites (probably mercenaries), only to suffer what he took to be the humiliation of being put in command of Tachôs' mercenaries. It was not long therefore before he deserted Tachôs for Nektanebis II and helped him drive Tachôs out of Egypt and into the arms of Artaxerxes. For this and other services Agesilaos was rewarded to the tune of 230 talents – only a fraction of the booty he had brought back to Sparta from Asia in 394 but very much better than nothing at all (which is what was left in Sparta's war-chest).

En route home, however, Agesilaos died aged about eighty-four at a place in Cyrenaica aptly called the Harbour of Menelaos. This was a Homeric echo that he might have approved, though it was to Menelaos' brother that he had had the foolhardiness to compare himself half a lifetime before. The body of the old king was embalmed in wax and transported thus to Sparta to receive – justly or unjustly, it is not for us perhaps to say – the last rites of a hero.

PART FOUR

Conclusions

21

Agesilaos and the Crisis of Sparta

When a war has been lost, a political system overthrown, or an empire shattered and dispersed, there is certain to be a post-mortem inquiry, and the discussion is seldom closed with the decease of the survivors: it may be perpetuated to distant ages, and, as strife is the father of all things, so is dispute and contention the soul of history. (Syme 1950, 3)

In other days I've seen men put their trust
in their own strength and manhood, or in numbers,
and hold their realms, beyond the will of Zeus
                    (Homer, *Iliad* 17.328-30; trans R. Fitzgerald)

In the preceding, narrative section of this book the process whereby the crisis of Sparta was resolved has been summarily traced. The present chapter aims to suggest answers equally briefly to the question why the crisis was and had to be resolved in that way. This question has two main components. Generally speaking, it raises the issue of the historian's peculiar concern with causation (cf. Carr 1964, 87). More specifically, this study has throughout been informed by the much debated problem of the role played by 'great' individuals in determining the course of history – or what is taken to count as 'history'.

Causation or causality is a notoriously snare-infested concept for the philosopher of history or indeed any other would-be explanatory discipline. Aristotle (*Phys.* 194b-195a3) isolated four different kinds of cause, or rather 'tells us that things are called "causes" in four different ways' (Barnes 1982, 52); but his account now seems excessively simplified. It is a fair measure of the topic's currently perceived opacity that one of the most lucid of recent enquiries culminates in cumbersome periphrasis: causation, concluded J.L. Mackie (1974, 296), is 'the way in which [events] follow one another. It involves regularities, universal or statistical ... but it is not exhausted by them; it includes also ... spatio-temporal continuity ..., qualitative or structural continuity, or partial persistence, ... and the features which constitute the direction of causation'. In the circumstances it is perhaps fortunate that practitioners of history, who (unlike their 'hard' scientist colleagues) can at best produce claims about causation that are justified, rather than backed by some covering law, 'do not have to be able to say what an explanation *is* ... but ... what is in practice to count as one' (Runciman 1983, 149 – emphasis original; cf. Hart/Honoré 1959, 9).

Explanations of what, though? Roughly speaking, what happened in history is an amalgam of singular events – not just 'great' events: there can also be a history of the uneventful, as Braudel and others have demonstrated – with more or less complex combinations of events, that is processes. In principle a societal crisis could be either an event or a process, a brief and not necessarily fatal conjuncture or an incurable malaise penetrating to the deepest foundations of the social structure. With the benefit of hindsight, one of the historian's most precious assets, and of the accurate observations of a contemporary like Aristotle (wearing his 'social scientist' hat) we may confidently assert that the Spartan crisis under study here was of the second, terminal variety.[1] In a way, however, that only renders our explanatory task more difficult. Clearly what we are seeking to pin down is the factor or factors that made the difference, the factor(s) but for which the crisis would either not have occurred in the form it in fact took or not have been resolved in the way it in fact was (cf. Runciman 1983, 175 for the general point). But equally it is clear – at least to some historians – that 'the historian must not claim to give the explanation of a complex historical phenomenon' (Badian 1976, 36).

To those who share Badian's rather pessimistic view it may perhaps be conceded that a confident claim to have discovered what is allegedly beyond doubt 'the' explanation of such a phenomenon is in itself suspect. Yet surely it is also the historian's duty to attempt more than 'constantly to discover the conditions making possible what actually happened' (W.H. Dray, quoted by Hunter 1982, 143). Indeed, 'the contrast of cause with mere conditions is an inseparable feature of all causal thinking' (Hart/Honoré 1959, 11, cf. 30); and such thinking is or should be second nature to the historian, who must try to distinguish practically between necessary conditions and sufficient causes. In the case of complex processes like the crisis of Sparta, besides, allowance should also be made for the likelihood of 'overdetermination', that is the operation of two or more distinct sufficient causes (cf. Elster 1983, 184; Powell 1980, 106-10). Our task, in short, is to attempt some sort of ranking or relative weighting of the demonstrably relevant and/or causally sufficient contributory variables – the factors that have been unsystematically exposed in chronological rather than explanatory order in the thematic section of this book.

From causation in general we turn to the role of the individual in particular. Not just any random individual: this chapter is not primarily intended as a contribution to the properly philosophical debate between methodological individualists and methodological holists.[2] My concern is specifically with the type of individuals, usually male, who are variously dubbed 'superior', 'charismatic', 'heroic' or just plain 'great'. The problem of interpretation they pose is this: how far and in what ways do events or processes that are taken to be

---

[1] Only G.L. Cawkwell (1976a, 1983) has, I think, denied that Sparta was undergoing any sort of crisis; but his belief that Sparta should have won the Battle of Leuktra not only makes it unnecessarily hard for him to explain that defeat convincingly but also leaves him at a loss to account for the rapidity and severity of its consequences; cf. S. Hornblower, *CR* n.s. 32 (1982), 236.

[2] For which see now S. James, *The Content of Social Explanation* (Cambridge, 1984).

historically significant owe their existence, configuration or development to the intervention of one named person or rather personality?

Historiographically speaking, this problem arose acutely in the nineteenth century; Gibbon, for instance, was blissfully ignorant of it. It provoked equal and opposite reactions. 'The History of the World', Thomas Carlyle trumpeted in his 1840 lectures *On Heroes, Hero-Worship, and the Heroic in History*, 'was the Biography of Great Men'. To which Karl Marx quietly replied in the preface to *Capital* (1867) that he had taken individuals into account 'only in so far as they are the personifications of economic categories, embodiments of particular class-relations and class-interests'. At the very end of the nineteenth century G.V. Plekhanov, writing within the tradition of Marx rather than Carlyle, attempted to bring a semblance of scholarly order to the ideological confusion, though it has to be said that he was not himself conspicuously free from ideological dogmatism.

Plekhanov examined the problem of 'the individual' as it had been posed by nineteenth-century historians and political commentators. He was exercised in particular by the view of Sainte-Beuve that the course and outcome of the French Revolution had been determined by what he (Plekhanov) saw as minor and elusive phenomena, whether accidental or belonging to a different order of causality from the Revolution itself: namely, the timing of the deaths of certain peculiarly prominent individuals – Mirabeau, Robespierre, Bonaparte. To this view Plekhanov objected that these individual causes, or accidents, should be distinguished from particular causes, that is the historical situation as a whole, and that the latter situation was of primary explanatory significance. For it was, he held, the form of social organization that in any given period determines the role and consequently the social significance that may fall to the lot of an individual, no matter how competent or talented. The quality of such an individual, he argued, only becomes causally relevant to social change when, where and to the extent that social relations, specifically social relations of production, permit. The final causes of social relationships, in other words, lay in the state of development of the productive forces; and influential individuals, although they might alter individual features of events and some of their particular consequences, could not change their general trend, which was determined by factors beyond their individual control. 'Great' men indeed, were great only because they were best equipped to secure the great social needs of their times.

Plekhanov's was a rather dogmatic, conceptually naive and logically leaky account. In the twentieth century, though, it is not so much these intrinsic intellectual flaws as the march of real-world human history that may be thought to make reading of Plekhanov's pioneering pamphlet supererogatory. This, it is argued, has been an era of movers and shakers, men like Lenin, Stalin, Hitler, Mussolini or Mao who in some important sense have 'made' history, that is altered its course rather than (as Marx and Plekhanov would have it) merely accelerated or retarded its progress or regress. The suggestion is initially plausible, but is it ultimately convincing? Or is it rather the case that even these looming personalities merely presided over or constituted the most prominent and tangible embodiments of the events and processes indelibly associated with their names? The case of Lenin may perhaps serve as a test of rival hypotheses, not least because it is uniquely well documented.

Leon Trotsky's participant history of the Bolshevik Revolution must be given some precedence (esp. Trotsky 1967, I.310-11; cf. I.101-8, II.11, III.327). Trotsky was not obliged by his remit to conduct the same sort of abstracted analysis of our problem as Plekhanov, but he was bound to try to explain why the Revolution had occurred when, where and how it did. Partly because Trotsky had himself played a role as leader second only to that of Lenin, he sought to integrate the significance of the personal within the broader revolutionary process. He did not deny, he said, the significance of the personal in the mechanics of the historical process, or the significance of the accidental in the personal. What he did reject was the tendency of psychologizing historians and biographers to see something purely personal or accidental in what he took to be really the refraction of great historical forces through an individual personality. Leaders of great movements did not emerge through an accident of personality; they were generally chosen out and trained up over the course of decades. Lenin (for example) was 'a product of the whole past of Russian history' and, in this sense, could be said merely to have entered into a chain of objective forces. However, Trotsky did also have an enormous admiration for Lenin as statesman or politician, the kind of admiration that Thucydides had evinced for Themistokles (1.138.3) and Perikles (2.65.5-13). And Trotsky was prepared to concede that Lenin was a 'great' link in that chain. Indeed, by orienting and uniting the Bolshevik Party Lenin had enabled it to seize the revolutionary opportunity which might otherwise have been let slip for many years.

Trotsky thus applied concretely Plekhanov's slight refinement of Marx's view of the role of 'great' individuals. Neither Russian writer, however, convinced Sidney Hook, a self-confessed heretical Marxist in his salad days of the early 1930s but by the early 1940s a non- or even anti-Marxist reacting against the various totalitarian regimes of the day (Hook 1945). Hook subtitled his relatively brief but wide-ranging examination 'A study in limitation and possibility', but it was the latter that he was particularly concerned to stress against Plekhanov and Trotsky. For he argued that, where possible alternatives of development existed in a historic situation, an 'event-making hero' might so exploit his outstanding capacities of intelligence, will and character (rather than any mere accidents of circumstance) as to influence subsequent developments along a quite different course from the one that would have been followed had he not so intervened. Hook's 'hero', that is, might not only retard or speed up such development but actually redirect the course of history. Concerning the October Revolution it was (and is) Hook's opinion that there is no good reason to believe it would have taken place in the absence of Lenin. Indeed, Hook claims that even Trotsky came to agree with this non-Marxist conclusion. If so, that would be surprising. For it is hard to see why Trotsky should have been prepared to agree either that the event-making hero could be as fully independent of the conditions determining the historic alternatives as Hook's individualist thesis explicitly requires or that he could remain a free agent in any useful sense whatsoever, let alone in the strong sense assumed by Hook.

However that may be, this debate has recently been usefully summarized by

Miliband (1983, 131-53), even if his own positive contribution has naturally not put an end to it. The subject of the debate Miliband rightly considers to be crucial for any theory of history and politics, but especially for Marxism; and against what he takes to be the doctrine of Classical Marxism (Marx, Engels, Plekhanov, Trotksy) he argues three theses: first, that circumstances do not necessarily produce the required heroic individual – there is nothing inevitable or automatic about the emergence of so-called 'great men' at any particular conjuncture; secondly, that the identity of the individual who rises to or capitalizes upon a certain combination of circumstances *can* make a significant difference – France, for instance, might well have experienced a military dictatorship in the wake of the Revolution, but another dictator would have ruled with significantly different effects from Napoleon; and, thirdly, that the intervention of the required kind of 'great man' does not simply accelerate or delay the general course of development – Lenin, for example, did actually change the course of world history. Miliband does not mean thereby to claim that Lenin's persona was not itself a product of an endlessly complex combination of factors or that his intervention would have been possible or effectual regardless of the opportunity afforded him by a unique conjuncture of conditions and circumstances. What he does claim is that in the short run, in 'generational' as opposed to 'transgenerational' perspective, the actions of Lenin did make the difference. Suppose counterfactually that Lenin had not reached the Finland Station, then the Revolution would not have occurred in October 1917 and might not have taken place at all or had the world-shattering effects it did.

There are numerous imponderables here, or at least factors the causal weight of which cannot be precisely quantified. But the foregoing discussion should at any rate have raised serious doubts over the capacity of any individual, however 'great' or 'heroic', to 'make' history. No one, I trust, would argue that Agesilaos was Sparta's Lenin; if anything, he would have to be Sparta's Czar Nicholas. But in so far as any one individual presided over or guided Sparta's destiny in the first four decades of the fourth century, that individual was Agesilaos. In antiquity he was described, admittedly with some little exaggeration, as 'the greatest and most illustrious man of his time' (Theopompos, *FGrHist.* 115F321) and was alleged, no doubt falsely in fact, to have been fined by the Ephors 'for appropriating to himself citizens who were the property of the state' (Plut. *Ages.* 5.4). More recently and with greater justice he has been said to have 'united the kingship with the position of a party boss' (Niese 1894, 803) and to have been in the 380s 'nearly as much King of Greece as Philip was after 338' (Davies 1978, 253). It was therefore obligatory to raise explicitly the general problem of the role of the 'great' individual as a potential causal agency, something that has never to my knowledge been done in connection with Agesilaos and only very rarely (esp. Beloch 1924, 1-16) for ancient Greek history as a whole.

To recapitulate: Sparta in 400 at the accession of Agesilaos to one of the two Spartan thrones enjoyed *archê* (imperial rule) over wide swathes of the Greek world east of the Adriatic. Forty years later, at the death of Agesilaos, Sparta had been forcibly deprived of half her former nuclear territory and was without a seat among the Greek powers that were. Why? What was the factor (or factors)

but for the operation of which Sparta might have retained for longer or extended
further her *archê* or at least not suffered quite so comprehensive and traumatic a
reversal of her fortunes?

   Causation, as we have seen, is an enormously complex and multi-faceted
notion. For the historian of the Spartan crisis the task of explanation is
aggravated by the incompleteness as well as the biasses of the evidence. Easy,
unicausal explanations must therefore be treated with the utmost reserve. Yet
unfortunately that is precisely the only type offered by most of our ancient
sources, including the fullest, Xenophon, with whom we must begin. Xenophon
recognises what is at most a necessary condition of the fall of Sparta's empire
when he draws attention – via his Theban speakers at Athens in 395 (3.5.12-15)
and Autokles at Sparta in 371 (6.3.7-9) – to Sparta's combination of imperialistic
arrogance, greed, and fondness for intervening in the internal political affairs of
her subjects, with her small number of citizens and lack of clearcut military
superiority by land or sea. But on the larger question of why Sparta ceased to be
a great power or indeed any kind of power Xenophon prefers theological to
historical explanation (cf. Chapter 5).

   'It seems, too,' Jason of Pherai is reported as saying ironically to the Thebans
with reference to Sparta's Leuktra defeat (6.4.23), 'that Heaven [literally 'the
(male) god'] delights in making the small great and the great small'. The pious
language could be dismissed as a *façon de parler*, and the sentiment as
conventional Greek pessimism (cf. e.g. Hdt. 1.5.3;7.10e; Thuc. 2.64.3; Plat. *Rep.*
546a; Polyb. 6.57.1), were it not for Xenophon's own explicit personal
explanation of that defeat as divine retribution for Sparta's perjurious occupation
of the Theban akropolis in peacetime (5.4.1). This for Xenophon was but one of
the many instances that could be adduced from both Greek and non-Greek
history to illustrate the iron rule that the gods are not careless of those who are
impious or commit unholy deeds. The inherent weakness of all such theological
explanation needs no underlining: 'if gods intervene enough in human history,
anything can happen, and it ceases to be possible to judge one hypothesis more
probable than another' (Dover 1973, 43).

   His point about divine intervention is repeated in a different way and with a
significantly wider application in the condemnatory fourteenth chapter of the
Lak. Pol., which was written when Sparta was no longer an imperial power and
many Greeks were 'calling upon each other to prevent [the Spartans] from
achieving *archê* again' (*LP* 14.6). In bitter conclusion Xenophon observes that
the Spartans manifestly no longer 'obey either the commands of Heaven [again,
'the god'] or the laws of Lykourgos'. Regarding the secular laws Xenophon
refers explicitly only to breaches arising directly or indirectly from the exercise
of empire: the Spartans' desire to live, and more especially act as governors,
abroad; and their possession, indeed pride in the possession, of gold. This does
tie in to some extent with the attacks on Spartan imperialism made in the
speeches in the *Hellenika* (above), but in the *Lak. Pol.* Spartan imperialism is seen
as an effect, not a cause, an effect of the same disobedience to divine precept that
was given explanatory precedence at *Hell.* 5.4.1. For it was this impiety
(Xenophon thought) that accounted for the critical decay in Spartan morality,
which in turn explained both the Spartans' loss of *archê* and their immoral desire

to regain it at any cost rather than be worthy of it. Xenophon's trivializing treatment of the small number of Spartan citizens in the *Lak. Pol.* (1.1) corroborates this interpretative emphasis. He does single it out, but for praise rather than blame and not in any explanatory way.

Plutarch, our next fullest source, does if anything rather better than Xenophon. Not that he anywhere attempted systematically to explain the genesis and outcome of the Spartan crisis – that hardly fell within his biographical brief. But for all his moralizing he does point the way to a more sophisticated explanatory hypothesis than Xenophon's theological determinism. Like Xenophon Plutarch can sweepingly ascribe Sparta's downfall to the abandonment of 'Lykourgan' precepts (*Comp. Lyc. et Num.* 4.14) and more particularly to the foreign cash that flowed into Sparta after 404 and engendered excessive greed (*Lyk.* 30.1, *Mor.* 239ef). But unlike Xenophon he goes significantly further, and fruitfully so, in his *Life* of Agis IV (*Agis* 5.1-2) by linking this greed for cash with the concentration of landed wealth and consequent diminution in citizen numbers after the Athenian War. The alleged *rhêtra* of the Ephor Epitadeus that he cites in this context is either a forgery or not causally crucial (see Chapter 10), but the emphasis on the causative relevance of *oliganthrôpia*, shortage of citizen manpower, is one he shares with Aristotle (below). In a related vein a fascinating apopththegm is attributed to Lykourgos by Plutarch (*Lyk.* 19.11 = *Mor.* 228e), though without discussion of its relevance to the Spartan crisis: when asked how the Spartans might prevent or ward off an enemy invasion, Lykourgos replied (in Doric) that they would do so by remaining poor and not lusting to be more important or powerful (*mesdôn* = *meizôn*) than each other.

Besides his broadly economic explanation Plutarch proposes a second chain of explanation both in the main body of the *Agesilaos* (30.1,33.4; cf. 31.6) and in the appended comparison (*sunkrisis*) between the careers of Agesilaos and Pompey (*Comp. Ages. et Pomp.* 1.2, 2.1-2, 3.2). The truncated syllogism goes like this. Agesilaos gained his throne by methods abhorrent to both gods and men – that is, through Lysander's speciously metaphorical interpretation of the divinely inspired oracle warning the Spartans against a lame kingship. He should never have become king, and Sparta's fall was ultimately due to divine retribution. The agency of the fall was Agesilaos' imperialist policy aimed at first enslaving Thebes and then depopulating the refounded Messene. Agesilaos thereby literally 'threw away' the hegemony of Greece. Many steps in the argument are elided here; but, as we shall see, Plutarch has found modern support at least for the secular aspect of the postulated causal nexus.

From Plutarch in the second century AD we may retrace our steps to the fourth century BC. Three other contemporaries apart from Xenophon offer reflections bearing on the causes of the Spartan crisis. Those of the Athenian pamphleteer Isokrates need not long detain us. The *Archidamos*, as one might expect of a speech placed in the mouth of Agesilaos' son and heir-apparent for delivery before the Spartan Assembly in a context of 366/5, is a litany of exculpation (e.g. 6.9,47,59) and a plea for unremitting effort to regain Messenia, rather than a reasoned explanation of why Sparta had lost it in the first place. In so far as the speech does contribute to an explanation of the Spartan crisis, it does so unwittingly – chiefly through the characterization of the socio-political situation in the Peloponnese since 371 (6.64-9). This passage is no doubt redolent of Isokratean nostalgia and puffed up with Isokratean rhetoric, but by reading between the lines one may spot the essential breakdown in patron-client relations within the *poleis* of the Peloponnesian League that helps explain why even before Leuktra the League had become such a fragile instrument of Spartan domination (cf. Chapter 13). Intimately connected with this, although 'Archidamos' does not make the connection, is the admission *en passant* that during their supremacy the Spartans had engaged in more wars than had been strictly necessary, when it had been possible for them to enjoy a peaceable well-being (6.51).

Isokrates thought highly enough of the real Archidamos to ask him by open letter (*Ep.* 9) in the mid-350s if he would effect his (Isokrates') cherished project of a 'panhellenist' expedition to Asia in order to carve out *Lebensraum* for the hordes of wandering mercenaries and other displaced persons who haunted Isokrates' Biedemeier imagination. But the Spartan state in general, or rather its foreign policy in particular, he criticized freely from the *Panegyric Oration* of 380 to his death in 338 (Ollier 1933, esp. 181; Cloché 1933, 129-39). Once or twice his criticism teetered on the brink of explanation rather than the usual moral condemnation. *Archê* (empire) was for Sparta the *archê* (beginning, origin) of her misfortunes, he remarked in the *Peace* of the mid-350s (8.101) – a pun, of course, but perhaps masking a serious explanatory implication. A decade or so later in the *Philippos* of 346 (5.103) he employed another literary figure, personification, to give what may possibly be dignified as a psychological explanation of Sparta's fall. Power, he remarks, was a *hetaira* (up-market female prostitute) to Sparta, charming but ruinous.

However, these variations on the conceit that imperial power corrupts do not take us far along the road to an explanation of the Spartan crisis. Far more helpful, paradoxically, is the eighth Book of the *Republic*, where Plato presents his famous five-stage paradigm of constitutional and social change or rather degeneration. No doubt this is primarily an artificial construct, but as always with Plato it is heavily larded with his own distinctive perception of contemporary political realities. The first stage of degeneration from the ideally Just State ruled by Platonic philosopher-kings is characterized as timarchy (*timarchia*) or timocracy (*timokratia*), rule in accordance with status, rank or honour (*Rep.* 545c-551a). This is a polity shot through with competitiveness and ambition; and since these are the two qualities said to typify the Spartan form of society (*Rep.* 545a), it is legitimate to infer that Plato's timarchic state is a sort of contemporary Sparta writ large, with her salient characteristics magnified for expository clarity.

Thus Plato's timarchy is a state geared for war rather than peace; in fact, warfare against not only foreign enemies but also its internal subject population of serfs and menials is this state's constant preoccupation. Education, respect for authority, abstention by the warrior-class from non-military productive activities, common messes, physical and military training – all are designed to serve the identical, martial end. The results, however, are deleterious in two ways: an overvaluation of physical to the detriment of intellectual training; and a passionate though necessarily secret desire for wealth in gold and silver. The latter is guarded in strongrooms in private houses, for, in sharp contrast to the prohibition of private property to the rulers of Plato's own ideally Just State, the rulers of the timarchic polity have allowed to themselves the private ownership of land and houses. Indeed, it is this – or rather more specifically the concentration of private wealth in a few hands – that causes the destruction from within of the timarchic state. For rank or status becomes equated with possession of wealth, and the shreds of a concern for true goodness that were still apparent in the character of *homo timarchicus* are now completely overlaid by an all-consuming desire for profit and by the distribution of political power and social status on a strictly economic basis.

This brilliant passage should not of course be taken literally as a serious piece of historical explanation; it was in any case written some years before the Battle of Leuktra. Its significance lies rather in its suggestiveness. For it was this broadly sociological as opposed to narrowly moralistic approach that was to be developed most fully by Plato's ablest pupil, Aristotle. Aristotle and his own pupils at the Lyceum between them made two major contributions to a better understanding of the Spartan polity: in the Aristotelian *Lak. Pol.*, which survives only in truncated quotations and other later references, and Aristotle's *Politics*, the greatest ancient work of political theory and historical sociology.

The Aristotelian *Lak. Pol.*, like the surviving *Ath. Pol.*, appears to have combined exposition of present political and social realities with a largely antiquarian account of Sparta's earlier history. By far the most interesting product of the Lyceum's antiquarian research on Sparta is the so-called 'Great Rhetra' preserved by Plutarch (*Lyk.* 6), who undoubtedly found it in the *Lak. Pol.* (Murray 1980, 160; cf. Chapter 8). But also of interest, and of more direct relevance in this context, is another oracle the researchers discovered in the Spartan archives: 'Love of acquiring material possessions (*philochrêmatia*) and nothing else will destroy Sparta' (Arist. fr. 544 Rose). As cited by much later writers, the *Lak. Pol.* does not attribute this oracle to a particular oracular centre such as Delphi; and it is noteworthy that Plutarch (*Mor.* 239f) does not either. But Plutarch did claim to know that the oracle was delivered to Kings Theopompos and Alkamenes jointly, that is in the joint reign immediately preceding the one in which the 'Great Rhetra' was allegedly delivered to Sparta by Delphi; and Diodoros (7.12.5) and others (cited in Fontenrose 1978, 272, Q10) were sure that it too was Delphic. Delphic or not, genuine or *post eventum*, the oracle has a far more obvious relevance to the Spartan crisis of the fourth century than to its putative original context (presumably the land-grabbing operation in Messenia in the late eighth century, for which see Cartledge 1979, ch. 8). Aristotle, however, is the only known theorist of the fourth century to have been able to give *philochrêmatia* a plausible setting within an overall appraisal of Sparta's internal arrangements and foreign relations.

His severe appraisal is delivered in two passages of the *Politics* (1269a29-1271b19; 1333b5-1334a10). The second and shorter passage is the more purely Platonic of the two, an extended meditation (developing 1271a41-1271b11) on the theme that it is wrong for a constitution to be ordered by its legislator (*ex hypothesi* Lykourgos in this instance) exclusively with a view to war and conquest. But whereas Plato was bound to confine his criticisms to the realm of abstract theory, Aristotle was able to state outright that this view of the Spartan legislator not only was easy to refute theoretically but had also been refuted by the facts: theoretically – because military training should not be regularly practised solely for the purpose of unlimited imperial aggrandisement without regard to the benefit of those ruled; by the facts – because the lawgiver had failed to educate the Spartans to use properly the leisure they had attained by winning their empire. Aristotle does not spell out here precisely what he thinks the failure consists in, or how precisely it brought about Sparta's downfall. Craving for material wealth is mentioned as the usual motive for imperialism, but it is given no other explanatory force. Instead, Aristotle contents himself with drawing an analogy between the deterioration of military states in peacetime and the way iron loses its temper when not put to use and cites the case of Pausanias (despite Aristotle, this must be the Regent not the King) to illustrate the danger in instilling excessive ambition to rule others in the citizens. For the full explanatory works the reader must therefore turn back to the earlier passage.

Here in the second Book Aristotle mounts a general onslaught on the *hupothesis* or basic presupposition of the Spartan lawgiver; in detail he singles out the seven most blameworthy features of the hypertrophied Spartan polity. First comes the Helot system. This is criticized both for being intrinsically a weak spot for neighbouring enemies to exploit and for being badly managed by the Spartans. But Aristotle does not credit this feature with any special responsibility for Sparta's demise. That he attributed rather to the second major blameworthy feature of the Spartan polity, the position of women and more particularly rich, married women. Aristotle's lengthy critique is subdivided into seven individual charges. The women are allowed too much licence or (the Greek is ambiguous) are too licentious. Wealth therefore is too highly valued. The damage this causes to all constitutions is aggravated in Sparta's case by the fact that the women dominate the men: at the time of the Spartan *archê* women managed many things. Thus the women adversely affected even the martial spirit of the state, for example during the Theban invasion of Lakonia in 370/69. Women, too, made a significant contribution to the uneven distribution of landed property in Sparta: almost two fifths of the country is under their control. This concentration of land in a few hands has caused the adult male citizen body to sink below one thousand – fatally, since as a result Sparta was unable to withstand the single defeat at Leuktra and 'was destroyed through shortage of citizen military manpower' (*oliganthrôpia*). But rather than keep property more evenly distributed in order to maintain the citizen body at a higher numerical level, the Spartans resorted to official devices to encourage the procreation of males that merely aggravated the problems.

Not all these criticisms are either entirely accurate or apposite (cf. in more detail Cartledge 1981b, esp. 85-9). But there is no doubt but that Sparta did suffer acute *oliganthrôpia* during the crisis and that it was a causally relevant factor. The question rather is how the significance of *oliganthrôpia* is to be understood and whether it can bear the interpretative burden placed upon it by Aristotle. Before trying to answer that, let us consider finally the only surviving explanation of the genesis and outcome of the Spartan crisis that was penned by a man whom we may describe with few qualms as a historian, indeed a historian of more than average competence.

Polybios was an aristocratic leader from Arkadian Megalopolis who found himself removed to Italy as a Roman hostage in 167 BC and ended by siding with the conquerors of Greece. In the sixth Book of his History he tried to explain why it was that Rome had succeeded where none of her predecessors had in achieving domination of 'almost the whole world'. The answer, he contended in thoroughly Greek fashion, lay in Rome's *politeia*, not just in her formal political constitution but in her sociopolitical institutions generally, her mores as well as her laws. To make that contention stick, Polybios contrasted the success of the Roman Republic with the ultimate failure of other ancient states, especially the two which (he thought) like Rome had a 'mixed' political constitution: viz. Carthage (6.51-2) and Sparta (6.48-50).

To explain why Sparta had so quickly declined from a position of imperial power to one where she was in danger of losing her own liberty, Polybios invoked a sharp distinction between Sparta's domestic and foreign affairs. At home, thanks to the dispositions of Lykourgos regarding land-tenure, common messes and education, the Spartans were courageous and self-disciplined and lived in harmony. But abroad Lykourgos made them in the highest degree ambitious, imperialistic and covetous towards the rest of the Greeks. This was fine so long as they restricted their hegemonial attentions to the Peloponnese. However, once they embarked upon the acquisition of an overseas *archê* after the Athenian War their Lykourgan domestic arrangements (iron money, lack of a convertible currency, insufficient surplus of natural produce to exchange for the necessary imports) forced them into dependence on Persia and constrained them to impose tribute on their Greek subjects to raise cash. In short, the Lykourgan system and imperial hegemony over Greece were mutually incompatible; one or other had to go, in practice the empire.

Many of these suggested explanations have been variously endorsed or modified by modern students of Sparta. Space permits only a short selection of these before I conclude with my own hypothesis. David (1981, 59) finds the sources that associate Sparta's downfall with the influx of imperial wealth to be an 'impressive chorus'; more modestly, and more convincingly, de Romilly (1977, 59) speaks of the new wealth as 'one of the causes which ruined Sparta'. More generally, Spartan imperialism has been seen as a, or the, decisive causal agent by several historians. For example, Hahn (1969, esp. 285, 296) agreed with Polybios that Sparta's new postwar conception of power politics was shattered on the rock of Spartan economic traditionalism. But whereas Polybios appears to have thought that Lykourgan dispensations were still honoured at home, Parke (1930, 77) expressed the more Xenophontic view that: 'The Spartan passion for imperialism inevitably clashed with the Lycurgean system and brought about its collapse.'

There is, in fact, a tension in both ancient and modern thinking between the belief that Sparta collapsed because she observed 'Lykourgan' precepts all too faithfully and the contrary belief that the collapse was due to her abandonment of them. Murray (1980, 158), for example, has suggested that Spartan society was ultimately destroyed by 'exclusiveness and ability to engender subordinate statuses'. So far as the failure to maintain the empire is concerned, the Emperor Claudius, Francis Bacon and Max Weber (1978, 1364) might have agreed with him; and in similar vein Bommelaer (1981, 231-2) has argued that Lysander ought to have used the new imperial wealth to create new full citizens. On the other hand, Greenidge (1911, 89, 114-15) was of the opinion that different factors accounted for respectively the collapse of the empire and that of Spartan society generally. For the former he held chiefly responsible Sparta's penchant for narrow oligarchy as a method of imperial rule; but on the downfall of Spartan society he took an essentially Aristotelian position, agreeing that the Spartan state perished almost literally through a lack of citizens (brought about by a concentration of wealth which itself had been fostered by a new commercial spirit). In the same connection Jeanmaire (1939, 468-9) drew attention to the 'family politics' of certain prominent individuals especially after the Athenian War.

Others have privileged the military factor, though in very different ways. Macaulay (1860, 137n), for example, pointed the finger at military innovation: Sparta had been overtaken by the professionalization of warfare – a point of view spelled out by Cawkwell (1983; but see above). Far more sophisticated is the approach of Finley (1981a, 40). The origins of Sparta's 'tragedy' he traces to the fact that Sparta was drawn by the Athenian War into extensive and genuinely military activity which placed uncontrollable and unbearable strains on traditional social, economic and cultural structures – on Spartiate manpower, on relations between Spartiates and the subordinate statuses of Spartan society, on Spartan xenophobia and contempt for private luxury: 'the system could not and did not long survive.' More recently, Hodkinson (1983) has argued that even before the Athenian War the system was in any case full of conflicts and contradictions, psychological and ideological as well as material, and that what the War did was promote the breakdown of the internal compromise between rich and poor Spartans that had resolved the social crisis of the seventh century. Which reminds one somewhat of Wade-Gery's lapidary judgment (1925, 567): 'The unstable equilibrium at home ... made Sparta unequal to the responsibility of leading Greece. The Helot system or the empire must eventually be abandoned: at Leuktra she lost both.'

Mention of Leuktra and Sparta's subsequent loss of the Messenian Helots brings us back to Agesilaos, conspicuous only by his absence from the modern judgments (and all but Plutarch's among the ancient) cited so far. Estimates of his general historical significance (a separate matter from his moral worth) have fluctuated far more wildly in modern times than in antiquity. For Hertzberg (1856, 1) he was 'one of the most important warriors and statesmen of Greece', whereas Ehrenberg (1965, 36) considered him 'little more than a bold and gifted soldier'. Bury (in Bury/Meiggs 1975, 384) conceded that Agesilaos had 'conducted [Sparta's] policy during a great part of thirty years of supremacy' but saw him in the end as a tragic rather than a great figure. The fame of Agesilaos was of course eclipsed in his own day (despite Theopompos F321) by that of Epameinondas, but his influence on foreign policy remained paramount in Sparta even after 371 despite continuing internal opposition (cf. Smith 1953/4 for the period 394 to 371). Did he employ that influence wisely? The consensus of modern opinion is that he did not. From Hertzberg (1856, 127, 311n.102) to Hamilton (1982a) most scholars have been clear that his policy of reviving and extending Sparta's hegemony after 386, and above all attempting to destroy Thebes, was a disaster. Hamilton, indeed, holds that his anti-Theban policy 'was largely responsible for the failure of Sparta's hegemony in Greece'. To that sin of commission Zierke (1936, 54-9) would add one of omission: Agesilaos' failure to seize the opportunity provided by the Peace of Antalkidas to initiate necessary social reform in Sparta.

In response to such attacks Cawkwell, as we have seen, has sought to undermine the basis of these strictures and exonerate Agesilaos from all personal responsibility for Sparta's post-Leuktra collapse. But even if we were to grant for the sake of argument that Sparta should have won Leuktra, we would still have to ask why Sparta, having in fact comprehensively lost that battle, did not merely cease to be the single most powerful state in Greece but also within just half a dozen years was deprived of half her territory (including the more important portion of her economic base), and the last remnants of her Peloponnesian League alliance. It is not enough, in other words, to explain or explain away only Sparta's loss of the dominion and empire abroad that she acquired in and after 404. Any satisfactory explanation of the origins, evolution and resolution of the Spartan crisis must also explain why the chance of a battle had these further deleterious consequences.

My own explanation of the Spartan crisis, finally, would run like this, all necessary allowances being made for the state of the evidence, for the inevitable relativity and partiality of any historical judgment, and for the impossibility of reproducing the past for the purpose of inspecting it microscopically under laboratory conditions. Already well before the Athenian War broke out Spartan society had shown signs of extreme strain. The first major Spartan crisis since the seventh century fell roughly in the period 490 to 460. The deaths at Sparta in shady circumstances of a king and a regent and the exile of another king were the outward and visible marks of a deep-seated power-struggle within the Spartan political hierarchy involving major questions of foreign and domestic policy. In the bowels of Spartan society subversive rumblings exploded in a major Helot revolt in the later 460s following a devastating earthquake that may have caused serious loss of Spartan life. Disaffection within the Peloponnesian League culminated in the revolt of Megara about 460.

By 432 an unstable equilibrium had been restored. A new generation of largely untried Spartan warriors had grown up and was eager for the fray. Elite members of the Perioikoi had been brigaded with Spartiates as part of Sparta's regular hoplite establishment to compensate for falling citizen numbers. The Helots were superficially quiescent, kept down by a mixture of terror, indoctrination and incentive bonuses. The strength of the Peloponnesian League, though, was being sapped by the growing power of Athens, and the major allies were overwhelmingly in favour of following Sparta if she would lead them to war. The Spartan political hierarchy – Gerousia, Ephors, other office-holders, and in general those outstanding for birth or wealth – were more or less unanimous in advocating war. Only the old and experienced Eurypontid king, Archidamos II (father of Agis II and Agesilaos), is said to have counselled caution.

If so, he was prudent. The Athenian War (431-404, with interruptions) cruelly exposed Spartan deficiencies in many areas: manpower shortage, inability to respond swiftly or fully enough to changes in strategy and tactics by land and sea, rudimentary 'system' of public finances, incompatibility between a Spartan upbringing and the requirements of a prolonged foreign command, internecine behind-the-scenes struggles for power and influence at Sparta, failure to retain the loyalty of some of her prominent Peloponnesian League allies, and, not least, the constant threat posed by the enemy within, the Helots, lying in wait for and (as in 425) seizing upon their collective master's misfortune. In the end it was not so much that Sparta had won the war as that Athens lost it; and if Sparta eventually emerged victorious, that was due above all to Persian money and the use made of it by Lysander, whose position of power outside Sparta far outdistanced that attained by Regent Pausanias and was utterly incompatible with traditional Spartan notions of collective civic responsibility.

Lysander, however, could not have achieved this position simply by an act of will. Most Spartans now favoured the kind of imperialism he advocated: the rich and influential because they welcomed the chance to throw their weight around in the Aegean area as a whole and gain access to the coinage of gold and silver that a 'Lykourgan' ordinance banned from Sparta; the poor because with imperial booty they might better their economic lot at home and so perhaps (in the case of the poorest) prevent or delay the slide from Spartiate down to 'Inferior' status due to inability to pay mess-dues. But Sparta's social, economic, political, even military structures were not suited to the kind of imperial domination Lysander envisaged. Moreover, Sparta incurred great unpopularity within her old Peloponnesian League alliance as a result of her selfish refusal to share the profits of imperialism and Lysander's excessive fondness for installing puppet regimes of his friends and clients throughout the new empire. The cult of Lysander's personality exacerbated internal and external tensions.

Sensing their opportunity, Lysander's Spartan enemies led by King Pausanias began to pursue a more subtle policy of limited involvement in the Aegean and Asia Minor coupled with a balance-of-power approach to inter-state relations in the Peloponnese and central Greece in the hope that internal pressures on traditional mores and institutions might thereby be eased. But only for a very short time did they gain a respite. Sparta may have been as a rule slow to go to war, and moderate in the enjoyment of success, before the Athenian War. Thereafter she proved the reverse. In Agesilaos Lysander found at first an eager pupil and willing accomplice in his imperial designs. Later to his cost he discovered an exponent of patronal politics even more skilful than he, one who knew how to exploit the inbuilt advantages of the kingship in pursuit of an imperialist ideal not so very different in scope or methods from that of his mentor while at the same time proclaiming himself to be the humble and devoted servant of the Spartan authorities and the eternal laws of the all-wise Lykourgos.

For thirty years almost without sensible interruption Agesilaos presided over the most powerful single state in Old Greece. Despite outward appearances, however, the basis of Spartan power was being steadily eroded throughout this period, and the high level of political skill undoubtedly required to maintain Sparta's ever more precarious hegemony increasingly became that of the confidence trickster. Between 371 and 365 Sparta's bluff was irretrievably called. What had merely been hints of weakness were now exposed as unsealable cracks in the foundations of the edifice of power. The threats of revolt by Helots, Perioikoi and Inferior Spartans against the Spartiate ruling class, threats that had briefly surfaced in the abortive conspiracy of Kinadon in 399, were now realized in 370/69. Persia, unable to preserve and unwilling to restore Sparta's hegemony of Greece, quickly abandoned her former champion for Thebes in 367. Agesilaos was probably the best Spartan general of his time, but not even he could have won Leuktra. Not simply because his strategy and tactics would not have matched those of Epameinondas, but because he, no less than Kleombrotos, would have lacked the requisite mental and physical material to do the job. For in respect both of the numbers of first-rate hoplites and of the morale of their allies the Spartans were crucially inferior to the numerically inferior Theban side. The loss of allied morale is quite simply accounted for. For too long the Peloponnesians had been treated as subjects instead of partners, as pawns in a game from which only a small handful of Agesilaos' oligarchic friends and clients stood directly and unambiguously to gain. Even Xenophon felt obliged to reveal that some allies were actually not displeased by the result of Leuktra.

One of their principal complaints against Sparta, it would appear, was that the Spartans though few were dictating to their allies who were many. The question of numbers brings us, I believe, to the nub of any explanation of the Spartan crisis. Aristotle, it will be recalled, stated flatly that it was through *oliganthrôpia*, a shortage of citizen military manpower, that Sparta was destroyed. He did not say that it was simply the small number of Spartiate hoplites (in fact 700) at Leuktra that caused the Spartant defeat, for the obvious reason that the Spartiates had long constituted but a small proportion of any major Spartan army. What he in fact said was that because of *oliganthrôpia* Sparta was unable to withstand or bear up under a single blow – that is, could not recover from the effects of the Leuktra defeat. *Oliganthrôpia* thus had a much wider than purely operational, military significance in Aristotle's explanatory scheme. In this respect I am sure that Aristotle was thinking along the right lines. For *oliganthrôpia* was ultimately a function of the Spartan class struggle, and it is there that I would locate 'the' cause of Sparta's collapse.

Briefly, there had always been rich and poor Spartans, as there had always been rich and poor in the Greek world generally. But rich Spartans could not exploit poor Spartans either individually or collectively in the same ways or to the same degree that rich Greeks could and did exploit their poor compatriots in other states. This was for the simple reason that the Spartans collectively lived off the backs of the Helots, who were collectively enslaved to the Spartan state. In order to prevent the disparity between rich and poor Spartans from leading to the kind of political class struggle (*stasis*) that characterized many other Greek *poleis* from Archaic times onwards and so offering the Helots a chance to revolt, the Spartan rich made a self-denying compact to minimize differences of lifestyle between themselves and their poor fellow-citizens. Power and prestige were of course to remain in their hands, but they would not rub the noses of ordinary Spartans in their humble poverty. Instead, they would stress the collective representation of all Spartan citizens as in crucial respects equals – Homoioi or 'Peers', as they called themselves.

This compact, founded ultimately on fear of the Helots, had a remarkably long run, from about the mid-seventh century to the mid-fifth. But by the beginning of the fourth century it had clearly broken down. Like rich Greeks elsewhere the Spartan rich had always practised the normal strategies of heirship – family limitation, adoption, marriage alliance and so on – to keep their property power intact. But during the second half of the fifth century something went drastically wrong with the overall distribution of private landed property, so that by the time Aristotle wrote the *Politics* most of the privately owned land in Lakonia (Messenia being by then lost) was in the hands of a few, almost two fifths were owned by women, and there were less than a thousand full Spartan citizens. The wealth that flowed into Sparta after the Athenian War did not cause this concentration of landownership and diminution of citizen numbers; already by the beginning of the War there were only about 3,000 citizens as compared to about 8,000 in 480 (though part of this fall could have been due to the earthquake of the mid-460s). But the new wealth, which tended to find its way into the hands of the already rich and powerful, did help greatly to accelerate these two interrelated processes. Moreover, the gap between rich and poor did not only become more palpable on paper as it were but also in highly visible everyday reality in this face-to-face society: the rich, for example, began to contribute wheaten bread to their messes (probably elite groupings in any case) over and above the time-honoured obligatory contribution of the coarser and humbler barley meal (Xen. *LP* 5.3); and the private houses of the rich grew 'stuffed with valuables' (*Hell.* 6.4.27,30 – in a context of 370/69). In short, two of the cardinal tenets of the 'Lykourgan' dispensation had been decisively abandoned – the ideal of equality of lifestyle between rich and poor, and the notion that the interests of community solidarity should always *ceteris paribus* prevail over private considerations of family and self. The most important immediate consequence of the breakdown of the compact was *oliganthrôpia*, but this in its turn heightened the multiple tensions with which Spartan society was riven, weakened the cohesiveness and morale of the social system as a whole, and correspondingly gave heart to Sparta's thousands of internal and external enemies. In the circumstances it is perhaps not so much the collapse that occasions wonder but that it was so long delayed.

Agesilaos cannot of course be held solely or principally responsible for this state of affairs. On the contrary, he offers the best possible illustration of the insurmountable contradictions of Spartan society in this era of crisis. For on the one hand he vigorously advocated the maintenance of, indeed represented himself as the living incarnation of, the strict Lykourgan regimen, so far as his own ostentatiously abstemious lifestyle was concerned. Yet, on the other hand, in his unrestrained pursuit of empire and his gusty manipulation of patronal politics he both increased the pressures tending to the abandonment of Lykourgan ways and inevitably relied on the kind of economic resources available only to the very richest of the Spartans. It is also possible to accuse him of failing to remedy the ever more glaring disparities of wealth within the rapidly shrinking citizen body (it dropped by about a half between his accession and the eve of Leuktra); although the drastically radical reforms that this would have required (witness those of Agis IV and Kleomenes III in the third quarter of the next century) need not have been contemplated actively until the Leuktra defeat, by when it was too late to introduce them as a means of retaining Sparta's status as a great power. Above all, however, one is bound to criticize Agesilaos for using his unparalleled sway over Spartan policymaking in such a blinkered and counterproductive manner. For the adverse effects of *oliganthrôpia* were showing themselves in a threatening form at home as early as Kinadon's abortive conspiracy (399). Four or five years later the point was being picked up by Sparta's enemies in the Quadruple Alliance, not least by her former ally Corinth. By the early 370s the message had percolated through the Peloponnesian League. In 370/69 it was a major incentive both for the revolt of Perioikoi on the northern frontier of Lakonia and, consequently, for the massive Theban-led invasion of Lakonia which in turn provided the opportunity for another and in fact finally successful Messenian Helot revolt.

In these circumstances Agesilaos, one might think, would have been well advised to pursue a quieter foreign policy after 386. But was this feasible, was there really another way? The issue at stake then is still very much alive today. It concerns the degree of genuine autonomy that a great power can permit to its satellites and remain a great power. Like the Soviet Union in Poland or the United States in El Salvador today, Agesilaos believed that Sparta's selfish interests dictated an interventionist line within her sphere of influence, even if this meant breaking sworn treaties or contravening natural justice. However, with regard to Thebes and Boiotia this literally drastic (from Greek *drastikos*) policy came horribly unstuck. Agesilaos was not responsible for alienating the Boiotian Confederacy, a Peloponnesian League ally until 395 and an exception to Sparta's usual practice of not allying to multi-*polis* organizations, in the first place. But he does deserve the major portion of the discredit for repeated violations of the autonomy of Thebes and interventions in and around Thebes' legitimate sphere of interest in central Greece – actions that ultimately forced Thebes to take the extreme step of suspending her 'natural' hostility towards Athens to the extent of joining an alliance in which Athens was the dominant partner. Under cover of membership in the Second Athenian League Thebes was also able to rebuild the Boiotian Confederacy that Sparta had dismantled in 386 and, through Epameinondas, Pelopidas and Gorgidas, develop an army that could not only challenge but eventually defeat Sparta in pitched battle. Agesilaos may have been surprised by the outcome of Leuktra. Epameinondas was not. That was the measure of the gulf between the vision and statecraft of the two men. Rather than throw Athens and Thebes together willy-nilly, Agesilaos ought to have done all in his power to keep them apart and at loggerheads – as Kleomenes I had done in 519 and Pausanias in 403.

In case Agesilaos was still unaware of the true implications of Spartiate *oliganthrôpia*, they were thrust upon his consciousness in the aftermath of Leuktra. Not only had 400 full Spartan citizens perished on the battlefield, but many of the three hundred survivors had surrendered rather than fight to the death. Sparta had not suffered a major defeat in pitched battle since Hysiai (?669), so precedents were hard to come by. But the obvious interpretation of the relevant 'Lykourgan' law demanded that these men should be demoted from the ranks of the Spartiates and consigned to the ignominious status of 'tremblers' (*tresantes*). Agesilaos, however, who was appointed 'lawgiver' to interpret the law, humiliatingly found himself obliged to fudge the issue – a final, limp recognition that the model military state of yore was now a proper subject, not for the military handbooks, but for the nostalgic or wish-fulfilling literary creations known collectively as 'the Spartan mirage' (see next and final chapter).

22

Epilogue: Agesilaos and the 'Spartan Mirage'

Not unjustly are the Spartans leaders of the Greeks, on account both of their inbred virtue and of their understanding in matters of war. They alone continue to be inviolate, without walls, free from civil strife, undefeated, and keeping still to their time-honoured manner of life. (Lysias 33.7)

When Pfefferberg had first asked him about leaving the OD, the police chief had pronounced ... that the only way out was on your shield. (Thomas Keneally, *Schindler's Ark*)

On 1 October 1939, shortly after the outbreak of the Second World War, Mr Winston Churchill gave a broadcast talk in which he referred to Soviet Russia as 'a riddle wrapped in a mystery inside an enigma'. Pretty much the same would have been said of Sparta by most non-Spartans at the outbreak of the Athenian War in 431, some fourteen years after the birth of Agesilaos (Chapter 2), or indeed at all periods of Spartan history before the Roman era. By *most*, not all, non-Spartans. For there existed a privileged international circle of Greeks – wealthy, often aristocratic, always oligarchic in their politics – who were permitted an intimate knowledge of the workings of pre-Roman Sparta thanks to personal friendships with leading Spartan families or even first-hand experience of the Spartan *agôgê* (as in the case of Xenophon's two sons and other such *trophimoi xenoi*: Chapter 13).

Fortunately several of these foreign friends of Sparta also chose to write about her for publication, and the relevant writings of one of them, Xenophon, have survived the vicissitudes of textual transmission from the fourth century BC to our own day largely intact (Chapter 5). It is chiefly due to Xenophon that the riddle of Sparta at least in the age of Agesilaos is, potentially, soluble. However, this is not to say that Xenophon was a historian pure and simple who told the truth, all of it and nothing but it, about the real Sparta of his own and earlier epochs. On the contrary, Xenophon was just as preoccupied with peddling a particular vision of Sparta as were Sparta's other literary devotees – in his case, as we shall see, the view favoured by his patron and friend Agesilaos. Xenophon, in short, was no less a purveyor of what has been dubbed the 'Spartan mirage' than, say, Plutarch.

In French and, I think, English parlance 'mirage' can have two distinct but overlapping senses. Primarily, it is used to refer to a phenomenon which appears to exist but in fact does not, the classic instance being the sheet of water that seems to be lying on a road or in the desert under hot, dusty conditions. In its other sense 'mirage' may describe something the appearance of which belies its actual nature, like the shadows that the prisoners in Plato's Cave mistook for real objects or the straw that appears bent when placed in a glass of water. *Le mirage spartiate*, a happy phrase coined by the French scholar who went on to edit Xenophon's *Lak. Pol.* (Ollier 1933-43; 1934), involves both senses in roughly equal measures. To be more precise, 'Spartan mirage' is a convenient shorthand expression for the way in which from antiquity to the present non-Spartans have with not a little help from their Spartan soulmates created the Sparta of their dreams, whether by inventing or by distorting facts about the real Sparta. Typically these idealized Spartas have been used as sticks with which to beat one's enemies: at first for political purposes by oligarchs who happened to live unwillingly in democracies, soon afterwards by philosophers bent on the creation of ideal states, thenceforth from a mixture of motives. Xenophon, characteristically, sought to use the mirage to teach philosophy by examples – or rather by the example of Agesilaos. But before we look at Xenophon's specific contribution to the mirage and at the way in which Agesilaos was thereafter so closely tied to the transmission of the Spartan legend, it is necessary first to situate the mirage or legend within its wider intellectual and literary context.

When Thomas More invented the term 'Utopia' in 1516 he was perfectly well aware as a good classical scholar that the 'u' prefix was formally ambiguous, that it could stand either for Greek 'ou' (not) or 'eu' (well). But he left no doubt that, so far as his own essay was concerned, Utopia was conceived first and foremost as a 'No-Place' and only secondarily as a 'Place of Well-Faring' (cf. Logan 1983). However, although More invented the word 'utopia', he by no means invented the genre of literature to which his *Utopia* (published originally in Latin) belongs. That honour (in principle) belongs to ancient Greece, as More himself recognized and advertized through his bastardized Greek title (cf. Berneri 1950, esp. 9-51; Finley 1975, 178-92). Indeed, the debt of More to his Greek models was far greater than has often been supposed, especially by those who have regarded *Utopia* as some sort of working model of society rather than a figment of More's imagination. Specifically, it is the link between More and Plato that gives Sparta a uniquely privileged position within the entire utopian tradition in western literature.

The impulse or propensity to utopian writing, for all that it is always rooted in dissatisfaction with the perceived *status quo*, has expressed itself in remarkably different concrete proposals over the ages (cf. Manuel/Manuel 1979). As a rule utopian writers criticize existing forms of society indirectly by asking the reader to contemplate an alternative, *ex hypothesi* better society founded inorganically by an omniprovident and omniscient legislator; and they all more or less transcend the bounds of historical time and space by talking about love, aggression, the nature of work, the collective fulfilment of personality and so on *sub specie aeternitatis*. But they give radically disparate answers to the basic principled and pragmatic questions posed by the construction on paper or papyrus of a utopian society. This is principally because utopians, or rather Utopiographers, have different perceptions of their societies' present evils, distinct historical understandings, and diverse moral, political and social ideals. Nevertheless, underlying the multiplicity of discordant responses to questions about social cohesion, sexual morality, the place of religion and so forth there would seem to subsist three more fundamental unities. The first is a unity of form. Utopiographers prefer the more dramatic, fictional, even fantastic approach to social amelioration as exemplified in (say) Plato's *Republic* as opposed to the Aristotelian method of patiently devising means to bring existing social arrangements and mentalities into closer alignment with general principles of political philosophy. Secondly, there subsists a unity of totality: the totality of the vision and of the proposed solution to societal imperfection sets a Utopiographer apart from the theorist who advances individual criticisms and a piecemeal programme of reform. Finally, constructors of utopias somewhat paradoxically agree in a tidy-minded preference for order above freedom – paradoxically in that the utopian impulse or longing has characteristically been predicated upon discontent with the restrictions on freedom imposed by actually existing societies.

The earliest practitioner on record, though he is not necessarily the creator of the genre (whose origins may be traced back to Homer's Syrie), is Hippodamos of Miletos, a fifth-century BC townplanner (Arist. *Pol.* 1267b23ff., 1330b24-5). Urbanization, however, is not of the essence of ancient Greek utopias. If it were, Plato – and wall-less, un-synoecized Sparta – would be no part of the story. Their essence is to be sought rather in two qualities. The first is that they are strictly hierarchical with regard to the organization of basic productive labour. Unlike the incredible projections of Euhemeros (DS 5.41.4-56.7) and his kin, in which food and drink were permanently and automatically on tap, Greek utopias were 'realistic' rather than metaphysical or escapist (cf., for the Renaissance, Eliav-Feldon 1982). Given the apparently irremediable technological backwardness of the age (cf. Finley 1981a, 176-95), they therefore required a subject labour force of one kind or another, often enough a purely servile one (cf. Garlan 1982, 143-6), which permitted those who were not toiling the leisure to enjoy the morally good life. The second differentiating feature of ancient Greek utopias is that they are static or, more precisely, ascetic – need-satisfying rather than want-satisfying.

More's reactions to ancient Greek Utopiography nicely illustrate the complexity of the western utopian tradition. On one hand, he refused to allow more than a small place to slavery or other sorts of forced labour (though he did envisage the enslavement of his Utopians for certain crimes, such as the breaking of what look uncomfortably like South Africa's recent pass laws). On the other hand, in contrast to many of his successors, More agreed that Utopia should be a static, ascetic, need-satisfying society. In other words, from a not wildly dissimilar technological situation he drew a different social conclusion but the same general moral conclusion as his ancient models. It is the similarity rather than the difference that immediately affects my present concerns. From More a direct line of influence and inspiration can be traced back *via* Plutarch's *Life* of Lykourgos to Xenophor's *Lak. Pol.* and the *Republic* of Plato and thence to Sparta, the ultimate model and fountainhead of the entire western utopian tradition (cf. Africa 1979, though he privileges the influence of Plutarch upon More above that of Plato). For Sparta was at once 'the most rigidly hierarchical state in the Greek world' (Finley 1975, 187) and yet, so far as the full Spartan citizens were concerned, a society of 'Peers' (Homoioi) who by a self-denying ordinance had austerely reduced their material wants to the minimum deemed necessary to sustain an all-conquering but internally egalitarian warrior elite.

However, to speak of the claim of 'Sparta' to utopiographical paternity is of course to beg the question. The real, historical Sparta of the fifth and fourth centuries BC and *a fortiori* earlier periods (above all that of 'Lykourgos') is not available for our direct inspection in objective literary works of sustained description and analysis – not least because Sparta herself never produced anything like what we understand by a historian (cf. Cartledge 1979, 51-2). Rather, Sparta is presented to us in all but a couple of cases through the Spartan mirage, a compound of distorted reality and sheer imaginative fiction. But through the smokescreen one fact at any rate shines with sufficient clarity. Whatever true basis there may once have been for depicting Sparta as the most nearly perfect of all actually existing Greek societies, that basis had become etiolated to the point of evanescence at the very moment when the mirage first acquired literary form in the latter part of the fifth century. To the extent, therefore, that Sparta served as the location of utopian imaginings in literary guise, it did so from the start strictly as an *ou*-topia rather than *eu*-topia. Sparta thus acted as the fount and origin of utopian writing in a double sense.

Justice cannot be done here to all, or even all the more important, aspects of the Spartan mirage – for instance, the state regulation or restriction of private property, industry, commerce and foreign contacts; or the claimed equality between the sexes involving the direction of sex and marriage towards service of the community. Suffice it to say that within what has loosely been called 'the Spartan tradition' (Rawson 1969) the Spartan model for the creation of social virtue by education has remained central to European thinking (cf. Murray 1980, 154) and that from Kritias to the Nazis there runs, albeit jerkily and discontinuously, a thin line of authoritarian reaction. More trivially, the still frequent use of the epithet 'Spartan' bears witness to a continuing fascination with Spartan character, discipline and toughness (cf. Rawson 1969, 366; and for a discussion of the injunction 'with your shield or on it', Hammond 1979/80). In what remains of this chapter, however, it is just the course of Agesilaos through the mirage from antiquity to the rise of modern historical scholarship in the nineteenth century that we will attempt to chart.

Kritias, leader of the pro-Spartan junta nicknamed the 'Thirty Tyrants', is the first literary contributor to the Spartan mirage on attestation (cf. Lévy 1976, 197-203; and Chapter 14); the contrast between his approach to Sparta and that of his contemporary Thucydides (cf. Cloché 1943) is particularly striking. But Kritias was killed in 403, three years before the accession of Agesilaos (Chapter 17); and it is due to Xenophon, the 'central source for the genesis of the Agesilaus myth' (David 1981, 53; cf. Ollier 1933, 434; Zierke 1936, 15), that the posthumous fortunes of Agesilaos are so closely intertwined with those of the mirage as a whole. Indeed, there is good reason to suspect that the supposedly 'Lykourgan' Sparta depicted as an ideal by Xenophon in the *Lak. Pol.* was as much (if not more) the creation of the propaganda of Agesilaos (cf. Ollier 1934, xxxv-vi). This is certainly true of at least one institutional detail, the provision of double rations for the kings, as may be seen by comparing *Ages.* 5.1 with *Lak. Pol.* 15-4; and it would be odd if Agesilaos had not influenced Xenophon to interpret Spartan society in a 'Lykourgan' way. For a prime technique whereby Agesilaos cannily sought to conciliate all shades of Spartan opinion and so facilitate his sway over Spartan policy was to represent himself as the exemplar of all the 'Lykourgan' virtues – a man who had passed with flying colours through the *agôgê*, won the contest for the Eurypontid throne on merit, was a brave warrior and capable commander, a skilled statesman and yet (unlike Lysander) totally subservient to the officials of the day, laden with riches but simple almost to excess in his personal lifestyle, and above all else utterly and unquestioningly pious.

Religion was the dominant form of ideology in Sparta, as in most early class societies (cf. Hodkinson 1983, 40-2), although the Spartans – like that other quintessentially military people, the Romans – were perhaps unusually superstitious and prone to manipulate religion for political ends (cf. Rahe 1980b, 397n.43; Finley 1983, 26-7, 66, 92-5, 132). Xenophon therefore dutifully began his enumeration of Agesilaos' virtues with his *eusebeia* or pious observance of the religious proprieties (*Ages.* 3.2,5) and ended with his *deisidaimonia* (*Ages.* 11.8), his perpetually god-fearing disposition. Agesilaos, he implied, was an exception to the confession wrung from him in the *Lak. Pol.* (14.7; cf. Chapter 21) that the Spartans had clearly ceased to perform their religious obligations. But (despite Plezia 1982, 56) Xenophon was not concerned to praise Agesilaos as an individual of exemplary virtue rather than as leader of his state. Both in the *Agesilaos* (e.g. 1.4) and in the *Lak. Pol.* (esp. chs 13, 15) Xenophon lavishes emphasis on the Spartan *basileia*, kingship, in a manner 'very characteristic of a powerful trend of his epoch' (von Fritz 1941a, 70; cf. Stroheker 1953/4, esp. 404, 407; Carlier 1978, esp. 138-9, 155-6). Typically, though, Xenophon's monarchism took a strictly practical form. Agesilaos captivated him because, as T.R. Glover well put it (1917, 380), 'there was something of a man about him, something soldierly, something of a prince, and his career seemed to show that someday a prince might achieve a final victory over Persia'. Of his contemporaries perhaps only Isokrates would have seen Agesilaos the prince in quite this way, but he had less reason than Xenophon to spare his criticism (e.g. 5.86-7; cf. Cloché 1933), and in the *Panathenaïcus* delivered himself of the only extant full-length attack on the Spartan legend in general.

No other surviving author provides so complete a picture of Agesilaos as Xenophon, although we know that he was not the only one to write an encomium (cf. Isok. *Ep* 9.1). But elements of the Xenophontic portrait reappear at intervals over the centuries, often in the bizarrest settings, and only Diogenes the Cynic chose to express the perfectly correct view that Agesilaos, like Epameinondas, was 'doomed to lie in the mire' (quoted *ap.* Diog. Laert. 6.39; cf. Julian, *Or.* 7.238a). Indeed, the normally dyspeptic Theopompos casually cited the allegedly general view that Agesilaos was the most celebrated man of his day (*FGrHist.* 115F321). Isokrates, however, was not the only contemporary to express reservations. Ephorus, who was reportedly a fellow-pupil of Isokrates with

Theopompos, was less than wholly impressed, so far as we may fairly infer his opinions from Diodoros (esp. 15.19.4, where the eirenic Agesipolis is preferred to the interventionist Agesilaos, and 15.88, where the palm in all Greece is given to Epameinondas); although he did give credit to Agesilaos' courage and military intelligence as a commander (Diod. 15.92.2). Polybios (9.23.7-8), too, did not approve Agesilaos' imperialistic attitude towards Sparta's allies. Even so, the criticisms of Polybios, Ephorus and Isokrates stand out from the general run of more or less encomiastic ancient comments, most notably those to be found in the two ancient 'biographies' that survive.

Cornelius Nepos moved in the highest Roman literary circles of the Late Republic, but his life of Agesilaos not only is brief but is so heavily dependent on Xenophon's *Agesilaos* as to be of no interest as a reflection of current perceptions. Plutarch's *Life* is an altogether different matter. He brought to it a very wide range of reading and a cultivated and not entirely uncritical spirit. He found distasteful Agesilaos' uncomradely ingratitude to Lysander (*Ages.* 8.6), condemned the king's preference for honouring the obligations of friendship above the claims of legality and justice (*Ages.* 13.5-6; cf. *Mor.* 807d), and even tentatively connected Sparta's downfall with Agesilaos' illegitimate accession and his harsh foreign policy (cf. Chapter 21). On the whole, though, Plutarch's presentation of Agesilaos' personal morality is as favourable as that of Xenophon; clearly he meant his readers to approve of a great man who in private rode a hobby-horse for the amusement of his children (*Ages.* 25.11). To the same end there are included throughout the *Life* examples of Agesilaos' supposed apophthegms drawn by Plutarch from an earlier (fourth-century?) collection of such brief, pointed and witty sayings. Since Agesilaos in fact easily outscores all other Spartans, Lykourgos included, in the collection of Spartan apophthegms that goes under Plutarch's name (*Mor.* 208b-236e), it would seem that for the sage of Chaironeia, as for the original compilers (and inventors) of the sayings, Agesilaos was *the* embodiment of the peculiarly Spartan virtues of simplicity, piety and self-reliance.

A slightly younger contemporary of Plutarch, the sophist Dio of Prusa and of the golden mouth, praised Agesilaos extravagantly for refusing to allow any portrait of himself to be created in any medium (*Or.* 37.43). The original of this story occurs in the concluding chapter of Xenophon's *Agesilaos* (11.7) and as such offers a revealing commentary on the life and times of Agesilaos, since that was the era when individual portraiture and self-advertisement were beginning to supplant the strictly idealized, generalized and as it were civic portraits of Perikles and other leading generals and politicians of the fifth century (cf. Chapters 15 and 16). But the story recurs in Cicero (*Ep.* 5.12.7) and Plutarch (*Ages.* 2.4, *Mor.* 191d, 215a), and to men writing in a world littered with bombastic portrait statues it must have seemed a particularly striking case of self-denial, especially by a king. Yet elsewhere (*Or.* 56) Dio could with magnificent inconsistency dismiss the Spartan kingship as no true kingship anyway, because (for example) Agesilaos was obliged to return from Asia when recalled by the Ephors (in 395/4: Chapter 11).

A constitutional detail like that did not trouble a later member of Dio's profession, the second-century rhetorician Maximus of Tyre. What especially impressed him (*Or.* 19(25).5), as it had impressed Xenophon (*Ages.* 5.4-7; cf. Cartledge 1981a, 19 and n.12), was the sexual self-control of Agesilaos. Indeed, for this reason Maximus placed Agesilaos above Leonidas as the supreme Spartan hero of old. Aelian, too, author of a 'Motley History' (*Varia Historia*) towards the end of the second century, gave Agesilaos a good press, praising for instance the simple way of living that he maintained even into old age (*VH* 7.13; cf. Plut. *Mor.* 210b) and echoing Plutarch's admiration of Agesilaos' paternal horse-play (*VH* 14.2). The warm approval given to Agesilaos' generalship by a contemporary of Aelian, Polyainos, compiler of a handbook of strategems, has been noted elsewhere (Chapter 12); worth adding here is that for Polyainos Agesilaos was the central character, featuring so prominently (in fact thirty-three times) that a picture of Agesilaos' character as well as his generalship is conveyed (esp. 2.1.4, 2.1.32-3; cf. Tigerstedt 1974, 192).

By the fourth century pagnism was firing its last literary salvoes in its death struggle with the various versions of Christianity, and Sparta unsurprisingly provided the pagan propagandists with suitable models. For example, the Hellenizing pagan Roman emperor Julian, who had a Spartan grammar teacher, lauded the Spartans on the interested ground that they 'appear to have enjoyed the best of governments, that of their kings' (*Or.* 1.13, 16); but his faulty scholarship unfortunately undermined the thesis, since he falsely believed that all Spartan kings went through the *agôgê* (*Or.* 1.14cd) whereas in fact Agesilaos had been exceptional in having done so (Chapter 3). At the very end of the fourth century Synesius of Cyrene composed an *On Kingship* for the edification of the emperor Arcadius in which he cited Agesilaos as a splendid model: he knew how to win friends, not mere flatterers; though lame he avoided becoming a subject of mockery; rather, his military prowess was such that he virtually deprived the Persian Great King of his throne (chs 12, 17).

This ludicrous overstatement was taken up again a century later in 501 by Procopius of Gaza. Addressing a panegyric to the emperor Anastasius Procopius made bold to hail his suzerain as 'the new Agesilaos, thanks to whom the barbarian remains quiet' (ch.26). In harsh reality, of course, the barbarian refused to remain quiet for long, and the hollowness of these classicizing tributes from the late antique world has been neatly exposed by Tigerstedt (1974, 270): 'While hordes of barbarians march through the empire, burning, plundering, murdering, the rhetoricians declaim intrepidly about Marathon, Thermopylae, Salamis, and compare their lords to Leonidas and Agesilaos. Classical civilization does not descend silently into the tomb; it dies, loudly proclaiming its past grandeur.'

After the sixth century Agesilaos, it would seem, suffered a *longa oblivio*; but then opinion on ancient Sparta generally 'became submerged until the revival of learning in the fourteenth century' (Epps 1960, 39). Nikephoros Gregoras, for instance, was well aware of Agesilaos as a great man and statesman and – though Agesilaos of course took part in neither – cited the Battles of Haliartos and Leuktra (*Hist. Byz.* 10.4.4). In the first half of the fifteenth century Gemistos Plethon in the course of a distinguished career combining learning with high office at Mistra (capital of the Despotate of the Morea) found occasion to mention, and overpraise, the last campaigns of Agesilaos (Chapter 15). Among

Plethon's many visitors was Cyriac of Ancona, rediscoverer of Greek antiquities for the Renaissance (cf. Cartledge 1983, 130); Cyriac spoke slightingly of the 'Byzantine vassalage' represented by the Despotate and movingly lamented in verse the absence of Agesilaos and other Spartan heroes of yore. But once Greece lost its last tatters of liberty to the Ottoman Turks, this lament was transmuted into a regular paean of eulogy, as Agesilaos became the Renaissance's favourite ancient Spartan – 'a triumphant example of temperance, affability, of military virtue, of magnanimity, of respect for fortune, and of kingly *brevitas loquendi* ... summing up in himself all the Renaissance virtues (except beauty)' (Rawson 1969, 135). The admiration of Machiavelli (cf. Berlin 1979, 44, 52, 60) was representative.

This lionization of Agesilaos did not outlast the seventeenth century. Already Pierre Bayle, the 'sceptic of Rotterdam' as Gibbon dubbed him, had suggested that Agesilaos' excessive passion for war had harmed his country. In the eighteenth century Rousseau could still speak of Sparta as 'this republic of demigods' (an allusion to Isok. 12.41; cf. Arnheim 1977, 72), but it was the beneficent and constructive legislation of Lykourgos rather than the martial virtuosity of Agesilaos that inspired this view of Sparta and his *Gouvernement de Pologne* (cf. Epps 1960, 41). From the eighteenth-century reaction against the type of the princely warrior the reputation of Agesilaos has never completely recovered, partly for moral reasons (Sir Frederick Pollock, quoted in Whibley 1896, 58, could discover only two Spartans who were gentlemen as well as officers – and neither of them was Agesilaos), partly for political ones (for example, Philip of Macedon not Agesilaos was the nineteenth-century's model of a nation-state builder). The best – or worst – efforts of Buttmann and others to rehabilitate him have not succeeded (cf. end of Chapter 1 and Appendix I).

It is true that Sparta has had her fervent admirers even in the present century, not least in Nazi Germany. But now we can all, I hope, agree thankfully with Rawson (1969, 170) that 'No one today would think of taking Agesilaus as a model, either for himself or for his rulers'. That last assertion would doubtless have mortified, if indeed it would have been comprehensible to, Xenophon. Which may be thought to sound the appropriate note of radical paradox on which to end this study of Agesilaos and the crisis of Sparta.

Appendices

Appendix I

Hertzberg's *Agesilaos*: a retrospect

Believers in the uniform and inevitable progress of scholarship will derive scant comfort and satisfaction from reading Hertzberg 1856 a century and quarter after its publication. On the other hand, those who take it to be axiomatic that all the best ideas were anticipated by some German scholar or other somewhere in the nineteenth century will not have that faith irretrievably shaken by it. This is not to say that the work is perfect: new evidence and new approaches have served to highlight its imperfections. But Hertzberg did make a remarkably impressive stab at the impossible, a biography of Agesilaos II.

Biography, of course, meant something very different in 1856 from what is now ordinarily comprehended by the term. Lytton Strachey's *Queen Victoria*, which shows the influence of Freud and is often hailed as the first 'modern' biography of a public figure, was still sixty-five years in the future. Hertzberg, however, did not attempt merely a 'political' biography, and it is, paradoxically, perhaps the chief structural flaw of his study that he took as his major theme the development or rather gradual deterioration of Agesilaos' moral character. There are two main reasons why this approach is an unsatisfactory one, in 1856 no less than today.

In the first place it turns the historian into a moralist. No doubt moral judgment is an unavoidable aspect of the historian's craft, but it should be a subordinate element kept rigorously in check rather than the historian's primary aim. It would have been well if Hertzberg's intimate familiarity with German ancient historical scholarship had been leavened by the spirit of von Ranke's 'wie es eigentlich gewesen' dictum (however impossible it may in fact be to observe that dictum to the letter). Secondly, Hertzberg's preoccupation with Agesilaos' moral decline placed him too squarely on the viewpoint and at the mercy of his two preferred ancient sources, the *Hellenika* of Xenophon and Plutarch's *Life* of Agesilaos. When criticizing, as was his wont, the author of the *Agesilaos* attributed to Xenophon (whose authorship Hertzberg conventionally denied), he could quite properly write: 'Our judgment of Agesilaos can naturally be based solely on facts, not on mere phrases.' But he was considerably more, indeed excessively, tolerant of the phrases employed in Xenophon's *Hellenika* and Plutarch's *Agesilaos*.

However, Hertzberg's excessive moralism is almost compensated for by his intimate knowledge of all the ancient literary sources then available and by his application to them of the techniques of *Quellenforschung* freshly pioneered in ancient history by Barthold Niebuhr (cf. Christ 1972). Almost, but not quite.

For Hertzberg is too tender towards the manifest deficiencies of Xenophon's *Hellenika*. This is not because he was ignorant of them. He rightly saw the work as a species of 'memoir literature', having all the advantages and disadvantages of the genre (cf. Chapter 5). Rather, he was forced to play down its defects because of his views on the historical value of Diodoros and the authenticity of the Xenophontic encomium.

In the case of Diodoros, Hertzberg lays down the general principle that, where he and Xenophon conflict irreconcilably on military matters, the contemporary and expert Xenophon is always to be preferred except where his pro-Spartan bias is blatant. That principle may seem admirable in the abstract, since the faults of Diodoros as a compiler, let alone as a military historian, are many and glaring. But a freak of chance discovery has undermined the principle, possibly irreparably. The recovery from Oxyrhynchos in Egypt of papyrus fragments from the work of the as yet anonymous 'Oxyrhynchos Historian' has given limited access to an author far more worthy than Xenophon to inherit the mantle of Thucydides. Unhappily for Xenophon, the longest fragment concerns events of 395, and the judgment of Cawkwell (1979, 406) after a comparison of 3.4.24 with DS 14.80 (clearly derived ultimately from Hell. Ox.) is just: 'Only those who believe that Xenophon was a "really well-informed and truthful reporter" [the belief of Eduard Meyer] will shrink from the awful truth that here at least he has seriously failed us, a case of *inextricabilis error.*'

As for the panegyric ascribed in antiquity to Xenophon, Hertzberg belonged to the then dominant school of thought that condemned it as an inept forgery. It was really, he believed, a compilation by a later Sophist or grammarian, culled from the *Hellenika* above all and perhaps composed in a spirit of Greek 'nationalist' reaction to the Macedonian conquest. This judgment is almost certainly false (cf. Chapter 5) and it inevitably prevented Hertzberg from making extensive use of the *Agesilaos*. Moreover, what use he did make of it missed the essential point. For he criticized the work for its choice and disposition of subject-matter – a long exposition of the Persian expedition, but only brief mentions of isolated episodes thereafter; two 'historical' chapters followed by eight extolling uncritically Agesilaos' manifold moral virtues – while failing to see how, once the moralizing veneer was stripped away, the work could bring us as close as may be to the mainsprings of its hero's long and nearly unbroken period of influence over Spartan and so Greek affairs (cf. Chapter 9).

There were other shortcomings, not all excusable by the date of composition. Hertzberg made no use of epigraphical or archaeological evidence, despite the example set by August Boeckh. In the ticklish matter of chronology, a particularly difficult problem for this period, Hertzberg's reconstructions were not always convincing, especially for the Corinthian War (cf. Chronological Table, below). He did not consistently hit the golden mean in the amount of space allotted to events of the period in which Agesilaos was not personally and directly involved; for example, he gave too much descriptive detail of the Corinthian War, whereas his account of the Boiotian Confederacy was exiguous to a degree. His touch, finally, was perhaps least sure when dealing with Persia and the succession of Peaces that followed what he rightly called the Peace of Antalkidas (which, however, he discussed very fully indeed).

In retrospect, though, these grave shortcomings are overbalanced by the wealth of learning and sound judgment that Hertzberg consistently displayed. *Agesilaos* was not his first book. Three years earlier he had produced a study of the germane topic of Alkibiades as general and politician, a highly suitable *Vorarbeit*. Nor was *Agesilaos* by any means his last work. In the 1870s there flowed from his pen a veritable torrent of general histories of Greece which between them spanned all the centuries from the fifth BC to the nineteenth AD. The *Agesilaos* shows incipient signs of this ability to take a broad view, and Hertzberg largely succeeded within his imposed limitations in turning his biography of Agesilaos into a history of Greece in the first four decades of the fourth century, which should be a goal of any historian of Agesilaos.

Over and above these personal qualities, it was Hertzberg's – and our – great good fortune to have written the *Agesilaos* when and where he did. More than once he calls the roll of his impressive forerunners in the field, beginning with J.C.F. Manso. With the exception of George Grote, whose debt in this regard was comparable (as J.S. Mill remarked with surprise and admiration), Hertzberg cites in his voluminous notes only German ancient historians; and he envisaged himself as standing 'in the Forum of German scholarship'. This flourishing period of German historical scholarship has been admirably surveyed with special reference to Sparta by Elizabeth Rawson, who wrote (1969, 326): 'If we turn to the great classical historians, whose influence spread beyond learned circles and beyond their own country, we shall find no special enthusiasm for Sparta here ..., though she received all the attention that the problems of her development deserved.' Unlike Buttmann's Agesilaos (1872), therefore, that of Hertzberg was very far from being the compleat ancient Greek hero.

To summarize adequately the overall purport of Hertzberg's 379-page monograph in a few words is not possible. But, briefly, he saw Agesilaos' career as king (the first forty-five or so years of his life he perforce virtually ignored) as falling into three unequal segments. First, there were the successful inaugural years, from his unexpected accession (wrongly dated 397) to the victory at Koroneia in 394. Then followed the period of 394 to 379 punctuated by the Peace of Antalkidas; during this Agesilaos achieved the pinnacle of his power. Finally, there ensued the years of decline initiated by the liberation of Thebes and terminated bathetically by Agesilaos' death on the coast of Libya. Leaving aside the obtrusive moralizing, Hertzberg does an excellent job of situating Agesilaos' reign within its Spartan and wider Greek context. He properly stresses the significance of the connection with Lysander, not excluding Agesilaos' early pederastic attachment and attributing to their friendship a deal of emotion. Hertzberg rightly observed that Agesilaos came to wield more influence over Spartan policy than any king before or after him, despite constant opposition; and he was also correct to attribute this unparalleled sway in part to Agesilaos' outward reverence for traditional Spartan norms and forms of domestic and public life. Agesilaos' passion for restoring oligarchic exiles and the full horror of his unreasoning and unremitting hostility to Thebes are graphically portrayed; the suggestion that after 371 this hostility was transferred from Thebes to newly resurrected Messene is cogent. The scene of Agesilaos' death is conveyed with a certain incongruous lyricism, the more sharply to underline the futility of his latter years and the more completely to douche the 'Panhellenist' ardour with which the scene is portrayed in the Xenophontic encomium. Hertzberg's general conclusion that the foreign policy of Agesilaos placed an intolerable burden on the shoulders of a state that was internally weak is fundamentally true.

In short, Hertzberg's *Agesilaos* is still a study to be reckoned with by the ancient historian. A biography, even a 'political' biography, of Agesilaos is in fact an impossibility (cf. Chapter 1). But Hertzberg deserves the credit for seeing that the years of Agesilaos' reign form an important historical subject and for being the first historian in modern times to write the history of those years illuminatingly around the life of this Spartan king.

Appendix II

Changes in Spartan Army Organization

We begin with the army's organization in its broadest sense, the way in which Spartan citizens were allocated their place in the hoplite phalanx. Thanks to a fragment of the Spartan hortatory poet Tyrtaios (fr. 19.8), who was active around 650, we happen to know that once upon a time the Spartan army was organized on the basis of the standard three Dorian tribes – Hylleis, Dymanes and Pamphyloi. The same poet makes it clear that the Spartans to whom he was addressing his elegies were by then marshalled in hoplite phalanx formation (cf. Cartledge 1977). What is not certain, unfortunately, is whether the Dorian tribal organization of the army survived the implementation of the hoplite reform at Sparta in the first half of the seventh century, and if so for how long. The matter is important, since the organization of the developed Spartan hoplite army was obviously one of the cardinal features conducing to its pre-eminence.

Both Herodotus and Xenophon, writing nearly a century apart, attribute the organization of the army together with all other essentials of the Spartan *politeia* to Lykourgos. But in the details of the organization these two writers differ rather dramatically. In Xenophon's day the largest units of the army, of which there were six, were called *morai* or 'divisions'; and the *mora* depended on a principle of grouping that cut across ties of both kinship and locality. It was neither tribal, in the sense that each Dorian tribe might theoretically have constituted two *morai*, nor local in the way that regiments were and are typically recruited more or less regionally in the British army. Herodotus, however, whose brief did not of course cover the period after 479, makes no mention of the *mora*. In an introductory passage on Spartan 'prehistory' (1.65.4-5) he reports the view of 'the Spartans' that Lykourgos introduced the existing social order (*kosmos*) from Crete. 'So far as arrangements for war were concerned, he established sworn brotherhoods (*enômotiai*), "thirties" (*triêkades*) and common messes (*sussitia*).' The 'thirties' are almost wholly mysterious to us on present evidence (despite the guesswork of, for example, Pareti 1958 (1910b), 91 or Forrest 1980, 45-6; cf. Jones 1980, 181-5 for possibly comparable units at Corinth); though units that are *prima facie* a multiple of three would fit a system based on the Dorian tribes. On the other hand, both the *enômotiai* and the *sussitia* do reappear in Xenophon. Only the former, however, are specifically reported by Xenophon as part of the army organization in the field, as they are by Thucydides too (5.66). For although the *sussitia*, technically also called *suskania* ('common tents'), are clearly also military in ethos and function, they were not apparently subsumed under the distribution of Spartan soldiers into *morai* for purposes of delivering battle. This suggests that they were now performing a rather different rôle.

It seems clear, therefore, that Herodotus and Xenophon cannot both be referring to the same putatively 'Lykourgan' military reform. Further, although the evidence of Herodotus could be harmonized with that of Tyrtaios so as to yield a Spartan hoplite army organized about 650 on the basis of the three Dorian tribes, the evidence of Xenophon could not be thus interpreted. There must, that is to say, have been at least one change in Spartan army organization between the introduction of the hoplite reform to which Tyrtaios is witness and Xenophon's day. This is a vital point to establish since it shows that not even the notoriously conservative Spartans were immune from all change and suggests that the pressures for change in this uniquely sensitive (and in very many societies ferociously tradition-bound) sphere must have been great if not overwhelming.

The evidence of Herodotus is fortunately not confined to a single sweeping reference to the army-reform of 'Lykourgos'. As part of his retailing of the 'great and wondrous deeds of both Greeks and non-Greeks' (to quote his Preface) it was inevitable that he should feature prominently the deeds of Spartan hoplites during the Persian Wars of 480-479. Both at Thermopylai (480) and at Plataia (479) they displayed collectively what Herodotus (7.211.3; 9.62.3) characterizes as knowledge or understanding and knack or professional skill; and Herodotus' Spartan information was sufficiently intimate and precise for him to name several individuals whose achievements the Spartans themselves had deemed worthy of record whether for praise or blame. But as so often with Herodotus, problems multiply as he moves from people to institutions. For our immediate purposes the most crucial item at issue is the status of what he calls (9.53.3) 'the Pitanate *lochos*' or '*lochos* of Pitana'.

Thucydides (1.20.3) categorically denied that such a unit existed or had ever existed, citing its mention as an example of the lamentably general disposition of people to believe the first story they heard rather than checking it by independent personal research at first hand. Almost certainly this allusive barb was aimed at the heart of Herodotus, since only his *Histories* could be thought to have given so esoteric a piece of information such wide currency. Generally speaking, on matters of institutional detail the modern historian is surely right to prefer Thucydides to Herodotus in case of a clash, other things being equal. But in this instance other things are not as equal as they may seem.

Only three times in his whole work does Herodotus name his informants individually. One of the three named was a certain Archias (3.55.2). He was a leading Spartan, clearly among those whom Herodotus could elsewhere describe as 'well-born and exceptionally wealthy' (7.134.2), and Herodotus had almost certainly been given an introduction to him through mutual Samian aristocratic friends (Cartledge 1982, 250). For some reason or other Herodotus does not merely tell us the name of Archias: he also makes a point of stating where he met him in Sparta and why he met him there.

He met him, he says, in Pitana, because that was the *dêmos* of Archias. *Dêmos* in this sense of a locality or local grouping is not known from any Spartan text. But since the information about Archias' provenance is being given for the benefit of non-Spartan readers or listeners, it would be reasonable to expect Herodotus to have translated a Spartan word into language more widely familiar. The correct Spartan technical term was in fact *ôba* (originally with a preceding *digamma*). Pitana does not happen to be attested as such in the fifth century; Thucydides (1.10.2), for example, speaks untechnically of *kômai* ('villages') and names no names. But *ôbai* appear in the Great Rhetra (not later than the fourth century if forged, probably seventh-century if this document preserved in Plut. *Lyk.* 6 is genuine: Cartledge 1980b), and Pitana is listed as an *ôba* or obe in Spartan public documents of the Hellenistic period and later. It seems perfectly legitimate therefore to extrapolate backwards to the fifth century and identify Pitana as an obe in Herodotus' day. Why, then, did Herodotus choose to describe Pitana as a *dêmos* of Sparta rather than, as Thucydides was to do, a *kômê*?

The answer, I suggest, is that Herodotus wished to convey the notion that Pitana was not merely a geographical entity but also a political unit, a constituent element of the *polis* of Sparta. Had Herodotus been writing specifically for an Athenian public, we might have interpreted him to mean that citizen rights in Sparta depended on being enrolled on the register of one's obe, just as citizenship at Athens depended on being enrolled on the register of a *dêmos* or deme. But since in fact the equivalent criterion in Sparta was enrolment and membership in a common mess, the parallel cannot be pressed in this way. Instead, we should take Herodotus to be implying a more general correspondence, namely that Pitana had some kind of political as opposed to purely topographical significance. In Sparta, as in any Greek *polis* known to Herodotus only more so, the army and the city were conceived as one. There could be no more 'political' function for Pitana to perform than to serve as a unit of recruitment for the Spartan citizen army. On this interpretation Herodotus was being perfectly consistent in speaking of the Pitanate *lochos* as a military unit and in calling Pitana a *dêmos*. In short, given his express mention of Archias, who ought to have known what he was talking about, the onus of proof is firmly on those who (like Kelly 1981b) wish to support Thucydides in denying that such a unit had ever existed.

The question, rather, is what sort of a unit this *lochos* was, for the word could be applied to a wide range of very different kinds (cf. Boucher 1912, 300n.1). Was it, like the *mora* later, the largest unit of division in the Spartan regular army? Or was it, like the famed Theban 'Sacred Band' (*hieros lochos*) an elite corps? Or something intermediate between these two? Here the tables are turned, and the pressure of questioning shifts from Herodotus on to Thucydides, specifically to his detailed and apparently exhaustive enumeration of the Spartan army at the (First) Battle of Mantineia of 418 (5.66). For Thucydides the *lochos* in action here was the largest unit of division of 'the Lakedaimonians' (who were not necessarily all full Spartan citizens). Since there were six such regular *lochoi*, which are to be distinguished from an irregular seventh *lochos* recruited *ad hoc* from ex-Helots, and since none of these was called 'Pitanate', the contempt of Thucydides for the allegedly general belief in the current existence of a 'Pitanate *lochos*' is readily comprehensible. But why was he so sure that there never had been such a *lochos* at any time before 418 or at any rate in the relatively recent past covered by Herodotus? The answer seems to be that, like many of his more easily gulled contemporaries, he believed that Sparta had enjoyed the same *politeia* for rather more than 400 years (1.18.1), and *politeia* for him as for Herodotus and Xenophon would embrace the military organization of the citizen army as well as the more narrowly 'constitutional' arrangements of a *polis*.

Yet despite its initial impression of plausibility and comprehensiveness Thucydides' account of the Spartan army at Mantineia is deeply unsatisfactory. The reasons for this have been repeatedly canvassed (e.g. by A. Andrewes in Gomme 1970, *ad loc.*). Unease arises first from his numerical computation, which would seem to give a much too low total for the Spartan side as a whole. No less troubling is his use of what are ostensibly Spartan technical terms. Thucydides calls a *lochos* what Xenophon, writing not much later and also describing a sixfold army organization ascribed to the dim and distant past, labels a *mora*; and in his listing of Spartan officers – he took it to be an essential ingredient of Spartan success that 'nearly the whole army, except for a small part, consists of officers serving under other officers' (5.66.4) – he contrives to leave the *lochagoi* without a unit to command. I have set out my views on these problems already in print (1979,254-7) and shall have little to add here.

For I am still convinced that Thucydides, baffled by what he candidly called 'the secrecy of the system' (5.68.2), committed the basic mistake of confusing the *lochos* with the *mora*. This error fatally undermines his critique of Herodotus' 'Pitanate *lochos*' and makes it possible for us to find room for a unit answering that description in some other form of army organization. We have already seen that Sparta certainly made at least one fundamental change, from an organization based on the Dorian kinship (or notional kinship) tribes to one based neither on kin nor on locality. It is, I submit, both a logical inference and an economical hypothesis that can be supported by the available evidence to postulate that between these two there intervened a third, which was based not on real or supposed kinship but on locality, and that this reform in organization coincided more or less with the adoption of the hoplite reform in Sparta. This change in its turn was premised on a political and economic transformation of Spartan society that also, I believe, belongs in the first half of the seventh century

First, the supporting evidence. Even if Herodotus' reference to the 'Pitanate *lochos*' had stood alone, I would have been willing to believe that the principle of local recruitment had been operative among Spartan citizens at the time of the Persian Wars. For it is clear to me from Thucydides' admittedly mistaken use of *lochos* in the Spartan context and from Herodotus' representation of the role played by the commander of the Pitanate *lochos* at Plataia that this *lochos* was not some small elite unit like the Theban Sacred Band but one of the largest divisions of the regular Spartan citizen army establishment. Our only source apart from Thucydides and Xenophon who gives a figure for the number of *lochoi* is Aristotle as reported by late scholiasts (fr. 541); indeed, Aristotle – or whichever of his pupils actually compiled the *Politeia of the Lakedaimonians* – actually cited the five *lochoi* by name. The names are of course important, as we shall see. But the number is no less so. For in another surviving fragment from this sadly lost work (fr. 540) Aristotle refers to the sixfold organization by *morai*. What is more, in this latter passage the writer emphasizes by his word-order that *all Lakedaimonians* were distributed among the six *morai*. By implication only *some* Lakedaimonians were grouped under the fivefold organization by *lochoi*, so that the difference in organizational units was a difference not just of names and number but of kind.

Of the five *lochos* names reported with variant spellings by the scholiasts only one is instantly recognizable and meaningful: Messoatês or Mesoagês. This can only be the *lochos* of Mes(s)oa, which is attested as an obe precisely like Pitana. The non-appearance by name of a 'Pitanate *lochos*' in the Aristotelian list is not by itself sufficient to warrant Thucydides' derisory denial of its very existence. Rather, the terminology of Herodotus may and should be explained on the same lines as *dêmos*, as an 'ordinary language' translation of the current Spartan name (or nickname) for the unit – if indeed Archias or whoever his informant was bothered to tell him the specific as opposed to generic name of the unit commanded by the heroic but literal-minded Amompharetos at Plataia. The other three names besides Messoatês/Mesoagês and the one concealing the *lochos* of Pitana would then refer to the *lochoi* raised from the other three obes constituting the Spartan *polis*, namely Kynosoura or Konöoura, Limnai and – physically separated from the other four but undoubtedly integrated politically and militarily: see esp. 4.5.10-11 – Amyklai. Corroboration of the hypothesis that the military organization of Sparta was at one time based on the five obes may be sought in the recurrence of fives in other aspects of *polis* administration before the fifth century: the five Ephors, the five Agathoergoi (Hdt. 1.67.5), both annually selected, and the five arbitrators chosen to resolve the disputed possession of Salamis (Plut. *Sol.* 10.6), and no doubt others. But more immediately relevant to Herodotus' account of the Battle of Plataia are the 5000 Spartans called out. This figure can only be rejected on *a priori* grounds and is most straightforwardly understood as five 'obal' regiments of 1000 men each.

So much for the evidence, direct and indirect, in favour of a change in army organization from a tribal, that is notionally kin-related, basis to a basis that was local-cum-political. The argument from logic depends partly on comparative evidence. For precisely such a change is known for certain to have occurred at Athens in the late sixth century with spectacular results in terms of solid military success. Herodotus (5.78) interprets this too narrowly as a function of the Athenians' newly-won 'equal freedom of speech' (*isêgoriê*); we may ascribe the success also to the great increase in efficiency and co-ordination promoted by the reform in the regimentation of the army. None the less, I would not wish to exclude *élan* and morale from the Spartan picture either. If my hypothesis about the date of the change is correct, it was part of a package that stimulated the Spartan *damos* to crush a Messenian Helot revolt and enabled it to receive somewhat belatedly the fruits of its military exertions in the form of economic and political guarantees. The military reform, in other words, is inseparable from the political context in the broadest sense – a lesson that modern military historians, obsessed with the technicalities of ever more specialized warfare, are sometimes rather too quick to overlook. Precisely the same connection may be posited for the further organizational reform which (I have argued in Chapter 4) was made at some time between 479 and 425.

Chronological Table*†

(spr. = spring   s. = summer   aut. = autumn   w. = winter   e. = early   l. = late   ? = year uncertain   c. = time of year uncertain)

Year (Julian Calendar)	Approximate age of Agesilaos	Agesilaos and Family	Greece and Aegean	Persian Empire	West
405	39	Agis II (half-brother) in 22nd or 23rd year of reign; in garrison at Dekeleia (since 413)	e.spr. Lysander returns to Aegean Lysander establishes extreme oligarchy at Miletos after executions and expulsions; interview with Agis aut. Battle of Aigospotamoi in Hellespont: Lysander destroys last Athenian fleet and remains of Athenian Empire; installation of dekarchies (accompanied by massacres) in Thasos and elsewhere w. Blockade of Athens begins, Konon flees to Euagoras (I) of Cypriot Salamis	s. Cyrus, plenipotentiary of Western Asia Minor, summoned to Media by father Darius II, entrusts revenues of his provinces to Lysander	spr. Dionysios (I) elected stratēgos autokratōr to resist Carthaginian take-over of Sicily (launched 409) Dionysios becomes tyrant of Syracuse Peace between Syracuse and Carthage

* Ancient systems of time-reckoning are discussed well in Bickerman 1980: see esp. 27-33 (Greek calendars), 47-51 (Julian Year) and 67-70 (dating by eponyms). The Spartan civil year was dated by the Eponymous Ephor in our period and began in Julian terms about the end of September or beginning of October, perhaps specifically with the heliacal rising of Arktouros (roughly the end of the traditional campaigning and sailing seasons): Ste. Croix 1972, 320.

† Bibliographical note: for 404-386 I have generally followed Funke 1980a; for 371-362 Buckler 1980c, Appendix 1; it is also a pleasure to acknowledge publicly the instruction I derived from G.L. Cawkwell's 'Age of Xenophon' lectures delivered at Oxford in 1971 which were accompanied by most helpful chronological charts. The chronological tables appended to CAH VI[1] are far from utterly reliable. Many dates, it has to be stressed, must necessarily remain controversial, even if the sequence of events in the various areas is usually secure.

	Greece	Athens	Persia / East	West
404	*spr.* Agis returns to Sparta	*spr.* Surrender of Athens to Lysander: Sparta and Peloponnesian League decide to preserve defence-less Athens	*c. spr.* Death of Darius II, accession of Artaxerxes II	Spartans send aid to Dionysios
		s. Long Walls and Peiraieus fortifications demolished	?Cyrus returns to Sardis, reappointed to super-satrapy: Asiatic Greeks revolt from Tissaphernes to Cyrus – except Miletos (seized and garrisoned by Tissaphernes)	Alliance of Katane and Leontinoi
		Rule of Thirty installed at Athens, soon supported by Spartan garrison; allies defy Spartan edict not to harbour Athenian exiles from Thirty	Death of Alkibiades in Hellespontine Phrygia (satrapy of Pharnabazus)	
		Dekarchy established on Samos, supported by harmost Thorax; divine honours for Lysander	Revolt of Egypt under Amyrtaeus II	
		Trial and execution of Thorax, Lysander in Chalkidike		
40(3)		?Spartan intervention in Thessaly (or 400)		
		w. Thrasyboulos seizes Phyle, advances to Peiraieus		

Year (Julian Calendar)	Approximate age of Agesilaos	Agesilaos and Family	Greece and Aegean	Persian Empire	West
403	41	w. Agis votes for condemnation of Pausanias	l.w. Battle of Peiraieus (Mounychia): death of Kritias, remnant of Thirty flee to Eleusis 'bunker' s. Lysander appointed harmost for Athens, aims to reinstate Thirty with aid of brother Libys (navarch), but overruled by Pausanias aut. General Amnesty and restoration of democracy at Athens, but recognition of Eleusis statelet w. Trial and acquittal of Pausanias 'Fall' of Lysander: Sparta withdraws official support from dekarchies ? visits of Lysander to Siwah oasis, Delphi and Dodona	? Lysander plunders territory of Pharnabazus	Revolt at Syracuse against Dionysios, but D. wins authority over Sicels (403–400) Reduction of Katane and Naxos by Dionysios

402	42	s. Agis begins Peloponnesian League campaign against Elis (402–400)	Thebes seizes Oropos Klearchos harmost of Byzantion recalled and exiled	Sparta agrees to aid Cyrus in revolt against Artaxerxes; Klearchos becomes Cyrus' principal mercenary recruiting sergeant
401	43	s. Agis attacks Elis, leaves harmost with garrison and oligarchic Eleian exiles at Epitalion	s. Eleusis reincorporated in Athenian state	spr. Cyrus collects army against Artaxerxes at Sardis, joined by fleet (including Spartan ships) at Issos s. Cyrus killed and defeated at Cunaxa north of Babylon Return march of Cheirisophos, Xenophon and 'Ten Thousand' mercenaries begins

Year (Julian Calendar)	Approximate age of Agesilaos	Agesilaos and Family	Greece and Aegean	Persian Empire	West
400	44	*spr./s.* Death of Agis *l.s.* Accession of Agesilaos (II) after dispute with Latychidas (A. probably by now married to Kleora and perhaps father of Archidamos)	End of war with Elis ? Expulsion of Messenians from Naupaktos and Kephallenia ? Archelaos of Macedon master of Thessalian Larissa Sparta intervenes at Herakleia Trachinia and establishes close relations with Lykophron of Thessalian Pherai	*l.w.* 'Ten Thousand' reach Black Sea at Trapezous *s.* Tissaphernes returns to Asia Minor coast, besieges Kyme *aut.* Sparta responds to Asiatic Greeks' appeal, declares war on Artaxerxes *w.* Thibron begins Spartan campaign in Asia Minor ? Nepherites I founds Dynasty XXIX of (still revolted) Egypt	Messenians settled by Dionysios with mercenaries at Tyndaris
399	45	Agesilaos helps abort Kinadon's conspiracy	Sparta instals garrison at Thessalian Pharsalos, now controls area from N. border of Boiotia to S. border of Achaia Phthiotis Death of Archelaos Conspiracy of Kinadon Trial and condemnation of Sokrates	*spr.* Remnant of 'Ten Thousand' incorporated in Thibron's army *aut.* Thibron fails to take Larissa, allows troops to plunder allies, replaced by Derkylidas Derkylidas makes truce with Tissaphernes, recovers cities of Aiolis and	

398	46	First Carthaginian War of Dionysios (398-2) begins, siege and capture of Motya Dionysios permitted to recruit mercenaries within Lakonia	*spr.* Renewal of truce between Derkylidas and Pharnabazus Derkylidas rebuilds wall across Thracian Chersonese, begins siege of Atarneus	Embassy of Ktesias (doctor to Artaxerxes) to Sparta and Cyprus	*w.* Pharnabazus (with Konon) appointed to command fleet against Sparta, supported by Euagoras Ktesias' *Persika* ends here
397	47	Carthage besieges Syracuse Lilybaion founded Dionysios recruits more mercenaries from Sparta	*s.* Athenian embassy to Artaxerxes intercepted by Pharax (navarch)	Pharnabazus bases naval effort on Cyprus and Phoenicia Derkylidas takes Atarneus, instals governor	*e.s.* Derkylidas concludes armistice with both Pharnabazus and Tissaphernes

Year (Julian Calendar)	Approximate age of Agesilaos	Agesilaos and Family	Greece and Aegean	Persian Empire	West
396	48	spr. Sparta and Peloponnesian League appoint Agesilaos to command of revitalised Persian campaign		Agesilaos renews truce with Tissaphernes, campaigns against Pharnabazus	Sparta sends relieving squadron to besieged Dionysios
				Konon intercepts aid from Sparta's ally Nepherites I to Agesilaos	Dionysios starts another war against Sicels (396-3)
			s./aut. Konon secures revolt of Rhodes from Sparta; Artaxerxes makes offerings to Lindian Athena	Lysander secures defection of Spithridates from Pharnabazus	Lakonian mercenaries at Leontinoi
		l.s. Kyniska (sister of Agesilaos) first woman to win four-horse chariot-race at Olympia		aut./w. Pharnabazus sends Rhodian Timokrates to Greece with funds for anti-Spartans	
			Return of Lysander to Sparta, ? prosecutes Naukleidas (Ephor of 403)	Dorieus of Rhodes in Peloponnese (? as Persian agent)	
395	49	spr./e.s. Agesilaos campaigns against Tissaphernes	spr. Demainetos affair at Athens	Pharnabazus' money doled out in Athens, Argos, Thebes and Corinth	

Agesilaos wins battle near Sardis: Tissaphernes executed at Kolossai, succeeded by Tithraustes

Truce between Agesilaos and Tithraustes (T. perhaps sends money to anti-Spartans in Greece)

l.s./aut. Agesilaos campaigns against Pharnabazus, enters Great Phrygia and Paphlagonia (Spithridates returns to Persian allegiance)

w. Agesilaos at Daskyleion

Konon receives further subvention from Artaxerxes

s. Thebes supports (West?) Lokrians against Phokians (allies of Sparta)

Lysander sent to aid Phokians, secures defection of Orchomenos from Boiotian Confederacy

Democratic revolution in Rhodes

Alliance between Boiotia and Athens

Battle of Haliartos: death of Lysander, deposition and exile of Pausanias (succeeded by under-age son Agesipolis)

Alliance between Boiotia, Athens, Corinth, Argos and others (Lokrians, Euboians, Akarnanians, Chalkidians and most Thessalians): beginning of Corinthian War proper

Spartans expelled from Herakleia Trachinia and Pharsalos

? Athens begins rebuilding Peiraieus walls

s. Agesilaos appoints brother-in-law Peisandros to command of Spartan fleet

Year (Julian Calendar)	Approximate age of Agesilaos	Agesilaos and Family	Greece and Aegean	Persian Empire	West
394	50	*e.spr.* Agesilaos recalled *s.* Agesilaos at Hellespont *Aug.* Battle of Koroneia (preceded by solar eclipse 14 Aug.): Agesilaos enabled to dedicate tithe of booty at Delphi and bring rest to Sparta ? Agesilaos secures estate for Xenophon at Skillous	*s.* Battle of Nemea River Gylis killed in Lokris after Battle of Koroneia: Sparta fails to recover central Greece	*e.spr.* Parley between Agesilaos and Pharnabazus *s.* Battle of Knidos: Pharnabazus and Konon defeat and kill Peisandros; islands and Asiatic Greek cities relieved of harmosts and garrisons Theopompos ends *Hellenika* Athens sends embassy to Artaxerxes ? Akoris succeeds Nepherites I	
393	51		*e.spr.* Pharnabazus and Konon garrison Kythera *s.* Konon returns to Athens: Long Walls and Peiraieus walls rebuilt with Persian money Athens reoccupies Delos (and perhaps now Lemnos, Imbros and Skyros)		*Jan./Feb.* Athens honours Dionysios, two brothers and brother-in-law but fails to win him from Sparta

392

52

l.s. Kyniska wins four-horse chariot-race at Olympia for second time running

Iphikrates commands 'Foreign Legion' in Corinthia (393-89), anti-Spartan alliance gains control of Corinthian Gulf

Amyntas III (newly acceded) driven from Macedonian kingdom by Illyrians: Chalkidians led by Olynthos resist Illyrians, gain control of Pella

March Massacre of pro-Spartans at Corinth: Union of Corinth with Argos begun (and completed?)

Sparta wins Battle of Long Walls of Corinth

Panhellenic Oration of Gorgias at Olympia

? Isokrates founds school of rhetoric at Athens

s. Antalkidas' mission to Tiribazus (successor of Tithraustes) at Sardis

s./aut. Sardis conference: arrest and death of Konon, recall of Tiribazus to Susa, Strouthas appointed to new satrapy of Ionia, Hekatomnôs to new satrapy of Caria

Dionysios makes peace with Carthage

Year (Julian Calendar)	Approximate age of Agesilaos	Agesilaos and Family	Greece and Aegean	Persian Empire	West
391	53	*spr.* Agesilaos ravages Argolid		*l.w./e.spr.* Peace Conference at Sparta (Andokides, *De Pace*) fails	Dionysios active in South Italy, conquers Rhegion, Lokroi, Kroton (391-87)
		s. Agesilaos and half-brother Teleutias (navarch?) co-operate in Corinthian Gulf, capture Lechaion	*s.* Knidos and Samos return to Spartan fold	*e.s.* Sparta renews war against Persia under recalled Thibron	
		July/Aug. Agesilaos ordinary member of chorus at Amyklaian Hyakinthia	*l.s./aut.* Rhodian appeal to Sparta: Ekdikos (navarch) sent	Death of Thibron succeeded by Diphridas	
390	54	*e.s.* Agesilaos celebrates Isthmian Games, captures Oinoe and Peiraion, retreats to Sparta on news of Lechaion disaster	*s.* Iphikrates' peltasts aided by Kallias' hoplites destroy Spartan *mora* near Lechaion; I. retakes Sidous, Krommyon, Peiraion, Oinoe – Corinthia secured but Sparta retains Lechaion	War between Euagoras (now master of Cyprus) and Persia begins	
		Teleutias replaces Ekdikos at Knidos, assures Spartan control of Samos	Expedition of Thrasyboulos begins	? Alliance of Euagoras, Athens and Akoris	
			Spartans harass Attika and Athenian shipping from Aigina		

Iphikrates replaced by Chabrias at Corinth		Iphikrates defeats Anaxibios (successor to Derkylidas) near Abydos (in satrapy of Pharnabazus): twelve harmosts killed, end of Sparta's involvement in Asia	Dionysios wins Battle of Elleporos
Expedition of Thrasyboulos recovers Thasos, Chalkedon, Byzantion (democratic revolution, re-establishment of Bosporos toll), parts of Chersonese (treaty with Thracian kings) and of Lesbos			
	s./aut. Expedition of Agesilaos to Akarnania in support of Achaian allies		
Thrasyboulos killed at Aspendos en route to Rhodes, succeeded by Agyrrhios			
	Teleutias returns to Sparta		
l.s./aut. Oligarchic counter-revolution (391-89) completed at Rhodes with assistance of Hierax (navarch)			

Year (Julian Calendar)	Approximate age of Agesilaos	Agesilaos and Family	Greece and Aegean	Persian Empire	West
388	56	*e.s.* Akarnanians submit under threat of renewed expedition by Agesilaos, join Peloponnesian League	*spr.* Agesipolis consults oracles at Olympia and Delphi, invades Argolid *e.s.* Antalkidas appointed navarch Gorgopas (harmost of Aigina) defeated and killed by Chabrias (en route to Cyprus) replaced by Eteonikos (ex-navarch) and (388/7) Teleutias	Antalkidas' mission to Susa (*via* Aigina and Ephesos): Artaxerxes replaces Pharnabazus with Ariobarzanes, restores Tiribazus Chabrias appointed to aid Euagoras	
387	57	*spr.* Teleutias (navarch) boldly attacks Peiraieus from Aigina, cuts grain-route between Athens and Egypt	*s.* Antalkidas gains control of Hellespont, cuts off Athens' wheat-supply from Black Sea	*spr.* Tiribazus and Ariobarzanes aid Antalkidas *aut./w.* Peace conference at Sardis to work out terms	*spr.* Dionysios sends ships to Antalkidas Plato visits Dionysios

386	58	*spr./s.* Agesilaos presides over Peace Congress in Sparta, compels Argos, Corinth and Thebes to submit to Peace on his terms	Peace of Antalkidas 'Union' of Corinth and Argos dissolved, Boiotian Confederacy dissolved, Athens retains Lemnos, Imbros and Skyros only	King's Peace sworn Artaxerxes receives all Asia including Greek cities, *plus* Euagoras' Cyprus and Athens' ally Klazomenai	Further Italian ventures of Dionysios (386-3) ? Sack of Rome by Gauls
385	59	*spr./le.s.* Agesilaos declines command against Mantineia	Agesipolis desynoecizes Mantineia ? Spartan intervention in Thasos	Euagoras, despite aid from Akoris and Hekatomnôs, loses great sea-fight Artaxerxes sends Tithraustes, Orontes and Pharnabazus against Egypt (385-0) Tyre and Cilician cities revolt from Artaxerxes	
384	60		Phleiasian exiles appeal to Sparta: Ephors request their restoration *s.* Athens allies with Chios *l.s.* Lysias delivers *Olympiakos* warning Greeks assembled at Olympia of danger from Persia and Sicily		Dionysios sends splendid legation to Olympic Games

Year (Julian Calendar)	Approximate age of Agesilaos	Agesilaos and Family	Greece and Aegean	Persian Empire	West
383	61		Negotiations between Athens, Thebes and Olynthos *aut./w.* Appeals to Sparta from Amyntas of Macedon and from Akanthos and Apollonia: Peloponnesian League decides to campaign against Olynthos and Chalkidian Confederacy	? Revolt of Tyre	Second Carthaginian War of Dionysios (383-78) begins
382	62	Phoibidas and brother Eudamidas appointed to command first forces against Olynthos, succeeded by Teleutias Phoibidas seizes Kadmeia Agesilaos defends action of Phoibidas at trial	Change in terms of Peloponnesian League Trial and execution of Hismenias; ? refoundation of Plataia (or 386)	Tiribazus unsuccessful against Euagoras	
381	63	*s.* Death of Teleutias at Olynthos *l.s./aut.* Agesilaos appointed to command against Phleious, siege begins	*s.* Agesipolis succeeds Teleutias at Olynthos	Euagoras finally defeated at sea off Kition	

380	64	Agesilaos continues siege of Phleious throughout year	s. Death of Agesipolis at Olynthos, succeeded by Polybiadas as commander, by brother Kleombrotos as king	Truce negotiated by Orontes between Euagoras and Artaxerxes; Euagoras retained as vassal ruler of Cyprus
			l.s. Panegyrikos of Isokrates urges Athens and Sparta to campaign jointly against Persia	Nektanebis I founds Dynasty XXX (following death of Akoris and brief rule of Nepherites II)
				Successes and failures of Dionysios against Carthage in Sicily
379	65	c.spr. Agesilaos reduces Phleious after twenty months, imposes oligarchy	s. Fall of Olynthos: Chalkidians incorporated individually in Peloponnesian League	Datames appointed to command against Egypt but diverted and removed, flees to Cappadocia, bases himself on Sinope
			Amyntas recovers kingdom	
			w. Liberation of Thebes by Pelopidas and other exiles	

Year (Julian Calendar)	Approximate age of Agesilaos	Agesilaos and Family	Greece and Aegean	Persian Empire	West
378	66	*Jan./Feb.* Agesilaos declines command against liberated Thebes	Kleombrotos fails to recapture Thebes	Iphikrates sent by Athens to serve with Persian forces under Pharnabazus against Egypt (until 375 or 374)	Peace between Syracuse and Carthage
			Thebes becomes democracy, refounds Boiotian Confederacy on democratic lines		
		spr. Sphodrias acquitted through Agesilaos (mediation of Archidamos, lover of Sphodrias' son)	*Feb./March.* Sphodrias (harmost of Thespiai) fails in raid on Peiraieus		
			Athens allies with Thebes, founds Second Athenian League (by midsummer)		
		s./aut. Agesilaos fails to recapture Thebes but ravages Theban land			
377	67	*spr./s.* Agesilaos leads second Peloponnesian League expedition against Thebes	*Feb./March* Decree of Aristoteles advertises Second Athenian League	Maussollos succeeds father Hekatomnôs as satrap of Caria	
		Agesilaos sustains serious leg injury at Megara (out of action until 370)	Euboians (except Histiaia/Oreos – under a Spartan harmost still) join Second Athenian League		

376	68	s. Expedition of Kleombrotos against Thebes abortive: Peloponnesian League transfers attention to Athens by sea	*Periplous* of Timotheos round Peloponnese, secures Kephallenia and Kerkyra for Athenian alliance
		Thebes seeks to recover remaining Boiotian cities from Spartan control	Battle of Alyzeia (Akarnania): Timotheos defeats Spartan fleet
		Sept. Battle of Naxos: Chabrias smashes Peloponnesian fleet	
375	69	Chabrias secures most of Chalkidike and Thrace for Athenian alliance	
		Battle of Tegyra: Pelopidas defeats Sparta's Orchomenos garrison	
		Thebes by now has recovered all Boiotia except Orchomenos, Thespiai and Plataia	
		Boiotians invade Phokis: Kleombrotos aids Phokians	

Year (Julian Calendar)	Approximate age of Agesilaos	Agesilaos and Family	Greece and Aegean	Persian Empire	West
			Sparta declines to aid Polydamas of Pharsalos: Jason of Pherai becomes *tagos* of all Thessaly Athenians commission 'Peace and Wealth' statue-group from Kephisodotos, dedicate statues of Konon and Timotheos on Akropolis, admit many new members to Second League	*aut.* Congress at Sparta: first renewal of King's Peace	
374	70			Death of Euagoras (Isokrates composes *Euagoras*), succeeded by son Nikokles	Dionysios promises aid to Sparta against Kerkyra Timotheos restores Zakynthian exiles, war with Sparta flares again (fleets under Aristokrates to Zakynthos, under Alkidas to Kerkyra)

Date			
373 71	Expedition of Timotheos to Thessaly, Macedon and Thrace Timotheos replaced by Chabrias, Kallistratos and Iphikrates ? Athens snatches back Oropos *l.s.* Thebes destroys Plataia (Isokrates' *Plataikos*) and fortifications of Thespiai *w.* Trial of Timotheos (Kallistratos appears for prosecution, Jason and Alketas of Epeiros for defence) Earthquakes in central Greece, Apollo temple at Delphi destroyed	*spr./s.* Persian attack on Egypt repulsed	Expedition of Mnasippos to Kerkyra Iphikrates intercepts small squadron sent by Dionysios to help Sparta against Kerkyra Failure and death of Mnasippos
372 72	*s.* A Theban presides over Congress of Second Athenian League Iphikrates threatens Messenia	Datames begins Satraps' Revolt Timotheos commands Greek mercenaries in Persian service in Egypt Antalkidas envoy to Artaxerxes to treat for renewal of Peace	

Year (Julian Calendar)	Approximate age of Agesilaos	Agesilaos and Family	Greece and Aegean	Persian Empire	West
371	73	*June.* Agesilaos presides over Peace conference at Sparta, contretemps with Epameinondas	*spr.* Boiotians threaten Phokis Kleombrotos despatched to aid Phokians		
			June. Spartans recall harmosts. Athenians recall Iphikrates, Boiotians excluded from Peace	*June.* Second renewal of King's Peace ('Peace of Kallias')	
			July. Battle of Leuktra: defeat and death of Kleombrotos (with Sphodrias and son), succeeded by Agesipolis II		
		Archidamos with allied support leads back defeated Spartan army	Jason, ally of Boiotians and *proxenos* of Spartans at Pherai, mediates at Leuktra but destroys fortifications of Herakleia Trachinia		
			aut. Peace conference at Athens: Elis excluded, recovers lower Alpheios valley	*aut.* Third renewal of King's Peace (perhaps following Athenian embassy to Susa)	
			Sparta fired by Delphic amphiktyony for seizing Kadmeia		

Civil disturbances at Argos, Tegea, Phleious, Phigaleia, Corinth, Sikyon

Re-synoecism of Mantineia: walls rebuilt (with Eleian help)

spr./s. Agesilaos fails to prevent re-synoecism of Mantineia

Democratic, anti-Spartan revolution at Tegea prelude to formation of Arkadian Confederacy (minus Orchomenos and Heraia): Sparta unable to prevent

s. Assassination of Jason

Thebes recovers Orchomenos, dispossesses Thespians

w. Agesilaos campaigns in Arkadia, takes defenceless Eutaia but precipitates ...

Appeal of Arkadians, Eleians and Argives to Athens (rejected) and Boiotians (accepted): Theban alliance (Boiotia, Phokis, Euboia, Lokris, Akarnania, Herakleia, Malis) invades Peloponnese and Lakonia Defection of N. Lakonian Perioikoi; liberation of Messenian Helots, foundation of New Messene

Defence of Sparta by Agesilaos, enlistment of Helots, suppression of conspiracies

Year (Julian Calendar)	Approximate age of Agesilaos	Agesilaos and Family	Greece and Aegean	Persian Empire	West
369	75		*spr.* Iphikrates blocks Isthmus but fails to prevent return of Epameinondas (late: trial and acquittal of E.)	Ariobarzanes meditates revolt, sends Philiskos of Abydos to convene Peace conference	Dionysios sends over twenty triremes and 2000 Gaulish and Iberian mercenaries for Sparta
			Alexander succeeds at Pherai		
			First expedition of Pelopidas to Thessaly: reorganization of Thessalian confederacy, Pelopidas intervenes in Macedon, alliance between Thebes and Alexander II (successor of Amyntas)		
			July. Second Theban invasion of Peloponnese under Epameinondas: Pellene and Sikyon detached from Sparta, foundation of Megalopolis begun		
			? Euphron seizes tyranny at Sikyon		

368	76	*spr.* Alliance between Athens and Alexander of Pherai	*s.* Archidamos with mercenaries from Dionysios destroys Karyai, ravages Parrhasia, wins 'Tearless Battle'	*spr./s.* Peace conference fails, Ariobarzanes promises mercenaries for Sparta	? Third Carthaginian War of Dionysios begins
		Iphikrates appointed to recover Amphipolis (368-5)			*June.* Dionysios receives Athenian citizenship
		Pelopidas captured by Alexander of Pherai			*s.* Arrival of second force from Dionysios for Sparta
		Foundation of Megalopolis largely completed			
367	77	*spr./e.s.* Epameinondas rescues Pelopidas from Thessalian captivity		*s.* Susa conference involving principal Greek states: Artaxerxes abandons Sparta for Pelopidas and Thebes (Messene and Amphipolis to be autonomous, Athens to lay up ships, Elis to receive Triphylia)	Dionysios allies with Athens, wins tragic prize at Lenaia, dies, succeeded by Dionysios II
		Pammenes in Arkadia			Peace between Syracuse and Carthage
					Plato fails to turn Dionysios II into a 'philosopher-king'
		w./spr. Congress at Thebes fails, Lykomedes leads Arkadian resistance		? Revolt of Ariobarzanes	

Year (Julian Calendar)	Approximate age of Agesilaos	Agesilaos and Family	Greece and Aegean	Persian Empire	West
366	78	spr./s Sparta refuses to make peace on condition of granting autonomy to Messene, dramatic date of Isokrates' *Archidamos* c. Aug. Agesilaos sails with Timotheos to Hellespont to help Ariobarzanes	spr. Murder of Euphron Third invasion of Peloponnese by Epameinondas, Achaia won for Theban alliance Themison of Eretria seizes Oropos from Athens, hands over to Thebes aut. Athens allies with Arkadians, death of Lykomedes aut. (or spr. 365). Corinth rejects Athenian garrison, seeks peace with Thebes Tyranny of Timophanes at Corinth	spr. Artaxerxes fails to frighten Greeks into swearing to Peace c. Aug. Timotheos sails to help revolt of Ariobarzanes ? Revolt in Phoenicia and Cilicia	
365	79	Agesilaos relieves Assos (Ariobarzanes under siege from Autophradates satrap of Lydia)	spr. End of Peloponnesian League: Corinth and other Spartan allies (incl. Phleious and Epidauros) make separate peace with Thebes	spr. Common Peace (or peace based generally on rescript of 367) Artaxerxes perhaps recognizes Athens' title to Amphipolis	spr. Dionysios II sends mercenaries for Sparta, help recapture Sellasia

364	80	spr. Archidamos takes Kromnos (in S.W. Arkadia), threatens Megalopolis, defeated by Arkadians and allies (incl. Thebes, Argos and Messene, but not Athens); Chilon (son-in-law of Agesilaos) killed	Outbreak of war between Elis (back in Spartan camp) and Arkadians ? Beginning of split within Arkadian Confederacy Timotheos replaces Iphikrates as general for Amphipolis	Athenian citizenship for Ariobarzanes and Philiskos c. July. Timotheos captures Samos after ten-month siege, expels Persian garrison, plants cleruchy Timotheos receives Sestos and Krithote from Ariobarzanes, lays claim to much of Thracian Chersonese
			spr./s. Epameinondas' naval expedition: Byzantion defects to Thebes from Athens (as do Naxos and Keos) 13 July. Solar eclipse July Battle of Kynoskephalai: death of Pelopidas Thebes destroys Orchomenos (and perhaps Koroneia) Pisatans celebrate Olympics: fighting in Altis between Eleians and Arkadians, Argives and Athenians		Satraps' revolt continues

Year (Julian Calendar)	Approximate age of Agesilaos	Agesilaos and Family	Greece and Aegean	Persian Empire	West
363	81		*spr./s.* Arkadians split: Tegea and Megalopolis stay Theban (as do Argos and Messene), Mantineia now supported by Sparta, Athens and Elis	Tachôs (co-regent since 365) succeeds Nektanebis I Satraps' revolt continues	
			Delphi cor.fers *promanteia* on Thebes		
			Timotheos recovers Byzantion		
			w. Timotheos still in command of war for Amphipolis		

362

spr. Elis and Arkadians
conclude truce

Beginning of 'Great Satrap
Revolt' under Orontes

e.s. Theban alliance
(Boiotia, Euboia, many
Thessalians, Lokris, Malis,
Ainianes but not Phokis)
invades Peloponnese

Athens recovers Keos

c. June. Battle of Mantineia:
Epameinondas defeats
Athens, Sparta, Mantineia
et al. but is killed, Common
Peace sworn on battlefield
(except Sparta), end of
Xenophon's *Hellenika*

Greeks refuse to aid
revolted satraps

Agesilaos and Archidamos
defend Sparta against
Epameinondas immediately
before Battle of Mantineia

Alliance of Athens, Achaia,
Phleious and Mantineia

Ariobarzanes crucified

Year (Julian Calendar)	Approximate age of Agesilaos	Agesilaos and Family	Greece and Aegean	Persian Empire	West
361	83		*s.* Pammenes prevents dismemberment of Megalopolis Athens plants cleruchy at Poteidaia, regains most of Chersonese	Tachôs summons Agesilaos and Chabrias	
360	84	*spr.* Agesilaos sails for Egypt with 30 Spartiate 'advisers' and 1000 hoplites, put in command of mercenaries by Tachôs *s.* Agesilaos deserts Tachôs (who flees to Artaxerxes) for Nektanebis II *w.* Agesilaos dies in Libya, succeeded by Archidamos (III)	*s.* Timotheos again fails to recapture Amphipolis Kephisodotos deposed while besieging Alopekonnesos	Artaxerxes re-establishes authority in Asia Minor: death of Datames	

Bibliography

This bibliography is consciously selective, aiming primarily to list all those works referred to by author and date in the text above. It is also somewhat biased towards recent works in English, especially those which provide full reference to the ancient and modern literature. Abbreviations follow the conventions of the 'Index des périodiques dépouillés' printed in the relevant volume of *L'année philologique*.

ABRAMS, P. (1982), *Historical Sociology*, West Compton House, Near Shepton Mallet (U.K.)

ACCAME, S. (1946), *L'imperialismo ateniense all' inizio del secolo IV a.c. e la crisi della polis*, 2nd edn, Naples

ACCAME, S. (1951), *Ricerche intorno alla guerra corinzia*, Naples

ACCAME, S. (1978a), 'Cratippo', in *Sesta miscellanea greca e romana*, Rome, 185-212

ACCAME, S. (1978b), 'Ricerche sulle Elleniche di Ossirinco', in ibid. 125-83

ADAMS, W.L. and E.N. BORZA (1982), eds, *Philip II, Alexander the Great and the Macedonian Heritage*, Washington, D.C.

ADCOCK, F.E. (1924), 'Some aspects of ancient Greek diplomacy', *PCA* 21, 92-116

ADCOCK, F.E. (1948), 'The development of ancient Greek diplomacy', *AC* 17, 1-12

ADCOCK, F.E. (1953), 'Greek and Macedonian kingship', *PBA* 39, 163-80

ADCOCK, F.E. and D.J. MOSLEY (1975), *Diplomacy in Ancient Greece*, London & New York

ADKINS, A.W.H. (1963), ' "Friendship" and "self-sufficiency" in Homer and Aristotle', *CQ* n.s. 13, 30-45

AFRICA, T.W. (1960), 'Phylarchus, Toynbee and the Spartan myth', *JHI* 21, 266-72

AFRICA, T.W. (1961), *Phylarchus and the Spartan Revolution*, Berkeley

AFRICA, T.W. (1979), 'Thomas More and the Spartan mirage', *Historical Reflections/- Réflexions historiques* 6, 343-52

AFRICA, T.W. (1982a), 'Homosexuals in Greek history', *Journal of Psychohistory* 9.4, 401-20

AFRICA, T.W. (1982b), 'Worms and the death of kings: a cautionary note on disease and history', *ClAnt* 1, 1-17

ALEXIOU, M. (1974), *The Ritual Lament in Greek Tradition*, Cambridge

ALFIERI TONINI, T. (1975), 'Il problema dei "neodamodeis" nell' ambito della società spartana', *RIL* 109, 305-16

ALMAGOR, U. (1978), *Pastoral Partners. Affinity and bond partnership among the Dassanetch of South-West Ethiopia*, Manchester. See also BAXTER, P.T.W.

AMIT, M. (1965), *Athens and the Sea. A study in Athenian sea-power*, Brussels

AMIT, M. (1973), *Great and Small Poleis. A study in the relations between the great powers and the small cities in ancient Greece*, Brussels

AMIT, M. (1974), 'A peace treaty between Sparta and Persia', *RSA* 4, 55-63

AMPOLO, C. (1980), 'Le condizioni materiali della produzione. Agricoltura e paessagio agrario', *DArch* 1, 16-46

ANDERSON, J.K. (1954), 'A topographical and historical study of Achaea', *ABSA* 49, 72-92

ANDERSON, J.K. (1961), *Ancient Greek Horsemanship*, Berkeley

ANDERSON, J.K. (1970), *Military Theory and Practice in the Age of Xenophon*, Berkeley

ANDERSON, J.K. (1974a), 'The battle of Sardis in 395 B.C.', *CSCA* 7, 27-53

ANDERSON, J.K. (1974b), *Xenophon*, London

ANDREADES, A.M. (1915), 'Hê dêmosia oikonomia tôn Spartiatôn', *Epetêris Parnassou*, 101-64, repr. in his *Erga* I (Athens, 1938) 179-224

ANDREADES, A.M. (1931), 'La mort de Sparte et ses causes démographiques', *Metron* 9, 99-105, repr, in op. cit. 225-30

ANDREADES, A.M. (1933), *A History of Greek Public Finance*, Cambridge, Mass.

ANDREWES, A. (1938), 'Eunomia', *CQ* 32, 89-102

ANDREWES, A. (1952), 'Sparta and Arcadia in the early fifth century', *Phoenix* 6, 1-5

ANDREWES, A. (1954), *Probouleusis. Sparta's contribution to the technique of government*, Oxford (inaugural lecture)

ANDREWES, A. (1961), 'Thucydides and the Persians', *Historia* 10, 1-18

ANDREWES, A. (1966), 'The government of Classical Sparta', in E. Badian (ed.), *Ancient Society and Institutions. Studies presented to Victor Ehrenberg on his 75th birthday*, Oxford, 1-20

ANDREWES, A. (1971), 'Two notes on Lysander', *Phoenix* 25, 206-26

ANDREWES, A. (1978), 'Spartan imperialism?', in Garnsey/Whittaker 1978, 91-102 with 302-6

ANDREWES, A. (1982), 'Notion and Kyzikos: the sources compared', *JHS* 102, 15-25. See also GOMME, A.W. and HILL, G.F.

ANDRONIKOS, M. (1956), 'Lakônika anaglypha', *Peloponnêsiaka* 1, 253-314

ARDEN, John (1982), *Silence Among the Weapons*, London

ARNHEIM, M.T.W. (1977), *Aristocracy in Greek Society*, London & New York

ASHERI, D. (1961), 'Sulla legge di Epitadeo', *Athenaeum* n.s. 49, 45-68

ASHERI, D. (1963), 'Laws of inheritance, distribution of land and political constitutions in ancient Greece', *Historia* 12, 1-21

ATHANASSIADI-FOWDEN, P. (1981), *Julian and Hellenism. An intellectual biography*, Oxford

AYMARD, A. (1967), *Études d'histoire ancienne*, Paris

BADIAN, E. (1966), 'Alexander the Great and the Greeks of Asia', in Badian (ed.), *Ancient Society and Institutions. Studies presented to Victor Ehrenberg on his 75th birthday*, Oxford, 37-69

BADIAN, E. (1976), 'Lucius Sulla: the deadly reformer', in Dunston 1976, 35-74 (originally Sydney, 1970)

BADIAN, E. (1981), 'The deification of Alexander the Great', in *Ancient Macedonian Studies in honor of Charles F. Edson*, Thessaloniki, 27-71

BALOGH, E. (1943), *Political Refugees in Ancient Greece. From the period of the tyrants to Alexander the Great* (with F.M. Heichelheim), Johannesburg

BALSDON, J.P.V.D. (1950), 'The "divinity" of Alexander', *Historia* 1, 363-88

BARBER, G.L. (1935), *The Historian Ephorus*, Cambridge

BARBU, N.I. (1934), *Les procédés de la peinture des caractères et la vérité historique dans les biographies de Plutarque*, Strasbourg

BARNES, J. (1982), *Aristotle*, Oxford & New York ('Past Masters' series)

BARTH, F. (1965), *Political Leadership among Swat Pathans*, London

BARTOLETTI, V. (1959), ed., *Hellenika Oxyrhynchia* (Teubner), Leipzig

BAUER, A. (1890), 'Der zweimalige Angriff des Epameinondas auf Sparta', *HZ* 65, 240-74

BAXTER P.T.W. and U. ALMAGOR (1978), eds, *Age, Generation and Time. Some features of East African age organizations*, London

BAYNES, N.H. (1955), *Byzantine Studies and Other Essays*, London

BEAN, G.E. (1979), *Aegean Turkey*, 2nd edn, London & Tonbridge

BEISTER, H. (1970), 'Untersuchungen zu der Zeit der thebanischen Hegemonie', diss. Munich

BELOCH, K.J. (1886), *Die Bevölkerung der griechisch-römischen Welt*, Leipzig

BELOCH, K.J. (1905-6), 'Griechische Aufgeböte I-II', *Klio* 5,341-74; 6, 34-78

BELOCH, K.J. (1924), *Griechische Geschichte* I.1, 2nd edn, Berlin & Leipzig

BENDIX, R. and S.M. LIPSET (1966/7), eds, *Class, Status and Power. Social stratification in comparative perspective*, 2nd edn, New York (1966) & London (1967)

BENGTSON, H. (1962), 'Die griechische Polis bei Aeneas Tacticus', *Historia* 11, 458-68

BENGTSON, H. (1969), *The Greeks and the Persians from the sixth to the fourth centuries* (with E. Bresciani, W. Caskell, M. Meuleau and M. Smith), London

BENGTSON, H. (1975), ed., *Die Staatsverträge des Altertums* II. *Die Verträge der griechisch-römischen Welt von 700 bis 338 v. Chr.*, 2nd edn, Munich

BENGTSON, H. (1977), *Griechische Geschichte, von den Anfängen bis in die römische Kaiserzeit*, 5th edn, Munich

BERLIN, I. (1978), *Concepts and Categories. Philosophical Essays*, ed. H. Hardy, Oxford

BERLIN, I. (1979), *Against the Current. Essays in the history of Ideas*, ed. H. Hardy, Oxford

BERNERI, M.L. (1950), *Journey through Utopia*, London

BERTHIAUME, G. (1976), 'Citoyens spécialistes à Sparte', *Mnemosyne* 29, 360-4

BERVE, H. (1937), *Sparta*, Leipzig (repr. in Berve 1966, 58-207)

BERVE, H. (1966), *Gestaltende Kräfte der Antike. Aufsätze und Vorträge zur griechischen und römischen Geschichte*, 2nd edn, Munich

BEST, J.G.P. (1969), *Thracian Peltasts and their Influence on Greek Warfare*, Groningen

BETHE, E. (1907), 'Die dorische Knabenliebe – ihre Ethik und ihre Ideale', *RhM* 62, 438-75

BICKERMAN, E.J. (1958), 'AUTONOMIA. Sur un passage de Thucydide (I,144,2)', *RIDA* 5, 313-44

BICKERMAN, E.J. (1980), *Chronology of the Ancient World*, 2nd edn, London & New York

BIELEFELD, E. (1964), 'Gott, Heros oder Feldherr?', *Gymnasium* 71, 519-34

BLISS, C.J. and N.H. STERN (1982), *Palanpur: the economy of an Indian village*, Oxford

BLOCH, H. (1940), 'Studies in the historical literature of the fourth century B.C.', *HSPh* Supp. I, 303-76

BLOCH, Marc (1954), *The Historian's Craft*, Manchester (repr. 1976)

BLOCH, Maurice (1981), 'Tombs and states', in Humphreys/King 1981, 137-47

BLOCH, Maurice and J. PARRY (1982), eds, *Death and the Regeneration of Life*, Cambridge

BLOEDOW, E.F. (1981), 'The speeches of Archidamus and Sthenelaidas at Sparta', *Historia* 30, 129-43

BLUM, R. and E. BLUM (1970), *The Dangerous Hour. The lore and culture of crisis and mystery in rural Greece*, London & Toronto

BOARDMAN, J. (1980), *The Greeks Overseas. Their early colonies and trade*, London & New York

BOCKISCH, G. (1965), '*Harmostai* (431-387)', *Klio* n.f. 46, 129-239

BOCKISCH, G. (1967), 'Die Harmostie Herakleia Trachis (Ein Kolonisationsversuch der Lakedaimonier vom Jahre 426)', *AAntHung* 15, 311-17

BOCKISCH, G. (1968), 'Die Politik der Lakedaimonier in Ionien von 412-405', *Helikon* 8, 139-60

BOCKISCH, G. (1974), 'Die sozial-ökonomische und politische Krise der Lakedaimonier und ihrer Symmachoi im 4. Jahrhundert v. u. Z.', in Welskopf 1974, I, 199-230

BOISSEVAIN, J. (1974), *Friends of Friends. Networks, manipulations and coalitions*, Oxford

BOLGAR, R.R. (1969), 'The training of élites in Greek education', in R. Wilkinson (ed.), *Governing Elites. Studies in training and selection*, New York, 23-49

BOMMELAER, J.-F. (1981), *Lysandre de Sparte. Histoire et traditions*, Paris

BONAMENTE, G. (1973), *Studio sulle Elleniche di Ossirinco. Saggio sulla storiografia della prima metà del IV sec. a. C.*, Perugia

BONNER, R.J. and G. SMITH (1942), 'Administration of justice in Sparta', *CPh* 37, 113-29

BORDES, J. (1982), *Politeia dans la pensée grecque jusqu'à Aristote*, Paris

BORING, T.A. (1979), *Literacy in Ancient Sparta*, Leiden

BÖRKER, G. (1980), 'König Agesilaos von Sparta und der Artemis-Tempel in Ephesos', *ZPE* 37, 69-75

BORZA, E.N.: see ADAMS, W.L.

BOUCHER, A. (1912), 'La tactique grecque à l'origine de l'histoire militaire', *REG* 25, 300-17

BOURDIEU, P. (1970), *Outline of a Theory of Practice*, Cambridge

BOURGUET, E. (1927), *Le dialecte laconien*, Paris

BRAUDEL, F. (1981-82-84), *Civilization and Capitalism 15th-18th Century*, 3 vols, London & New York

BREITENBACH, H.R. (1967), 'Xenophon', *RE* IXA, 1569-2052

BREITENBACH, H.R. (1970), 'Hellenika Oxyrhynchia', *RE* Supp. XII, 383-426

BRELICH, A. (1969), *Paides e Parthenoi* I, Rome

BRESCIANI, E.: see BENGTSON, H.

BRIANT, P. (1980), 'Forces productives, dépendance rurale et idéologie religieuse dans l'empire Achéménide', in *Religions, pouvoir, rapports sociaux = Annales littéraires de l'Université de Besançon* 237, 17-68

BRIANT, P. (1982), *Rois, tributs et paysans. Études sur les formations tributaires du Moyen-Orient ancien*, Besançon & Paris

BRINGMANN, K. (1971), 'Xenophons Hellenika und Agesilaos. Zu ihrer Entstehungsweise und Datierung', *Gymnasium* 78, 224-41

BRINGMANN, K. (1975), 'Die grosse Rhetra und die Entstehung des spartanischen Kosmos', *Historia* 24, 513-38

BRINGMANN, K. (1980), 'Die soziale und politische Verfassung Spartas – ein Sonderfall der griechischen Verfassungsgeschichte?', *Gymnasium* 87, 465-84

BROWN, E.A.R. (1980), 'The ceremonial of royal succession in Capetian France: the funeral of Philip V', *Speculum* 55, 266-93

BROWN, T.S. (1949), 'Callisthenes and Alexander', *AJPh* 70, 225-48

BROWN, T.S. (1973), *The Greek Historians*, Lexington, Mass., Toronto & London

BROWN, T.S. (1978), 'Suggestions for a Vita of Ctesias of Cnidus', *Historia* 27, 1-19

BRUCE, I.A.F. (1967), *An Historical Commentary on the Hellenica Oxyrhynchia*, Cambridge

BRUNS, I. (1896), *Das literarische Porträt der Griechen in fünften und vierten Jht. v. Christi Geburt*, Berlin

BRUNT, P.A. (1965), 'Spartan policy and strategy in the Archidamian War', *Phoenix* 19, 255-80

BRUNT, P.A. (1966), 'Athenian settlements abroad in the fifth century B.C.', in E. Badian (ed.), *Ancient Society and Institutions. Studies presented to Victor Ehrenberg on his 75th birthday*, Oxford, 71-92

BRUNT, P.A. (1979), *JRS* 69, 168-75 (review of Fears 1977)

BRUNT, P.A. (1980), 'On historical Fragments and Epitomes', *CQ* n.s. 30, 477-94

BUCK, R.J. (1970), 'The Athenian domination of Boeotia', *CPh* 65, 217-27

BUCK, R.J. (1979), *A History of Boeotia*, Edmonton

BUCKLER, J. (1971), 'Dating the Peace of 375/4', *GRBS* 12, 353-61

BUCKLER, J. (1972), 'A second look at the monument of Chabrias', *Hesperia* 41, 466-74

BUCKLER, J. (1977a), 'Land and money in the Spartan economy – a hypothesis', *Research in Economic History* 2, 249-79

BUCKLER, J. (1977b), 'Plutarch and the fate of Antalkidas', *GRBS* 18, 139-45

BUCKLER, J. (1978a), 'The alleged Achaian arbitration after Leuktra', *SO* 53, 85-96
BUCKLER, J. (1978b), 'Plutarch on the trials of Pelopidas and Epameinondas (369 B.C.)', *CPh* 73, 36-42
BUCKLER, J. (1979), 'The re-establishment of the *Boiotarchia* (378 B.C.)', *AJAH* 4, 50-64
BUCKLER, J. (1980a), 'The alleged Theban-Spartan alliance of 386 B.C.', *Eranos* 78, 179-85
BUCKLER, J. (1980b), 'Plutarch on Leuktra', *SO* 55, 75-93
BUCKLER, J. (1980c), *The Theban Hegemony, 371-362 B.C.*, Cambridge, Mass., & London
BUCKLER, J. (1982a), 'Alliance and hegemony in fourth-century Greece: the case of the Theban Hegemony', *AncW* 5, 79-89
BUCKLER, J. (1982b), 'Xenophon's speeches and the Theban Hegemony', *Athenaeum* n.s. 60, 180-204
BUFFIÈRE, F. (1980), *Eros adolescent. La pédérastie dans la Grèce antique*, Paris
BULLOCK, A. (1979), 'Is history becoming a social science?', *History Today*, 760-7
BURKERT, W. (1965), 'Demaratos, Astrabakos und Herakles. Königsmythos und Politik zur Zeit der Perserkriege (Herodot VI, 67-69)', *MH* 22, 166-77
BURKERT, W. (1975), 'Apellai und Apollon', *RhM* 118, 1-21
BURN, A.R. (1960), *The Lyric Age of Greece*, London (repr. with bibliographical addendum 1978)
BURNETT, A.P. (1962), 'Thebes and the expansion of the Second Athenian Confederacy: *IG* II² 40 and *IG* II² 43', *Historia* 11, 1-17
BURTON, G.P.: see HOPKINS, K.
BURY, J.B. (1898), 'The double city of Megalopolis', *JHS* 18, 15-22
BURY, J.B. (1909), *The Ancient Greek Historians*, London
BURY, J.B. and R. MEIGGS (1975), *A History of Greece*, London
BUSOLT, G. (1905), 'Spartas Heer und Leuktra', *Hermes* 40, 387-449
BUSOLT, G. and H. SWOBODA (1926), *Griechische Staatskunde* II: *Darstellung einzelner Staaten und der zwischenstaatlichen Beziehungen*, 3rd edn. Munich, 633-737
BUTLER, D. (1962), 'Competence of the demos in the Spartan Rhetra', *Historia* 11, 385-96
BUTTMANN, A. (1872), *Agesilaus sohn des Archidamus. Lebensbild*, Halle
CAMPBELL, J.K. (1974), *Honour, Family and Patronage. A study of institutions and moral values in a Greek mountain community*, Oxford
CARGILL, J. (1981), *The Second Athenian League. Empire or Free Alliance?*, Berkeley, Los Angeles & London
CARGILL, J. (1982), 'Hegemony not empire: the Second Athenian League', *AncW* 5, 91-102
CARLIER, P. (1977), 'La vie politique à Sparte sous le règne de Cléomène Iᵉʳ: essai d'interprétation', *Ktema* 2, 65-84
CARLIER, P. (1978), 'L'idée de monarchie impériale dans la *Cyropédie* de Xénophon', *Ktema* 3, 133-63
CARLYLE, Thomas (1841), *On Heroes, Hero-Worship and The Heroic in History*, London
CARPENTER, E. (1919), *Intermediate Types among Primitive Folk. A study in social evolution*, 2nd edn, London
CARR, E.H. (1964), *What is History?*, Harmondsworth (originally London 1960)
CARTLEDGE, P.A. (1975), 'Toward the Spartan revolution', *Arethusa* 8, 59-84
CARTLEDGE, P.A. (1976a), 'A new 5th-century Spartan treaty', *LCM* 1, 87-92
CARTLEDGE, P.A. (1976b), 'Did Spartan citizens ever practise a manual *technē*?', *LCM* 1, 115-19
CARTLEDGE, P.A. (1976c), 'Seismicity and Spartan society', *LCM* 1, 25-8
CARTLEDGE, P.A. (1977), 'Hoplites and heroes: Sparta's contribution to the technique of ancient warfare', *JHS* 97, 11-27 (revised German trans. forthcoming in a 'Wege der Forschung' vol. on Sparta ed. K. Christ)

CARTLEDGE, P.A. (1978a), 'Literacy in the Spartan oligarchy', *JHS* 98, 25-37
CARTLEDGE, P.A. (1978b), 'The new 5th-century Spartan treaty again', *LCM* 3, 189-90
CARTLEDGE, P.A. (1979), *Sparta and Lakonia. A regional history c.1300-362 BC*, London & Boston
CARTLEDGE, P.A. (1980a), 'Euphron and the *douloi* again', *LCM* 5, 209-11
CARTLEDGE, P.A. (1980b), 'The peculiar position of Sparta in the development of the Greek city-state', *PRIA* 80C, 91-108
CARTLEDGE, P.A. (1981a), 'The politics of Spartan pederasty', *PCPhS* n.s. 30, 17-36
CARTLEDGE, P.A. (1981b), 'Spartan wives: liberation or licence?', *CQ* n.s. 31, 84-105
CARTLEDGE, P.A. (1982), 'Sparta and Samos: a special relationship?', *CQ* n.s. 32, 243-65
CARTLEDGE, P.A. (1983), 'Archaeology in Greece', in T. Winnifrith and P. Murray (eds), *Greece Old and New*, London & Basingstoke, 129-52
CARY, M. (1922), 'Notes on the *aristeia* of Thebes', *JHS* 42, 184-91
CARY, M. (1926), 'Notes on the history of the fourth century', *CQ* 20, 186-91
CARY, M. (1927), 'The ascendancy of Sparta', in The *Cambridge Ancient History* VI¹, 25-54
CASKELL, W.: see BENGTSON, H.
CATLING, H.W. (1976), 'New excavations at the Menelaion, Sparta', in *Neue Forschungen in griechischen Heiligtümern*, Tübingen, 77-90
CATLING, H.W. (1977), 'Excavations at the Menelaion, Sparta, 1973-76', *AR*, 24-42
CATLING, H.W. and H. CAVANAGH (1976), 'Two inscribed bronzes from the Menelaion, Sparta', *Kadmos* 15, 145-57
CAVAIGNAC, E. (1912), 'La population du Péloponnèse aux Vᵉ et IVᵉ siècles', *Klio* 12, 261-80
CAVAIGNAC, E. (1924), 'Les Dékarchies de Lysandre', *Revue des Etudes Historiques* 90, 285-316
CAVANAGH, H.: see CATLING, H.W.
CAWKWELL, G.L. (1961), 'The Common Peace of 366/5 B.C.', *CQ* n.s. 11, 80-6
CAWKWELL, G.L. (1963), 'Notes on the Peace of 375/4', *Historia* 12, 84-95
CAWKWELL, G.L. (1968), 'The power of Persia', *Arepo* 1, 1 5
CAWKWELL, G.L. (1972a), 'Epaminondas and Thebes', *CQ* n.s. 22, 254-78
CAWKWELL, G.L. (1972b), ed., *Xenophon. The Persian Expedition*, trans. R. Warner, Harmondsworth
CAWKWELL, G.L. (1973), 'The foundation of the Second Athenian Confederacy', *CQ* n.s. 23, 47-60
CAWKWELL, G.L. (1976a), 'Agesilaus and Sparta', *CQ* n.s. 26, 62-84
CAWKWELL, G.L. (1976b), 'The imperialism of Thrasybulus', *CQ* n.s. 26, 270-7
CAWKWELL, G.L. (1979), ed., *Xenophon. A History of My Times*, trans. R. Warner, Harmondsworth
CAWKWELL, G.L. (1981a), 'The King's Peace', *CQ* n.s. 31, 69-83
CAWKWELL, G.L. (1981b), 'Notes on the failure of the Second Athenian Confederacy', *JHS* 101, 40-55
CAWKWELL, G.L. (1983), 'The decline of Sparta', *CQ* n.s. 33, 385-400
CHADWICK, J.: see VENTRIS, M.G.F.
CHRIMES, K.M.T. (1948), *The Respublica Lacedaemoniorum Ascribed to Xenophon*, Manchester
CHRIMES, K.M.T. (1949), *Ancient Sparta. A re-examination of the evidence*, Manchester
CHRIST, K. (1972), *Von Gibbon zu Rostovtzeff; Leben und Werk führender Althistoriker der Neuzeit*, Darmstadt
CHRISTIEN, J. (1974), 'La loi d'Épitadeus: un aspect de l'histoire économique et sociale à Sparte', *RD* 52, 197-221
CHRISTOU, Chr. (1964), 'Spartiatikoi arkhaïkoi taphoi kai epitaphios met' anagluphôn amphoreus tou Lakônikou ergastêriou', *AD* 19.1, 123-63 (Eng. summ. 283-5)

CHUBB, J. (1982), *Patronage, Power and Poverty in Southern Italy. A tale of two cities*, Cambridge

CLAUSS, M. (1983), *Sparta. Eine Einführung in seine Geschichte und Zivilisation*, Munich

CLOCHÉ, P. (1919-20), 'La Grèce et l'Égypte de 405/4 à 342/1 avant J.-C.', *Revue Égyptologique* n.s. 1, 210-58; 2, 82-127

CLOCHÉ, P. (1933), 'Isocrate et la politique lacédémonienne', *REA* 35, 129-45

CLOCHÉ, P. (1942), 'Aristote et les institutions de Sparte', *LEC* 11, 289-313

CLOCHÉ, P. (1943), 'Thucydide et Lacédémone', *LEC* 12, 81-113

CLOCHÉ, P. (1944), 'Les "Helléniques" de Xénophon (Livres III-VII) et Lacédémone', *REA* 46, 12-46

CLOCHÉ, P. (1949), 'Sur le rôle des rois de Sparte', *LEC* 17, 113-38, 343-81

COLDSTREAM, J.N. (1976), 'Hero-cults in the age of Homer', *JHS* 96, 8-17

COLEMAN-NORTON, P.R. (1941), 'Socialism at Sparta', in *The Greek Political Experience. Studies in honor of W.K. Prentice*, Princeton, 61-77

COLIN, G. (1933), *Xénophon historien d'après le livre II des Helléniques, hiver 406/5 à 401/0. Annales de l'Est*, mém. 2, Paris

CONNOLLY, P. (1981), *Greece and Rome at War*, London

CONNOR, W.R. (1968), *Theopompus and Fifth-century Athens*, Washington, D.C.

CONNOR, W.R. (1979), 'Pausanias 3.14.1: a sidelight on Spartan history, c. 440 B.C.?', *TAPhA* 109, 21-7

COOK, J.M. (1983), *The Persian Empire*, London

COOK, R.M. and A.G. WOODHEAD (1958), 'Speculations on the origins of coinage', *Historia* 7, 257-62

COSTA, E.A., jr. (1974), 'Evagoras I and the Persians, ca. 411 to 391 B.C.', *Historia* 23, 40-56

COZZOLI, U. (1978), 'Sparta e l'affrancamento degli iloti nel V e nel IV secolo', in *Sesta miscellanea greca e romana*, Rome, 213-32

COZZOLI, U. (1979), *Proprietà fondiaria ed esercito nello stato spartano dell'età classica*, Rome

CRAWFORD, M.H. (1983), ed., *Sources for Ancient History*, Cambridge

CRICK, B. (1982), *George Orwell. A life*, rev. edn, Harmondsworth

DANDAMAYEV, M. (1969), 'Achaemenid Babylonia', in I.M. Diakonoff (ed.), *Ancient Mesopotamia, Socio-Economic History. A collection of studies by Soviet scholars*, Moscow, 296-311

DAÜBLER, T. (1923), *Sparta. Ein Versuch*, Leipzig

DAUX, G. (1937), 'Alcibiade, proxène de Lacédémone (Thucydide V,43,2 et VI,89,2)', in *Mélanges offerts à A.M. Desrousseaux par ses amis et ses élèves en l'honneur de sa cinquantième année d'enseignement supérieur, 1887-1937*, Paris, 117-22

DAVID, E. (1979a), 'The conspiracy of Cinadon', *Athenaeum* n.s. 57, 239-59

DAVID, E. (1979b), 'The pamphlet of Pausanias', *PP* 34, 94-116

DAVID, E. (1979/80), 'The influx of money into Sparta at the end of the fifth century B.C.', *SCI* 5, 30-45

DAVID, E. (1980), 'Revolutionary agitation in Sparta after Leuctra', *Athenaeum* n.s. 58, 299-308

DAVID, E. (1981), *Sparta between Empire and Revolution, 404-243 B.C. Internal problems and their impact in contemporary Greek consciousness*, New York

DAVIES, J.K. (1977/8), 'Athenian citizenship: the descent-group and the alternatives', *CJ* 73, 105-21

DAVIES, J.K. (1978), *Democracy and Classical Greece*, Glasgow (corr. impr. 1981)

DAVIES, J.K. (1981), *Wealth and the Power of Wealth in Classical Athens*, New York (companion to his *Athenian Propertied Families 600-300 B.C.*, Oxford 1971)

DAVIS, J.C. (1983), *Utopia and the Ideal Society. A study of English Utopian writing 1516-1700*, Cambridge

DECKER, J. de (1913), 'La genèse de l'organisation civique des Spartiates', *25th Bulletin Instituts Solvay* = *Archives Sociologiques* 4, Brussels, 306-13

DELBRÜCK, H. (1975), *History of the Art of War within the framework of political history*, Westport, Conn. (German original Berlin 1920)

DELEBECQUE, E. (1946/7), 'Xénophon, Athènes et Lacédémone. Notes sur la composition de l'*Anabase*', *REG* 59/60, 71-138

DELEBECQUE, E. (1957), *Essai sur la vie de Xénophon*, Paris

DEMAND, N.H. (1982), *Thebes in the Fifth Century. Heracles resurgent*, London & Boston

DEN BOER, W. (1954), *Laconian Studies*, Amsterdam

DEN BOER, W. (1979), *Private Morality in Greece and Rome*, Leiden

DICKINS, G. (1912), 'The growth of Spartan policy', *JHS* 32, 1-42

DICKINS, G. (1913), 'The growth of Spartan policy – a reply', *JHS* 33, 111-12

DIHLE, A. (1956), *Studien zur griechischen Biographie*, Göttingen

DODDS, E.R. (1933), 'The portrait of a Greek gentleman', *G & R* 2, 97-107

DÖRIG, J. (1980), 'Quelques remarques sur l'origine ionienne du portrait grec', in *Eikones. Fest. H. Jucker (AK* Beiheft 12), 89-95

DÖRRIE, H. (1972), 'Die Wertung der Barbaren im Urteil der Griechen. Knechtsnaturen? Oder Bewahrer und Künder heilbringendes Weisheit?', in R. Strehl and G.A. Lehmann (eds), *Antike und Universalgeschichte. Fest. H.E. Stier*, Münster, 146-75

DOVER, K.J. (1973), *Thucydides* (*G & R* New Surveys in the Classics 7), Oxford

DOVER, K.J. (1974), *Greek Popular Morality in the time of Plato and Aristotle*, Oxford

DOVER, K.J. (1978), *Greek Homosexuality*, London & Cambridge, Mass. See also GOMME, A.W.

DRAY, W.H. (1964), *Philosophy of History*, Englewood Cliffs, N.J.

DREWS, R. (1962), 'Diodorus and his sources', *AJPh* 83, 383-92

DREWS, R. (1963), 'Ephorus and history written *kata genos*', *AJPh* 84, 244-55

DREWS, R. (1973), *The Greek Accounts of Eastern History*, Cambridge, Mass.

DREWS, R. (1979), 'Phoenicia, Carthage and the Spartan *Eunomia*', *AJPh* 100, 45-58

DREWS, R. (1983), *BASILEUS: the evidence for kingship in Geometric Greece*, New Haven & London

DU BOULAY, J. (1974), *Portrait of a Greek Mountain Village*, Oxford

DUCAT, J. (1974), 'Le mépris des hilotes', *Annales (ESC)* 29, 1451-64

DUCAT, J. (1978), 'Aspects de l'hilotisme', *AncSoc* 9, 5-46

DUCAT, J. (1983), 'Sparte Archaïque et Classique. Structures économiques, sociales, politiques (1965-1982)', *REG* 96, 194-225

DUCREY, P. (1968), *Le traitement des prisonniers de guerre dans la Grèce antique des origines à la conquête romaine*, Paris

DUGAS, Ch. (1910), 'La campagne d'Agésilas en Asie Mineure (395). Xénophon et l'Anonyme d'Oxyrhynchos', *BCH* 34, 58-95

DULL, C.J. (1977), 'Thucydides 1.113 and the leadership of Orchomenus', *CPh* 72, 305-14

DÜMMLER, F. (1901), *Kleine Schriften*, 3 vols, Leipzig (includes at II.359-73 the previously unpublished 'Das Königtum der Spartaner')

DUNSTON, A.J. (1976), ed., *Essays on Roman Culture. The Todd Memorial Lectures*, Toronto & Sarasota (lectures originally delivered at and published by the University of Sydney)

EBERT, J. (1972), *Griechische Epigramme auf Sieger an gymnischen und hippischen Agonen*, *ASAW* 63.2, Berlin

EDELMANN, H. (1974), 'Volksmassen und Einzelpersönlichkeit im Spiegel von Historiographie und Publizistik des 5. und des 4. Jahrhunderts', *Klio* 56, 415-54

EHRENBERG, V (1924), 'Spartiaten und Lakedaimonier', *Hermes* 59, 23-72 (repr. in Ehrenberg 1965, 161-201)

EHRENBERG, V. (1927), 'Asteropos', *Philologische Wochenschrift* 47, 27-9

EHRENBERG, V. (1929), 'Sparta (Geschichte)', *RE* IIIA, 1373-1453

EHRENBERG, V. (1937), '*Tresantes*', *RE* VIA, 2292-7

EHRENBERG, V. (1965), *Polis und Imperium. Beiträge zur alten Geschichte*, ed. K.F. Stroheker and A.J. Graham, Zurich

EHRENBERG, V. (1969), *The Greek State*, 2nd edn, London

EHRENBERG, V. (1974), *Man, State and Deity*, London

EHRHARDT, C. (1970), 'Xenophon and Diodorus on Aegospotami', *Phoenix* 24, 225-8

EISENSTADT, S.N. and L. RONIGER (1980), 'Patron-client relations as a model of structuring social exchange', *CSSH* 22, 42-77

EISENSTADT, S.N. and R. LEMARCHAND (1981), eds, *Political Clientelism, Patronage and Development*, Beverly Hills

ELIAV-FELDON, M. (1982), *Realistic Utopias: the ideal imaginary societies of the Renaissance 1516-1630*, Oxford

ELSTER, J. (1983), *Explaining Technical Change. A case study in the philosophy of science*, Cambridge.

EPPS, P.H. (1933), 'Fear in Spartan character', *CPh* 28, 12-29

EPPS, P.H. (1960), 'Opinions of the Spartans since the second century B.C.', in L.B. Lawler et al. (eds), *Studies in Honor of B.L. Ullmann presented to him on the occasion of his 75th birthday*, Saint Louis, 35-47

FALLERS, L.A. (1956), *Bantu Bureaucracy. A study of integration and conflict in the political institutions of an East African people*, Cambridge

FARBER, J.J. (1979), 'The *Cyropaedia* and hellenistic kingship', *AJPh* 100, 497-514

FEARS, J.R. (1977), *Princeps a diis electus: the divine election of the Emperor as a political concept at Rome*, Rome

FELLMANN, B. and H. SCHEYHING (1972), eds, *100 Jahre deutsche Ausgrabung in Olympia*, Munich

FERGUSON, J. (1975), *Utopias of the Classical World*, London & New York

FERGUSON, W.S. (1918), 'The Zulus and the Spartans: a comparison of their military systems', *Harvard African Studies* 2, 197-234

FIGUEIRA, T.J. (1981), 'Aiginetan membership in the Peloponnesian League', *CPh* 76, 1-24

FINLEY, M.I. (1964), 'Between slavery and freedom', *CSSH* 6, 233-49 (repr. in Finley 1981a, 116-32 with 265)

FINLEY, M.I. (1975), *The Use and Abuse of History*, London

FINLEY, M.I. (1978), 'Empire in the Greco-Roman world', *G & R* n.s. 25, 1-15

FINLEY, M.I. (1979), *The World of Odysseus*, rev. edn, Harmondsworth

FINLEY, M.I. (1980), *Ancient Slavery and Modern Ideology*, London

FINLEY, M.I. (1981a), *Economy and Society in Ancient Greece*, ed. B.D. Shaw and R.P. Saller, London

FINLEY, M.I. (1981b), 'The elderly in Classical Antiquity', *G & R* n.s. 28, 156-71

FINLEY, M.I. (1982), 'Problems of slave society: some reflections on the debate', *Opus* 1, 201-11

FINLEY, M.I. (1983), *Politics in the Ancient World*, Cambridge

FISHER, N.R.E. (1976), ed., *Social Values in Classical Athens*, London & Toronto

FONTENROSE, J. (1978), *The Delphic Oracle. Its responses and operations with a catalogue of responses*, Berkeley, Los Angeles & London

FORBES, H.A.: see FOXHALL, L.

FORNARA, C.W. (1983), ed., *Archaic Times to the End of the Peloponnesian War*, 2nd edn, Cambridge

FORREST, W.G.G. (1960), 'Themistokles and Argos', *CQ* n.s. 10, 221-40

FORREST, W.G.G. (1967), 'Legislation in Sparta', *Phoenix* 21, 11-19

FORREST, W.G.G. (1980), *A History of Sparta c.950-192 B.C.*, London (repr., with new Preface, of 1968 original)

FOSSEY, J.M.: see TOMLINSON, R.A.

FOUCAULT, M. (1977), *Discipline and Punish*, London

FOXHALL, L. And H.A. FORBES (1982), '*Sitometreia*: the role of grain as a staple food in Classical Antiquity', *Chiron* 12, 41-90

FRANKFORT, H. (1970), *The Art and Architecture of the Ancient Orient*, 4th edn, Harmondsworth

FRANKLIN, S.H. (1971), *Rural Societies*, London

FREEMAN, E.A. (1893), *History of Federal Government in Greece and Italy*, 2nd edn, ed. J.B. Bury, London & New York

FREEMAN, K.J. (1907), *Schools of Hellas. An essay on the practice and theory of ancient Greek education from 600 to 300 B.C.*, London

FREESE, W.L. (1844), 'Wie lange erhielt sich die Gleichheit der lakedämonischen Bürger in ihrer politischen Berechtigung und in ihrem Grundbesitz?', *Gymnasium zu Stralsund*, 1-14

FREL, J. (1981), *Greek Portraits in the J. Paul Getty Museum*, Malibu

FRITZ, K. von (1941a), 'Conservative reaction and one man rule in ancient Greece', *Political Science Quarterly* 56, 51-83

FRITZ, K. von (1941b), 'The historian Theopompos', *AHR* 46, 761-85

FROLOV, E. (1974a), 'Das Problem der Monarchie und der Tyrannis in der politischen Publizistik des 4. Jahrhunderts v. u. Z.', in Welskopf 1974, I, 401-34

FROLOV, E. (1974b), 'Die späte Tyrannis im Balkanischen Griechenland', in Welskopf 1974, I, 231-400

FROLOV, E. (1975-6), 'Organisation und Charakter der Herrschaft Dionysios des Älteren', *Klio* 57, 103-22; 58, 377-404

FUKS, A. (1972), 'Isokrates and the social-economic situation in Greece', *AncSoc* 3, 17-44 (repr. in his *Social Conflict in Ancient Greece*, ed. M. Stern and M. Amit, Jerusalem & Leiden 1984, 52-79)

FUNKE, P. (1980a), *Homónoia und Arché. Athen und die griechische Staatenwelt vom Ende des Peloponnesischen Krieges bis zum Königsfrieden (404/3-387/6 v. Chr.)*, Wiesbaden

FUNKE, P. (1980b), 'Stasis und politischer Umsturz im Rhodos zu Beginn des IV. Jhdts. v. Chr.', in *Fest. F. Vittinghoff*, Köln-Graz, 59-70

FUQUA, C. (1981), 'Tyrtaeus and the cult of heroes', *GRBS* 22, 215-26

FUSTEL DE COULANGES. N.D. (1888), 'Étude sur la propriété à Sparte', *Mémoires de l'Académie des Sciences morales et politiques de l'Institut de France* 16, 835-930

FUSTEL DE COULANGES, N.D. (1904), 'Lacedaemoniorum Respublica', in Ch. Daremberg and E. Saglio (eds), *Dictionnaire des antiquités grecques et romaines* III.2, 886-900

GABBA, E. (1957), 'Studi su Filarco. Le biografie plutarchee di Agide e di Cleomene', *Athenaeum* n.s. 35, 3-55, 193-239

GABELMANN, H. (1982), 'Die Inhaber des Lykischen und des Satrapensarkophages', *AA*, 493-5

GARLAN, Y. (1968), 'Fortifications et histoire grecque', in Vernant 1968, 245-60

GARLAN, Y. (1972), *La guerre dans l'antiquité*, Paris

GARLAN, Y. (1974), *Recherches de poliorcétique grecque*, Paris

GARLAN, Y. (1982), *Les esclaves en Grèce ancienne*, Paris

GARLAND, R.S.J. (1982), '*Geras thanontôn*: an investigation into the claims of the Homeric dead', *BICS* 29, 69-80

GARNSEY, P.D.A. and C.R. WHITTAKER (1978), eds, *Imperialism in the Ancient World*, Cambridge

GAUTHIER, Ph. (1966), 'Les clérouques de Lesbos et la colonisation athénienne au Vᵉ siècle', *REG* 79, 64-88

GAUTHIER, Ph. (1973), 'A propos des clérouquies athéniennes au Ve siècle', in M.I. Finley (ed.), *Problèmes de la terre en Grèce ancienne*, Paris & The Hague, 163-78

GAWANTKA, W. (1975), *Isopolitie. Ein Beitrag zur Geschichte der zwischenstaatlichen Beziehungen in der griechischen Antike*, Munich

GELLNER, E. and J. WATERBURY (1977), eds, *Patrons and Clients in Mediterranean Societies*, London

GENOVESE, E.D. (1979), *From Rebellion to Revolution. Afro-American slave revolts in the making of the modern world*, Baton Rouge, Louisiana

GERNET, L. (1983), *Les grecs sans miracle. Textes 1903-1960 réunis par R. Di Donato*, Paris. See also GORDON, R.L.

GEYL, P. (1965), *Napoleon: For and Against*, Harmondsworth (first Eng. trans. London 1949)

GIARIZZO, G. (1950), 'La diarchia di Sparta', *PP* 5, 192-201

GIGON, O. (1973), 'Der Begriff der Freiheit in der Antike', *Gymnasium* 80, 8-56

GILBERT, G. (1895), *The Constitutional Antiquities of Sparta and Athens = Greek Constitutional Antiquities* I, 2nd edn, London

GIRARD, P. (1898), 'Un texte inédit sur la Cryptie des Lacédémoniens', *REG* 11, 31-8

GIRARD, P. (1900), '*Krypteia*', in *Daremberg-Saglio* III.1, 871-3

GITTINGS, R. (1978), *The Nature of Biography*, London

GLOTZ, G. (1968), *La cité grecque*, Paris (repr. with 'Bibliographie Complémentaire' of 1928 edn)

GLOVER, R.P. (1950), 'Some curiosities of ancient warfare', *G & R* 19, 1-9

GLOVER, T.R. (1917), *From Pericles to Philip*, London

GLOVER, T.R. (1945), *Springs of Hellas*, Cambridge

GOMME, A.W. (1945-56-81), *A Historical Commentary on Thucydides*, 5 vols, Oxford (vols IV and V with A. ANDREWES and K.J. DOVER)

GOODY, J. (1966), ed., *Succession to High Office*, Cambridge

GOODY, J. (1976a), 'Inheritance, property and women: some comparative considerations', in J. Goody, J. Thirsk and E.P. Thompson (eds), *Family and Inheritance. Rural Society in Western Europe 1200-1800*, Cambridge, 10-36

GOODY, J. (1976b), *Production and Consumption. A comparative study of the domestic domain*, Cambridge

GOODY, J. and I.P. WATT (1963), 'The consequences of literacy', *CSSH* 5, 304-45 (repr. in J. Goody, ed., *Literacy in Traditional Societies*, Cambridge 1968, 27-68)

GORDON, R.L. (1981), ed., *Myth, Religion & Society. Structuralist essays by M. Detienne, L. Gernet, J.-P. Vernant and P. Vidal-Naquet*, Cambridge

GOUKOWSKY, P.: see WILL, Ed.

GOULDNER, A.W. (1960), 'The norm of reciprocity: a preliminary statement', *American Sociological Review* 25, 161-78 (repr. in Schmidt et al. 1977, 28-43)

GOULDNER, A.W. (1965), *Enter Plato*, New York (London edn 1967)

GRAEFE, F. (1935), 'Die Operationen des Antialkidas im Hellespont', *Klio* 28, 262-70

GRAHAM, A.J. (1982), 'The colonial expansion of Greece', in *The Cambridge Ancient History* III.3², 83-162

GRAHAM, A.J. (1983), *Colony and Mother City in Ancient Greece*, 2nd edn, Chicago

GRAY, V.J. (1973), 'The Treatment of Military Operations and Military Leaders in Xenophon's *Hellenika*: the Paradigmatic Factor', diss. Cambridge

GRAY, V.J. (1979), 'Two different approaches to the Battle of Sardis in 395 B.C.', *CSCA* 12, 183-201

GRAY, V.J. (1980), 'The years 375 to 371 BC: a case study in the reliability of Diodorus Siculus and Xenophon', *CQ* n.s. 30, 306-26

GRAY, V.J. (1981), 'Dialogue in Xenophon's *Hellenica*', *CQ* n.s. 31, 321-34

GREENIDGE, A.H.J. (1911), *A Handbook of Greek Constitutional History*, London (repr. of 1896 edn)

GRENFELL, B.P. and A.S. HUNT (1908), eds, *The Oxyrhynchus Papyri Part V. Nos. 840-844*, London (P. Oxy. 842 = Hell. Ox.)

GRIFFIN, A. (1982), *Sikyon*, Oxford

GRIFFITH, G.T. (1935), *Mercenaries of the Hellenistic World*, Cambridge (repr. Chicago 1975)

GRIFFITH, G.T. (1950), 'The Union of Corinth and Argos (392-386 B.C.)', *Historia* 1, 236-56

GRIFFITH, G.T. (1978), 'Athens in the fourth century', in Garnsey/Whittaker 1978, 127-44 with 310-14. See also HAMMOND N.G.L.

GROTE, G. (1888), *History of Greece*, new edn in 10 vols, London

GRUNDY, G.B. (1894), *The Topography of the Battle of Plataea: The City of Plataea. The Field of Leuctra*, London

GRUNDY, G.B. (1908), 'The population and policy of Sparta in the fifth century', *JHS* 28, 77-96

GRUNDY, G.B. (1912), 'The policy of Sparta', *JHS* 32, 261-9

GRUNDY, G.B. (1948), *Thucydides and the History of his Age*, 2 vols, Oxford

GSCHNITZER, F. (1958), *Abhängige Orte im griechischen Altertum*, Munich

GSCHNITZER, F. (1973), 'Proxenos', *RE* Supp. XIII, 629-730

GSCHNITZER, F. (1978), *Ein neuer spartanischer Staatsvertrag und die Verfassung des Peloponnesischen Bundes*, Meisenheim/Glan

GUASTI, L.: see SCHMIDT, S.W.

GUIRAUD, P. (1893), *La propriété foncière en Grèce jusqu'à la conquête romaine*, Paris

HABICHT, Chr. (1970), *Gottmenschentum und griechische Städte*, 2nd edn, Munich

HACK, H.M. (1978), 'Thebes and the Spartan hegemony, 386-382 B.C.', *AJPh* 99, 210-27

HAHN, I. (1969), 'Aspekte der spartanischen Aussenpolitik im 5. Jh', *AAntHung* 17, 285-96

HALLOCK, R.T. (1969), *Persepolis Fortification Texts*, Chicago

HALLOCK, R.T. (1971), 'The evidence of the Persepolis tablets' (advance publication in fascicle form of I. Gershevitch (ed.), *The Cambridge History of Iran* II, 1985, ch. 11)

HAMDORF, F.W. (1964), *Griechische Kultpersonifikation der vorhellenistischen Zeit*, Mainz

HAMILTON, C.D. (1970), 'Spartan politics and policy 405-401 B.C.', *AJPh* 91, 294-314

HAMILTON, C.D. (1979a), 'On the perils of extraordinary honors: the cases of Lysander and Conon', *AncW* 2, 87-90

HAMILTON, C.D. (1979b), *Sparta's Bitter Victories. Politics and diplomacy in the Corinthian War*, Ithaca & London

HAMILTON, C.D. (1980), 'Isocrates, IG ii² 43, Greek propaganda and imperialism', *Traditio* 36, 83-109

HAMILTON, C.D. (1982a), 'Agesilaus and the failure of Spartan hegemony', *AncW* 5, 67-78

HAMILTON, C.D. (1982b), 'The early career of Archidamus', *EMC* n.s. 1, 5-20

HAMILTON, C.D. (1982c), 'Philip II and Archidamus', in Adams/Borza 1982, 61-83

HAMILTON, C.D. (1982d), 'Problems of alliance and hegemony reconsidered', *EMC* n.s. 1, 297-318 (rev. of Buckler 1980c and Cargill 1981)

HAMILTON, J.R. (1969), *Plutarch Alexander. A commentary*, Oxford

HAMMOND, M. (1979/80), 'A famous *exemplum* of Spartan toughness', *CJ* 75, 97-109

HAMMOND, N.G.L. (1982), 'The evidence for the identity of the royal tombs at Vergina', in Adams/Borza 1982, 111-27

HAMMOND, N.G.L. and G.T. GRIFFITH (1979), *A History of Macedonia* II. *550-336 B.C.*, Oxford

HAMPL, F. (1937), 'Die lakedämonischen Perioken', *Hermes* 72, 1-49

HANSON, V.D. (1980) 'Warfare and Agriculture in Ancient Greece', diss. Stanford

HARDING, P. (1973), 'The purpose of Isokrates, *Archidamos* and *On the Peace*', *CSCA* 6, 137-49

HARLEY, T.R. (1934), 'The Public School of Sparta', *G & R* 3, 129-39

HARRIS, M. (1978), *Cannibals and Kings. The origins of cultures*, Glasgow

HARRISON, R. (1973), *Warfare*, Minneapolis

HART, H.L.A. and A.M. HONORÉ (1959), *Causation in the Law*, Oxford (2nd edn 1985)

HART, J. (1982), *Herodotus and Greek History*, London & New York

HARTOG, F. (1982), 'La mort de l'autre: les funérailles des rois scythes', in G. Gnoli and J.-P. Vernant (eds), *La mort, les morts dans les sociétés anciennes*, Cambridge, 143-54

HARVEY, F.D. (1967), 'Oxyrhynchus Papyrus 2390 and early Spartan history', *JHS* 87, 62-73

HARVEY, F.D. (1979), 'Leonidas the regicide? Speculations on the death of Kleomenes I', in *Arktouros. Hellenic Studies presented to B.M.W. Knox*, Berlin, 253-60

HATZFELD, J. (1946), 'Agésilas et Artaxerxès II', *BCH* 70, 238-46

HATZFELD, J. (1951), *Alcibiade. Étude sur l'histoire d'Athènes à la fin du Ve siècle*, 2nd edn, Paris

HAVELOCK, E.A. (1972), 'War as a way of life in classical culture', in E. Gareau (ed.), *Classical Values and the Modern World*, Ottawa, 19-78

HEICHELHEIM, F.M.: see BALOGH, E.

HEISSERER, A.J. (1980), *Alexander the Great and the Greeks: the epigraphic evidence*, Norman, Oklahoma

HEITLAND, W.E. (1921), *Agricola. A study of agriculture and rustic life in the Greco-Roman world from the point of view of labour*, Cambridge

HELBIG, W. (1884), *Das homerische Epos aus den Denkmälern erlautert. Archäologische Untersuchungen*, Leipzig

HENIGE, D.P. (1974), *The Chronology of Oral Tradition: quest for a chimera*, Oxford

HENIGE, D.P. (1982), *Oral Historiography*, London, New York & Lagos

HENNIG, D. (1974), 'Orchomenos', *RE* Supp. XIV, 333-55

HENRY, W.P. (1967), *Greek Historical Writing. A historiographical essay based on Xenophon's Hellenica*, Chicago

HEREWARD, D. (1956), 'Doubts on the dates of some Spartan kings', *BICS* 3, 56 (summary)

HERMANN, G. (1980-81), 'The "Friends" of the early Hellenistic rulers: servants or officials?', *Talanta* 12-13, 103-49

HERRENSCHMIDT, C. (1982), 'Sur l'inscription de Bisotun', *Annales (ESC)* 37, 813-23

HERTZBERG, G.F. (1856), *Das Leben des Königs Agesilaos II von Sparta*, Halle

HERZFELD, E. (1969), *The Persian Empire. Studies in the geography and ethnography of the ancient Near East*, Wiesbaden

HICKS, E.L. and G.F. HILL (1901), *A Manual of Greek Historical Inscriptions*, 2nd edn, Oxford

HIGGINS, W.E. (1977), *Xenophon the Athenian. The problem of the individual and the society of the polis*, Albany, N.Y.

HILL, G.F. (1951), *Sources for Greek History between the Persian and Peloponnesian Wars*, a new edn by R. MEIGGS and A. ANDREWES, Oxford. See also HICKS, E.L.

HOBSBAWM, E.J. (1947), 'The hero in history', *Modern Quarterly* n.s. 2.2, 185-9 (rev. of Hook 1945).

HODKINSON, S.J. (1983), 'Social order and the conflict of values in Classical Sparta', *Chiron* 13, 239-81

HODKINSON, S.J. and H. HODKINSON (1981), 'Mantineia and the Mantinike: settlement and society in a Greek polis', *ABSA* 76, 239-96

HOFSTETTER, J. (1978), *Die Griechen in Persien. Prosopographie der Griechen im persischen Reich vor Alexander*, Berlin

HOLLADAY, A.J. (1977), 'Spartan austerity', *CQ* n.s. 27, 111-26

HOLLADAY, A.J. (1982), 'Hoplites and heresies', *JHS* 102, 94-103

HONORÉ, A.M.: see HART, H.L.A.

HOOK, S. (1945), *The Hero in History. A study in limitation and possibility*, London (originally Boston 1943)

HOOKER, J.T. (1980), *The Ancient Spartans*, London

HOPKINS, K. (1983), *Death and Renewal. Sociological Studies in Roman History* II, Cambridge (with G.P. BURTON and M. LETTS)

HORNBLOWER, J. (1981), *Hieronymus of Cardia*, Oxford

HORNBLOWER, S. (1982), *Mausolus*, Oxford

HORNBLOWER, S. (1983), *The Greek World 479-323 BC*, London (corr. impr. 1985)

HORSLEY, G.H.R. (1982), ed., *Hellenika. Essays on Greek history and politics*, North Ryde, N.S.W.

HOWARD, M. (1976), *War in European History*, Oxford

HOWARD, M. (1983), *The Causes of Wars*, London

HUMPHREYS, S.C. (1978), *Anthropology and the Greeks*, London & Boston

HUMPHREYS, S.C. (1983), *The Family, Women and Death. Comparative studies*, London etc.

HUMPHREYS, S.C. and H. KING (1981), eds, *Mortality and Immortality. The anthropology and archaeology of death*, London

HUNT, A.S.: see GRENFELL, B.P.

HUNT, D. (1982), 'Lessons in diplomacy from Classical Antiquity', *PCA* 79, 7-19

HUNTER, L.W. (1927), ed., *Aineas on Siegecraft*, revised by S.A. Handford, Oxford

HUNTER, V.J. (1982), *Past and Process in Herodotus and Thucydides*, Princeton

HUNTINGTON, R. and P. METCALF (1979), *Celebrations of Death. The anthropology of mortuary ritual*, Cambridge

HUTTER, H. (1979), *Politics as Friendship. The origins of Classical notions of politics in the theory and practice of friendship*, Waterloo, Ontario

HUXLEY, G.L. (1978), 'Simonides and his world', *PRIA* 78C, 231-47

IRWIN, T.H. (1974), rev. of L. Strauss, *Xenophon's Socrates* (Ithaca 1972), in *Philosophical Review* 83, 409-13

JACOBY, F. (1944), '*Chrêstous Poiein* (Aristotle fr. 592R)', *CQ* 38, 15-16

JACOBY, F. (1955), *FGrHist*. IIIb, 2 vols (Text, Noten), Leiden

JEANMAIRE, H. (1913), 'La Kryptie lacédémonienne', *REG* 26, 121-50

JEANMAIRE, H. (1939), *Couroi et Courètes. Essai sur l'éducation spartiate et sur les rites d'adolescence dans l'antiquité grecque*, Lille

JEFFERY, L.H. (1961a), *The Local Scripts of Archaic Greece. A study of the origin of the Greek alphabet and its development from the eighth to the fifth centuries B.C.*, Oxford

JEFFERY, L.H. (1961b), 'The pact of the first settlers at Cyrene', *Historia* 10, 139-47

JENKINSON, E.M. (1973), 'Cornelius Nepos and biography at Rome', *ANRW* I.3, 703-19

JEVONS, F.B. (1895), 'Greek burial laws', *CR* 9, 247-50

JONES, A.H.M. (1952/3), 'Two synods of the Delian and Peloponnesian Leagues', *PCPhS* n.s. 2, 43-6

JONES, A.H.M. (1964), *The Later Roman Empire 284-602*, 3 vols, Oxford (repr. in 2 vols 1974)

JONES, A.H.M. (1966), 'The Lycurgan Rhetra', in E. Badian (ed.), *Ancient Society and Institutions. Studies presented to V. Ehrenberg on his 75th birthday*, Oxford, 165-76

JONES, A.H.M. (1967), *Sparta*, Oxford

JONES, C.P. (1966), 'Towards a chronology of Plutarch's works', *JRS* 56, 61-74

JONES, N.F. (1980), 'The civic organization of Corinth', *AJPh* 101, 161-93

JORDAN, B. (1969), 'The meaning of *Hyperesia* in naval contexts', *CSCA* 2, 183-207

JUDEICH, W. (1892), *Kleinasiatische Studien*, Marburg

KAHRSTEDT, U. (1919), 'Die spartanische Agrarwirtschaft', *Hermes* 54, 279-94

KAHRSTEDT, U. (1922), *Griechische Staatsrecht* I. *Sparta und seine Symmachie*, Göttingen

KARWIESE, S. (1980), 'Lysander as Herakliskos Drakonopnigon', *NC* 20, 1-27

KEEGAN, J. (1978), *The Face of Battle. A study of Agincourt, Waterloo and the Somme*, Harmondsworth (originally London 1976)

KELLY, D.H. (1975), 'Sources and Interpretations of Spartan History in the Reigns of Agesilaus II, Archidamus III and Agis III', diss. Cambridge

KELLY, D.H. (1978a), 'Agesilaus' strategy in Asia Minor, 396-395 B.C.', *LCM* 3, 97-8

KELLY, D.H. (1978b), 'The new Spartan treaty', *LCM* 3, 133-41

KELLY, D.H. (1979), 'Lysias XII 72', *Historia* 28, 98-101

KELLY, D.H. (1981a), 'Policy-making in the Spartan Assembly', *Antichthon* 15, 47-61

KELLY, D.H. (1981b), 'Thucydides and Herodotus on the Pitanate *lochos*', *GRBS* 22, 31-8

KELLY, D.H. (1982), 'Sparta. Some myths, ancient and modern', in Horsley 1982, 9-19

KESSLER, E. (1910), *Plutarchs Leben des Lykurgos*, Berlin

KIECHLE, F. (1959), *Messenische Studien. Untersuchungen zur Geschichte der messenischen Kriege und der Auswanderung der Messenier*, Kallmünz

KIENAST, D. (1973), 'Presbeia', *RE* Supp. XIII, 499-628

KIENITZ, F.K. (1953), *Die politische Geschichte Ägyptens vom 7. bis zum 4. Jahrhundert vor der Zeitwende*, Berlin

KING, H.: see HUMPHREYS, S.C.

KLUCKHOHN, C. (1961), *Anthropology and the Classics*, Providence, R.I.

KNAUTH, W. (1933), 'Die spartanische Knabenerziehung im Lichte der Völkerkunde', *Zeitschrift für Geschichte der Erziehung und des Unterrichts* 23, 151-85

KOENEN, L. (1976), 'Fieldwork of the International Photographic Archive in Cairo', *StudPap* 15, 55-76

KOERNER, R. (1974), 'Die staatliche Entwicklung in Alt-Achaia', *Klio* 56, 457-95

KRENTZ, P. (1982), *The Thirty at Athens*, Ithaca & London

KROMAYER, J. (1903), 'Studien über Wehrkraft und Wehrverfassung der griechischen Staaten, vornehmlich im 4. Jahrhundert v. Chr.', *Klio* 3, 47-67, 173-212

KRÖMER, D. (1971), 'Xenophons Agesilaos: Untersuchungen zur Komposition', diss. Berlin (Freie Universität)

LACEY, W.K. (1968), *The Family in Classical Greece*, London & New York (repr. Auckland 1980)

LAIX, R.A. de (1974), 'Aristotle's conception of the Spartan constitution', *Journal of the History of Philosophy* 12, 21-30

LANDÉ, C.H.: see SCHMIDT, S.W.

LANE FOX, R.J. (1973), *Alexander the Great*, London

LANE FOX, R.J. (1980), *The Search for Alexander*, London & New York

LARSEN, J.A.O. (1932), 'Sparta and the Ionian Revolt: a study of Spartan foreign policy and the genesis of the Peloponnesian League', *CPh* 27, 136-50

LARSEN, J.A.O. (1933-4), 'The constitution of the Peloponnesian League', *CPh* 28, 257-76; 29, 1-19

LARSEN, J.A.O. (1937), 'Perioikoi', *RE* XIX, 816-33

LARSEN, J.A.O. (1955), 'The Boeotian Confederacy and fifth-century oligarchic theory', *TAPhA* 86, 41-50

LARSEN, J.A.O. (1960), 'Orchomenus and the formation of the Boeotian Confederacy', *CPh* 55, 9-18

LARSEN, J.A.O. (1968), *Greek Federal States. Their institutions and history*, Oxford

LAUFFER, S. (1959), 'Die Diodordublette XV 38=50 über die Friedenschlüsse zu Sparta 374 und 371 v. Chr.', *Historia* 8, 315-48

LECRIVAIN, Ch. (1900), 'Helotae', in *Daremberg-Saglio* III.1, 67-71

LEGON, R.P. (1967), 'Phliasian politics and policy in the early fourth century B.C.', *Historia* 16, 324-37

LEGON, R.P. (1981), *Megara. The political history of a Greek city-state to 336 B.C.*, Ithaca & London

LEHMANN, G.A. (1972), 'Die revolutionäre Machtergreifung der "Dreissig" und die staatliche Teilung Attikas (404-401/0 v. Chr.)', in *Antike und Universalgeschichte. Fest. H.E. Stier*, Münster, 201-33

LEHMANN, G.A. (1976), 'Ein Historiker namens Kratippos', *ZPE* 23, 265-88

LEHMANN, G.A. (1977), 'Ein neues Fragment der Hell. Oxy.: einige Bemerkungen zu P. Cairo (Temp. Inv. No.) 26/6/27/1-35', *ZPE* 26, 181-91

LEHMANN, G.A. (1978a-b), 'Spartas *archê* und die Vorphase des Korinthischen Krieges in den Hellenica Oxyrhynchia I-II', *ZPE* 28, 109-26; 30, 73-93

LEMARCHAND, R.: see EISENSTADT, S.N.

LENGAUER, W. (1979), *Greek Commanders in the Fifth and Fourth Centuries B.C. – politics and ideology: a study of militarism*, Warsaw

LE ROY LADURIE, E. (1973), *Le territoire de l'historien* I, Paris

LE ROY LADURIE, E. (1981), *The Mind and Method of the Historian*, Hassocks

LETTS, M.: see HOPKINS, K.

LÉVY, E. (1976), *Athènes devant la défaite de 404. Histoire d'une crise idéologique*, Paris

LÉVY, E. (1977), 'La Grande Rhètra', *Ktema* 2, 85-103

LÉVY, E. (1978), 'La monarchie macédonienne et le mythe d'une royauté démocratique', *Ktema* 3, 201-35

LÉVY, E. (1983), 'Les trois traités entre Sparte et le Roi', *BCH* 107, 221-41

LEWIS, A.W. (1982), *Royal Succession in Capetian France. Studies in familial order and the State*, Cambridge, Mass.

LEWIS, D.M. (1958), 'The Phoenician fleet in 411', *Historia* 7, 392-7

LEWIS, D.M. (1977), *Sparta and Persia*, Leiden

LEWIS, D.M. and R.S. STROUD (1979), 'Athens honors King Euagoras of Salamis', *Hesperia* 48, 180-93

LINDHOLM, C. (1982), *Generosity and Jealousy. The Swat Pukhtun of Northern Pakistan*, New York & Guildford (U.K.)

LINS, H. (1914), 'Kritische Betrachtungen der Feldzüge des Agesilaos in Kleinasien', diss. Halle

LINTOTT, A.W. (1982), *Violence, Civil Strife and Revolution in the Classical City 750-330 BC*, London & Canberra

LIPSET, S.M.: see BENDIX, R.

LITTMAN, R.J. (1969), 'A new date for Leotychidas', *Phoenix* 23, 269-77

LOGAN, G.M. (1983), *The Meaning of More's 'Utopia'*, Guildford

LONIS, R. (1969), *Les usages de la guerre entre Grecs et Barbares*, Paris

LONIS, R. (1980), 'La valeur du serment dans les accords internationaux en Grèce classique', *DHA* 6, 267-86

L'ORANGE, H.P. (1947), *Apotheosis in Ancient Portraiture*, Oslo

LORAUX, N. (1977), 'La "belle mort" spartiate', *Ktema* 2, 105-20

LORING, W. (1895), 'Some ancient routes in the Peloponnese', *JHS* 15, 25-89

LOTZ, W. (1935), 'Bericht über den neuesten Stand der Forschungen über öffentliche Finanzen Athens und Spartas in der klassischen Zeit', *Archiv für Kulturgeschichte* 25, 327-37

LOTZE, D. (1959), *Metaxu Eleutherôn kai Doulôn. Studien zur Rechtsstellung unfreier Landbevölkerung bis zum 4. Jht. v. Chr.*, Berlin

LOTZE, D. (1962), '*Mothakes*', *Historia* 11, 427-35

LOTZE, D. (1970), 'Selbstbewusstsein und Machtpolitik. Bermerkungen zur Machtpolitischen Interpretation spartanischen Verhaltens in den Jahren 479-477 v. Chr.', *Klio* 52, 255-75

LOTZE, D. (1971), 'Zu einigen Aspekten des spartanischen Agrarsystems', *JWG*/II, 63-76

LOTZE, D. (1982), 'Varianten der Produktionsweise in der griechischen Landwirtschaft der archaischen Periode', in J. Herrmann and I. Sellnow (eds), *Produktivkräften und Gesellschaftsformen in vorkapitalistischen Zeit*, Berlin, 303-11

LURIA, S. (1927), 'Zum politischen Kampf in Sparta gegen Ende des 5. Jahrhunderts', *Klio* 21, 404-20

MACAULAY, T.B. (1860), 'On the Athenian Orators' (August 1824), repr. in *The Miscellaneous Writings* I, London, 125-40

MACDONALD, A. (1972), 'A note on the raid of Sphodrias', *Historia* 21, 38-44

McKAY, K.L. (1953), 'The Oxyrhynchus Historian and the outbreak of the Corinthian War', *CR* n.s. 3, 6-7

MACINTYRE, A. (1981), *After Virtue. A study in moral theory*, London

MACKIE, J.L. (1974), *The Cement of the Universe. A study of causation*, Oxford (repr. with Addenda 1980)

MAHAFFY, J.P. (1906), *The Silver Age of the Greek World*, Chicago

MANDEL, J. (1978-9), 'Timophane: un commandant de mercénaires devenu tyran', *Euphrosyne* n.s. 9, 151-9

MANDEL, J. (1980), 'Jason: the tyrant of Pherae, Tagus of Thessaly, as reflected in ancient sources and modern literature: the image of the "new" tyrant', *RSA* 10, 47-77

MANFREDINI, M. and L. PICCIRILLI (1980), eds, *Plutarco. Le Vite di Licurgo e di Numa*, Florence

MANNHEIM, K. (1936), *Ideology and Utopia. An introduction to the sociology of knowledge*, London

MANSO, J.C.F. (1800-02-05), *Sparta. Ein Versuch zur Aufklärung der Geschichte und Verfassung dieses Staates*, 3 vols, Leipzig

MANUEL, F.E. and F. MANUEL (1979), *Utopian Thought in the Western World*, Oxford

MARASCO, G. (1978), 'La leggenda di Polidoro e la ridistribuzione di terre di Licurgo nella propaganda spartana del III sec.', *Prometheus* 4, 115-27

MARASCO, G. (1980), 'La retra di Epitadeo e la situazione sociale di Sparta nel IV secolo', *AC* 49, 131-45

MARINOVIĆ, L.P. (1968), 'Die Söldner in der Zeit des Peloponnesischen Krieges', *VDI* 106, 70-90 (in Russian: German summary in *Historia* 21, 1972, 383)

MARROU, H.-I. (1965), *Histoire de l'éducation dans l'antiquité*, 6th edn, Paris

MARSCHALL, Th. (1928), 'Untersuchungen zur Chronologie der Werke Xenophons', diss. Munich.

MARTIN, R. (1951), *Recherches sur l'agora grecque. Études d'histoire et d'archéologie urbaines*, Paris

MARTIN, V. (1944), 'Le traitement de l'histoire diplomatique dans la tradition littéraire du IVᵉ siècle avant J.-C.', *MH* 1, 13-30

MARTIN, V. (1949), 'Sur une interprétation nouvelle de la "Paix du Roi" ', *MH* 6, 127-39

MATHIEU, G. (1946), 'Le mirage spartiate de Diogène à Lucien', *RPh* 72 = 20³, 144-52 (rev. of Ollier 1943)

MEIGGS, R. (1983), *Trees and Timber in the Ancient Mediterranean*, Oxford. See also BURY, J.B. and HILL, G.F.

MELONI, P. (1949), 'Il contributo di Dionisio I alle operazioni di Antalcida del 387 av. Cr.', *RAL* 4, 191-203

MELONI, P. (1950), 'Tiribazo satrapo di Sardi', *Athenaeum* n.s. 28, 292-339

METCALF, P.: see HUNTINGTON, R.

MEULEAU, M.: see BENGTSON, H. (1969)

MEYER, Ernst (1978), 'Messenien', *RE* Supp. XV, 155-289

MICHELL, H. (1952), *Sparta. To krypton tês politeias tôn Lakedaimoniôn*, Cambridge

MILIBAND, R. (1983), 'Political action, determinism and contingency' (1980), repr. in his *Class Power and State Power*, London, 131-53

MITSOS, M. (1983), 'Une inscription d'Argos', BCH 107, 243-9

MOCKLER, A. (1969), Mercenaries, London

MOGGI, M. (1974), 'Il sinecismo di Megalopoli', ASNP³ 4, 71-107

MOGGI, M. (1976), I sinecismi interstatali greci I. Dalle origini al 338 a. C., Pisa

MOMIGLIANO, A.D. (1932), 'Sparta e Lacedemone e una ipotesi sull' origine della diarchia spartana', A & R 13, 3-11

MOMIGLIANO, A.D. (1934), 'Il re di Sparta e le leve dei perieci', Athenaeum n.s. 12, 255-6 (repr. in his Quinto contributo alla storia degli studi classici e del mondo antico, Rome 1979, 473-4)

MOMIGLIANO, A.D. (1963), Sommario di storia delle civiltà antiche I. L'oriente e la Grecia, Florence

MOMIGLIANO, A.D. (1966), Studies in Historiography, London

MOMIGLIANO, A.D. (1971), The Development of Greek Biography, Cambridge, Mass.

MOMIGLIANO, A.D. (1975), Alien Wisdom. The limits of Hellenization, Cambridge

MOMIGLIANO, A.D. (1979), 'Persian empire and Greek freedom', in A. Ryan (ed.), The Idea of Freedom. Essays in honour of Isaiah Berlin, Oxford, 39-51

MOOREY, P.R.S. (1975), Biblical Lands, Oxford

MORETTI, L. (1957-70), Olympionikai, i vincitori negli antichi agoni olympici = Atti Accad. Naz. Lincei, cl. sci. mor., stor. e filol.⁸ 8.2, Rome, 53-198, with supplement in Klio 52, 295-303

MORETTI, L. (1962), Ricerche sulle leghe greche (Peloponnesiaca-Beotica-Licia), Rome

MOSCHOU, L. and T. MOSCHOS (1981), 'To arkhaio phrourio tês Teuthrônês', AE, 10-22

MOSLEY, D.J. (1962), 'The Athenian embassy to Sparta in 371 B.C.', PCPhS n.s. 6, 41-6

MOSLEY, D.J. (1963), 'Pharax and the Spartan embassy to Athens in 370/69', Historia 12, 247-50

MOSLEY, D.J. (1971a), 'Cimon and the Spartan proxeny', Athenaeum n.s. 49, 431-2

MOSLEY, D.J. (1971b), 'Spartan kings and proxeny', ibid. 433-5

MOSLEY, D.J. (1972a), 'Euthycles: one or two Spartan envoys?', CR n.s. 22, 167-9

MOSLEY, D.J. (1972b), 'Timagoras' bed-makers', ibid. 12

MOSLEY, D.J. (1973), Envoys and Diplomacy in Ancient Greece, Wiesbaden

MOSLEY, D.J. (1979), 'Spartanische Diplomatie', in E. Olshausen (ed.), Antike Diplomatie, Darmstadt, 183-203. See also ADCOCK, F.E.

MOSSÉ, Cl. (1953), 'Sur un passage de l'"Archidamos" d'Isocrate', REA 55, 29-35

MOSSÉ, Cl. (1962), La fin de la démocratie athénienne. Aspects sociaux et politiques du déclin de la cité grecque au IVᵉ siècle avant J.-C., Paris (repr. New York 1979)

MOSSÉ, Cl. (1968), 'Le rôle politique des armées dans le monde grec à l'époque classique', in Vernant 1968, 221-9

MOSSÉ, Cl. (1977), 'Les périèques lacédémoniens. A propos d'Isocrate, Panathénaïque 177sqq.', Ktema 2, 121-4. See also WILL, Ed.

MOURLON-BEERNAERT, P. (1961), 'Tyrtée devant la mort', LEC 29, 391-9

MOXON, I. (1978), 'Thucydides' account of Spartan strategy and foreign policy in the Archidamian War', RSA 8, 7-26

MURRAY, O. (1966), 'Ho archaios dasmos', Historia 15, 142-56

MURRAY, O. (1980), Early Greece, Glasgow

MURRAY, O. (1981), 'The Greek symposion in history', TLS 6 November, 1307-8

NELLEN, D. (1972), 'Zur Darstellung der Schlacht bei Sardes in den Quellen', AncSoc 3, 45-54

NICCOLINI, G. (1900-01-02), 'Il re e gli efori a Sparta nei secoli IV e III A.C.', Rivista di storia antica 5, 524-51; 6, 281-315; 7, 363-79

NICCOLINI, G. (1905), 'Per la storia di Sparta. La confederazione del Peloponneso', RIL 38, 538-57

NICHOLAS, R.W. (1965), 'Factions: a comparative analysis', in M. Gluckman and F.

Eggan (eds), *Political Systems and the Distribution of Power*, London, 21-61 (repr. in Schmidt 1977, 55-73)

NICKEL, R. (1979), *Xenophon*, Darmstadt

NIESE, B. (1894), 'Agesilaos (4)', *RE* I, 796-804

NIESE, B. (1906), 'Neue Beiträge zur Geschichte und Landeskunde Lakedämons. Die lakedaimonischen Periöken', *Göttingische Gelehrte Nachrichten*, 101-42

NIESE, B. (1910), 'Drei Kapitel eleischer Geschichte', in *Fest. C. Robert*, Berlin, 1-47

NILSSON, M.P. (1912), 'Die Grundlagen des spartanischen Lebens', *Klio* 12, 308-40 (repr. in his *Opera Selecta* II, Lund 1952, 826-69)

NIPPEL, W. (1980), *Mischverfassungs-Theorie und Mischverfassungs-Realität in der Antike und Fruhe Neuzeit*, Stuttgart

NYLANDER, C. (1979), 'Achaemenid imperial art', in M.T. Larsen (ed.), *Power and Propaganda. A symposium on ancient empires*, Copenhagen, 345-59

OBER, J. (1978), 'Views of sea power in the fourth-century Attic orators', *AncW* 1, 119-30

OBER, J. (1983), 'Two ancient watchtowers above Aigosthena in the Northern Megarid', *AJA* 87, 387-92

OELSNER, J. (1974), 'Krisenerscheinungen im Achaimenidenreich im 5. und 4. Jht. v.u. Z.', in Welskopf 1974, II, 1014-73

OLIVA, P. (1971), *Sparta and her Social Problems*, Amsterdam

OLIVA, P. (1981), 'Heloten und Spartaner', *Index* 10, 43-54

OLLIER, F. (1933-43), *Le mirage spartiate. Étude sur l'idéalisation de Sparte dans l'antiquité grecque* I. *De l'origine jusqu'aux cyniques*; II. *Du début de l'école cynique jusqu'à la fin de la cité*, Paris (repr. in 1 vol. New York 1973)

OLLIER, F. (1934), ed., *Xénophon. La République des Lacédémoniens* (*Annales de l'Université de Lyon* n.s. II, Fasc. 47), Lyon & Paris

OLMSTEAD, A.T. (1939), 'Persia and the Greek frontier problem', *CPh* 34, 305-22

OLMSTEAD, A.T. (1948), *History of the Persian Empire*, Chicago & London

O'NEIL, J.L. (1981), 'The exile of Themistokles and democracy in the Peloponnese', *CQ* n.s. 31, 335-46

OSBORNE, M.J. (1971), 'Athens and Orontes. *IG* II² 207, *SEG* XV.92, XXI.261', *ABSA* 66, 297-321

OSBORNE, M.J. (1975), 'The satrapy of Mysia', *GB* 3, 291-309

OSBORNE, M.J. (1981-2-3), *Naturalization in Athens*, 4 vols in 3, Brussels

OSTWALD, M.P. (1969), *Nomos and the Beginnings of the Athenian Democracy*, Oxford

OSTWALD, M.P. (1982), *Autonomia. Its genesis and early history*, New York

PAGE, D.L. (1981), ed., *Further Greek Epigrams* ..., Cambridge

PANAGOPOULOS, A. (1975), ' "Apêllagêsan ek tês Hellados" (hê tukhê tôn arkhaiôn Messêniôn tês diasporas)', *Platon* 27, 263-8

PARETI, L. (1908/9), 'Ricerche sulla potenza marittima degli Spartani e sulla cronologia dei nauarchi', *MAT* 59, 71-159 (repr. in Pareti 1961, 1-131)

PARETI, L. (1910a), 'Origine e sviluppo dell' eforato spartano', *Studi Spartani*, Turin, 25-153 (repr. in Pareti 1958, 101-220)

PARETI, L. (1910b), 'Le tribù personali e le tribù locali a Sparta', *RAL* 19, 455-73 (repr. in Pareti 1958, 77-92)

PARETI, L. (1911), 'Per la storia di alcuni dinaste greche dell' Asia minore', *AAT* 46, 132-44 (repr. in Pareti 1961, 179-91)

PARETI, L. (1911/12), 'Elementi formatori e dissolventi dell' egemonia Spartana in Grecia', *AAT* 48, 108-26 (repr. in Pareti 1961, 193-211)

PARETI, L. (1913), 'Le imprese di Tibrone in Asia nel 400-399 e nel 391 av Cr', in *Entaphia. In memoria di E. Pozzi*, Turin (repr. in Pareti 1961, 259-77)

PARETI, L. (1932), 'Sulle origini della diarchia spartana', *A & R* 13, 11-13 (repr. in Pareti 1958, 93-5)

PARETI, L. (1950), 'Le "leggende" spartane di Senofonte', _Idea_ 2, 15-19 (repr. in Pareti 1958, 97-100)

PARETI, L. (1958-61), _Studi minori di storia antica_, 2 vols, Rome

PARKE, H.W. (1927), 'Herippidas, harmost at Thebes', _CQ_ 21, 159-65

PARKE, H.W. (1930), 'The development of the Second Spartan Empire (405-371 B.C.)', _JHS_ 50, 37-79

PARKE, H.W. (1931), 'The evidence for harmosts in Laconia', _Hermathena_ 46, 31-8

PARKE, H.W. (1932), 'The tithe of Apollo and the harmost at Decelea, 413 to 404 B.C.', _JHS_ 52, 42-6

PARKE, H.W. (1933), _Greek Mercenary Soldiers from the earliest times to the Battle of Ipsus_, Oxford

PARKE, H.W. (1945), 'The deposing of Spartan kings', _CQ_ 39, 106-12

PARKE, H.W. (1957), 'A note on the Spartan embassy to Athens (408/7 B.C.)', _CR_ n.s. 7, 106-7

PARKE, H.W. and D.E.W. WORMELL (1956), _The Delphic Oracle_, 2 vols, Oxford

PARKER, R.C.T. (1983), _Miasma. Pollution and purification in early Greek religion_, Oxford

PARRY, J.: see BLOCH, Maurice

PASSMORE, J. (1970), _The Perfectibility of Man_, London

PAYRAU, S. (1961), 'Sur un passage d'Andocide (_Paix_ 27)', _REA_ 63, 15-30

PAYRAU, S. (1971), 'Eirenika. Considérations sur l'échec de quelques tentatives panhelléniques au IVᵉ siècle avant Jésus-Christ', _REA_ 73, 24-79

PEARSON, L. (1962a), _Popular Ethics in Ancient Greece_, Stanford

PEARSON, L. (1962b), 'The pseudo-history of Messenia and its authors', _Historia_ 11, 397-426

PEEK, W. (1974), 'Ein neuer spartanischer Staatsvertrag', _ASAW_ 65.3, 3-15

PELLING, C.B.R. (1976), rev. of Wardman 1974 in _JHS_ 96, 189-90

PELLING, C.B.R. (1980), 'Plutarch's adaptation of his source-material', _JHS_ 100, 127-40

PERLMAN, S. (1957), 'Isocrates' "Philippus" – a reinterpretation', _Historia_ 6, 307-16

PERLMAN, S. (1964), 'The causes and the outbreak of the Corinthian War', _CQ_ n.s. 14, 64-81

PERLMAN, S. (1968), 'Athenian democracy and the revival of imperialistic expansion at the beginning of the fourth century B.C.', _CPh_ 63, 257-67

PERLMAN, S. (1976), 'Panhellenism, the Polis and imperialism', _Historia_ 25, 1-30

PERLMAN, S. (1976-7), 'The Ten Thousand. A chapter in the military, social and economic history of the fourth century', _RSA_ 6-7, 241-84

PICARD, O. (1980), _Les grecs devant la ménace perse_, Paris

PICCIRILLI, L. (1976), _Gli arbitrati interstatali greci_, Pisa. See also MANFREDINI, M.

PITT-RIVERS, J. (1968), 'The stranger, the guest and the hostile host: introduction to the study of the laws of hospitality', in J.G. Peristiany (ed.) _Contributions to Mediterranean Sociology_, Paris & The Hague, 13-30.

PITT-RIVERS, J. (1971), _The People of the Sierra_, 2nd edn, Chicago

PLEKHANOV, G.V. (1940), _The Role of the Individual in History_, London (Russian original 1898)

PLEZIA, M. (1982), 'Agesilaos und Timotheos: zwei Staatsmännerporträts aus der Mitte des IV. Jhs.', _ICS_ 7, 49-61

POPP, H. (1957), _Die Einwirkung von Vorzeichen, Opfern und Festen auf die Kriegführung der Griechen in 5. und 4. Jahrhundert v. Chr._, Erlangen

PORALLA, P. (1913), _Prosopographie der Lakedaimonier bis auf die Zeit Alexanders des Grossen_, Breslau (a revised and augmented edn by A.S. Bradford has been published by Ares, Chicago, 1985)

PORTER, W.H. (1935), 'The antecedents of the Spartan revolution of 243 B.C.', _Hermathena_ 49, 1-15

POUILLOUX, J. and F. SALVIAT (1983), 'Lichas, Lacédémonien, Archonte à Thasos et le

Livre VIII de Thucydide', *CRAI*, April-June, 376-403

POWELL, C.A. (1980), 'Athens' difficulty, Sparta's opportunity: causation and the Peloponnesian War', *AC* 49, 87-114

PRANDI, L. (1976), 'La liberazione della Grecia nella propaganda spartana durante la guerra del Peloponneso', in M. Sordi (ed.), *I canali della propaganda nel mondo antico*, Milan, 72-83

PRENTICE, W.K. (1934), 'The character of Lysander', *AJA* 38, 37-42

PRITCHETT, W.K. (1965-69-80-82), *Studies in Ancient Greek Topography*, 4 vols, Berkeley

PRITCHETT, W.K. (1974-9), *The Greek State at War*, 3 vols, Berkeley

RAHE, P. (1977), 'Lysander and the Spartan Settlement, 407-403 B.C.', diss. Yale

RAHE, P. (1980a), 'The military situation in Western Asia Minor on the eve of Cunaxa', *AJPh* 101, 79-96

RAHE, P. (1980b), 'The selection of Ephors at Sparta', *Historia* 29, 385-401

RAHN, P.J. (1981), 'The date of Xenophon's exile', in G.S. Shrimpton and D.J. McCargar (eds), *Classical Contributions. Studies in honour of M.F. McGregor*, Locust Valley, N.Y., 103-19

RAWLINGS, H.R. III (1981), *The Structure of Thucydides' History*, Princeton

RAWSON, E. (1969), *The Spartan Tradition in European Thought*, Oxford

READ, M. (1938), 'The moral code of the Ngoni and their former military state', *Africa* 11, 1-24

REDFIELD, J. (1977/8), 'The women of Sparta', *CJ* 73, 146-61

REINA, R.E. (1959), 'Two patterns of friendship in a Guatemalan community', *American Anthropologist* 61, 44-50

RENEHAN, R.: see SANSONE, D.

RHODES, P.J. (1981a), *A Commentary on the Aristotelian Athenaion Politeia*, Oxford

RHODES, P.J. (1981b), 'The selection of Ephors at Sparta', *Historia* 30, 498-502

RICE, D.G. (1974), 'Agesilaus, Agesipolis, and Spartan politics, 386-379 B.C.', *Historia* 23, 164-82

RICE, D.G. (1975), 'Xenophon, Diodorus and the year 379/78 B.C.: reconstruction and reappraisal', *YCS* 24, 95-130

RICHARDS, H. (1907), *Notes on Xenophon and Others*, London

RICOEUR, P. (1980), *The Contribution of French Historiography to the Theory of History*, Oxford (Zaharoff Lecture for 1978-9)

RIDLEY, R.T. (1974), 'The economic activities of the Perioikoi', *Mnemosyne* 27, 281-92

RIDLEY, R.T. (1981), 'Exegesis and audience in Thucydides', *Hermes* 109, 25-45

ROBERTSON, N. (1980), 'The sequence of events in the Aegean in 408 and 407 B.C.', *Historia* 29, 282-301

ROEBUCK, C.A. (1941), 'A History of Messenia from 369 to 146 B.C.', diss. Chicago

ROEBUCK, C.A. (1945), 'A note on Messenian economy and population', *CPh* 40, 149-65

ROLLEY, Cl. (1977), *Fouilles de Delphes* V.3. *Les trépieds à cuve clouée*, Paris

ROLOFF, G. (1903), *Probleme aus der griechischen Kriegsgeschichte*, Berlin

ROMILLY, J. de (1958), 'Eunoia in Isocrates or the political importance of creating good will', *JHS* 78, 92-101

ROMILLY, J. de (1968), 'Guerre et paix entre cités', in Vernant 1968, 207-20

ROMILLY, J. de (1977), *The Rise and Fall of States according to Greek Authors*, Ann Arbor

ROMILLY, J. de (1979), *La douceur dans la pensée grecque*, Paris

RONIGER, L.: see EISENSTADT, S.N.

RONNET, G. (1981), 'La figure de Callicratidas et la composition des "Helléniques" ', *RPh* 55, 111-21

ROOBAERT, A. (1977), 'Le danger hilote?', *Ktema* 2, 141-55

ROSTOVTZEFF, M.I. (1941), *The Social and Economic History of the Hellenistic World*, 3 vols, Oxford (corr. impr. 1953)

ROUSSEL, P. (1960), *Sparte*, 2nd edn, Paris

ROUX, G. (1979), *L'amphictionie, Delphes et le temple d'Apollon au IV* siècle*, Lyon & Paris

ROY, J. (1967), 'The mercenaries of Cyrus', *Historia* 16, 287-323

ROY, J. (1971), 'Arcadia and Boeotia in Peloponnesian affairs, 370-362 B.C.', *Historia* 20, 569-99

ROY, J. (1973), 'Diodorus Siculus XV.40 – the Peloponnesian revolutions of 374 B.C.', *Klio* 55, 135-9

RUNCIMAN, W.G. (1983), *A Treatise on Social Theory* I. *The methodology of social theory*, Cambridge

RUSSELL, D.A. (1966), 'On reading Plutarch's *Lives*', *G & R* n.s. 13, 139-54

RUSSELL, D.A. (1973), *Plutarch*, London

RUSSELL, D.A. (1983), *Greek Declamation*, Cambridge

RUSSELL, D.A. and N.G. WILSON (1981), eds, *Menander Rhetor*, Oxford

RYDER, T.T.B. (1965), *Koine Eirene. General peace and local independence in ancient Greece*, Oxford

SACCO, G. (1978), 'Due note epigrafiche', *RFIC* 106, 75-81

SACHSE, A. (1888), *Die Quellen Plutarchs in der Lebenbeschreibung des Königs Agesilaos*, Schwerin

SAGLIO, E. (1911), 'Syssitia', in *Daremberg-Saglio* IV.2, 1600-01

SAHLINS, M.D. (1963), 'Poor man, rich man, Big-man, chief: political types in Melanesia and Polynesia', *CSSH* 5, 285-303 (repr. in Schmidt 1977, 220-31)

STE. CROIX, G.E.M. de (1953), 'Demosthenes' *timêma* and the Athenian *eisphora* in the fourth century B.C.', *C & M* 14, 30-70

STE. CROIX, G.E.M. de (1954/5), 'The character of the Athenian Empire', *Historia* 3, 1-41

STE. CROIX, G.E.M. de (1972), *The Origins of the Peloponnesian War*, London & Ithaca

STE. CROIX, G.E.M. de (1981), *The Class Struggle in the Ancient Greek World from the Archaic Age to the Arab Conquests*, London & Ithaca (corr. impr. 1983)

SALLER, R.P. (1982), *Personal Patronage under the Early Empire*, Cambridge

SALMON, J.B. (1977), 'Political hoplites?', *JHS* 97, 84-101

SALMON, P. (1981), *Études sur la confédération béotienne (447/6-386)*, Brussels

SALVIAT, F. (1984), 'Les Archontes de Thasos', *Praktika tou H' Diethnous Sunedriou Hellênikês kai Latinikês Epigraphikês* (Athens, 3-9 October 1982), Athens, 233-58. See also POUILLOUX, J.

SANSONE, D. (1981), 'Lysander and Dionysius (Plut. *Lys.* 2)', *CPh* 76, 202-6 (with addendum by R. RENEHAN, 206-7)

SAUNDERS, T.J. (1981), ed., *Aristotle. The Politics*, rev. edn, Harmondsworth

SCHAEFER, H. (1957), 'Das Eidolon des Leonidas', in *Charites. Studien zur Altertumswissenschaft ... E. Langlotz*, Bonn, 223-33

SCHEYHING, H.: see FELLMANN, B.

SCHMIDT, S.W., L. GUASTI, C.H. LANDÉ and J.C. SCOTT (1977), eds, *Friends, Followers and Factions. A reader in political clientelism*, Berkeley, Los Angeles & London

SCOTT, J.C. (1977), 'Patronage or exploitation?', in Gellner/Waterbury 1977, 21-39. See also SCHMIDT, S.W.

SCOTT, M. (1981), 'Some Greek terms in Homer suggesting non-competitive attitudes', *AClass* 24, 1-15

SCOTT, M. (1982), '*Philos, Philotês* and *Xenia*', *AClass* 25, 1-19

SEAGER, R.J. (1967), 'Thrasybulus, Conon and Athenian imperialism, 396-386 B.C.', *JHS* 87, 95-115

SEAGER, R.J. (1974), 'The King's Peace and the balance of power in Greece, 386-362 B.C.', *Athenaeum* n.s. 52, 36-63

SEAGER, R.J. (1977), 'Agesilaus in Asia: propaganda and objectives', *LCM* 2, 183-4

SEAGER, R.J. and C.J. TUPLIN (1980), 'The freedom of the Greeks of Asia', *JHS* 100, 141-57

SEALEY, B.R.I. (1969), 'Probouleusis and the sovereign Assembly', *CSCA* 2, 247-69

SEALEY, B.R.I. (1976), 'Die spartanische Nauarchie', *Klio* 58, 335-58

SEALEY, B.R.I. (1977), *A History of the Greek City-states ca. 700-338 B.C.*, Berkeley, Los Angeles & London

SECK, F. (1976), ed., *Isokrates*, Darmstadt ('Wege der Forschung')

SEIBERT, J. (1979), *Die politische Flüchtlinge und Verbannten in der griechischen Geschichte*, 2 vols, Darmstadt

SERGENT, B. (1976), 'La représentation spartiate de la royauté', *RHR* 189, 3-52

SHATZMAN, I. (1968), 'The meeting place of the Spartan Assembly', *RFIC* 96, 385-9

SHIMRON, B. (1979), 'Ein Wortspiel mit HOMOIOI bei Herodot', *RhM* n.F. 122, 131-3

SINCLAIR, R.K. (1978), 'The King's Peace and the employment of military and naval forces 387-378', *Chiron* 8, 29-54

SMITH, G.: see BONNER, R.J.

SMITH, M.: see BENGTSON, H. (1969)

SMITH, R.E. (1948), 'Lysander and the Spartan empire', *CPh* 43, 145-56

SMITH, R.E. (1953/4), 'The opposition to Agesilaus' foreign policy 394-371 B.C.', *Historia* 2, 274-88

SNODGRASS, A.M. (1965), 'The hoplite reform and history', *JHS* 85, 110-22

SNODGRASS, A.M. (1967), *Arms and Armour of the Greeks*, London & New York

SORDI, M. (1950-1), 'I caratteri dell' opera storiografica di Senofonte nelle Elleniche', *Athenaeum* n.s. 28, 3-53; 29, 273-348

SPAHN, P. (1977), *Mittelschicht und Polisbildung*, Frankfurt

STADTER, P. (1965), *Plutarch's Historical Methods. An analysis of the* Mulierum virtutes, Cambridge, Mass.

STANTON, G.R. (1982), 'Federalism in the Greek world. An introduction', in Horsley 1982, 183-90

STARR, C.G. (1975), 'Greeks and Persians in the fourth century B.C. I. A study of cultural contacts before Alexander', *IA* 11, 39-99

STARR, C.G. (1977-78), 'Greeks and Persians in the fourth century B.C. II. The meeting of two cultures', *IA* 12, 49-115

STEIN, H.K. (1863), *Das Kriegswesen der Spartaner*, Konitz

STERN, E. von (1884), *Geschichte der spartanischen und thebanischen Hegemonie vom Königsfrieden bis zur Schlacht bei Mantineia*, Dorpat

STERN, N.H.: see BLISS, C.J.

STEWART, F.H. (1977), *Fundamentals of Age-Group Systems*, New York

STIBBE, C.M. (1978), 'Dionysos auf den Grabreliefs der Spartaner', *Castrum Peregrini* 132/133, 6-26

STRAUSS, B.S. (1979), 'Division and Conquest: Athens, 403-386 B.C.', diss. Yale

STRAUSS, B.S. (1983), 'Aegospotami reexamined', *AJPh* 104, 24-35

STRAUSS, L. (1939), 'The spirit of Sparta and the taste of Xenophon', *Social Research* 6.4, 502-36

STRAUSS, L.: see also IRWIN, T.H.

STROHEKER, K.F. (1953/4), 'Zu den Anfängen der monarchischen Theorie in der Sophistik', *Historia* 2, 381-412

STRONACH, D. (1980), 'Iran under the Achaemenians and Seleucids', in A. Sherratt (ed.), *The Cambridge Encyclopaedia of Archaeology*, Cambridge, 206-11 with 459

STROUD, R.S. (1971), 'Greek inscriptions. Theozotides and the Athenian orphans', *Hesperia* 40, 280-301. See also LEWIS, D.M.

STUART, D.R. (1928), *Epochs of Greek and Roman Biography*, Berkeley

SWOBODA, H: see BUSOLT, G.

SYME, R. (1939), *The Roman Revolution*, Oxford

SYME, R. (1950), 'A Roman Post-Mortem: an inquest on the fall of the Roman Republic', Sydney (repr. in Dunston 1976, 139-57, and Syme 1979, 205-17)

SYME, R. (1974), 'History or biography: the case of Tiberius Caesar', *Historia* 23, 481-96 (repr. in Syme 1984, 937-52)

SYME, R. (1979-84), *Roman Papers*, 3 vols (I-II ed. E. Badian; III ed. A.R. Birley), Oxford

SYMONS, J. (1982), 'The art of biography', in M. Holroyd (ed.), *Essays by Divers Hands. Transactions of the Royal Society of Literature* 42, 163-78

SZEGEDY-MAZSAK, A. (1981), *The* Nomoi *of Theophrastus*, New York

TAEGER, F. (1935), 'Charismatische Ideen bei Herodot', *Klio* 28, 255-61

TAEGER, F. (1957-60), *Charisma. Studien zur Geschichte des antiken Herrscherkultes*, 2 vols, Stuttgart

TAÏPHAKOS, I.G.: see VAGIAKAKOS, D.V.

TARN, W.W. (1927), 'Persia from Xerxes to Alexander', in *The Cambridge Ancient History* VI¹, 1-24

TARN, W.W. (1930), *Hellenistic Military and Naval Developments*, Cambridge (repr. Chicago 1975)

TARN, W.W. (1948), *Alexander the Great*, 2 vols, Cambridge

TAZELAAR, C.M. (1967), '*Paides kai epheboi*. Some notes on the Spartan stages of youth', *Mnemosyne* 20, 127-53

THOMAS, C.G. (1974), 'On the role of the Spartan kings', *Historia* 23, 257-70

THOMAS, L.-V (1980), *Le cadavre. De la biologie à l'anthropologie*, Paris

THOMPSON, W.E. (1970), 'The politics of Phlius', *Eranos* 68, 224-30

THOMPSON, W.E. (1973-74), 'Observations on Spartan politics', *RSA* 3-4, 47-58

THOMPSON, W.E. (1983a), 'Arcadian factionalism in the 360's', *Historia* 32, 149-60

THOMPSON, W.E. (1983b), 'Isocrates on the Peace treaties', *CQ* n.s. 33, 75-80

TIGERSTEDT, E.N. (1965-74-78), *The Legend of Sparta in Classical Antiquity*, 2 vols and Index vol., Stockholm, Göteborg & Uppsala

TOD, M.N. (1948), *A Selection of Greek Historical Inscriptions* II. *403-323 B.C.*, Oxford

TOMLINSON, R.A. and J.M. FOSSEY (1970), 'Ancient remains on Mt Mavrovouni, South Boeotia', *ABSA* 65, 243-63

TOYNBEE, A.J. (1969), *Some Problems of Greek History*, Oxford (Part III: 'The Rise and Decline of Sparta', 152-417)

TREVES, P. (1944), 'The problem of a history of Messenia', *JHS* 64, 102-6

TRIEBER, K. (1871), 'Zum Kriegswesen der Spartaner', *Neue Jahrbücher für Philologie* 103, 443-7

TROTSKY, L. (1967), *History of the Russian Revolution*, Sphere Books edn in 3 vols, London (a repr. of Max Eastman's 1932-3 trans.)

TUMARKIN, N. (1983), *Lenin Lives! The Lenin cult in Soviet Russia*, Cambridge, Mass.

TUPLIN, C.J. (1976), 'Aeneas Tacticus: Poliorketika 18.8', *LCM* 1, 127-31

TUPLIN, C.J. (1977a), 'The Athenian embassy to Sparta 372/1', *LCM*, 2, 51-6

TUPLIN, C.J. (1977b), 'Kyniskos of Mantinea', *LCM* 2, 5-10

TUPLIN, C.J. (1977c), 'Xenophon: a didactic historian?', *PCA* 74, 26-7 (summary)

TUPLIN, C.J. (1981), rev. of Cawkwell 1979 in *CR* n.s. 31, 6-9

TUPLIN, C.J. (1982), 'The date of the union of Corinth and Argos', *CQ* n.s. 32, 75-83. See also SEAGER, R.J.

TURNER, E.G. (1952), 'Roman Oxyrhynchus', *JEA* 38, 78-87

TURNER, F.M. (1981), *The Greek Heritage in Victorian Britain*, New Haven & London

UNDERHILL, G.E. (1900), *A Commentary on the Hellenica of Xenophon*, Oxford

USHER, S. (1969), *The Historians of Greece and Rome*, London

USHER, S. (1979), ' "This to the fair Critias" ', *Eranos* 77, 39-42

VAGIAKAKOS, D.V. and I.G. TAÏPHAKOS (1975), 'Lakônikê Bibliographia', *Lakônikai*

Spoudai 2, 417-87

VAN GENNEP, A. (1960), *The Rites of Passage*, London & Henley (French original 1909)

VATIN, C. (1981), 'Monuments votifs à Delphes. IV. Le portique de Tégée', *BCH* 105, 453-9

VENTRIS, M.G.F. and J. CHADWICK (1973), *Documents in Mycenaean Greek*, 2nd edn, Cambridge

VERBRUGGHE, G.P.: see WICKERSHAM, J.

VERMEULE, E.T. (1979), *Aspects of Death in early Greek art and poetry*, Berkeley, Los Angeles & London

VERNANT, J.-P. (1968), ed., *Problèmes de la guerre en Grèce ancienne*, Paris & The Hague

VERNANT, J.-P. (1982), 'Lameness, tyranny, incest in legend and history', *Arethusa* 15, 19-38. See also GORDON, R.L.

VIAL, Cl. (1977), ed., *Diodore de Sicile Livre XV*, Budé edn, Paris

VIDAL-NAQUET, P. (1981), *Le chasseur noir. Formes de pensée et formes de société en Grèce ancienne*, Paris (corr. repr. 1983). See also GORDON, R.L.

VILLARD, P. (1981), 'Sociétés et armées civiques en Grèce; de l'union à la subversion', *RH* 266/2, 297-310

VOKOTOPOULOU, I. (1980), 'Pilos Lakônikos', in *STELE. Fest. N. Kondoleon*, Athens, 236-41

VOLQUARDSEN C.A. (1868), *Untersuchungen über die Quellen der griechischen und sizilischen Geschichte bei Diodor XI bis XVI*, Kiel

von FRITZ, K.: see FRITZ, K. von

WACE, A.J.B. (1937), 'A Spartan hero relief', *AE*, 217-20

WADE-GERY, H.T. (1925), 'The growth of the Dorian states', *The Cambridge Ancient History* III¹, 527-70

WADE-GERY, H.T. (1943-4), 'The Spartan Rhetra in Plutarch *Lycurgus* VI', *CQ* 37, 62-72; 38, 1-9, 115-26 (repr. in Wade-Gery 1958, 37-85)

WADE-GERY, H.T. (1945), 'Kritias and Herodes', *CQ* 39, 19-33 (repr. in Wade-Gery 1958, 271-92)

WADE-GERY, H.T. (1958), *Essays in Greek History*, Oxford

WALBANK, F.W. (1957-67-79), *A Historical Commentary on Polybius*, 3 vols, Oxford

WALBANK, F.W. (1968-9), 'The historians of Greek Sicily', *Kokalos* 14-15, 476-98

WALBANK, F.W. (1976/77), 'Were there Greek federal states?', *SCI* 13, 27-51

WALBANK, M.B. (1978), *Athenian Proxenies of the Fifth Century B.C.*, Toronto & Sarasota

WALBANK, M.B. (1982a), 'A correction to *IG* ii² 65', *ZPE* 48, 261-3

WALBANK, M.B. (1982b), 'An Athenian decree re-considered: honours for Aristoxenos and another Boiotian', *EMC* n.s. 1, 259-74

WALBANK, M.B. (1983), 'Herakleides of Klazomenai: a new join at the Epigraphical Museum', *ZPE* 51, 183-4

WALLACE, M.B. (1970), 'Early Greek *proxenoi*', *Phoenix* 24, 189-208

WALSER, G. (1975), 'Zum griechisch-persischen Verhältnis vor dem Hellenismus', *HZ* 220, 529-42

WALTER, E.V. (1969), *Terror and Resistance. A study of political violence with case studies of some primitive African communities*, New York

WARDMAN, A.E. (1971), 'Plutarch's methods in the *Lives*', *CQ* n.s. 21, 254-61

WARDMAN, A.E. (1974), *Plutarch's Lives*, London. See also PELLING, C.B.R. (1976)

WASSERMANN, F.M. (1952/3), 'The speeches of King Archidamus in Thucydides', *CJ* 48, 193-200

WASSERMANN, F.M. (1963/4), 'The voice of Sparta in Thucydides', *CJ* 59, 289-97

WATERBURY, J.: see GELLNER, E.

WATT, I.: see GOODY, J.

WEBER, M. (1978), *Economy and Society. An outline of interpretive sociology*, 2 vols, ed. G. Roth and C. Wittich, Berkeley, Los Angeles & London

WEHRLI, F. (1968), 'Zur politischen Theorie der Griechen: Gewaltherrschaft und Hegemonie', *MH* 25, 214-25

WELLES, C.B. (1966), 'Isocrates' view of history', in *The Classical Tradition. Literary and historical essays in honor of H. Caplan*, Ithaca, 3-25

WELSKOPF, E.C. (1974), ed., *Hellenische Poleis. Krise-Wandlung-Wirkung*, 3 vols, Berlin

WELWEI, K.-W. (1974-7), *Unfreie im antiken Kriegsdienst* I. *Athen und Sparta*; II. *Die kleineren und mittleren griechischen Staaten und die hellenistische Reiche*, Wiesbaden

WELWEI, K.-W. (1979), 'Die spartanische Phylenordnung im Spiegel der Grossen Rhetra und des Tyrtaios', *Gymnasium* 86, 178-96

WESENBERG, B. (1981), 'Agesilaos im Artemision', *ZPE* 41, 175-80

WEST, M.L. (1978), ed., *Hesiod. Works and Days*, Oxford

WESTLAKE, H.D. (1935), *Thessaly in the Fourth Century B.C.*, London

WESTLAKE, H.D. (1938), 'Alcibiades, Agis and Spartan policy', *JHS* 58, 31-40

WESTLAKE, H.D. (1966), 'Individuals in Xenophon, *Hellenica*', *BRL* 49, 246-69 (repr. in Westlake 1969, 203-25)

WESTLAKE, H.D. (1968), *Individuals in Thucydides*, Cambridge

WESTLAKE, H.D. (1969), *Essays on the Greek Historians and Greek History*, Manchester

WESTLAKE, H.D. (1975), 'Xenophon and Epaminondas', *GRBS* 16, 23-40

WESTLAKE, H.D. (1976), 'Reelection to the Ephorate?', *GRBS* 17, 343-52

WESTLAKE, H.D. (1979), 'Ionians in the Ionian War', *CQ* n.s. 29, 9-44

WESTLAKE, H.D. (1981), 'Decline and fall of Tissaphernes', *Historia* 30, 257-79

WESTLAKE, H.D. (1983a), 'The progress of Epiteichismos', *CQ* n.s. 33, 12-24

WESTLAKE, H.D. (1983b), 'Rival traditions on a Rhodian stasis', *MH* 40, 239-50

WHALEY, J. (1981), ed., *Mirrors of Mortality. Studies in the social history of death*, London

WHATLEY, N. (1964), 'On the possibility of reconstructing Marathon and other ancient battles', *JHS* 84, 119-39

WHEELER, E.L. (1982), '*Hoplomachia* and Greek dances in arms', *GRBS* 23, 223-33

WHIBLEY, L. (1896), *Greek Oligarchies. Their character and organisation*, London (repr. Chicago 1975)

WHITEHEAD, D. (1979), 'Ant<i>alkidas, or, the case of the intrusive iota', *LCM* 4, 191-3

WHITEHEAD, D. (1981), 'The serfs of Sicyon', *LCM* 6, 37-41

WHITEHEAD, D. (1982/83), 'Sparta and the Thirty Tyrants', *AncSoc* 13/14, 105-30 (in fact published 1984)

WHITTAKER, C.R.: see GARNSEY, P.D.A.

WICKERSHAM, J. and G.B. VERBRUGGHE (1973), eds, *The Fourth Century*, Toronto

WICKERT, K. (1961), 'Der peloponnesische Bund von seiner Entstehung bis zum Ende des archidamischen Krieges', diss. Erlangen-Nürnberg

WIDE, S. (1893), *Lakonische Kulte*, Leipzig

WIESEHÖFER, J. (1980), 'Die "Freunde" und "Wohltäter" des Grosskönigs', *Studia Iranica* 9, 7-21

WILAMOWITZ-MOELLENDORF, U. von (1881), *Antigonos von Karystos*, Berlin

WILAMOWITZ-MOELLENDORF, U. von (1884), *Homerische Untersuchungen*, Berlin

WILL, Ed. (1960), 'Chabrias et les finances de Tachôs', *REA* 62, 254-75

WILL, Ed. (1972), *Le monde grec et l'orient* I. *Le Ve siècle (510-403)*, Paris (rev. impr. 1980)

WILL, Ed., Cl. MOSSÉ and P. GOUKOWSKY (1975), *Le monde grec et l'orient* II. *Le IVe siècle et l'époque hellénistique*, Paris

WILLEMSEN, F. (1977), 'Zu den Lakedämoniergräbern im Kerameikos', *MDAI(A)* 92, 117-57

WILSON, J.B. (1979), *Pylos 425 B.C. A historical and topographical study of Thucydides' account of the campaign*, Warminster

WILSON, N.G. (1983), *Scholars of Byzantium*, London. See also RUSSELL, D.A.

WISEMAN, J. (1969), 'Epaminondas and the Theban invasions', *Klio* 51, 177-99

WISEMAN, J. (1978), *The Land of the Ancient Corinthians*, Göteborg

WISEMAN, T.P. (1979), *Clio's Cosmetics. Three studies in Greco-Roman literature*, Leicester

WOLF, E.R. (1966), 'Kinship, friendship and patron-client relations in complex societies', in M. Banton (ed.), *The Social Anthropology of Complex Societies*, London, 1-22 (repr. in Schmidt 1977, 167-77)

WOOD, N. (1964), 'Xenophon's theory of leadership', *C & M* 25, 33-66

WOODHEAD, A.G.: see COOK, R.M.

WORMELL, D.E.W.: see PARKE, H.W.

ZAHRNT, M. (1971), *Olynth und die Chalkidier. Untersuchungen zur Staatenbildung auf der Chalkidischen Halbinsel im 5. and 4. Jahrhundert v. Chr.*, Munich

ZEILHOFER, G. (1959), 'Sparta, Delphoi und die Amphiktyonen im 5. Jahrhundert vor Christus', diss. Erlangen

ZIEHEN, L. (1933), 'Das spartanische Bevölkerungsproblem', *Hermes* 68, 218-37

ZIERKE, E. (1936), 'Agesilaos. Beiträge zum Lebensbild und zur Politik des Spartanerkönigs', diss. Frankfurt/Main

ZINSERLING, G. (1965), 'Persönlichkeit und Politik Lysanders im Lichte der Kunst', *WZJena* 14, 35-43

Index locorum

Compiled by N.M. de Courcy.
Numbers in **bold** type refer to the pages of this book.

General index

Athenians/Athens, 11, 16, 38, 63, 71, 85, 121, 151, 160, 168, 194, 225, 230, 249, 336, 431; democracy, 27, 72, 123-4, 129, 130, 247, 281, 285, 297, 298, 349, 429; empire/ imperialism, 8-9, 51, 53, 87, 89, 196, 286, 287, 292-3, 294, 295, 298, 299, 302, 311, 318, 349, 367, 376; ephebic training, 30; grain-supply, 47, 274-5, 293, 294, 304, 348, 365, 367, 367-8; navy, 16, 34, 48, 274-5, 280, 287, 293, 299, 318, 357, 359; and Persia, 49, 187, 287, 291, 302, 311; and Sicily, 48, 49, 187, 310, 367, 379; and Sparta, 8, 61, 82, 93, 136, 161-2, 210, 212, 218-25, 235, 253, 254, 274-313, 324, 358, 360-8, 371, 382, 384, 385-6, 388, 391; and Thebes, 136, 137, 157, 231, 235, 270, 271, 274-313, 382, 390; 'Thirty' at, 90, 91, 118, 280, 281-3, 349-51, 373; walls, 65, 90, 280, 281, 287, 293, 299, 349, 357, 362
  see also 'dual hegemony' thesis; Leagues; Peiraieus
Attika, 47, 93, 123, 279-80, 301, 350; Spartan invasions of, 17, 45, 46, 47, 54, 106, 160-1
Augustus (Roman emperor), 98, 120
Aulis, 212, 279, 290, 291, 357, 369
Autokles (Athenian), 306, 400
autonomy, 9-10, 49, 191, 194, 213, 242, 243, 249-50, 268, 273, 284-5, 295, 301, 302, 351, 370, 378; Spartan interpretations of, 10, 49, 226, 250, 251, 255, 258, 261, 280, 297, 308, 369, 370, 373, 374, 379, 379-80, 382-3, 388, 392
Autophradates (Persian), 389

Babyka (Spartan bridge), 124
Babylon/Babylonia, 184, 185, 189, 334
Bacon, Francis, 20, 77, 99, 406
barley, 108, 131, 173, 178, 410
Belmina/Belminatis, 389
Bias (Spartiate), 224
biography: ancient, 5, 56, 70, 418; modern, 5-6, 423, 425, 426
  see also historiography; individuals
Bithynia, 210, 211
Boiotia (region), 54, 188, 276, 354, 377, 384; and Sparta, 13, 146, 156, 192
  see also federalism; Thebans
Boiotios (Spartiate), 80, 189-90
booty, *see* warfare
Bosporos, 47, 59, 295, 304, 367
Brasidas (Spartiate), 18, 45, 48, 49, 85, 114, 207, 288; heroization at Amphipolis, 185, 337, 338; Thracian expedition, 39, 45, 49, 50, 91-2, 93, 210, 216, 224, 268-9, 317, 318
  see also Akanthos; Helots, manumission
bribery, by and of Spartans, 17, 51, 88, 96, 122, 126, 127, 153, 228, 234-5, 352

burials, *see* dead, disposal of
Byzantion, 92, 191, 289, 295, 298, 311, 320, 349, 352, 367, 376, 390

camels, 59, 216
Caria, 193, 195, 209, 211, 349, 365
  see also Hekatomnôs; Maussollos
Carlyle, Thomas, 397
Carthage, 117, 318, 320, 329, 349, 405
Chabrias (Athenian), 231, 303, 304, 329, 377
Chaironeia, 69, 279; battle of (338), 43, 205, 274, 330
Chalkedon, 92, 191, 367
Chalkideus (Spartiate), 187-8
Chalkidians/Chalkidike, 45, 52, 85, 226, 268, 269, 283, 288, 296, 323, 360
  see also federalism
Charilaos (Eurypontid king), 23, 102, 103, 111
Charmides (Athenian), 350
Charon (of Lampsakos), 71
Cheirisophos (Spartiate), 191, 320
Chians/Chios, 93, 145, 170-1, 211, 296, 298, 299, 311, 356, 370, 372, 375-6
Chilon (Spartan Ephor), 107, 110, 149, 339
Chilon (son-in-law of AGESILAOS), 149
Cicero, 5, 49
civil strife/war, *see* stasis
class/class struggle, 13, 119, 165-6, 247, 409
  see also stasis
Claudius (Roman emperor), 192, 406
Clausewitz, General von, 48, 207, 240
coinage, 225, 276, 279, 315-16, 350
  see also Sparta/Spartans, money
colonization, 315, 338
Corcyra, *see* Kerkyra
Corinth/Corinthians, 12, 47, 48, 61, 228, 242, 254, 293, 363-4, 375, 383; and Athens, 52, 253-4, 285, 293; and Persia, 254; and Sparta, 11, 12, 47, 51, 53, 132, 212, 220, 249, 251, 253-7, 266, 269, 272, 275, 282, 283, 285, 290, 348, 349, 351, 356, 358, 360-8, 385, 388
  see also Argives/Argos; Isthmus; Lechaion
Corinthia, 5, 321, 361, 363
Corinthian Gulf, 8, 17, 48, 310, 353, 362, 364
Corinthian War, 54, 61, 62, 218-26, 253, 255, 263, 269, 283, 289, 290, 292-5, 358-63, 373
Cretans/Crete, 117, 315, 330
crisis, defined, 3; of fourth century, 6, 317; of Sparta, 4, 6, 36-7, 165, 178-9, 395-412
Cunaxa, battle of (401), 59, 186, 191, 209, 353
Cyprus, 274, 277, 348; and Persia, 198, 356, 370, 375
  see also Euagoras I
Cyrenaica, *see* Libya
Cyriac (of Ancona), 420
Cyrus II 'the Great' (Persian king), 3, 24, 153,

78, 81, 94-6, 105, 114, 162-3, 179, 337, 352, 358

see also AGESILAOS; Cyrus the Younger; Pausanias (Agiad king)

Lysandros (Spartiate), 127

Lysanoridas (Spartiate), 150, 297, 375

Lysias (Attic orator), 61, 372

Macedon/Macedonians, 4, 8, 49, 100, 112, 181, 224, 268, 270-1, 273, 386, 424

Machiavelli, 263, 314, 420

Maiandrios (Samian tyrant), 244

Mandeville, Bernard, 8

Mantineia/Mantineians, 11, 222, 224, 368, 374, 383, 390-1; battles of: (418), 39, 41, 46, 130, 154, 204, 207, 220, 258, 429-30; (362), 63, 235, 253, 257, 262, 274, 312, 314, 324, 391-2; democracy, 248, 258, 371, 383; and Sparta, 13, 53, 90, 156, 222, 226, 235, 249, 256, 258, 259-62, 280, 284, 285, 296, 298, 325, 366, 370-1, 389; and Tegea, 257-62, 386, 390-1

Marathon, battle of (490), 34

Mardonius (Persian), 193

Marx, Karl, 3, 7, 397

Maussollos (ruler of Caria), 193, 201, 326-7, 376n.1, 389

meat, 154, 218, 223

Media, 49, 89, 184, 185

medism/medizers, 47, 60, 187, 276, 280, 296, 369-70

Megalopolis, 261-2, 273, 310, 312, 347, 385, 386, 389-90

Megara/Megarians: and Athens, 8, 17, 254, 277; and Sparta, 11, 17, 52, 53, 254, 256, 263, 272, 276, 282, 285, 349, 385

Megillos (Spartiate), 31

Melesippidas (grandfather of AGESILAOS), 22, 145

Melos, 52, 93, 275

Menekrates (Syracusan), 332

Menelaion (sanctuary of Menelaos and Helen), 147, 339

Menelaos (Homeric king of Lakedaimon), 244

mercenaries, 80, 201, 209, 222, 305, 314-30, 364, 378, 386, 389, 402; Spartan employment of, 39, 210, 211, 213, 219, 224, 231, 234, 271, 306, 314-30, 348, 350, 355, 373, 387, 392; 'Ten Thousand', 59, 185, 191, 209, 289, 316, 320-1, 355, 361

see also AGESILAOS; peltasts; Xenophon

Mes(s)oa, *see* Sparta (town), obes/villages

Messene, New, 235, 257, 273, 310, 312, 347, 387, 390, 391; foundation of (369), 35, 63, 200, 310, 385; Spartan refusal to recognize, 200, 201, 257, 262, 325, 385, 388, 389, 392, 401, 425

Messenia, 31, 38, 39, 40, 200, 232, 262, 333, 353, 360, 362, 384, 385, 386, 403

see also Helots, Messenian; Naupaktos; Perioikoi, Messenian; Sparta/Spartans, land-tenure

Messenian Wars: First, 14-15, 104, 315; Second, 14-15, 173, 431; Third, 13, 16-17, 31, 176, 260, 353, 371

Methymna, 376

Milesians/Miletos, 91, 188, 189, 337, 365

Mnasippos (Spartiate), 306, 323-4, 379

morai, *see* Sparta/Spartans, army organization

More, Thomas, 414, 415-16

mothakes, *see* Lysander; Sparta/Spartans, citizenship

Mounychia, 350

Mykale, battle of (479), 47, 86

Myron (of Priene), 175

Mysia/Mysians, 210, 217

Mytilenaians/Mytilene, 46-7, 255, 311, 376, 387

Nabis (Eurypontid 'tyrant'), 110, 114

Napoleon, 206, 224, 236, 240

Narthakion (Thessaly), 218, 219, 362

Naubates (Spartiate), 210-11

Naukleidas (Spartiate), 97, 126, 135, 271

Naupaktos, 17, 322, 353

Naxos, 311, 390; battle of (376), 304, 305, 377

Nektanebis II (Egyptian ruler), 329, 392

Nemea River, battle of (394), 146, 218, 220-1, 240, 272, 361

Neodamôdeis, *see* Helots, manumission

Neon (Perioikos), 320

Nepherites I (Egyptian ruler), 218, 328, 358

Nepos, Cornelius, 70, 71, 93, 418

Niebuhr, B.G., 62, 423

Nikias (Athenian), 99

see also Peaces

Nisaia, 91

Notion, battle of (407/6), 80, 81

Odrysoi, 295

Oiniadai, 225

Oion (Skiritis), 234

Oita/Oitaians, 288, 292

Okyllos (Spartiate), 157, 299, 301

oliganthrôpia, *see* Sparta/Spartans, citizenship

oligarchy, 37, 122, 143; Sparta as special kind of, 32, 72, 117, 131-2, 167

see also Lysander, and dekarchies; Sparta/Spartans, support for oligarchy

olives, 335

Olympia, 8, 12, 49, 60, 61, 86, 253, 324, 330, 372; Sparta and, 248

Olympic Games, 8, 29, 84, 249; control of disputed, 248, 252, 390; Spartan victors at,